www.wadsworth.com

www.wadsworth.com is the World Wide Web site for Wadsworth and is your direct source to dozens of online resources.

At *www.wadsworth.com* you can find out about supplements, demonstration software, and student resources. You can also send email to many of our authors and preview new publications and exciting new technologies.

www.wadsworth.com
Changing the way the world learns®

From the Wadsworth Series in Speech Communication

THE BASICS OF COMMUNICATION RESEARCH

Leslie A. Baxter

The University of Iowa

Earl Babbie

Chapman University

THOMSON ™

WADSWORTH

Australia • Canada • Mexico • Singapore • Spain • United Kingdom • United States

Publisher: Holly J. Allen
Editor: Annie Mitchell
Assistant Editor: Amber Fawson
Editorial Assistant: Breanna Gilbert
Technology Project Manager: Jeanette Wiseman
Media Assistant: Bryan Davis
Marketing Manager: Kimberly Russell
Marketing Assistant: Neena Chandra
Advertising Project Manager: Shemika Britt

Project Manager, Editorial Production: Cathy Linberg
Print/Media Buyer: Doreen Suruki
Permissions Editor: Kiely Sexton
Production Service: Greg Hubit Bookworks
Copyeditor: Donald Pharr
Cover Designer: Belinda Fernandez, Studio B
Cover Images: Getty Images
Compositor: G&S Typesetters
Printer: Transcontinental Printing/Louiseville

Printed in Canada
3 4 5 6 7 07 06 05

For more information about our products, contact us at:
Thomson Learning Academic Resource Center
1-800-423-0563

For permission to use material from this text, contact us by:
Phone: 1-800-730-2214 **Fax:** 1-800-730-2215
Web: http://www.thomsonrights.com

Library of Congress Control Number: 2003102373

Student Edition: ISBN 0-534-50778-6
Instructor's Edition: ISBN 0-534-50836-7

Wadsworth/Thomson Learning
10 Davis Drive
Belmont, CA 94002-3098
USA

Asia
Thomson Learning
5 Shenton Way #01-01
UIC Building
Singapore 068808

Australia/New Zealand
Thomson Learning
102 Dodds Street
Southbank, Victoria 3006
Australia

Canada
Nelson
1120 Birchmount Road
Toronto, Ontario M1K 5G4
Canada

Europe/Middle East/Africa
Thomson Learning
High Holborn House
50/51 Bedford Row
London WC1R 4LR
United Kingdom

Latin America
Thomson Learning
Seneca, 53
Colonia Polanco
11560 Mexico D.F.
Mexico

Spain/Portugal
Paraninfo
Calle/Magallanes, 25
28015 Madrid, Spain

Leslie dedicates the book to her daughter, Emma, the best question asker she knows.

Earl dedicates the book to Aaron and Ara Babbie, who keep finding new ways to enrich his life.

CONTENTS IN BRIEF

CONTENTS

Chapter 11

The Basics of Quantitative Data Analysis   256

Chapter 12

Inferential Statistics in Quantitative Data Analysis   271

LIST OF BOXES

PREFACE

Mikhail Bakhtin, a favorite social theorist of one of us, argues that no discourse is ever originary; instead, it is always animated by traces of prior discourses. Certainly, Bakhtin's claim holds true for this book. *The Basics of Communication Research* is based on Earl Babbie's *The Basics of Social Research,* which in turn dates back to the first appearance of his *The Practice of Social Research* in 1975. The goal of this book is to provide a paperback book (sensitive to student economics) that retains the many strengths of Babbie's *Basics* while concentrating on the unique features of research about communication.

Many issues and methods relevant to communication research are common throughout the social sciences. Yet these issues and methods have different textures to them from one discipline or field to another. Thus, our goal was to flesh out the unique textures of social scientific methods when they are used to answer questions about communication. The book strives to continue the Babbie tradition of user-friendly prose and a multitude of concrete examples—all grounded in the study of communication phenomena.

Although quantitative research methods dominated the social scientific study of communication through the third quarter of the 20th century, the century ended with a growing interest in qualitative research. Today, communication researchers are increasingly relying on both quantitative methods and qualitative methods in understanding communication forms, functions, processes, and outcomes. Our goal was to produce a book in which quantitative methods and qualitative methods are presented on their own terms. Too often in research methods books, qualitative methods are presented in a token chapter and framed within the logic system and evaluative standards of quantitative research. We think that these practices have often positioned qualitative methods as somehow secondary to quantitative methods. Our position is that both kinds of methods are necessary for a comprehensive understanding of communication. Both methods need to be trustworthy—consumers of research

need to have confidence in the researcher's conclusions. However, as we shall see, these two kinds of methods accomplish trustworthiness in different ways. Both quantitative methods and qualitative methods have strengths and limitations. Both are valuable to the project of understanding communication. Both merit attention to their unique, yet complementary, ways of achieving explanation and understanding.

This book is designed with two additional goals in mind: to help readers learn how to *do* communication research and to help readers learn how to *read and evaluate* others' communication research. In our view, these two goals are interconnected in a complementary way. Researchers rarely conduct studies on a topic of interest without first reading and evaluating what is already known on the topic from past research. Further, researchers benefit from knowing in advance of conducting a study the standards by which its trustworthiness will be assessed. At the same time, consumers of research learn how to read and evaluate research studies by knowing the details of how they are done. In short, producers of research need to know how to be effective consumers of research, and consumers of research need to understand how research is done. We view producers/consumers of communication research as the book's primary audience.

The book is organized into three main parts. Part 1 examines introductory issues of interest to both quantitatively oriented and qualitatively oriented producers/consumers. Chapter 1 continues Babbie's user-friendly style of demonstrating to research newcomers that they have been doing research all of their lives, although perhaps less systematically than the rigors of scientific inquiry. Chapter 1 also introduces readers to the domain of communication, discussing the kinds of issues addressed by communication researchers and how students can access published communication research.

Chapter 2 offers an overview of the research process, providing a step-by-step discussion of the major kinds of decisions that face researchers as they plan a study. It discusses how to conduct a review of literature and how to read both quantitatively oriented and qualitatively oriented communication research. The APA style is discussed. This chapter concludes by presenting two checklists of questions important to ask in conducting and evaluating research—one focused on quantitatively oriented research and one focused on qualitatively oriented research. Several appendices complement issues developed in this chapter, including a list of communication-related journals, advice on how to conduct electronic searches in abstracts and indexes, research in cyberspace, a sample research report/proposal laid out in APA style, and advice on how to handle citations in APA style. Much of this chapter is new to instructors familiar with Babbie's *Basics*.

We view research as a way of knowing. Ways of knowing cannot be evaluated outside of the researcher's underlying assumptions about the nature of reality, what counts as a knowledge claim, and how we can come to know something. We call these assumptions *paradigms of knowing,* and Chapter 3 discusses four of the major sets of assumptions in which communication research is grounded: the positivist paradigm, the systems paradigm, the interpretive paradigm, and the critical paradigm. Although the correspondence is not absolute, quantitatively oriented research and qualitatively oriented research tend to be embedded in different paradigms of knowing. We think it is important for students to understand the basic assumptions that undergird research, because these assumptions lead to differences in how trustworthy research is defined. We are unaware of other communication research books that treat the issue of paradigms of knowing as comprehensively as you will find in this chapter.

Chapter 4 emphasizes the role of logic and reasoning in the research process. In Chapter 1, we indicate that scientific inquiry is built on two pillars: logic and observation. This chapter focuses on the pillar of logic, providing a detailed treatment of inductive reasoning and deductive reasoning. How these two forms of reasoning are used in quantitative research and qualitative research is illustrated in depth. The linkages between reasoning and theory are developed, demonstrating that different kinds of theory are used for different purposes in communication research. We are unaware of other communication research books that devote such detailed attention to reasoning and logic in the research enterprise.

Chapter 5 presents an in-depth discussion of the ethics that guide communication research. We review the ethical standards that guide research, discuss some controversial violations of those standards in past research, and provide detailed discussion of institutional review

boards (IRBs), including presenting a sample informed consent form and a list of questions commonly asked by IRBs.

With the backdrop of introductory issues in hand, Part 2 of the book is devoted to issues and methods of particular relevance to producers/consumers of quantitatively oriented communication research. The introduction to Part 2 provides an overview of how trustworthiness is assessed in quantitatively oriented communication research. Four criteria are developed, which are woven into all of the chapters of Part 2: internal validity, measurement reliability, measurement validity, and external validity.

Chapter 6 continues the Babbie tradition of a lucid discussion of conceptualization and operationalization. We now focus that lucidity on communication concepts. We provide a comprehensive discussion of exactly how reliability and validity of communication measures are established.

Chapter 7 is devoted largely to probability-based sampling methods, although nonprobability sampling methods are previewed for a return performance in Part 3 of the book. The Babbie tradition of establishing the logical framework that guides probability sampling has been retained because it provides such a fruitful foundation for the discussion of inferential statistics, now developed in Chapter 12.

Chapter 8 is devoted to standardized questionnaires and interviews. It is organized into three sections: criteria for question development, question format and organization, and administration. Because the details of constructing indexes and scales may be too advanced for some instructors' purposes, we have developed these issues in depth in a separate appendix (H).

Chapter 9 discusses pre-experiments, quasi-experiments, and classic experiments. We frame the chapter using the design symbol notations and formats of the classic work by Campbell and Stanley (1963) on this subject. For more advanced students, we include factorial experiments in addition to the simpler designs in which a single independent variable is studied. Because evaluation research most commonly uses experimental designs (quasi-experimental designs more particularly), we fold discussion of this applied method into this chapter as well.

Chapter 10 provides detailed treatment of the two text-analysis methods most commonly found in communication research: content analysis and interaction analysis. The two methods are presented as close cousins, although different in several respects. We provide step-by-step instructions on how to calculate unitizing reliability and coding reliability. We are unaware of other communication research methods books that probe these two methods in the detail found in this chapter.

Chapters 11 and 12 function as an introductory "primer" of sorts to descriptive and inferential statistics. Of course, the goal here is not to present a mini statistics book; rather, our goal is to emphasize the logic of statistics. We provide concrete step-by-step instructions and examples in the calculation of several basic descriptive and inferential statistics, including measures of central tendency (mean, median, mode), measures of dispersion (range, standard deviation), standardized (z) scores, how to construct and interpret contingency (percentage) tables, chi square, t-test, one-way ANOVA, two-way ANOVA, and Pearson correlation. Although we are aware that students can calculate these statistics using statistical software, we believe that it is important for students to have "hands-on" experience with some basic statistics, thereby underscoring the logic of how statistics function in decision making by researchers.

Part 3 shifts our attention to issues and methods relevant to producers/consumers of qualitative communication research. The introduction to this part details four criteria by which the trustworthiness of qualitative research is assessed: dependability, credibility, confirmability, and transferability. These four criteria are woven throughout all of the chapters in this part of the book. Part 2 emphasizes three methods (surveys, experiments, quantitative text analysis), and Part 3 develops three methods as well: participant observation (Chapter 13), qualitative interviewing (Chapter 14), and social text analysis (Chapter 15). Issues of sampling and conceptualization, as understood and applied by qualitative researchers, are woven throughout these three chapters. Much of this part of the book is new to instructors familiar with Babbie's *Basics*.

Participant observation takes many forms, and these are presented and illustrated in Chapter 13. A popular form of participation-observation research, the ethnography of communication, is presented in this chapter. This chapter frames participant observation as a dance, complete with warm-up, execution, and closure phases. Each of these phases is discussed in detail, with concrete discussions of the various issues that field researchers face in the study of communication. Attention is given to the nitty-gritty details of how to take field notes as well.

Chapter 14 presents unstructured and semi-structured interviewing. This method surfaces in many forms, including ethnographic interviews, in-depth interviews, narrative interviews, focus group interviews, and postmodern interviews. The chapter discusses and illustrates the range of types of questions found in qualitative interviewing, in addition to a discussion of some important steps in executing the qualitative interview.

Chapter 15 examines how qualitative researchers study naturally occurring communication messages and symbols—what we call *social texts*. Communication criticism, discourse analysis, conversation analysis, narrative analysis, performative analysis, and semiotics are discussed as different ways to approach the analysis of social texts.

Chapter 16 can be thought of as the qualitative counterpart of Chapters 11 and 12; it is devoted to a detailed treatment of the step-by-step process of how to analyze textual data qualitatively rather than statistically. Two specific analytic methods are illustrated in depth: the Developmental Research Sequence (DRS) and Grounded Theory Development (GTD).

Each of the book's chapters contains several boldfaced terms that are gathered in a glossary at the end of the book. Each chapter also includes several italicized words and phrases, marking their importance as additional technical terms that the reader should note.

Each chapter concludes with a detailed summary of main points, review questions and exercises, a list of key words boldfaced throughout the chapter, terms to explore through InfoTrac College Edition (an electronic repository of complete articles and abstracts relevant to communication researchers), and a suggested continuity project. The continuity project follows one topic—gender/sex differences in communication—throughout the book. In each chapter, the reader can pursue how the subject matter of that chapter is relevant to the study of gender/sex differences in communication.

Acknowledgments

We thank two former editors at Wadsworth/Thomson Learning: Todd Armstrong, who approached us with the idea for this book, and Deirdre Anderson, who worked with us during the book's lengthy gestation. Leslie thanks the University of Iowa for a sabbatical during which much of the writing of this book took place. In addition, Leslie thanks Erin Sahlstein, now a communication studies professor in her own right, for invaluable library assistance in searching for examples of various concepts in the book. Last, Leslie thanks Earl Babbie for his good humor and his intellectual generosity. Earl, for his part, is overjoyed by the opportunity to be Leslie's partner in sharing the excitement of social research methods with communication faculty and students.

A NOTE FROM THE AUTHORS

Leslie A. Baxter

I started off college as a mathematics major but moved on to study communication because I wanted to understand the human condition better. During my junior year, I walked into a research methods class followed by an introductory statistics class, and I realized that I could bring both interests together in the scientific study of communication. When I conducted a quantitative research study for my senior honors thesis, I knew I was hooked for life. In graduate school, I was fortunate enough to encounter professors who urged me to gain expertise in qualitative methods as well as in quantitative methods. Throughout my career as a scholar, I have used both kinds of methods (often in the same study), and I've always been grateful for multi-method training. I am particularly interested in finding out how communication works in personal and familial relationships.

As a teacher, I've taught research methods to both undergraduate and graduate students for twenty-five years now—first at the University of Montana, then Lewis & Clark College, then the University of California–Davis, and now at the University of Iowa. I have used Earl Babbie's research methods books for a good number of those years. Thus, when Wadsworth approached me about writing *The Basics of Communication Research* with Earl, it was a joy to accept their offer.

When I'm not doing research or teaching, I'm busy raising my seven-year-old daughter. I have hopes of someday producing a perennial flower bed that will be the envy of the neighborhood. When it's not gardening season, I like reading murder mysteries and books about U.S. history.

Earl Babbie

Writing is my joy, sociology my passion. I delight in putting words together in a way that makes people learn or laugh or both. Sociology shows up as a set of words, also. It represents our last, best hope for planet-training our race and finding ways for us to live together. I feel a special excitement at being present when sociology, at last, comes into focus as an idea whose time has come.

I grew up in small-town Vermont and New Hampshire. When I announced I wanted to be an auto-body mechanic, like my dad, my teacher told me I should go to college instead. When Malcolm X announced he wanted to be a lawyer, his teacher told him a colored boy should be something more like a carpenter. The difference in our experiences says something powerful about the idea of a level playing field. The inequalities among ethnic groups run deep.

I ventured into the outer world by way of Harvard, the USMC, U.C. Berkeley, and 12 years teaching at the University of Hawaii. Along the way, I married Sheila two months after our first date, and we created Aaron three years after that: two of my wisest acts. I resigned from teaching in 1980 and wrote full-time for seven years, until the call of the classroom became too loud to ignore. For me, teaching is like playing jazz. Even if you perform the same number over and over, it never comes out the same twice, and you don't know exactly what it'll sound like until you hear it. Teaching is like writing with your voice.

At last, I have matured enough to rediscover and appreciate my roots in Vermont each summer. Rather than a return to the past, it feels more like the next turn in a widening spiral. I can't wait to see what's around the next bend.

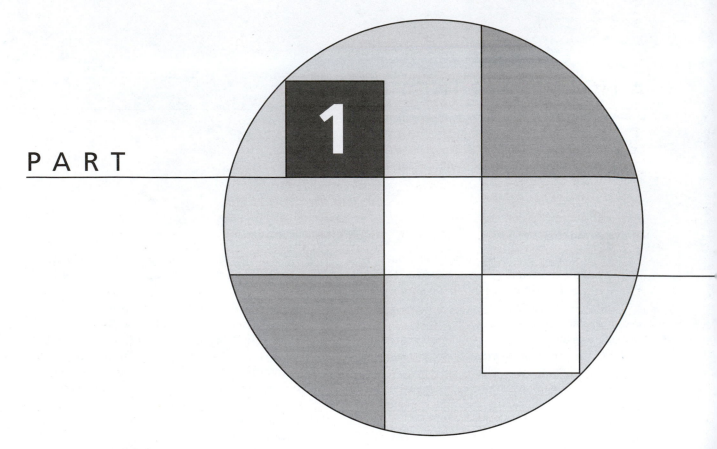

An Introduction to Scientific Inquiry about Communication

Science is a familiar word used by everyone. Yet images of science differ greatly. For some, science is mathematics; for others, it's white coats and laboratories. It's often confused with technology or equated with tough high school or college courses.

Science is, of course, none of these things per se. However, it's difficult to specify exactly what science is. Scientists, in fact, disagree on the proper definition. For the purposes of this book, we'll look at science as a method of inquiry—a way of developing knowledge claims about the world. Contrasted with other ways of learning and knowing about the world, science has some special characteristics. We'll examine these traits in this opening set of chapters.

Dr. Benjamin Spock, the renowned author and pediatrician, began his books on child care by assuring new parents that they already knew more about child care than they thought they did. We want to begin this book on a similar note. It will become clear to you before you've read very far that you already know a great deal about the practice of scientific research about communication. In fact, you've been conducting scientific research all your life. From that perspective, the purpose of this book is to help you sharpen skills that you already have and perhaps to show you some tricks that may not have occurred to you.

Part 1 of this book is intended to lay the groundwork for the discussions that follow in the rest of the book—to examine the fundamental characteristics and issues that make the scientific approach different from other ways of knowing things. In Chapter 1, we'll begin with a look at native human inquiry, the sort of thing you've been doing all your life. In the course of that examination, we'll see some of the ways that people go astray in trying to understand the world around them, and we'll summarize the primary characteristics of scientific inquiry that guard against those errors. We'll also introduce the field of communication. We'll present an overview of the range of topics of interest to communication researchers. In addition, we'll discuss how knowledge production is organized in the communication field. We'll provide you with a guide to the major journals useful in locating published research about communication.

Chapter 2 gets you started in conducting research of your own. We discuss the basic building blocks of this process: selecting and narrowing your research topic, conducting a review of related research literature, formulating your research design, and writing up a proposal for the study. Even if you don't plan on conducting research, this chapter will be useful to you. A skilled consumer of research needs to know the issues involved in conducting a research study.

Chapter 3 deals with social scientific paradigms in communication research. We'll look at the primary theoretical paradigms that shape the nature of inquiry about communication and that largely determine what communication researchers look for and how they interpret what they see.

In Chapter 4, we'll consider the two logic systems used by all communication researchers: deduction and induction. In addition, we'll see how these logic systems involve theory. Theory? Yes, you read that correctly! Central to the research enterprise is theory, and we'll see how theories about communication are constructed and used in the conduct of research.

Chapter 5, the final chapter in this introductory section, is an overview of the ethical principles that guide communication researchers. We'll discuss institutional review boards (IRBs) and professional codes of ethics, which are the two main formalized guidance systems used to ensure that research is conducted in such a way that the human rights of study participants are protected.

The overall purpose of Part 1 is to construct a backdrop against which to view more specific aspects of research design and execution. By the time you complete Part 1, you should be ready to look at some of the more concrete aspects of communication research.

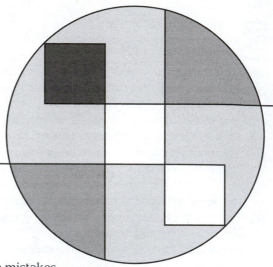

CHAPTER 1

Human Inquiry and Scientific Inquiry about Communication

What You'll Learn in This Chapter

We'll examine the way people learn about their world and the mistakes they make along the way. We'll also begin to see what makes science different from other ways of knowing things.

INTRODUCTION

The subject matter of this book is how to make knowledge claims about communication. Our primary purpose is to help you look at *how* to make claims about communication, not *what* to know about it. Let's start by examining a few things you probably already know about communication.

You probably know that the first electronic medium of communication was the telegraph. You probably know that the early years of TV broadcast only black-and-white images. You probably know that American Sign Language (ASL) is a manual language used by many hearing-disabled persons.

How do you know? If you think for a minute, you'll see you know these things because somebody told them to you. Perhaps your instructor in a course on the history of mass media told you about the telegraph and early TV, or maybe you read it on a web-based encyclopedia page under "communication." Maybe you saw someone signing in ASL at a public lecture and asked the person next to you what that was. That's how you know.

Some of the things you know seem absolutely obvious to you. If we asked you how you know astronauts in space can communicate with people on Earth, you'd probably say, "Everybody knows that." There are a lot of things everybody knows. Of course, at one time, everyone "knew" that people were confined to the planet Earth.

Most of what you know is a matter of agreement and belief. Little of it is based on personal experience. A big part of growing up in any society, in fact, is the process of learning to accept what everybody around you "knows" is so. If you don't know those same things, you can't really be a part of the group. If you were to question seriously the ability of astronauts to communicate while in space, you'd quickly find yourself set apart from other people. You might be sent to live in a hospital with other people who share your suspicion.

Although it's important for you to see that most of what you know is a matter of believing what you've been told, we also want you to see that there's nothing wrong with you in that respect. That's simply the way human societies are structured. The basis of knowledge is agreement. Because you can't learn through personal experience all you need to know, things are set up so you can simply believe what others tell you. You know some things through tradition, others from "experts."

There are other ways of knowing things, however. In contrast to knowing things through agreement, you can know them through direct experience—through **observation.** If you dive into a glacial stream flowing through the Canadian Rockies, you don't need anyone to tell you it's cold. You notice that all by yourself (although you learned from others to label the sensation "cold").

When your experience conflicts with what everyone else knows, though, there's a good chance you'll surrender your experience in favor of the agreement. For example, imagine you've come to a party. You think it's a high-class affair, and the drinks and food are excellent. In particular, you're taken by one of the appetizers the host brings around on a tray: a breaded, deep-fried tidbit that's especially zesty. You have a couple—they're delicious! You have more. Soon you are subtly moving around the room to be wherever the host is offering this tray of nibbles. Finally, you can't contain yourself anymore. "What are they?" you ask. "How can I get the recipe?" And the host lets you in on the secret: "You've been eating breaded, deep-fried worms!" Your response is dramatic: Your stomach rebels, and you promptly throw up all over the living room rug. Awful! What a terrible thing to serve guests!

The point of the story is that both feelings about the appetizer would be quite real to you. Your initial liking for them was certainly genuine, but so was the feeling you had when you found out what you'd been eating. However, it should be evident that the feeling of disgust you had when you discovered you were eating worms was strictly a product of the agreements you have with those around you that worms aren't fit to eat. That's an agreement you began the first time your parents found you sitting in a pile of dirt with half of a wriggling worm dangling from your lips. You learned that worms are not acceptable food in our society when your parents pried your mouth open and reached down your throat for the other half of the worm.

Aside from these agreements, what's wrong with worms? They're probably high in protein and low in calories. Bite-sized and easily packaged, they're a distributor's dream. They are also a delicacy for some people who live in societies that lack our agreement that worms are disgusting. Some people might love the worms but be turned off by the deep-fried breading.

Thus, the question of making knowledge claims about worm eating is a complicated business. Making knowledge claims about anything is complicated. This book studies how we can make claims about what we know about communication.

SEARCHING FOR KNOWLEDGE ABOUT COMMUNICATION

Knowledge about reality is a tricky business. You've probably already gotten the suspicion that some of the things you "know" may not be "true," but how can you really know what's "real"? People have grappled with this question for thousands of years.

One answer that has arisen out of that grappling is science, which offers an approach to both agreement reality and experiential reality. Scientists have certain criteria that must be met before they'll accept a knowledge claim about something they haven't personally experienced. In general, an assertion must have both *logical* and *empirical* support: It must make sense, and it must not contradict actual observation. Why do earthbound scientists accept the assertion that it's cold on the dark side of the moon? First, it makes sense, because the surface heat of the moon comes from the sun's rays. Second, the scientific measurements made on the moon's dark side confirm the expectation. So scientists accept claims about things they don't personally experience—they accept an agreement reality—but they have special standards for doing so.

More to the point of this book, however, science offers a special approach to generating knowledge claims about communication through personal experience. *Epistemology* is the science of knowing; *methodology* (a subfield of epistemology) might be called the science of finding out. This book is an examination and presentation of social science methodology used by communication researchers.

In the rest of this chapter, we'll look at inquiry as an activity. We'll begin by examining inquiry about communication as a natural human activity, one we all have engaged in every day of our lives. Next, we'll look at some kinds of errors we make in normal inquiry about communication, and we'll conclude by examining what makes the scientific approach different. We'll see some of the ways the scientific approach guards against common human errors in inquiry. We will end the chapter by discussing in general terms the field of communication studies, focusing on the kinds of claims about communication made by communication researchers.

Ordinary Human Inquiry about Communication

Practically all people exhibit a desire to understand their present communicative circumstances and to predict their future circumstances. Our experience of the world would be utter chaos—an overwhelming stream of unrelated sounds, sights, and sensations—if we were unable to sort it out by attaching meaning. Meaning making, or understanding, is a process of identifying relationships among phenomena. When a baby gazes at a face and comes to understand that upturned corners of the mouth accompanied by a slight narrowing of the eyes form a "smile," meaning has replaced chaos. Whenever we enter a strange and familiar situation, we are anxious to understand it—to render it intelligible.

We seek to identify patterns and relationships not only to render intelligible our immediate communicative experiences but also to predict future circumstances. Children learn to pay careful attention to the way their parents summon them (e.g., "Sweetheart, can you come here for a minute?" versus "Elizabeth Katherine Smith, come here right this instant!"), based on the perception that summons language is usually related systematically to the kind of encounter they are likely to have with that parent.

Moreover, we seem quite willing to undertake this prediction business using *causal* and *probabilistic* reasoning. First, we generally recognize that future circumstances are somehow caused or conditioned by present ones. We learn as children that *how* we ask parents to get us things affects their likelihood of compliance. An artfully expressed "Please can I have a spinner toy? I'll work extra hard to pay you back! All my friends' parents have gotten them for their kids. I wouldn't be drooping around the house saying 'I'm bored' if I had one" sure beats "I want a spinner right now!" for its ability to persuade a parent to comply and purchase the toy.

Second, people also learn that such patterns of cause and effect are probabilistic in nature: The effects occur more often when the causes occur than when the causes are absent—but not always. Thus, children learn that verbal politeness is usually important in making a successful request for a new toy but that it doesn't always work. ("No, honey, I can't get you anything new right now because of a lot of unexpected expenses we've had this month.")

In looking at ordinary human inquiry about communication, we need to distinguish prediction and causal explanation. Often, we can make predictions without an explanation of why or how something will happen—perhaps you can predict how a conversation with a friend will go based on whether the friend arches his eyebrows a certain way when greeting you. And often, even if we can't explain why, we're willing to act on the basis of a demonstrated predictive ability. You don't know how or why that eyebrow arches, but past experience has led you to choose your words carefully when you see it!

Sometimes, communication researchers are interested in questions of prediction and causal explanation about communicative phenomena. Other times, researchers are more interested in questions about how meaning is accomplished or what something means. Sometimes, researchers are interested in understanding how the various parts of communication systems work together. What makes a question interesting or important is determined by many things, including the basic set of assumptions that a researcher holds about the world and what counts as a knowledge claim. We'll discuss this issue at greater length in Chapter 3.

As we suggested earlier in the chapter, our attempts to learn about the world are only partly linked to direct, personal inquiry or experience. Another, much larger, part comes from the agreed-on knowledge that others give us. This agreement reality both assists and hinders our attempts to find out for ourselves. Two important sources of our secondhand knowledge—tradition and authority—deserve brief consideration here.

Tradition

Each of us inherits a culture made up, in part, of firmly accepted knowledge about the workings of communication. We may learn from others that silence is golden in formal events such as funerals. Or we may learn from others that insulting people is regarded as rude. We may test a few of these "truths" on our own, but we simply accept the great majority of them, the things that "everybody knows."

Tradition, in this sense of the term, offers some clear advantages to human inquiry. By accepting what everybody knows, you are spared the overwhelming task of starting from scratch in your search for regularities, meaning, prediction, and explanation. Knowledge is cumulative, and an inherited body of information and understanding is the jumping-off point for the development of more knowledge. We often speak of "standing on the shoulders of giants"—that is, of previous generations.

At the same time, tradition may be detrimental to human inquiry. If you seek a fresh understanding of something that everybody already understands and has always understood, you may be marked the fool for your efforts. More to the point, it will probably never occur to you to seek new knowledge of something already accepted as obvious. For example, it is common knowledge that "birds of a feather stick together." If you choose to research the role of similarity in communication encounters, you may be criticized for studying "the obvious." However, researchers who have systematically studied the role of similarity have discovered that it functions in quite complicated ways: Sometimes, perceived similarity attracts parties to interaction with one another; other times, parties are attracted to differences (remember the adage that "opposites attract"?). Further, it is important to pay attention to exactly what is the basis of the similarity or difference; it's one thing to differ on preferred ice cream flavors and quite another to differ on basic lifestyles.

Authority

Despite the power of tradition, new knowledge claims about communication appear every day. Aside from your own personal inquiries, throughout your life you will benefit from new knowledge produced by others. Often, acceptance of these new acquisitions will depend on the status of the person who claims to know. For example, you're more likely to believe the communication researcher who declares that fear appeals of moderate intensity can be very persuasive than to believe your Uncle Pete, whose evidence is an anecdotal story of how he scared your father into doing something when they were both kids.

Like tradition, authority can both assist and hinder human inquiry. We do well to trust in the judgment of the person who has special training, expertise, and credentials in a given matter, especially in the face of controversy. At the same time, inquiry can be greatly hindered by the legitimate authority who errs within his or her own special province. Scientists, after all, do make mistakes. As we shall see, there is never such a thing as a "perfect study," free of limitations. In addition, scientific knowledge changes over time.

Inquiry is also hindered when we depend on the authority of experts speaking outside their realm of expertise. For example, consider the political or religious leader with no biochemical expertise who declares that marijuana is a dangerous drug. The advertising industry plays heavily on this misuse of authority by having popular athletes discuss the nutritional value of breakfast cereals, having movie actors evaluate the performance of automobiles, and using other similar tactics. In fact, communication researchers with an interest in understanding the phenomenon of speaker credibility have a long history of studying the link between speaker expertise and persuasion.

Both tradition and authority, then, are double-edged swords in the search for knowledge about communication. Simply put, they provide us with a starting point for our own inquiry, but they may lead us to start at the wrong point and push us off in the wrong direction.

Errors in Ordinary Inquiry about Communication and Some Solutions

Quite aside from the potential dangers of tradition and authority, we often stumble and fall when we set out to learn for ourselves. We're going to mention some of the common errors we make in our casual inquiries about communication and look at the ways a scientific approach guards against those errors.

Inaccurate Observations   Quite frequently, we all make mistakes in our observation. How often did your research methods instructor use a filled pause (e.g., "uh," "uhm") the first time your class met, for example? If you have to guess, that's because most of our daily observations are casual and semiconscious. That's why we often disagree about what really happened.

In contrast to casual human inquiry, scientific observation is a conscious activity. Simply making observation more deliberate helps reduce error. For example, you probably don't recall your instructor's use of filled pauses during your initial class meeting. If you had to guess now, you'd probably make a mistake. If you had gone to the first class meeting with a conscious plan to observe your instructor's speech, however, you'd be more accurate.

In many cases, both simple and complex measurement devices help guard against inaccurate observations. Moreover, they add a degree of precision well beyond the capacity of the unassisted human senses. Suppose, for example, that you had taken detailed notes about your instructor's speech or used a tape recorder to record his or her remarks.

Overgeneralization   When we look for patterns among the specific things we observe around us, we often assume that a few similar events are evidence of a general pattern. Probably the tendency to overgeneralize is greatest when the pressure to arrive at a general understanding is high. Yet it also occurs without such pressure. Whenever overgeneralization does occur, it can misdirect or impede inquiry.

Imagine you are a news reporter covering an animal-rights demonstration. You have orders to turn in your story in just two hours, and you need to know the reasons that people are demonstrating. Rushing to the scene, you start interviewing them, asking for their reasons. If the first two demonstrators you interview give you essentially the same reason, you may simply assume that the other 3,000 are also there for that reason.

Sometimes, communication researchers guard against overgeneralization by committing themselves in advance to a sufficiently large sample of observations. Other researchers guard against overgeneralization by employing a sampling plan designed to ensure that they capture the diversity in a sample. The replication of inquiry provides another safeguard. Basically, this means repeating a study, checking to see if the same results are produced each time. Then the study may be repeated under slightly varied conditions.

Selective Observation   One danger of overgeneralization is that it may lead to selective observation. Once you have concluded that a particular pattern exists and have developed a general understanding of or explanation for it, you'll tend to focus on future events and situations that fit the pattern and ignore those that don't. For example, if you have concluded that people are telling a lie if they avert their eyes, you might miss a lot of good conversations with shy truth-tellers because you didn't take them seriously.

Sometimes, a research design will specify in advance the number and kind of observations to be made as a basis for reaching a conclusion. If we wanted to learn whether women are more likely than men to interrupt during a conversation, we'd commit ourselves to making a specified number of observations on that question in a research project. We might select a hundred conversations to observe. Alternately, when making direct observations of a given conversation, communication researchers would make a special effort to find "deviant cases"—precisely those that do not fit into the general pattern.

Illogical Reasoning   There are other ways of handling observations that contradict our conclusions about the way communication happens in daily life. Surely one of the most remarkable creations of the human mind is "the exception that proves the rule." That idea doesn't make any sense at all. An exception can draw attention to a rule or to a supposed rule, but in no system of **logic** can it prove the rule it contradicts. Yet we often use this pithy saying to brush away inconsistencies with a simple stroke of illogic.

What statisticians have called the *gambler's fallacy* is another illustration of illogic in day-to-day reasoning. A consistent run of either good or bad luck is presumed to foreshadow its opposite. Thus, the person who has been rejected from three job interviews feels that his or her luck is bound to turn with the fourth interview.

Although all of us sometimes fall into embarrassingly illogical reasoning in day-to-day life, communication researchers avoid this pitfall by using systems of logic consciously and explicitly. Chapter 4 will examine the logic(s) of scientific inquiry about communication in more depth. For now, it's enough to note that logical reasoning is a conscious activity for researchers and that they always have their colleagues around to keep them honest.

These, then, are a few of the ways that all of us go astray in our attempts to know about communication and some of the ways that the scientific approach protects inquiry from these pitfalls. **Scientific inquiry** is more conscious and careful than our casual efforts. In scientific inquiry, we are more wary of making mistakes and take special precautions to avoid error.

We hope the preceding comments underscore the point that making knowledge claims about anything, including communication, is not an obvious or trivial matter. Indeed, it's even more complicated than we've suggested so far.

What's Really "Real"?

Philosophers sometimes use the phrase *naive realism* to describe the way most of us operate in our daily lives. When you are speaking, you probably don't spend a lot of mental energy focusing on the neural connectors in the brain that lead your mouth and tongue to take particular positions to produce particular sounds. You take "speaking" pretty much for granted. When you are watching a movie on your new DVD player, you're not reflecting on the binary {0, 1} codes of which the images are made. Instead, you're enjoying the images for their entertainment value. We all live with a view that what's real is pretty obvious—and that view usually gets us through the day.

We don't want this book to interfere with your ability to deal with everyday life. However, we hope that the preceding discussions have demonstrated that the nature of "reality" is perhaps more complex than we tend to assume. Here are three views on reality that will provide a philosophical backdrop for the discussions of scientific inquiry to follow. Let's look at what are sometimes called premodern, modern, and postmodern views of reality (Anderson, 1990).

The Premodern View   This view of reality has guided most of human history. Our early ancestors all assumed that they saw things as they really were. In fact, this assumption was so fundamental that they didn't even see it as an assumption. No cavemom said to her cavekid, "Our tribe makes an assumption that evil spirits reside in the Old Twisted Tree." No, she said, "STAY OUT OF THAT TREE, OR YOU'LL TURN INTO A TOAD!"

As humans evolved and became aware of their diversity, they came to recognize that others did not always share their views of things. Thus, they may have discovered that another tribe didn't buy the wicked tree thing; in fact, the second tribe felt that the spirits in the tree were holy and beneficial. The discovery of this diversity led members of the first tribe to conclude that "some tribes I could name are pretty stupid." For them, the tree was still wicked, and they expected some misguided people to be moving to Toad City.

The Modern View   What philosophers call the modern view accepts such diversity as legitimate, a philosophical "different strokes for different folks." As a modern thinker, you would say, "I regard the spirits in the tree as evil, but I know others regard them as good. Neither of us is right or wrong. There are simply spirits in the tree. They are neither good nor evil, but different people have different ideas about them."

It's probably pretty easy for you to adopt the modern view. Some might regard a dandelion as a beautiful flower whereas others see only an annoying weed. To the premoderns, a dandelion has to be either one or the other. If you think it is a weed, it is *really* a weed, though you may admit that some people have a warped sense of beauty. In the modern view, a dandelion is simply a dandelion. It is a plant with yellow petals and green leaves. The concepts "beautiful flower" and "annoying weed" are subjective points of view imposed on the plant by different people. Neither is a quality of the plant itself, just as "good" and "evil" are concepts imposed on the spirits in the tree.

The Postmodern View   Increasingly, philosophers speak of a *postmodern* view of reality. In this view, the spirits don't exist. Neither does the dandelion. All that's "real" are the images we get through our points of view. Put differently, there's nothing *out there*; it's all *in here*. As Gertrude Stein said of Oakland, California, "There's no there, there."

No matter how bizarre the postmodern view may seem to you on first reflection, it has a certain ironic inevitability. Take a moment to notice the book you're reading; notice specifically what it looks like. Since you're reading these words, it probably looks like Figure 1-1A.

But does Figure 1-1A represent the way your book "really" looks? Or does it merely represent what the book looks like from your current point of view? Surely, Figures 1-1B, C, and D are equally valid representations. But these views of the book are so different from one another. Which is the "reality"?

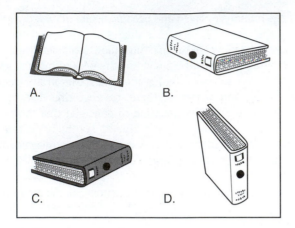

FIGURE 1-1 **A Book**

As this example should illustrate, there is no answer to the question "What does the book *really* look like?" All we can offer is the different ways that it looks from different points of view. Thus, according to the postmodern view, there is no "book," only various images of it from different points of view. And all the different images are equally "true."

Now let's apply this logic to a social situation. Imagine a husband and wife arguing. When the wife looks over at her quarreling husband, Figure 1-2 is what she sees. Take a minute to imagine what you would feel and think if you were the woman in this drawing. How would you explain later to an outsider, to your best friend, what had happened? What solutions to the conflict would seem appropriate if you were this woman? Perhaps you have been in similar situations, and your memories of those events can help you answer these questions.

Now let's shift gears dramatically. What the woman's husband sees is another matter altogether, as shown in Figure 1-3.

Take a minute to imagine experiencing the situation from his point of view. What thoughts and feelings would you have? How would you tell your best friend what had happened? What solutions would seem appropriate for resolving the conflict?

Now consider a third point of view. Suppose you're an outside observer, watching this interaction between a wife and husband. What would it look like to you now? Unfortunately, we can't easily portray the third point of view without knowing something about the personal feelings, beliefs, past experiences, and so forth that you would bring to your task as "outside" observer. (Though we call you an *outside* observer, you are, of course, observing from *inside* your own mental system.)

To take an extreme example, if you were a confirmed male chauvinist, you'd probably see the fight pretty much the same way the husband sees it. On the other hand, if you were committed to the view that men are unreasonable bums, you'd see things the way the wife sees them.

But consider this. Imagine that you look at this situation and see two unreasonable people quarreling irrationally with each other. Could you get the feeling that they are equally responsible for the conflict?

Or imagine that you see two people facing a difficult human situation, each doing the best he or she can to resolve it. Imagine feeling compassion for them and noticing how each of them attempts to end the hostility, even though the gravity of the problem keeps them fighting.

Notice how different these last two views are. Which is a "true" picture of what is happening between the wife

FIGURE 1-2 **Wife's Point of View**

FIGURE 1-3 **Husband's Point of View**

and the husband? You win the prize if you notice that the personal baggage you brought along to the observational task would again color your perception of what is happening here.

The postmodern view represents a critical dilemma for scientists. Although their task is to observe and understand what is "really" happening, they are all human and, as such, bring along personal orientations that will color what they observe and how they explain it. There is ultimately no way people can totally step outside their humanness to see and understand the world as it "really" is.

Whereas the modern view acknowledges the inevitability of human subjectivity, the postmodern view suggests there is no "objective" reality to be observed in the first place. There are only our several subjective views.

We're going to let you ponder these views on your own for a while. We'll return to this discussion in Chapter 3, when we focus on more specific scientific paradigms that organize communication research. In particular, we'll introduce different approaches to social scientific thinking in communication research. What you'll see, ultimately, is that (1) established scientific procedures sometimes allow you to deal effectively with this dilemma—that is, you can study people and help them through their difficulties without being able to view "reality" directly—and (2) the philosophical stances we've presented suggest a powerful range of possibilities for structuring your research.

Let's turn now to the foundations of the scientific approach to understanding communication.

THE FOUNDATIONS OF SCIENTIFIC INQUIRY ABOUT COMMUNICATION

The two pillars of scientific inquiry about any phenomenon, including communication, are logic and observation. A scientific understanding of communication must (1) make sense and (2) correspond with what we observe. Both elements are essential to the scientific approach and relate to three major aspects of the overall scientific enterprise: *theory, data collection,* and *data analysis.*

As a gross generalization, **theory** deals with the logical aspect of scientific inquiry, and **data collection** deals with the observational aspect. **Data analysis** brings logical and observational aspects together in the search for patterns in what is observed. Though most of this book deals primarily with data collection and data analysis—demonstrating how to conduct empirical research about communication—you must recognize that a scientific approach involves all three elements. As such, Part 1 of this book deals largely with the theoretical context of research; Parts 2 and 3 focus on data collection and analysis.

Let's turn now to some of the fundamental issues that distinguish the scientific approach—theory, data collection, and analysis—from other ways of looking at communication phenomena.

An Empirical Enterprise

A scientific approach to communication is an **empirical enterprise**, which means that communication researchers base their knowledge claims on observations rather than their "armchair speculations" or their own personal values. In casual conversations we sometimes hear people say things like "Oh, that's just a theory!" when they wish to criticize someone for engaging in idle speculation that is out of touch with the world. To communication researchers, "theory" is neither idle speculation nor removed from empirical observation; scientific theory has to do with knowledge claims about communication phenomena, and it occupies a central place in the logic of a scientific approach.

This means that theory—and science itself—cannot settle debates about value. Communication researchers cannot determine whether negative political campaign ads are better or worse than positive political campaign ads except in terms of agreed-on criteria. We could determine scientifically whether negatively or positively oriented political campaign ads most supported the interests of democracy only if we could agree on some definition of what those interests are; our conclusion in that case would depend totally on this agreement. The conclusions would have no general meaning beyond that.

By the same token, if we could agree that the absence of divorce, say, is an acceptable measure of a good marriage, then we could determine scientifically whether couples who talk about the state of their relationship or couples who refrain from such talk have better marriages. Again, our conclusion would be inextricably tied to the given criterion. As a practical matter, people seldom agree on criteria for determining issues of value, so scientific research is seldom useful in settling such value-based debates.

We'll consider this issue in more detail in Chapter 9, when we look at *evaluation research.* As you'll see, communication researchers have become increasingly involved in studying programs that reflect ideological points of view, so one of the biggest problems researchers face is getting people to agree on criteria of success and failure. Yet such criteria are essential if communication research is to tell us anything useful about matters of value. By analogy, a stopwatch can't tell us if one sprinter is better than another unless we can agree that speed is the critical criterion.

Although scientifically based communication research is not well equipped to make value-laden knowledge claims (e.g., claims about good–bad, right–wrong, success–failure), the conduct of scientific research itself is shaped by ethical values in order to protect the rights and interests of all human participants. We discuss the ethical values of research in Chapter 5.

Social Regularities

In large part, communication researchers aim to find patterns of regularity in communication phenomena. Without patterns, there is no meaning, no prediction, no explanation. That aim, of course, applies to all science, but it is sometimes a barrier for people when they first approach the scientific study of communication. What about the exceptions, you might ask? It's not important that a particular woman self-discloses less than a particular man if women more so than men disclose more personal information about themselves overall. The pattern still exists. **Social regularities** represent probabilistic patterns, and a general pattern need not be reflected in 100 percent of the observable cases.

This rule applies in physical science as well as social scientific communication research. In genetics, for example, the mating of a blue-eyed person with a brown-eyed person will *probably* result in a brown-eyed offspring. However, the birth of a blue-eyed child does not challenge the observed regularity, since the geneticist states only that the brown-eyed offspring is more likely and, further, that brown-eyed offspring will be born in a certain percentage of the cases. The communication researcher makes a similar, probabilistic prediction—that women overall are more likely to disclose personal information.

Aggregates, Not Individuals

Therefore, social regularities in communication do exist; further, they are both susceptible to and worthy of theoretical and empirical study. As such, communication researchers primarily study social patterns rather than individual ones. All the regular patterns we've mentioned have reflected the **aggregate** or collective actions and situations of many individuals. Although communication researchers often study motivations that affect individuals' communication, the individual per se is seldom the subject of communication research.

Social scientific communication theories deal then, typically, with aggregated, not individual, behavior. Their purpose is to render intelligible or to explain aggregated patterns of human communicative action even when the individuals participating in them may change over time. It could be said that communication researchers don't even seek to study *people*. Instead, they study the *systems* in and through which people operate, the systems that explain why people do what they do.

An emphasis on aggregate patterns can be difficult to understand at first; our most natural attempts at understanding usually take place at the level of the concrete and idiosyncratic. That's just the way we think.

Imagine that someone says to you, "Women ought to get back into the kitchen where they belong." You are likely to hear that comment in terms of what you know about the speaker. If it's your old Uncle Harry, who, you recall, is also strongly opposed to daylight saving time, zip codes, and electricity, you are likely to think his latest pronouncement simply fits into his rather dated point of view about things in general.

If, on the other hand, the statement issues forth from a politician who is trailing a female challenger and who has also begun making statements about women being emotionally unfit for public office, not understanding politics, and the like, you may hear his latest comment in the context of this political challenge and the politician's rhetorical strategy to win the election.

In both examples, you're trying to understand the thoughts of a particular individual. In a scientific approach, however, communication researchers go beyond that level of understanding to seek insights into classes or types of individuals. Regarding the two examples just described, they might use terms such as *old-fashioned* or *bigot* to describe the kind of person who made the comment. In other words, they try to identify the concrete individual with some set of similar individuals, and that identification operates on the basis of abstract concepts.

One implication of this approach is that when this venture into understanding and explanation ends, communication researchers will be able to make sense out of more than one person. This is not to say that communication researchers don't care about real people. They certainly do. Most of the researchers we know were attracted to the enterprise of communication research because of their abiding awe of, and respect for, the richness and complexity of the communication experience.

In Chapter 3, we will demonstrate that communication researchers theorize about and observe communication in very different ways. None of these ways is better or worse than the others—they simply reflect different assumptions about the two prongs of the scientific enterprise: logic and observation. All communication researchers are empirical, and all of them study regularities of aggregates.

KNOWLEDGE CLAIMS ABOUT COMMUNICATION

Thus far, we've introduced the field of communication through example by suggesting some possible questions and issues that could be studied scientifically by communication researchers. In this section, however, we want to discuss more systematically the sorts of knowledge claims of interest to communication researchers. Think of this section as your navigational sailing guide to the waters of communication research.

What Communication Researchers Study

If you're a communication studies major, you probably have some inkling about the range of phenomena of interest to communication researchers. But if you're new to the field of communication, or if you still find yourself getting that "deer in the headlights" feeling when your friends or family members ask you what a communication studies major is about, this section is for you.

Communication studies is a field of research on the production and uses of symbols (both linguistic and nonverbal, whether face to face or mediated) in concrete social and cultural contexts to enable the dynamics of systems, society, and culture. Three key terms of this definition—*production, uses,* and *dynamics*—underscore that communication is a process. Considered as a whole, communication studies is a broad field, one that encompasses both social scientific and humanistically oriented research. In this book, we're concentrating on social scientific approaches. However, when we turn to qualitative methods in Part 3 of the book, the distinction between "scientific" and "humanistic" approaches becomes easily blurred, as we shall see.

Researchers in fields other than communication studies often study communication phenomena. In this sense, the study of communication is truly a multidisciplinary undertaking. However, researchers in communication studies generally position communication as the primary phenomenon they seek to understand. By contrast, researchers from other fields tend to study communication because it is a means toward understanding other phenomena. For example, a psychologist might study how individuals produce messages because of an interest in understanding how individual dispositions or personality characteristics affect behavior. By contrast, a communication researcher would be more likely to study how in-

dividuals produce messages because of an interest in understanding the message production process.

Communication researchers typically study communication with three interests in mind. First, researchers are interested in studying the processes of message production, transmission, and meaning making. Such a focus could be examined in a variety of contexts and levels. One researcher might be interested in the processes by which individuals produce messages responsive to particular goals such as impression management or social influence. Another researcher might be interested in the joint meaning making that transpires in such dyads as friendships. Yet another researcher might focus at the societal level by studying the institutional and organizational processes of producing TV shows.

Second, communication researchers systematically examine the content or form of communicative messages. Again, a range of contexts can be studied with this particular focus. For example, a family communication researcher might study the content of family talk at the dinner table, perhaps with an eye toward understanding how children become socialized to think about "current events" in the world around them. A researcher with interests in television might examine the content of network programming to determine its portrayal of such societal institutions as the law.

Third, communication researchers are interested in studying the functions and effects of messages. For example, one researcher might have an interest in studying the persuasive effects of anti-smoking public service messages targeted at young adolescents. Another researcher might be interested in examining cultural differences in how people save face in giving verbal accounts of their actions. Someone else might study how adolescents co-opt various symbols from the popular music scene in order to construct certain identities.

Another way to get a feel for the range of interests held by communication researchers is to examine the range of contexts in which communication is examined. If you leaf through several communication journals or the proceedings of professional communication conferences, you will see that scientific inquiry about communication addresses a wide range of issues, including (but not limited to) the following:

- Communication policy and law: inquiry into the role of lawmaking and policy making relevant to various communication systems. Wackwitz (2002), for instance, engaged in a critical textual analysis of the majority opinions of Supreme Court Justice Warren Burger in the Miller obscenity cases, identifying underlying assumptions about the potential influence of mass media in the interpretation of freedom of speech.

- Communication and technology: inquiry into the communication process in existing or emerging new technologies. Wright (2002), for example, recently conducted an online survey to study the motives of participants in 20 different online support groups, finding that a desire to pass the time correlated with daily time spent online with the support group.
- Comparative media systems: inquiry into the structures and functions of media systems in various nations. Tanner (2001) conducted a content analysis of an online forum devoted to discussion of the arrest of the Chilean ex-dictator Augusto Pinochet. Tanner argued that this forum functioned as a public space to shape public opinion and collective memories.
- Cross-cultural communication: inquiry into the communication practices of people of different national cultures. Oetzel and his colleagues (2001) examined face and facework during conflicts across four national cultures: China, Germany, Japan, and the United States.
- Development communication: inquiry into communication in national development. Papa and his colleagues (2000) employed several methods to study how the education content of a radio soap opera achieved social change in a village in India.
- Family communication: inquiry into communication between family members. Miller and Lee (2001) studied how parents communicate disappointment to sons and daughters.
- Group communication: inquiry into the communication between members of task groups or work teams. Pavitt and Johnson (2002) examined the extent to which group discussions feature "spiraling," returning to proposals discussed earlier in the course of a meeting.
- Health communication: inquiry into communicative messages focused on health promotion and health care. Morgan and Miller (2002) examined factors relevant to successful communication campaigns to encourage the public to participate in organ donation (giving the "gift of life").
- Instructional communication: inquiry into the communication process associated with learning contexts. Braun (2001) presented a case study about service learning in an organizational communication course.
- Interpersonal communication: inquiry into the communication between people in everyday social and personal relationships, including acquaintances, friends, romantic partners, and marital partners. Caughlin (2002) examined the relationship between a demand–withdraw pattern of communication between spouses and their marital satisfaction.
- Intrapersonal communication: inquiry into the cognitive processes related to the production or interpretation of behavior. Smith and Ellis (2001) examined people's reports of "memorable messages" from others that came to mind when self-assessing their own actions—for example, a message to "do your best" after achieving a major accomplishment.
- Language and social interaction: inquiry into the particulars of how talk is enacted in specific situations or cultural groups. We learn about the cultural meaning of "listening" among Blackfeet people in Montana in Carbaugh's (1999) ethnographic study.
- Legal communication: inquiry into communication in legal contexts. Reinard and Arsenault (2000) recently conducted an experiment on *voir dire,* the questioning of potential jurors to determine their fitness to serve on a given jury. The researchers found that certain kinds of questions affected jurors' perceptions of defendant guilt.
- Mass communication: inquiry into the mediated communication process, including the electronic, cinematic, and print media. Berger (2001) examined how news media use quantitative depictions of trends in ways calculated to increase their drama, thereby making things seem worse than they are.
- Organizational communication: inquiry into the communicative messages between organizational members. Kirby and Krone (2002) recently conducted a qualitative study of how organizational members' talk about various work–family benefits affected the use of such benefits. Among other findings, the researchers found that when co-workers complained about having to work harder to cover for those using family leave, they could affect fellow workers' decisions against use of those initiatives in the future.
- Political communication: inquiry into the communication associated with politics and public argument. Benoit and Hansen (2001) determined that the questions journalists ask of presidential candidates during televised debates do not reflect the issues of interest to voters as represented in issue-based public opinion polls.

- Popular communication: inquiry into the communication associated with contemporary popular culture. Acosta-Alzuru and Kreshel (2002) interviewed mothers and daughters about the "American Girl" marketing of a line of dolls, accessories, and books, inquiring about an identity as an "American girl."
- Public communication: inquiry into the communication between speakers and their audiences in public speaking contexts. Behnke and Sawyer (2001) examined the role of physiological arousal in speech anxiety.
- Public relations: inquiry into the communication between organizations and specified publics. Boyd (2001) used Boeing's corporate rhetoric as a case study to examine how the rhetorical boundary between public and private spheres is fuzzy.

Whew! It should be evident from this partial list that knowledge claims about communication are to a large extent organized by the context of the message—for example, who is communicating, the medium of communication, and the purpose of the communicative exchange. However, these distinctions often get fuzzy. For example, a study of how people initiate or sustain their relationships through the use of e-mail bridges both interpersonal communication and new technologies. A study of the interaction patterns of workers in a TV newsroom bridges both mass communication and organizational communication. And so on.

But how can you access the knowledge claims that researchers have already made about communication? Well, you might say "That's what textbooks are for!" To a certain extent, you are right—the purpose of a textbook is to bring together existing knowledge claims about a given subject matter. But the knowledge claims that appear in a textbook are the ones decided upon by the author of the text, based on his or her reading of the research. You might desire more independence than this, wanting to decide for yourself whether a certain knowledge claim about communication should be accepted. In addition, especially given the costs of textbooks these days, you might not want to invest in an entire book when the question of interest to you is more narrowly focused. And if you want the latest knowledge "hot off the press," you will need to know how to access conference proceedings or scholarly journals; textbooks often have a longer production time than is characteristic of proceedings or journals. Should you want to do a research project on your own—for example, a senior thesis—one of the first tasks that awaits you is a "review of literature," an integrative summary of existing research on your topic of interest. The next section should provide some initial help as you figure out how to locate existing knowledge claims about communication that are based on social scientific research. We'll return to this subject in greater detail in Chapter 2.

The Dissemination of Communication Research

Researchers interested in studying communication tend to be affiliated with colleges and universities or affiliated with various public or private research-based organizations. They typically belong to at least one professional society or association whose mission is to support the generation of knowledge about communication. These professional societies or associations sponsor annual conferences or meetings where researchers gather to present their latest research findings to one another. These societies or associations also sponsor scholarly journals, which publish research four to six times annually. In addition, communication researchers often publish their research in interdisciplinary journals sponsored by professional associations or by publishers outside of the communication studies field per se.

Sometimes, communication researchers don't disseminate their research findings in proceedings or journals because the findings are not designed for public consumption. Many researchers conduct proprietary research—that is, research sponsored by a private source and technically owned by that source. For example, a communication researcher may be an organizational consultant who conducts research in a given organization at the request of its top management; the researcher submits the research report to the organizational client, and its findings are exclusively for use by the organization that paid for the research services. For example, Corporation ABC might be experiencing a lot of employee turnover and the communication difficulties that can arise when there is an influx of new employees all at once. A communication researcher could be hired to find out how well the new employee orientation program is working and ways it could be improved.

Some Dissemination Sites for Communication Research

Communication researchers tend to be located in any of several academic departments, including communication, communication studies, information sciences, mass communication, speech, and speech communication, just to name a few. And communication researchers have several professional associations with which to affiliate.

The list below provides a sense of the range of associations or societies, and the journals they sponsor:

- National Communication Association (NCA) (www.natcom.org). This professional organization was the first to sponsor research publications in communication. Originally founded in 1914 as the National Association of Academic Teachers of Public Speaking, this organization has grown as scholarly interests have expanded beyond public speaking. Name changes have indexed this growth: Until 1970, this association was called the Speech Association of America; from 1970 to 1997, it was known as the Speech Communication Association; and in 1997, it became the National Communication Association. This organization is one of the two primary professional associations that serve the full range of communication research topics of inquiry. Affiliated with the NCA are four regional associations that tend to parallel the national organization in structure and purpose: the Central States Communication Association (CSCA), the Eastern Communication Association (ECA), the Southern States Communication Association (SSCA), and the Western States Communication Association (WSCA).
- The International Communication Association (ICA) (www.icahdq.org). This is the second primary professional association for communication researchers that serves the full range of topics of inquiry. Founded in 1949 as the National Society for the Study of Communication, this organization changed its name to the current one in the 1960s.

In addition to these two associations, which serve all communication researchers, any number of more-specialized professional organizations focus on particular aspects of communication. Here are a few of these more specialized organizations, just to give you an idea of what we're referring to:

- Association for Education in Journalism and Mass Communication (AEJMC). Founded in 1912 as the American Association of Teachers of Journalism, this organization focuses on mass communication, especially journalistic media.

- Broadcast Education Association (BEA). This organization held its first convention in 1954 as the Association of Professional Broadcast Education. This association is of particular interest to researchers who study the electronic media and the effects of mediated messages on audiences.
- The Public Relations Society of America and the Foundation for Public Relations Research. Formed in 1945 and 1975, respectively, these two professional associations are of particular interest to people interested in research on public relations.
- The World Association of Public Opinion Research. This organization is an international association devoted to research on the opinions, attitudes, and behaviors of people in the various countries of the world.
- The International Association for Relationship Research. Two interdisciplinary groups for the study of social and personal relationships merged in 2002 to form this new association. This association holds particular relevance for interpersonal and family communication scholars.
- The International Society for Intercultural Education Training and Research, the International and Intercultural Communication Association, the Pacific and Asian Communication Association, and the World Communication Association. These professional associations are of special interest to communication researchers with interests in cross-cultural communication, cultural communication, and international communication.
- The Organization for Research on Women and Communication; Women in Communication, Inc.; and the Organization for the Study of Communication, Language, and Gender. All of these professional associations share a focus on gender and communication.

These professional associations, both general and specialized, sponsor a number of journals where communication research is published. In addition, communication researchers publish their findings in other scholarly outlets. Appendix A provides a summary of some of the key publication outlets where you can locate communication research.

Main Points

- Inquiry about communication is a natural human activity.

- We know much of what we know by agreement rather than by experience.
- Tradition and authority are important sources of understanding.

❏ When we understand through experience, we make observations and seek patterns of regularities in what we observe.

❏ In day-to-day inquiry about communication, we often make mistakes. Science offers protection against such mistakes.

❏ Whereas people often observe inaccurately, such errors can be avoided in science by making observation a careful and deliberate activity.

❏ We sometimes jump to general conclusions on the basis of only a few observations. Communication researchers can avoid overgeneralization through replication, or repeating studies.

❏ Once a conclusion has been reached, we sometimes ignore evidence that contradicts that conclusion, paying attention only to evidence that confirms it. Communication researchers commit themselves in advance to a set of observations to be made regardless of apparent patterns, or they devise a research plan to seek "deviant cases," if any exist.

❏ People sometimes reason illogically. Communication researchers avoid this by being as careful and deliberate in their reasoning as in their observations. Moreover, the public nature of communication research means that researchers have their colleagues looking over their shoulders.

❏ Social scientific theory and research about communication do not engage in value judgments of good–bad or right–wrong.

❏ Communication researchers look for regularities in social life.

❏ Communication researchers are interested in human aggregates, not individuals.

❏ Although communication researchers observe people, they seek to study underlying systems or patterns, not individuals.

❏ Communication researchers study the production and uses of symbols by using the methods of social science.

❏ Communication researchers study the processes of message production, transmission, and meaning making; message forms and content; and the functions and effects of communication.

❏ Communication research is either proprietary or conducted in the public domain.

❏ Public-domain communication research is disseminated through a number of publication outlets, many of which are scholarly journals sponsored by professional associations and societies to which communication researchers belong.

Key Terms

observation	data analysis
logic	empirical
scientific inquiry	social regularities
theory	aggregate
data collection	communication studies

Review Questions and Exercises

1. Review the common errors of human inquiry discussed in this chapter. Find a magazine or newspaper article, or perhaps a letter to the editor, that illustrates one of these errors. Discuss how a scientist could have avoided it.

2. Go to one of the communication journals listed in Appendix A. Examine the Contents page for a couple of issues of this journal to gain a sense of the range of topics addressed by communication researchers.

3. Identify someone who is active in the conduct of communication research, and e-mail him or her to find out a bit more about the kinds of issues that interest him or her in research. (Your instructor may be able to suggest researchers you could interview.)

Continuity Project

To demonstrate the interconnections among the various elements of communication research, you might want to apply the materials of each successive chapter to a single research project. We'll suggest here the topic of communication and gender/sex, but your instructor may suggest something different. Why the reference to "gender/sex"? "Gender" refers to socially prescribed meanings for the sexes—for example, the social expectations attached to being a male or female in society. "Sex" is a category based on genetic and biological characteristics. When our goal is to compare men and women on some characteristic or phenomenon, we're probably talking about studying a sex difference. When we want to examine how masculinity and femininity relate to communication (that is, how to be a "man" and a "woman," respectively), we're probably talking about a gender difference. Some of the continuity projects in this book will address communication differences between males and females, whereas other continuity projects will examine socially prescribed meanings for being male and female.

In the context of this first chapter, you might consider these issues: Write down all that you think you know about gender/sex and communication—how males communicate, how females communicate, and how they communicate together. For each of your beliefs, ask yourself how you formed this belief. Did you come to this belief through personal experience? Through watching men and women portrayed on television while you were growing up? Through sage advice from your "aunt Sophie"? How might a communication researcher go about finding out how males and females communicate? See if you can locate any existing research on gender/sex and communication in the sources identified in Appendix A.

Additional Readings

Cole, S. (1992). *Making science: Between nature and society.* Cambridge, MA: Harvard University Press. If you're interested in a deeper examination of science as a social enterprise, you may find this book to be a fascinating analysis.

Nisbett, R., & Ross, L. (1980). *Human inference: Strategies and shortcomings of social judgment.* Englewood Cliffs, NJ: Prentice-Hall. If you're interested in finding out more about the kinds of perceptual errors we make in everyday life, this volume is a classic.

Trent, J. S. (Ed.) (1998). *Communication: Views from the helm for the 21st century.* Needham Heights, MA: Allyn & Bacon. Here's a recent volume in which several leading scholars in communication studies talk about future directions for communication research in many of the areas of inquiry mentioned in this chapter.

InfoTrac College Edition
http://www.infotrac-college.com/ wadsworth/access.html

Access the latest news and journal articles with InfoTrac College Edition, an easy-to-use online database of reliable, full-length articles from hundreds of top academic journals. Conduct an electronic search using the following search terms:

- communication
- postmodernism
- modernism
- perception
- meaning
- empirical

CHAPTER 2

Basic Building Blocks in Conducting Communication Research

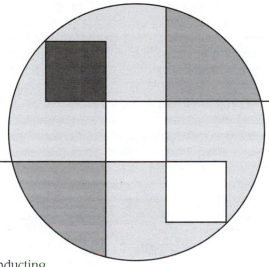

What You'll Learn in This Chapter

Here you'll learn about some basic issues that you face in conducting a research study. Planning a study requires you to make several decisions, and we'll review these choices. Planning a study also requires reading existing research, and this chapter discusses how to read a communication research report. Writing up a research proposal is often part of the planning process, and we'll discuss some basic writing issues. You should leave this chapter with an overview of the issues addressed in depth in the remaining chapters.

INTRODUCTION

Social science is an enterprise dedicated to "finding out." No matter what you want to find out, though, there will likely be a great many ways of doing it. That's true in life generally. Suppose, for example, that you want to find out whether a particular automobile—say, the new Burpo-Blasto—would be a good car for you. You could, of course, buy one and find out that way. You could talk to a lot of B-B owners or to people who considered buying one and didn't. You might check the classified ads to see if there are a lot of B-Bs being sold cheap. You could read a consumer magazine's evaluation of Burpo-Blastos, and so on. The same situation occurs in scientific inquiry.

This chapter addresses the planning of scientific inquiry—designing a strategy for finding out something about communication. Although the special details vary according to what you wish to study, there are two major things to consider. First, you must specify as clearly as possible what you want to find out. Second, you must determine the best way to do it. Interestingly, if you can handle the first consideration fully, you'll probably handle the second in the same process. As mathematicians say, a properly framed question contains the answer.

Ultimately, scientific inquiry comes down to making observations and interpreting what you've observed. (Parts 2 and 3 of this book deal with these aspects of communication research in depth.) Before you can observe and analyze, however, you need a plan. You need to determine what you're going to observe and analyze: why and how.

Although developing a research plan occurs at the beginning of a research project, it involves all the steps of the subsequent project. The comments that follow, then, should (1) give you some guidance on how to start a research project and (2) provide an overview of the topics that follow in later chapters of the book. Ultimately, you need to grasp the research process as a *whole* to create a research plan or design. Unfortunately, both textbooks and human cognition operate on the basis of sequential parts.

We'll start by briefly examining how you go about selecting a topic to study. Key to this selection is your ability to narrow the topic down so that you are adequately focused when you undertake the data-gathering phase of the study. Central to this process of topic selection is your ability to read existing research literature in your topic area. Figuring out the main purpose of your study is also of central importance in narrowing down your topic area. Once you have narrowed your topic and determined your purpose, you need to formulate your research question or research hypothesis. Then we'll turn to various issues related to your research design. We'll consider various options in your units of analysis—the what or whom you want to study. Next, we'll consider different orientations toward time and space in the study you are planning. As you'll see, it is sometimes appropriate to examine a static cross-section of communicative life, but other studies follow communication processes across time. In addition, some research is dependent on the physical setting in which the phenomenon is situated, whereas other research is relatively independent of the particular setting or situation. Last, you need to decide which methods are best suited to your particular research purpose.

Finally, we discuss how to write research proposals. Often, the actual conduct of research needs to be preceded by this detailing of your intentions—to obtain funding for a major project or to get your instructor's approval for a class project. You'll see that this step offers an excellent excuse and forum for ensuring that you have considered all aspects of your research in advance.

Our brief overview of the overall research process serves three purposes: (1) It gives you a map to the remainder of this book, (2) it helps you see how you might go about designing a study, and (3) it helps you see how you might go about evaluating a study conducted by someone else.

SELECTING AND NARROWING YOUR TOPIC AREA

Choosing a topic sounds like the easiest step in planning a research study, but in truth, it's the most challenging. Once you have figured out what it is that you want to study, the rest of the process sorts itself out fairly readily. We assume because you're taking a course in communication inquiry that the subject matter of communication holds some inherent interest value for you. Why so? What about communication interests you and has attracted you to begin with to this field of study? If you can answer this question, you have taken your first step toward selecting your topic area—the best research comes from researchers who seek answers to the questions that hold high interest value for them.

A useful exercise to locate topics of interest is to reflect on your recent communication experiences. Maybe you're really attracted to someone and don't know how to make a good impression on this person. There's a good research topic area lurking in this state of affairs—impression management through verbal and nonverbal communication. Or perhaps you just received a particularly vicious e-mail message—you wonder why people say things through e-mail that they probably wouldn't say face to face. Another good topic has just emerged here—the perceived norms of appropriate conduct over e-mail versus face-to-face communication. Perhaps you took a break from reading this book to catch a couple of music videos on MTV and were struck by their portrayals of men and women. Aha! Another topic possibility: gender portrayals on MTV. Maybe you're having a lot of arguments and disagreements with your roommate right now, and you'd like to find out how you can handle these conflicts more constructively. Your everyday communicative experiences are a gold mine of possible topics to explore. The key is to locate a topic area that interests you.

If you're having trouble identifying a topic area based on personal reflection, go on a reconnaissance mission and find out what has interested other communication researchers. We have already referred you to Appendix A, a list of journals and other references where communication research is published. Go and peruse a few issues of some journals to see if your interest and curiosity about a topic are aroused. You might also find it helpful to access handbooks or other references whose purpose is to survey and distill a large quantity of material. Appendix B provides some suggestions on how to use the library, and Appendix C provides some insights into Web-based research. Rebecca Rubin, Alan Rubin, and Linda Piele (2000) have written a very helpful book titled *Communication Research: Strategies and Sources* that provides a comprehensive list of resources and searching strategies to find existing communication research.

Usually, when a topic interests us, it's not quite "ready for prime time" yet and needs to be narrowed down so that it is researchable. By researchable, we mean that it is capable of being answered (even if tentatively) in a single study. In general, we use this rule of thumb to guide the narrowing-down process for researchers new to the process: If you are working in the tradition of variables, narrow the study down to two variables (three at the utmost); if you are working with semantic relationships or rules, narrow the study down to one. What are "variables," "semantic relationships," and "rules," you might ask. We'll return to this issue in depth in Chapter 3.

In short, in order for you to narrow down your topic area, you're going to have to come to grips with several of the issues we will discuss in this and the next three chapters. What is your purpose in conducting the research? Do you want to describe some state of affairs, explore some phenomenon, examine why something occurs, examine how something functions, or understand what (and how) something means? When you figure out your basic purpose, this will help guide you to the appropriate kind of methods—either the quantitative methods tool kit, the qualitative methods tool kit, or some combination thereof, as in multi-method research.

What unit of analysis do you want to study? Are you interested in examining some characteristic about individuals? Groups? Organizations? Maybe you're interested in studying social artifacts of some kind. You will find that what you want to know is tied up with the question of units of analysis.

Essential to your narrowing-down process will be library and Web work in which you uncover what other researchers have published on your topic of interest and the methods they have used. We'll start with the review of literature and then return to other factors that are important to your task of narrowing down your topic.

CONDUCTING A LITERATURE REVIEW

A **review of literature** is a comprehensive survey of what researchers have already done in your topic area. Depending on your topic area, a review of literature is either a fairly limited exercise, with only a handful of studies, or an overwhelming task in which you are faced with the prospects of thousands of published research studies. Once you dig into the body of existing work in your topic area, you will get a sense of the number of studies you are dealing with. Obviously, the larger the domain of existing studies on a given topic, the greater the importance of narrowing down your topic, thereby winnowing down the number of relevant studies that you will need to read and digest.

Usually, the research relevant to your literature review is published in scholarly journals (see Appendix A). These are the so-called primary sources in your literature review. Occasionally, an author summarizes a large number of studies in a book chapter or in an entire book; such summaries are known as secondary sources. Such secondary sources are very useful to read, especially at the beginning of a literature review, because they provide you with a general overview of the range of issues, and their complexities, on a given topic. A secondary summary of a body of literature can also give you insight into key researchers in a topic area, thereby positioning you to conduct a literature search not just by subject but by author as well. Ultimately, however, a good review of literature works with primary sources—original research studies published in scholarly journals.

When students new to the research process undertake a library search for relevant research literature, a typical response we hear is "I couldn't find anything on my topic." While this might well be so, it is often the case that students do not cast a wide enough net in locating existing research. Figuring out keywords by which to conduct the search is very important. Let's suppose that you're interested in how people get their way with others, gaining their compliance with various kinds of requests. If you use the keywords "getting your way" in searching catalog holdings of titles or subjects or in conducting an electronic search of abstracted or indexed journals, you might come up short, with no citations. If you concluded at this point that no research exists on your topic area, you would unfortunately be making a huge error! A great deal of research exists on this topic; you simply need to figure out the keywords by which you can gain access to it in your searching. Usually, a given phenomenon is captured in the research literature through multiple keywords. Once you identify one keyword, you can springboard to other related keywords by studying the published studies that surface through your initial keyword. For example, most journals require that researchers identify four or five keywords to be associated with each published study. These are printed on the first page of a published article and are picked up in the primary abstracts and indexes relevant to communication research (see Appendix B). Your instructor or a reference librarian is a wonderful resource in helping you identify initial keywords to use in conducting your subject searches. On the topic area of "getting your way," for example, you will quickly identify a wealth of relevant keywords, including "persuasion," "social influence," "compliance-gaining," "requests," "attitude change," "parent–child discipline," "manipulation," and "coercion."

Another way in which the beginning researcher erroneously concludes that "nothing has been done on my topic" is to define the population of participants or the setting too narrowly. For example, suppose that a student wants to know what University of Iowa students think about a required public speaking class for entering first-year students. A survey of the literature is likely to turn up nothing on this particular topic with this particular population—University of Iowa students. However, if you search more broadly—say, with such keywords as "public speaking," "public speaking classes," "communication anxiety," "university requirements," "communication skills"—you might uncover research relevant to the broader issue of the value of public speaking courses. Your task would be sorting out which research studies hold greatest relevance to your desire to find out what University of Iowa students think about a required public speaking course.

What do you do when you discover that the study in mind has already been done? Perhaps you'll decide to use a previous researcher's method or even replicate an earlier study. The independent **replication** of research projects is a standard procedure in the physical sciences, and it's just as important in communication, although communication researchers tend to overlook that.

Here's another approach closely related to replication that you might take. Suppose a topic has been studied previously using field research methods. Can you design an experiment that would test the findings those earlier researchers produced? Did a survey yield results that you'd like to explore in greater detail through some qualitative observations and in-depth interviews? The use of several different research methods to test the same finding is sometimes called **triangulation,** and you should always keep it in mind as a valuable research strategy. Because each research method has particular strengths and weaknesses, there is always a danger that research findings will reflect, at least in part, the method of inquiry. In the best of all worlds, your own research design should bring more than one research method to bear on the topic.

You might want to go beyond replication or triangulation and study some aspect of the topic that you feel previous researchers have overlooked. A primary way you narrow your topic area is to identify gaps or absences in existing research: What has not yet been studied? When you are reading existing research, it is very important to ask yourself "What is missing from this body of work?" Often, researchers will help you figure out gaps, particularly as you read the "Discussion" section of published research studies. One of the obligations of a researcher in this section of an article is to indicate directions for future research—that is, current gaps that need to be addressed in the future.

Sometimes when you read a body of existing literature, you uncover equivocal findings: Half the studies have found X, and the other half have found Y. Such pockets of equivocality provide fruitful directions for narrowing down your research topic. Specifically, you can focus on one possible reason for the equivocality of findings and pursue that in your research study.

When you undertake a review of literature, it is important to survey the relevant research for each facet of your proposed study. If your topic area is focused on the relationship between two factors or characteristics, for example, then you need to review the literature for each factor separately and then locate research in which the factors were considered together in a single study. If your topic seeks to understand situated meanings, you need to review separately, and then together, the specific phenomenon you are studying (e.g., politeness rules, rules of gender construction) as well as the situation, setting, or group (e.g., the working class, young adults).

It makes intuitive sense that you would want to search for combination studies—studies in which both of your factors were studied together or studies in which the phenomenon of interest has been studied in the situation/group of interest. But what's the logic of undertaking literature reviews of each component separately? The operative word here is *logic*. If you discover that no one has engaged in research in which your factors have been combined or your phenomenon has not been studied in the situation/setting/group of interest to you, it is up to you to build an argument, using deductive reasoning, for why and how your proposed study makes sense. (We'll elaborate on this kind of reasoning and its close cousin, inductive reasoning, in Chapter 4.) You will share this reasoning when you write up your proposal for research, and again when you seek to publish the findings of your study.

We'll return to this point when we discuss the formulation of research questions and hypotheses. For now, let's turn to some nitty-gritty details of how to read a published research study.

READING COMMUNICATION RESEARCH REPORTS

In order to be an informed consumer of existing communication research, you need to know how to read a study. Just like English literature, where it is important to understand different genres of writing such as the poem or the novel, so it is important to understand the scientific report as a genre of writing. In particular, you need to understand the different forms that a report can take and have a sense of how a research report is organized.

Different Forms of Communication Research Reports

Each form affects the nature of the report. It's useful to think about the variety of reports that you might encounter in reading existing research.

Often, researchers must prepare proprietary reports for the sponsors of their research. These are not readily available in the public domain, but you may have located one through other means (e.g., maybe the manager of the firm where you propose to conduct a study has handed you a copy of a proprietary study that the firm had conducted recently). In reading such a report, you should bear in mind the sponsors of the report and their reasons for having the study conducted in the first place. Don't be surprised if the write-up doesn't summarize all of the relevant literature on the general topic or if it fails to address how the findings have advanced basic scientific knowledge (if they have). Proprietary research is generally focused on providing a narrow answer to a question provided by the parties that contracted the research.

Working papers are another form of research reporting. A working paper constitutes a tentative presentation of findings with an implicit request for comments. Working papers can vary in length, and they may present all of the research findings of the project or only a portion of them. Because a researcher's professional reputation is not at stake in a working paper, he or she generally feels free to present tentative interpretations that can't be altogether justified—identifying them as such and asking for evaluations.

Many research projects result in papers delivered at professional meetings. Often, these serve the same purpose as working papers. Although the length of professional papers may vary depending on the organization of the meetings, most professional conferences in communication studies allow submissions of 25–30 pages in length. Oral presentations of these written papers tend to be 8–15 minutes in length, depending on the particular convention program.

A short research note for publication in an academic or technical journal is another report form. Such reports are concise and direct—about half the length of a full journal article. In a short amount of space, a researcher can't present the state of the field in any detail, and methodological notes must be somewhat abbreviated as well. Basically, a research note should tell the reader why a brief note is justified by the findings, then tell what those findings are.

Probably the most popular research report is the article published in a scholarly journal. Again, lengths vary, and you should examine the lengths of articles previously published by the journal in question. As a rough guide, however, the typical length of a study submitted for publication in a journal is 25–30 double-spaced typed pages.

Sometimes, researchers present the results of a study in a book chapter that appears in an edited volume. Generally, book chapters are not merely journal articles appearing in chapter form. Usually, book chapters have a goal of summarizing a body of work, and the results of a single study may be presented to illustrate an analytical point being made by the author.

A book, of course, represents the most complex form of research report. It has all the advantages of the working paper—length and detail—but it is generally a more polished document, more or less like a published article only substantially longer.

Probably the research report you will most frequently encounter as you conduct your review of literature is the published journal article. Your reading will be easier if you understand how journal articles are organized. Most of the journals of communication studies abide by the publication guidelines that appear in the *Publication Manual of the American Psychological Association,* 5th edition (APA, 2001), often referred to as the **APA style.** A useful Web page for finding out more about the APA style is the APA Style Helper, found at www.apastyle.org. We're not going into all of the details on organization, just those important to help you generally understand what to expect. In Appendix D, we present portions of a hypothetical research report in order to provide you with a visual display of how one is laid out. The organization differs somewhat for quantitative and qualitative research. We'll discuss quantitative research reports first, then turn to qualitative research reports. What's the difference between quantitative and qualitative research? Basically, **quantitative research** presents findings in numerical form—frequencies, averages, and so forth. By contrast, **qualitative research** presents findings in textual form—usually words. We'll discuss other differences in these two kinds of research in the next two chapters.

Organization of the Quantitative Research Report

The Title The title should capture the essence of the study in a concise and clear manner, generally no longer than 10–12 words. The title is a very important element of a research article because it is used for abstracting and indexing purposes. For example, if a researcher conducted a study with an interest in two communication characteristics (say, communicator style and communicator competence), those characteristics should be folded into the title so that a reader could easily detect from the title alone what the study was about. Titles also provide you with your first hint about the basic assumptions on which the study was based. For example, if you encounter a title such as "The Effects of Guilt Appeals on Compliance among Marital Spouses," you have your first hint that this is a positivist study. Why? The word *effects* suggests an interest in causal explanation. We'll address the importance of locating a study according to its basic assumptions in Chapter 3.

The Byline The byline contains the author's name and institutional affiliation, informing the reader how the author could be contacted. This information is very helpful if you would like to find out something about the study that was not published in the text of the article (e.g., a copy of all of the questions used in an interview), or to ask the author about additional publications he or she has undertaken on the topic.

The Abstract The abstract is a concise (not to exceed 120 words) summary of the study. A good abstract is the most important single paragraph of a study. It is used in abstracting and indexing an article because it provides a thumbnail sketch of the study. A useful abstract tells the reader the following things: (1) the problem under investigation, (2) characteristics of the participants in the study (e.g., marital spouses), (3) the methods employed in the study (e.g., an experiment, a survey, an in-depth interview), (4) major findings, and (5) major implications of the findings (e.g., addresses an important absence in existing work). It is helpful to read an abstract before reading the entire article in order to gain an overview of what the study was about. In fact, when you undertake a search for research literature using the various abstracting and indexing sources (see Appendix B), you can access abstracts directly and read them to determine whether you should go to the trouble of getting a copy of the complete articles.

The Introduction The first section of an article is its introduction. It rarely has a heading, because it begins the article. The introduction contains four things. First, an opening paragraph or two should introduce the problem and its significance. Some unanswered questions are too trivial to merit study, and a researcher will present an argument for the importance of the study, either for society and/or for the research community. For example, a researcher who is examining correlates of marital satisfaction might point to the soaring divorce rate in the society and cite scholars who argue that this is a problem that needs attention. A researcher who has identified a gap in the research literature on a given topic could argue that the importance of the study lies in addressing that gap and the theoretical importance of doing so.

Second, the researcher will indicate the purpose of the study. Is the researcher interested in describing some communication phenomenon? Determining whether two factors are systematically related to each other? Examining the causes or effects of some phenomenon? Understanding how some phenomenon functions? Understanding what something means or how it comes to mean? A good purpose paragraph indicates how the researcher is responding to the problem introduced in the opening paragraphs of the article.

Third, the researcher will provide the reader with background information in the form of a review of related literature. Because every research report should be placed in the context of the general body of scientific knowledge, you must indicate where your report fits in that picture. That's the purpose of a review of literature. Having presented the general purpose of your study, you should bring the reader up to date on the previous research in the area.

We like to view a literature review as evidence for an argument the researcher is making. This argument should culminate in the statement of the research question or research hypothesis of the study. Thus, the review of literature should position the researcher to build a rationale for the study's research question/hypothesis. A poorly written review of literature is one in which the research question/hypothesis seems to appear "out of thin air." An effective review of literature is one in which the reader is not surprised by the formal statement of the research question/hypothesis. Instead, the logical scaffold has been built for the reader to perceive the question/hypothesis as logically appropriate.

To an extent, a review of the literature serves a bibliographical function for readers, indexing the previous research on a given topic. This approach can be overdone, however, and the effective literature review avoids mention of every previous study in the field. The review of literature should focus only on those studies that have direct relevance to the present one.

Sometimes, researchers opt for a straight chronological ordering of prior research literature: "Research X was the first to study this in year A. In year B, this was followed up with a series of studies. Subsequent research in the next five-year period elaborated upon earlier themes." This might work on occasion, but our general experience with this way of organizing the review of literature is that it makes it difficult for a reader to see the argument that is being made. An effective review of literature features a researcher who has figured out the argument for why the study needs to be done and then presented relevant research citations as evidence to support his or her claims.

In some cases, the argument that the researcher wants to make challenges previously accepted ideas. He or she should carefully review the studies that had led to the acceptance of those ideas, then indicate the factors that have not been previously considered or the logical fallacies present in the previous research.

Sometimes, a researcher's argument attempts to resolve a disagreement among previous researchers or inconsistency in findings from one study to another. He or she should organize the review of literature around the opposing or discrepant points of view or findings: summarizing the research supporting one view, then summarizing the research supporting the other, and finally suggesting the reasons for the disagreement.

A researcher's argument sometimes points to a gap in existing research. His or her review of literature will summarize what has been studied with an eye toward pointing out unanswered questions. The researcher's argument will address why it is important that identified gaps in the literature be addressed.

Fourth, and last, the introduction section should culminate in the presentation of the research questions and/or hypotheses that guided the study. These should not materialize out of the blue. Rather, they should flow logically from the argument you presented in the review of literature. In Chapter 3 we'll discuss in greater detail the different kinds of questions and hypotheses that can be found in communication research.

In citing prior research in a review of literature, APA style is followed. We'll elaborate on this in the section on writing research proposals.

Method A research report containing interesting findings and conclusions can be very frustrating when the reader can't determine the methodological design and execution of the study. The worth of all scientific findings depends heavily on the manner in which the data were collected and analyzed.

Researchers find it helpful to employ subheadings that flag the following information contained in a method section of a research report: *Participants, Materials,* and *Procedures.* The *Participants* subheading introduces a section that contains information about the number of participants; who they were, as a group; and how they were recruited for participation in the study. In general, it is helpful to readers if a researcher provides a basic demographic profile of the group of participants: the gender breakdown, average age, racial and ethnic composition, education level, and so forth. Recruitment information assures the reader that the procedures were in compliance with the ethical standards that guide the conduct of research (more on this topic in Chapter 5), at least with respect to voluntary informed consent and assurances of anonymity/confidentiality. Recruitment information also provides readers with information that will help them judge whether the study's findings are applicable only to the immediate sample included in the study or generalizable to a larger population.

The other two sections under the *Method* heading provide the reader with the details of how the study was executed. The *Materials* subheading introduces a section that contains a brief description of any apparatus or materials used in the study. For example, if participants filled out various survey measures, each would be described in this section. The *Procedures* subheading introduces a section in which the reader is provided with a detailed summary of what was done in executing the study.

The reader should be in a position to replicate the entire study independently after reading the Method section of a research report. Recall that replicability is an essential norm of science. A single study does not prove a point; only a series of studies can begin to do so. And unless studies can be replicated, there can be no meaningful series of studies.

Results Having set the study in the perspective of previous research and having described the design and execution of it, the researcher then presents the study's findings.

An effective presentation of a study's results or findings features several characteristics. The presentation of findings should be integrated into a logical whole. It's frustrating to the reader to discover a collection of seemingly unrelated analyses and findings with a promise that all the loose ends will be tied together later in the report. In general, results should be presented as answers to the posed research questions and/or hypotheses. Every step in the analysis should make sense—at the time it is taken. The researcher should present a rationale for a particular analysis and then present the findings relevant to it.

The presentation of data analyses should provide a maximum of detail without being cluttered. An effective presentation of results achieves the following aims:

- The researcher should present data so the reader can recompute them. In the case of percentage tables, for example, readers should be able to collapse categories and recompute the percentages. Readers should receive sufficient information to permit them to compute percentages in the table in the opposite direction from that of the initial presentation.
- The researcher should describe all aspects of a quantitative analysis in sufficient detail to permit a secondary analyst to replicate the analysis from the same body of data. This means that the reader should be able to create the same indexes and scales, produce the same tables, arrive at the same regression equations, and so forth. This will seldom be done, of course, but if the report allows for it, the reader will be far better equipped to evaluate the report than if it does not.

- The researcher should integrate tables, charts, and figures, if any, into the text of the Results section. The researcher should summarize the "bottom line" of any tabled information. Tables, charts, and figures do not speak for themselves, and it the researcher's job to make certain that interpretations are provided of tabled information. At the same time, however, it is important that a researcher not duplicate tabled information in the text of the article—page space is precious in journals.

Discussion The report should conclude with a statement of what the researcher has discovered about the subject matter and where future research might be directed. A quick review of recent journal articles will probably indicate a high frequency of this concluding statement: "It is clear that much more research is needed." This is probably always a true conclusion, but it's of little value unless the researcher can offer pertinent suggestions about the nature of that future research. In addition, the researcher should review the particular shortcomings of the study and suggest ways those shortcomings might be avoided in future research.

A researcher should draw explicit conclusions. Although research is typically conducted for the purpose of drawing general conclusions, the researcher should carefully note the specific basis for such conclusions. Otherwise, he or she may lead the reader into accepting unwarranted conclusions.

The researcher should point to any qualifications or conditions warranted in the evaluation of conclusions. The researcher knows best the shortcomings and tentativeness of the study's conclusions, and he or she should give the reader the advantage of that knowledge. Failure to do so can misdirect future research and result in a waste of research funds.

References After the Discussion section, the researcher presents a list of cited references. This list is alphabetized, using the APA style we mentioned above. We'll describe this citation form under the section on writing research proposals. A list of cited references isn't necessarily the same as a bibliography of sources. The References list is limited to sources cited in the body of the article. A researcher may well have consulted a wide range of resources in planning or executing the study. This broader list would be the researcher's bibliography.

A typical example of a quantitative research report is an experiment reported by Michael Slater and his colleagues (2002) titled "Effects of Threatening Visuals and Announcer Differences on Responses to Televised Alcohol Warnings." The article's title informs the reader about the factors examined in the study. The article's abstract informs the reader about the study's purpose: "This study examined threatening background visuals and voice-over differences in televised alcohol warnings" (Slater et al., 2002). The abstract tells us that the study had 401 participants. It also informs us about the method used—an experiment. The reader is given a brief summary of the study's findings and their implications.

Following the abstract is a list of keywords provided by the authors to assist abstracting and indexing of their study: "warning," "television advertising," "fear appeals," "alcohol," "threat messages," and "visual images" (Slater et al., 2002, p. 27). If a researcher entered any of these keywords in a literature search with any of the major abstracts and indexes, this article should pop up.

The introduction to the article addresses the social significance of the topic: the growing interest in mandating health warnings on television alcohol advertising just as has already been done for cigarette packages and alcohol beverage containers. Then the authors give us their gap argument for the current study: Although there is substantial research on product warnings, it has focused on print warnings to the neglect of audiovisual presentations. The authors then review relevant research in persuasion to logically deduce four research hypotheses and three research questions.

The Method section contains subsections in which the authors describe their participants and the recruiting procedures employed, the design used in the study, the production and presentation of message stimuli, how responses to the message stimuli were measured, and the statistics they used to analyze the data.

The Results section provides a description of the study's findings, organized by research hypothesis and research question. The Discussion section provides a brief summary of the study's findings and the implications of those findings in light of the argument and the literature review presented in the Introduction. The authors address the limitations of their study and end by suggesting directions for future research.

The organization of a qualitative research report is both similar to and different from that of a quantitative research report.

Organization of the Qualitative Research Report

The APA style does not distinguish qualitative from quantitative research for purposes of presentation. Thus, the same sections we used above—Introduction, Method, Results, Discussion, and References—will often be used by qualitative researchers to present their research study.

But, for reasons we will elaborate in Chapters 13–16, this organization is an awkward fit for qualitative researchers, much more than for quantitative researchers. In qualitative research, the process of inquiry integrates the processes of data gathering, analysis, and interpretation organically into a whole.

Although the same basic organizational structure is likely to be used by qualitative researchers, the contents of the sections differ from those of the quantitative research report.

Qualitative researchers, like quantitative researchers, have an introductory section in which the study is placed in a conversation with other literature and a rationale is provided for the study. But differences exist in the two kinds of introductory sections. Qualitative research generally studies the details of meaning making in particular situations or groups. An introduction in a qualitative study often provides a rationale for why the particular group or setting merits study. In addition, the introduction situates the findings of the study in an appropriate conversation with other relevant work, either theoretical or empirical.

Thus, for example, if a researcher is doing a qualitative study on rules of conversational politeness in a particular retirement home, he or she might introduce the study by discussing other related literature on community life in retirement homes, politeness theory and research, and perhaps communication and aging.

Qualitative researchers typically start the research process using inductive reasoning—that is, moving from specific observations to infer more general patterns or principles (to be discussed in detail in Chapter 4). Thus, the introduction sections of qualitative studies generally work with more general research questions than those found in quantitative studies, along the lines of "what is going on here?" With respect to our retirement home example, a qualitative researcher might indicate that he or she entered the field with a goal of understanding communication practices in general; the focus on politeness might have emerged empirically from field observation work. Alternatively, the researcher might have entered the field with a more focused goal of understanding how politeness is enacted among residents of a retirement home.

Qualitative researchers, like quantitative researchers, need to inform their readers about the methods they used to conduct the study. Participants are described largely in terms of their membership in the particular group under study or their presence in a particular situation or setting of interest. In qualitative research, the primary research instrument is the researcher. Although qualitative researchers describe how they gathered their data, the goal is not one of positioning the reader to replicate the study exactly. For reasons that we shall see in Chapter 3, qualitative research embraces the subjective stance of the researcher; it is understood in qualitative research that a second researcher who studied the same group or setting might interpret it differently.

Results and Discussion sections are often integrated in a qualitative study. The qualitative researcher often addresses the significance and implications of his or her interpretations as they are being presented. In quantitative research, the Results section is presumably the more objective rendering of what was discovered, whereas the Discussion section is the place where the thoughts and opinions of the researcher can be brought to bear. In a qualitative study, the objective–subjective divide is less distinct, which results in the seamless integration of traditional Results and Discussion sections.

The challenge facing qualitative researchers hinges on how they tell the story of what they learned in the study. The presentation of qualitative findings is a narrative tale. Qualitative studies are textual constructions about textual data. As Thomas Lindlof (1995, p. 259) tells us, "Narrative, in qualitative writing, is a foundational concept." But not all narratives are alike.

John van Maanen (1988) has identified three basic genres of narrative tales that ethnographers employ in writing about what they learned in the field; these basic genres easily apply to all forms of qualitative research.

The Realist Tale   This narrative form is probably the most common in qualitative communication research. The researcher views the narrative as an accurate representation of the phenomenon. In this genre, the narrative ideally is a mirror that reflects the reality of what was observed.

According to van Maanen (1988), the realist approach to the qualitative narrative has four characteristics. First, the authorial voice is third person ("People of group X do such and such."). The voice of the author (the "I") has been stripped from the narrative; you don't read statements like "I saw people doing such and such" or "I experienced such and such like the people of group X." The presence of the researcher is evident only in the portion of the manuscript where his or her methods are described.

Within the genre of the realist tale, findings are organized according to emergent themes and the researcher's conceptual/theoretical interests.

The second characteristic of the realist tale, according to van Maanen (1988, p. 48), is "a documentary style focused on minute, sometimes precious, but thoroughly mundane details of everyday life among the people studied." The watchwords here are *details* (as opposed to generalities) and *everyday* (on the assumption that a group is best understood by paying attention to the mundane rather than the unusual).

The third characteristic of the realist tale is attention to the native's point of view. The researcher's task is to present the everyday life of the participant through his or her own eyes: "Extensive, closely edited quotations characterize realist tales, conveying to readers that the views put forward are not those of the fieldworker but are rather authentic and representative remarks transcribed straight from the horse's mouth" (van Maanen, 1988, p. 49).

The fourth, and final, characteristic of the realist tale is what van Maanen (1988, p. 51) calls "interpretive omnipotence." The researcher has the final say on how the textual data are written up and interpreted. Thus, although the native's voice is captured through extensive quotations, it is the researcher in the end who decides who will be quoted and which excerpt will be selected for inclusion. It is the researcher who determines what those quotations mean.

Illustrative of the realist tale is the participant-observation study of a utility company experiencing a merger, conducted by Lisa Howard and Patricia Geist (1995). The researchers observed how company employees coped with the stability and change that characterized the merger process. The voice of the article is third person—we read about "CGPC employees," "an employee," "a supervisor," but not "we, the researchers," apart from a short description of their participant-observation methods. The article is peppered with quotations from employees, which the researchers present by way of capturing the natives' point of view surrounding the contradictions they experienced during the merger and how they responded. The researchers make sense of patterns they observe using a particular theoretical lens known as structuration theory, positioning their analysis as the only view presented in the article.

The Confessional Tale   The second genre of narrative writing discussed by van Maanen (1988) is the confessional tale, which contrasts sharply from the realist tale. Three features typify this kind of narrative.

First, the narrative features "personalized author(ity)" (van Maanen, 1988, p. 74). The researcher is present in the narrative text. The voice of the narrative is first person instead of third person. That is, instead of the realist statement "People in this group do X," we encounter statements like "I saw people in this group do X." In the confessional tale, the researcher is a presence in the scene.

Second, the researcher's point of view is present in the text—not as the accepted backdrop for the analysis as in the realist tale. The researcher writes of how his or her point of view developed and changed over time. The researcher shares his or her surprises, uncertainties, and so forth, as they evolved over the course of the fieldwork.

Third, the confessional tale is characterized by naturalness. This feature is a tricky one to execute, because the reader has just been presented with the subjectivities of the researcher through an autobiographical rendering of his or her point of view. In the end, the researcher strives to persuade the reader that his or her rendering of the phenomenon under study is still representationally accurate. Often, confessional writers achieve naturalness by demonstrating how they were accepted by the natives or how they gained sufficient understanding of the group to behave competently like a member. In addition, by providing insight into the experience of the researcher while in the field, we are provided with explicit information relevant to the trustworthiness of the study.

The ethnographic study of the Lowell Bennion Community Service Center by Connie Della-Piana and James Anderson (1995) provides a confessional contrast to the realist presentation of organizational merger discussed above. The first-person voice permeates this article, as Della-Piana shares with her reader her thoughts and feelings while undertaking the fieldwork in this community-service organization. However, by the article's end, we emerge with a vivid portrait of what "community" means to the volunteers who work at this organization. By our gaining insight into the experiences of the field researcher, her insights have credibility for us, as readers.

The Impressionist Tale The third genre of narrative writing identified by van Maanen (1988) is the impressionist tale. The name comes from impressionist painting, which

> sets out to capture a worldly scene in a special instant or moment of time. The work is figurative, although it conveys a highly personalized perspective. What a painter sees, given an apparent position in time and space, is what the viewer sees. (van Maanen, 1988, p. 101)

Four characteristics typify this approach. First, the impressionist tale features dramatic recall. Events are told chronologically, in as much detail as the researcher can remember. The reader experiences the narrative as a story—with a beginning, a middle, an end, a cast of characters, and a story line.

Second, and relatedly, knowledge is fragmented. The researcher's obligation is to tell a story, event by event. The tidy organization by theme that characterizes the realist tale is supplanted by the more disorderly nature of a chronology.

The third characteristic of the impressionist tale is the construction of characters—individuals who are given names, lives, and feelings. We aren't told about groups of participants; instead, a story is crafted in which specific characters are created to personify the group's membership.

Fourth, and finally, the impressionist tale features dramatic control. The story is often told in the first person. It has dramatic tension to it, which builds to a climax. The goal of dramatic control is to make the readers feel as if they are there, living the experience told in the tale.

The final chapter of Kristine Fitch's (1998) book on interpersonal communication in urban Colombia provides us with an excellent example of an impressionist tale. This chapter, presented as an epilogue to an ethnography that is otherwise presented in a realist manner, grabs the reader with its dramatic first-person story, in which Fitch tells a story about Aurelio, someone who was senselessly murdered. The narrative reads like a novel, complete with dialogue between characters.

Of the three genres identified by van Maanen (1988), doubtless it is the realist tale that is most compatible with the APA style of Introduction-Method-Results-Discussion, whereas the impressionist tale is least compatible with this presentation structure. All three kinds of tales contain introductory rationales, information about methods, and presentation of interpretations, but the "packaging" varies from genre to genre.

Organization of the Multi-Method Research Report

Increasingly, communication researchers are engaging in multi-method research. This kind of research uses more than one method in gathering data, triangulating the insights of one method with the insights of another method. Because no method is perfect, multi-method research offsets the limitations of one method with the strengths of another. Multi-method research takes three basic forms: multiple quantitative methods, multiple qualitative methods, and a combination of quantitative and qualitative methods. When all of the methods are of the same basic family (quantitative or qualitative), the research report takes one of the two basic shapes we have just discussed.

Qualitative–quantitative multi-method research is a hybrid, and thus the research reports based on this kind of research are also hybrids of the two kinds of reports we have just discussed. Sometimes, a single journal article contains two more or less self-contained studies, with separate introductions, research questions/hypotheses, method sections, results sections, and discussion sections. Usually, however, there is an overall introduction that provides a rationale for both studies and an overall discussion that integrates the findings from both studies. Daena Goldsmith's (2000) article on how utterance sequencing mitigates possible face threats in soliciting advice illustrates this type of organization. She provides an overall introduction that provides a rationale for both studies. Then she presents two "self-contained" studies—the first qualitative and the second quantitative— linked together because the second study is based on the findings from the first study. She concludes the article with an overall discussion.

Alternatively, researchers write up the results of their hybrid study in traditional Introduction-Method-Results-Discussion format. Quantitative and qualitative methods are both described in the Method section. The Results section presents both quantitative and qualitative findings interwoven together. Michael Papa and his colleagues (2000) used this format in presenting their study of the effects of a radio soap opera in India, based on survey, content analysis, and interview methods.

Regardless of which form hybrid multi-method research takes, the qualitative portion of the data tends to be reported in a realist manner.

Checklists for Reading Communication Research Reports

Our basic philosophy in writing this book is that the best preparation we can provide for becoming a literate reader of communication research reports is to understand how the research was conducted. The remainder of the book is designed to give you the knowledge you need to become that literate reader. Having said that, however, we'll provide you here with two tools that should assist you in reading research reports in communication. Figure 2-1 presents a checklist of questions to ask when reading a quantitative report. Figure 2-2 presents a checklist of questions to ask when reading a qualitative report. Obvi-

---

1. Is this study quantitative or qualitative in nature? If qualitative, see Figure 2-2.
2. What is the basic paradigm of knowing in which this study is embedded? What is the basic purpose or goal of research in this tradition?
3. What is the purpose of this particular study? Try to locate the researcher's purpose statement.
4. What is the rationale for why this study needed to be done? See if you can summarize the researcher's argument in a few sentences.
5. What are the variables in the study? Which are the independent variables? The dependent variables?
6. What are the study's research questions or research hypotheses? Are they directional or nondirectional? Questions/hypotheses of difference or association between variables?
7. Do the research questions/hypotheses flow logically out of the review of literature provided by the researcher?
8. How was each variable operationalized, or measured? For each operationalization, are you given information to persuade you that it had adequate measurement reliability and measurement validity? How was reliability determined? Validity?
9. What was the unit of analysis in the study?
10. How were units sampled for inclusion in the study? Do the sampling procedures allow you to generalize from the immediate sample used in the study to a larger population? In other words, did the sampling plan have adequate external validity?
11. How would you describe the basic design employed in the study: survey research, experimental research, quasi-experimental research, content analysis, or interaction analysis?
12. Were the procedures used in implementing the design adequate to allow confidence in the explanatory claims made by the researcher? In other words, did the design display adequate internal validity?
13. Was the conduct of the study ethical?
14. Were statistical inferences made from the data? Did statistical tests examine differences or relationships between variables?
15. Did the results of the statistical tests achieve a significance level of $\leq .05$?
16. What were the results of the study with respect to the initial research questions and/or research hypotheses?
17. Was the study presented in a thorough and readable manner? Were you given enough information to allow for replication of the study?
18. What are the weaknesses of the study?
19. What are the strengths of the study?
20. What are the implications of the study? That is, what's the "so what?" value of the study?

FIGURE 2-1 **Checklist of Questions to Ask in Reading Quantitative Research Reports**

1. Is this study quantitative or qualitative in nature? If quantitative, see Figure 2-1.
2. What is the basic paradigm of knowing in which this study is embedded? What is the basic purpose or goal of research in this tradition?
3. What is the purpose of this particular study? Try to locate the researcher's purpose statement.
4. What is the rationale for why this study needed to be done? See if you can summarize the researcher's argument in a few sentences.
5. Did this study use participant-observation methods? If "no," proceed to question 9 below. If "yes," continue.
6. How did the researcher gain access to the field site?
7. What role(s) did the researcher occupy? For how long?
8. How were field notes taken? Was a reflexive journal maintained?
9. Did this study use qualitative interviewing? If "no," proceed to question 12 below. If "yes," continue.
10. What kind of qualitative interviewing was conducted?
11. What questions were asked of participants?
12. Did this study use discourse analysis? How was transcription conducted?
13. Did this study rely on social texts as data? What were they?
14. What was the study's sampling plan?
15. Was the study conducted in an ethical manner?
16. What was the researcher's analytic framework that guided data analysis?
17. How were the data analyzed?
18. Are the researcher's interpretive findings dependable, or trackable?
19. Are the researcher's interpretive findings confirmable—characterized by a systematic, coherent reasoning process from evidence to conclusions?
20. Are the researcher's interpretive findings credible—do they ring true to the native?
21. Does the study provide "thick description" to allow you to determine the transferability of the findings?
22. What is the narrative style of the study's write-up—realist, confessional, or impressionist?
23. What are the weaknesses of the study?
24. What are the strengths of the study?
25. What are the implications of the study? That is, what's the "so what?" value of the study?

FIGURE 2-2   **Checklist of Questions to Ask in Reading Qualitative Research Reports**

ously, in the case of quantitative–qualitative hybrid research, you will need to use both checklists. You don't yet know how to answer most of these questions—that's what the rest of the book is for. You may find it useful to return to these checklists as you progress through remaining chapters. As you use these checklists, it is important to recognize three overarching principles:

1. *Try not to evaluate a study outside the parameters of the approach to knowing in which it is positioned.* Don't critique a quantitative study because it's not qualitative, and vice versa. Don't critique an experiment because it's not a survey, and so forth. Figure out where the study is positioned, and evaluate it against the criteria appropriate for that research approach.

2. *Try not to reject findings because a study and its method are not perfect.* We have never read a "perfect study" or encountered "the perfect method." All research methods have limitations. Hopefully,

the limitations of one method or study are offset by the strengths of a second method or study, whose own weaknesses are offset by the strengths of a third method or study, and so forth. Research is an imperfect business. Make a judgment call about a study based on an overall assessment of its strengths and limitations. Each study has something to contribute, just as each study has weaknesses. Because of this fact, our own preference is multi-method research.

3. *Try not to confuse form with substance.* Many consumers of research reports experience qualitative reports as easy to read, whereas quantitative reports are experienced as more challenging because of their technical terminology. For some readers, this means that quantitative reports must be somehow better because they seem more scientific than qualitative reports. By contrast, other readers conclude that qualitative reports must be better because they can be understood more

readily. We find both kinds of judgments to be flawed. Qualitative reports are just as scientific as quantitative reports, but they present different ways of being scientific. Qualitative reports may employ fewer technical terms than quantitative reports in the write-up of the study, but they require just as much technical knowledge to evaluate (compare Figures 2-1 and 2-2).

At this point in your reading, you should be prepared to read communication research, at least in a cursory manner, in order to find out what we already know. This will help you in narrowing down your topic area. You will also narrow your topic depending on your research purpose.

DETERMINING YOUR PURPOSE

Communication research, of course, serves many purposes. Four of the most common and useful purposes are *exploration, description, causal/functional explanation,* and *understanding.* Although a given study can have more than one of these purposes—and most do—examining them separately is useful because each has different implications for other aspects of research design.

Exploration

Sometimes, communication research is conducted to explore a topic, or to provide a beginning familiarity with that topic. This approach is typical when a researcher examines a new interest or when the subject of study itself is relatively new.

As an example, let's suppose that widespread taxpayer dissatisfaction with the government erupts into a taxpayers' revolt. People begin refusing to pay their taxes, and they organize themselves around that issue. You might like to learn more about the swirl of political discourse that surrounds this movement. What are the arguments employed by members of the movement? How persuasive are their messages in recruiting others to join their cause? What are the counterarguments by the government? You might undertake an exploratory study to obtain at least approximate answers to some of these questions. You might talk to people who define themselves in taxpayer revolt, analyzing their arguments. You might interview other people to gain insight into what they find persuasive—or not—about the movement's rhetoric. You might systematically analyze the arguments of the movement and of the government that have appeared in selected national newspapers since the revolt began.

Exploratory studies are also appropriate for more persistent phenomena. Suppose that you're unhappy with your college's graduation requirements for the communication studies major and want to help change them. You might study the history of these requirements at the college and meet with college officials to learn the reasons for the current standards. You could talk to several students who currently are majors to get a rough idea of their sentiments on the subject. Although this last activity would not necessarily yield an accurate picture of student opinion, it could suggest what the results of a more extensive study might be.

Sometimes, exploratory research is pursued through the use of *focus groups,* or guided small-group discussions. This technique is frequently used in market research; we'll examine it further in Chapter 14.

Exploratory studies are typically done for three purposes: (1) to satisfy the researcher's curiosity and desire for better understanding, (2) to test the feasibility of undertaking a more extensive study, and (3) to develop the methods to be employed in any subsequent study.

Not long ago, for example, one of us became aware of the growing popularity of something called "channeling," in which a person known as a *channel* or *medium* enters a trance state and begins speaking with a voice that claims it originates outside the channel. Some of the voices say they come from a spirit world of the dead, some say they're from other planets, and still others say they exist on dimensions of reality difficult to explain in ordinary human terms. You may be familiar with channeling through the "Seth" books of Jane Roberts (1974) or more recent books by Shirley MacLaine (1983).

The channeled voices, often referred to as *entities,* sometimes use the metaphor of radio or television for the phenomenon they represent. "When you watch the news," one said in the course of an interview, "you don't believe Dan Rather is really inside the television set. The same is true of me. I use this medium's body the way Dan Rather uses your television set."

The idea of channeling is interesting from several perspectives, not the least of which is the methodological question of how to study scientifically something that violates so much of what we take for granted, including scientific staples such as space, time, causation, and individuality.

Lacking any rigorous theory or precise expectations, the initial goal was merely to learn more. Using some of the techniques of qualitative research discussed in Part 3, information was collected and preliminary categories were formed for making sense of the observations. Books and articles about the phenomenon were read, and people who had attended channeling sessions were interviewed. Channeling sessions were attended, observing others who attended as well as the channel and entity.

Subsequently, personal interviews were conducted with numerous channels and entities.

Many interviews began by asking the human channels questions about how they first began channeling, what it was like, and why they continued, as well as standard biographical questions. The channel would then go into a trance, whereby the interview continued with the entity speaking. "Who are you?" might be asked. "Where do you come from?" "Why are you doing this?" Although these interview sessions were entered with several questions prepared in advance, each of the interviews followed whatever course seemed appropriate in the light of answers given.

This example of exploration illustrates where inductive research often begins. Whereas researchers working from deductive theories have the key phenomena of interest laid out in advance, inductive research begins with a relatively "blank slate." Basic questions that guide the inductive process are "What is going on here?" and "What's this all about?" For example, differences were noted in the circumstances of channeling sessions. Some channels said they must go into deep trances, some use light trances, and others remain conscious. Most sit down while channeling, but others stand and walk about. Some channels operate under pretty ordinary conditions; others seem to require metaphysical props such as dim lights, incense, and chanting. Many of these differences became apparent only in the course of initial observations. We'll discuss inductive and deductive reasoning in detail in Chapter 4.

Exploratory studies are quite valuable in communication research. They're essential whenever a researcher is breaking new ground, and they can almost always yield new insights into a topic for research.

The chief shortcoming of exploratory studies is that they seldom provide satisfactory answers to research questions, though they can hint at the answers and can give insights into the research methods that could provide more definitive answers. Exploratory studies are small in scale and preliminary in nature.

Description

A major purpose of many social scientific studies is to describe something about the communication process. The researcher observes and then describes what was observed. Because scientific observation is careful and deliberate, however, scientific descriptions are typically more accurate and precise than casual ones.

A Gallup poll conducted during a political election campaign describes the voting intentions of the electorate. A researcher who carefully chronicles the percentage of television characters who are minority group members has, or at least serves, a descriptive purpose. A researcher who depicts the communication among management team members in a specific corporate organization also serves a descriptive purpose. In fact, most qualitative studies aim primarily at description.

Causal/Functional Explanation

The third general purpose of communication research is to explain things. Reporting the voting intentions of an electorate is a descriptive activity, but reporting why the televised campaign ads for Candidate A are more persuasive than the ads for candidate B is an explanatory activity. Reporting why some television shows have higher viewer ratings than others involves explanation, but simply reporting the different viewer ratings is a case of description.

In Chapter 3, we will distinguish causal explanation from functional explanation. Both types of explanations are sought in communication research. Suppose that you are a researcher interested in studying eye-contact patterns among members of decision-making groups. If you simply describe that speakers glance up when they are nearing the end of their utterances, you are serving a descriptive purpose. If, however, you observe that eye contact is part of the communicative system of coordinated turn-taking, and the function of speaker eye contact is to signal that the floor is about to become open and that the person looked at is being designated as the next speaker, you have entered the realm of functional explanation. That is, you have described the function of eye contact in the system of communicative behaviors through which turn-taking is coordinated, and thereby you have explained it. If, however, you want to explain why certain types of group members are designated as the next speaker more often than other types of members—say, why high-status members are designated more so than members of lower status—you are entertaining a question of causal explanation. Causal explanation addresses *why* questions, and functional explanation addresses *how* questions.

Understanding

In Chapter 3, we will discuss a third type of explanation—reason-based. Most scholars refer to this kind of explanation as *understanding*. When you understand a human communicative action, you know what it means and the rules that guide its enactment.

Most qualitative communication researchers move beyond description and strive for understanding. It is *description* to observe that people usually greet someone they know. It is *understanding* when the researcher knows the social group's rules that produce this pattern of action and when the researcher can claim, say, that the greeting means the participants had a prior relationship of some sort and were signaling their recognition of their familiarity with one another.

Although it is useful to distinguish the four purposes of research, it bears repeating that most studies will have multiple purposes. Many researchers combine description with causal/functional explanation. Other researchers combine description with understanding. When researchers—both qualitative and quantitative—undertake exploratory work, it is usually descriptive and is intended as a preliminary step to either explanation or understanding.

When you are undertaking a study, it is important for you to determine what your purpose is. Similarly, when you are evaluating the research of someone else, it is important for you to ask yourself "What is the researcher's purpose in this study?" It is unreasonable to criticize a study whose goal is understanding because it did not provide insight into causal explanation. Similarly, it is unreasonable to reject a study designed to address *why* questions if it failed to provide in-depth understanding of meanings. Part of becoming a sophisticated consumer or producer of communication research is appreciating the several purposes that research can serve. An important skill to develop is the ability to distinguish apples from oranges when it comes to research purposes, and never to criticize an apple merely because it is not an orange.

Let's turn now to a consideration of whom or what you want to explore, describe, explain, or understand.

DETERMINING YOUR UNIT OF ANALYSIS

There is virtually no limit to what or who you can study, or the **units of analysis.** Presumably, however, the focus of your research study will be communication in some fashion or another. Are you interested in studying the intricacies of messages? Predispositions of individuals that lead them to communicate in certain ways? The system of rules that guide members of a certain social group to communicate in specific ways? Media systems as economic institutions? Obviously, there are many different things that could be studied about communication. You need to decide what your focus will be, and an important part of that decision is the unit of analysis.

Communication researchers perhaps most typically choose individual people as their units of analysis. More specifically, researchers study the communication characteristics of individual people—their levels of speech anxiety, their levels of politeness, their accents, their willingness to disclose, their conflict styles, and so forth. Often, an individual's communication is studied in conjunction with some other feature about the individual—the gender, age, education level, personality, and so forth. The researcher then combines these descriptions to provide a composite picture of the group the individuals represent: whether members of a certain social group or culture, all people who are male, all persons who have completed at least four years of college, and so on.

For example, you may note the conflict style of each student enrolled in Communication Studies 100 and then characterize the group of students as being 30 percent competitive, 30 percent collaborative, and 40 percent avoidance oriented. Although the final description would be of the class as a whole, the individual characteristics are aggregated for purposes of describing some larger group.

The same aggregation would occur in an explanatory study. Suppose that you wished to discover whether students with lower speech anxiety received better grades in Communication Studies 100 than did students with a higher speech anxiety level. You would measure the speech anxiety levels and the course grades of individual students. You might then aggregate students with low anxiety and those with high anxiety and see which group received the best grades in the course. The purpose of the study would be to explain why some students do better in the course than others (looking at levels of speech anxiety as a possible explanation), but individual students would still be the units of analysis.

Units of analysis in a study are typically also the units of observation. Thus, to study voting intentions, we would interview ("observe") individual voters. Sometimes, however, we "observe" our units of analysis indirectly. For example, we might ask husbands and wives their individual voting intentions, for the purpose of distinguishing couples who agree and disagree politically. We might want to find out whether political disagreements tend to cause divorce, perhaps. In this case, our units of analysis would be married couples, though the units of observation would be the individual wives and husbands.

Units of analysis, then, are those things we examine in order to create summary descriptions and to explain or understand differences among them. This concept should be clarified further as we now consider several common units of analysis in communication research.

Individuals

As mentioned previously, individual human beings are perhaps the most typical units of analysis for communication research. We tend to describe, explain, and understand social groups by aggregating the descriptions of individuals.

Any type of individual may be the unit of analysis for communication research. In practice, communication researchers seldom study all kinds of people. At the very least, their studies are typically limited to the people living in a single country, though some comparative studies stretch across national boundaries. Often, however, studies are quite circumscribed.

Examples of specific groups whose members may be units of analysis—at the individual level—include students, gays and lesbians, parents, consumers, TV viewers, and faculty members. Note that each of these terms implies some population of individual persons. (See Chapter 7 for more on populations.) At this point, it's enough to realize that studies with individuals as their units of analysis typically aim to describe the population that comprises those individuals.

As the units of analysis, individuals may be characterized in terms of their membership in social groupings. Thus, an individual may be described as belonging to a rich family or to a poor one, or a person may be described as having a college-educated mother or not. We might examine in a research project whether people with college-educated mothers communicate differently than those with non-college-educated mothers. In each case, the individual would be the unit of analysis—not the family or the mother.

As the units of analysis, individuals may also be characterized in terms of their categorization on psychological attributes. For example, we can describe an individual as being high or low in cognitive complexity (i.e., whether a person uses a greater or smaller number of mental categories when he or she thinks about things). We might examine in a research study whether people who are high in cognitive complexity are more likely to display empathic communication than those who are low in cognitive complexity. Because we are studying the relationship between individual level of cognitive complexity and individual empathic communication, the individual is our unit of analysis.

Groups

Social groups themselves may also be the units of analysis for communication research. Realize how this differs from studying the individuals within a group. If you were to study the members of management teams to learn about managers, for example, the individual (manager) would be the unit of analysis. But if you studied all the management teams in several corporations to learn the differences in communication, say, between effective teams and ineffective ones, between those with low turnover versus those with high turnover, and so forth, the unit of analysis would be the *management team,* a social group.

Here's another example. You might describe families in terms of their style of parent–child communication and whether or not they own computers. You could aggregate families and describe the most frequent style and the percentage with computers. You would then be in a position to determine whether families with certain styles of parent–child communication were more likely to have computers than those with different parent–child communication styles. The individual family in such a case would be the unit of analysis.

Other units of analysis at the group level could be friendship cliques, married couples, neighborhoods, chatrooms, and cancer support groups. Each of these terms also implies a population. *Married couples* implies a population that includes all married couples. The population of married couples could be described, say, in terms of its satisfaction level, its frequency of conflict, or its longevity, and an explanatory study of married couples might discover whether long-term married couples were more likely than newlyweds to engage in conflict.

A particular kind of qualitative researcher known as an ethnographer of communication specializes in understanding the communication of a particular social or cultural group. For example, Kristine Fitch (1998) conducted fieldwork with the goal of understanding the code of communication of urban residents of Colombia. When qualitative researchers focus on a single social or cultural group, they are not viewing that group as representative of a larger population of groups. They usually refer to the social or cultural group they are studying as a *speech community*—that is, a group of persons who share a code of communication.

Organizations

Formal social organizations may also be the units of analysis in communication research. An example would be corporations, implying, of course, a population of all corporations. Alternatively, a researcher might be interested in understanding a single organization or corporation. Individual corporations might be characterized in terms of their number of employees, their legitimation of bottom-up innovation, communication satisfaction, and so forth. We might determine whether large corporations legitimate bottom-up innovation more so than smaller corporations. Other examples of formal social organizations suitable as units of analysis would be church congregations, colleges, army divisions, academic departments, supermarkets, hospitals, crisis centers, and hospices.

As with other units of analysis, we can derive the characteristics of organizations from those of their individual members. Thus, we might describe a hospice center in terms of the average number of years of nursing experience among staff members, or the average satisfaction that families of hospice patients experience with staff members. In a descriptive study, then, we might find the percentage of all hospices in which the average experience of staff members exceeds five years. In an explanatory study, we might determine whether the average experience level of a hospice's staff relates systematically to the communication satisfaction experienced by patient families. In each of these examples, however, the *hospice* would be the unit of analysis. Had we asked whether satisfaction is greater with more-experienced hospice nurses than with less-experienced hospice nurses, then the individual nurse would have been the unit of analysis.

If all this seems unduly complicated, rest assured that in most research projects you are likely to undertake, the unit of analysis will be relatively clear to you. When the unit of analysis is not so clear, however, it is absolutely essential to determine what it is; otherwise, you cannot determine what observations are to be made about whom or what.

Some studies try to describe or explain more than one unit of analysis. In these cases, the researcher must anticipate what conclusions she or he wishes to draw with regard to which units of analysis.

Social Artifacts

Another unit of analysis is the *social artifact,* or any product of social beings or their behavior. In 1966, Eugene Webb and three colleagues published an ingenious little book on social research (revised in 1981) that has become a classic: *Nonreactive Measures in the Social Sciences.* It focuses, as you might have guessed, on the idea of nonreactive research, or **unobtrusive research**—research in which the focus of study is unaware of being studied. Webb and his colleagues have provided us with many examples of types of social artifacts that can be examined fruitfully.

Some social artifacts are *physical traces.* Webb and his colleagues discussed two types of physical traces: *erosion traces* and *accretion traces.* Want to know what exhibits are the most popular at a museum? You could conduct an opinion poll, but people might tell you what they thought you wanted to hear or what might make them look more intellectual and serious. You could stand by different exhibits and count the viewers who came by, but people

might come over to see what you were doing. Webb and his colleagues suggest you check the wear and tear on the floor tiles in front of various exhibits—an example of an erosion trace. Basically, erosion traces are based on the erosion of some social artifact—floor tiles, in this instance. Want to know which exhibits are the most popular with little kids? You might choose an accretion trace—physical remnants or deposits—such as fingerprints, mucous deposits, sticky food residues, and so forth, on the glass cases.

Webb and his colleagues discuss various kinds of *archival records* as a different kind of social artifact. Archives can be *public* or *private* in nature. You might want to assess the effects of no-fault divorce laws by examining the actuarial records of divorce before and after the change in divorce laws. You might use the white pages of telephone directories to gauge a population's mobility. You might examine the society pages of local newspapers as a way to tap into the power elite of communities—who is seen with whom, and so forth. The possibilities are virtually endless in the use of public records of one kind or another.

Sometimes, privately owned archival records are fruitful social artifacts to study. You might study the rate at which physicians prescribe a new drug as an index of the rate of diffusion of a new product. You might study historical diaries and letters for insights into social rules of the time. For example, Ellen Rothman published a book in 1984 titled *Hands and Hearts: A History of Courtship in America 1770–1920,* based on her systematic analysis of diaries, journals, and letters in various state historical societies and university archives.

Communication *messages* of one kind or another can be regarded as social artifacts. One class of artifacts includes concrete objects, such as newspaper editorials, television programs, music videos, interoffice memos, presidential campaign ads, personal dating ads, and e-mail messages. Usually, researchers interested in uttered talk derive audiotapes or videotapes of conversation, or they work with written transcripts of conversations between people.

Each social object implies a set of all such objects: all editorials, all television programs, all music videos, and so on. An individual editorial might be characterized by its partisanship, frequency of emotive words, or readability. The population of all editorials or of a particular kind of editorial could be analyzed for the purpose of description or explanation.

A communication researcher could analyze whether minority representation among soap opera characters has changed over the past ten years, in which case the soap opera would be the unit of analysis. You might examine the personal ads of your local newspaper to see if female-seeking-male ads differ in their content from male-seeking-female ads. The unit of analysis would be the individual personal ad. You might study the ads on Saturday-morning children's cartoons to assess the extent to which toys are gender stereotyped for boys or for girls. The individual ad would be the unit of analysis.

Social interactions form another class of social artifacts suitable for social scientific investigation by communication researchers. For example, we might characterize wedding ceremonies as traditional or not, religious or secular in nature, ending in divorce or not, or by descriptions of one or both of the marriage partners (such as, "previously married, Oakland Raider fan, wanted by the FBI"). Realize that when a researcher reports that weddings between partners of different religions are more likely to be performed by secular authorities than those between partners of the same religion, the weddings are the units of analysis, not the individuals involved.

Other examples of such units of analysis are court cases, traffic accidents, fistfights, ship launchings, race riots, student demonstrations, and congressional hearings. The congressional hearings could be characterized by whether they occurred during an election campaign or not, whether the committee chairs were running for a higher office and/or had been convicted of a felony, and so forth.

Units of Analysis in Review

The purpose of this section has been to stretch your imagination somewhat regarding possible units of analysis for your research study. Although individual human beings are typical units of analysis, this need not be the case. Indeed, many research questions can be answered more appropriately through the examination of other units of analysis. (This discussion should point out once more that communication researchers can study absolutely anything.)

Realize further that the units of analysis we've named and discussed here are not the only possibilities. John and Lyn Lofland (1995) speak of practices, episodes, encounters, roles, relationships, groups, organizations, settlements, social worlds, lifestyles, and subcultures as suitable units of study. Grasping the logic of units of analysis is more important than repeating a particular list.

The concept of the unit of analysis may seem more complicated than it needs to be. What you call a given unit of analysis—a group, a formal organization, or a social artifact—is irrelevant. However, you must be clear about what your unit of analysis is. You must decide whether you are studying marriages or marriage partners, editorials or newspapers, corporations or corporate

executives. Unless you keep this point in mind, you run the risk of making assertions about one unit of analysis based on the examination of another.

To test your grasp of the concept of units of analysis, here are some examples of real research topics from published communication research. See if you can determine the unit of analysis in each. (The answers are at the end of this chapter.)

[1] Older adults have larger companionship networks than social support networks on the Internet. (Wright, 2000, p. 110)

[2] The growth of foreign TV programming took off shortly after the reforms started. Within the first decade of reforms, the proportion of imported TV programs jumped significantly from 9.5% in 1980 to 29.7% in 1990 and the number grew almost ten times. The most impressive increase occurred between 1985 and 1990, when the Chinese society became more dynamic and volatile and eventually culminated in the 1989 Tiananmen Square crackdown. (Wang & Chang, 1996, pp. 200–201)

[3] Seven major types of marital rituals were identified on the basis of responses of all 99 participating married couples. (Bruess & Pearson, 1997, p. 33)

[4] A pattern of black images in these advertisements emerges: only 19.27 percent of the advertisements during these black athlete dominated sporting events had any identifiable black images, and only 9.5 percent of the advertisements had major black spokespersons or images. (Wonsek, 1992, p. 455)

[5] Younger people were more likely than older people to discuss AIDS, but older people were more likely to use any noninterpersonal channel of AIDS information, regardless of its involvement level. (Engelberg, Flora, & Nass, 1995)

[6] Group performance is enhanced when groups engage in the "evaluation of task relevant issues." That is, the greater the attention given by groups to the positive and negative aspects of various choices, the more likely they are to make a correct choice. (Salazar, Hirokawa, Propp, Julian, & Leatham, 1994, p. 547)

[7] We have focused on advice, both in the examples we have offered thus far and in the study we will subsequently report, because we believe advice is a useful type of act on which to focus in developing a communicative approach to the study of social support. (Goldsmith & Fitch, 1997, p. 457)

[8] The excessively feminine displays of Mary Kay Cosmetics consultants exemplify a kind of performance

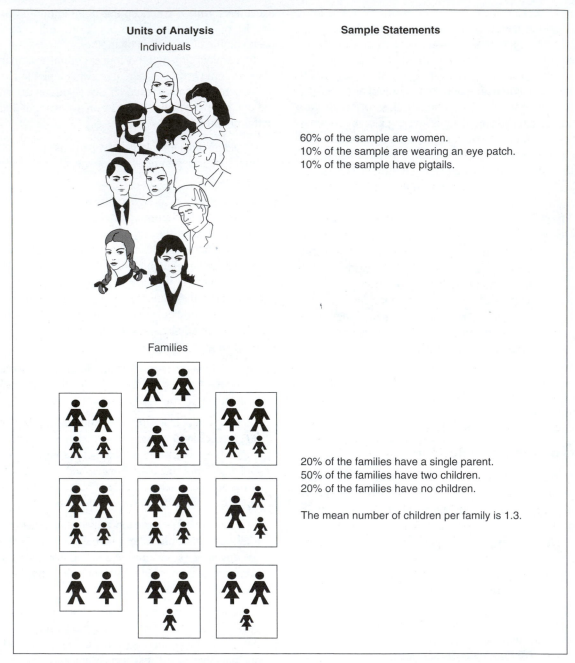

FIGURE 2-3 **Illustrations of Units of Analysis**

often associated with women in traditional women's cultures. (Waggoner, 1997, p. 256)

[9] Using a sample of 1,050 Dutch elementary school-children who were in Grades 2 and 4 at the outset of the research, this study investigated the longitudinal effects of television viewing on the frequency with which children read books and comic books at home. (Koolstra & Van Der Voort, 1996, p. 4)

[10] This study found that people who report high communication apprehension with regard to employment interviews are recommended to be hired less frequently than those who report less apprehension. (Ayres & Crosby, 1995, p. 148)

Figure 2-3 gives you a graphic illustration of some different units of analysis and the statements that might be made about them.

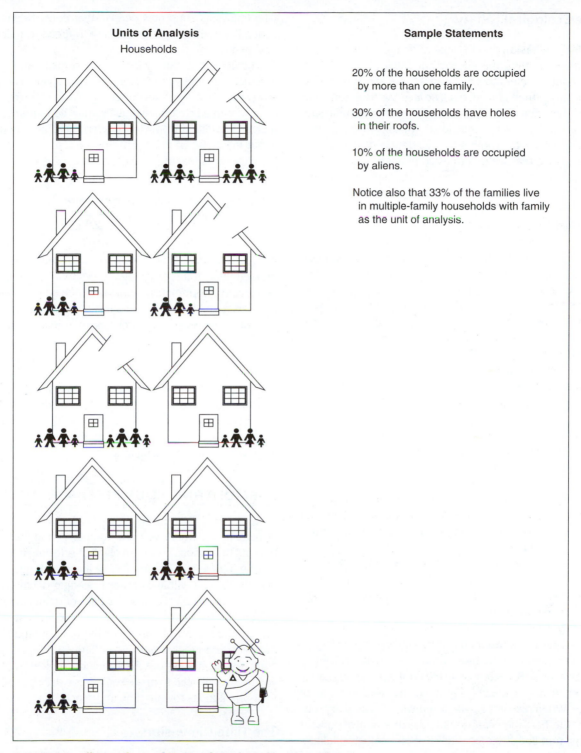

Units of Analysis
Households

Sample Statements

20% of the households are occupied by more than one family.

30% of the households have holes in their roofs.

10% of the households are occupied by aliens.

Notice also that 33% of the families live in multiple-family households with family as the unit of analysis.

FIGURE 2-3   **Illustrations of Units of Analysis (*continued*)**

The Ecological Fallacy

A clear understanding of units of analysis will help you avoid committing the **ecological fallacy.** *Ecological* in this context refers to groups or sets or systems: something larger than individuals. The *fallacy* is to assume that something learned about such an ecological unit says something about the individuals making up that unit. Let's consider a hypothetical illustration of this fallacy.

Suppose that we're interested in learning something about the effects of a mass media campaign against drinking alcohol while pregnant that was conducted in rural counties through a series of public service announcements. Let's assume that prior to the airing of the public service announcements (PSAs), we have access to some baseline data that provide us with information on the drinking behavior of clients who visit health-care clinics in those counties. Thus, we can tell which counties are characterized at the outset by more or less drinking among their residents. Assume also that we have demographic data describing some characteristics of residents of those counties. Our analysis of such data might show that counties with a higher average level of education featured less drinking behavior than counties with lower average education levels. We might be tempted to conclude from these findings that well-educated pregnant women are less likely to drink than are less-educated pregnant women. In reaching such a conclusion, we run the risk of committing the ecological fallacy because it may have been the less-educated women in those "well-educated" counties who refrained from drinking alcohol while pregnant. Our problem is that we have examined *counties* as our units of analysis but wish to draw conclusions about *pregnant women.*

The same problem would arise if we found TV viewing rates higher in Protestant countries than in Catholic ones. We still could not know for sure that more Protestants than Catholics watched more TV.

Very often, the communication researcher must address a particular research question through an ecological analysis. Perhaps the most appropriate data are simply not available. For example, in the drinking and pregnancy example, maybe the only data available are at the county level. When researchers are faced with this kind of problem, the best they can do is to reach tentative conclusions, mindful of the possibility of an ecological fallacy.

Don't let these warnings against the ecological fallacy lead you into committing what we might call an *individualistic fallacy.* Some students approaching communication research for the first time have trouble reconciling general patterns of attitudes and actions with individual exceptions they know of. If you know a painfully shy person who enjoys meeting new people, that doesn't deny the general pattern of shyness relating to dread in meeting new people.

The ecological fallacy deals with something else altogether—drawing conclusions about individuals based solely on the observation of groups. Although the patterns observed among variables may be genuine, the danger here lies in drawing unwarranted assumptions about the cause of those patterns—assumptions about the individuals making up the groups.

FORMULATING YOUR RESEARCH QUESTION OR HYPOTHESIS

If you have worked your way through the issues addressed thus far in this chapter, you should find yourself better able to formulate a formal research question or hypothesis to guide your data collection and analysis. The difference between a research question and a research hypothesis is that the latter advances a prediction about some phenomenon, whereas the former simply inquires about some phenomenon.

Depending on your purpose, your review of literature, and the kind of research you are undertaking, you will be attracted to different ways of formulating a research question/hypothesis. We will address this matter at length in the next two chapters.

FORMULATING YOUR RESEARCH DESIGN

Depending on where you end up in working your way through the various issues involved in selecting and narrowing a topic and in formulating a research question/hypothesis, you will find yourself heading down one of three methodological paths: the path of quantitative research (the subject of Part 2), the path of qualitative research (the subject of Part 3), or the multi-method path in which you employ both quantitative and qualitative methods. Regardless of which methodological "tool kit" you use, you'll need to make some basic decisions about your orientations toward time and space.

The Time Dimension

Time plays many roles in the design and execution of research, quite aside from the time it takes to do research. For example, in Chapter 3 we'll find that the time sequence of events and situations is critical to determining causation. Time also affects the generalizability of research findings. Do the descriptions and explanations resulting from a particular study accurately represent the situation of ten years ago, ten years from now, or only the present? Many field-based studies involve extended periods of time in the field, observing a group or culture day in and day out in order to identify patterned communicative practices. In short, researchers need to come to grips with how time enters into their designs. You need to do the same in planning your research study.

So far in this chapter, we have regarded research design as a process for deciding *what aspects* we shall observe, *of whom,* and *for what purpose.* Now we must consider a set of time-related options that cuts across each of these earlier considerations. We can choose to make observations more or less at one time or over a long period.

Cross-Sectional Studies   Many research projects are designed to study some phenomenon by taking a cross-section of it at one time and analyzing that cross-section carefully. Exploratory and descriptive studies are often **cross-sectional.** For example, a single public opinion poll is a study aimed at describing the U.S. population at a given time.

Many cause–effect explanatory studies are also cross-sectional. A researcher conducting a large-scale national survey to examine sources of sexual harassment would probably collect data from many different individuals or organizations at one point in time.

Cause–effect explanatory cross-sectional studies have an inherent problem. Although they typically aim at understanding causal processes that occur over time, their conclusions are based on observations made at only one time. This problem is somewhat akin to that of determining the speed of a moving object on the basis of a high-speed, still photograph that freezes the movement of the object.

The problem of speaking about communication in general, based on a snapshot in time, is one we will address repeatedly throughout this book. One solution is to collect data at several points in time.

Longitudinal Studies   Some research projects, called **longitudinal studies,** are designed to permit observations over an extended period. For example, a researcher can participate in and observe the communicative activities of a radical political group from its inception to its demise. In analyses of newspaper editorials or Supreme Court decisions over time, it would be irrelevant whether the researcher's actual observations and analyses were made at one time or over the course of the actual events under study; however, the studies would still be considered longitudinal.

Most field research projects, involving direct observation and perhaps in-depth interviews, are naturally longitudinal. Thus, for example, when Carolyn Ellis (1995) wanted to provide a qualitative understanding of what happens to a personal relationship, and to the two individuals, when one of the parties is dying from emphysema, she provided us a longitudinal glimpse over time as the illness progressed.

Longitudinal studies can be more difficult for quantitative studies such as large-scale surveys. Nonetheless, they are often undertaken, so three special types of longitudinal studies should be noted here:

- *Trend studies.* When we study changes within some general population over time, we engage in a **trend study.** Examples include a comparison of televised violence for each of several decades, showing us trends in the portrayal of violent acts, or a series of Gallup polls during the course of an election campaign, showing trends in the relative strengths and standing of different candidates. An additional example is a study conducted by Kevin Barnhurst and Diana Mutz (1997), who argued that the definition of "news" has changed in the 20th century. They conducted a content analysis of the news stories in selected U.S. newspapers from the years 1894, 1914, 1934, 1954, 1974, and 1994. In particular, they monitored the traditional five *W*'s of journalistic reporting: the who, what, when, where, why (and how) of news events. Over time, they noticed that stories grew longer, included more analysis, expanded from specific locations to broader regions, placed more emphasis on time frames other than the present, and named fewer individuals but more groups, officials, and outside sources. Thus, the basic "recipe" for news—the report of events new to the reader—has broadened over time to include contextualization and interpretations.

- *Cohort studies.* When we examine relatively specific subpopulations or *cohorts* as they change over time, we engage in a **cohort study.** Typically, a cohort is an age group, such as those people born during the 1920s, but it can also be based on some other time grouping, such as people born during the Vietnam War or people who got married in 1964. An example of a cohort study would be a series of national surveys, conducted perhaps every 10 years, to study attitudes toward open communication in marriage of the cohort that reached adulthood at the time of the Vietnam War. A sample of people 21–25 years of age might be surveyed in 1970, another sample of those 31–35 years of age in 1980, another sample of those

41–45 years of age in 1990, and another sample of those 51–55 years of age in 2000. Although the specific set of people studied in each survey would differ, each sample would represent the survivors of the cohort who reached adulthood around the time of the Vietnam War.

- *Panel studies*. Though similar to trend and cohort studies, **panel studies** examine the same set of people each time. For example, we could interview the same sample of voters every month during an election campaign, asking for whom they intended to vote. Although such a study would allow us to analyze overall trends in voter preferences for different candidates, it would also show the precise patterns of persistence and change in intentions. For example, a trend study that showed that Candidates A and B each had exactly half of the voters on September 1 and on October 1 as well could indicate that none of the electorate had changed voting plans, that all of the voters had changed their intentions, or something in between. A panel study would eliminate this confusion by showing what kinds of voters switched from A to B and what kinds switched from B to A, as well as other facts. Joseph Veroff, Elizabeth Douvan, and Shirley Hatchett (1995) wanted to learn about marital adjustment among newlyweds, looking for differences between white and African American couples. To get participants to study, they selected a sample of couples who applied for marriage licenses in Wayne County, Michigan, April through June 1986.

Concerned about the possible impact their research might have on the couples' marital adjustment, the researchers divided their sample in half at random: an *experimental* group and a *control* group (concepts we'll explore further in Chapter 9). Couples in the former group were intensively interviewed over a four-year period, whereas the latter group was contacted only briefly each year.

By studying the same couples over time, the researchers could follow the specific problems that arose and the way the couples dealt with them. As a by-product of their research, they found that those studied the most intensely seemed to achieve a somewhat better marital adjustment. The researchers felt that the interviews may have forced couples to discuss matters they may have otherwise buried.

Because the distinctions among trend, cohort, and panel studies are sometimes difficult to grasp at first, let's contrast the three study designs in terms of the same

phenomenon: attitudes toward sexual harassment. A trend study might look at shifts over time in society's attitudes toward sexual harassment, say a Gallup poll every 10 years across a 50-year period of time. A cohort study might follow shifts in attitudes toward sexual harassment among "the hippie generation" specifically, say, people who were between 18 and 25 in 1970. We could study a sample of people 28–35 years old in 1980, a new sample of people aged 38–45 in 1990, and so forth. A panel study could start with a sample of the whole population or of some special subset and study those specific individuals over time. Notice that only the panel study would give a full picture of the shifts in attitude. Cohort and trend studies would uncover only net changes.

Longitudinal studies have an obvious advantage over cross-sectional ones in providing information about communication processes over time. But this advantage often comes at a heavy cost in both time and money, especially in a large-scale survey. Observations may have to be made at the time events are occurring, and the method of observation may require many research workers.

Panel studies, which offer the most comprehensive data on changes over time, face a special problem: *panel attrition*. Some of the respondents studied in the first wave of the study may not participate in later waves. (This is comparable to the problem of experimental mortality discussed in Chapter 9.) The danger is that those who drop out of the study may not be typical, thereby distorting the results of the study.

Approximating Longitudinal Studies Often, we can draw approximate conclusions about processes that take place over time, even when only cross-sectional data are available. Here are some ways to do that.

Sometimes, cross-sectional data imply processes over time on the basis of simple logic. For example, in a study of student drug use that one of us was involved in, students were asked to report whether they had ever tried each of several illegal drugs. Regarding marijuana and LSD, it was found that some students had tried both drugs, some had tried only one, and others had not tried either. Because these data were collected at one time, and because some students presumably would experiment with drugs later on, it would appear that such a study could not tell whether students were more likely to try marijuana or LSD first.

However, a closer examination of the data showed that although some students reported having tried marijuana but not LSD, there were no students in the study who had tried only LSD. From this finding it was inferred—as common sense suggested—that marijuana use preceded LSD use. If the process of drug experimentation occurred in the opposite time order, then a study at a given time should have found some students who had tried LSD but not marijuana, and it should have found no students who had tried only marijuana.

Logical inferences may also be made whenever the time order of variables is clear. If we discovered in a cross-sectional study of college students that those educated in private high schools could craft more persuasive arguments than those educated in public high schools, we would conclude that the type of high school attended affected persuasiveness, not the other way around. Thus, even though our observations were made at only one time, we would feel justified in drawing conclusions about processes taking place across time.

Very often, age differences discovered in a cross-sectional study form the basis for inferring processes across time. Suppose that you're interested in developing public health campaigns targeted at people across the life span. Thus, you're interested in the pattern of worsening health over the course of the typical life cycle. You might study the results of annual checkups in a large hospital. You could group health records according to the ages of those examined and rate each age group in terms of several health conditions—sight, hearing, blood pressure, and so forth. By reading across the age-group ratings for each health condition, you would have something approximating the health history of individuals. Thus, you might conclude that the average person develops vision problems earlier in life than hearing problems, for example. You would need to be cautious in this assumption, however, since the differences might reflect society-wide trends. Perhaps improved hearing examinations instituted in the schools had affected only the young people in your study.

Asking people to *recall* their pasts is another common way of approximating observations over time. We use that method when we ask people where they were born or when they graduated from high school or whom they voted for in 2000.

The danger in this technique is evident. People sometimes have faulty memories; sometimes they lie. When people are asked in post-election polls whom they voted for, the results inevitably show more people voting for the winner than actually did so on election day. As part of a series of in-depth interviews, such a report can be validated in the context of other reported details; however, results based on a single question in a survey must be regarded with caution.

These, then, are some of the ways that time figures into communication research and some of the ways that

researchers have learned to cope with them. In designing any study, you need to look at both the explicit and the implicit assumptions you are making about time. Are you interested in describing some process that occurs over time, or are you simply going to describe what exists now? If you want to describe a process occurring over time, you will have to make observations at different points in the process, or you will have to approximate such observations—drawing logical inferences from what you can observe now. Unless you pay attention to questions like these, you'll probably end up in trouble. The box titled "The Time Dimension and Aging" explores this issue further.

The Space Dimension

Just as you need to think through the issue of time, you also need to think through the issue of space. In particular, you need to think through how the physical setting matters (if it does) in your research. In general, we can identify research in which the setting matters from research that is fairly independent of issues related to physical setting.

Field-Dependent Research   Often, researchers are interested in research topics in which the physical setting for the research is an integral part. For example, suppose that you are interested in how college roommates use their personal space in their dorm room: how bulletin boards are used to display individual identities, how beds are positioned to construct privacy, and so forth. You might be interested in whether roommates who are closer have greater communal space as opposed to space that is divided up into "mine" and "yours." An interest in personal space is part of a broad topic in nonverbal communication known as *proxemics.* But field-dependent research isn't limited to those with an interest in the topic of proxemics.

In general, researchers who conduct so-called *naturalistic field research* are interested in how people communicate in the natural surroundings of their everyday lives. In order to study people living their normal lives, researchers need to study them in their normal settings. For example, James Lull (1990) wanted to know how families viewed and used television. In order to answer this question, he had to spend time in the living rooms of actual families while they were watching TV. We'll have more to say about this kind of research in Part 3.

Researchers with an interest in *evaluation research* also conduct field-dependent research. We'll discuss evalua-

THE TIME DIMENSION AND AGING

By Joseph J. Leon
Behavioral Science Department
California State Polytechnic University, Pomona

One way to identify the type of time dimension used in a study is to imagine a number of different research projects on growing older in U.S. society. If we studied a sample of individuals in 1990 and compared the different age groups, the design would be termed *cross-sectional.* If we drew another sample of individuals using the same study instrument in the year 2000 and compared the new data with the 1990 data, the design would be termed *trend.*

Suppose we wished to study only those individuals who were 51–60 in the year 2000 and compare them with the 1990 sample of 41–50-year-old persons (the 41–50 age cohort); this study design would be termed *cohort.* The comparison could be made for the 51–60 and 61–70 age cohorts as well. Now, if we desired to do a panel study on growing older in America, we would draw a sample in the year 1990 and, using the same sampled individuals in the year 2000, do the study again. Remember, there would be fewer people in the year 2000 study because all the 41–50-year-old people in 1990 are 51–60 and there would be no 41–50-year-old individuals in the year 2000 study. Furthermore, some of the sampled individuals in 1990 would no longer be alive in the year 2000.

CROSS-SECTIONAL STUDY
1990
↕ 41–50
↕ 51–60
↕ 61–70
↕ 71–80

COHORT STUDY

1990	2000
41–50	41–50
51–60	51–60
61–70	61–70
71–80	71–80

TREND STUDY

1990	2000
41–50 ⟷	41–50
51–60 ⟷	51–60
61–70 ⟷	61–70
71–80 ⟷	71–80

PANEL STUDY

1990	2000
41–50*	41–50
51–60*	51–60*
61–70*	61–70*
71–80*	71–80*
	+81*

⟷ Denotes comparison
*Denotes same individuals

---

tion research in greater depth in Chapter 9, but we introduce it here to give another example of research in which the setting matters. Evaluation research—also known as program evaluation—assesses the impact of social interventions such as public health media campaigns and crisis management. Evaluation researchers are interested in specific actions in particular contexts. Do these specific public service announcements aired in Johnson County, Iowa, during March and April work in deterring young adolescents from smoking? Does the ABC system of conflict management work in facilitating a cooperative, working relationship between environmental factions in Oregon?

Field-Independent Research Researchers are also interested in a variety of topics that are independent of the setting. Often, when researchers ask study participants to fill out a questionnaire or complete an interview, the setting in which the responses are elicited doesn't matter very much, as long as it permits the participant to focus on the research task at hand. Thus, for example, when the U.S. Census mails a survey to all households, census officials don't care whether it is filled out in the kitchen or on the back patio, or on an airplane at 30,000 feet in the air. We will return to the topic of surveys in Chapter 8.

Researchers who conduct experimental research for purposes of inferring cause-and-effect relationships between variables are also engaged in field-independent research. Experimental researchers conduct tightly controlled studies in which variables are manipulated in order to study their effects; the setting of the experiment is regulated so that it cannot affect the responses of participants in the study. To experimental researchers, thus, the setting is not integral to the topic under study; instead, the setting is something to be controlled in order to determine the effects of an independent variable on a dependent variable. We will have more to say about experiments in Chapter 9.

As a beginning researcher, you need to think through whether the research topic that interests you is field-dependent or field-independent. How you answer this question will affect the methods you choose to study your topic.

Quite often, in the design of a research project, you'll have to lay out the details of your plan for someone else's review and/or approval. If your research involves human participants, you will need clearance from your institution's IRB (institutional review board) or your instructor, who may be functioning as the ethical clearinghouse for student research projects. We have more to say about IRBs in Chapter 5. In the case of a course project, your instructor might very well want to see a "proposal" before you set off to work in order to provide you with feedback. Later in your career, if you wanted to undertake a major project, you might need to obtain funding from a foundation or governmental agency, which would most definitely want a detailed proposal that described how you would spend its money. Sometimes, you will respond to a Request for Proposals (RFP), which both public and private agencies often circulate in search of someone to do research for them.

WRITING UP YOUR RESEARCH PROPOSAL

We'll conclude this chapter with a brief discussion of how you might prepare a research proposal. Although some funding agencies (or your instructor, for that matter) may have specific requirements for the elements and/or structure of a research proposal, we think of a research proposal as an abbreviated research report, with the obvious exception that you have not yet gathered your observations and thus have no results to report. You will have a title, a byline, an abstract (minus a summary of results and their implication), an introduction that presents a literature review and a rationale for the proposed study, a statement of your research questions/hypotheses, a de-

tailed description of your proposed methods, and a list of references. Because we have already discussed these components earlier in the chapter, we will not repeat ourselves here. In the Methods section, however, your proposal will address two issues not typically found in a research report: schedule and budget.

It's often appropriate to provide a schedule for the various stages of research. Unless you have a timeline for accomplishing the several stages of research and keeping track of how you're doing, you may end up in trouble.

When you ask someone to cover the costs of your research, you need to provide a specific budget. Large, expensive projects include budgetary categories such as personnel, equipment, supplies, telephones, and postage. Even for a project you'll pay for yourself, it's a good idea to spend some time anticipating expenses: office supplies, photocopying, computer disks, telephone calls, transportation, and so on.

Now let's turn to the matter of writing style and presentation. Before proceeding further, we should suggest one absolutely basic guideline. Good writing requires good English (or Spanish or whatever language you use). Whenever we ask the figures "to speak for themselves," they tend to remain mute. Whenever we use unduly complex terminology, communication is reduced. Every researcher should read and reread (at approximately three-month intervals) an excellent small book by William Strunk, Jr., and E. B. White, *The Elements of Style*. If you do this faithfully, and if even 10 percent of the contents rub off, you stand a rather good chance of making yourself understood and your findings appreciated.

In addition to having a writing style that is both literate and lucid, research proposals typically follow the presentation rules of the APA style. Appendix D provides a sample research report, whose layout and format you will need to modify in the ways we have discussed to propose a research study. It is important to pay attention to the details of this sample report—placement on a page, capitalization, and so forth.

The APA style also provides detailed guidelines for how to cite others' research in the body of the proposal and in the References list, among other issues involved in the preparation of a written research report. Appendix E presents a summary of some important citation guidelines in the APA style.

Now that you've had a broad overview of social scientific research in communication, let's move on to the remaining chapters in this book and learn exactly how to design and execute each specific step. If you've found a research topic that really interests you, you'll want to keep it in mind as you see how you might go about studying it.

Main Points

- Designing a research study involves seven basic steps: selecting and narrowing a topic area, conducting a review of research literature, determining your purpose, determining your unit of analysis, formulating a research question or hypothesis, formulating a research design, and preparing a research proposal.

- A review of literature is a survey of existing primary research relevant to your topic. A review of literature is an argument or rationale for the study. Research questions or hypotheses must flow logically from the review of literature.

- There are several different kinds of research reports, depending on the researcher's purpose and audience: the proprietary report, the working paper, the conference paper, the research note, the research article, and the scholarly book.

- Most research in communication journals employs the APA style for the organization and presentation of a research study.

- Qualitative studies present findings in the form of a narrative tale, whereas quantitative studies present findings through quantitative and statistical summaries.

- Exploration is the attempt to develop an initial, rough understanding of some phenomenon.

- Description is the precise reporting of the characteristics of some population or phenomenon under study.

- Causal explanation is the discovery and reporting of relationships among different aspects of the phenomenon under study. Whereas descriptive studies answer the question "what's so?" causal explanatory ones tend to answer the question "why?"

- Functional explanation is the discovery and reporting of how parts of systems function interdependently. Instead of focusing on "why?" functional explanatory studies tend to answer the question "how?"

- Understanding is the attempt to render intelligible what and how something means.

- Units of analysis are the people or things the characteristics of which communication researchers observe, describe, explain, and understand. Typically, the unit of analysis in communication research is the individual person, but it may also be a group or a social artifact.

- The ecological fallacy involves conclusions drawn from the analysis of groups (e.g., corporations) that are then assumed to apply to individuals (e.g., the employees of corporations).

- Cross-sectional studies are based on observations made at one time. Although such studies are limited by this characteristic, inferences can be made about processes that occur over time.

- In longitudinal studies, observations are made at many times. Such observations may be made of samples drawn from general populations (trend studies), samples drawn from more specific subpopulations (cohort studies), or the same sample of people each time (panel studies).

- In field-dependent studies, the physical setting is an integral part of the phenomenon of interest to the researcher. By contrast, in field-independent studies, the physical setting is either irrelevant or tightly controlled.

- A research proposal provides a preview of why a study will be undertaken and how it will be conducted. A useful device for planning, it may also be required in most circumstances.

Key Terms

review of literature	unobtrusive research
replication	ecological fallacy
triangulation	cross-sectional study
APA style	longitudinal study
quantitative research	trend study
qualitative research	cohort study
units of analysis	panel study

Review Questions and Exercises

1. Consult the communication journals listed in Appendix A in order to locate studies that illustrate exploration, description, causal explanation, functional explanation, and understanding.

2. Make up a research example—different from those discussed in the text—that would illustrate a researcher falling into the trap of the ecological fallacy. Then modify the example to avoid this trap.

3. Consult communication journals to locate examples of cross-sectional and longitudinal research.

4. Consult communication journals to locate examples of field-dependent and field-independent research.

5. Identify a research topic in communication. Write up a literature review of a minimum of five research studies on the topic, using the citation guidelines of the APA style.

Continuity Project

With the general topic area of gender/sex and communication in mind, try to formulate several research questions that vary in their purpose and in their unit of analysis.

Additional Readings

American Psychological Association (2001). *Publication manual of the American Psychological Association* (5th ed.). Washington, DC: Author. The standard reference book on how to write up communication research for publication in journals. It includes many excellent suggestions on writing style, in addition to the discussion of presentation and formatting guidelines.

Cooper, H. M. (1989). *Integrating research: A guide for literature reviews.* Newbury Park, CA: Sage. The author leads you through each step in the literature review process.

Katzer, J., Cook. K. H., & Crouch, W. W. (1991). *Evaluating information: A guide for users of social science research.* New York: McGraw-Hill. A very useful book that provides an extended discussion of how to read a research report, particularly for quantitative research reports.

Rubin, R. B., Rubin, A. M., & Piele, L. J. (2000). *Communication research: Strategies and sources* (5th ed.). Belmont, CA: Wadsworth. This is an outstanding book in describing how to conduct a literature review in communication and how to plan a research study.

Strunk, W., Jr., & White, E. B. (1979). *The elements of style* (3rd ed.). New York: Macmillan. An excellent little book on how to write well. Read, reread, and reread it again.

InfoTrac College Edition
http://www.infotrac-college.com/
wadsworth/access.html

Access the latest news and journal articles with Info-Trac College Edition, an easy-to-use online database of reliable, full-length articles from hundreds of top academic journals. Conduct an electronic search using the following search terms:

- replication
- triangulation
- unit of analysis
- cross-sectional study
- longitudinal study
- quantitative research
- qualitative research

Answers to Units of Analysis Exercise (pages 35–36)

1. Individuals (older adults)
2. Social artifacts (Chinese TV programming by year)
3. Social artifacts (marital rituals)
4. Social artifacts (advertisements)
5. Individuals (younger vs. older persons)
6. Groups (decision-making groups)
7. Social artifacts (advice)
8. Individuals (Mary Kay consultants)
9. Individuals (Dutch children)
10. Individuals (interviewees)

CHAPTER 3

Paradigms of Knowing in Communication Research

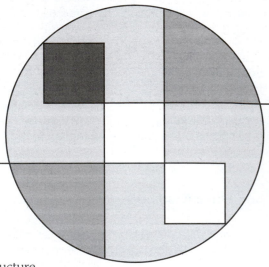

What You'll Learn in This Chapter

You'll see some of the basic theoretical points of view that structure social scientific inquiry about communication. This chapter will lay the groundwork for your understanding of the specific research techniques discussed throughout the rest of the book.

INTRODUCTION

Imagine Researcher A, who is interested in finding out why people differ in their anxiety levels when they speak in public. She wonders whether early life experiences with adult caregivers have anything to do with anxiety levels experienced later in life. She locates a prominent theory of caregiver–child interaction, attachment theory. After reading about early-life attachment, she predicts that people with secure early-life attachment experiences are likely to be characterized by less communication anxiety in public than will characterize people with insecure attachment experiences. In order to test this prediction, she locates a group of 200 first-year university students on the first day of their required class in public speaking and collects quantitative data from them using already established measures of speaking anxiety when speaking in public and early-life attachment. She examines statistically the extent to which people with secure and insecure early-life attachment experiences vary in their speech anxiety levels.

Now imagine Researcher B, who is also interested in people's anxiety levels when they speak publicly. He is interested in how the communication system functions for people who are very high in speaking anxiety. In particular, he wants to know how the verbal, or linguistic, communication of such speakers functions in conjunction with their nonverbal communication (for example, their body movements, their eye contact, and their facial expressions). He videotapes speakers known to be high in public speech anxiety and examines whether the verbal and nonverbal messages are synchronized and consistent with one another.

Now imagine Researcher C, who is also interested in learning more about people's anxiety levels when they speak in public. This researcher takes out an ad in a local newspaper, seeking volunteers who perceive themselves to experience high anxiety when they speak in public. He interviews each volunteer in depth, seeking to understand, from their point of view and in their own words, what anxiety feels like to them. Do their palms sweat? Do they feel nauseated? He looks for commonalities among his interviewees in what anxiety means to them as they experience it. He writes up his findings by describing these common themes in detail, quoting from his interviews in order to illustrate these themes.

Researcher D also has an interest in public speaking anxiety. She spends a year in a kindergarten classroom, observing the details of when and how children talk aloud. For example, she notes how these children come to understand the boundary between "private talk" (for example, whispering with the child seated in the adjacent chair) and "public talk" (talking in front of the whole class). She comes to understand that a key marker of this boundary, to the children and the teacher alike, is whether hand raising is required in order to speak. She notices who is encouraged and allowed to talk "privately" and "in public," and who is discouraged from doing so. Over the course of the year, she talks with the children about their anxieties in talking in various ways and in various contexts in the classroom. She writes up her observations in the form of a critique of the early-education system, arguing that it systematically silences girls more so than boys in speaking in public, citing her observations as supporting evidence for her claims.

You may be wondering how we can describe these four researchers as interested in the same general topic when their research inquiries appear so different! These four examples illustrate typical kinds of research you are likely to find in communication studies. Taken as a set, these four examples illustrate the four basic research traditions, or paradigms, that dominate social scientific research about communication: the positivist tradition, the systems tradition, the interpretive tradition, and the critical tradition. The purpose of this chapter is to introduce you to these four paradigms, traditions that can be identified within most social scientific fields, not just communication.

Why is it important for you to understand these research traditions? Several reasons come to mind. First, we want you to appreciate the diversity of approaches that communication researchers can take in studying what is seemingly the same general topic of interest. Second, the criteria by which we determine valid research vary somewhat from tradition to tradition. It is important to know which tradition grounds a particular study in order to know the criteria by which we can appropriately evaluate its knowledge claims. Third, different paradigms of knowing are associated with different methods of research. When you read about a particular method, it is important to understand the tradition of knowing typically associated with it.

FOUR SOCIAL SCIENCE PARADIGMS: AN OVERVIEW

Because theories organize our observations and make sense of them, there is normally more than one way to make sense of things. Different points of view usually yield different explanations and understandings. This is true in daily life: Liberals and conservatives, for example, often explain the same phenomenon quite differently; so do atheists and fundamentalists.

We begin our examination, then, with some of the major points of view that communication researchers employ in the search for explanation and understanding. Thomas Kuhn (1970) refers to the fundamental points of view characterizing a science as its **paradigms.** In the history of the natural sciences, major paradigms include Newtonian mechanics, Einsteinian relativism, Darwin's evolutionary theory, and Copernicus's heliocentric theory of heavenly motion, to name a few.

While we sometimes think of science as developing gradually over time, marked by important discoveries and inventions, Kuhn says that it was typical for one paradigm to become entrenched, resisting any substantial change. Eventually, however, as the shortcomings of that paradigm became obvious, a new paradigm would emerge and supplant the old one. Thus, the view that the sun revolves around the earth was supplanted by the view that the earth revolves around the sun. Kuhn's classic book on this subject is titled, appropriately enough, *The Structure of Scientific Revolutions.*

Social scientists have developed several paradigms for understanding social behavior. However, the fate of supplanted paradigms in the social sciences has differed from what Kuhn has observed in the natural sciences. Natural scientists generally believe that the succession from one paradigm to another represents progress from a false view to a true one. No modern astronomer believes that the sun revolves around the earth.

In the social sciences, on the other hand, theoretical paradigms may gain or lose popularity, but they're seldom discarded. As you'll see shortly, the paradigms in communication research offer a variety of views, each of which offers insights that the others lack—but ignores aspects of communication that the others reveal.

Thus, each of the paradigms we're about to examine offers a different way of looking at communication. Each makes certain assumptions about the nature of social reality. We advise you to examine each in terms of how it might open up new understandings for you, rather than to try to decide which is true and which is false. Ultimately, paradigms cannot be true or false; as ways of looking, they can only be more or less useful. Try to find ways that these paradigms might be useful to you. We'll return to this point at the end of the chapter.

THE POSITIVIST PARADIGM

When the French philosopher Auguste Comte (1798–1857) argued that society could be studied in the same way that scientists studied natural phenomena, he launched an intellectual adventure that is still unfolding today. (Initially, he wanted to label his enterprise "social physics," but that term was co-opted by another scholar.)

Prior to Comte's time, society simply *was*. To the extent that people recognized different kinds of societies or changes in society over time, religious paradigms generally predominated in explanations of the differences. The state of social affairs was often seen as a reflection of God's will. Alternatively, people were challenged to create a "City of God" on earth to replace sin and godlessness.

Comte separated his inquiry from religion. He felt that society could be studied scientifically, that religious belief could be replaced with scientific objectivity. His "positive philosophy" postulated three stages of history. A "theological stage" predominated throughout the world until about 1300. During the next five hundred years, a "metaphysical stage" replaced God with ideas such as "nature" and "natural law."

Finally, Comte felt he was launching the third stage of history, in which science would replace religion and metaphysics—basing knowledge on observations through the five senses rather than on belief. Comte felt that society could be studied and understood logically and rationally, and that such study could be as scientific as biology or physics.

Comte's view came to form the foundation for subsequent development of the social sciences. In his optimism for the future, he coined the term *positivism* to describe this scientific approach—in contrast to what he regarded as negative elements of the Enlightenment.

The **positivist paradigm** has undergone many refinements, revisions, and criticisms since its articulation by Comte in the mid-19th century. This tradition is one of the mainstays of communication research today.

Positivist research is marked by certain features: the belief in an objective reality knowable only through empirical observation; the study of variables; the development of theories that enable prediction, explanation, and control; the search for generalized laws; and observations in the form of quantitative data. Researcher A in our opening section illustrates someone grounded in the positivist research tradition. She was interested in identifying the underlying causes of speech anxiety, focusing in particular on early-life attachment experiences with adult caregivers such as parents.

An Objective Reality

In Chapter 1 we note that researchers hold different beliefs about reality. Positivist researchers believe that there is an objective reality "out there," independent of the researcher. Knowledge claims about this reality rest on empirical observations. Positivist researchers place an emphasis on objective ways to gather empirical observations in order to minimize the subjectivity of the researcher. We will return to this point in greater detail in Chapter 6. Furthermore, reality is characterized by a pattern of relations between phenomena such that everything can be explained as a result (effect) of a real cause that precedes it. This reality is fragmentable, which means that a researcher can discover one cause-and-effect law at a time. These laws are discoverable through the use of systematic, rigorous methods that minimize the subjective biases of the researcher. Communication researchers who adopt the positivist tradition believe that communication practices and patterns have an objective reality to them that awaits discovery through valid methods. The primary methods used by positivist researchers are surveys (Chapter 8), experiments (Chapter 9), and quantitative text analysis (Chapter 10).

The Study of Variables

Positivist researchers don't study individuals or other social phenomena per se; instead, they study features or characteristics about individuals or phenomena. These features or characteristics are known as variables.

In the instance of Researcher A in the introduction to this chapter, the variables under study were speech anxiety and early-life attachment. People vary in their level of speech anxiety, just as they vary in the kinds of early-life attachment experiences they had with their adult caregivers.

Because the idea of variables may be foreign to you, here's an analogy to demonstrate what we mean. The subject of a physician's attention is the patient. If the patient is ill, the physician's purpose is to help that patient get well. By contrast, a medical researcher's subject matter is different: a disease, for example. The medical researcher, adopting the positivist tradition, may study the physician's patient, but for the researcher that patient is relevant only as a carrier of the disease. The disease would be the variable for the medical researcher.

That is not to say that medical researchers don't care about real people. They certainly do. Their ultimate purpose in studying diseases is to protect people from them. But in their actual research, patients are directly relevant only for what they reveal about the disease under study. In fact, when they can study a disease meaningfully without involving actual patients, medical researchers do so.

Positivist communication research involves the study of variables and the attributes that compose them. Positivist theories are written in a language of variables, and people get involved only as the carriers of those variables. Here's a closer look at what positivist communication researchers mean by variables and attributes.

Attributes or values are characteristics or qualities that describe an object or phenomenon—in this case, the communicative behaviors of a person. Examples include *chatty, high-pitched,* and *rapid.* Anything you might say to describe how you communicate or how someone else communicates involves an attribute.

Variables, on the other hand, are logical groupings of attributes. Thus, for example, *chatty* and *reticent* are attributes, and *level of talkativeness* is the variable composed of these two attributes. The variable *pitch level* is composed of attributes such as *high, moderate,* and *low.* And the variable of *rate of speaking* is composed of attributes such as *rapid* and *slow.* Instead of using adjectives such as *rapid* or *slow,* we might want to substitute the number of words spoken per minute, with each number representing a possible attribute for the speaking rate variable. Sometimes it helps to think of attributes as the "categories" or "quantities" that can make up a variable. Figure 3-1 provides a schematic review of some sample variables often studied by communication researchers. Figure 3-1A provides a list of some concepts you might encounter in communication research. Figure 3-1B indicates whether the elements in this list are variables or attributes. For each variable identified in 3-1B, Figure 3-1C indicates its possible attributes. For each attribute identified in 3-1B, Figure 3-1C indicates the underlying variable. Thus, for example, *advice* is an attribute of the underlying variable *kind of social support,* along with such other attributes as *monetary assistance.* However, the designation of variables and attributes is not absolute. To the researcher interested in discovering all of the kinds of social support, advice is an attribute. However, to the researcher interested in studying advice as a variable, the attributes might be whether the form of the advice was direct or indirect, or whether the advice was transmitted in face-to-face or mediated channels.

A. Some Communication Concepts

Advice
Indirect
Nonverbal
Verbal
Violent acts per hour
E-mail
Face-to-face
Speech anxiety
Conflict style
Submissive
% Female characters

B. Different Kinds of Concepts

Variables	Attributes
	Advice
	Indirect
	Nonverbal
	Verbal
Violent acts per hour	
	E-mail
	Face-to-face
Speech anxiety	
Conflict style	
	Submissive
% Female characters	

C. The Relationship between Variables and Attributes

Variables	Attributes
Kind of social support	Advice, monetary assistance . . .
Directness of talk	Direct, indirect
Channel of communication	Verbal, nonverbal
Violent acts per hour	0, 1, 2, 3, 4 . . .
Medium of communication	E-mail, face-to-face, telephone, letter . . .
Speech anxiety	Low, medium, high . . .
Conflict style	Competitive, submissive, collaborative . . .
% female characters	0%, 10%, 20%, . . . 100%

FIGURE 3-1 **Variables and Attributes**

The relationship between attributes and variables lies at the heart of description in positivist science. For example, we might describe television shows in terms of the variable *sex* by reporting the observed frequencies of the attributes *male* and *female:* "Prime-time television shows for the Monday–Friday period were composed of 60 percent male and 40 percent female characters." We might also describe television shows in terms of their portrayal of violence. If we summarized our observations by saying that "TV show X portrayed 15 acts of physical violence, and TV show Y portrayed 5 acts of physical violence," the numbers *15* and *5* are attributes of the *violence* variable.

Sometimes, the meanings of the concepts that lie behind social scientific concepts are pretty clear. Other times, they aren't. This is discussed in the box "The Hardest Hit Was . . ."

The relationship between attributes and variables is more complicated in the case of explanation and gets to the heart of the variable language of positivist social scientific theory. Here's an example involving two variables, *sex of speaker* and *level of self-disclosure.* For the sake of simplicity, let's assume that the self-disclosure variable has only two attributes: *high* and *low* (Chapter 6 will address the issue of how such things are defined and measured). And sex of speaker also has two attributes: *female* and *male.*

Now let's suppose that 90 percent of the females are high in self-disclosure and the other 10 percent are low in self-disclosure. And let's suppose that 30 percent of the males are high in self-disclosure and the other 70 percent are low in self-disclosure. This is illustrated graphically in Figure 3-2A.

Figure 3-2A illustrates a *relationship* or *association* between the variables *sex of speaker* and *level of self-disclosure.* This relationship can be seen in terms of the pairings of attributes on the two variables. There are two predominant pairings: (1) females who are high in self-disclosure and (2) males who are low in self-disclosure. Here are two other useful ways of viewing that relationship.

First, let's suppose that we play a game in which we bet on your ability to guess whether a person is high or

THE HARDEST HIT WAS . . .

In early 1982, a deadly storm ravaged the San Francisco Bay Area, leaving an aftermath of death, injury, and property damage. As the mass media sought to highlight the most tragic results of the storm, they sometimes focused on several people who were buried alive in a mud slide in Santa Cruz. Other times, they covered the plight of the 2,900 made homeless in Marin County.

Implicitly, everyone wanted to know where the worst damage was done, but the answer was not clear. Here are some data describing the results of the storm in two counties: Marin and Santa Cruz. Look over the comparisons, and see if you can determine which county was "hardest hit."

	Marin	Santa Cruz
Businesses destroyed	$15.0 million	$56.5 million
People killed	5	22
People injured	379	50
People displaced	370	400
Homes destroyed	28	135
Homes damaged	2,900	300
Businesses destroyed	25	10
Businesses damaged	800	35
Private damages	$65.1 million	$50.0 million
Public damages	$15.0 million	$56.5 million

Certainly, in terms of the loss of life, Santa Cruz was the "hardest hit" of the two counties. Yet more than seven times as many people were injured in Marin as in Santa Cruz; certainly, Marin County was "hardest hit" in that regard. Or consider the number of homes destroyed (worse in Santa Cruz) or damaged (worse in Marin): It matters which you focus on. The same dilemma holds true for the value of the damage done: Should we pay more attention to private damage or public damage?

So which county was "hardest hit"? Ultimately, the question as posed has no answer. While we and you both have images in our minds about communities that are "devastated" or communities that are only "lightly touched," these images are not precise enough to permit rigorous measurements.

The question can be answered only if we can specify what we mean by "hardest hit." If we measure it by death toll, then Santa Cruz was the hardest hit. If we choose to define the variable in terms of people injured and/or displaced, then Marin was the bigger disaster. The simple fact is that we cannot answer the question without specifying exactly what we mean by the term *hardest hit*. This is a fundamental requirement that will arise again and again as we attempt to measure social science variables.

Data source: San Francisco Chronicle, January 13, 1982, p. 16.

---

low in self-disclosure—that is, a guess about whether the person is likely to reveal a lot or a little personal information about himself or herself. We'll pick the people one at a time from Figure 3-2A (not telling you which ones we've picked), and you have to guess whether each person is likely to be high or low in self-disclosure. We'll do it for all 20 people in Figure 3-2A. Your best strategy in this case would be to guess highly self-disclosive each time, since 12 out of the 20 are categorized that way. Thus, you'll get 12 right and 8 wrong, for a net success of 4.

Now let's suppose that when we pick a person from the figure, we have to tell you whether the person is a male or a female. Your best strategy now would be to guess high in self-disclosure for each female and low in self-disclosure for each male. If you followed this strategy, you'd get 16 right and only 4 wrong. Your improvement in guessing level of self-disclosure by knowing the sex of the person is an illustration of what we mean by the variables being related. (This procedure, by the way, provides the basis for the statistic known as *lambda*.)

Second, by contrast, let's consider how the 20 people would be distributed if sex of speaker and level of self-disclosure were *unrelated* to each other. This is illustrated in Figure 3-2B. Notice that half the people are female and half are male. Also notice that 12 of the 20 (60 percent) are high in self-disclosure. If 6 of the 10 people in each group were high in self-disclosure, we would conclude that the two variables were unrelated to each other. Knowing a speaker's sex would not be of any value to you in guessing whether that person was likely to be high or low in self-disclosure.

You'll be looking at the nature of relationships among variables in some depth in a later section of this book. In particular, you'll see some of the ways relationships can

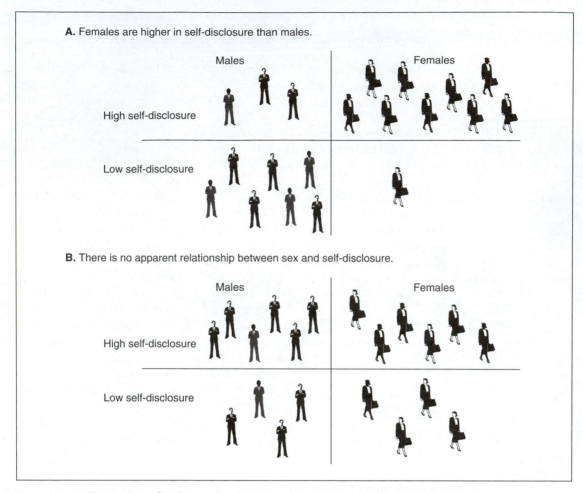

FIGURE 3-2 **Illustration of Relationship between Two Variables (Two Possibilities)**

be discovered and interpreted in research analysis. However, you need a general comprehension of the relationship between variables to appreciate the logic of positivist communication theories.

Positivist Theory

In the positivist tradition of social scientific research, *theories* describe the relationships we might logically expect among variables. When variables are related, we have the ability to predict one variable with knowledge of the other variable. Usually, however, positivist researchers have a goal greater than prediction. They seek to explain the cause–effect relationship between variables. A person's attributes on one variable are expected to cause, predispose, or encourage a particular attribute on another variable. In the example just illustrated, it appeared that a speaker's sex predisposed that person to be high or

low in self-disclosure. It seems that there is something about being male or female that leads people to be less disclosive if they are male, or at least this is the pattern presented in Figure 3-2A.

As we'll discuss in more detail later in the book, sex of speaker and level of self-disclosure in this example would be regarded as the **independent variable** and the **dependent variable,** respectively. In the example of Figure 3-2A, we assume that the likelihood of disclosing personal information is determined or caused by something. Self-disclosure depends on something; hence, it is called the dependent variable, which depends on an independent variable, in this case the speaker's sex. Although people's sex varies from one person to another, such variation is independent of their level of self-disclosure.

The discussion of Figure 3-2A has involved the interpretation of data. We looked at the distribution of the 20 people in terms of the two variables. In constructing a positivist theory, we would derive an expectation regarding the relationship between the two variables based on what we know about each. We know, for example, that in U.S. society males and females are socialized to different kinds of behaviors. Females are socialized more so than males to share their emotions and innermost feelings. Females are portrayed on the media as "relationship specialists" more so than males are portrayed, and they are shown engaged in self-disclosure as a kind of "social glue" that builds and sustain personal intimacy. When people are high in self-disclosure, they are involved in sharing their emotions and innermost feelings, often for purposes of creating or maintaining intimacy with others. Logically, then, we would expect that a person's sex and likelihood of high self-disclosure would be related. This expectation would be tested by observations of the communicative behaviors of males and females in real-life settings.

Whereas Figure 3-2 illustrates two possibilities—(a) that one's sex is related to one's level of self-disclosure or (b) that there is no relationship between a person's sex and level of self-disclosure—you might be interested in knowing what actual research has found. According to Kathryn Dindia and Mike Allen (1992), who conducted a meta-analysis (a statistical analysis of the findings across several research studies) of over 205 studies on sex differences in self-disclosure, females are slightly more likely than males to be high in self-disclosure. However, they found that this slight difference is moderated by the sex of the person to whom the speaker is talking, the closeness of the personal relationship between them, and how the researcher chose to measure self-disclosure. In other words, our theory that links sex of speaker with level of self-disclosure is probably too simplistic. If we are trying to create a theory that enables us to predict and explain people's levels of self-disclosure, we probably need to take into account several independent variables, including, at a minimum, the variables of speaker sex (with attributes female and male), the sex of the interaction partner (with attributes female and male), and the closeness of the relationship between the speaker and his or her partner (with attributes such as "close" and "distant").

Remember Researcher A, with whom we began this chapter? She was interested in the two variables of speech anxiety and early-life attachment. Her theory of speech anxiety led her to predict a relationship between level of speech anxiety and type of early-life attachment, and she explained this relationship as a causal one. Her expectation was that early-life attachment experiences caused a person to experience more or less comfort, and thus anxiety, when speaking in public to others. That is,

Researcher A thought that early-life attachment was the independent variable and that speech anxiety was the dependent variable. To our knowledge, this theory has not yet been put to the test through empirical observation. Thus, we don't know whether Researcher A's theory of speech anxiety adequately fulfills our criteria of prediction and **causal explanation.** Demonstrating causality is a complicated business.

Paul Lazarsfeld (1959) suggested three specific criteria for demonstrating causality among variables. *The first requirement in a causal relationship between two variables is that the cause precede the effect in time.* It makes no sense in positivist science to imagine something being caused by something else that happens later on. A bullet leaving the muzzle of a gun does not cause the gunpowder to explode; it works the other way around.

As simple and obvious as this criterion may seem, you'll discover endless problems in this regard in the analysis of communication data. Often, the order of two variables is simply unclear. In a study to examine the relationship between marital satisfaction and the expression of negativity, which comes first? Dissatisfied marital partners might express more negativity toward each other than would their satisfied counterparts, to be sure. But it is also quite possible that when negativity is expressed, satisfaction dwindles in marital couples.

Even when the time order seems essentially clear, exceptions can often be found. For example, in a study to examine the effects of parenting style on child behavior, it is easy to assume that the parental behavior is the cause of the child's behavior. But, as any parent can tell you, the causal direction may go in reverse: how the parent behaves may be the result, not the cause, of the child's behavior.

The second requirement in a causal relationship is that the two variables be empirically related to each other. It would make no sense to say that exploding gunpowder causes bullets to leave the muzzles of guns if, in observed reality, bullets did not come out after the gunpowder exploded.

Again, communication research has difficulties in regard to this apparently obvious requirement. At least in the probabilistic world of explanations, there are few perfect relationships. Most of the time, the amount of studying for an exam is related to exam performance, but not always. Therefore, we are forced to ask how great the empirical relationship must be for that relationship to be considered causal.

The third requirement for a causal relationship is that the observed empirical correlation between two variables cannot be explained in terms of some third variable related

to both of them. For example, there is a positive relationship between ice cream sales and deaths due to drowning: the more ice cream sold, the more drownings, and vice versa. The third variable at work here is season or temperature. Most drowning deaths occur during summer—the peak period for ice cream sales. There is no direct causal relationship between ice cream sales and drowning, however.

Any relationship satisfying all three of these criteria is causal, and these are the only criteria. To emphasize this point more strongly, let's briefly examine some inappropriate criteria sometimes employed, especially by non-scientists. In this discussion, we are indebted to Travis Hirschi and Hanan Selvin for an excellent article on this subject and its later expansion in their book *Principles of Survey Analysis* (1973, pp. 114–136).

First, to review a point made earlier, a perfect relationship between variables is not a criterion of causality in communication research (or in science generally, for that matter). Put another way, exceptions, although they do not prove the rule, do not necessarily deny the rule either. In probabilistic models, there are almost always exceptions to the posited relationship. If a few people got higher exam scores in the absence of studying and a few people who studied hard received lower exam scores, that would not deny the general causal relationship between amount of studying and exam grade.

Within this probabilistic model, it is useful to distinguish two types of causes: necessary and sufficient. A *necessary cause* represents a condition that must be present for the effect to follow. For example, it is necessary for you to take college courses in order to get a degree, but simply taking the courses is not sufficient. (You need to take the right ones and pass them.)

A *sufficient cause,* on the other hand, represents a condition that, if it is present, will pretty much guarantee the effect in question. Thus, for example, getting married is a sufficient cause for becoming sex partners, though it's not the only way. Or skipping an exam in this course would be a sufficient cause for failing it, though you could fail it other ways as well.

The discovery of a necessary and sufficient cause is, of course, the most satisfying outcome in communication research. If marital satisfaction were the dependent variable or the effect under examination, it would be nice to discover a single communication behavior between spouses that (1) had to be present for satisfaction to occur and (2) always resulted in satisfaction. In such a case, you would surely feel that you knew precisely what caused marital satisfaction.

Unfortunately, we never discover single causes that are absolutely necessary and absolutely sufficient when analyzing the relationships among variables. However, it is not uncommon to find causal factors that are either 100-percent necessary (for example, you must be female to become pregnant) or 100-percent sufficient (pleading guilty in a court of law will result in your conviction).

In communication research, either necessary or sufficient causes—even imperfect ones—can be the basis for concluding there is a causal relationship between variables. However, in order to claim that one variable causes another, the researcher must be able to demonstrate that (1) the cause precedes the effect in time, (2) there is an observed empirical relationship between them, and (3) the relationship is not found to be the result of some third variable.

Generalized Laws

Notice that our theory of speaker sex and level of self-disclosure had to do with two variables, not with people per se. People are, as we indicated before, the carriers of these two variables, so the relationship between the variables can be seen only when we observe people. Ultimately, however, the theory uses a language of variables. It describes the associations we might logically expect to exist between particular attributes of different variables, and it explains why those associations exist. Our theory illustrates a **nomothetic** type of explanation, in contrast to an **idiographic** explanation.

We actually use both nomothetic and idiographic types of explanations as we go through life explaining things around us every day. You explain why you did poorly or well on an exam, why your favorite team is winning or losing, why you may be having trouble getting dates you enjoy.

Sometimes, we attempt to explain a single situation exhaustively. Thus, for example, you may have done poorly on an exam because (1) you had forgotten there was an exam that day, (2) it was in your worst subject, (3) a traffic jam made you late for class, (4) your roommate had kept you up the night before the exam with loud music, (5) the police kept you until dawn demanding to know what you had done with your roommate's stereo—and with your roommate, for that matter—and (6) a wild band of coyotes ate your textbook. Given all these circumstances, it is no wonder that you did poorly.

This type of causal explanation is called an idiographic explanation. *Idio* in this context means unique, separate, or distinct, as in the word *idiosyncrasy.* When we have completed an idiographic explanation, we feel that we fully understand the causes of what happened in this particular instance. At the same time, our explanation is limited to the case at hand. While parts of the idiographic explanation might apply to other situations, our intention is to explain one case fully.

Now consider a different kind of explanation. (1) Every time you study with a group, you do better on the exam than if you study alone. (2) Your favorite team does better at home than on the road. (3) Athletes get more dates than members of the Biology Club. This type of explanation—labeled nomothetic—seeks to explain a class of situations or events rather than a single one. Moreover, it seeks to explain "economically," using only one or just a few explanatory factors. Finally, it settles for a partial rather than a full explanation.

In each of these examples, you might qualify your causal statements with such words or phrases as *on the whole, usually,* or *all else being equal.* Thus, you usually do better on exams when you've studied in a group, but not always. Similarly, your team has won some games on the road and lost some at home. And the good-looking head of the Biology Club may get lots of dates, while the defensive lineman Pigpen-the-Terminator may spend a lot of Saturday nights alone punching heavy farm equipment. Such exceptions are acceptable within a broader range of overall explanation.

Both the idiographic and nomothetic approaches to explanation can be useful to you in your daily life. The nomothetic patterns you discover might offer a good guide for planning your study habits, but the idiographic explanation is more convincing for your parents when you account for your failing grade on an exam.

By the same token, both idiographic and nomothetic explanation have their place in social scientific communication research. The researcher who seeks an exhaustive explanation of the communication breakdown that led a particular company to recall a product from the market is engaged in fruitful idiographic research. She or he is trying to understand one incident in one company as comprehensively as possible.

In the positivist tradition, however, researchers usually aim at a more generalized explanation across an entire class of events, even though the level of explanation is inevitably more superficial. For example, positivist researchers might seek to understand the primary communication variables implicated in product recalls. They might discover, for example, that product recalls are more likely when there is limited lateral communication across the various divisions or departments of corpora-

tions. Although this explanation would extend well beyond a single organization and a single instance of a product's recall, it would do so at the expense of a complete explanation.

Returning to our Researcher A, we would describe her goal as that of nomothetic explanation. She is not interested in understanding the speech anxiety of a single person in light of everything about that person's background and life experiences, as would a researcher with an idiographic goal. Instead, she is seeking to explain a primary cause of speech anxiety in general by positing early-life attachment as her independent variable.

Similarly, in our example above of speaker sex and level of self-disclosure, we were interested in understanding the relationship between these two variables for all males and females. Our goal was nomothetic explanation because we were seeking to explain self-disclosure levels in general, in light of a person's sex. If, instead, we had been trying to understand all of the reasons why Cousin Juan is never forthcoming about the personal details of his life, we would have been engaged in an idiographic enterprise.

In general, then, positivist research seeks to predict and explain variables in a way that maximizes generalization to the largest possible class of phenomena. Researchers who subscribe to the positivist tradition strive to discover **laws** that generalize beyond particular instances to encompass the entire class of phenomena of relevance. Sometimes, scholars refer to this feature of positivist research as a "covering law" approach, meaning that the laws that are theorized are intended to "cover" or "include" the broadest possible range of phenomena. Probability sampling is the key way researchers attempt to generalize to a broad class of phenomena by collecting data from a representative sample of those phenomena. We'll have more to say about sampling in Chapter 7.

Quantitative Data

Most simply put, the distinction between **quantitative data** and **qualitative data** in communication research is the distinction between numerical and nonnumerical data. When you say someone is beautiful, you've made a qualitative assertion. When you say he or she is a "9" on a scale of 1 to 10, you are attempting to quantify your qualitative assessment.

Every observation is qualitative at the outset, whether it be your experience of someone's beauty, the location of a pointer on a measuring scale, or a check mark entered on a questionnaire. None of these things is inherently numerical or quantitative, but sometimes it is useful to convert them to a numerical form. Joel Smith (1991, p. 3) describes the distinction between qualitative and quantitative data in terms of uniqueness and categorization:

> No one seriously argues that events or groups or people are not unique in at least some minor detail. Rather, the issue is whether objects share attributes so important for one's concerns that their unique features can be ignored. The real issue is whether we can categorize. After all, categorizing permits grouping, grouping permits case enumeration, and counts are intrinsically quantitative.

Quantification can make our observations more explicit. It can also make it easier to aggregate and summarize data. Further, it opens up the possibility of statistical analyses, ranging from simple frequency counts to simple averages to complex formulas and mathematical models.

Thus, our Researcher A, with interests in studying speech anxiety, might ask people to indicate their degree of felt anxiety on a 1 to 10 scale. Or she might hook the speaker up to a heart-rate monitor and gauge anxiety with a measure of heartbeats per minute.

Our interest in self-disclosure among males and females might measure self-disclosure as the number of times in an hour that a person expresses personal information about himself or herself—that is, information not readily known to others. If Jake and Tyler are in a conversation and Jake spends the entire conversation discussing the basketball game televised on TV the night before, we would probably give him a self-disclosure score of "0." By contrast, if over the course of the conversation Tyler mentions that he tried out for basketball in junior high but was told he would always be too short to make the grade, if he shares that this incident was so ego crushing that it makes him uneasy when he approaches a taller female to ask for a date, and if he shares that all of his siblings are at least 4 inches taller than he is, we might give him a self-disclosure score of "3" because of his revelation of three personal bits of information about himself.

Now, researchers may quibble over whether we quantified self-disclosure in the best way. One researcher might give males and females a questionnaire and ask them to circle on a 1 to 5 scale how often they talk about various topics that ranged in disclosiveness, such as politics, sexual exploits, greatest fears, and career goals. Another researcher might assess disclosiveness by asking the partner of the speaker to rate the speaker's disclosiveness during their conversation on a scale of 1 to 10.

The challenge of sorting out which way to quantify a given variable is a complicated matter and the subject of Chapter 6. For our purposes now, however, the important point to note is that the positivist tradition usually emphasizes a quantitative approach to variables, rather than a qualitative approach.

Researchers grounded in the positivist tradition seek to study variables objectively through quantitatively based empirical observations for purposes of nomothetic prediction and explanation that take the form of cause-and-effect laws. How do you know a positivist study when you see one? Let's consider an example, a study titled "The Impact of an Adult Parent on Communicative Satisfaction and Dyadic Adjustment in the Long-Term Marital Relationship: Adult-Children and Spouses' Retrospective Accounts" conducted by Lisa Bethea (2002). The title alone gives us a hint of the positivist assumptions that guide the study. We are told that the study focuses on the impact of one variable on another—this suggests an interest in cause–effect relations. The independent variable in the study was whether an elderly parent lived with a marital couple in order to be cared for. The dependent variables in the study were the marital partners' reports of their satisfaction with their communication (communication satisfaction) and their overall satisfaction with their marriage (dyadic adjustment). The study has a nomothetic goal; although the researcher studied only about 60 couples, she was interested in making generalized claims about all marital couples who care for an elderly parent. The researcher used survey research, asking married partners to fill out quantitatively oriented questionnaires about their degree of satisfaction.

But the positivist paradigm is only one way that social scientific communication research gets done. We started our discussion of paradigms with the positivist tradition, because it was the first to stake a foothold in the social sciences. Subsequent paradigms emerged in response to the positivist paradigm.

THE SYSTEMS PARADIGM

The social **systems paradigm** grows out of a notion pioneered by a Viennese professor of biology named Ludwig von Bertalanffy. In his statement of general systems theory, von Bertalanffy argued that a social entity, such as a social group, an organization, or a whole society, can be viewed as an *organism*. As a biologist, von Bertalanffy understood that organisms are dynamic wholes that function through the organized interaction of their parts. For example, the human body is an organism that sustains itself through the ongoing interaction of its various body organs. When something happens to challenge the well-being of the body system—for example, invasion by a virus—the body's various parts marshal a united front to restore the body to its normal state. Like an organism, a social system is made up of parts, each of which contributes to the functioning of the whole. By analogy, consider an automobile, composed of tires, steering wheel, gas tank, spark plugs, and so forth. Each of the parts serves a function for the whole; taken together, that system can get us across town. None of the individual parts would be of much use to us by itself, however.

Researcher B in the introduction to this chapter was grounded in the systems paradigm. He viewed an individual's communication as a system composed of two parts—the verbal or linguistic part and the nonverbal part. His research purpose was to examine how these parts fit together for people high in speech anxiety. Of course, each of these two parts is, in turn, made up of subsystems: nonverbal communication, for example, includes body gestures, facial expressions, vocal characteristics, and so on.

Characteristics of Systems

Communication researchers presume that communication is a *system:* a group of interrelated parts that functions as a whole. We cannot study an individual's words in isolation of his or her nonverbal actions, nor can this individual's words and actions be understood outside of the larger interactional system of which he or she is a part—that is, the communication behavior of the other people with whom our individual is speaking.

Similarly, we cannot understand, say, the popular music industry without recognizing its interdependence with the radio industry and now the industry of Web-based music: All of these parts are interdependent with one another.

When researchers adopt a systems perspective, they recognize that the parts of the system are characterized by **interdependence.** This means that a change in one part results in changes elsewhere in the system. As a student, you probably have often been graded "on the curve." "Curve grading" is a system. If one person's score on an exam gets changed because of an error in reading a certain answer, this change affects the overall class average, and this in turn could affect the cut-offs for who receives an A, a B, and so forth.

Communication systems, like all systems, are *organized wholes.* This means that researchers cannot understand one part in isolation of other parts; the system must be studied as a whole. Anyone who has ever been a member of an athletic team understands this feature of wholeness very well. It is impossible to understand the actions of one player on the team without taking into account the actions of fellow teammates. The team functions as a totality, a whole.

Researchers of communication systems appreciate that *the whole is more than the sum of its parts.* Two atoms of hydrogen added together with one atom of water do not sum to three atoms. Instead, they form one molecule of water. The whole—the water—is a new characteristic that emerged out of the relation of the constituent parts. Similarly, a family's communication system is more than the sum of the individual communication characteristics of each family member; the family system is the synergy that comes from their interactions together.

Communication systems, like all systems, are characterized by *dynamic equilibrium.* This means that the various system parts function to sustain the system in a state of balance. When a family has a big argument over something—say, whether to go to a fancy resort or camping on its vacation—its communication system is probably thrown out of kilter to some extent. After heads cool off and family members calm down, they probably say and do things to make amends and to repair damaged feelings so that the family can get back to things the way they were prior to the big argument. Equilibrium is not the absence of change; rather, it means ongoing adjustment to sustain the system's balance. Family members never go back to exactly where they were before their big fight; they always have a memory of the fight and may act differently in subsequent family arguments because of what happened in the "vacation fight." Thus, the family system is dynamic, not static. But it strives to sustain itself on an even keel, a condition of equilibrium.

Systems vary in their *openness* to external influences. For the most part, social systems are open systems, meaning that the system is constantly responding to external factors that can influence what happens to it.

When communication researchers adopt the systems tradition, then, they ask these questions: What is the system? What are the boundaries of the system? That is, what is considered "outside" the system, and what is "inside" the system? What are the parts of the system? How do the parts function interdependently? What is equilibrium for the system? How do the system parts function jointly in response to external factors in order to sustain dynamic equilibrium for the system?

A Comparison of Systems and Positivist Paradigms

Researchers who adopt the systems paradigm share some features in common with the positivist tradition, yet significant differences exist as well. Systems researchers, like positivist researchers, believe in an objective reality. However, the reality they examine is not the patterned relationships of causes and effects among variables. Instead, systems researchers believe that the social world is organized into systems composed of parts. The research agenda is that of discovering how the parts function together to sustain the system.

Most systems researchers use the language of variables. Equilibrium states are usually defined in terms of variables. For example, equilibrium for a marriage might be conceived as a couple's satisfaction with their bond. Disruptions to equilibrium would be reflected in lowered levels of satisfaction.

The interdependence of system parts and the functioning of these parts are also described in the language of variables. For example, the communication of marital partners can be described with respect to its degree of symmetry. If a husband makes a controlling statement (e.g., "Get your coat; let's go!"), which is met with another controlling statement by the wife (e.g., "Calm down! There's no hurry!"), the communication system in the marriage is high in symmetrical, or matching, responses.

Systems researchers, like positivist researchers, often work with quantitative data, relying on a quantitative text analysis method known as interaction analysis (see Chapter 10). Thus, to continue our example of the husband–wife pair, we could describe the percentage of times that the wife responds to her husband's control efforts through symmetrical control statements of her own. Sometimes, however, systems researchers prefer to describe functional interdependencies among system parts nonnumerically, through words. For example, we might find this qualitative summary of our husband–wife communication system: "The husband and the wife tend to mirror each other in their talk, particularly when it comes to utterances that have implications for power and control."

Some research from the systems tradition is idiographic in nature. For example, a researcher might be interested in studying the U.S. television industry as a system composed of economic, legal, and artistic components. Such a research project focuses on one system, not all television industries in the world.

However, much systems research features a nomothetic approach. For example, family communication researchers often adopt a systems perspective with the goal of explaining how all families function, not just one particular family.

The positivist and systems traditions differ in their approaches to explanation. Whereas the positivist researcher explains something by identifying generalized laws of cause and effect, the systems researcher explains something by identifying how it functions. The positivist researcher believes that one can discover reality variable by variable, whereas a systems researcher is committed to understand phenomena more holistically.

How can you spot a systems study when you see one? Let's consider an example: Paul Taylor's (2002) descriptive study of hostage negotiations between hostage suspect and police negotiator. The researcher tells us in the Abstract to the article that his purpose was to "formulate a comprehensive definitional model of the interrelationships among communication behaviors in crisis negotiation" (p. 7). Utterances were coded into several behavioral types to enable Taylor to examine patterns of sequencing and interrelationship between behavioral types. His focus was not on hostage suspects and police negotiators per se; rather, he was interested in the interaction between suspects and negotiators. His results pointed to an unfolding cylindrical structure in the interactions that characterize hostage negotiations. Although the term *system* does not feature prominently in the study, it is grounded in the systems paradigm nonetheless. Taylor is interested in describing a communication system—the interaction between suspects and negotiators in hostage situations. His focus is not on the separate parts (e.g., suspect talk and negotiator talk) but rather on the interrelationships between these interaction parts. He examines how utterances function in producing the model of unfolding that he identified. The study relied on quantitative text analysis (interaction analysis, to be exact), and the system's functioning was described by applying statistical tests to the quantitative data.

Although they have some differences, systems and positivist traditions can be viewed as close cousins, at least in communication research. A radically different tradition is the interpretive paradigm.

THE INTERPRETIVE PARADIGM

In contrast to both systems and positivist researchers, who believe that the social world is basically similar to the natural world, interpretive researchers believe that the human experience is profoundly different from the natural world. The **interpretive paradigm** encompasses a broad range of orientations, each with its own historical roots. However, in general, researchers who embrace the interpretivist tradition believe that human action stands apart from the rest of the physical and biological world because of the reflective capacity of human beings.

Human action is purposive; it is action intended to accomplish some purpose. Humans act based on the social web of meanings in which they are embedded, and their actions are attributed meaning by others from within that same system of meaning. Humans are accountable for their actions to others in their shared social world, and they make sense (to others and to themselves) on the basis of their capacity to render their actions intelligible.

Think of the last time you did something that you regard as less than healthy for your body. Perhaps you overindulged with a wickedly sweet dessert at dinner last night. Perhaps you broke your training regimen and skipped a day of jogging. Why did you do this? As you answered this question, you probably found yourself in the meaning-laden world of purposive action: "I earned that dessert as a reward because of all my hard work this week." "I skipped jogging because I faced an important deadline at school and didn't have time." These expressed reasons are intelligible to us because we share, at least to some extent, a system of meanings as members of the U.S. society at the beginning of the 21st century. You acted purposively, and your actions were guided by the webs of meaning to which you have been socialized.

To interpretivists, thus, humans act not because some external variable caused them to behave a certain way. Similarly, humans act not because they occupy a certain niche in a bigger social system of which they are an interdependent part. Humans act the way they do because they are attempting to do something purposive, and such action is made intelligible or meaningful in this light. Human action is meaning-making activity.

Given this orientation to human action, the primary goal of the interpretive researcher is to understand the web of meanings in which humans act. Because people from different cultures or social groups are embedded in different systems of meaning, the researcher must attempt to understand the particular systems of meaning of those whose actions are being understood. Key to such understanding is the capacity to "walk a mile in their shoes." That is, interpretive researchers embrace the subjective world of the people they are studying, and they try to see the world through their eyes. Interpretive researchers rely on the qualitative methods of participant observation (Chapter 13), qualitative interviewing (Chapter 14), and qualitative text analysis (Chapters 15 and 16).

Recall Researcher C in the introductory section of this chapter. His research typifies work in the interpretive tradition. He was interested in finding out what speech anxiety meant to those who experienced it. By gaining an in-depth understanding of how his interviewees made sense of their experience, he hoped to gain insights into why they took the actions they did, such as avoiding situations where they might be called upon in public.

Key markers of the interpretive paradigm are meanings, rules, an idiographic focus, and use of qualitative data.

The Study of Meanings

Because of their belief that human action is centered in meaning, not in causes or functions, the goal of interpretive researchers is to understand what action means to people. That is, they seek to render human action intelligible. In contrast to positivist and systems researchers, who use the language of variables, interpretivist researchers think and write in terms of what something means to those whose actions they are trying to understand.

The interpretive counterpart to the variable is the **semantic relationship.** A semantic relationship can be thought of as a unit, kernel, category, or "chunk" of meaning. The ethnographer James Spradley (1979, p. 111) has identified several basic types of semantic relationships that collectively represent a system of meaning:

- Strict inclusion: "X is a kind of Y."
- Spatial: "X is a place in Y"; "X is a part of Y."
- Cause–effect: "X is a result of Y"; "X is a cause of Y."
- Rationale: "X is a reason for doing Y."
- Location for action: "X is a place for doing Y."
- Function: "X is used for Y."
- Means–end: "X is a way to do Y."
- Sequence: "X is a step or stage in Y."
- Attribution: "X is an attribute or characteristic of Y."

Let's imagine that we didn't know what an "apple" was, and we asked you to help us understand what it meant. You might start off describing what an apple looks like—it can be red, yellow, green; its size is kind of roundish with a diameter of about 3 to 4 inches, on average; its taste can range from sweet to tart; its meat is white and juicy. You have helped us understand what an apple is by relying largely on the semantic relationship of *attribution*—you have told us what an apple ("Y") means by describing its various attributes ("X's").

But you probably wouldn't stop here, especially if we still seemed confused or curious. You might go on to tell us that an apple is a kind of fruit and belongs to the same food group as oranges, strawberries, bananas, and so forth. You have added to our understanding of what an apple is by invoking the semantic relationship of *strict inclusion:* An apple ("X") is a kind of fruit ("Y"). You might tell us about places in the United States where apples are a primary agricultural product, say, the Yakima Valley in the state of Washington. You've just added to our understanding of what an apple is by using the *spatial* semantic relationship: The Yakima Valley ("X") is a place where apples are grown ("Y"). How do farmers grow apples, we might inquire? You would invoke the *means–end* semantic relationship to describe for us all the steps in growing an apple. You might distinguish organic from nonorganic apples at this point in the tutorial (calling upon another *strict inclusion* semantic relationship) and tell us your views on the results of pesticide use in apple growing (invoking the *cause–effect* semantic relationship in the process). "So why are apples so popular?" we ask. You might answer our question by telling us all the things you can do with apples—eat them raw, bake an apple pie, give one to your favorite teacher, make cider —and thereby use the *function* semantic relationship. And so on.

In other words, the meaning of an "apple" is pretty complex, particularly if we want to understand it as completely as possible. Every time you uttered a statement about apples, you gave us a "chunk" of meaning. And these various kernels of meaning informed us about different facets of what an apple is.

All meaning making is similarly complex. In order to understand something comprehensively, we weave together all of the bits of knowledge we can that tell us about it.

But meaning making varies depending on whom you talk to. If you asked an apple grower to tell you what an apple is, he or she would probably rely on different kernels of meaning than someone who was not an expert in apples. One of us has a six-year-old, and when asked what an apple was, this little girl said simply "You send them in my lunch sometimes. I like the red ones, but the green ones are yucky."

Whose meaning of an apple is right, and whose is wrong? Obviously, neither meaning is right or wrong; the two attempts to tell us about apples are merely different from each other. And so it is with all meanings. To interpretivist researchers, there is no single reality, because there are different meanings that can guide differ-

ent people's actions. The goal of an interpretivist researcher is to understand the web of meanings that characterize a given group of people or a given situation or setting. Interpretivist researchers seek to understand this web of meanings by describing its component semantic relationships.

You probably noticed that two of the semantic relationships identified by Spradley appear similar to issues we have discussed for the positivist and the systems paradigms: cause–effect and function. Although the words are the same, these semantic relationships are quite different from the approaches to causation and function that we discussed above. Interpretive researchers are interested in people's subjective perceptions of cause and effect and of function, whereas positivists assume an objective reality of cause-and-effect relations and systems researchers assume an objective reality of system functions.

The Study of Rules

Meanings, and actions, are inherently social in nature. Although part of your meaning for an apple no doubt rests on your own experience eating apples, you certainly can't describe that experience to us without relying on language. Language is acquired through others—it is social. Even if you are thinking silently to yourself about apples, your silent thoughts are probably put into words; thus, even thinking is a social activity because it is language based. Furthermore, much of what you know about apples you probably learned from others or read about or watched on TV—all social ways that you arrived at your current understanding of what an apple is.

Human actions are also social in nature. Even actions that we execute in private are social in that their meanings stem from our experiences in the social world.

Because meanings and human actions are social, they are guided by rules. If people did not have agreement on what things meant and how to communicate meanings through words and actions, the social world would be utter chaos. Thus, in the interpretive tradition, the study of meanings is closely linked to the study of rules.

But what exactly is a rule in the interpretive tradition? A **rule** is a commonly shared belief among members of a group or subculture about appropriate action. Rules inform us about what is prohibited, allowed, encouraged, or required in the social worlds in which we occupy membership.

For example, we have rules of language use that we all learned through our years of formal schooling. We learned requirements of expression—how to write and talk in grammatical ways, which vocabulary words hold what meanings, and so forth. We also learned at school and in our everyday lives how to communicate with others beyond the technicalities of vocabulary and grammar. We learned rules of politeness, rules of greeting, rules for delivering "bad news" to others, rules of being supportive—in short, all of our communication practices are guided by what we know about appropriate or required social conduct.

The rules of conduct that guide our communication behaviors are part of the meaning-making process. At a minimum, rules of appropriate and required action provide a moral backdrop against which others evaluate our actions as "good," "bad," "correct," "inappropriate," and so forth. Such judgments form part of the meaning of our actions.

Rules that guide communication behavior obviously differ from setting to setting and from social group to social group. It is OK to yell at a soccer match but not in a public library. It is probably acceptable among some friendship cliques to engage in verbal teasing, whereas this practice may be frowned upon in other friendship groups. It may be expected in one organization to employ "team talk"—that is, to talk in ways that emphasize the organizational members as team players—whereas another organization's culture may view "team talk" as hokey.

The goal of interpretive communication researchers is to identify the rules that guide communicative actions in a given setting or social group. In identifying the rules that guide communication, interpretive researchers render those actions intelligible.

Interpretive Theory

Theory occupies an important place in the interpretive tradition, just as it does in the positivist and systems traditions. However, the kinds of theory valued by interpretive researchers are different from those valued by positivist and systems researchers. Both positivist and systems researchers are interested in abstract theories of explanation—either cause-and-effect explanation or functional explanation. And both positivist and systems researchers are interested in generalized claims—about relations among variables or about systems. By contrast, interpretive researchers are interested in theories of understanding.

In the interpretive tradition, theories of understanding take one of two forms. One form of interpretive theory is

local knowledge. Because rules and meanings are specific to the setting or social group under study, it is impossible to generalize. Instead, the goal of some interpretive researchers is to give us a comprehensive understanding of meaning making in that single setting or group.

For example, Gerry Philipsen (1975) provided us with a local-knowledge theory of talk among working-class males in a southside Chicago neighborhood that he called "Teamsterville." Talking (as opposed to other forms of action) was allowed only among males who were friends or same-status peers. Deviations from this rule meant that a male's masculinity was challenged by fellow Teamsterville residents. For example, if a bully from outside the neighborhood insulted the girlfriend of a Teamsterville male, he should not try to talk rationally to the bully and ask him to stop. Instead, he needed to act, probably with a physical threat in this circumstance. By providing us with detailed insight into the code of communication that guided Teamsterville males, Philipsen provided us with a theory of communication—claims about local knowledge in Teamsterville.

A second form of interpretive theory is the *heuristic framework.* A heuristic framework is a set of statements designed to guide our efforts to understand meaning making regardless of the specific setting or group. For example, the ethnographer Dell Hymes (1972) developed a heuristic theory of communication codes that can usefully be summarized in the acronym SPEAKING. For example, Hymes suggests that all communication codes are organized, in part, around rules organized by situation (S rules)—what kinds of talk are encouraged or required in specific settings or situations—and participant rules (P rules)—what kinds of talk are encouraged or required between people depending on their relationship to one another. (We'll return in greater detail to the theory of SPEAKING in a later chapter.)

Regardless of the setting or group one is studying, Hymes's theory is a useful tool that guides the researcher in how to look. Guided by the "S" and the "P" components of Hymes's theory, for example, a researcher would ask "How does communication vary by the situation for this cultural group?" and "How is communication organized depending on who is involved in the interaction?" An interpretive theory is heuristic if it is useful in guiding the researcher's attempt to understand a specific setting or social group. Of course, the specific answers to these heuristic questions will differ locally.

Local-knowledge theories are obviously idiographic in nature. By contrast, heuristic frameworks operate at a nomothetic level.

Qualitative Data

Interpretive researchers generally prefer to work with nonnumerical data, typically words or visual images. Their goal is to provide understanding in as rich and detailed a manner as possible; in the interpretive tradition, this is usually referred to as *evocativeness*. Interpretive researchers strive to paint a verbal picture so rich that readers of the study feel as if they had walked that mile in the shoes of the group members.

It's not that you can't summarize meanings quantitatively. As we will see in a later chapter devoted to surveys and questionnaires, positivist researchers often solicit numerical data from study participants on their beliefs and perceptions about any number of things. For example, researchers could ask study participants to circle a number from 1 to 5 indicating the extent to which they believe that "When people tell lies, they don't look you squarely in the eye." The circled number—and the average of circled numbers across a group of participants—provide a numerical summary of what averted eye contact means. Typically, positivist researchers are interested in determining whether people's perceptions are caused by antecedent, independent variables of one kind or another. For example, a positivist researcher might want to know whether people with different family backgrounds (divorced versus intact, for example) vary in their belief that averted eye contact means that a person is lying.

However, interpretive researchers generally believe that numerical data are relatively "thin" compared to the evocativeness of words. To interpretive researchers, a circled number on a questionnaire is but the tip of the iceberg; they prefer to describe in detail the rest of the iceberg. An interpretive researcher might give us this rendering of a social group's strong belief that eye aversion means lying: "To members of this community, the failure to 'look someone in the eye' is a sure give-away that a lie is being told. Children are often told by their elders 'Look me in the eye when you talk to me,' and a failure to comply is often punished. When people are gossiping about others, they often refer to tongue–eye images to comment on whether the person being gossiped about was lying; e.g., 'His tongue said one thing, but his eyes told the truth.' However, there's a fine line between 'looking someone in the eye' and 'staring down' someone. If a person 'stares down' someone, the truth of their words is also questioned." This qualitative description is an attempt to flush out in greater depth the meaning of eye aversion. This description is certainly compatible with a quantitative statement that "On average, '4.9' was circled by the group of participants." The two kinds of claims—qualitative and quantitative—simply provide us with different kinds of information about the participants.

Interpretive research reveals its paradigm through several clues. Let's consider the clues in a study one of us recently published along with several co-authors (2002): "Contradictions of Interaction for Wives of Elderly Husbands with Adult Dementia." We were interested in understanding, and describing richly, wives' communication experiences with their elderly husbands who were in nursing homes because of dementia-related illnesses, typically Alzheimer's. We relied on open-ended qualitative interviews with several wives in order to hear their reports in their own words of how they experienced communication with a husband who was physically present yet often cognitively and emotionally absent. We found that these wives experienced communication in contradictory ways, and the results were presented in prose form by quoting extensively from the wives. This study was interpretive for several reasons. First, it was interested in the subjective experiences of the wives; the goal of the study was to attempt to "walk a mile in their shoes" by conducting in-depth interviews with them. Our purpose was thus understanding, not prediction, causal explanation, or functional explanation. We weren't interested in variables; instead, we were interested in meanings and the rules that guided these wives' communication encounters with their husbands.

The interpretivist tradition differs substantially from the positivist and systems traditions. But there's a fourth paradigm in communication research—the critical.

THE CRITICAL PARADIGM

Historical roots of the **critical paradigm** are several, and they are diverse in origin. However, critical scholars share in common two beliefs. First, they challenge the presumption that empirical observation is the only pathway to knowledge, believing instead that reflection can produce knowledge. In fact, when critical researchers gather data, whether quantitative or qualitative, they do not accept the data and their analysis as sufficient grounds for knowledge claims. Rather, it is the critical reflection on those data that enables knowledge.

Critical Reflection

What is "critical reflection"? It is not the mere interpretation of the data with a goal of providing an accurate and complete summary of them. Instead, it refers to an interrogation of a data set with an eye toward identifying its ideological bias and the implications of this bias for power relations.

Scholars who endorse the critical paradigm believe that **ideology** and power characterize the social experience. Critical scholars engage in critical reflection with a goal of exposing the values implicit in social practices in order to enlighten and emancipate members of a society or group. Typical questions asked by critical scholars include "What are the underlying values of a given communicative practice?" and "Whose interests are served (and whose interests are not served) by this ideological practice?"

By unmasking implicit ideologies and power imbalances, critical scholars believe that they are functioning to liberate all social agents from the oppression of the status quo. Critical scholars, thus, are committed to emancipatory social change.

Let's return to the introduction to this chapter for one final visit, this time to researcher D. Researcher D gathered empirical data about talk and silence patterns in a classroom context. However, her task as a scholar was not done when she collected and analyzed her data. Instead, she took the next step of criticizing the gender ideology of that classroom for its bias against girls. In mounting this critique, researcher D was attempting to emancipate all members of society—both males and females—from an ideology that she had unmasked.

Scholars who align with the critical paradigm believe that the scientific enterprise is part of the social world, not removed from it. Thus, the practices of science are subject to the same critical reflection as other facets of the social world. In the past 20 years in particular, critical scholars have been active in unmasking the ideological biases they see in the conduct of social scientific research.

For example, in an intriguing 1991 essay titled "Interpersonal Research as Ideological Practice," John Lannaman critiqued scholars of interpersonal communication for their implicit endorsement of individualism and their systematic denial of the communal and social bases of face-to-face interaction. The study of interpersonal communication, he argued, is steeped in the ideology of a capitalist society.

Some Critical Approaches

Critical scholars approach the task of ideological critique from any number of perspectives. Some ground their critical reflection in the work of Karl Marx (1818–1883), who suggested that social behavior could best be seen as a process of conflict—the attempt to dominate others and to avoid being dominated. Marx primarily focused on the struggle among economic classes. Specifically, he examined the way capitalism produced the oppression of workers by the owners of industry. A communication researcher from this tradition might examine how social class is reproduced in the communication practices of working-, middle-, and upper-class persons. For example, Michael Huspek (1989) examined the power implications of "You know" and "I think" expressions in working-class speech.

Other critical scholars ground their critiques in feminist theory. In part, feminists (of both sexes) have focused on gender differences and how these relate to the rest of social organization. This body of work has drawn attention to the oppression of women in society. Researcher D was engaged in this kind of feminist critique.

Because men and women have had very different communication experiences throughout history, they have come to see things differently, with the result that their conclusions about communication may vary in many ways. In perhaps the most general example, feminist scholars have challenged the prevailing notions concerning consensus in society. Most descriptions of the predominant beliefs, values, and norms of a society are written by people representing only portions of society. In the United States, for example, such analyses have typically been written by middle-class white men—not surprisingly, they have written about the beliefs, values, and norms that they share.

Our growing recognition of the intellectual differences between men and women led the psychologist Mary Field Belenky and her colleagues to speak of *Women's Ways of Knowing* (1986). In-depth interviews with 45 women led the researchers to distinguish five perspectives on knowing that should challenge the view of inquiry as obvious and straightforward:

- *Silence:* Some women, especially early in life, feel themselves isolated from the world of knowledge, their lives largely determined by external authorities.
- *Received knowledge:* From this perspective, women feel themselves capable of taking in and holding knowledge originating with external authorities.
- *Subjective knowledge:* This perspective opens up the possibility of personal, subjective knowledge, including intuition.
- *Procedural knowledge:* Some women feel they have mastered the ways of gaining knowledge through objective procedures.
- *Constructed knowledge:* The authors describe this perspective as "a position in which women view all knowledge as contextual, experience themselves as

creators of knowledge, and value both subjective and objective strategies for knowing." (Belenky et al., 1986, p. 15)

"Constructed knowledge" is particularly interesting in the context of our previous discussions. For example, the positivist paradigm of Comte would have a place neither for "subjective knowledge" nor for the idea that truth might vary according to its context. The interpretive paradigm, on the other hand, would accommodate these notions easily.

The critical paradigm is centered in reflection and critique rather than empirical observation. However, when critical scholars engage in empirical work, they typically use the methods of qualitative research.

PARADIGMS REVISITED: SOME CONCLUDING REMARKS

We began with Comte's assertion that an objective reality exists and that we can discover its laws of cause and effect through systematic and rigorous empirical observation. Since his time, social scientists have reacted to this position in different ways. In this chapter, we have discussed the primary paradigms that organize these reactions in communication research. Let's discuss two of the main issues or fault lines that distinguish the paradigms from one another.

Objectivity and Subjectivity

To begin, *all our experiences are inescapably subjective.* There is no way out. You can see only through your own eyes, and anything peculiar to your eyes will shape what you see. You can hear things only through the way your particular ears and brain transmit and interpret sound waves.

Despite the inescapable subjectivity of our experience, we humans seem to be wired to seek an agreement on what is *really real,* what is *objectively* so. Objectivity is a *conceptual* attempt to get beyond our individual views. It is ultimately a matter of communication, as we attempt to find a common ground in our subjective experiences. Whenever we succeed in our search, we say we are dealing with objective reality. This is the *agreement reality* discussed in Chapter 1.

While our subjectivity is individual, our search for objectivity is social. This is true in all aspects of life, not just in science. While we prefer different foods, we must agree to some extent on what is fit to eat and what is not, or else

there could be no restaurants, no grocery stores, no food industry. The same argument could be made regarding every other form of consumption. There could be no movies or television, no sports.

From the 17th century through the middle of the 20th century, the belief in an objective reality that people could see predominated in science. For the most part, it was not simply held as a useful paradigm but as *The Truth.* This is the view challenged today by many scholars.

Some say that the ideal of objectivity conceals as much as it reveals. As we saw earlier, much of what was agreed on as scientific objectivity in years past was actually an agreement primarily among white, middle-class, European men. Subjective experiences common to women, to ethnic minorities, or to the poor were not necessarily represented in that reality.

The early anthropologists are now criticized for often making modern, Westernized "sense" out of the beliefs and practices of nonliterate tribes around the world—sometimes portraying their subjects as superstitious savages. We often call nonliterate tribal beliefs about the distant past "creation myths," whereas we speak of our own beliefs as "history." Increasingly today, there is a demand to find the native logic by which various peoples make sense out of life.

Ultimately, we'll never know whether there is an objective reality that we experience subjectively or whether our concepts of an objective reality are illusory. So desperate is our need to know just what is going on, however, that both the positivists and the nonpositivists are sometimes drawn into the belief that their view is real and true. There is a dual irony in this. On the one hand, the positivist's belief in the reality of the objective world must ultimately be based on faith; it cannot be proven by "objective" science, since that's precisely what's at issue. And critics, who say nothing is objectively so, do at least feel that the absence of objective reality is *really* the way things are.

The Nature of Explanation

Three basic types of explanation have been advanced in these paradigms: cause-and-effect explanation, function explanation, and reason explanation. The cause-and-effect explanation of positivism is a popular one in the natural sciences. For example, growth is caused by several factors. We can affect the growth of plants by varying the amount of light, water, and nutrients they receive. Similarly, positivist researchers seek to identify the causes of human behavior through rigorous empirical observation.

Sometimes, people protest cause-and-effect explanations of human behavior by arguing that individuals have free will and make choices about how they will behave. Didn't you choose to go to school? No set of factors forced your presence in school, right? You are in school because you want to be there. That is, your actions can be explained by your reasons.

But we suspect that you wouldn't be in school unless you had enough money to pay the tuition. If you hadn't had enough money to pay your tuition, that factor would have forced you to stay out of school. But then suppose your desire to learn about the world around you was so powerful that you overcame the lack of money—maybe you got a scholarship or went to work for a while or took out loans. In that case, we're back to your powerful desires and goals as reasons you are in school.

Ah, argue positivists, but why do you have a desire to go to school? Perhaps you grew up in a family where everyone had gone to college and you felt you were letting your family down by not attending college yourself. Or perhaps you came from a family where nobody had ever gone to college before, and they were all proud of the fact that you might be the first. That is, family background factors caused, or predisposed, you to have certain goals and desires. Well, yes, you might agree, you certainly faced family pressures of one kind or another, but in the end the choice was yours—your family didn't force you to attend school.

Positivists do not believe that all human actions, thoughts, and feelings are determined, nor do they lead their lives as though they believed it. Furthermore, the tradition of cause-and-effect explanation does not assume we are all controlled by the same factors and forces: Your reasons for going to college surely differed somewhat from ours. Moreover, cause-and-effect explanation does not suggest that we now know all the answers about what causes what or that we ever will.

Finally, positivists operate on the basis of a probabilistic causal model, not an absolute causal model. Rather than predicting that a particular person will attend college, they say that certain factors make attending college more or less likely within groups of people. Thus, high school students whose parents attended college are more likely to attend college themselves than those students whose parents did not attend college. This does not mean that all of the former and none of the latter will attend college. Thus, cause-and-effect explanation does not deny free will on the part of human actors.

Although interpretive scholars embrace the notion that humans are capable of choosing their actions, they seek to answer a different question from that of cause and effect. Interpretive scholars are interested in meanings. They would be much more interested in finding out what a college education means to students as a way of understanding why they are attending.

Systems scholars would intersect with the discussion of explanation in yet another way. They might be interested in the functions of a college education for individuals as members of society. Individuals would be viewed as parts of a larger societal system. For example, college education might function to enhance lifetime earning power, which has implications for the society's economic growth.

Critical scholars would introduce yet a different question. They might critique the fact that success in U.S. public education is predicated on a communication code that favors people from white, middle-class backgrounds. Persons socialized to different codes of communication would thus be handicapped. Shirley Heath (1983) made exactly this argument in noting that formal education is oriented to a code of literacy rather than orality, thereby positioning lower-working-class whites and African Americans to be evaluated less favorably in school.

So which approach to explanation is correct? The answer is "none." Cause–effect, function, and reason explanations are not right or wrong; they are simply very different ways to approach human activity.

The Advantages of Multi-Method Research

Rather than align yourself with any of the approaches discussed in this chapter, we encourage you to treat them as distinct tools in your communication inquiry tool kit. Each approach brings special strengths, and each compensates for the weaknesses of the other. Why choose? Work both sides of the street.

Communication researchers often work both sides of the street when they conduct **multi-method research.** As we indicated in the prior chapter, multi-method research is research in which the researcher uses more than one methodological tool from his or her inquiry kit in conducting a study. Sometimes, multi-method research draws on tools that share grounding in the same paradigm. More relevant to the point we are making here, however, is multi-method research in which the researcher employs tools drawn from different paradigmatic backgrounds. Such work usually mixes both quantitative and qualitative data in a single research project. This can be done in several ways. Sometimes, researchers start with quantitative data and supplement them with qualitative data in order to "flesh out" in a more detailed manner some of the quantitative findings they have uncovered. This is exactly what Dawna Ballard and David Seibold (2000) did in their study of how orientations toward time were related to group communicative practices. The researchers developed a quantitatively based survey measure to assess different orientations toward time—for example, whether a group regarded time as flexible or rigid. Discussions with work group members were relied on to elaborate on the various orientations, supplementing the quantitative portion of the study with qualitative insights.

Other times, qualitative data are gathered initially and followed up with quantitative methods designed to provide numerical precision for the qualitative findings. For example, Daena Goldsmith (2000) employed this combination in studying the sequence of communicative acts in advice-giving episodes. She used the qualitative method of participant observation to take careful field notes on advice-giving sequences. From these data, she identified six different types of sequences. Then Goldsmith asked a sample of participants to quantitatively rate sample dialogues illustrating these six types on their facework implications.

Sometimes, quantitative and qualitative methods are used simultaneously. For example, when Michael Papa and his colleagues (2000) studied how a radio soap opera resulted in social change in an Indian village, they gathered quantitative survey data, quantitative content analysis data, and qualitative interview data.

The advantage of quantitative–qualitative multi-method research is that it provides a more complete picture of the phenomenon under study. However, a cautionary note is in order. As we have seen in this chapter and will realize again in Chapter 4, the different paradigms make different assumptions about reality and knowledge claims about it. It is important to evaluate each method in a manner consistent with its paradigmatic background.

This chapter on paradigms of knowing is intended to illustrate the rich variety of theoretical perspectives that can be brought to bear on the study of communication. But regardless of which tradition frames a given study, all researchers employ the logic systems of deduction and induction in the task of constructing theory. This is the topic of our next chapter.

Main Points

- A paradigm is a fundamental model or scheme that organizes our view of something.

- Communication researchers use a variety of paradigms to organize how they understand and inquire into communication.

- Positivism assumes we can scientifically discover through objective empirical observation the laws of cause and effect that determine communication.

- The systems paradigm seeks to discover what functions the many elements of a communication system perform for the whole system.

- The interpretive paradigm seeks to understand the webs of meaning that guide human communication.

- The critical paradigm seeks to unmask the ideological practices and sources of domination in communication, thereby emancipating the oppressed.

- The basic conceptual units of study for communication researchers are variables (positivists), systems (systems researchers), semantic relationships and rules (interpretivists), and ideologies (critical communication researchers).

- The goals of communication research are to predict and causally explain (positivists), to explain function (systems researchers), to understand meanings and meaning making (interpretivists), or to emancipate (critical communication researchers).

- Communication researchers construct either idiographic or nomothetic knowledge claims.

- The research task is that of quantitative observation (positivists or systems researchers), qualitative observation (systems researchers, interpretive researchers, critical researchers), or critical reflection (critical researchers).

Key Terms

paradigm	quantitative data
positivist paradigm	qualitative data
attributes	systems paradigm
variables	interdependence
independent variable	interpretive paradigm
dependent variable	semantic relationship
causal explanation	rule
nomothetic	critical paradigm
idiographic	ideology
laws	multi-method research

Review Questions and Exercises

1. Peruse an issue of one of the communication journals listed in Appendix A and locate a social scientific study. Try to identify the paradigm that frames the researcher's study. What about the article led you to align the study with your selected paradigm?

2. Go to an issue of one of the communication journals listed in Appendix A and locate a social scientific study. After trying to identify the paradigm in which the study is positioned, ask yourself how researchers whose assumptions reflect the alternative paradigms might study the phenomenon differently.

3. Using one of the many search engines (such as Lycos, WebCrawler, Excite, Google, and Infoseek), find information on the Web concerning some of the paradigms or concepts discussed in this chapter. Record the web site and what you found there.

Continuity Project

Show how the four paradigms discussed in this chapter might structure your inquiry into the topic of gender/sex and communication. What aspects of the subject would the paradigm lead you to focus on? How might you interpret observations within each paradigm?

Additional Readings

Bochner, A. P. (1985). Perspectives on inquiry: Representation, conversation, and reflection. In M. L. Knapp and G. R. Miller (Eds.), *Handbook of interpersonal communication* (pp. 27–58). Beverly Hills, CA: Sage. This book chapter offers a concise discussion of the primary paradigms that organize communication research. The discussion speaks to all areas of communication and is not limited to interpersonal communication.

Burrell, G., & Morgan, G. (1988). *Sociological paradigms and organizational analysis.* Portsmouth, NH: Heinemann. Although this book is grounded in organizational sociology, it offers a quite readable discussion of the same paradigm issues addressed in this chapter. However, Burrell and Morgan provide a different organizational framework for paradigms than what is provided in this chapter.

Casmir, F. L. (1994). The role of theory and theory building. In F. L. Casmir (Ed.), *Building communication theories* (pp. 7–41). Hillsdale, NJ: Erlbaum. A useful discussion of what a communication theory is and why it is important to understand theory in a course in research methods.

Denzin, N. K., & Lincoln, Y. S. (Eds.) (1994). *Handbook of qualitative research.* Newbury Park, CA: Sage. Various authors discuss the process of qualitative research from the perspective of various paradigms, showing how they influence the nature of inquiry. The editors also critique positivism from a postmodern perspective.

Kuhn, T. (1970). *The structure of scientific revolutions.* Chicago: University of Chicago Press. An exciting and innovative recasting of the nature of scientific development. Kuhn disputes the notion of gradual change and modification in science, arguing instead that established "paradigms" tend to persist until the weight of contradictory evidence brings their rejection and replacement by new paradigms. This short book is at once stimulating and informative.

Polkinghorne, D. (1983). *Methodology for the human sciences: Systems of inquiry.* Albany, NY: State University of New York Press. A classic book on the paradigms that organize the social scientific enterprise.

Putnam, L., & Pacanowsky, M. (Eds.) (1983). *Communication and organizations: An interpretive approach.* Newbury Park, CA: Sage. Although this book deals with organizational communication, its discussion of interpretive approaches is excellent and applies to interpretive approaches in contexts other than organizations.

Reinharz, S. (1992). *Feminist methods in social research.* New York: Oxford University Press. This book explores several social research techniques (such as interviewing, experiments, and content analysis) from a feminist perspective.

Wood, J. (1997). *Communication theories in action: An introduction.* New York: Wadsworth. A very readable introduction to some of the primary theories that organize communication research. These theories reflect basic paradigm differences as discussed in this chapter.

InfoTrac College Edition
http://www.infotrac-college.com/ wadsworth/access.html

Access the latest news and journal articles with InfoTrac College Edition, an easy-to-use online database of reliable, full-length articles from hundreds of top academic journals. Conduct an electronic search using the following search terms:

- paradigms
- positivist research
- interpretive research
- systems research
- critical theory
- causality
- functionalism
- rules
- power

CHAPTER 4

Logic Systems and Theory in Communication Research

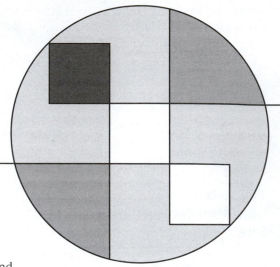

What You'll Learn in This Chapter

Here you'll see how two systems of reasoning—deduction and induction—function in communication research. You'll also learn how theory fits into the reasoning process.

INTRODUCTION

This chapter is about two types of reasoning that are used in social scientific communication research—induction and deduction. Remember from Chapter 1 that logic is one of the two elements central to the scientific enterprise (the other is observation).

Induction and deduction are already familiar to you— you rely on both kinds of reasoning as you go through the typical day. For example, suppose you find yourself puzzling, part of the way through your college career, why it is that you do so well on exams sometimes but poorly at other times. You might list all the exams you've ever taken (!), noting how well you did on each. Then you might try to recall any circumstances shared by all the good exams and by all the poor ones. Did you do better on multiple-choice exams or essay exams? Morning exams or afternoon exams? Exams in the natural sciences, the humanities, or the social sciences? Times when you studied alone or SHAZAM! It occurs to you that you have almost always done best on exams when you studied with others. This mode of inquiry is known as **induction.**

Inductive reasoning moves from the particular to the general, from a set of specific observations to the discovery of a pattern that represents some degree of order among all the given events. Notice, incidentally, that your insight doesn't necessarily tell you why or how the pattern exists—just that it does.

Here's a different way you might have arrived at the same conclusion about studying for exams. Imagine approaching your first set of exams in college. You wonder about the best ways to study—how much to review, how much to focus on class notes. You learn that some students prepare by rewriting their notes in an orderly fashion. Then you consider whether to study at a measured pace or pull an all-nighter just before the exam. Among these musings, you might ask whether you should get together with other students in the class or just study on your own. You could evaluate the pros and cons of both options.

Studying with others might not be as efficient, because a lot of time might be spent on things you already understand. On the other hand, you can understand something even better when you've explained it to someone else. And other students might understand parts of the course you haven't gotten yet. Several minds can reveal perspectives that might have escaped you. Also, making a new commitment to study with others makes it more likely that you'll study rather than decide to watch the special eight-hour *Brady Bunch* marathon on TV.

In this fashion, you might add up the pros and cons and conclude, logically, that you'd benefit from studying with others. It seems reasonable to you, the way it seems reasonable that you'll do better if you study rather than not. Sometimes, we say things like this are true "in theory." To complete the process, we test whether they're true in practice. For a complete test, you might study alone for half your exams and study with others for the other exams. This procedure would test your logical reasoning. This second mode of inquiry is known as **deduction.**

Deductive reasoning moves from the general to the specific. It moves from (1) a pattern that might be logically or theoretically expected to (2) observations that determine whether the expected pattern actually occurs.

These two very different approaches are both valid avenues for scientific inquiry into communication. Moreover, they work together to provide ever more powerful and complete explanations and understandings. The first purpose of this chapter is to understand these two logic systems in greater depth.

Notice, by the way, that the deductive/inductive process is not necessarily linked to the nomothetic and idiographic perspectives. In our example so far, we've been operating at an idiographic level—your exam performances. However, we might go through the same reasoning process if we wondered about the link between group studying and exam performance for all students. If we were interested in all students as a group, we would be operating at the nomothetic level.

Whether your reasoning was inductive or deductive, you arrived at the same conclusion, what we will be calling a **theory.** Your theory is that studying in a group is associated with higher exam scores than is studying alone. For our purposes, a theory is a set of statements that renders intelligible some phenomenon or process.

Theory is central to all scientific reasoning about communication, regardless of the paradigm in which a study is framed. Why is theory so important to the research enterprise? Theory functions three ways in research.

First, it prevents us being taken in by random flukes. Let's return to our research topic of speech anxiety posed at the beginning of Chapter 3. Someone may be promoting a remedy for speech anxiety, a pill that is taken an hour before speaking in public. The evidence to support the promoter's claim might be that he tried it out with some folks who were uptight about giving speeches; more than half of them reported being calmer after taking the pill. If we can't explain why the pill seemed to work, we run the risk of supporting a fluke claim.

Second, theories make sense of observed patterns in a way that can suggest other possibilities. If we understand the reasons people feel anxious when they speech in public, we will be better positioned to devise remedial actions, perhaps in the form of treatment programs that will help people who are chronically anxious whenever they talk in public.

Finally, theories can shape and direct research efforts. If you were looking for your lost keys on a dark street, you could whip your flashlight around randomly, hoping to chance upon the errant keys—or you could use your memory of where you had been to limit your search to more likely areas. If you were trying to identify a treatment to reduce people's anxiety levels when they speak in public, you could try out a number of things through trial and error, hoping to stumble onto something that worked. Theory, by analogy, directs researchers' flashlights where they are most likely to "pay off" and away from areas that might be less fruitful.

A second goal of this chapter is to understand how theory fits into the research enterprise and to understand the logic systems by which theory and empirical observation are linked.

TWO LOGIC SYSTEMS

We opened this chapter with an idiographic example of the two systems of logic that are used in scientific reasoning. It's time for a more formal definition of induction and deduction. W. I. B. Beveridge, a philosopher of science, describes these two systems of logic in a way that should already seem familiar to you:

> Logicians distinguish between inductive reasoning (from particular instances to general principles, from facts to theories) and deductive reasoning (from the general to the particular, applying a theory to a particular case). In induction one starts from observed data and develops a generalization which explains the relationships between the objects observed. On the other hand, in deductive reasoning one starts from some general law and applies it to a particular instance. (Beveridge, 1950, p. 113)

Let's shift to a nomothetic example of deduction and induction, one we will illustrate graphically. We're still on the general topic of exam performance. But we've shifted our interest from your experience studying in a group to the relationship, for students as a whole, between the number of hours spent studying for an exam and the grade earned on that exam.

Using the deductive method, we would begin by examining the matter logically. Doing well on an exam re-

flects a student's ability to recall and manipulate information. Both of these abilities should be increased by exposure to the information before the exam. In this fashion, we would arrive at a **hypothesis** suggesting a positive relationship between the number of hours spent studying and the grade earned on the exam. In this example, our two variables are *number of hours spent studying* and *the earned exam grade*. Because this example is framed within the tradition of cause-and-effect explanation, we might refer to the number of hours spent studying as our independent variable and the earned exam grade as our dependent variable. We hypothesize a *positive* relationship because we expect grades to increase as the hours of studying increase. If increased hours produced decreased grades, that would be called a *negative* relationship. The hypothesis is represented by the line in part 1(a) of Figure 4-1.

Our next step, using the deductive method, would be to make observations relevant to testing our hypothesis. The shaded area in part 1(b) of the figure represents perhaps hundreds of observations of different students, noting how many hours they studied and what grades they got. Finally, in part 1(c), we compare the hypothesis and the observations. Because observations in the real world seldom if ever match our expectations perfectly, we must decide whether the match is close enough to consider the hypothesis confirmed. Put differently, can we conclude that the hypothesis describes the general pattern that exists, granting some variations in real life?

Now let's turn to addressing the same research question, using the inductive method. In this case, we would begin—as in part 2(a) of the figure—with a set of observations. Curious about the relationship between hours spent studying and grades earned, we might simply arrange to collect some relevant data. Then we'd look for a pattern that best represented or summarized our observations. In part 2(b) of the figure, the pattern is shown as a curved line running through the center of the curving mass of points.

The pattern found among the points in this case suggests that with 1 to 15 hours of studying, each additional hour generally produces a higher grade on the exam. With 15 to about 25 hours, however, more study seems to slightly lower the grade. Studying more than 25 hours, on the other hand, results in a return to the initial pattern: More hours produce higher grades. Using the inductive method, then, we end up with a *tentative* conclusion about the pattern of the relationship between the two variables. The conclusion is tentative because the observations we have made cannot be taken as a test of the pattern—those observations are the *source* of the pattern we've created.

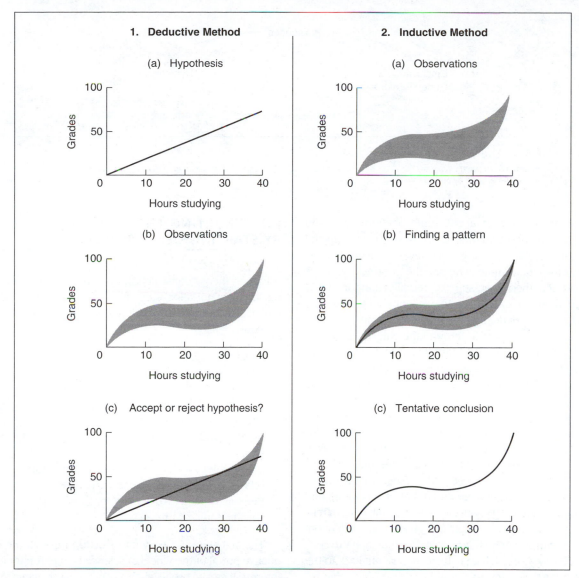

FIGURE 4-1   **Deductive and Inductive Methods**

While both inductive and deductive methods are valid in scientific inquiry, individuals may feel more comfortable with one approach than the other. Consider this exchange in Sir Arthur Conan Doyle's *A Scandal in Bohemia,* as Sherlock Holmes answers Dr. Watson's inquiry (Doyle, 1891/1892, p. 13):

> "What do you imagine that it means?"

> "I have no data yet. It is a capital mistake to theorise before one has data. Insensibly one begins to twist facts to suit theories, instead of theories to suit facts."

Some communication researchers would more or less agree with this inductive position, while others would take a deductive stance. Most, however, concede the legitimacy of both approaches. In actual practice, theory and research interact through a never-ending alternation of deduction, induction, deduction, and so forth. Walter Wallace (1971) has represented this process nicely as a wheel, which is presented in a modified form in Figure 4-2. Both quantitative research and qualitative research engage the full circle of deductive and inductive reasoning. However, researchers typically enter the wheel at different points depending on their basic paradigmatic approach to research.

Quantitative researchers, both positivists and systems researchers, tend to enter the wheel of science through the gateway of deduction. They start with a theory (a set

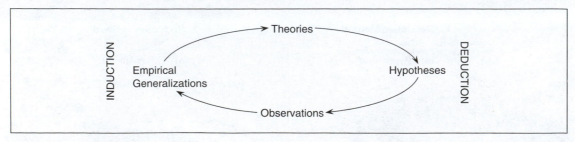

FIGURE 4-2 **The Wheel of Science**

Source: Adapted from Walter Wallace, *The Logic of Science in Sociology* (New York: Aldine deGruyter, 1971). Copyright © 1971 by Walter L. Wallace. Used by permission.

of general statements about some phenomenon) and work toward observations. Then they reason from the observations back to the general level of theory. For example, they determine whether the observed findings support the theory or suggest modifications in it. Of course, there are exceptions to this tendency to enter the wheel through deduction—sometimes, quantitative researchers enter the circle through the gateway of induction, gathering specific quantitative observations from which they reason a theory. Then this theory is directed toward specific observations. Either way, the full circle is completed.

Qualitative researchers, both interpretivist and critical, tend to enter the wheel through the gateway of induction. They start with specific observations and, based on the patterns present in those data, infer more general conclusions (theory). These more general conclusions are then examined against additional observations and modified as needed. However, some qualitative researchers enter the circle through the gateway of deduction, starting with a general theory that they then apply to concrete observations, which in turn are brought back to the general level of theory again. Either way, qualitative researchers, like quantitative researchers, progress through the full circle of the wheel of science.

In summary, the scientific norm of logical reasoning provides a bridge between theory and research—a two-way bridge. Scientific inquiry in practice typically involves an alternation between deduction and induction. During the deductive phase, we reason *toward* observations; during the inductive phase, we reason *from* observations. Both logic and observation are essential. In practice, both deduction and induction are routes to the construction of communication theories.

Having gotten an overview of the deductive and inductive linkages between theory and research, let's look just a little deeper into how theories are constructed and used in these two logic systems.

CONSTRUCTING THEORY BY STARTING DEDUCTIVELY

Although theory construction that starts with deductive reasoning is not a lockstep affair, the following list of elements in theory construction summarizes the activity for you:

1. Specify the topic.
2. Specify the range of phenomena the theory addresses. Will the theory apply to all of human social life, will it apply only to U.S. citizens, only to young people, or what?
3. Identify and specify the major concepts and variables.
4. Find out what is known (propositions) about the relationships among those variables.
5. Reason logically from those propositions to the specific topic of interest.

The first step in theory construction through the deductive portal of the wheel of science is to pick a topic of interest. It can be broad, such as "What are the keys to effective communication?" or narrower, as in "Why are some people good listeners and other people poor listeners?" Whatever. In general, the narrower the topic, the easier it will be to study.

Sometimes, topics come from a researcher's own curiosity about personal experiences or the experiences of those around him or her. Other times, topics emerge from the findings of the researcher's prior research or from the research conducted by others.

Related to the selection of a topic area is the statement of the scope conditions of the topic—is the researcher interested in knowledge claims about all of the human condition, communication in U.S. society, communication among university students, employees of organization X?

Once the topic has been selected, the researcher undertakes an inventory of what is known or thought about it. In part, this means writing down his or her own observations and ideas about it. Beyond that, the researcher learns what other scholars have said about the topic.

This preliminary work will probably uncover consistent patterns discovered by prior scholars. For example, cognitive variables and personality variables have often been linked to communication competence by researchers. Findings such as these are very useful in creating a theory.

As the researcher identifies the relevant concepts and discovers what has already been learned about them, he or she begins to create a propositional structure that explains the topic under study. It is useful to look at a well-reasoned example. We draw our example from positivist communication research, because this approach to theory construction is valued in that paradigmatic perspective.

A Detailed Example

In 1975, Charles Berger and Richard Calabrese published a deductively derived theory of initial interaction between strangers and acquaintances. This theory, known as uncertainty reduction theory (URT), has had an important role in much research in interpersonal communication and in intercultural communication. Although the scope of the theory as originally stated was initial interactions, subsequent work with the theory extended it to interactions between people who are in established relationships.

Berger and Calabrese noted that when strangers or acquaintances meet, they are motivated to reduce uncertainty about each other: What is the other person like? Will he or she like me? What topics are "safe" to discuss, and what topics will be embarrassing or insulting to the other person? Central to their theory was the presumption that communication in initial interaction is driven by the effort to reduce uncertainty.

Based on a wide range of research published by various scholars, Berger and Calabrese (1975, pp. 101–107) felt confident in advancing URT in the form of seven propositions or axioms, which served as the theoretical cornerstones of their deductive reasoning process. We paraphrase these axioms here:

- Axiom 1: As the amount of verbal communication between strangers increases, the level of uncertainty for each person will decrease. As uncertainty is further reduced, the amount of verbal communication will increase. (In other words, the more two people talk together, the less uncertain they are about each other, and vice versa.)

- Axiom 2: As the nonverbal expression of liking increases, uncertainty will decrease. In addition, decreases in uncertainty level will cause increases in the nonverbal expression of liking. (In other words, when the other person smiles at you, you feel more certain about him or her, and vice versa.)

- Axiom 3: High levels of uncertainty increase information-seeking behavior. As uncertainty declines, information seeking decreases. (In other words, when you're uncertain about the other person, you ask a lot of questions; once you have some certainty about the person, you stop being so inquisitive.)

- Axiom 4: High uncertainty results in decreased intimacy in communication content. Low levels of uncertainty produce high levels of intimacy. (In other words, when you're uncertain about someone, you don't reveal very much about the personal details of your life.)

- Axiom 5: High uncertainty results in high rates of reciprocity. Low uncertainty results in low reciprocity rates. (In other words, when you're uncertain about the other, you tend to mirror his or her communication. For example, the person describes his or her pet dog, so you describe your pet dog.)

- Axiom 6: Similarities between persons reduce uncertainty, while dissimilarities increase uncertainty. (In other words, when two people feel that they share something in common, it reduces their uncertainty about each other.)

- Axiom 7: Increases in uncertainty level decrease liking; decreases in uncertainty increase liking. (In other words, if you feel uncertain about someone, you aren't going to like him or her.)

Notice that our parenthetical statements are worded quite informally, in contrast to the more formalized wording of URT's axioms. That's because axiomatic theories are worded as precisely as possible. More specifically, theories are worded in terms of the relationship between variables. URT uses this core set of variables: level of uncertainty, amount of verbal communication, degree of nonverbally expressed liking, amount of information seeking, level of expressed intimacy, reciprocity rate, degree of similarity, degree of liking. These variables are conceived in quantitative terms—high, low; more, less;

increased, decreased. The axiomatic statements provide mathematical links between variables: "If variable X is high (low), then variable Y is low (high)."

Using the deductive logic of syllogisms, Berger and Calabrese (1975) derived 21 testable theorems from their seven axioms. We won't list all 21 of these theorems, just one for purposes of illustration:

- Theorem 14: "Intimacy level of communication content and similarity are positively related" (p. 109).

This theorem was deduced as follows from logically combining axioms 6 and 4: Increased similarity decreases uncertainty, and decreased uncertainty increases intimacy of communication content. Therefore, increased similarity is linked to increased intimacy of communication content. Because similarity and intimacy of content both increase, Theorem 14 states that the two variables are positively related.

Realize that a theory guarantees none of its given predictions. The role of research is to determine whether what makes sense (theory) occurs in practice (research). There are two important elements in science, then: logical integrity and empirical observation. Both are essential to scientific inquiry and discovery. Logic alone is not enough, but on the other hand, the mere observation and collection of empirical facts do not provide understanding—a telephone directory, for example, is not a scientific conclusion. Let's turn to the matter of how a deductively derived theory is linked to empirical observations. In doing so, we will see how a researcher who enters the wheel of science on the deduction side moves to the induction side, and back again to another iteration of deduction.

LINKING DEDUCTIVELY DERIVED THEORY TO OBSERVATION, AND BACK AGAIN

When a deductively derived theory moves toward observation, two general theory-observation linkages can be identified in communication research: hypothesis testing and heuristic application.

Hypothesis Testing

A hypothesis is a statement in which a specific empirical outcome is predicted. The prediction is deduced logically from the researcher's theory. Hypotheses (plural form of *hypothesis*) need to be worded carefully so that they can be tested clearly. A good hypothesis must be **falsifiable;** that is, the researcher must allow for the possibility of

concluding that the hypothesis will not gain empirical support. If we hypothesize that "Tomorrow it will rain or not," our hypothesis is not falsifiable. Instead, if we hypothesize "It will rain tomorrow" or if we hypothesize "It will not rain tomorrow," either hypothesis is falsifiable.

Hypotheses tend to be worded in some basic, almost formulaic ways. In general, a hypothesis can be described as a prediction of relationship or a prediction of difference. A hypothesis of relationship predicts that two variables are statistically related, either positively or negatively. If two variables are related positively, they both increase together and decrease together. If two variables are related negatively, one variable increases in value while the other decreases, or vice versa.

For example, if we predict that exam scores are positively related to study time, we have a hypothesis of relationship—a positive relationship, to be exact. If we predict that exam scores are negatively related to partying the night before the exam, we still have a hypothesis of relationship—this time a negative relationship because as partying increases, exam scores are predicted to decrease.

We sometimes work with variables whose attributes are not numbers that range from lower to higher values. The variable of gender, for example, has attributes masculine and feminine. If we predict that feminine persons more so than masculine persons will disclose personal information, we have a hypothesis of difference. In this kind of hypothesis, we predict that the attributes of one variable differ with respect to the attributes of a second variable.

Sometimes, our deductive reasoning does not logically allow us to predict the direction of a relationship or difference; instead, we can reason only that a relationship or a difference of some kind will be observed. For example, suppose we hypothesize that exam scores will be related to partying. If our observations find either a positive or a negative relationship between these two variables, we will conclude that our hypothesis has been supported. After all, our hypothesis does not predict whether the relationship will be positive or negative—it simply predicts that partying and exam scores will relate in some way. Similarly, if we had hypothesized that masculine and feminine persons will differ in their amount of self-disclosure, our hypothesis would be supported whether masculine persons disclosed more than feminine persons or vice versa. Our hypothesis did not predict the direction of the difference, simply that there would be a difference of some kind.

When a hypothesis specifies a direction of outcome, it is known as a directional, or one-tailed, hypothesis. By

TABLE 4-1   **Sample Research Hypotheses**

Research Hypothesis	Hypothesis of Relationship or Difference?	Directional or Nondirectional?
"The more television viewers watch, the more fearful they are of the world."	Relationship (positive, to be exact)	Directional
"The more supportive an organization's work climate, the lower its employee turnover."	?	?
"Persuasive messages to limit alcoholic consumption during pregnancy will be more effective if they arouse fear in the viewer as opposed to messages that do not arouse fear."	?	?
"Subjects exposed to the foot-in-the-door appeal will respond differently than subjects not exposed to the appeal."	?	?
"Marital couples who are high in mutual negativity will have a greater likelihood of divorce than will marital couples who are low in mutual negativity."	?	?
"Males and females will differ in the frequency with which they request advice from others."	?	?

contrast, when a hypothesis simply predicts that a relationship of some sort will be observed or that a difference of some sort will be found, it is known as a nondirectional, or two-tailed, hypothesis. In general, the more specific a hypothesis is, the better. Thus, directional hypotheses are generally preferable to nondirectional ones, if reasoning allows a researcher to make a directional prediction. Table 4-1 gives you some sample hypotheses—test your understanding by trying to determine whether each hypothesis is (a) directional or nondirectional, and (b) a prediction of relationship or a prediction of difference.

A hypothesis is always a prediction about the empirical outcome of a specific study. Thus, before a hypothesis can be worded properly, it is necessary to know how each variable will be **operationalized,** or measured. Let's return to our example of URT.

URT—with its 7 axioms and its 21 deduced theorems —positions a researcher to derive a hypothesis that could be tested in a study. But first, the researcher would need to operationalize the relevant variables. That is, the researcher would need to figure out how the attributes of the variables would be measured.

A researcher might craft a study in which people will be brought to an observation lab to interact with strangers. Prior to their participation, the participants in the study will fill out a series of questionnaires on their values and interests. The researcher will then inform some of the research participants that they will be communicating with someone very similar to them in basic values and interests, whereas other participants will be told that they will be communicating with someone very different from them in basic values and interests. The participants will then be taken one at a time into a room equipped with a video camera to record the conversation that transpires between the research participant and the similar (or dissimilar) stranger. (Actually, the same person will role-play the stranger and interact with all of the research participants, although participants will not be aware of this at the time.) The researcher plans to measure the intimacy level of communication content as the number of personal statements uttered by the participant over the course of the half-hour videotaped conversation between the research participant and the stranger.

With these very specific operationalizations in mind, the researcher would be poised to advance, and test, the following hypothesis derived from Theorem 14 of URT: "Participants paired with a stranger thought to be similar to themselves will disclose more personal information than will participants paired with a stranger thought to be dissimilar to themselves." (Note that this is a directional hypothesis of difference.)

If our researcher actually conducted this study with 100 research participants, 50 paired with a bogus similar stranger and 50 paired with a bogus dissimilar stranger, the following results might have been found:

	Similarity Condition	Dissimilarity Condition
Average number of personal statements	10.4	6.7

Descriptively, participants paired with someone they thought was similar to themselves appear to have engaged in more disclosive communication than did participants paired with someone they thought was dissimilar to themselves (10.4 statements versus 6.7 statements, respectively).

Whether the difference between these two numbers is a one-time fluke or a finding that the researcher can have confidence in is a matter of data analysis using

inferential statistics. In general, statistics operate with the baseline presumption that only random chance is operating in a set of data; this presumption is known as the **null hypothesis,** the implicit presumption that there is no difference between groups or no relationship between the variables being studied. Only when the observed pattern in the data is sufficiently large in magnitude can the researcher reject the null hypothesis. In rejecting the null hypothesis of no difference/relationship, inferential statistics have found the pattern in the data to be statistically significant at some level of confidence (usually 95 percent confidence). When the null hypothesis is rejected, the research hypothesis is supported at the same level of confidence (usually 95 percent confidence). We will examine in greater detail in Chapter 12 how inferential statistics are used in deciding whether or not to reject the null hypothesis. For now, let's presume that our statistical test found this difference to be statistically significant at the 95-percent confidence level, and we conclude that the research hypothesis is supported. This means that we are 95 percent confident that the differences we observed are not a one-time fluke occurrence; that is, our observations do not reflect mere random fluctuations in our numerical data.

But let's imagine a different outcome from our hypothetical study:

	Similarity Condition	Dissimilarity Condition
Average number of personal statements	8.5	8.4

Descriptively, the difference between the similarity condition and the dissimilarity condition is very small—probably trivial (although we would want a statistical test to make the judgment of whether the one-tenth difference is within the normal variation we would expect by random chance alone). For now, let's presume that our statistical test found this difference trivial at the 95-percent confidence level; that is, there was no difference between these two conditions. We would not reject the null hypothesis, thereby failing to support our research hypothesis. But what are the implications of our findings for the underlying theory? To pose this question brings us full circle in the wheel of science. After moving toward data (the deductive portion of the circle), we are now moving back again from our observations to the theory.

What are the implications of these two hypothetical outcomes to our hypothesis-testing exercise? If a hypothesis deduced from a theory is empirically supported, then the theory is supported as well. If a deduced hypothesis is

not supported, neither is the theory, assuming that the study's methods are otherwise sound.

Notice that we are discussing the implications of hypothesis testing in the language of support for the theory. We are not using the language of proof. That is, if a deduced hypothesis is supported, we have not proven the theory, just supported it. Why can't we prove a theory if we find support for a hypothesis that is deduced from that theory? We can point to two primary reasons why communication researchers are not in the business of proof.

First, inferential statistics in quantitative research are used probabilistically. When an inferential statistic concludes at the 95-percent confidence level that the null hypothesis can be rejected, there is a 5-percent likelihood that the null hypothesis is actually the true state of affairs. Thus, any conclusion from inferential statistics is never absolute.

Second, there could be other, rival theories that would predict the very same outcome. For example, some theorists argue that expected rewards drive communication, not uncertainty reduction per se. To these theorists, uncertainty is often unrewarding, but it can sometimes be very rewarding—otherwise, how could we ever be pleasantly surprised? This alternative theory might go something like this at the axiomatic level:

- Axiom 1: As the amount of reward expected from the other increases, a person's intimacy level of communication content also increases. (This axiom is based on the presumption that when we expect the other person to like and affirm us, we are more willing to open up to the person and disclose personal information about ourselves.)
- Axiom 2: As similarity increases, so does the expectation for reward. (This axiom presumes that people who are similar to us will agree with and affirm us, whereas such affirmation will be less from someone who is dissimilar.)

A theorem that can be deduced from these two axioms would be this: "As similarity increases, the intimacy level of communication content increases." And the research hypothesis we would put to the test from this theorem would be the same one we tested above for URT. If the hypothesis were supported, we would face the dilemma of deciding which theory is a better explanation of our findings—a theory of uncertainty reduction or a theory of reward.

The deductive-to-inductive-to-deductive process is a complex one, requiring many studies on a given topic. In general, confidence in a certain theory grows as more and more studies support hypotheses derived from the theory; reciprocally, confidence in a certain theory wanes as hypotheses deduced from the theory fail to gain empirical support.

In the case of two competing theories, researchers ideally seek studies that pit the two explanations against each other in as direct a fashion as possible. For example, if we wanted to find out whether uncertainty reduction or reward was at the heart of the matter, we might conduct a study with two conditions—one in which certainty was rewarding and another in which certainty was not rewarding. Then we could observe whether certainty or reward drives communication behavior. In general, however, it is exceedingly difficult for researchers to craft studies that pit competing theoretical explanations against each other so directly.

Often, the results of empirical observation are used to revise a theory. Many of the theorems of URT have been supported empirically, but some have not. Thus, the theory has been modified or revised in ways that account for the empirical findings. These revisions have also been put to the empirical test, thereby moving full circle again in the wheel of science.

Using Deductively Derived Theories Heuristically

Often, researchers use deductively derived theory heuristically as a basis of organizing the questions asked and observations made about a phenomenon. The heuristic use of deductively derived theory is especially common among systems, interpretive, and critical researchers. When deductively derived theory is being used heuristically, formal hypothesis testing is rarely involved. Instead, the researcher reasons specific research questions to guide the kinds of things looked for in the empirical study. At the conclusion of the study, the theory is not evaluated with respect to whether the findings support it. Rather, the theory is judged as either more or less useful in producing insight about a phenomenon.

In 1984, Anthony Giddens presented social scientists with his structuration theory. This theory was designed to account for both societal structures and human actions. In particular, Giddens argued in his theory that human actions function to reproduce societal structures or to create, or produce, new structures. For example, whenever politicians give speeches to urge voters to turn out on election day, they are functioning to reproduce the structure of democratic elections. Politicians who urge the overthrow of the voting process are attempting to challenge the existing democratic structure and perhaps to replace it with some new societal system or structure. Although our actions often function to reproduce existing social structures, humans have a choice to reproduce or to change those structures whenever they act. This process of (re)producing societal structures is what Giddens labeled *structuration*.

Communication researchers Marshall Scott Poole, David Seibold, and Robert McPhee (1996) have adapted structuration theory to the context of decision-making group communication. Using deductive reasoning, they built a logical bridge to move down the ladder of abstraction from the general theory of structuration to a more narrowly constructed theory of group decision making. In particular, they argued that the rules, resources, and structures that groups face are not fixed but are instead subject to the same process of reproduction and production that Giddens posited for society in general. This process of decision-making structuration became their focus of study, and they have undertaken 15 years of research designed to understand how structures become real to group members through their talk.

Group members create structures unique to their group, import structures from outside the group, and adapt outside structures. For example, a group may decide to import the structure of parliamentary procedure to guide their deliberations and decision making, but simplify it somewhat. Another group may decide to suspend its normal structure of "majority vote rules" in favor of a goal of reaching consensus among group members. In much of their research activity, Poole and his colleagues have examined the details of interaction among group members in order to study the structuration process. In fact, some studies have developed elaborate coding systems to observe on an utterance-by-utterance basis the kind of structuration work that is enacted by group members.

The work of Poole and his colleagues in the structuration process of decision-making groups is an excellent exemplar to illustrate how researchers use deductively derived theories heuristically. Researchers reason from a general theory toward more detailed contexts and phenomena. Poole and his colleagues reasoned that decision-making groups are small societies and function as Giddens argued in his original statement of structuration theory. They then used various features of Giddens's theory to guide their more specific reasoning about group communication processes. Poole and his colleagues do not ask whether structuration theory is supported or not by the results of a given study. They do not subject structuration theory to hypothesis testing. Instead, they argue that the theory is heuristic because it provides us with a useful lens through which to understand the process by which group members reach decisions. If they had found that structuration theory did not produce insight about group decision making, they would have concluded that it lacked heuristic value for the specific phenomenon of interest to them.

CONSTRUCTING THEORY BY STARTING INDUCTIVELY

Quite often, communication researchers begin constructing a theory by entering the inductive portal of the wheel of science. These researchers use the inductive method of reasoning by observing aspects of communicative life and then looking for patterns that may point to more abstract or general principles. Although the process starts inductively, it more accurately involves a process of moving back and forth from induction to deduction to induction again. This back-and-forth reasoning process thus characterizes all of theory construction, whether a researcher enters through the deductive or the inductive portal. Inductively derived theories can be found in both qualitative and quantitative communication research, but they are more commonly found in qualitative research.

A Detailed Qualitative Example

What exactly is the process of reasoning used by researchers when they identify rules, including the rules of meaning that we called semantic relationships in Chapter 3? The qualitative researcher begins the process by observing some communicative phenomenon until a pattern can be discerned. Second, the researcher then formulates this pattern as a hypothesized rule: "If X conditions are present, then Y [a specific behavior or meaning] is obligated, preferred, or prohibited." In terms of a rule statement, "Xs" can refer to an actor's goals, a situation or context, or a particular set of circumstances. Thus, for example, we could express a greeting rule as follows: "If you meet someone you know, you should acknowledge his or her presence with a greeting." We might have additional rules for the kind of greeting. For example, "If the person you meet is of higher status, your greeting should be a title-plus-last-name."

When a researcher forms a tentative or hypothesized rule statement, he or she has moved inductively from specific observations to the formulation of a more general statement of the rule. But once a tentative rule has been formulated, the researcher moves deductively in the same study to determine whether the rule has been accurately identified. This third step in the process—a deductive move—seeks to determine the validity of the rule statement when examined against additional observational activity.

These subsequent observations are very focused in nature. Rule statements take the logical form of a conditional: "If X, then Y." According to formal logic, a conditional is validated by either affirming the antecedent (the "If X . . ." clause) or by denying the consequent clause (the "then Y . . ." clause). When a researcher affirms the antecedent, he or she looks for X situations and then observes whether Y is also present. To continue with the greeting rule ("If you meet someone you know, you should acknowledge his or her presence with a greeting"), the researcher would take note of what people did when they encountered someone they knew. For the rule to gain support, the researcher should notice that greetings are enacted.

The researcher would also undertake observations with the logical intent of denying the consequent. That is, he or she would observe when greetings were absent, expecting to find that the person encountered was not known to the actor.

But a rule is not merely a pattern of co-occurrence between X and Y clauses of a conditional logic statement. Rules are judgments of appropriateness. If the researcher undertakes additional observations designed to affirm the antecedent and to deny the consequent, and concludes that the pattern holds, then the researcher needs to undertake the fourth step in the process—observations to demonstrate that the pattern is criticizable.

According to Susan Shimanoff (1980), a given X–Y pattern is rule-governed if it is criticizable. Three kinds of evidence demonstrate that a behavioral action is subject to criticism: (1) people can evaluate the action's appropriateness, (2) negative sanctions are employed in instances in which an actor deviates from or violates the rule, and (3) repair efforts are undertaken when a violation has occurred, either by the actor who engaged in the deviant act or by someone acting on behalf of the violator.

Let's continue with our greeting rule example. In order to demonstrate that the greeting rule is criticizable, the researcher needs to undertake observations to satisfy at least one of the three kinds of evidence of criticizability. The researcher might ask people through interviewing what they would think of people who failed to greet someone they knew and what they would think of people who always greeted someone they knew. ("Would you regard people like this as polite or rude?") If people judged others in terms of politeness/rudeness, it would provide the first kind of evidence listed above—evidence that people can evaluate the action's appropriateness. Any evaluation will do—judged correctness or incorrectness, a judgment of right/wrong, and so forth.

The researcher might observe what happened to people who failed to greet someone they knew. If the greeting rule is criticizable, then deviations from it should be reacted to negatively by others, and the actor should be sanctioned in some way—criticized, teased, reprimanded, punished. If no one deviated from the rule, the researcher might intentionally deviate from the rule and refrain from greeting known others in order to observe whether he or she received negative sanctioning from others. If deviations from the rule evoked negative sanctioning of some sort, the second kind of evidence suggested by Shimanoff (1980) has been demonstrated.

The researcher would also observe whether repair attempts took place when the greeting rule was violated. Did the actor apologize for the oversight, thereby attempting a social repair? ("I'm really sorry—I don't know where my mind was just now.") Did others provide excuses on behalf of the actor? ("Forgive him; he's really preoccupied today.") Efforts to repair, or correct, a rule violation demonstrate the third kind of criticizability evidence.

If the researcher's observations support the X–Y pattern and demonstrate that the pattern is criticizable, then he or she can conclude that a rule has been identified. The logical move here is inductive: from concrete observations to a conclusion of a general rule statement. The rule is no longer posited as tentative, because it has been put to the test of additional, more focused, observations.

But what if the tentative hypothesized rule is not supported in subsequent observations? In qualitative research, the researcher revises his or her statement of the rule as many times as necessary, always collecting additional observations to determine whether the rule statement is consistent with observations. A researcher stops making additional observations when the tentative rule statement gains consistent support empirically, with no need for additional revision of or refinement in the statement of the rule. This is known as the point of **saturation.**

In 1975, Gerry Philipsen published a classic ethnography of communication about a southside Chicago neighborhood that he dubbed "Teamsterville." He posited this basic rule that guided male communicative action: "When the social identity relationship of the participants in a situation is symmetrical, the situation can appropriately re-

alize a great amount of talking by a Teamsterville man. . . . A high quantity of speaking is considered inappropriate in situations in which the participants' identity relationship is asymmetrical" (1975, p. 15). A symmetrical relationship was one between peers—either long-time friends or people with the same status levels. An asymmetrical relationship was interaction with a stranger or with someone who was higher or lower in status than the participant.

Philipsen spent two-and-a-half years engaged in field observations to first formulate this rule tentatively and then to test it against subsequent observations. His observations supported the X clause of his X–Y conditional rule statement—the symmetrical or asymmetrical nature of relationships. His observations also supported the Y clause of his X–Y rule statement—variations in the quantity of talk displayed by males.

Philipsen also presented his reader with evidence of criticizability. He observed that when males violated the rule, their masculinity was questioned. Thus, clear evidence of evaluation was provided. In addition, Philipsen reported an example of social rejection of a man who violated the rule—clear evidence of negative sanctioning. Finally, he recounted a detailed example of an older Teamsterville man who was attempting to make sense of someone who had violated the rule, in essence offering several repair attempts that would absolve the violator of ridicule.

What's the theory that Philipsen presented in his ethnographic work? It is a local knowledge theory—a theory of "speaking like a man in Teamsterville."

A Detailed Quantitative Example

Qualitative research is not the only method of observation appropriate to the development of theory by starting inductively. Here's another detailed example to illustrate further the construction of theory by entering the induction portal, this time an example taken from quantitative research.

Mary Anne Fitzpatrick (1988) has conducted inductive research on marital communication. She began with a large pool of more than 200 questionnaire items that dealt with a wide range of issues in marriage. More than 1,400 married people filled out the questionnaire, subsequently named the Relational Dimensions Instrument. From the pattern of responses to the questions, Fitzpatrick inductively identified three underlying dimensions: a conventional/unconventional ideology of marriage, the interdependence/autonomy of marital partners, and conflict engagement/avoidance.

Based on how married couples responded to questions representing these underlying dimensions, Fitzpatrick inductively derived a typology of marital types. *Traditional* marriages are those in which the husband and wife report that they endorse a traditional ideology of marriage (e.g., "A woman should take her husband's last name when she marries"), conduct their day-to-day marriage through high interdependence and sharing, and are willing to engage in open conflicts, especially on important issues. By contrast, *independent* marriages are those in which husbands and wives share an unconventional ideology of marriage (e.g., "In marriage/close relationships, there should be no constraints or restrictions on individual freedom"), sustain high interdependence and sharing in their day-to-day lives, and experience quite a bit of conflict because they do not seek to avoid it. *Separate* marriages are those in which husbands and wives share a conventional ideology of marriage, conduct their day-to-day lives with substantial independence and autonomy from each other, and strive to avoid open conflicts.

In addition to these three "pure types," in which husbands and wives agreed in their responses to the three underlying dimensions that organized the questionnaire items, Fitzpatrick identified several "mixed types" in which husbands and wives held different attitudes and beliefs on one or more of the dimensions.

In the more than 25 years since her initial research, Fitzpatrick and her associates have uncovered many systematic differences among the marital types, especially the three "pure types." In her initial work, Fitzpatrick operated inductively—she did not know the number of marital types that existed or the underlying dimensions that distinguished them from one another. Her typology of marital types was derived from her initial observational work using questionnaires. Subsequent work has been more deductively centered. Fitzpatrick and her colleagues have deduced hypotheses of difference among the marital types based on her typological theory, and have empirically tested these hypotheses through a range of quantitative methods.

USING INDUCTIVE AND DEDUCTIVE REASONING TO GET STARTED IN RESEARCH

As a consumer of communication research, you will often encounter theories. As a beginning producer of research, you probably will not be asked to construct a full-blown theory right away. However, you will experience the wheel of science, with its inductive and deductive components. In this section, we're going to illustrate how you might use both of these forms of reasoning in formulating a topic for research. In Parts 2 and 3 of this book, you'll study the methods by which you can systematically gather data relevant to your selected topic.

Let's suppose that your research methods instructor has assigned you the task of conducting an empirical study. You must begin the task by making a decision about what will be the focus of your study: What do you want to find out?

You might start your decision-making process using inductive reasoning. In particular, you might reflect on your own communication experiences in order to identify a phenomenon in which you have a genuine interest. Maybe you've just experienced a terrible conflict with your roommate; thus, the topic of roommate conflict is one you'd like to know more about. As you ponder your past conflict experiences with this roommate and with former roommates, and your observations about how other roommate pairs get along, you try to identify common patterns. That is, you are reasoning inductively from specific experiences toward a more general pattern or principle. Let's suppose that you spot this tentative pattern in your experience: Roommates handle conflict poorly during midterm and final examination weeks.

You could undertake observations directly to examine whether your tentatively identified pattern is supported empirically. But you decide to review the research literature to see what other researchers have done. You don't want to "rediscover the wheel" by addressing a question that others have already answered. Plus, you want to see how others have gone about studying this phenomenon.

You conduct a review of literature on roommate conflict. Nobody has examined roommate conflict during exam and nonexam weeks of the semester. In fact, not very much research has been done with roommates. However, you find that a great deal of study has been undertaken on conflict in a variety of kinds of interpersonal relationships, including friendships, romantic relationships, marriage, and family relationships. You review this body of work in search of established findings (we'll call these propositions) that might be relevant to your interest.

You find that many researchers have identified a link between stress levels and conflict management in interpersonal relationships. In particular, as stress levels increase for the parties in interpersonal relationships, conflict is managed less constructively. This is a proposition from which you can deductively reason to the particular matter of roommate conflicts during exam weeks.

First, you reason that roommates are a kind of interpersonal relationship because they are characterized by the same features that typify the interpersonal relationships already examined in the research literature—they are characterized by a frequency of interaction across time and interdependence between the parties. How do you know this? You read the research literature on the characteristics of interpersonal relationships to determine if the roommate relationship qualifies. You want to be able to reason that the conflict findings identified for other types of relationships should logically apply to the roommate relationship.

Remember the if–then conditional from earlier in the chapter? Well, we're going to "affirm the antecedent" in a different way than we did earlier. We'll start with this if–then conditional proposition:

> If a relationship is characterized by interdependence and frequency of interaction across time, then it is an interpersonal relationship.

> The roommate relationship is characterized by interdependence and frequency of interaction across time.

> THEREFORE, the roommate relationship is an interpersonal relationship.

We have used deductive reasoning to argue that findings for friendships, romantic relationships, marriage, and family relationships should also apply to the roommate relationship because it is an interpersonal relationship. Therefore, we can take our general proposition from the research literature and reword it as follows: "As stress levels increase for roommates, they manage their conflicts less constructively."

But we're not done yet. We still need to reason a logical connection between stress levels and examination weeks. Let's work with a different syllogism, as follows:

> All situations that increase stress levels for parties in interpersonal relationships [roommates] are characterized by less constructive conflict management.

> Midterm and final exam weeks are situations that increase stress levels for parties in interpersonal relationships [roommates].

> THEREFORE, midterm and final exam weeks are situations that are characterized by less constructive conflict management for parties in interpersonal relationships [roommates].

Our first proposition in this syllogism is simply a restatement of the pattern identified in the conflict literature, logically generalized to the roommate relationship. Our second statement is one we would argue after examining relevant research—maybe we found research literature suggesting that exams make people doubt their abilities, get fewer hours of sleep per night, and increase susceptibility to colds and flu, all of which are indicators that stress levels are heightened.

We have now deductively reasoned ourselves to this testable hypothesis:

> H: The conflicts between roommates that occur during midterm and final examination weeks will be handled less constructively than the conflicts that occur during other weeks of the semester.

This is a directional hypothesis of difference that involves two variables: The independent variable is time of the semester (with attributes "midterm and final exam weeks" and "weeks other than midterm and final exams"), and the dependent variable is the extent to which roommates handle their conflict constructively (presumably measured on some quantitative indicator that ranges from low to high).

As you get started in the research process, you will probably employ inductive and deductive reasoning in ways similar to this example. Of course, when you are gathering and analyzing your data, you will return to these modes of reasoning once again.

RELATING THEORY TO PRACTICE: SOME CONCLUDING THOUGHTS

In some minds, theoretical and practical matters are virtual opposites. Communication researchers committed to the use of science know differently, however. No matter how practical and/or idealistic your aims, a theoretical understanding of the terrain may very well be the difference between success and failure.

For example, let's suppose that you are deeply concerned about the media's portrayal of thinness in the female body. You think that the ideal of thinness presented in TV, films, and magazines is responsible for eating disorders among females, particularly adolescents. This sounds like a logical argument on your part. But when we turn to empirical research on this issue, we see that it grows complicated very quickly. Some scholars have found that young adolescents who are concerned about their body image seek out media images of thinness—that is, media portrayals don't cause female concern with body image; instead, female concern with body image causes media consumption. Other scholars have found that images of thinness do not affect females' attitudes and behavior, but fat images do produce an effect, depending on the particular medium in which the image appears. Other scholars have found that the effects of media portrayals depend on the ethnicity of the female viewer/reader. In short, what appears simple on the surface can in fact become very complicated when we undertake systematic observations. Our theories help to guide us through this maze of empirical findings so that we can explain or understand what is going on.

We hope the various discussions in this chapter make clear that there is no simple recipe for conducting social scientific research in communication. Ultimately, science rests on two pillars: logic and observation. As you'll see throughout this book, they can be fit together in many patterns.

Main Points

- Two logic systems are employed in communication research—deduction and induction. All research employs both kinds of reasoning.

- Deduction is reasoning from a general principle or statement to a particular incident or set of observations.

- Induction is reasoning from a specific or particular incident or set of observations to a more general statement or conclusion.

- A theory is a set of statements about some phenomenon with a goal of rendering it intelligible. Theory represents the logic side of scientific inquiry, and it complements the observation side of scientific inquiry.

- Theories can be constructed by starting with either deductive reasoning or inductive reasoning.

- Positivistic and systems researchers tend to construct theories by starting deductively, whereas interpretivist and critical researchers tend to construct theories by starting inductively.

- Research hypotheses are deduced from theory and are tested through empirical observation.

- Research hypotheses are either predictions of difference or predictions of relationship between variables.

- Research hypotheses are either directional or nondirectional in nature.

- The null hypothesis is the presumption of no difference or relationship between variables. Inferential statistics are employed in quantitative research to determine whether the null hypothesis can be rejected at the 95-percent confidence level. If the null hypothesis is rejected, the research hypothesis is supported.

- A communication rule takes the form of an if–then statement: "If X [e.g., a condition, situation, or goal] is present, then Y [a communication phenomenon] is appropriate."

Key Terms

induction
deduction
theory
hypothesis
falsifiable

operationalized
inferential statistics
null hypothesis
saturation

Review Questions and Exercises

1. Identify some communication phenomenon of interest to you. Prepare a deductive approach to studying it, as well as an inductive approach.

2. Select a social scientific study from one of the communication journals listed in Appendix A. Identify all of the ways in which inductive and deductive reasoning are used by the researcher.

3. Keep a diary record of how you use inductive reasoning and deductive reasoning during the course of a single day.

Continuity Project

How might you approach the issue of gender and communication using deductive and inductive reasoning? Observe how "masculinity" and "femininity" are accomplished through communicative practices. Using inductive reasoning, infer at least one pattern or principle from your observations. Go to the research literature on gender and communication, and locate studies in which the construction of gender has been examined. See if you can use deductive reasoning to infer one hypothesis from this body of work.

Additional Reading

Berger, C. R., & Calabrese, R. J. (1975). Toward a developmental theory of interpersonal communication. *Human Communication Research, 1,* 99–112. This article is the original presentation of Uncertainty Reduction Theory. It is an excellent example of deductive theory construction.

Fitzpatrick, M. A. (1988). *Between husbands and wives: Communication in marriage.* Beverly Hills, CA: Sage. This volume presents a complete summary of Fitzpatrick's program of research through 1988 on her typological theory of marital types. Examine the book to see how her work has progressed from inductive to deductive research.

Philipsen, G. (1992). *Speaking culturally: Explorations in social communication.* Albany, NY: State University of New York Press. This book is a summary of Philipsen's inductively derived theory of two speech codes that organize some communication in the United States. The book nicely illustrates a theory of local knowledge.

Poole, M. S., Seibold, D. R., & McPhee, R. D. (1996). The structuration of group decisions. In R. Y. Hirokawa & M. S. Poole (Eds.), *Communication and group decision making* (2nd ed.; pp. 114–146). Thousand Oaks, CA: Sage. This essay provides a more complete illustration than the discussion in this chapter of how structuration theory can be used heuristically. It nicely displays how a deductive theory can guide observational work.

Shimanoff, S. B. (1980). *Communication rules: Theory and research.* Beverly Hills, CA: Sage. This is a classic volume on what a rule is and how a qualitative researcher goes about the iterative process of identifying rules of meaning and action.

InfoTrac College Edition
http://www.infotrac-college.com/
wadsworth/access.html

Access the latest news and journal articles with Info-Trac College Edition, an easy-to-use online database of reliable, full-length articles from hundreds of top academic journals. Conduct an electronic search using the following search terms:

- deductive
- inductive
- hypothesis
- hypothesis testing
- null hypothesis
- saturation
- theory

CHAPTER **5**

The Ethics of Communication Research

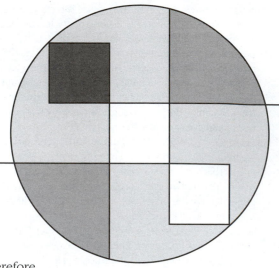

What You'll Learn in This Chapter

Communication research takes place in a social context. Therefore, researchers must take into account many ethical considerations alongside scientific ones in designing and executing their research. Often, however, clear-cut answers to thorny ethical issues are hard to come by.

INTRODUCTION

Our purpose in Part 1 of this book is to present a useful introduction to doing communication research. However, no introduction to research methods in communication could be complete without a discussion of research ethics. You may be saying to yourself "Hey, I'm an ethical person who knows right from wrong, so I don't need a whole chapter on the topic!" But research ethics can be subtle and complicated. Here's a story to illustrate what we mean.

Several years ago, one of us was invited to sit in on a planning session to design a study of legal education in California. The joint project was to be conducted by a university research center and the state bar association. The purpose of the project was to improve legal education by learning which aspects of the law school experience were related to success on the bar exam. Essentially, the plan was to prepare a questionnaire that would get detailed information about the law school experiences of individuals. People would be required to answer the questionnaire when they took the bar exam. By analyzing how people with different kinds of law school experiences did on the bar exam, we could find out what sorts of things worked and what didn't. The findings of the research could be made available to law schools, and legal education could ultimately be improved.

The exciting thing about collaborating with the bar association was that all the normally irritating logistical hassles would be handled. There would be no problem getting permission to administer questionnaires in conjunction with the exam, for example, and the problem of nonresponse could be eliminated altogether.

The prospects for the study were exciting! However, when a colleague was told about it, she said "That's unethical. There's no law requiring the questionnaire, and participation in research has to be voluntary." The study wasn't done.

In retelling this story, it's obvious that requiring participation would have been inappropriate. You may have seen this even before we told you about the colleague's comment. But we had a specific purpose in telling this story.

All of us consider ourselves ethical—not perfect, perhaps, but as ethical as anyone else and perhaps more so than most. The problem in communication research, as probably in life, is that ethical considerations are not always apparent to us. As a result, we often plunge into things without seeing ethical issues that may be apparent to others and may even be obvious to us when pointed out. When the colleague's reactions were reported back to the others in the planning group, for example, no one disagreed with the inappropriateness of requiring participation. Everyone was a bit embarrassed about not having seen it.

Any of us can immediately see that a study that requires small children to be tortured is unethical. We know you'd speak out immediately if we suggested that we interview people about their sexual communication and then publish what they said, by name, in the local newspaper. But, as ethical as you are, you'll totally miss the ethical issues in some other situations—we all do.

This chapter deals with the ethics of communication research. In part, it presents some of the broadly agreed-upon norms describing what's ethical in all social scientific research and what's not. More important than simply knowing the guidelines, however, is becoming sensitized to the ethical component in research so that you'll look for it whenever you plan or read a study. Even when the ethical aspects of a situation are debatable, you should know that there's something to argue about.

THE ORIGINS OF RESEARCHER AGREEMENTS ABOUT ETHICAL CONDUCT

In most dictionaries and in common usage, *ethics* is typically associated with morality, and both deal with matters of right and wrong. But what is right and what wrong? What is the source of the distinction? For individuals, the sources vary. They may be religious doctrines, political ideologies, or the pragmatic observation of what seems to work and what doesn't.

Webster's New World Dictionary is typical among dictionaries in defining *ethical* as "conforming to the standards of conduct of a given profession or group." Although this definition may frustrate those in search of moral absolutes, what we regard as morality and ethics in day-to-day life is a matter of agreement among members of a group. And, not surprisingly, different groups agree on different codes of conduct. Part of living successfully in a particular society is knowing what that society considers ethical and unethical. The same holds true for the community of social scientists, including communication researchers. Anyone involved in social scientific research, then, needs to be aware of the general agreements shared by all social scientists, including communication researchers, about what is proper and improper in the conduct of scientific inquiry. These ethical agreements didn't just materialize out of thin air. So before we turn to a discussion of each ethical agreement, we want to discuss a brief history of their origins.

Concerns over the treatment of human participants in research arose after evidence of gross mistreatments was made public. Current ethical agreements can be traced to the Nuremberg Code, adopted during the Nuremberg military tribunal on Nazi war crimes after World War II. Civilian and military prisoners in Nazi concentration camps were subjected to freezing; malaria; mustard gas; sulfanilamide; bone, muscle, and nerve transplantations; jaundice; sterilization; spotted fever; various poisons; and phosphorus burns, among other tortures. Many died, and others were permanently maimed; all suffered tremendous physical and psychological pain. (For more on the ethics of Nazi experiments, see http://www.ushmm .org/research/doctors/indiptx.htm.) The Nuremberg Code committed to several ethical principles in the conduct of biomedical research:

- The importance of gaining the voluntary content of research participants
- The avoidance of unnecessary physical or psychological suffering
- The avoidance of research where death or disabling injury was likely
- The commitment to end any experiment if its continuation would likely kill, injure, or disable participants
- The importance of having research conducted only by highly qualified researchers
- The commitment to research only for the good of society

Although the Nuremberg Code applied only to biomedical research, similar codes were developed in the international community for the conduct of social scientific research—for example, the 1948 Universal Declaration of Human Rights by the United Nations. Over time, the U.S. government has adopted a number of regulations and laws to protect human participants in research (participants are often referred to as "human subjects" in these regulations). Most of the current regulations have evolved from policies developed by the Public Health Service beginning in 1966. In 1974 the National Research Act established the National Commission for the Protection of Human Subjects in Biomedical and Behavioral Research. This body significantly expanded the range of regulations and assigned responsibility for ethical conduct to institutional review boards (**IRBs**) in research institutes and universities. The Department of Health and Human Services issued regulations in 1981 that are still in force, along with subsequent additions and revisions. We'll re-

turn to the topic of IRBs and human subjects regulations later. For now, let's discuss ethical principles that are commonly accepted throughout the biomedical and social scientific research community.

ETHICAL ISSUES IN CONDUCTING COMMUNICATION RESEARCH

This section summarizes the four most important ethical agreements that prevail in all social scientific research, including communication research.

Voluntary Participation

Often, though not always, communication research represents an intrusion into people's lives. The interviewer's knock on the door or the arrival of a questionnaire in the mail signals the beginning of an activity that the respondent has not requested and that may require significant time and energy. Participation in a communication experiment disrupts the participant's regular activities.

Moreover, communication research often requires that people reveal personal information about themselves—information that may be unknown to their friends and associates. And communication research often requires that such information be revealed to strangers. Other professionals, such as physicians and lawyers, also ask for such information. However, their requests may be justified by their aims: They need the information in order to serve the personal interests of the respondent. Communication researchers can seldom make this claim. Like medical scientists, they can argue only that the research effort may ultimately help all humanity.

A major tenet of medical research ethics is that experimental participation must be **voluntary.** The same norm applies to communication research. No one should be forced to participate. This norm is far easier to accept in theory than to apply in practice, however. Again, medical research provides a useful parallel. Many experimental drugs are tested on prisoners. In the most rigorously ethical cases, the prisoners are told the nature and the possible dangers of the experiment, they are told that participation is completely voluntary, and they are further instructed that they can expect no special rewards—such as early parole—for participation. Even under these conditions, it's often clear that volunteers are motivated by the belief that they will personally benefit from their cooperation.

When the instructor in an introductory communication class asks students to fill out a questionnaire that he or she hopes to analyze and publish, students should always be told that their participation in the survey is completely voluntary. Even so, most students will fear that nonparticipation will somehow affect their grade. Therefore, the instructor should be especially sensitive to such implications and make special provisions to eliminate them. For example, the instructor could ensure anonymity by leaving the room while the questionnaires are being completed. Or students could be asked to return the questionnaires by mail or to drop them in a box near the door just before the next class meeting.

This norm of voluntary participation, though, goes directly against several scientific concerns. In the most general terms, the scientific goal of generalizability is threatened if participants in an experiment or survey study are all the kinds of people who willingly participate in such things. Because this orientation probably reflects more general personality traits, the results of the research might not be generalizable to all kinds of people. Most clearly, in the case of a descriptive survey, a researcher cannot generalize the sample survey findings to an entire population unless a substantial majority of the scientifically selected sample actually participates—the willing respondents and the somewhat unwilling.

As you'll see in Chapter 13, field research has its own ethical dilemmas in this regard. Very often, the researcher cannot even reveal that a study is being done, for fear that such a revelation might significantly affect the communication processes being studied. Clearly, the participants in such studies are not given the opportunity to volunteer or refuse to participate.

Although the norm of voluntary participation is important, it is sometimes impossible to follow. In cases where you feel ultimately justified in violating it, it is all the more important that you observe the other ethical norms of scientific research. Furthermore, you are obligated to inform people after their participation that they were observed, usually giving them the option of having their data withdrawn should they feel uncomfortable with the study.

Sometimes, people volunteer to participate and then change their minds once their participation in the study has begun. Whenever possible, research participants should be given the opportunity to withdraw from a study.

No Harm to the Participants

Communication research should never injure the people being studied, regardless of whether they volunteer for the study. Perhaps the clearest instance of this norm in practice concerns the revealing of information that would embarrass participants or endanger their home life, friendships, jobs, and so forth. We'll discuss this aspect of the norm more fully in a moment.

Because participants can be harmed psychologically in the course of a communication research study, the researcher must look for the subtlest dangers and guard against them. Quite often, research participants are asked to reveal deviant behavior, attitudes they feel are unpopular, or personal characteristics that may seem demeaning, such as the absence of friends. Revealing such information usually makes subjects feel uncomfortable at best.

Communication research projects may also force participants to face aspects of themselves that they don't normally consider. This can happen even when the information is not revealed directly to the researcher. In retrospect, a certain past behavior may appear unjust or immoral. The project, then, can cause continuing personal agony for the participant. If the study concerns codes of ethical conduct in everyday communication, for example, the participant may begin questioning his or her own morality, and that personal concern may last long after the research has been completed and reported. Probing questions on any topic can potentially injure a fragile self-esteem.

It should be apparent from this discussion that just about any research you might conduct runs the risk of injuring other people in some way. It isn't possible to guard against all these possible injuries, but some study designs make such injuries more likely than do others. If a particular research procedure seems likely to produce unpleasant effects for participants—asking survey respondents to report deviant behavior, for example—the researcher should have the firmest of scientific grounds for doing it. If the research design is essential and also likely to be unpleasant for participants, you'll find yourself in an ethical netherworld and may go through some personal agonizing. Although agonizing has little value in itself, it may be a healthy sign that you've become sensitive to the problem.

Increasingly, the ethical norms of voluntary participation and no harm to participants have become formalized in the concept of **informed consent.** This means that participants must base their voluntary involvement in research projects on a full understanding of the possible risks involved. In a medical experiment, for example, prospective participants will be presented with a discussion of the experiment and all the possible risks to themselves. They will be required to sign a statement indicating that they are aware of the risks and that they choose to participate anyway. While the value of such a procedure is obvious when participants will be injected with drugs designed to produce physical effects, for example, it's hardly appropriate when a participant observer rushes to the scene of a demonstration to study communication behavior. The researcher in this latter case is not excused from the norm of not bringing harm to those observed, but gaining informed consent is not the means to achieving that end.

Like voluntary participation, avoiding harm to people is easy in theory but often difficult in practice. However, sensitivity to the issue and experience with its applications should improve the researcher's tact in delicate areas of research. Federal and other funding agencies typically require an independent evaluation of the treatment of human participants for research proposals, and most universities now have human-subject committees to serve this evaluative function. Although sometimes troublesome and inappropriately applied, such requirements not only guard against unethical research but can also reveal ethical issues overlooked by even the most scrupulous researchers.

Anonymity and Confidentiality

The clearest concern in the protection of the participants' interests and well-being is the protection of their identity. If revealing their behavior or responses would injure them in any way, adherence to this norm becomes all the more important. Two techniques—anonymity and confidentiality—assist researchers in this regard, although people often confuse the two.

Anonymity   A research project guarantees **anonymity** when the researcher—not just the people who read about the research—cannot link a given response to a given participant. This means, for example, that a typical interview respondent can never be considered anonymous because an interviewer collects the information from an identifiable respondent. An example of anonymity is a mail survey in which no identification numbers are put on the questionnaires before their return to the research office.

As we'll see in Chapter 8, on survey research, assuring anonymity can make it difficult to keep track of who has or hasn't returned the questionnaires. Despite this problem, there are some situations in which you may be advised to pay the necessary price. In one study of drug use among university students, for example, one of us decided specifically against knowing the identity of respondents. It was felt that honestly assuring anonymity would increase the likelihood and accuracy of re-

sponses. Also, knowledge of respondent identity would have placed the researcher in the position of being asked by authorities for the names of drug offenders. In the few instances in which respondents volunteered their names, such information was immediately obliterated on the questionnaires.

Confidentiality   A research project guarantees **confidentiality** when the researcher can identify a given person's responses but essentially promises not to do so publicly. In an interview, for example, the researcher would be in a position to make public the income reported by a given respondent, but the respondent is assured that this will not be done. Whenever a research project is confidential rather than anonymous, it is the researcher's responsibility to make that fact clear to the respondent. Moreover, researchers should never use the term *anonymous* to mean *confidential*.

With few exceptions (such as surveys of public figures who agree to have their responses published), the information that respondents give must at least be kept confidential. This is not always an easy norm to follow because, for example, the courts have not recognized social scientific research data as the kind of "privileged communication" accepted in the case of priests and attorneys.

This unprotected guarantee of confidentiality produced a near disaster in 1991. Two years earlier, the *Exxon Valdez* supertanker had run aground near the port of Valdez in Alaska, spilling ten million gallons of oil into the bay. The economic and environmental damage was widely reported.

Less attention was given to the psychological and sociological damage suffered by residents of the area. There were anecdotal reports of increased alcoholism, family violence, and other secondary consequences of the disruptions caused by the oil spill. Eventually, 22 communities in Prince William Sound and the Gulf of Alaska sued Exxon for the economic, social, and psychological damages suffered by their residents.

To determine the amount of damage done, the communities commissioned a San Diego research firm to undertake a household survey asking residents very personal questions about increased problems in their families. The residents in the sample were asked to reveal painful and embarrassing information under the guarantee of absolute confidentiality. Ultimately, the results of the survey confirmed that a variety of personal and family problems had increased substantially following the oil spill.

When Exxon learned that survey data would be presented to document the suffering, the company took an unusual step: It asked the court to subpoena the survey questionnaires! The court granted the defendant's request and ordered the researchers to turn over the questionnaires—with all identifying information. It appeared that Exxon's intention was to call survey respondents to the stand and cross-examine them regarding answers they had given interviewers under the guarantee of confidentiality. Moreover, many of the respondents were Native Americans, whose cultural norms made such public revelations all the more painful.

Happily, the *Exxon Valdez* case was settled before the court decided whether it would force survey respondents to testify in open court. Unhappily, the potential for disaster remains.

The seriousness of this issue is not limited to established research firms. Rik Scarce was a graduate student at Washington State University when he undertook participant observation among animal-rights activists. In 1990, he published a book based on his research titled *Ecowarriors: Understanding the Radical Environmental Movement*. In 1993, Scarce was called before a grand jury and asked to identify the activists he had studied. In keeping with the norm of confidentiality, the young researcher refused to answer the grand jury's questions and spent 159 days in the Spokane County jail.

You can use several techniques to guard against such dangers and ensure better performance on the guarantee of confidentiality. To begin, interviewers and others with access to respondent identifications should be trained in their ethical responsibilities. Beyond training, the most fundamental technique is to remove identifying information as soon as it's no longer necessary. In a survey, for example, all names and addresses should be removed from questionnaires and replaced by identification numbers. An identification file should be created that links numbers to names to permit the later correction of missing or contradictory information, but this file should not be available except for legitimate purposes.

Similarly, in an interview you may need to identify respondents initially so that you can recontact them to verify that the interview was conducted and perhaps to get information that was missing in the original interview. As soon as you've verified an interview and assured yourself that you don't need any further information from the respondent, however, you can safely remove all identifying information from the interview booklet. Often, interview booklets are printed so that the first page contains all the identifiers—it can be torn off once the respondent's identification is no longer needed. J. Steven Picou (1996) points out that even removing identifiers from data files does not always sufficiently protect respondent confidentiality, a lesson he learned during nearly a year in federal court. A careful examination of all the responses of a particular respondent sometimes allows others to deduce that person's identity. Imagine, for example, that someone said he or she was a former employee of a particular company. Knowing the person's gender, age, ethnicity, and other characteristics could make it possible for the company to identify that person.

Even if you intend to remove all identifying information, suppose you have not yet done so. What do you do when the police or a judge orders you to provide the responses given by your research participants?

Deception

We've seen that the handling of participants' identities is an important ethical consideration. Handling your own identity as a researcher can also be tricky. Sometimes it's useful and even necessary to identify yourself as a researcher to those you want to study. You'd have to be an experienced con artist to get people to participate in a laboratory experiment or complete a lengthy questionnaire without letting on that you were conducting research.

Even when you must conceal your research identity, you need to consider the following. Because deceiving people is unethical, deception within social scientific research needs to be justified by compelling scientific or administrative concerns. Even then, the justification will be arguable.

Sometimes, researchers admit that they're doing research but fudge about why they're doing it or for whom. Although it's difficult to conceal the fact that you're conducting research, it's usually a simple—and sometimes appropriate—matter to conceal your purpose or sponsorship. For example, many studies conceal their real purpose in order to avoid eliciting biased responses from study participants. This is especially an issue when the study involves behaviors or attitudes that might be judged as socially desirable or undesirable.

Consider, for example, an experiment designed to test the extent to which people will abandon the evidence of their own observations in favor of the views expressed by others. Figure 5-1 shows the stimulus from the classic Asch experiment in which participants were shown three lines of differing lengths (A, B, and C) and asked to compare them to a fourth line (D). Participants were then asked "Which of the first three lines is the same length as the fourth?"

You'd probably find it a fairly simple task to identify "B" as the correct answer. However, your job would be

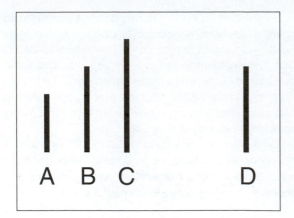

FIGURE 5-1   **Asch Experiment: Lines of Differing Lengths**

complicated by the fact that several other "participants" sitting beside you all agreed that A is the same length as D! In reality, of course, the others in the experiment were all confederates of the researcher, told to agree on the wrong answer. The purpose of the experiment was to see whether you'd give up your own judgment in favor of the group agreement. We think you can see that conformity is a useful phenomenon to study and understand, and it couldn't be studied experimentally without deceiving the participants. We'll examine a similar situation in the discussion of a famous experiment by Stanley Milgram later in this chapter. The question is this: How do we get around the ethical issue that deception is necessary for an experiment to work?

One appropriate solution that researchers have found is to debrief participants following an experiment. **Debriefing** entails interviews to discover any problems generated by the research experience so that those problems can be corrected. Even though participants can't be told the true purpose of the study prior to their participation in it, there's usually no reason they can't know afterward. Telling them the truth afterward may make up for having to lie to them at the outset. This must be done with care, however, making sure that the participants aren't left with bad feelings or doubts about themselves based on their performance in the experiment. If this seems complicated, it's simply the price we pay for using other people's lives as the subject matter for our research.

As a communication researcher, then, you have many ethical obligations to the participants as you conduct your study. But ethical obligations don't end once you have your data in hand.

ETHICAL ISSUES IN ANALYZING AND REPORTING COMMUNICATION RESEARCH

Ethical concerns do not end with the collection of data from participants. Researchers face ethical issues, as well, in the analysis and reporting of their findings. We will emphasize four issues in particular.

Objectivity and Ideology

In Chapter 1, we suggested that social scientific research can never be totally objective, because researchers are human and therefore necessarily subjective. Science, as a collective enterprise, achieves the equivalent of objectivity through intersubjectivity. That is, different scientists, having different subjective views, can and should arrive at the same results when they employ accepted research techniques. Essentially, this will happen to the extent that each can set personal values and views aside for the duration of the research.

The classic statement on objectivity and neutrality in social science is Max Weber's lecture "Science as a Vocation" (1925/1946). In this talk, Weber urged social scientists to engage in value-free research—that is, research unencumbered by personal values. Liberals and conservatives alike could recognize the "facts" of social science, regardless of how those facts were in accordance with their personal politics.

Many communication researchers have agreed with this abstract ideal, but not all. For example, you may recall from Chapter 3 that researchers from a critical paradigm of knowing have argued that communication research and social action cannot and should not be separated. Explanations of the status quo in society, they contend, shade subtly into defenses of that same status quo. Merely studying the role and function of communication in society without a commitment to making society more humane has been called irresponsible and unethical. For example, in 1997 the *Western Journal of Communication* published a special series of invited essays in which a variety of scholars questioned the ways in which academic research in the communication discipline privileges some perspectives while excluding others. Taken as a whole, this series of essays argued that all research is embedded in social values and that those values reproduce social injustices. Contributors argued that researchers should "own up" to their values and that the research community should work harder to fulfill its ethical obligations to work for the good of society.

Clearly, this issue is not one that we can settle. However, we urge you as a researcher to grapple with the ethical issues raised by researchers who align with the critical paradigm of knowing. It is important for researchers to decide for themselves the extent to which their research functions perpetuate the status quo and the extent to which their research bears an ethical obligation for social action and change.

Protection of Study Participants

Every now and then, research participants read the books published about the studies they participated in. Reasonably sophisticated participants can locate themselves in the various indexes and tables. Having done so, they may find themselves characterized—though not identified by name—as communicatively incompetent, lacking in empathy, and so forth. At the very least, such characterizations are likely to trouble them and threaten their self-images. Yet the whole purpose of the research project may be to explain why some people are communicatively incompetent and others are not. As a researcher, you need to take great care to describe participants in such a way that participants cannot identify themselves, or to provide balanced presentations so that negatives can be offset with positives in your portrayals of them.

One of the most important ways you can protect the identity of your participants is to substitute pseudonyms when you describe particular participants. For example, you may know that a particular participant was "Susan" and her husband was "Sam." However, when you provide a quotation from Susan, you could refer to her as "Samantha" and to her husband as "Henry." However, sometimes, pseudonyms don't work well in protecting participant identity if you provide other details about the participant that enable identification. For example, a statement such as "'Samantha' was the only female employed in top management in this firm. The firm, the only one of its kind where the ABVZ product can be found . . ." allows someone to identify who "Samantha" really is because of two kernels of information provided: the firm (the only one of its kind where a very specific product can be obtained) and the fact that "Samantha" is the only female in top management. Generally, researchers are best served by describing their study participants as a group, rather than individually. When individual descriptions of participants are necessary, they should be worded carefully so that no "insider" could figure out who's who.

The same principle of camouflaged identity applies when dealing with units of analysis other than individuals. For example, if you conduct a field study of intercultural communication in a particular town where long-time residents of one cultural heritage face an influx of new residents from a different cultural background, you would be ethically wise to provide the town, as well as its residents, with pseudonyms. The town might be called "Clashville," for example, if cultural clash between these two groups proved to be a prominent theme in your analysis.

Honesty and Integrity

In addition to their ethical obligations to society as a whole and to participants in particular, researchers have ethical obligations to their colleagues in the scientific community. First and foremost, a researcher bears the ethical obligation to be true to his or her data. Even in a qualitative impressionist tale—the narrative form that most reads like a fictionalized story—the researcher is obliged to do his or her best to capture the phenomenon under study with utmost honesty and integrity. Falsification is simply not allowed in good communication research.

In any rigorous study, the researcher should be more familiar than anyone else with the study's technical limitations and failures. Researchers have an obligation to make such shortcomings known to their readers—even if admitting qualifications and mistakes makes them feel foolish. For example, negative findings should be reported if they are at all related to the analysis. There is an unfortunate myth in scientific reporting that only positive discoveries are worth reporting (journal editors are sometimes guilty of believing this as well). In science, however, it's often as important to know that two variables are *not* related as to know that they are.

Similarly, researchers must avoid the temptation to save face by describing their findings as the product of a carefully preplanned analytical strategy when that is not the case. Many findings arrive unexpectedly—even though they may seem obvious in retrospect. An interesting relationship was uncovered by accident—so what? Embroidering such situations with descriptions of fictitious hypotheses is dishonest. It also does a disservice to less-experienced researchers by leading them into thinking that all scientific inquiry is rigorously preplanned and organized.

In general, science progresses through honesty and openness; ego defenses and deception retard it. Researchers can best serve their peers—and scientific discovery as a whole—by telling the truth about what they observed and all the pitfalls and problems they've experienced in a particular line of inquiry. Perhaps they'll save others from the same problems.

Avoiding Plagiarism

As we discussed in Chapter 2, in writing up a research report you must place your research in the context of what others have done and said. The improper use of their materials is a serious ethical offense. Mastering this matter is a part of your "coming of age" as a scholar.

Whenever you're reporting on the work of others, you must be clear about who said what. That is, you must avoid **plagiarism:** the theft of another's words and/or ideas—whether intentional or accidental—and the presentation of those words and ideas as your own. Because this is a common and sometimes unclear problem, let's take a minute to examine it in some detail. Here are the main ground rules regarding plagiarism:

- You cannot use another writer's exact words without using quotation marks and giving a complete citation, which indicates the source of the quotation such that your reader could locate that quotation in its original context. As a general rule, taking a passage of eight or more words without citation is a violation of federal copyright laws.
- It's also not acceptable to edit or paraphrase another's words and present the revised version as your own work.
- Finally, it's not even acceptable to present another's *ideas* as your own—even if you use totally different words to express those ideas.

The following examples should clarify what is or is not acceptable in the use of another's work.

The Original Work:

Laws of Growth

Systems are like babies: once you get one, you have it. They don't go away. On the contrary, they display the most remarkable persistence. They not only persist; they grow. And as they grow, they encroach. The growth potential of systems was explored in a tentative, preliminary way by Parkinson, who concluded that administrative systems maintain an average growth of 5 to 6 percent per annum regardless of the work to be done. Parkinson was right so far as he goes, and we must give him full honors for initiating the serious study of this important topic. But what Parkinson failed to perceive, we now enunciate—the general systems analogue of Parkinson's Law.

The System Itself Tends to Grow at 5 to 6 Percent per Annum

Again, this Law is but the preliminary to the most general possible formulation, the Big-Bang Theorem of Systems Cosmology.

Systems Tend to Expand to Fill the Known Universe (Gall, 1975, pp. 12–14)

Now let's look at some of the *acceptable* ways you might make use of Gall's work in your own paper:

- Acceptable: One scholar draws a humorous parallel between systems and infants: "Systems are like babies: once you get one, you have it. They don't go away. On the contrary, they display the most remarkable persistence. They not only persist; they grow" (Gall, 1975, p. 12).
- Acceptable: Gall (1975, p. 12) warns that systems are like babies. Create a system, and it sticks around. Worse yet, Gall notes, systems keep growing larger and larger.
- Acceptable: It has also been suggested that systems have a natural tendency to persist, even grow and encroach (Gall, 1975, p. 12).

Here now are some *unacceptable* uses of the same material, reflecting some common errors:

- Unacceptable: In this paper, I want to look at some of the characteristics of the social systems we create in our organizations. First, systems are like babies: once you get one, you have it. They don't go away. On the contrary, they display the most remarkable persistence. They not only persist; they grow. [It is unacceptable to quote directly someone else's materials without using quotation marks and giving a full citation.]
- Unacceptable: In this paper, I want to look at some of the characteristics of the social systems we create in our organizations. First, systems are a lot like children: once you get one, it's yours. They don't go away; they persist. They not only persist, in fact: they grow. [It is unacceptable to edit another's work and present it as your own.]
- Unacceptable: In this paper, I want to look at some of the characteristics of the social systems we create in our organizations. One thing I've noticed is that once you create a system, it never seems to go away. Just the opposite, in fact: they have a tendency to grow. You might say systems are a lot like children in that respect. [It is unacceptable to paraphrase someone else's ideas and present them as your own.]

Each of the preceding unacceptable examples is an example of plagiarism and represents a serious offense. Admittedly, there are some "gray areas." Some ideas are more or less in the public domain, not "belonging" to any one person. Or you may develop an idea on your own that someone else has already put in writing. If you have a question about a specific situation, discuss it with your instructor before you prepare your paper.

INSTITUTIONAL REVIEW BOARDS

As we mentioned earlier, the issue of research ethics in studies involving humans is now governed by federal law (the "Protection of Human Subjects" law may be found online at http://ohrp.osophs.dhhs.gov/humansubjects/guidance/45cfr46.htm). Any agency (such as a university or a hospital) wishing to receive federal research support must establish an "institutional review board" (IRB), a panel of faculty (and possibly others) who review all research proposals involving human participants so that they can guarantee that the participants' rights and interests will be protected. The law applies specifically to federally funded research, but many universities apply the same standards and procedures to all research, including that funded by nonfederal sources and even research done at no cost, such as student projects.

The chief responsibility of an IRB is to ensure that the risks faced by human participants in research are minimal. In some cases, the IRB may ask the researcher to revise the study design; in other cases, the IRB may refuse to approve a study. Where some minimal risks are deemed unavoidable, researchers are required to prepare an "informed consent" form that describes those risks clearly. Participants may be involved in the study only after they have read the statement and signed it as an indication that they know the risks and voluntarily accept them.

In order for an IRB to evaluate a proposed study for its ethics, a researcher must prepare an IRB proposal. Typically, this is an abbreviated research proposal organized around core questions. Figure 5-2 presents a list of questions that appear in a typical IRB proposal form. Figure 5-3 presents a sample "Informed Consent" form, submitted as part of the IRB proposal for one of the research projects one of us recently conducted on communication in stepfamilies (Baxter, Braithwaite, Bryant, & Wagner, 2001). Participants in this interview study read and signed the informed consent document before the interview could begin.

Much of the impetus for establishing IRBs had to do with biomedical experimentation on humans, and many social scientific research study designs are generally regarded as exempt from IRB review. An example is an anonymous survey sent to a large sample of respondents. The guidelines to be followed by IRBs, as contained in the Federal Exemption Categories (45 CFR 46.101 [b]), exempt a variety of research situations:

(1) Research conducted in established or commonly accepted educational settings, involving normal educational practices, such as (i) research on regular and special education instructional strategies, or (ii) research on the effectiveness of or the comparison among instructional techniques, curricula, or classroom management methods.

---

1. Who are the researchers affiliated with the project, and what are their qualifications to conduct research?
2. Who is sponsoring the research?
3. Does the project involve special populations (under 18 minors; pregnant women/fetuses; cognitively impaired persons; prisoners) whose human rights require extra protections?
4. How will participants be recruited? What is the exact language that will appear in any advertisements or announcements for volunteers?
5. How will informed consent be obtained? What is the exact language that will appear in the informed consent document?
6. What is the purpose of the study?
7. What are the procedures involved in the study? What exact measures will be used? What exact questions will be asked? Will deception be employed?
8. What methods will be used to protect participant confidentiality?
9. What emotional, psychological, legal, social, financial, and/or physical risks are possible for participants? What measures will be undertaken to minimize these risks?
10. What are the benefits of the study to participants and/or to society as a whole?

FIGURE 5-2 **Questions Included in a Typical IRB Review Form**

Project Title: Perceptions of Communication in Stepfamilies

Principal Investigators: Leslie A. Baxter, Professor, Communication Studies, University of Iowa
                           Amy Wagner, doctoral student, Communication Studies, University of Iowa

PURPOSE

This study involves research. The purpose of the research is to solicit perceptions of what communication is like in stepfamilies among young-adult stepchildren.

   We are inviting people to participate in this research because they have voluntarily expressed an interest in being interviewed and are eligible for participation. Eligibility includes being part of a stepfamily for no less than 4 years and living in the same home as that family for the majority of that time. Because we are interested in interviewing people who can recall what happened in their stepfamily, we are seeking participants whose stepfamilies did not begin before they are able to recall what happened; for most people, this probably means a stepfamily that began no more than 10 years ago. This project will last for 45–60 minutes.

PROCEDURES

Those agreeing to participate can expect the following to occur. After completing this Informed Consent Form, we will turn on the tape recorder to record the interview. You will first be asked to complete a "Family Tree" sheet that provides us with a demographic sketch of who is in your stepfamily and in your original biological or adoptive family; only first names will be listed. This sheet helps the interviewer keep various family members straight during the interview. Next, you will be asked to fill out a 30-item questionnaire that asks you questions about how your stepfamily functions. Next, we will ask you to describe the formation and development of your stepfamily. Last, we will ask you to tell us about the most positive aspects and the most challenging aspects of communication in your stepfamily, including various members of your stepfamily. There are no right or wrong answers here; we are simply interested in your perceptions.

RISKS

This section of the form describes possible risks that might accompany participation in the study. Because we are asking you to think aloud about the challenging aspects of communication in your stepfamily, this may cause you some discomfort. You are free not to answer any question that is asked of you, should you choose. In addition, you are free to withdraw from participating in the study at any time, should you choose. If you would like a referral to a professional counselor who could talk to you about your stepfamily experiences, please feel free to contact Dr. Leslie Baxter, principal investigator, and she can put you in contact with appropriate services. Her phone number is xxx-xxxx, e-mail address is xxxxxxxxxxxx.

BENEFITS

There may be no personal benefits for participating in this study, beyond the experience of sharing experiences with the interviewer. However, it is hoped that, in the future, society could benefit from this study because of the information we may gain about communication among stepfamily members.

COSTS AND COMPENSATION

There will not be any costs to the participant for being involved in this research project. Participants will be compensated for their time and inconvenience for participating in the study. If a participant signed up for participation in exchange for extra credit, the instructor of the appropriate course will be notified before the end of the current semester. If a participant signed up for participation after referral by someone else, their name will be entered into a lottery, the winner of which will receive a free coupon for a dinner-for-two at a local Iowa City restaurant.

CONFIDENTIALITY

Records of participation in this research project will be maintained and kept confidential to the extent permitted by law. However, federal government regulatory agencies and the University of Iowa Institutional Review Board may inspect and copy a subject's records pertaining to the research, and these records may contain personal identifiers.

FIGURE 5-3   **A Sample Informed Consent Form**

(2) Research involving the use of educational tests (cognitive, diagnostic, aptitude, achievement), survey procedures, interview procedures or observation of public behavior, unless: (i) information obtained is recorded in such a manner that human subjects can be identified, directly or through identifiers linked to the subjects; and (ii) any disclosure of the human subjects' responses outside the research could reasonably place the subjects at risk of criminal or civil liability or be damaging to the subjects' financial standing, employability, or reputation.

(3) Research involving the use of educational tests (cognitive, diagnostic, aptitude, achievement), survey procedures, interview procedures, or observation of public behavior that is not exempt

The interview will be audiotaped. By initialing in the space provided below, you are verifying that you have been told that audio materials will be generated during the course of this study. These recordings will be used for purposes of obtaining a complete record of the interview. The audiotapes of the interview will not contain any personal identifiers that could be linked to the participant or his/her stepfamily; only first names will be allowed throughout the interview and participants are free to use pseudonyms if they desire. The tapes will be transcribed by the principal investigator and her assistants, and then the tapes will be destroyed. No personal identifiers will be linked to the transcripts.

_____ Subject's initials

The demographics sheet and questionnaire will not contain personal identifiers and will be linked to the interview only through a common interview number. Participants receiving extra credit will record their ID# on a separate extra credit sheet that will be given to the appropriate course instructor; no link will be made between this record and the interview. Participants who are eligible for enrollment in the lottery will record their name, mailing address, and phone number on a separate lottery ticket, which the participant will place in the entry box so that a winner can be drawn at the conclusion of the study; this lottery ticket will not be linked in any way to the interview. In the event of any report or publication from this study, the identity of subjects will not be disclosed. Results will be reported in a summarized manner in such a way that subjects cannot be identified.

VOLUNTARY PARTICIPATION

All participation is voluntary. There is no penalty to anyone who decides not to participate. Nor will anyone be penalized if he or she decides to stop participation at any time during the research project. You can elect not to answer a given question that is asked of you simply by leaving it blank or by telling the interviewer you do not want to answer that question. You can elect to withdraw completely from the study at any point, should you choose, simply by notifying the interviewer. You will forfeit your extra credit or lottery enrollment should you withdraw completely from the study.

QUESTIONS

Questions are encouraged. If there are any questions about this research project, please contact Professor Leslie A. Baxter, Communication Studies Department, phone xxxxxxx, e-mail address xxxxxxxxx. Questions about the rights of research subjects or research related injury may be addressed to the Human Subjects Office, xxxxxxxxxxxxx.

Subject's name (printed) _____

Signature of subject _____

Date _____

INVESTIGATOR STATEMENT

I have discussed the above points with the subject or the legally authorized representative, using a translator when necessary. It is my opinion that the subject understands the risks, benefits, and obligations involved in participation in this project.

Signature of Investigator _____

Date _____

Note: This is the approved Informed Consent form used by Leslie Baxter and Amy Wagner to gather data subsequently analyzed and reported (Baxter, Braithwaite, Bryant, & Wagner, 2001). Because this research project involved a team of researchers from two different institutions, researchers associated with the second institution were required to submit a separate IRB form, including an Informed Consent form, to their IRB.

FIGURE 5-3   **A Sample Informed Consent Form (*continued*)**

under paragraph (b)(2) of this section, if: (i) the human subjects are elected or appointed public officials or candidates for public office; or (ii) Federal statute(s) require(s) without exception that the confidentiality of the personally identifiable information will be maintained throughout the research and thereafter.

(4) Research involving the collection or study of existing data, documents, records, pathological specimens, or diagnostic specimens, if these sources are publicly available or if the information is recorded by the investigator in such a manner that subjects cannot be identified, directly or through identifiers linked to the subjects.

(5) Research and demonstration projects which are conducted by or subject to the approval of Department or Agency heads, and which are designed to study, evaluate, or otherwise examine: (i) Public benefit or service programs; (ii) procedures for obtaining benefits or services under

those programs; (iii) possible changes in or alternatives to those programs or procedures; or (iv) possible changes in methods or levels of payment for benefits or services under those programs.

(6) Taste and food quality evaluation and consumer acceptance studies, (i) if wholesome foods without additives are consumed or (ii) if a food is consumed that contains a food ingredient at or below the level and for a use found to be safe, or agricultural chemical or environmental contaminant at or below the level found to be safe, by the Food and Drug Administration or approved by the Environmental Protection Agency or the Food Safety and Inspection Service of the U.S. Department of Agriculture.

Paragraph (2) of the excerpt exempts some of the communication research described in this book. However, it is typically not the researcher who independently determines whether his or her research project is exempt from IRB review. Often, a researcher is required by his or her university to submit a research proposal to the IRB, or some representative thereof, so that it can be judged exempt from full formal review by the board.

What guides the conduct of research sponsored outside the auspices of a research institute or university— say, a consulting firm not eligible for federal research monies that engages in contracted proprietary research? Most professional associations have professional codes of ethics to guide researchers who are not otherwise controlled by IRBs.

PROFESSIONAL CODES OF ETHICS

Ethical issues in communication research are both important and ambiguous. For this reason, most of the professional associations of communication researchers rely on formal codes of conduct describing what is considered acceptable and unacceptable professional behavior. As one example, Figure 5-4 presents the code of conduct of the American Association for Public Opinion Research (AAPOR), an interdisciplinary research association in the social sciences to which some communication researchers belong. Most professional associations have such codes of ethics, and they are quite similar to one another in their commitment to the core principles of ethical conduct we discussed earlier in the chapter. You can find many of these on the associations' web sites.

TWO ETHICAL CONTROVERSIES

As you may already have guessed, the adoption and publication of professional codes of conduct have not totally resolved the issue of research ethics. Researchers still disagree on some general principles, and those who agree in principle often debate specifics. This section briefly describes two research projects that have provoked ethical controversy and discussion throughout the social sciences. The first project studied homosexual behavior in public restrooms, and the second examined obedience in a laboratory setting.

Trouble in the Tearoom

As a graduate student, Laud Humphreys became interested in the study of homosexual behavior. He developed a special interest in the casual and fleeting same-sex acts engaged in by some male nonhomosexuals. In particular, his research interest focused on homosexual acts between strangers meeting in the public restrooms in parks, called "tearooms" among homosexuals. The result was the publication in 1970 of *Tearoom Trade*.

What particularly interested Humphreys about the tearoom activity was that the participants seemed otherwise to live conventional lives as "family men": accepted members of the community. They did nothing else that might qualify them as homosexuals. Thus, it was important to them that they remain anonymous in their tearoom visits. How would you study something like that?

Humphreys decided to take advantage of the social structure of the situation. Typically, the tearoom encounter involved three people: the two men actually engaging in the sexual act and a lookout, called the "watchqueen." Humphreys began showing up at public restrooms, offering to serve as watchqueen whenever it seemed appropriate. Since the watchqueen's payoff was the chance to watch the action, Humphreys was able to conduct field observations as he would in a study of political rallies or jaywalking behavior at intersections.

To round out his understanding of the tearoom trade, Humphreys needed to know something more about the people who participated. Since the men probably would not have been thrilled about being interviewed, Humphreys developed a different solution. Whenever possible, he noted the license numbers of participants' cars and tracked down their names and addresses through the police. Humphreys then visited the men at their homes, disguising himself enough to avoid recognition, and announced that he was conducting a survey. In that fashion,

CODE OF PROFESSIONAL ETHICS AND PRACTICES

We, the members of the American Association for Public Opinion Research, subscribe to the principles expressed in the following code.

Our goal is to support sound practice in the profession of public opinion research. (By public opinion research we mean studies in which the principal source of information about individual beliefs, preferences, and behavior is a report given by the individual himself or herself.)

We pledge ourselves to maintain high standards of scientific competence and integrity in our work, and in our relations both with our clients and with the general public. We further pledge ourselves to reject all tasks or assignments which would be inconsistent with the principles of this code.

THE CODE

I. *Principles of Professional Practice in the Conduct of Our Work*

  A. We shall exercise due care in gathering and processing data, taking all reasonable steps to assume the accuracy of results.

  B. We shall exercise due care in the development of research designs and in the analysis of data.

    1. We shall employ only research tools and methods of analysis which, in our professional judgment, are well suited to the research problem at hand.

    2. We shall not select research tools and methods of analysis because of their special capacity to yield a desired conclusion.

    3. We shall not knowingly make interpretations of research results, nor shall we tacitly permit interpretations, which are inconsistent with the data available.

    4. We shall not knowingly imply that interpretations should be accorded greater confidence than the data actually warrant.

  C. We shall describe our findings and methods accurately and in appropriate detail in all research reports.

II. *Principles of Professional Responsibility in Our Dealings with People*

  A. The Public:

    1. We shall cooperate with legally authorized representatives of the public by describing the methods used in our studies.

    2. We shall maintain the right to approve the release of our findings whether or not ascribed to us. When misinterpretation appears, we shall publicly disclose what is required to correct it, notwithstanding our obligation for client confidentiality in all other respects.

  B. Clients or Sponsors:

    1. We shall hold confidential all information obtained about the client's general business affairs and about the findings of research conducted for the client, except when the dissemination of such information is expressly authorized.

    2. We shall be mindful of the limitations of our techniques and facilities and shall accept only those research assignments which can be accomplished within these limitations.

  C. The Profession:

    1. We shall not cite our membership in the Association as evidence of professional competence, since the Association does not so certify any persons or organizations.

    2. We recognize our responsibility to contribute to the science of public opinion research and to disseminate as freely as possible the ideas and findings which emerge from our research.

  D. The Respondent:

    1. We shall not lie to survey respondents or use practices and methods which abuse, coerce, or humiliate them.

    2. We shall protect the anonymity of every respondent, unless the respondent waives such anonymity for specified uses. In addition, we shall hold as privileged and confidential all information which tends to identify the respondent.

FIGURE 5-4   **Code of Conduct of the American Association for Public Opinion Research**

Source: American Association for Public Opinion Research, *By-Laws* (May 1977). Used by permission.

he collected the personal information he couldn't get in the restrooms.

As you can imagine, Humphreys's research provoked considerable controversy both inside and outside the social scientific community. Some critics charged Humphreys with a gross invasion of privacy in the name of science. What men did in public restrooms was their own business. Others were mostly concerned about the deceit involved—Humphreys had lied to the participants by leading them to believe he was only a voyeur. Even people who felt that the tearoom participants were fair game for observation because they used a public facility protested the follow-up survey. They felt it was unethical for Humphreys to trace the participants to their homes and to interview them under false pretenses.

Still others justified Humphreys's research. The topic, they said, was worth study. It couldn't be studied any other way, and they regarded the deceit as essentially harmless, noting that Humphreys was careful not to harm his participants by disclosing their tearoom activities.

The tearoom trade controversy has never been resolved. It's still debated, and it probably always will be, since it stirs emotions and involves ethical issues that people disagree about. What do you think? Was Humphreys ethical in doing what he did? Are there parts of the research that you believe were acceptable and other parts that were not?

Observing Human Obedience

The second illustration differs from the first in many ways. Whereas Humphreys's study involved participant observation (a method we describe in detail in Chapter 13), the setting of this study was in the laboratory. And whereas Humphreys examined behavior considered by some to be a form of deviance, the researcher in this study examined obedience and conformity.

One of the more unsettling clichés to come out of World War II was the German soldier's common excuse for atrocities: "I was only following orders." From the point of view that gave rise to this comment, any behavior—no matter how reprehensible—could be justified if someone else could be assigned responsibility for it. If a superior officer ordered a soldier to kill a baby, the fact of the order supposedly exempted the soldier from personal responsibility for the action. Although the military tribunals that tried the war crime cases did not accept this excuse, researchers and others have recognized the extent to which this point of view pervades social life. People often seem willing to do things they know would be considered wrong by others if they can claim that some higher authority ordered them to do it. Such was the pattern of justification in the My Lai tragedy of Vietnam, when U.S. soldiers killed more than 300 unarmed civilians—some of them young children—simply because their village, My Lai, was believed to be a Viet Cong stronghold. This sort of justification appears less dramatically in day-to-day civilian life. Few would disagree that this reliance on authority exists, yet Stanley Milgram's study (1963, 1965) of the topic provoked considerable controversy.

To observe people's willingness to harm others when following orders, Milgram brought 40 adult men from many different walks of life into a laboratory setting designed to create the phenomenon under study. If you had been a participant in the experiment, you would have had something like the following experience.

You've been informed that you and another person are about to participate in a learning experiment. Through a draw of lots, you're assigned the job of "teacher" and your fellow participant the job of "pupil." The "pupil" is led into another room and strapped into a chair; an electrode is attached to his wrist. As the teacher, you're seated in front of an impressive electrical control panel covered with dials, gauges, and switches. You notice that each switch has a label giving a different number of volts, ranging from 15 to 315. The switches have other labels, too, some with the ominous phrases "Extreme-Intensity Shock," "Danger—Severe Shock," and "XXX."

The experiment runs like this: You read a list of word pairs to the learner and then test his ability to match them up. Because you can't see him, a light on your control panel indicates his answer. Whenever the learner makes a mistake, you're instructed by the experimenter to throw one of the switches—beginning with the mildest—and administer a shock to your pupil. Through an open door between the two rooms, you hear your pupil's response to the shock. Then you read another list of word pairs and test him again.

As the experiment progresses, you administer ever more intense shocks, until your pupil screams for mercy and begs for the experiment to end. You're instructed to administer the next shock anyway. After a while, your pupil begins kicking the wall between the two rooms and continues to scream. The implacable experimenter tells you to give the next shock. Finally, you read a list and ask for the pupil's answer—but there is no reply whatever, only silence from the other room. The experimenter informs you that no answer is considered an error and instructs you to administer the next higher shock. This continues up to the "XXX" shock at the end of the series.

What do you suppose you really would have done when the pupil first began screaming? When he began kicking on the wall? Or when he became totally silent and gave no indication of life? You'd refuse to continue giving shocks, right? And surely the same would be true of most people.

So we might think—but Milgram found out otherwise. Of the first 40 adult men Milgram tested, nobody refused to continue administering the shocks until they heard the pupil begin kicking the wall between the two rooms. Of the 40, 5 did so then. Two-thirds of the subjects, 26 of the

40, continued doing as they were told through the entire series—up to and including the administration of the highest shock.

As you've probably guessed, the shocks were phony, and the "pupil" was a confederate of the experimenter. Only the "teacher" was a real participant in the experiment. As a participant, you wouldn't actually have been hurting another person, but you would have been led to think you were. The experiment was designed to test your willingness to follow orders to the point of presumably killing someone.

Milgram's experiments have been criticized both methodologically and ethically. On the ethical side, critics have particularly cited the effects of the experiment on the participants. Many seem to have experienced personally about as much pain as they thought they were administering to someone else. They pleaded with the experimenter to let them stop giving the shocks. They became extremely upset and nervous. Some had uncontrollable seizures.

How do you feel about this research? Do you think the topic was important enough to justify such measures? Would debriefing the participants be sufficient to ameliorate any possible harm? Can you think of other ways the researcher might have examined obedience?

This chapter concludes our introduction to communication research. We have considered how social scientific research about communication is, and is not, like everyday inquiry. We have introduced the two pillars of good science: logic and observation. We have introduced you to the process of planning a research study and the importance of a literature review in that undertaking. We have discussed how researchers from different paradigms of knowing approach the research enterprise differently. Despite their differences, we have realized that all researchers embrace both deductive and inductive reasoning. Last, we have emphasized the ethical backdrop against which all communication should be evaluated. We now turn to a detailed treatment of the primary kinds of communication research—quantitative and qualitative. As we have emphasized in this part of the book, we see quantitative and qualitative research as two sides of the same coin and strongly encourage researchers to engage in multi-method research, in which both kinds of research are employed. However, to simplify our presentation, we are going to divide our discussion into two parts: Part 2, devoted to quantitative communication research, and Part 3, devoted to qualitative communication research.

Main Points

- What is ethical and unethical in research is ultimately a matter of what a community of people agree is right and wrong.

- Researchers agree that participation in research should normally be voluntary. However, this norm can conflict with the scientific need for generalizability.

- Researchers agree that research should not harm those who participate in it unless they willingly and knowingly accept the risks of harm by giving their informed consent.

- Whereas anonymity refers to the situation in which even the researcher cannot link specific information to the individuals it describes, confidentiality refers to the situation in which the researcher promises to keep information about participants private. The most straightforward way to ensure confidentiality is to destroy identifying information as soon as it's no longer needed.

- Many research designs involve a greater or lesser degree of deception of participants. Because deceiving people violates common standards of ethical behavior, deception in research requires a strong justification—and even then the justification may be challenged.

- Researchers have ethical obligations in analyzing and reporting their data, in addition to the obligations that guide the conduct of research. Depending on a researcher's paradigm of knowing, he or she may have an ethical obligation to use research to bring about social change. All communication researchers should strive to protect the identity of their participants in their reporting of findings. Communication researchers are ethically bound to display both honesty and integrity in their analysis and reporting of data. Finally, they are ethically obligated to write in a manner that credits others appropriately for their ideas and words.

- Institutional review boards (IRBs) evaluate proposed research when researchers are affiliated with research institutes or universities.

❑ Professional associations in several disciplines publish codes of ethics to guide researchers. These codes are necessary and helpful, but they do not resolve all ethical questions.

❑ Laud Humphreys's study of "tearoom" encounters and Stanley Milgram's study of obedience raise ethical issues that are debated to this day.

Key Terms

IRB (institutional review board)	confidentiality
voluntary participation	debriefing
informed consent	plagiarism
anonymity	

Review Questions and Exercises

1. Review the discussion of the Milgram experiment on obedience. How would you design a study to accomplish the same purpose while avoiding the ethical criticisms leveled at Milgram? Would your design be equally valid? Would it have the same effect?

2. Another very famous study from the standpoint of research ethics is the Stanford Prison Experiment. Visit this web site to read about the study as it unfolded: www.prisonexp.org. When, if at all, would you have closed the study on ethical grounds? On what ethical grounds is your decision based?

3. Evaluate the following examples with respect to their research ethics:

   a. A communication instructor asks students in an introductory communication class to complete questionnaires needed in order for the instructor to complete her dissertation and graduate on time.

   b. After a field study of the interaction between pro-choice and pro-life protestors at an abortion clinic, law enforcement officials demand that the researcher identify those people who were observed to engage in violence. Rather than risk arrest as an accomplice after the fact, the researcher complies.

   c. After completing the final draft of a book reporting a research project, the researcher/author discovers that 25 of the 2,000 survey interviews were falsified by interviewers but chooses to ignore that fact and publishes the book anyway.

   d. Researchers obtain a list of "problem employees" provided by corporate management. They contact the employees with the explanation that each has been selected "at random" from among the corporation's employees to take a sampling of "employee opinion."

   e. A college instructor who wants to test the effect of unfair berating administers an hour exam to both sections of a specific course. The overall performance of the two sections is essentially the same. The grades of one section are artificially lowered, however, and the instructor berates them for performing so badly. The instructor then administers the same final exam to both sections and discovers that the performance of the unfairly berated section is worse. The hypothesis is confirmed, and the research report is published.

   f. In a study of sexual behavior, the investigator wants to overcome participants' reluctance to report what they might regard as shameful behavior. To get past their reluctance, participants are asked "Everyone masturbates now and then; about how much do you masturbate?"

   g. A researcher studying roommate communication in campus dorms discovers that 60 percent of the residents regularly violate restrictions on alcohol consumption. Publication of this finding would probably create a furor in the campus community. Because no extensive analysis of alcohol use is planned, the researcher decides to ignore the finding and keep it quiet.

   h. To test the extent to which people may try to save face by expressing attitudes on matters they are wholly uninformed about, the researcher asks for their attitudes regarding a fictitious issue.

   i. A researcher's questionnaire is circulated among students as part of their registration packet. Although students are not told they must complete the questionnaire, the hope is that they will believe they must—thus ensuring a higher completion rate.

   j. A field researcher pretends to join a radical political group in order to understand its communication strategies and is successfully accepted as a member of the inner planning circle. State what you think the researcher should do if the group makes plans for the following: (1) a peaceful, though illegal, demonstration; (2) the bombing of a public building during a time it is sure to be unoccupied; (3) the assassination of a public official.

Continuity Project

In 1994, Carole Blair and her colleagues published an essay titled "Disciplining the Feminine," in which they argued that some of the research practices in the communication discipline reproduced a masculinist ideology. They argued that such practices functioned to exclude other voices, particularly feminist ones. Read their essay and react to it in light of the ethical issues discussed in this chapter, especially the "Objectivity and Ideology" section.

Additional Readings

Bower, R. T., & de Gasparis, P. (1978). *Ethics in social research: Protecting the interests of human subjects.* New York: Praeger. This study provides an excellent overview of the ethical issues involved in social scientific research and discusses the ways those issues are dealt with. It contains an extensive bibliography.

Lee, R. (1993). *Doing research on sensitive topics.* Newbury Park, CA: Sage. This book examines the conflicts between scientific research needs and the rights of the people involved—with guidelines for dealing with such conflicts.

Picou, J. S., Gill, D. A., & Cohen, M. J. (Eds.) (1999). *The* Exxon Valdez *disaster: Readings on a modern social problem.* Dubuque, IA: Kendall-Hunt. An interesting book on all facets of the disaster, including the ethical obligations of researchers who studied the matter.

Scarce, R. (1994). (No) trial, (but) tribulations: When courts and ethnography conflict. *Journal of Contemporary Ethnography, 23,* 123–149. A more detailed discussion of Scarce's experiences with the court when he refused to turn over his field notes when they were subpoenaed.

InfoTrac College Edition
http://www.infotrac-college.com/ wadsworth/access.html

Access the latest news and journal articles with InfoTrac College Edition, an easy-to-use online database of reliable, full-length articles from hundreds of top academic journals. Conduct an electronic search using the following search terms:

- anonymity
- code of ethics
- confidentiality
- informed consent
- IRB (institutional review board)
- plagiarism

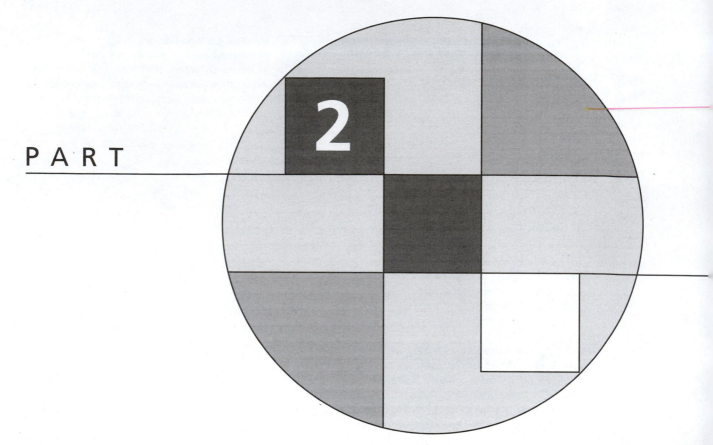

PART 2

Quantitative Communication Research

The introductory issues addressed in Part 1 of the book are integral to the research process, whether quantitative or qualitative. Although quantitative research and qualitative research share many things in common, we are separating them for purposes of in-depth discussion. In this part of the book, we'll consider communication research that is quantitative in nature. These methods are typically used by researchers who adopt positivist or systems perspectives on communication. In Part 3 of the book, we'll turn to qualitative methods, often used by interpretive and critical communication researchers. This division is somewhat arbitrary on our part—as we have indicated before, we think the strongest communication research is multi-method, in which both quantitative and qualitative methods are used to study a given communication phenomenon.

All researchers agree that research must meet the standard of trustworthiness. Put simply, all researchers want to persuade their audiences that the findings of their research are believable and should be taken seriously. When researchers plan a research study, they make careful methodological decisions with this criterion in mind. As consumers of others' research, we ask ourselves if we can believe a study's findings. But what makes one study trustworthy and another less so? The criteria by which trustworthiness is judged differ somewhat for quantitative research and qualitative research. At this point, we want to introduce you to the criteria by which most quantitative research is judged trustworthy (or not). We urge you to keep these criteria in mind as you read the chapters in this part of the book.

Four criteria are important in evaluating the trustworthiness of quantitatively oriented communication research: internal validity, measurement reliability, measurement validity, and external validity.

INTERNAL VALIDITY

Internal validity addresses the "truth value" of a study's findings. How can you establish confidence in the "truth" of the findings? This criterion is used in evaluating the research design employed by the researcher. With a goal of description, the issue of internal validity revolves around the researcher's conceptualization and operationalization of the study's variables. With a goal of explanation, internal validity refers to the extent to which variations in the dependent (outcome) variable can be attributed to the independent variable within the confines of a given study. Thus, an explanatory study has high internal validity if its methods allow the researcher to make a confident claim about what caused a certain outcome in the study. With a goal of functional explanation, internal validity refers to the extent to which the researcher can be confident in identifying how system parts function as a whole in sustaining dynamic equilibrium for the system.

What can get in the way of a study's internal validity? Social science researchers have identified three broad categories of threats to internal validity. First, a study's claims can be threatened by researcher-related factors. For example, in an interview, a participant may answer questions based on the appearance of the person conducting the interview. Second, a study's claims can be threatened by participant-related factors. Participants may be highly motivated to provide what they think is a socially desirable answer, for instance. Or participants might grow tired or bored with the study and cease giving it their full attention. Third, a researcher's claims can be threatened by the research procedures used in the study. For example, a survey researcher could pose a question in a confusing or biased manner, thereby reaping an invalid response from the participants. Or a researcher interested in causal explanation could fail to control for alternative explanations for why two variables, X and Y, are correlated to each other in addition to the possibility that X is a cause of Y. In discussing the three primary methods used in quantitative communication research—surveys, experiments, and quantitative text analysis—we're going to elaborate on the ways researchers try to minimize these threats to internal validity.

Chapter 8 examines in depth one of the most frequently used methods in communication research—the survey. Whether a paper-and-pencil questionnaire or a structured interview, survey research is designed to elicit people's attitudes, beliefs, and perceptions, self-reports of their behaviors, and self-reports of their behavioral intentions. Survey research is a primary form of measurement in quantitative communication research, and our concern is how to maximize the trustworthiness of claims made using this method.

Chapter 9 examines a primary method employed to examine questions of cause and effect: the experiment. Experiments are usually thought of in connection with the physical sciences, but in this chapter, we'll see how communication researchers use experiments. This is the most rigorously controllable of the methods we'll examine. We'll emphasize trustworthiness again in this chapter.

Chapter 10 is devoted to two methods commonly known as quantitative text analysis—content analysis and interaction analysis. These two methods quantify content, themes, or functions of messages of a variety of types—from face-to-face talk to TV programs to music lyrics. We'll examine how these methods can lead to trustworthy conclusions.

A particular subset of procedural threats deals with the conceptualizations and operationalizations, or measures, of a study's variables. Two special criteria are used in judging the trustworthiness of a study's measures—measurement reliability and measurement validity.

MEASUREMENT RELIABILITY

Measurement reliability speaks to consistency: How can you establish that your observations would be repeated if your methods were replicated, or repeated, with the same participants in the same context? To quantitatively oriented researchers, it seems reasonable that each time you apply a given instrument or measure to the same thing, the observation should result in the same findings. If you stand on a scale to be weighed, you should get the same reading each time (assuming that you haven't gained or lost any weight in between the readings!). The same applies to the measurement of variables—you want your measure to be consistent.

MEASUREMENT VALIDITY

Measurement validity addresses whether or not you measure what you say you are measuring. Let's suppose you claim to have a measure of "TV appreciation," the extent to which someone appreciates and values TV viewing. The way you measure this is to simply count up the number of hours the person spends in front of a TV in a typical day. You argue that if someone is appreciative of TV, he or she will spend a lot of time viewing it. But have you really measured TV appreciation or something else instead—say, boredom or loneliness? When people are bored, they might watch a lot of TV, not because they appreciate or value it but because there's nothing better to do. And lonely people might watch a lot of TV because they don't have many friends to join them in alternative leisure pursuits. In short, hours spent in watching TV may measure a person's opportunity for alternative pursuits, not appreciation of TV. Measurement validity speaks to whether researchers measure the variables they claim to be studying.

Beginning researchers often confuse measurement reliability and validity. It's easy to confuse the two, because they are integrally related to each other. Measurement reliability is a necessary precondition of validity: To be valid, a measure must be reliable. But reliability alone is insufficient evidence to give us confidence of validity. Any two people could probably use a stopwatch to assess the time someone spends watching TV—our two observers would be reliable with each other. But, as we just discussed, the fact that they reliably measured TV watching doesn't mean that they were measuring what was claimed—TV appreciation.

We'll have much more to say about measurement reliability and validity in Chapter 6, which deals with the specification of what it is you want to study—a process called *conceptualization*. We're going to look at some of the terms we use quite casually in everyday life and see how essential it is to clarify what we really mean by such terms when we do quantitative research. Once we can conceptualize a phenomenon we wish to study, we can then develop a set of procedures to identify the variable and measure its attributes—a process called *operationalization*. Conceptualization and operationalization address measurement reliability and measurement validity in some detail.

EXTERNAL VALIDITY

External validity speaks to a study's generalizability. How can you establish confidence that the findings of a particular study have applicability in other contexts or with people other than those who participated in the study? Positivist and systems researchers are usually interested in advancing generalizable explanations—either causal or functional—that extend beyond the boundaries of the particular study. Positivist researchers are interested in making statements about causal laws that apply whenever and wherever the independent variable and the dependent variable are present. Systems researchers are interested in making statements of functional explanation that apply to all systems that are like those examined in a particular study.

Beginning researchers often confuse internal validity and external validity. The key to keeping them straight lies in the words *internal* and *external.* External validity directs our attention externally, beyond the boundaries of a given study, to ask if the study's findings are applicable outside the study to other contexts and to other people. By contrast, internal validity looks inside a given study to see if its methods and procedures allow confident claims about description and explanation.

Chapter 7, on sampling, addresses the fundamental scientific issue of generalizability, or external validity. As you'll see, we can select a few people or things for observation and then apply what we observe to a much larger group. For example, by surveying 2,000 U.S. citizens about whom they favor for president of the United States, we can accurately predict how tens of millions will vote. In this chapter, we'll examine techniques that increase the generalizability of what we observe.

When quantitatively oriented communication researchers analyze their data, they are usually interested in making claims beyond the immediate sample included in the study. The process of making statistical claims about populations from samples is an issue we examine in our introduction to statistics in Chapters 11 and 12. Chapter 11 discusses some basic issues in how to work with quantitative data and how quantitatively to describe a sample with respect to some variable. Chapter 12 introduces you to the logic of inferential statistics and introduces you to basic statistics often found in communication research.

Before we turn to the chapters in this part of the book, two points should be made. First, you'll probably discover that you've been using these scientific methods casually in your daily life for as long as you can remember. You employ a crude form of content analysis every time you judge an author's motivation or orientation from her or his words. You engage in at least casual experiments frequently. The chapters in Part 2 will show you how to improve your use of these methods to avoid the pitfalls of casual, uncontrolled observation.

Second, none of the data-collection methods described in the following chapters are appropriate to all research topics and situations. We've tried to give you some ideas of when a given method might be appropriate. Still, we could never anticipate all the possible research topics that may one day interest you. As a general guideline, you should always use a variety of techniques in the study of any topic. Because each method has its weaknesses, the use of several methods can help fill in any gaps. If the different, independent approaches to the topic all yield the same conclusion, you've achieved a form of replication.

CHAPTER 6

Conceptualization and Operationalization

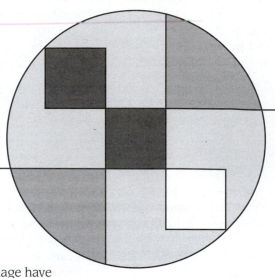

What You'll Learn in This Chapter

You'll discover that most of the words used in everyday language have vague, unspecified meanings. In science, however, it's essential to specify exactly what we mean (and don't mean) by the terms we use. This is known as conceptualization. We'll go from conceptualization to the next step in measurement—seeing how communication researchers find concepts reflected in the real world. This step is known as operationalization.

INTRODUCTION

This chapter deals with the process of moving from vague ideas about what you want to study to recognizing it and measuring it in the real world. In this chapter, we deal with the general issues of *conceptualization* and *operationalization*. *Conceptualization* is the refinement and specification of abstract concepts, and *operationalization* is the development of specific research procedures (operations) that will result in empirical observations representing those concepts in the real world.

We want to begin this chapter with a frontal attack on the hidden concern that people sometimes have about whether it's possible to measure the stuff of life: love, hate, prejudice, alienation, verbal abuse, satisfaction, and things like that. The answer is yes, but it will take a few pages for us to make that point. Once you see that we can measure anything that exists, we'll turn to the steps involved in doing so.

MEASURING ANYTHING THAT EXISTS

It seems altogether possible to us that you may have some reservations about the ability of science to measure the really important aspects of human social existence. You may have read research reports dealing with something like TV violence, and you may have been dissatisfied with the way the researchers measured whatever they were studying. You may have felt they were too superficial, that they missed the aspects that really matter most. Maybe they measured *TV violence* as the number of times a character used, or threatened to use, physical force directed at another character, or maybe they measured it as the number of weapons of destruction shown on the screen per hour. Your dissatisfaction would surely have been increased if you found your favorite TV programs being misclassified by the measurement system. People often have that experience.

Or you may have looked up the definition of a word such as *compassionate* in the dictionary and found the definition wanting. You may have heard yourself muttering, "There's more to it than that." In fact, whenever you look up the definition of something you already understand well, you can probably see ways that people might misunderstand the term if they had only that definition to go on.

Earlier in this book, we said that one of the two pillars of science is *observation*. Because this word can suggest a rather casual, passive activity, quantitative researchers often use *measurement* instead, meaning careful, deliberate observations for the purpose of describing objects and events in terms of the attributes composing a variable. If the variable under study were *comfort with e-mail,* we might give people a survey and ask them to report on a series of 1–10 scales how comfortable they felt communicating each of several kinds of information through e-mail—comfort in expressing affection toward another, comfort in breaking bad news, comfort in criticizing someone, and so forth. In this fashion, we would have measured their level of comfort. Or in an in-depth interview about their uses of a computer, we might simply ask people whether they would classify themselves in general as comfortable or uncomfortable in using e-mail. There is usually more than one way to measure a variable. If it exists, we can measure it.

How Do You Know?

To demonstrate to you that communication researchers can measure anything that exists, we'd like you to imagine that we're discussing the matter. We'll write the script, but feel free to make substitutions for your side of the dialogue as you see fit.

US: Communication researchers can measure anything that exists.

YOU: Hah! Betcha can't.

US: Tell me something that exists, and we'll tell you how to measure it.

YOU: OK, let's see you measure love.

US: Good choice. Now, we're not willing to waste our time trying to measure something that doesn't exist. So tell us if it exists.

YOU: Yes, of course it exists. Everybody knows that love exists. Everybody knows that. If you're so smart, I would have thought you'd know that. Even stupid people know that.

US: Everybody used to "know" the world was flat, too. We want to know *how* you know love really exists.

YOU: OK, OK. Since you seem to get off on "observation," how about: "I've *seen* love."

US: What have you seen that proves love exists?

YOU: Well, my brother just told me that he's met his soulmate and that he can't imagine living the rest of his life without her. How's that?

US: Great! That sounds like love to us, so I guess we can assume love exists. We are now prepared to measure love. Ready?

YOU: Ready.

US: We will quietly observe our acquaintances, families, and friends, talking to them about life. Whenever they tell us that they have a soulmate and can't imagine living the rest of life without this person, we'll count that as a case of love. Whenever we're not told that, we'll count the conversation as a case of nonlove. When we finish, we'll be able to classify all the people we've talked to as either in love or not in love.

YOU: Wait a minute! That's not a very good measure of love. We're going to miss a lot of love that way. All we'll measure is some people who are vocal in expressing a certain way that love feels to them. That's precisely why I doubt that you can really measure love.

US: We see what you mean. But your comment also means that the situation you described before proves only that an expression of having met a soulmate exists. We'd better reconsider whether love exists. Does it?

YOU: Of course it does. I was just giving you one example of love. There are hundreds of other examples.

US: Give us one that proves love exists.

YOU: OK, try this for size. I was at a football game last Saturday, and some guy had hired a pilot to write "I love you Susan marry me" in the sky at halftime. Is that enough love for you?

US: Suits us. That would seem to prove that love exists, so we're ready again to measure love. We will split up and start touring the country and attending Saturday football games. We'll keep our eyes open for halftime skywriting that says "I love you . . . marry me."

YOU: Hold it! I see where this is headed, and that's not going to do it either. A person who did that would be in love, but we're going to classify a lot of people who are in love as if they weren't just because they don't happen to get carried away and use skywriting at football games.

US: All of which brings us back to our original question. Does love really exist, or have you been just stringing us along?

YOU: Yes, it exists!

US: Well, we're not sure any longer. You persuaded us that people exist who report having a soulmate with whom they want to spend the rest of their lives, because you saw that, and we believe you. You persuaded us that there are people who hire skywriters at halftime to express "I love you . . . marry me" in the sky. But we're not so sure *love* exists. We'd sure like to track it down so we can show you that we can measure it. To be honest, though, we're beginning to doubt that it really exists. Have you ever seen a love? What color is it? How much does it weigh? Where is it located?

YOU: What are you talking about? Hello. Earth to Baxter and Babbie: phone home.

The point of this dialogue, as you may have guessed, is to demonstrate that *love doesn't exist.* We don't know what a love looks like, how big it is, or what color. None of us has ever touched a love or ridden in one. But we do talk a lot about love. Here's how that came about.

As we wandered down the road of life, we observed a lot of things and knew they were real through our observations. We heard about a lot of other things that other people said they observed, and those things seemed to have existed. Someone reported seeing a young couple in love and described it in great detail—the nonstop hand holding, the eyes fixed on each other, the close proximity, the smiling.

With additional experience, we noticed something more. Pairs who enjoy close physical proximity also think about each other in the partner's absence. They experience a physiological "high" when they are with their partner and experience a feeling deep in the pit of their stomachs when they are separated from their partner for an extended period of time. They are concerned about each other's welfare to the point of making sacrifices themselves in order to bring happiness to the partner. Eventually, we began to get the feeling that there was a certain kind of emotional bond that people could experience. When we discussed the couples we'd observed, it was appropriate to identify them in terms of those tendencies. We used to say a couple was "one of those pairs who enjoys close physical proximity, misses each other when separated, and shows concern for the partner's welfare." After a while, however, it got pretty clumsy to say all of that, and you had a bright idea: "Let's use the word *love* as a shorthand notation for people like that. We can use the term even if they don't do all those things—as long as they're pretty much like that."

Being basically agreeable and interested in efficiency, we agreed to go along with the system. That's where love came from. It never really existed. We never saw it. We just made it up as a shortcut for talking behind people's backs. Ultimately, *love* is merely a term we have agreed to use in communication: a name we use to represent a whole collection of apparently related phenomena that we've each observed in the course of life. Each of us developed his or her own mental image of what the real phenomena we've observed represent in general and what they have in common.

When we say the word *love,* we know it evokes a mental image in your mind, just as it evokes one in our minds. It's as though file drawers in our minds contain thousands of sheets of paper, with each sheet of paper labeled in the upper-right-hand corner. A sheet of paper in each of your file drawers has the term *love* on it. On your sheet are all the things you were told about love and everything you've observed that seemed to be an example of it. Our sheets have what we were told about it plus all the things we've observed that seemed to be examples of it.

Conceptions and Concepts

The technical term for those mental images, those sheets of paper in our mental file drawers, is *conception.* That is, each sheet of paper is a conception. Now, we can't communicate these mental images directly. There's no way we can directly reveal to you what's written on our mental sheets. So we use the terms written in the upper-right-hand corner as a way of communicating about our conceptions and the things we observe that are related to those conceptions. The terms associated with the conceptions in our separate minds make it possible for us to communicate and eventually agree on specifically what we will mean by those terms. The process of coming to an agreement is **conceptualization,** and the result is called a **concept.**

Let's suppose we're going to meet someone named Pat, whom you already know. We ask you what Pat is like. Now suppose you've seen Pat help lost children find their parents and put a tiny bird back in its nest. Pat got you to take turkeys to poor families on Thanksgiving and to visit a children's hospital on Christmas. You've seen Pat weep in a movie about a mother overcoming adversities to save and protect her child. As you search through your mental file drawer, you may find all or most of those phenomena recorded on a single sheet labeled *compassionate.* You look over the other entries on the page, and you find they seem to provide an accurate description of Pat. So you say, "Pat is compassionate."

Now we leaf through our own mental file drawers until we find sheets marked *compassionate.* We then look over the things written on our sheets and say, "Oh, that's nice." We now feel we know what Pat is like, but our expectations in that regard reflect the entries on our file sheets, not yours. Later, when we meet Pat, we happen to find that our own experiences correspond to the entries we have on our *compassionate* file sheets, and we say that

you sure were right. But suppose that our observations of Pat contradict the things we have on our file sheets. We tell you that we don't think Pat is very compassionate, and we begin to compare notes with you.

You say, "I once saw Pat weep in a movie about a mother overcoming adversity to save and protect her child." We look at our *compassionate* sheets, and neither one of us can find anything like that. Looking elsewhere in our files, each one of us locates that sort of phenomenon on a sheet labeled *sentimental,* and we retort, "That's not compassion. That's just sentimentality."

To further strengthen our case, we tell you that we saw Pat refuse to give money to an organization dedicated to saving the whales from extinction. "That represents a lack of compassion," we argue. You search through your files and find saving the whales on two sheets—*environmental activism* and *cross-species dating*—and you say so. Eventually, we all set about comparing the entries we have on our respective sheets labeled *compassionate.* We may discover that we have quite different mental images represented by that term.

In the big picture, language and communication work only to the extent that we all have considerable overlap in the kinds of entries that are on our corresponding mental file sheets. The similarities we have on those sheets represent the agreements existing in our society. As we grow up, we're told approximately the same thing when we're first introduced to a particular term. Dictionaries formalize the agreements our society has about such terms. Each of us, then, shapes his or her mental images to correspond with such agreements, but because all of us have different experiences and observations, no two people end up with exactly the same set of entries on any sheet in their file systems. Returning to the assertion made at the outset of this chapter, we can measure anything that's observable. For example, we can measure whether Pat actually puts the little bird back in its nest, visits the hospital on Christmas, weeps at the movie, or refuses to contribute to saving the whales. All of those things exist, so we can measure them. But is Pat really compassionate? We can't answer that question; we can't measure compassion in that sense, because compassion doesn't exist the way those things we just described exist.

Compassion as a *term* does exist. We can measure the number of letters it contains and agree that there are ten. We can agree that it has three syllables and that it begins with the letter *C.* In short, we can measure those aspects of it that are observable.

Some aspects of our conceptions exist also. Whether or not you have a mental image associated with the term *compassion* is real. When an elementary school teacher asks a class how many know what *compassion* means, those who raise their hands can be counted. The presence of particular entries on the sheets bearing a given label is also real, and that can be measured. We could measure how many people do or do not associate giving money to save the whales with their conception of compassion. About the only thing we cannot measure is what compassion *really* means, because compassion isn't real. Compassion exists only in the form of the agreements we have about how to use the term in communicating about things that are real.

If you recall our earlier discussions of postmodernism, you'll recognize that some people would object to the degree of "reality" we've allowed in the preceding comments. Although we're not going to be radically postmodern in this chapter, we think you'll recognize the importance in many researchers' minds of an intellectually tough view of what's real and what's not.

In this context, Abraham Kaplan (1964) distinguishes three classes of things that scientists measure. The first class is *direct observables:* those things we can observe rather simply and directly, like the color of an apple or the check mark made in a questionnaire. *Indirect observables* require "relatively more subtle, complex, or indirect observations" (1964, p. 55). We note a person's check mark beside *female* in a questionnaire and have indirectly observed that person's sex. History books or minutes of corporate board meetings provide indirect observations of past social actions. Finally, *constructs* are theoretical creations that are based on observations but that cannot be observed directly or indirectly. Scholastic aptitude is a good example. It is constructed mathematically from observations of the answers given to a large number of questions on a scholastic aptitude test.

Kaplan (1964, p. 49) defines *concept* as a "family of conceptions." A concept is, as Kaplan notes, a construct. The concept of compassion, then, is a construct created from your conception of it, our conceptions of it, and the conceptions of all those who have ever used the term. It cannot be observed directly or indirectly, because it doesn't exist. We made it up.

Conceptualization

Day-to-day communication usually occurs through a system of vague and general agreements about the use of terms. Usually, others do not understand exactly what we wish to communicate, but they get the general drift of our meaning. Although we do not agree completely about the use of the term *compassionate,* we're probably safe in assuming that Pat won't pull the wings off flies. A wide range of misunderstandings and conflict—from the interpersonal to the international—is the price we pay for our imprecision, but somehow we muddle through. However, science aims at more than muddling; it cannot operate in a context of such imprecision.

Catherine Marshall and Gretchen Rossman (1995, p. 18) speak of a "conceptual funnel" through which a researcher's interest becomes increasingly focused. Thus, a general interest in compassion could narrow to "individuals who are concerned about the welfare of others" and further focus on discovering "what experiences shaped the development of compassionate people." This focusing process is inescapably linked to the language we use.

As you've seen, conceptualization is the process through which we specify what we will mean when we use particular terms. Suppose we want to find out, for example, whether women are more compassionate than men. We suspect many people assume this is the case, but it might be interesting to find out if it's really so. We can't meaningfully study the question, let alone agree on the answer, without some working agreements about the meaning of *compassion.* They are *working* agreements in the sense that they allow us to work on the question. We don't need to agree or even pretend to agree that a particular specification is ultimately the best one.

Indicators and Dimensions

The product of this conceptualization process is the specification of one or more **indicators** of what we have in mind, indicating the presence or absence of the concept we're studying. Here's a fairly simple example.

We might agree that visiting children's hospitals during Christmas and Hanukkah is an indicator of compassion. Putting little birds back in their nests might be agreed on as another indicator, and so forth. If the unit of analysis for our study were the individual person, we could then observe the presence or absence of each indicator for each person under study. Going beyond that, we could add up the number of indicators of compassion observed for each individual. We might agree on ten specific indicators, for example, and find six present in our study of Pat, three for John, nine for Mary, and so forth.

Returning to our original question, we might calculate that the women we studied had an average of 6.5 indicators of compassion, the men an average of 3.2. Therefore, we might conclude on the basis of our quantitative analysis of group difference that women are, on the whole, more compassionate than men. Usually, though, it's not that simple.

Whenever we take our concepts seriously and set about specifying what we mean by them, we discover disagreements and inconsistencies. Not only do we disagree, but each of us is likely to find a good deal of muddiness within our own mental images. If you take a moment to look at what *you* mean by compassion, you'll probably find that your image contains several *kinds* of compassion. The entries on your file sheet can be combined into groups and subgroups, and you'll even find several different strategies for making the combinations. For example, you might group the entries into feelings and actions.

The technical term for such groupings is *dimension:* a specifiable aspect or facet of a concept. Thus, we might speak of the "feeling dimension" of compassion and the "action dimension" of compassion. In a different grouping scheme, we might distinguish "compassion for humans" from "compassion for animals." Or we might see compassion as helping people have what we want for them versus what they want for themselves. Still differently, we might distinguish "compassion as forgiveness" from "compassion as pity."

Thus, we could subdivide *compassion* according to several sets of **dimensions.** Conceptualization involves both specifying dimensions and identifying the various indicators for each.

Specifying the different dimensions of a concept often paves the way for a more sophisticated understanding of what we're studying. We might observe, for example, that women are more compassionate in terms of feelings and men more so in terms of actions—or vice versa. Whichever the case, we would not be able to say whether men or women are really more compassionate. Our research, in fact, would have shown that there is no single answer to the question.

The Interchangeability of Indicators

Suppose, for the moment, that we have compiled a list of 100 indicators of compassion and its various dimensions. Suppose further that we disagree widely on which indicators give the clearest evidence of compassion or its absence. If we pretty much agree on some indicators, we could focus our attention on those, and we would probably agree on the answer they provided. But suppose we don't really agree on any of the possible indicators. We can still reach an agreement on whether men or women are the more compassionate.

If we disagree totally on the value of the indicators, one solution would be to study all of them. Now, suppose that women turn out to be more compassionate than men on all 100 indicators—on all the indicators on our composite list. Then we would be able to agree that women are more compassionate than men even though we still disagree on what compassion means in general.

The *interchangeability of indicators* means that if several different indicators all represent, to some degree, the same concept, then all of them will behave the same way that the concept would behave if it were real and could be observed. Thus, if women are generally more compassionate than men, we should be able to observe that difference by using any reasonable measure of compassion.

You have now seen the fundamental logic of conceptualization and measurement. The discussions that follow are mainly refinements and extensions of what we've just presented. Before turning to more technical elaborations on the main framework, however, we want to cover a few useful general topics.

First, we know that the previous discussions may not fit exactly with your previous understanding of the meaning of such terms as *love* and *compassion*. We tend to operate in daily life as though such terms have real, ultimate meanings. In the next subsection, then, we want to comment briefly on how we came to that understanding.

Second, lest this whole discussion create a picture of anarchy in the meanings of words, we will describe some of the ways researchers have organized the confusion to provide standards, consistency, and commonality in the meaning of terms. You should come away from this latter discussion with a recaptured sense of order—but one based on a conscious understanding rather than on a casual acceptance of common usage.

The Confusion over Definitions and Reality

First, here's a brief review. Concepts are derived from the mental images (conceptions) that summarize collections of seemingly related observations and experiences. Although the observations and experiences are real, at least subjectively, concepts are only mental creations. The terms associated with concepts are merely devices created for the purposes of filing and communication. For example, *love* is only a collection of letters and has no intrinsic meaning.

Usually, however, we fall into the trap of believing that terms have real meanings. That danger seems to grow stronger when we begin to take terms seriously and attempt to use them precisely. Further, the danger is all the greater in the presence of experts who appear to know more than you do about what the terms really mean: It's very easy to yield to authority in such a situation.

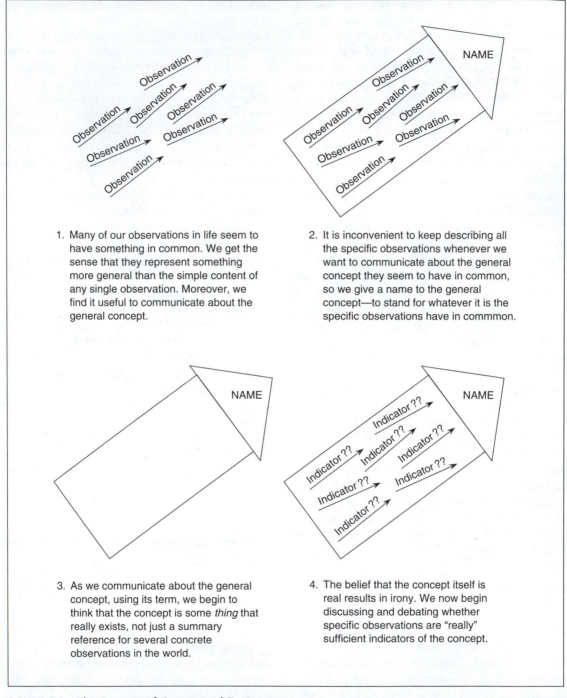

1. Many of our observations in life seem to have something in common. We get the sense that they represent something more general than the simple content of any single observation. Moreover, we find it useful to communicate about the general concept.

2. It is inconvenient to keep describing all the specific observations whenever we want to communicate about the general concept they seem to have in common, so we give a name to the general concept—to stand for whatever it is the specific observations have in commmon.

3. As we communicate about the general concept, using its term, we begin to think that the concept is some *thing* that really exists, not just a summary reference for several concrete observations in the world.

4. The belief that the concept itself is real results in irony. We now begin discussing and debating whether specific observations are "really" sufficient indicators of the concept.

FIGURE 6-1 **The Process of Conceptual Entrapment**

Once we have assumed that terms have real meanings, we begin the tortured task of discovering what those real meanings are and what constitutes a genuine measurement of them. Figure 6-1 illustrates the history of this process. We make up conceptual summaries of real observations because the summaries are convenient. However, they prove to be so convenient that we begin to think they are real. Regarding as real those things that are not is called **reification,** and the reification of concepts in day-to-day life is quite common.

The design and execution of communication research require us to clear away the confusion over concepts and reality. In the midst of disagreement and confusion over what a term really means, researchers can specify a nominal definition for the purposes of an inquiry. Wishing to examine *TV violence* in a study, for example, we may simply specify that we're going to treat it as a frequency count of the number of times per hour that physical force is used. In this decision, we rule out other possible aspects of televised violence: threats of physical force, distinctions between milder and harsher forms of violence (e.g., a slap as opposed to a fatal shooting), physical force used in self-defense as opposed to premeditated physical force, and so forth.

Creating Conceptual Order

Although conceptualization is a continuing process, it's vital in quantitative research that you specifically address it at the beginning of the study design. In a survey, for example, **operationalization** results in a commitment to a specific set of questionnaire items that will represent the concepts under study. Without that commitment, the study could not proceed further.

Let's explore initial conceptualization the way it applies to structured inquiries such as surveys, experiments, and quantitative text analysis. Although specifying nominal definitions focuses our observational strategy, it does not allow us to observe. As a next step, we must specify exactly what we are going to observe, how we will do it, and what interpretations we are going to place on various possible observations. All these further specifications make up what is called the operational definition of the concept—a definition that spells out precisely how the concept will be measured. Strictly speaking, an *operational definition* is a description of the "operations" that will be undertaken in measuring a concept.

Pursuing the example of TV violence, we might want to provide two coders with a checklist of different kinds of physical violence and ask them to place a check mark beside the appropriate action when they see it portrayed in a TV program. Our checklist might contain such physically violent actions as slapping, hitting, use of a physical object to hit another, use of a gun or knife, and creation of an unsafe environment to cause injury to another (e.g., planting a bomb in a car).

Though others might disagree with our conceptualization and operationalization, the definition would have one essential scientific virtue: It would be absolutely specific and unambiguous. Even if someone disagreed with our definition, that person would have a good idea of how to interpret our research results, because what we meant by TV violence—reflected in our analyses and conclusions—would be clear.

Here's a diagram showing the progression of measurement steps from our vague sense of what a term means to specific measurements in a fully structured scientific study:

Conceptualization
↓
Nominal Definition
↓
Operational Definition
↓
Measurements in the Real World

We devote the rest of this chapter to some considerations and alternatives involved in the creation of useful definitions and measurements.

OPERATIONALIZATION

We'll begin with an overview of some of the operationalization choices you have in organizing the business of observation and measurement: what range of variation to consider, what levels of measurement to use, and whether to depend on a single indicator or on several. Then we'll illustrate some different ways to measure a given variable that we hope will broaden your imagination and vision. Last, we'll discuss operationalization as a process that continues throughout a research project. Although we've discussed it in the context of research design—gearing up for the collection of data—you'll see that concepts are also operationalized when these data are analyzed.

Operationalization Choices

The communication researcher has a number of choices to make when measuring a concept. These choices are intimately interconnected, but we've separated them for the sake of discussion. However, please realize that operationalization does not proceed through a systematic checklist.

Range of Variation In operationalizing any concept, you must be clear about the range of variation that interests you in your research. To what extent are you willing to combine attributes in fairly gross categories?

Let's suppose you want to measure people's incomes in a study designed to determine whether people's anxiety about speaking in groups and public settings is negatively correlated with income. The highest annual incomes that people receive run into the millions of dollars, but not many people get that much. Unless you're studying the very rich, it probably wouldn't be worth much to allow for and keep track of extremely high categories. Depending on whom you study, you'll probably want to establish a highest-income category with a much lower floor—maybe $100,000 or more. Although this decision will lead you to throw together people who earn a trillion dollars a year with paupers earning a mere $100,000, they'll survive it, and that mixing probably won't hurt your research any, either. The same decision faces you at the other end of the income spectrum. In studies of the general U.S. population, a cutoff of $5,000 or less usually works just fine.

Many communication researchers study the persuasiveness of messages—the extent to which communication messages change attitudes or beliefs. In measuring attitudes and beliefs, the question of range of variation has another dimension. Unless you're careful, you may end up measuring only half an attitude without really meaning to. Here's an example of what we mean.

Suppose you've been contracted to develop a series of persuasive messages designed to increase people's support for the expanded use of nuclear power generators. You'd anticipate in advance that some people consider nuclear power generators the greatest thing since the wheel, whereas other people have absolutely no interest in them whatsoever. Given that anticipation, it would seem to make sense to ask people how much they favor expanding the use of nuclear energy. You might give them answer categories ranging from "Favor it very much" to "Don't favor it at all."

However, this operationalization conceals half the attitudinal spectrum regarding nuclear energy. Many people have feelings that go beyond simply not favoring it: They are absolutely *opposed* to it. In this instance, there is considerable variation on the left side of zero. Some oppose it a little, some quite a bit, and others a great deal. To measure the full range of variation, then, you'd want to operationalize attitudes toward nuclear energy with a range from favoring it very much, through no feelings one way or the other, to opposing it very much.

This consideration applies to many of the variables that communication researchers study. Virtually any issue involves both support and opposition, each in varying degrees. Political orientations range from very liberal to very conservative, and depending on the people you study, you may want to allow for radicals on one or both ends.

We don't mean that you must measure the full range of variation in every case. However, you should consider whether you need to, given your research purpose. If the difference between *not liberal* and *anti-liberal* isn't relevant to your research, forget it. Someone has defined pragmatism as "any difference that makes no difference is no difference." Be pragmatic.

Finally, your decision on the range of variation should be governed by the expected distribution of attributes among your subjects of study. That is what we meant earlier when we said range depends on whom you are studying. In a study of college professors' attitudes toward the value of higher education, you could probably stop at *no value* and not worry about those who might consider higher education dangerous to students' health. (If you were studying students, however. . . .)

Variations between the Extremes   How fine will you make distinctions among the various possible attributes composing a given variable? Does it really matter whether a person is 16 or 19 years old, or could you conduct your inquiry by throwing them together in a group labeled 10- to 19-year-olds? Don't answer too quickly. If you wanted to study parent–child communication, the difference between 16 and 19 might be major—19-year-olds are more likely to have left their parents' home, and this factor might be related to parent–child communication in a systematic way.

If you're going to measure age, then, you must look at the purpose and procedures of your study and decide whether fine or gross differences in age are important to you. If you measure political affiliation as part of a study on the effectiveness of a political campaign, will it matter to your inquiry whether a person is a conservative Democrat rather than a liberal Democrat, or will it be sufficient to know the person's party? Do you simply need to know whether a person is married or not, or will it make a difference to know if he or she has never married or is separated, widowed, divorced, or remarried?

There is, of course, no general answer to such questions. The answers come out of the purpose of your study, or why you're making a particular measurement. We can mention a useful guideline, though. Whenever you're not sure how much detail to get in a measurement, get too much rather than too little. During the analysis of data, you can always combine precise attributes into more general categories, but you can never separate out any variations you lumped together during observation and measurement.

A Note on Dimensions   When people get down to the business of creating operational measures of variables, they often discover—or worse, never notice—that they're not exactly clear about which dimensions of a variable they're really interested in. In the prior section, we dealt with this to some degree, but now we want to look at it more closely.

Let's suppose you're studying communication and sexuality in dating pairs. You need to measure attitudes toward sexuality. Here are just a few of the dimensions you might examine (Hendrick & Hendrick, 1987):

- How permissive are people in accepting sexual activity prior to marriage?
- What is the range of sexually related behaviors that people engage in or condone?
- To what extent is sexuality viewed as a means for bonding emotionally with the partner?
- To what extent is sexuality viewed as an instrument for physical pleasure?

It's essential that you be clear about which dimensions are important in your inquiry; otherwise, you may measure how people feel about sex-as-physical-gratification instead of sex-as-emotional-bonding, or vice versa.

Once you've decided on the relevant range of variation, the degree of precision needed between the extremes of variation, and the specific dimensions of the variables that interest you, you may have another choice: a mathematical–logical one. That is, you may need to decide what *level* of measurement to use. To discuss this, we need to take another look at attributes and their relationship to variables. (See Chapter 3 for the first discussion of this topic.)

Levels of Measurement

An attribute, you'll recall, is a characteristic or quality of something. *Feminine* would be an example. So would *old* or *student.* Variables, on the other hand, are logical sets of attributes. Thus, *gender* is a variable composed of the attributes *feminine* and *masculine.*

The conceptualization and operationalization processes can be seen as the specification of variables and the attributes composing them. Thus, *group decision-making consensus* could be a variable having the attributes *member agreement* and *member disagreement;* the list of attributes could also be expanded to include other possibilities.

Every variable conceptualized and operationalized by a researcher must have two important qualities. First, the attributes composing it should be *exhaustive.* For the variable to have any utility in research, you must be able to classify every observation in terms of one of the attributes composing the variable. You'll run into trouble in a study of the effectiveness of political campaign ads on viewers of different political party affiliations if you conceptualize the variable *political party affiliation* in terms of the attributes *Republican* and *Democrat,* because some of the people you set out to study will identify with the Green Party, or some other organization, and some (often a large percentage) will tell you they have no party affiliation. You could make the list of attributes exhaustive by adding *other* and *no affiliation.* Whatever you do, you must be able to classify *every* observation.

At the same time, attributes composing a variable must be *mutually exclusive.* You must be able to classify every observation in terms of *one and only one* attribute. Thus, for example, in studying the variable *participation in an Internet chatroom,* you need to define *chatroom participant* and *chatroom nonparticipant* in such a way that nobody can be both at the same time. That means being able to handle the person who has entered a chatroom once or twice out of curiosity but doesn't consider herself a regular. In this case, you might define your attributes to distinguish the person who has never entered a chatroom from the person who has entered them fewer than half a dozen times from the person who has entered them six or more times.

Attributes operationalized as mutually exclusive and exhaustive may be related in other ways as well. For example, the attributes composing variables may represent different *levels of measurement.* In this section, we'll examine four levels of measurement: nominal, ordinal, interval, and ratio. It's important to note at the outset of our discussion of levels of measurement that variables are not automatically at a specific level. The level of measurement for a given variable depends on the attributes used.

Nominal Measures   Variables with attributes that have *only* the characteristics of exhaustiveness and mutual exclusiveness are being measured at the **nominal level.** Examples include *e-mail server, birthplace, college major,* and *hair color.* Although the attributes composing each of these variables—*blonde, brown, black,* and so forth composing the variable *hair color*—are distinct from one another (and exhaust the possibilities of hair color among people), they have no additional structures. Nominal measures merely offer names or labels for characteristics.

It might be useful to imagine a group of people being characterized in terms of one such variable and physically grouped by the applicable attributes. Imagine asking a large gathering of people to stand together in groups according to the states in which they were born: all those born in Vermont in one group, those born in California in another, and so forth. The variable would be *place of birth;*

the attributes would be *born in California, born in Vermont,* and so on. All the people standing in a given group would have at least one thing in common and would differ from the people in all other groups in that same regard. Where the individual groups formed, how close they were to one another, or how the groups were arranged in the room would be irrelevant. All that would matter would be that all the members of a given group share the same state of birth and that each group have a different shared state of birth.

The only mathematical procedure you can perform on variables measured at the nominal level is to count up the frequencies with which each attribute appears—for example, the number of Iowa-borns, the number of California-borns, and so forth in your sample (or the percentages or proportions of each place of birth).

Ordinal Measures   Variables with attributes we can logically rank-order are being measured at the **ordinal level.** The different attributes represent relatively more or less of the variable. Examples might include *social class, class standing (first year, sophomore, junior, senior),* and the like.

In the physical sciences, *hardness* is the most frequently cited example of an ordinal measure. We may say that one material (for example, diamond) is harder than another (say, glass) if the former can scratch the latter and not vice versa (that is, diamond scratches glass, but glass does not scratch diamond). By attempting to scratch various materials with other materials, we might eventually be able to arrange several materials in a row, ranging from the softest to the hardest. We could never say how hard a given material was in absolute terms, but only in relative terms—which materials it was harder than and which it was softer than.

Let's pursue the earlier example of grouping the people at a social gathering. Imagine that we asked all the people who had graduated from college to stand in one group, all those with only a high school diploma to stand in another group, and all those who had not graduated from high school to stand in a third group. This manner of grouping people would satisfy the requirements for exhaustiveness and mutual exclusiveness discussed earlier. Thus, we could have measured our *formal education* variable at the nominal level. In addition, however, we might logically arrange the three groups in terms of the relative amount of formal education each had. We might arrange the three groups in a row, ranging from most to least formal education. This arrangement would provide a physical representation of an ordinal measure. If we knew which groups two individuals were in, we

could determine that one had more, less, or the same formal education as the other. In a similar way, one individual object could be ranked as harder, softer, or of the same hardness as another object.

Note that in this example it would be irrelevant how close or far apart the educational groups were from one another. The college and high school groups could be 5 feet apart, and the less-than-high-school group might be 500 feet farther down the line. These actual distances would not have any meaning. However, the high school group should be between the less-than-high-school group and the college group, or else the rank order would be incorrect.

Interval Measures   For the attributes composing some variables, the actual distance separating those attributes matters. Such variables are being measured at the **interval level.** For these, the logical distance between attributes can be expressed in meaningful standard intervals. For example, in the Fahrenheit temperature scale, the difference, or distance, between 80 degrees and 90 degrees is the same as that between 40 degrees and 50 degrees in the Celsius scale. However, 80 degrees Fahrenheit is not twice as hot as 40 degrees, since the zero point in the Fahrenheit and Celsius scales is arbitrary; zero degrees does not really mean lack of heat, nor does −30 degrees represent 30 degrees less than no heat. (The Kelvin scale is based on an absolute zero, which does mean a complete lack of heat.)

Many of the variables used in communication research are used at the interval level. For example, we could measure communication competence on scale from 1 to 10, where "1" stands for "very little" and "10" stands for "a great deal." The difference between a person who scores "8" and a person who scores "6" is +2. Although some measurement experts might argue that at most we can interpret these scale values at the ordinal level (concluding simply that the first person scores higher than the second), most communication researchers choose to use such rating scale measures at the interval level. When you are using numbers at the interval level, you can perform most of the arithmetic functions on them. About the only thing you can't reasonably do is calculate ratios.

Ratio Measures   When a variable is being measured at the **ratio level,** the attributes composing it, besides having all the structural characteristics mentioned previously, are based on a true zero point. We have already mentioned the Kelvin temperature scale in contrast to the Fahrenheit and Celsius scales. Examples of variables

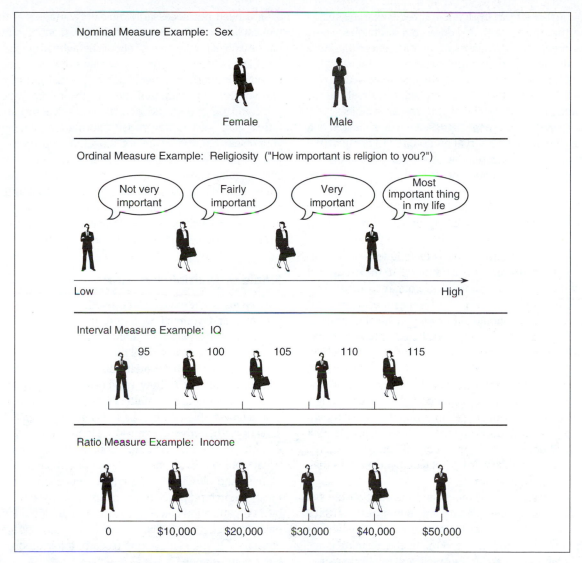

FIGURE 6-2   **Levels of Measurement**

measured at the ratio level in communication research might include *age, number of times married,* and *number of children.*

Returning to the illustration of methodological party games at a social gathering, we might ask people to group themselves by age. All the one-year-olds would stand (or sit, lie, or squirm) together, the two-year-olds together, the three-year-olds, and so forth. The fact that members of a single group share the same age and that each different group has a different shared age satisfies the minimum requirements for a nominal measure. Arranging the several groups in a line from youngest to oldest meets the additional requirements of an ordinal measure and lets us determine if one person is older than,

younger than, or the same age as another. If we space the groups equally far apart, we satisfy the additional requirements of an interval measure and will be able to say *how much* older one person is than another. Finally, because one of the attributes included in age represents a true zero (babies carried by women about to give birth), the phalanx of hapless partygoers also meets the requirements for a ratio measure, permitting us to say that one person is twice as old as another.

To review this discussion, Figure 6-2 presents a graphic illustration of the four levels of measurement.

Implications of Levels of Measurement   Because it's unlikely you will undertake the physical grouping of people just described (try it once, and you won't be invited to many parties), we should draw your attention to some of the practical implications of the differences that have been distinguished. Primarily, these implications appear in the analysis of quantitative data (discussed in Chapters 11 and 12), but such analytical implications should be anticipated in the structuring of your research project.

Ratio measures are the highest level of measurement, descending through interval and ordinal to nominal, the lowest level of measurement. A variable measured at a given level of measurement—say, ratio—may also be treated as representing a lower level of measurement—say, ordinal. Here, "high" and "low" refer to the number of assumptions you are making about what numerals mean.

Certain quantitative analysis techniques require certain minimum levels of measurement. To the extent that the variables to be examined in your research project were measured at a particular level of measurement—say, ordinal—you should plan your analytical techniques accordingly. More precisely, you should anticipate drawing research conclusions appropriate to the levels of measurement used in operationalizing your variables. For example, you might reasonably plan to determine and report the mean age of a population under study if you had their individual ages in years (add up all the individual ages and divide by the number of people), but you could not report the mean age if you had gathered only ordinal-level data from individuals (e.g., "less than 18," "18–25," and so on).

If you wished to examine only the relationship between age and some variable measured at the ordinal level—say, self-perceived communication effectiveness (high, medium, and low)—you might choose to treat age as an ordinal-level variable as well. You might characterize the participants of your study as being *young, middle-aged,* and *old,* specifying what age range composed each of these groupings. Finally, *age* might be used as a nominal-level variable for certain research purposes. People might be grouped as being born during the depression of the 1930s or not. Another nominal measurement, based on birth date rather than just age, would be the grouping of people by astrological signs.

The analytical uses planned for a given variable, then, should determine the level of measurement to be sought. If a variable is to be used in a variety of ways, requiring different levels of measurement, the study should be designed to achieve the highest level required. For example, if the participants in a study are asked their exact ages, these ages can later be organized into ordinal or nominal groupings.

You need not necessarily measure variables at their highest level of measurement, however. If you're sure to have no need for the ages of people at higher than the ordinal level of measurement, you may simply ask people to indicate their age range, such as 20 to 29, 30 to 39, and so forth. In a study of the wealth of corporations, you could use Dun & Bradstreet data to rank corporations rather than seek more precise information. Whenever your research purposes are not altogether clear, however, you should seek the highest level of measurement possible. Again, although ratio measures can later be reduced to ordinal ones, you cannot convert an ordinal measure to a ratio one. More generally, you cannot convert a lower-level measure to a higher-level one. This is a one-way street worth remembering.

Single or Multiple Indicators

With so many alternatives for operationalizing variables, you may find yourself worrying about whether you'll make the right choices. To counter this feeling, let us add a dash of certainty and stability.

Many variables have pretty obvious, straightforward measures. No matter how you cut it, *sex of participant* usually turns out to be a matter of *male* or *female:* a nominal-level variable that can be measured by a single observation—by either looking or asking a question. Although you'll want to think about foster children, it's usually pretty easy to find out how many children a family has. And although some fine-tuning is possible, for most research purposes the number of people employed by an organization can be obtained from their personnel office. A great many variables, then, have obvious single indicators. If you can get one piece of information, you have what you need.

Sometimes, however, there is no single indicator that will give you the measure of a variable you really want. Many concepts are subject to varying interpretations—each with several possible indicators. In these cases, you'll want to make several observations for a given variable. You can then combine the several pieces of information you've collected to create a *composite* measurement of the variable in question.

Consider the concept *college performance.* All of us have noticed that in terms of performance in courses, some students do well in college and others don't. In studying this, we might ask what characteristics and experiences are related to high levels of performance; many researchers have done just that. How should we measure overall performance? Each grade in any single course is a potential indicator of college performance, but in using any single course grade, we run a risk that the one used will not typify the student's general performance. The solution to this problem is so firmly established that it is, of course, obvious to you: the *grade point average* (GPA). We assign numerical scores to each letter grade, total the points earned by a given student, and divide by the number of courses taken to obtain a composite measure. (If the courses vary in number of credits, adjustments are made in that regard.) It's often appropriate to create such composite measures in communication research. Such composites are very common in survey research, and we'll return to this topic in greater depth in Chapter 8.

Some Operationalization Illustrations

To bring together all the operationalization choices available to the quantitatively oriented researcher and to show the potential in those possibilities, we want to take a little time to illustrate some of the ways in which you might address certain research problems. Our purpose here is to stretch your imagination just a bit further and demonstrate the challenge that communication research can present to your ingenuity. To simplify matters, we have not attempted to describe all the research conditions that would make one alternative superior to the others, though you should realize that in a given situation they would not all be equally appropriate. Let's look at specific research questions, then, and some of the ways you could address them. We'll begin with an example discussed at length in the first part of this chapter. It has the added advantage that one of the variables is reasonably straightforward.

1. *Are women more compassionate than men?*
    a. Select a group of participants for study. Present them with hypothetical situations that involve someone's being in trouble. Ask them what they would do if they were confronted with that situation. What would they do, for example, if they came across a small child who was lost and crying for his or her parents? Consider any answer that involves helping the child or comforting him or her to be compassionate, and count whether men or women are more likely to indicate they would be compassionate. If a given participant could be scored as either "compassionate" or "not compassionate," then, we would have operationalized our *compassion* variable at the nominal level.
    b. Set up an experiment in which you pay a small child to pretend that he or she is lost. Put the

kid to work on a busy sidewalk, and observe whether men or women are more likely to offer verbal assistance. Be sure to count how many men and women walk by, also, since there may be more of one than the other. If that's the case, simply calculate the percentage of men and the percentage of women who help. If a given man or woman was simply assigned a measure of "offered help" or "did not offer help," we would again have a nominal-level measure of *compassion*. However, suppose that we counted for each man and woman the number of helpful statements they uttered (from zero to the largest number uttered in our sample). If we calculated the mean number of helpful statements uttered by men and the mean number uttered by women, we would have operationalized *compassion* at the ratio level.
    c. Select a sample of people and do a survey in which you ask them what organizations they belong to. Calculate whether women or men are more likely to belong to those that seem to reflect compassionate feelings. To take account of men belonging to more organizations than women in general—or vice versa—do this: For each person you study, calculate the *percentage* of his or her organizational memberships that reflect compassion. See if men or women have a higher average percentage. Because percentage could vary from 0 to 100, we would have another ratio-level measurement of our *compassion* variable.
    d. Watch your local newspaper for a special feature on some issue involving compassion—the slaughter of baby seals, for example. In the days that follow, keep a record of all letters to the editor on the subject. See whether men or women are the more likely to express their compassion in the matter—making the necessary adjustments for one sex writing more letters to the editor than the other in general. We'd have a percentage of all letters written by men that were on the compassion subject and a percentage of all letters written by women that were on the compassion subject. Percentages are ratio-level measures.

2. *Are people in California more friendly than people in New York?*
    a. Plant confederates on randomly selected street corners in comparably sized cities in each state. Have the confederates appear lost and

approach people to ask for directions. Count the number of people in each state (or the percentage of people approached in each state) who attempt to provide directions. This would be a ratio-level measurement, since we could conceivably have values from zero upwards.

b. Take out classified ads in newspapers in each state asking for volunteers to participate in a survey. To qualify for participation, people should have lived part of their adult years in each state. Ask them to indicate through a series of questions whether they experienced California or New York to be friendlier and why they think this is so. The level of measurement here would depend on how the questions were worded. If we asked people to circle which state overall, we'd have a nominal measure (whose two attributes would be *New York* and *California*).

c. Have observers stationed on randomly selected street corners in comparably sized cities in each state. Observers should count the number of people who walk by them with smiles on their faces (alternatively, use the percentage of people who pass by who are smiling). This would be ratio-level measurement.

3. *Are communication students or accounting students more effective in communicating information?*

a. Devise a task in which people have to communicate information to someone—perhaps giving directions to some local park. Have a confederate approach both kinds of students and request directions to the park. Tape-record the directions, and have a group of neutral judges evaluate the directions on a 1–10 scale of clarity and brevity. Average the scores for the directions given by the communication students and the scores for the accounting students' directions. Most communication researchers would regard this as an interval-level measurement.

b. Bring communication students and accounting students into a laboratory one at a time. Ask them to give an informational presentation on some topic about which they should have comparable knowledge. Videotape the presentations. Have advanced students in public speaking classes view and rate the presentations on their effectiveness on a 1–10 scale. This would be interval-level measurement again.

The point of these illustrations has been to broaden your vision of the many ways variables can be operationalized, not necessarily to suggest respectable research projects. When you think about it, absolutely everything you see around you can already be regarded as an operationalized measure of some variable. Most are measures of more than one variable, so all you have to do is pick the ones you want and decide what they will represent in your particular study. Usually, you'll want to use more than one measure for each variable in the inquiry.

DEFINITIONS AND RESEARCH PURPOSES

Recall from Chapter 2 that two of the general purposes of research are *description* and *causal/functional explanation.* The distinction between them has important implications for definition and measurement. If you've formed the opinion that description is a simpler task than explanation, you'll be surprised to learn that definitions are more problematic for descriptive research than for explanatory research. Before we turn to issues of measurement quality, you'll need a basic understanding of why this is so.

The importance of definitions for descriptive research should be clear. If we want to describe and report the amount of physical violence presented on television, our definition of *physical violence* is critical. This is more challenging than it might appear at first glance. Must the act be physical, or will it suffice to verbally threaten someone? Is the statement "Turn over your wallet, or I'll kill you" of the same order as a physical attempt to remove someone's wallet while holding a gun to the chest? Must the threat be real or merely illusory? What if a robber merely holds his hand in his pocket to make it look like there's a gun, and the character being held up believes there is a gun, but the viewer has knowledge that there is no gun in the robber's pocket. Are intentional acts of physical violence to be treated the same as unintended accidents in which someone suffers from physical violence? If a hired hit man kills a victim, should this be counted the same as a gun accidentally left in an unlocked cabinet that goes off when a child plays with it? When there's a fistfight in a bar, how many acts of physical violence are there? Should we count each punch, or count the entire violent episode as one instance of physical violence? As you can readily see, the question of what counts as physical violence quickly becomes a complicated matter. The researcher of physical violence in the media needs to have a clear conception of what he or she is going to study and make claims about.

We have spelled out these considerations in some detail so you can see that the conclusion of a descriptive study about televised physical violence, for example, depends directly on how each issue is resolved. Working with a broad definition of physical violence might lead to an exaggerated claim about just how much violence there is on TV. But if we narrow our definition excessively, we could end up underestimating the amount of violence there is on TV, by definition alone.

Thus, the descriptive statement that the rate of physical violence on TV is five acts per hour, or ten acts per hour, or whatever it might be, depends directly on the operational definitions used. When researchers conduct quantitatively descriptive studies, they owe it to their readers to inform them as clearly as possible how they conceptualized and operationalized their variables. The reader is then positioned to decide for himself or herself whether the definition is useful.

Ironically, definitions are less problematic in the case of causal/functional explanatory research. Let's suppose we're interested in explaining the adoption of new technology. Why are some people quick to adopt such technological innovations as hand-held electronic organizers, digital cameras, and robotic devices, whereas others are not? More specifically, let's suppose we're interested in whether old people are generally more hesitant to adopt new technologies than are young people. What if we have 25 different operational definitions of *hesitancy to adopt new technologies,* and we can't agree on which definition is the best one? As we've already seen, this is not necessarily an insurmountable obstacle. Suppose, for example, that we found old people more hesitant than young people in terms of all 25 definitions! (Recall the earlier discussion of compassion in men and women.) Suppose that we found old people more hesitant than young people by every reasonable definition of *hesitancy to adopt new technologies* we could think of. It wouldn't matter what our definition was. We would conclude that old people are generally more hesitant than young people—even though we couldn't agree about what a hesitant adopter really was.

In practice, explanatory research seldom results in findings quite as unambiguous as this example suggests; nonetheless, the general pattern occurs a lot in actual research. There *are* consistent patterns of relationships in human communicative life that result in consistent research findings; however, such consistency does not appear in a descriptive situation. Changing definitions almost inevitably results in different descriptive conclusions.

CRITERIA FOR THE TRUSTWORTHINESS OF MEASURES

In this chapter, we've come some distance. We began with the bald assertion that researchers can measure anything that exists. Then we discovered that most of the things we might want to measure and study don't really exist. Next we learned that it's possible to measure them anyway. We want to conclude the chapter with a discussion of some of the yardsticks against which we judge our relative success or failure in measuring things—even things that don't exist. We introduced this topic in the introduction to Part 2 with the labels *measurement reliability* and *measurement validity.* Let's make another pass at these criteria, more detailed than before.

To begin, measurements can be made with varying degrees of precision, representing the fineness of distinctions made between attributes composing a variable. The description of a woman as "43 years old" is more precise than "in her forties." Saying an organization was formed in the summer of 1999 is more precise than saying "during the 1990s."

As a general rule, precise measurements are superior to imprecise ones, as common sense would dictate. There are no conditions under which imprecise measurements would be intrinsically superior to precise ones. Even so, precision is not always necessary or desirable. If knowing that a woman is in her forties satisfies your research requirements, then any additional effort invested in learning her precise age is wasted. The operationalization of concepts, then, must be guided partly by an understanding of the degree of precision required. If your needs are not clear, be more precise rather than less.

Don't confuse precision with accuracy, however. Describing someone as "born in Stowe, Vermont," is more precise than "born in New England"—but suppose the person in question was actually born in Boston. In this instance, the less precise description is more accurate, a better reflection of the world.

Precision and accuracy are obviously important qualities in research measurement, and they probably need no further explanation. When communication researchers construct and evaluate measurements, however, they pay special attention to two technical considerations: reliability and validity.

Reliability

In the abstract, **measurement reliability** is a matter of whether a particular technique, applied repeatedly to the same object, would yield the same result each time. Let's say you want to know how much a certain person weighs. As one technique, you might ask two different people to estimate the weight of the person. If the first person estimated 150 pounds and the other estimated 300, we would have to conclude that the technique of having people estimate weight isn't very reliable.

Suppose, as an alternative, that we use a bathroom scale as our measurement technique. The person steps on the scale twice, and we note the result each time. The scale would presumably report the same weight both times, indicating that the scale provided a more reliable technique for measuring a person's weight than did asking people to estimate it.

Reliability, however, does not ensure accuracy any more than precision does. Suppose we've set the bathroom scale to shave five pounds off weight estimates just to make people feel better. Although you would (reliably) report the same weight for the person each time, you would always be wrong. Be warned that reliability does not ensure accuracy.

Let's suppose we're interested in studying morale among factory workers in two different kinds of factories. In one set of factories, workers have specialized jobs, reflecting an extreme division of labor. Each worker contributes a tiny part to the overall process performed on a long assembly line. In the other set of factories, each worker performs many tasks, and small teams of workers complete the whole process.

How should we measure *morale*? Following one strategy, we could observe the workers in each factory, noticing such things as whether they joke with one another, whether they smile and laugh a lot, and so forth. We could ask them how they like their work and even ask them whether they think they would prefer their current arrangement or the other one being studied. By comparing what we observed in the different factories, we might reach a conclusion about which assembly process produced the higher morale.

Now let's look at some reliability problems inherent in this method. First, how we are feeling when we do the observing will likely color what we see. We may misinterpret what we see. We may see workers kidding each other but think they're having an argument. Or maybe we'll catch them on an off day. If we were to observe the same group of workers several days in a row, we might arrive

at different evaluations on each day. If several observers evaluated the same behavior, on the other hand, they too might arrive at different conclusions about the workers' morale.

Here's another strategy for assessing morale. Suppose we check the company records to see how many grievances have been filed with the union during some fixed period of time. Presumably, this would be an indicator of morale: the more grievances, the lower the morale. This measurement strategy would appear to be more reliable. Counting up the grievances over and over, we should keep arriving at the same number.

If you find yourself saying "Wait a minute" over the second measurement strategy, you're worrying about validity, not reliability. Let's complete the discussion of reliability, and then we'll handle validity.

In quantitative research, reliability problems crop up in many forms. Reliability is a concern every time a single observer is the source of data, because we have no certain guard against the effect of that observer's subjectivity. We can't tell for sure how much of what's reported originated in the situation observed and how much in the observer. This is not only a problem with single observers, however.

Survey researchers have known for a long time that because of their own attitudes and demeanors, different interviewers get different answers from respondents. Or, if we were to conduct a study of editorial positions on some public issue, we might create a team of coders to take on the job of reading hundreds of editorials and classifying them in terms of their position on the issue. Different coders would code the same editorial differently. Or we might want to classify a few hundred specific popular songs by their type, only to find that one coder classifies a given song as "rock" while another coder classifies it as "country."

Each of these examples illustrates problems of reliability. Similar problems arise whenever we ask people to give us information about themselves. Sometimes we ask questions that people don't know the answers to: How many times have you watched television? Sometimes we ask people about things they consider totally irrelevant: Are you satisfied with China's current relationship with Mexico? And sometimes we explore issues so complicated that a person who had a clear opinion on the matter might arrive at a different interpretation of the question when asked a second time.

How do you create reliable measures? There are several techniques. First, in asking people for information—if your research design calls for that—be careful to ask only about things the respondents are likely to know the answer to. Ask about things relevant to them, and be clear in what you're asking. The danger in these instances is that people *will* give you answers—reliable or not. People will tell you how they feel about China's relationship with Mexico even if they haven't the foggiest idea what that relationship is.

Fortunately, communication researchers have developed several techniques for dealing with the basic problem of reliability.

Test–Retest Method Sometimes, it's appropriate to make the same measurement more than once. If you do not expect the information to change, then you should expect the same response both times. Such consistency would demonstrate adequate **test–retest reliability.** If answers vary, the measurement method may, to the extent of that variation, be unreliable. Here's an illustration.

In their research on health hazard appraisal (HHA), a part of preventive medicine, Jeffrey Sacks, W. Mark Krushat, and Jeffrey Newman (1980) wanted to determine the risks associated with various background and lifestyle factors, making it possible for physicians to counsel their patients appropriately. By knowing patients' life situations, physicians could advise them on their potential for survival and on how to improve it. This purpose, of course, depended heavily on the accuracy of the information gathered about each participant in the study.

To test the reliability of their information, Sacks and his colleagues had all 207 participants complete a baseline questionnaire that asked about their characteristics and behavior. Three months later, a follow-up questionnaire asked the same participants for the same information, and the results of the two surveys were compared. Overall, only 15 percent of the participants reported the same information in both studies.

Sacks and his colleagues report the following (1980, p. 730):

> Almost 10 percent of subjects reported a different height at follow-up examination. Parental age was changed by over one in three subjects. One parent reportedly aged 20 chronologic years in three months. One in five ex-smokers and ex-drinkers have apparent difficulty in reliably recalling their previous consumption pattern.

Some participants erased all trace of previously reported heart murmur, diabetes, emphysema, arrest record, and thoughts of suicide. One participant's mother, deceased in the first questionnaire, was apparently alive and well in time for the second. One participant had one ovary missing in the first study but present in the second. In another case, an ovary present in the first study was missing in the second study—and had been for ten years! You have to wonder if the physician-counselors could ever have nearly the impact on their patients that their patients' memories did. Thus, the data-collection method was not especially reliable.

One of the variables of ongoing interest to communication researchers is cognitive complexity. People who are higher in cognitive complexity have a comparatively large number of finely articulated, well-integrated thoughts; by contrast, people who are lower in cognitive complexity tend to be drawn to black-and-white, dichotomous thinking. Cognitive complexity relates to a wide range of communication behaviors, including how much a person takes into account the perspectives of other people when communicating with them. Cognitive complexity is often measured with the Role Category Questionnaire (RCQ), which asks people to describe in open-ended fashion several persons, usually peers, known to them. The impressions that people provide in their answers are then scored for several features, including the number of different features or characteristics with which people are described (differentiation), the abstractness of the characteristics (abstractness), and the degree to which characteristics are interrelated with one another (integration). In the two-person version, people are asked to provide a description of someone they like and a description of someone they don't like. Daniel O'Keefe, Greg Shepherd, and Thomas Streeter (1982) gave the two-person RCQ to a large group of undergraduates on two occasions, separated by one month. This repeat testing allowed the researchers to determine whether the differentiation score at time 1 was repeated at time 2. Scores were highly consistent across the month, demonstrating that the RCQ had adequate test–retest reliability.

Alternate-Form Method This technique requires a researcher to develop two different forms or versions of the same measure from the same pool of measurement items. It is used particularly with paper-and-pencil questionnaires. The two versions of the questionnaire are used with the same group of people, and the researcher compares the measurements taken by the two versions. If the measure has acceptable **alternate-form reliability,** the same, or similar, scores will be derived for subgroups measured with each form. For example, let's suppose your research methods instructor developed an exam to determine your mastery of communication research methods. If the exam were taken in a very crowded room in which it was difficult for students to have privacy in their answers, the instructor might develop two or more alternative forms of the exam from a large pool of test items. If the exam has adequate alternate-form reliability, those who took Form A of the exam should score similarly to those who took Form B, Form C, and so forth. Of course, this presumes that students with comparable mastery of the material were in each subgroup. As we shall see in Chapter 7, this is a reasonable presumption provided that forms were distributed randomly to the students.

The study described above by O'Keefe and his colleagues (1982) also tested alternative-form reliability. The RCQ was given in a timed version, which controlled how much time people had to complete the open-ended questionnaire, and in an untimed version, which allowed people to take as long as they desired in completing the task. Scores were highly correlated between the timed and the untimed versions, thereby demonstrating that the RCQ had adequate alternate-form reliability in addition to its demonstrated test–retest reliability.

Internal Consistency Method As a general rule, it's always good to make more than one measurement of any subtle or complex communication concept, such as communication competence or romantic love. This procedure lays the groundwork for another check on reliability. This technique is based on the assumption that the various items in a given measure should correlate positively with one another. In other words, they should perform consistently.

The internal consistency method can take several forms. The first of these is **split-half reliability.** Let's say you've created a questionnaire that contains ten items you believe measure romantic love. Using the split-half technique, you would randomly (see Chapter 7) assign those ten items to two sets of five. Each set should provide a good measure of love, and the sets should correspond in the way they classify the respondents to the study. If the two sets of items measure people differently, that, again, points to a problem in the reliability of how you're measuring the variable.

The Communication Anxiety Inventory, a measure of how much communication apprehension someone experiences in a given context or situation, was assessed for the adequacy of its split-half reliability by dividing the inventory's items into two random halves (Booth-Butterfield & Gould, 1986). Results indicated that the halves correlated highly with each other, as you would expect in split-half reliability.

A second form of internal consistency is **item-total reliability.** This technique compares the consistency, or correlation, of each item in a measure with the total score across all items of the measure. It is used with questionnaire measures. When a measure has high item-total reliability, it means that its component items correlate positively with the total score, summed across all items. If a given item doesn't correlate very well with the total score, it is not performing reliably and should probably be dropped from the measure.

Mary Anne Fitzpatrick and L. David Ritchie (1994) used this form of reliability check to test their newly developed measure of family communication, the Family Communication Environment Measure. For both parents and children, results indicated that the scores on individual items contained in the instrument correlated positively with the total scores.

Using Established Measures Another way to help ensure reliability in getting information from people is to use measures that have proven their reliability in previous research. If you want to measure romantic love, for example, you might want to use the Love Attitudes Scale (Hendrick & Hendrick, 1992), a popular measure that has demonstrated reliability based on its use in prior research.

The heavy use of measures, though, does not guarantee their reliability. For example, the Scholastic Aptitude Test and the Minnesota Multiphasic Personality Inventory (MMPI) have been accepted as established standards in their respective domains for decades. In recent years, though, they've needed fundamental overhauling to reflect changes in society.

Reliability of Research Workers Research workers—interviewers and coders, for example—can also generate measurement unreliability. There are several solutions. To guard against interviewer unreliability, it is common practice in surveys to have a supervisor call a subsample of the respondents on the telephone and verify selected pieces of information.

Replication also works in other situations. If you're worried that newspaper editorials or occupations may not be classified reliably, why not have each independently coded by several coders? Those that generate disagreement should be evaluated more carefully and resolved. To the extent that independent observers or coders agree in their judgments, they have what is known as **inter-observer** or **inter-coder agreement.**

Finally, clarity, specificity, training, and practice will avoid a great deal of unreliability and grief. If we spent some time reaching a clear agreement on how to evaluate editorial positions on an issue—discussing various positions and reading through several together—we could probably do a good job of classifying them in the same way independently.

Brian Patterson and his colleagues (1996) provide us with an unusual illustration of inter-observer reliability. They observed that when researchers have transcribed the audiotapes of conversations in order to analyze them with a method known as conversation analysis (see Chapter 15), they historically have not determined whether the transcription work has been done reliably. So they asked multiple transcribers to listen to the same tapes, making transcription notations for such phenomena as pauses, interruptions, and simultaneous talk. Their findings suggested that trained transcribers agree at rates of 75 percent or better, demonstrating adequate inter-observer reliability (or perhaps we should say inter-transcriber in this instance).

Reliability Coefficients Notice that almost all of the methods of reliability are based on agreement or consistency between two or more phenomena: one observation with a second observation, one form with another form, one half with another half, one item with the total, a research worker at time 1 and the same research worker at time 2, two observers or coders. Researchers capture the extent of agreement or consistency with a statistical coefficient known as a reliability coefficient. Any of several statistics could be reported: the correlation coefficient, r; Kuder-Richardson formula 20, K-R 20; Cronbach's alpha; and Cohen's kappa. (In Chapter 12, we'll see how to calculate a correlation coefficient.) It is beyond our scope to discuss the differences among these variations. For our purposes, it is sufficient to note that a reliability coefficient can range from a value of 0 to a value of 1.00, with the latter indicating perfect agreement or consistency and the former indicating the total absence of agreement or consistency. Obviously, researchers hope to produce reliability coefficients as close to 1.00 as they can get, because this suggests greater reliability. In general, a good guideline to use in evaluating a measure's reliability is whether it can demonstrate a reliability coefficient at least equal to .70.

The reliability of measurements is a fundamental issue in communication research, and we'll return to it more than once in the chapters ahead. For now, however, let's recall that even total reliability doesn't ensure that our measures measure what we think they measure. Next, let's plunge into the question of validity.

Validity

In conventional usage, the term **measurement validity** refers to the extent to which an empirical measure adequately reflects the *real meaning* of the concept under consideration. Whoops! We've already committed to the view that concepts don't have real meanings. How can we ever say whether a particular measure adequately reflects the concept's meaning, then? Ultimately, of course, we can't. At the same time, as we've already seen, all of social life, including communication, operates on *agreements* about the terms we use and the concepts they represent. There are several criteria regarding our success in making measurements appropriate to these agreements.

First, there's something called **content validity,** which refers to how well a measure covers the range of meanings, or the dimensions, included within the concept. For example, Edward Carmines and Richard Zeller (1979) point out that a test of mathematical ability cannot be limited to addition alone but would also need to cover subtraction, multiplication, division, and so forth. Or, if we say we are measuring communication competence in general, do we measure competence in communicating with family members, friends, strangers, co-workers, and in public speaking contexts? If not, our measure has inadequate content validity because it fails to tap the full range of contexts in which communication takes place. Does our general communication competence capture different kinds of competence—for example, competence in conveying factual content, competence in conveying relational meanings, verbal competence, and nonverbal competence? Unless it covers different facets or dimensions of communication competence, it cannot be complete. Content validity is addressed in three ways.

The first way that content validity is addressed is through **face validity.** Particular empirical measures may or may not jibe with our common agreements and our individual mental images concerning a particular concept. We might quarrel about the adequacy of measuring worker morale by counting the number of grievances filed with the union, but we'd surely agree that the number of grievances has something to do with morale. If we were to suggest that we measure morale by finding out how many books the workers took out of the library during their off-duty hours, you'd undoubtedly raise a more serious objection: That measure wouldn't have much face validity.

Shereen Bingham and Brant Burleson (1996) developed a questionnaire measure of self-reported proclivity to engage in sexually harassing behavior. They developed 26 "date-getting strategies" in response to hypothetical scenarios (e.g, "Comment on how pretty Donna is," "Let Donna catch you looking at her body"). In order to assess face validity, they took the scenarios to a group of males and asked them to assess their plausibility. Such assessments told the researchers whether "on its face" the measure appeared to be tapping sexual harassment situations.

Second, there's a kind of validity known as **expert panel validity.** In this form of validity work, a group of experts in the area evaluates a measure's adequacy. Expert panel validity is face validity performed by a group of experts. Sometimes, these expert judgments are adopted in formally established agreements that define some concepts. For example, the Census Bureau has created operational definitions of such concepts as family, household, and employment status that seem to have a workable validity in most studies using these concepts.

Patrice Buzzanell and her colleagues (1996) were interested in the extent to which callers' talk converges stylistically with the talk that appears in answering machine messages. They consulted an expert panel—graduate students enrolled in a sociolinguistics seminar—in developing the answering machine messages that they used in the actual study.

Third, many researchers address content validity through statistical procedures such as factor analysis, analyzing the multidimensional structure of their measures. For example, Kathleen Ellis (2000) developed a measure of perceived teacher confirmation—the extent to which teachers communicate to their students that they are valued and important individuals. Ellis developed a questionnaire measure containing many items. She gave the measure to a large group of students, and then she analyzed statistically the inter-item patterns to see which items appeared to group together in people's minds. Her argument for content validity is based on her evidence that teacher confirmation appears to consist of three underlying dimensions, all of which were present in her measure: teachers' confirming responses to questions and comments from students, demonstrated interest in students' learning, and teaching style.

The second major form of validity is **criterion validity,** which takes two forms—**predictive validity** and **concurrent validity.** Common to both forms is assessing a measure's validity through its relation to some external criterion. For predictive validity, a measure must demonstrate that it predicts future behavior. For example, the validity of the College Boards is shown in its ability to predict the college success of students. The validity of a written driver's test is determined, in this sense, by the relationship between the scores people get on the test and their subsequent driving records. In these examples, college success and driving ability are the criteria.

To test your understanding of this concept, see if you can think of behaviors that might be used to validate each of the following attitudes:

- Is very health-conscious
- Supports equality of men and women
- Supports far-right militia groups
- Is concerned about the environment

Joe Ayres and Steve Crosby (1995) were interested in demonstrating the predictive validity of a measure of communication anxiety known as the Personal Report of Communication Apprehension—Employment Interviews (PRCAEI). They found that a participant's score on the PRCAEI correlated negatively with the rank that he or she received by an interviewer in a real job interview context. Specifically, people who scored higher in communication apprehension received lower rankings by the interviewer. The measure predicted future behavior in an expected manner, thereby demonstrating adequate predictive validity.

Sometimes, another valid measure exists for the variable you are seeking to measure—you may have developed an easier or less expensive way to measure the same variable. If your new measure assesses the variable you think it does, then how someone scores on your new measure should correspond to how he or she scores on the established measure. This form of criterion validity is known as concurrent validity. Suppose someone has a questionnaire measure of relationship closeness that involves 50 questions. Although this measure has demonstrated validity, it is long and cumbersome for couples to fill out. You may have developed a single question that you believe measures relationship closeness as well as the longer, more complex measure. If your single question is valid, then couples who are assessed as very close on your measure should also be very close when measured on the 50-question measure. Couples who are low in closeness should score as low on both measures. And so forth.

Let's return to that Sexual Harassment Proclivity Index developed by Bingham and Burleson (1996). The researchers pointed out that there was already a developed measure called the Likelihood of Sexual Harassment (LSH) measure. But they argued that it was cumbersome to administer. They developed the less cumbersome SHPI measure as a new measure. As part of their validation work, they asked people to respond to both the SHPI and the LSH measures. Scores on the two measures were positively correlated, thereby demonstrating that their measure had concurrent validity.

Sometimes, it's difficult to find behavioral criteria that can be taken to validate measures as directly as in our examples. In those instances, however, we can often approximate such criteria by considering how the variable in question ought, theoretically, to relate to other variables. The third kind of validity, **construct validity,** is based on the logical relationships among variables. In particular, two kinds of logical relationships are emphasized. In **convergent construct validity,** a researcher demonstrates that the measure converges, or correlates positively, with measures of theoretically related variables. In **discriminant construct validity,** the measure diverges from, or correlates negatively with, measures of theoretically different variables.

Let's suppose, for example, you want to study marital satisfaction—its sources and consequences. As part of your research, you develop a measure of marital satisfaction, and you want to assess its validity. In addition to developing your measure, you will have also developed certain theoretical expectations about the way the variable *marital satisfaction* relates to other variables. For example, you might reasonably conclude that satisfied husbands and wives will be less likely than dissatisfied ones to cheat on their spouses. If your measure relates to marital fidelity in the expected fashion, that constitutes evidence of your measure's construct validity. If satisfied marriage partners were as likely to cheat on their spouses as the dissatisfied ones, however, that would challenge the validity of your measure.

In addition to demonstrating the concurrent validity of their SHPI measure, Bingham and Burleson (1996) also demonstrated construct validity. How did they do that? With respect to convergent validity, they reasoned that a male who scores high in proclivity for sexual harassment should endorse an adversarial view toward women and accept traditional sex roles. With respect to discriminant validity, they reasoned that a high SHPI scorer should score low on a measure of dating competence. Results largely supported their theoretical arguments.

It's less important that you distinguish these types of validity than that you understand the logic of validation that they have in common: If we have been successful in measuring some variable, then our measures should relate in some logical fashion to other measures.

Who Decides What's Valid?

We began the preceding comments on validity by reminding you that we depend on agreements to determine what's real, and we've just seen some of the ways that communication researchers can agree among themselves that they have made valid measurements. However, there is yet another way of looking at validity.

Communication researchers sometimes criticize themselves and one another for implicitly assuming they are somewhat superior to those they study. Indeed, we often seek to uncover motivations that the social actors themselves are unaware of. You *think* you bought that new Burpo-Blasto because of its high performance and good looks, but *we know* you're really trying to establish a higher social status for yourself.

Although this implicit sense of superiority would fit comfortably with some communication researchers, it clashes with a different approach taken by other researchers. This has led some scholars to argue for another kind of validity known as **representational validity.** This form of validity asks whether a measure's categories are meaningful to the people who are being assessed. Representational validity is employed in many interaction coding measures, where people's communication behaviors are classified by observers into categories. As Marshall Scott Poole and Joseph Folger (1981) have argued, the coding categories should make sense to the people whose interaction is being classified. If, for example, interruption behavior is coded as "domination," then representational validity exists to the extent that the people observed regard all interruptions as instances of domination.

Ultimately, communication researchers should look both to their colleagues and to their research participants as sources of agreement on the most useful meanings and measurements of the concepts they study. Sometimes one source will be more useful, sometimes the other. Neither should be dismissed, however.

Tension between Reliability and Validity

A tension often exists between the criteria of reliability and validity, a trade-off between the two. If you'll recall the example of measuring morale in different factories, you'll see that the strategy of immersing yourself in the day-to-day routine of the assembly line, observing what goes on, and talking to the workers would provide a more *valid* measure of morale than would counting grievances. It just seems obvious that you'd get a clearer sense of whether the morale was high or low.

As we pointed out earlier, however, the counting strategy would be more *reliable*. This situation reflects a more general strain in quantitative research measurement. Most of the really interesting concepts we want to study have many subtle nuances, and it's hard to specify precisely what we mean by them. Researchers sometimes speak of such concepts as having a "richness of meaning." Although scores of books and articles have been written on the topic of romantic love, for example, they still haven't exhausted it.

Very often, then, the specification of reliable operational definitions and measurements seems to rob such concepts of their richness of meaning. After all, morale is much more than a lack of grievances filed with the union; romantic love is much more than a paper-and-pencil measure of it. Yet the more variation and richness we allow for a concept, the more opportunity there is for dis-

agreement on how it applies to a particular situation, thus reducing reliability.

By being forewarned, you'll be effectively forearmed against this persistent and inevitable dilemma. Be prepared for it, and deal with it. If there is no clear agreement on how to measure a concept, measure it several different ways. If the concept has several dimensions, measure them all. Above all, know that the concept does not have any meaning other than what we give it. The only justification for giving any concept a particular meaning is utility. You should measure concepts in ways that help us understand the world around us.

Main Points

- Conceptions are idiosyncratic mental images we use as summary devices for bringing together observations and experiences that seem to have something in common. We use terms or labels to reference these conceptions.

- Concepts are the agreed-on meanings we assign to terms, thereby aiding communication, measurement, and research.

- Our concepts do not exist in the real world, so they can't be measured directly.

- It *is* possible to measure the things that our concepts summarize.

- Conceptualization is the process of specifying the vague mental imagery of our concepts, sorting out the kinds of observations and measurements that will be appropriate for our research.

- The interchangeability of indicators permits us to study and draw conclusions about concepts even when we can't agree on how those concepts should be defined.

- Operationalization is an extension of the conceptualization process.

- In operationalization, we specify concrete empirical procedures that will result in measurements of variables.

- Operationalization is the final specification of how we would recognize the different attributes of a given variable in the real world.

- In determining the range of variation for a variable, we must consider the opposite of the concept. Will it be sufficient to measure communication competence

from "very much" to "none," or should we go past "none" to measure "incompetence" as well?

- Nominal approaches to measurement describe a variable's attributes categorically. Numbers being used nominally have no arithmetic functions associated with them.

- Ordinal measures allow us to rank-order a variable's attributes along some progression from more to less. An example is year in school.

- Interval measures allow us not only to rank-order a variable's attributes but also to quantify the distance that separates them.

- Ratio measures are the same as interval measures except that ratio measures are also based on a true zero point. Age is an example.

- Precision refers to the exactness of the measure used in an observation or description of an attribute. For example, the description of a person as being "six feet, one and three-quarters inches tall" is more precise than "about six feet tall."

- Reliability refers to the likelihood that a given measurement procedure will yield the same description of a given phenomenon if that measurement is repeated. There are several ways that researchers assess reliability: test–retest, alternate forms, internal consistency, using established measures, and intercoder or inter-observer agreement.

- Validity refers to the extent to which a specific measurement provides data that relate to commonly accepted meanings of a particular concept. There are numerous yardsticks for determining validity: content validity (face validity, expert panel validity, and statistical analyses of multidimensionality); criterion validity (predictive and concurrent); construct validity (convergent and discriminant); and representational validity.

❑ The creation of specific, reliable measures often seems to diminish the richness of meaning that our general concepts have. This problem is inevitable. The best solution is to use several different measures, tapping the different aspects of the concept.

Key Terms

conceptualization	item-total reliability
concept	inter-observer agreement
indicators	measurement validity
dimensions	content validity
reification	face validity
operationalization	expert panel validity
nominal-level measurement	criterion validity
ordinal-level measurement	predictive validity
interval-level measurement	concurrent validity
ratio-level measurement	construct validity
measurement reliability	convergent construct validity
test–retest reliability	discriminant construct
alternate-form reliability	validity
split-half reliability	representational validity

Review Questions and Exercises

1. Pick a communication concept such as supportiveness; then specify that concept so that it could be studied in a research project. Be sure to specify the dimensions you wish to include and those you wish to exclude in your conceptualization.

2. Take your selected communication concept from question 1, and brainstorm several possible ways to operationalize it. For example, how could you measure supportiveness, based on your conceptualization of it? Go to the social support research to discover how researchers have measured supportiveness.

3. Go to the social support research to discover how researchers have gone about demonstrating the trustworthiness of their measures of supportiveness. What reliability methods have been used? What validity approaches have been employed?

4. What level of measurement—nominal, ordinal, interval, or ratio—could be used to describe each of the following variables?

   a. Race (African American, Asian, Caucasian, and so forth)

   b. Number of children in families

   c. Attitudes toward nuclear energy (strongly approve, approve, disapprove, strongly disapprove)

   d. Stage of relationship development (dating stage, serious courtship stage, long-term commitment stage)

   e. Market size (the number of people in the viewing audience of a local TV station)

   f. State of residence (Alabama, Alaska, Arkansas, etc.)

   g. Speaker credibility (high, moderate, low)

Continuity Project

Males and females have been socialized to many possible dimensions of communication. List at least five different dimensions, and suggest how you might measure each. It's OK to use different research techniques for measuring the different dimensions.

Additional Readings

Bohrnstedt, G. W. (1983). Measurement. In P. H. Rossi, J. D. Wright, & A. B. Anderson (Eds.), *Handbook of survey research* (pp. 70–121). New York: Academic Press. This essay offers the logical and statistical grounding of reliability and validity in measurement.

Carmines, E. G., & Zeller, R. A. (1979). *Reliability and validity assessment.* Beverly Hills, CA: Sage. In this chapter, we've examined the basic logic of validity and reliability in social science measurement. Carmines and Zeller explore these issues in more detail and examine some of the ways to calculate reliability mathematically.

Emmert, P., & Barker, L. L. (Eds.) (1989). *Measurement of communication behavior.* New York: Longman. A useful volume that addresses key issues in the measurement of communication phenomena.

Gould, J., & Kolb, W. (1964). *A dictionary of the social sciences.* New York: Free Press. A primary reference to the social scientific agreements on various concepts. Although the terms used by social scientists do not have ultimately "true" meanings, this reference book lays out the meanings that social scientists have in mind when they use those terms.

Rubin, R. B., Palmgreen, P., & Sypher, H. E. (1994). *Communication research measures: A sourcebook.* New York: Guilford. A compendium of frequently used measures in communication research, with a focus on questionnaire measures.

Tardy, C. H. (Ed.) (1988). *A handbook for the study of human communication: Methods and instruments for observing, measuring, and assessing communication processes.* Norwood, NJ: Ablex. An excellent volume in which the reader is provided with summaries of the primary ways that communication is measured.

InfoTrac College Edition
http://www.infotrac-college.com/
wadsworth/access.html

Access the latest news and journal articles with Info-Trac College Edition, an easy-to-use online database of reliable, full-length articles from hundreds of top academic journals. Conduct an electronic search using the following search terms:

- inter-coder reliability
- test–retest reliability
- predictive validity
- construct validity
- representational validity
- conceptualization
- operationalization

CHAPTER 7

The Logic of Sampling

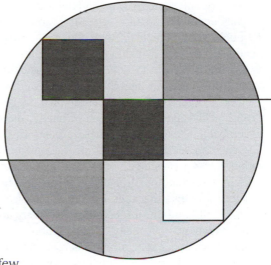

What You'll Learn in This Chapter

Now you'll see how communication researchers can select a few people for study—and discover things that apply to hundreds of millions of people not studied.

INTRODUCTION

The 2000 presidential election was one of the closest in U.S. history. Candidates Al Gore and George W. Bush were virtually tied in the popular vote. Many critics chastised the public opinion polls for their "failure" to predict the election's outcome. Actually, the polls performed as well as they have historically done—they predicted the outcome of the election within their margins of error.

Robert Worcester (in press) assembled the results of various public opinion polls taken within two days of the November 7, 2000, election; these are shown in Table 7-1. You can see that the polls' predictions are largely within 3 to 4 percentage points, the typical margin of error in a national political poll. The prediction of the pollsters was thus that the election was basically "too close to call," and this turned out to be a very accurate statement about an incredibly close election.

Public opinion pollsters have been successfully predicting the results of presidential elections for 50 years, within their margins of error. How can this be done?

How many interviews do you suppose it takes national pollsters to come within 3–4 percentage points of estimating the behavior of about one hundred million voters? Fewer than 2,000! In this chapter, we're going to find out how quantitatively oriented researchers can pull off such wizardry.

Although we've been talking a lot about observation, our discussions have omitted the question of what or who will be observed. When you think about it, you'll see that a communication researcher has a whole world of potential observations. Yet nobody can observe everything. A critical part of communication research, then, is the decision about what to observe and what not. If you want to study voters, for example, which voters should you study? That's the subject of this chapter.

Sampling is the process of selecting observations. After a brief history of social scientific sampling, the key section of this chapter discusses the logic and the skills of probability sampling. As you'll see, probability sampling techniques—involving *random sampling*—allow a researcher to make relatively few observations and generalize from those observations to a much wider population. We'll examine the requirements for generalizability. In the Part 2 introduction, we discussed generalizability in terms of the external validity criterion of trustworthiness.

As you'll discover, random selection is a precise, scientific procedure; there's nothing haphazard about it.

Specific sampling techniques allow us to determine and/or control the likelihood of specific individuals being selected for study. In the simplest example, flipping a coin to choose between two individuals gives each one exactly the same probability of selection—50 percent. Complex techniques also guarantee an equal probability of selection when substantial samples are selected from large populations.

You'll find sampling more rigorous and precise than some topics in this book. Communication research as a whole is both art and science, but probability sampling leans toward science. Because sampling is more "technical," some students find it more difficult than other aspects of research. At the same time, other students say the logical neatness of sampling actually makes it easier for them to comprehend it than, say, conceptualization.

Probability sampling is central to quantitative communication research today, but we'll introduce you to nonprobability sampling methods as well. Although not based on random selection, these methods have their own logic and can provide useful samples for social inquiry. We'll have more to say about nonprobability sampling in Part 3 of the book.

THE HISTORY OF SAMPLING

Sampling in social scientific research has developed hand in hand with political polling. This is the case, no doubt, because political polling is one of the few opportunities that social scientists have to discover the accuracy of their estimates. On election day, they find out how well or how poorly they did.

President Alf Landon

You may have heard about the *Literary Digest* in connection with political polling. The *Digest* was a popular news magazine published between 1890 and 1938 in the United States. In 1920, *Digest* editors mailed postcards to people in six states, asking them whom they were planning to vote for in the presidential campaign between Warren Harding and James Cox. Names were selected for the poll from telephone directories and automobile registration lists. Based on the postcards sent back, the *Digest* correctly predicted that Harding would be elected. In the elections that followed, the *Literary Digest* expanded the size of its poll and made correct predictions in 1924, 1928, and 1932.

TABLE 7-1　**Election Eve Polls Reporting Percentage of Population Voting for U.S. Presidential Candidates, 2000**

	Gore	Bush	Nader	Buchanan*
11/5: Hotline [Polling Co/GSG]	43%	51%	4%	1%
11/5: Marist College	46	51	2	1
11/5: Fox [Opinion Dynamics]	47	47	3	2
11/5: Newsweek [PRSA]	46	49	6	0
11/5: NBC/Wall St. Journal [Hart/Teeter]	45	48	4	2
11/5: Pew	46	49	3	1
11/5: ICR	44	46	7	2
11/5: Harris	47	47	5	1
11/5: Harris (online)	47	47	4	2
11/5: ABC/Washington Post [TNSI]	46	49	3	1
11/6: IDB/CSM [TIPP]	47	49	4	0
11/6: CBS	48	47	4	1
11/6: Portrait of America [Rasmussen]	43	52	4	1
11/6: CNN/USA Today [Gallup]	46	48	4	1
11/6: Reuters/MSNBC [Zogby]	48	46	5	1
11/6: Voter.com [Lake/Goeas]	45	51	4	0
November 7, 2000 Election Results	**48%**	**48%**	**3%**	**1%**

Source: Adapted from Robert Worcester, *WAPOR Newsletter,* Winter 2001 (in press).

* "Don't knows" have been apportioned so that the totals equal 100%. (Rounding error may result in totals of 99% or 101%.)

In 1936, the *Digest* conducted its most ambitious poll: Ten million ballots were sent to people listed in telephone directories and on lists of automobile owners. Over two million responded, giving the Republican contender, Alf Landon, a stunning 57 to 43 percent landslide over the incumbent, President Franklin Roosevelt. As the editors modestly cautioned,

> We make no claim to infallibility. We did not coin the phrase "uncanny accuracy" which has been so freely applied to our Polls. We know only too well the limitations of every straw vote, however enormous the sample gathered, however scientific the method. It would be a miracle if every State of the forty-eight behaved on Election Day exactly as forecast by the Poll. ("Landon," 1936a, p. 6)

Two weeks later, the *Digest* editors knew the limitations of straw polls even better: Voters gave Roosevelt a

second term in office by the largest landslide in history, with 61 percent of the vote. Landon won only 8 electoral votes to Roosevelt's 523. The editors were puzzled by their unfortunate turn of luck.

A part of the problem surely lay in the 22-percent return rate garnered by the poll. As the editors asked,

> Why did only one in five voters in Chicago to whom the *Digest* sent ballots take the trouble to reply? And why was there a preponderance of Republicans in the one-fifth that did reply? . . . We were getting better cooperation in what we have always regarded as a public service from Republicans than we were getting from Democrats. Do Republicans live nearer to mailboxes? Do Democrats generally disapprove of straw polls? ("What Went Wrong," 1936b, p. 7)

A part of the answer to these questions lay in the sampling frame used by the *Digest:* telephone subscribers and automobile owners. Such a design selected a disproportionately wealthy sample, especially coming in the middle of the worst economic depression in the nation's history. The sample effectively excluded poor people, and the poor people predominantly voted for Roosevelt's New Deal recovery program.

President Thomas E. Dewey

The 1936 election also saw the emergence of a young pollster whose name would become synonymous with public opinion. In contrast to the *Literary Digest,* George Gallup correctly predicted that Roosevelt would beat Landon. Gallup's success in 1936 hinged on his use of quota sampling, which we'll have more to say about later in the chapter. For now, you need know only that quota sampling is based on a knowledge of the characteristics of the population being sampled: what proportion are men, what proportion are women, what proportions are of various incomes, ages, and so on. People are selected to match the population characteristics: the right number of poor, white, rural men; the right number of rich, African American, urban women; and so on. The quotas are based on those variables most relevant to the study. By knowing the numbers of people with various incomes in the nation, Gallup selected his sample to ensure the right proportion of respondents at each income level.

Gallup and his American Institute of Public Opinion used quota sampling to good effect in 1936, 1940, and 1944—correctly picking the presidential winner in each of those years. Then, in 1948, Gallup and most political pollsters suffered the embarrassment of picking New York Governor Thomas Dewey over incumbent President Harry Truman. Several factors accounted for the 1948 failure. First, most of the pollsters stopped polling in early October despite a steady trend toward Truman during the campaign. In addition, many voters were undecided throughout the campaign, and they went disproportionately for Truman when they stepped in the voting booth. More important, Gallup's failure rested on the unrepresentativeness of his samples.

Quota sampling—which had been effective in earlier years—was Gallup's undoing in 1948. This technique requires that the researcher know something about the total population (of voters, in this instance). For national political polls, such information came primarily from census data. By 1948, however, World War II had produced a massive movement from country to city, radically changing the character of the U.S. population from what the 1940 census showed, and Gallup relied on 1940 census data. Moreover, city dwellers tended to vote Democratic;

hence, the overrepresentation of rural voters also underestimated the number of Democratic votes.

Two Types of Sampling Methods

In 1948, some academic researchers were experimenting with probability sampling methods. This technique involves the selection of a "random sample" from a list containing the names of everyone in the population you're interested in studying. By and large, the probability sampling methods used in 1948 were far more accurate than quota sampling techniques.

Today, probability sampling remains the primary method for selecting large, representative samples for social science research, such as the political polls described earlier. The bulk of this chapter will be addressed to the logic and techniques of probability sampling.

At the same time, many research situations often make probability sampling impossible or inappropriate. **Nonprobability sampling** techniques are often the most appropriate. We'll begin now with a discussion of some nonprobability sampling techniques used in communication research, and then we'll examine the logic and techniques of **probability sampling** techniques. We'll have more to say about nonprobability sampling in Chapter 13.

NONPROBABILITY SAMPLING

Communication research is often conducted in situations where you can't select the kinds of probability samples used in large-scale social surveys. Suppose that you wanted to study how romantic pairs convey their "coupleness" to others: There is no list of all romantic pairs, nor are you likely to create such a list. Moreover, as you'll see, there are times when probability sampling wouldn't be appropriate even if it were possible. Many such situations call for nonprobability sampling. We'll examine four types in this section: **reliance on available participants, purposive** or **judgmental sampling, snowball sampling,** and **quota sampling.**

Reliance on Available Participants

Convenience sampling relies on available participants, such as stopping people at a street corner or some other location. It is a risky sampling method, although it's used frequently. It's justified only if the researcher wants to study the characteristics of people passing the sampling point at specified times or if less risky sampling methods are not feasible. Even when this method is justified on grounds of feasibility, you must exercise great caution in generalizing from your data. Also, you should alert readers to the risks associated with this method.

University researchers frequently conduct surveys among the students enrolled in large lecture classes. The ease and low expense of such a method explain its popularity, but it is risky to generalize the results to a larger population of students or to people in general.

Purposive or Judgmental Sampling

Sometimes, it's appropriate for you to select your sample on the basis of your own knowledge of the population, its elements, and the nature of your research aims: in short, based on your judgment and the purpose of the study. Especially in the initial design of a questionnaire, you might wish to select the widest variety of respondents to test the broad applicability of questions. Although the study findings would not represent any meaningful population, the test run might effectively uncover any peculiar defects in your questionnaire. However, this situation would be considered a *pilot study* rather than a final study.

For example, one of us recently conducted a study on aesthetic relating—those interaction moments that the participants would describe as "beautiful." Although several theorists had argued that such interaction experiences existed, we conducted a pilot study with a small group of people to see if the concept "rang true" with their own communicative experiences and if our open-ended questionnaire was effective in eliciting descriptions of their aesthetic moments of relating. Only when it was clear from our pilot data that people had such experiences and could write about them in an open-ended survey did we undertake the full study with a much larger group of participants.

In some instances, you may wish to study a small subset of a larger population in which many members of the subset are easily identified but the enumeration of them all would be nearly impossible. For example, Kevin Wright (2000) wanted to examine the ways in which older adults use computer-mediated communication (CMC) for social support. Because he couldn't enumerate a list of all older adults who use CMC, he asked older adults using SeniorNet and other related web sites to complete an online questionnaire on the topic of social support. Although we cannot generalize his findings to all older adults who use CMC, we have some insights into the particular subset of individuals from whom Wright collected data.

Or let's say you want to examine the effects of nega-tive political campaign ads on voter turnout. Because you may not be able to enumerate and sample from all of the districts in which negative campaign ads were used, you might decide to sample voters from one particular district in which negative campaign ads were employed. James Lemert, Wayne Wanta, and Tien-Tsung Lee (1999) used this procedure, sampling voters who had, and had not, voted in a vote-by-mail special congressional election in which negative ads appeared. Although such a sample design would not provide a good description of the effects of negative campaign ads as a whole, it might suffice for general comparative purposes.

Snowball Sampling

Another nonprobability sampling technique, one that some consider to be a form of accidental sampling, is called *snowball sampling*. Snowball sampling is appropriate when the members of a special population are difficult to locate. This procedure is implemented by collecting data on the few members of the target population you can locate and then asking those individuals to provide the information needed to locate other members of that population whom they happen to know. *Snowball* refers to the process of accumulation as each located participant suggests other participants.

For example, one of us once conducted a study of long-term marital couples who decided to renew their marriage vows in some sort of ceremony (Braithwaite & Baxter, 1995). We used flyers in the community to solicit initial participants in our interview study, and we also followed up on announcements of renewal events in the local newspaper. Whenever we interviewed a couple about their marriage renewal, we asked them if they knew other couples who had renewed their vows or were planning to do so. In this way, we were able to broaden our sample.

If you wish to learn, say, the pattern of recruitment to a community organization over time, you might begin by interviewing fairly recent recruits, asking them who introduced them to the group. You might then interview the people named, asking them who introduced *them* to the group. You might then interview those people named, asking, in part, who introduced *them*.

Or, in studying a loosely structured group of volunteers involved in a community project, you might ask one of the participants who he or she believes to be the most influential members of the group. You might interview those people and, in the course of the interviews, ask who *they* believe to be the most influential. In each of these examples, your sample would "snowball" as each of your interviewees suggested others.

Quota Sampling

As you know, quota sampling is the method that helped George Gallup avoid disaster in 1936—and set up the disaster of 1948. Like probability sampling, *quota sampling* addresses the issue of representativeness, although the two methods approach the issue quite differently.

Quota sampling begins with a matrix, or table, describing the characteristics of the target population. You need to know what proportion of the population is male and what proportion is female, for example, and what proportions of each sex fall into various age categories, educational levels, ethnic groups, and so forth. In establishing a national quota sample, you would need to know what proportion of the national population is urban, eastern, male, under 25, white, working class, and all the other permutations of such a matrix.

Once such a matrix has been created and a relative proportion assigned to each cell in the matrix, you collect data from people having all the characteristics of a given cell. All the people in a given cell are then assigned a weight appropriate to their portion of the total population. When all the sample elements are so weighted, the overall data should provide a reasonable representation of the total population.

Quota sampling has several inherent problems. First, the *quota frame* (the proportions that different cells represent) must be accurate, and it is often difficult to get up-to-date information for this purpose. Gallup's failure to predict Truman as the presidential victor in 1948 was due partly to this problem. Second, biases may exist in the selection of sample elements within a given cell—even though its proportion of the population is accurately estimated. Instructed to interview five people who meet a given, complex set of characteristics, an interviewer may still avoid people living at the top of seven-story walkups, having particularly run-down homes, or owning vicious dogs.

In recent years, attempts have been made to combine probability and quota sampling methods, but the effectiveness of this effort remains to be seen. At present, you would be advised to treat quota sampling warily if your purpose is statistical description of a larger population.

At the same time, the *logic* of quota sampling can sometimes be applied usefully to a field research setting. In a study of flight attendants' performance of their roles, for example, Alexandra Murphy (2001) made sure that she interviewed both male and female attendants and attendants who were relatively new at their work as well as seasoned attendants. In general, whenever representativeness is desired, you should use the logic of quota sampling and interview both men and women, young people and old, and so forth.

Let's shift gears now and look at sampling in large-scale surveys, aimed at precise, statistical descriptions of large populations. Sometimes, we want to know the percentage of the population who plan to vote for Candidate X as part of a study on political campaign rhetoric, or we want to know what percentage of the population feel comfortable talking about their health problems with their physicians. These tasks are typically accomplished through the logic and techniques of probability sampling.

THE LOGIC OF PROBABILITY SAMPLING

If all members of a population were identical in all respects—all demographic characteristics, attitudes, experiences, behaviors, and so on—there would be no need for careful sampling procedures. In such a case, any sample would indeed be sufficient. In this extreme case of homogeneity, in fact, one case would suffice to study the characteristics of the whole population.

In fact, of course, the human beings who compose any real population are quite heterogeneous, varying in many ways. Figure 7-1 offers a simplified illustration of a heterogeneous population: The 100 members of this small population differ by sex and race. We'll use this hypothetical micropopulation to illustrate various aspects of sampling throughout the chapter.

To provide useful descriptions of the total population, a sample of individuals from a population must contain essentially the same variations that exist in the population. This isn't as simple as it might seem, however.

Let's take a minute to look at some of the ways researchers might go astray. Then we'll see how probability sampling provides an efficient method for selecting a sample that should adequately reflect variations in the population.

Conscious and Unconscious Sampling Bias

At first glance, it may seem as though sampling is pretty straightforward. To select a sample of 100 university students, you might simply interview the first 100 students you find walking around the campus. This kind of sampling method is often used by untrained researchers, but it has serious problems.

Figure 7-2 illustrates what can happen when you simply select people who are convenient for study. Although

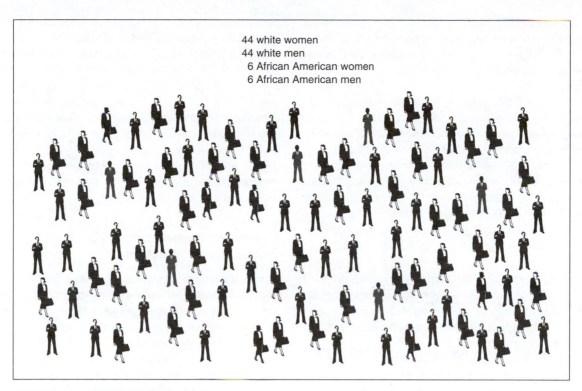

44 white women
44 white men
6 African American women
6 African American men

FIGURE 7-1   **A Population of 100 Folks**

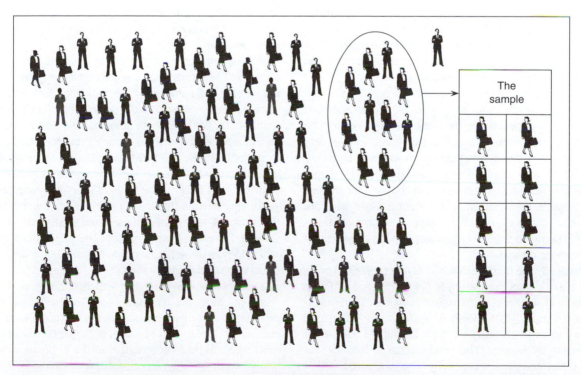

The sample

FIGURE 7-2   **A Sample of Convenience: Easy, but Not Representative**

women are only 50 percent of our micropopulation, those closest to the researcher (in the upper-right corner) happen to be 70-percent women, and although the population is 12-percent black, none were selected for the sample.

Beyond the risks inherent in simply studying people who are convenient, other problems can arise. To begin, your personal leanings may affect the sample to the point where it would not truly represent the student population. Suppose you're a little intimidated by students who look particularly "cool," feeling that they might ridicule your research effort. You might consciously or unconsciously avoid interviewing such people. Or you might feel that the attitudes of "super-straight-looking" students would be irrelevant to your research purposes and so avoid interviewing them.

Even if you sought to interview a "balanced" group of students, you wouldn't know the exact proportions of different types of students making up such a balance, and you wouldn't always be able to identify the different types just by watching them walk by.

And even if you made a conscientious effort to interview every tenth student entering the university library, you could not be sure of a *representative* sample, since different types of students visit the library with different frequencies. Your sample would overrepresent students who visit the library most often.

When we speak of *bias* in connection with sampling, this simply means those selected are not "typical" or "representative" of the larger populations they have been chosen from. This kind of bias is virtually inevitable when you pick people by the seat of your pants.

Similarly, the "public-opinion call-in polls"—in which television or radio stations ask people to call specified telephone numbers to register their opinions—cannot be trusted to represent general populations. At the very least, not everyone in the population will even be aware of the poll. This problem also invalidates polls by magazines and newspapers that publish coupons for readers to complete and mail in. Even among those who are aware of such polls, not all will express an opinion, especially if doing so will cost them a stamp, an envelope, or a telephone charge.

Ironically, the failure of such polls to represent all opinions equally was inadvertently acknowledged by Philip Perinelli (1986), a staff manager of AT&T Communications' DIAL-IT 900 Service, which offers a call-in poll facility to organizations. Perinelli attempted to counter criticisms by saying, "The 50-cent charge assures that only interested parties respond and helps assure also that

no individual 'stuffs' the ballot box." We cannot determine general public opinion while considering "only interested parties." This excludes those who don't care 50-cents' worth, as well as those who recognize that such polls are not valid. Both types of people may have opinions and may even vote on election day. Perinelli's assertion that the 50-cent charge will prevent ballot stuffing actually means that only the prosperous can afford to engage in that practice.

The possibilities for inadvertent sampling bias are endless and not always obvious. Fortunately, there are techniques that help us avoid bias.

Representativeness and Probability of Selection

Although the term **representativeness** has no precise, scientific meaning, it carries a commonsense meaning that makes it useful here. For our purpose, a sample will be representative of the population from which it is selected if the aggregate characteristics of the sample closely approximate those same aggregate characteristics in the population. (Samples need not be representative in all respects; representativeness is limited to those characteristics relevant to the substantive interests of the study, though you may not know which are relevant at first.) For example, if the population contains 50 percent women, then a representative sample would also contain "close to" 50 percent women. Later, we'll discuss "how close" in detail.

A basic principle of probability sampling is that *a sample will be representative of the population from which it is selected if all members of the population have an equal chance of being selected in the sample.* (We'll see shortly that the size of the sample selected also affects the *degree* of representativeness.) Samples that have this quality are often labeled **EPSEM samples** (equal probability of selection method). Later, we'll discuss variations of this principle, which forms the basis of probability sampling.

Moving beyond this basic principle, we must realize that samples—even carefully selected EPSEM samples—seldom if ever *perfectly* represent the populations from which they're drawn. Nevertheless, probability sampling offers two special advantages.

First, probability samples, although never perfectly representative, are typically *more representative* than other types of samples because the biases previously discussed are avoided. In practice, a probability sample is more likely to be representative of the population from which it is drawn than a nonprobability sample is.

Second, and more important, probability theory permits us to estimate the accuracy or representativeness of the sample. Conceivably, an uninformed researcher might, through wholly haphazard means, select a sample that nearly perfectly represents the larger population. However, the odds are against doing so, and we would be unable to estimate the likelihood that he or she has achieved representativeness. The probability sampler, on the other hand, can provide an accurate estimate of success or failure.

Following a brief glossary of sampling terminology, we'll examine the means that the probability sampler uses to estimate the representativeness of the sample.

SAMPLING CONCEPTS AND TERMINOLOGY

The following discussions of sampling theory and practice use many technical terms, which we'll quickly define here. For the most part, we'll employ terms commonly used in sampling and statistical textbooks so that you may better understand those other sources.

In presenting this glossary, we would like to acknowledge a debt to Leslie Kish and his excellent textbook *Survey Sampling*. Although we've modified some of the conventions used by Kish, his presentation is easily the most important source of this discussion.

Element   An *element* is that unit about which information is collected and that provides the basis of analysis. Typically, in survey research, elements are people or certain types of people. However, other kinds of units can constitute the elements for social research: Families, social clubs, television shows, magazine ads, or corporations might be the elements of a study. (*Note:* Elements and units of analysis are often the same in a given study, though the former refers to sample selection and the latter to data analysis.)

Population   A *population* is the theoretically specified aggregation of study elements. Whereas the vague term *Americans* might be the target for a study, the delineation of the population would include the definition of the element *Americans* (for example, citizenship, residence) and the time referent for the study (Americans as of when?). Translating the abstract *adult New Yorkers* into a workable population would require a specification of the age defining *adult* and the boundaries of *New York*. Specifying the term *college student* would include a consideration of full- and part-time students, degree candidates and nondegree candidates, undergraduate and graduate students, and so forth.

Although researchers must begin with careful specification of their population, poetic license usually permits them to phrase their reports in terms of the hypothetical universe. For ease of presentation, even the most conscientious researcher normally speaks of "Americans" rather than "resident citizens of the United States of America as of November 12, 2002." The primary guide in this matter, as in most others, is that you should not mislead or deceive your readers.

Study Population   A *study population* is that aggregation of elements from which the sample is actually selected. As a practical matter, you're seldom in a position to guarantee that every element meeting the theoretical definitions laid down actually has a chance of being selected in the sample. Even where lists of elements exist for sampling purposes, the lists are usually somewhat incomplete. Some students are always omitted, inadvertently, from student rosters. Some telephone subscribers request that their names and numbers be unlisted.

Often, researchers decide to limit their study populations more severely than indicated in the preceding examples. National polling firms may limit their national samples to the 48 adjacent states, omitting Alaska and Hawaii for practical reasons. A researcher wishing to sample communication professors may limit the study population to those in communication departments, omitting those in other departments. (In a sense, we might say that these researchers have redefined their universes and populations, in which case they must make the revisions clear to their readers.)

Sampling Unit   A *sampling unit* is that element or set of elements considered for selection in some stage of sampling. In a simple single-stage sample, the sampling units are the same as the elements and are probably the units of analysis. In more complex samples, however, different levels of sampling units may be employed. For example, you might select a sample of census blocks in a city, then select a sample of households on the selected blocks, and finally select a sample of adults from the selected households. The sampling units for these three stages of sampling are, respectively, census blocks, households, and adults, of which only the last of these are the elements. More specifically, the phrases *primary sampling units, secondary sampling units,* and *final sampling units* designate the successive stages.

Sampling Frame A *sampling frame* is the actual list of sampling units from which the sample, or some stage of the sample, is selected. In single-stage sampling designs, the sampling frame is simply a list of the study population, defined earlier. If a simple sample of students is selected from a student roster, the roster is the sampling frame. If the primary sampling unit for a complex population sample is the census block, the list of census blocks composes the sampling frame—in the form of a printed booklet, a magnetic tape file, or some other computerized record.

In a single-stage sample design, the sampling frame is a list of the elements composing the study population. In practice, existing sampling frames often define the study population rather than the other way around. We often begin with a population in mind for our study; then we search for possible sampling frames. The frames available for our use are examined and evaluated, and we decide which frame presents a study population most appropriate to our needs.

Although the relationship between populations and sampling frames is critical, it has not received sufficient attention. A later section will pursue this issue in greater detail.

Observation Unit An *observation unit,* or unit of data collection, is an element or aggregation of elements from which information is collected. Again, the unit of analysis and unit of observation are often the same—for example, the individual person—but this need not be the case. Thus, the researcher may interview heads of households (the observation units) to collect information about all members of the households (the units of analysis).

Our task is simplified when the unit of analysis and the observation unit are the same. Often, this isn't possible or feasible, however, and in such situations we need to exercise some ingenuity in collecting data relevant to our units of analysis without actually observing those units.

Variable As discussed earlier, a *variable* is a set of mutually exclusive attributes: sex, age, employment status, and so forth. The elements of a given population may be described in terms of their individual attributes on a given variable. Often, quantitative communication research aims at describing the distribution of attributes composing a variable in a population. Thus, a researcher may describe the age distribution of a population by examining the relative frequency of different ages among members of the population.

A variable, by definition, must possess *variation;* if all elements in the population have the same attribute, that attribute is a *constant* in the population rather than part of a variable.

Parameter A *parameter* is the summary description of a given variable in a population. The mean income of all families in a city and the age distribution of the city's population are parameters. An important portion of quantitative communication research involves the estimation of population parameters on the basis of sample observations.

Statistic A *statistic* is the summary description of a given variable in a sample. Thus, the mean income computed from a sample and the age distribution of that sample are statistics. Sample statistics are used to make estimates of population parameters.

Sampling Error Probability sampling methods seldom, if ever, provide statistics exactly equal to the parameters they are to estimate. However, probability theory permits us to estimate the degree of error to be expected for a given sample design. **Sampling error** is discussed in more detail later.

Confidence Levels and Confidence Intervals The two key components of sampling error estimates are *confidence levels* and *confidence intervals.* We express the accuracy of our sample statistics in terms of a level of confidence that the statistics fall within a specified interval from the parameter. For example, we may say we are 95-percent confident that our sample statistics (for example, 50 percent favor Candidate X) are within plus or minus 5 percentage points of the population parameter. As the confidence interval is expanded for a given statistic, our confidence increases, and we may say we are 99.9-percent confident that our statistic falls within 7.5 percentage points of the parameter. In the next section, we'll describe how sampling intervals and levels are calculated, making these two concepts even clearer.

PROBABILITY SAMPLING THEORY AND SAMPLING DISTRIBUTION

With definitions presented, we can now examine the basic theory of probability sampling as it applies to quantitative communication research. We'll also consider the logic of sampling distribution and sampling error with

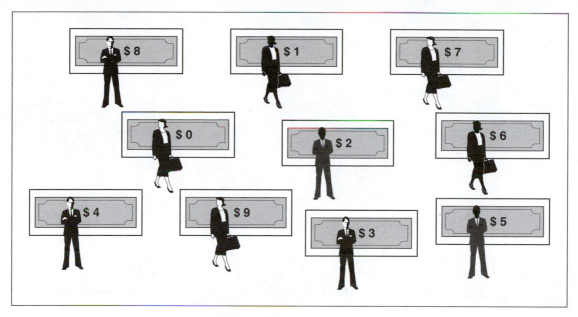

FIGURE 7-3   **A Population of Ten People with $0–$9**

regard to a *binomial variable*—a variable composed of two attributes.

Probability Sampling Theory

The ultimate purpose of sampling is to select a set of elements from a population in such a way that descriptions of those elements (statistics) accurately portray the parameters of the total population from which the elements are selected. Probability sampling enhances the likelihood of accomplishing this aim and also provides methods for estimating the degree of probable success.

Random selection is the key to this process. In random selection, each element has an equal chance of selection independent of any other event in the selection process. Flipping a perfect coin is the most frequently cited example: The "selection" of a head or a tail is independent of previous selections of heads or tails. Rolling a perfect set of dice is another example. Such images of random selection seldom apply directly to social scientific research sampling methods, however. The researcher more typically uses tables of random numbers or computer programs that provide a random selection of sampling units. Later in this chapter, we'll see how computers are used to select random telephone numbers for interviewing—called *random-digit dialing*.

The reasons for using random selection methods—random-number tables or computer programs—are two-

fold. First, this procedure serves as a check on conscious or unconscious bias on the part of the researcher. The researcher who selects cases on an intuitive basis might very well select cases that would support his or her research expectations or hypotheses. Random selection erases this danger. More important, random selection offers access to the body of probability theory, which provides the basis for estimates of population parameters and estimates of error. Let's now examine this probability theory in greater detail.

The Sampling Distribution of Ten Cases

To introduce the statistics of probability sampling, let's begin with a simple example of only ten cases.* Suppose there are ten people in a group, and each has a certain amount of money in his or her pocket. To simplify, let's assume that one person has no money, another has one dollar, another has two dollars, and so forth up to the person with nine dollars. Figure 7-3 presents the population of ten people.

Our task is to determine the average amount of money one person has: specifically, the mean number of dollars. If you simply add up the money shown in Figure 7-3, you'll find that the total is $45, so the mean is $4.50. Our

---

*We want to thank Hanan Selvin for suggesting this method of introducing probability sampling.

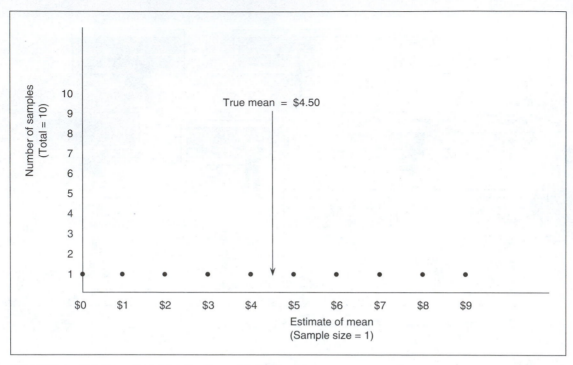

FIGURE 7-4   **The Sampling Distribution of Samples of 1**

purpose in the rest of this exercise is to estimate that mean without actually observing all ten individuals. We'll do that by selecting random samples from the population and using the means of those samples to estimate the mean of the whole population.

To start, suppose we were to select—at random—a sample of only *one* person from the ten. Depending on which person we selected, we'd estimate the group's mean as anywhere from $0 to $9. Figure 7-3 displays the ten possible samples.

The ten dots shown on the graph in Figure 7-4 represent the ten "sample" means we would get as estimates of the population. The distribution of the dots on the graph is called the *sampling distribution*. Obviously, it wouldn't be a very good idea to select a sample of only one, since we would stand a very good chance of missing the true mean of $4.50 by quite a bit.

But what if we take samples of two each? As you can see from Figure 7-5, increasing the sample size improves our estimations. There are now 45 possible samples: [$0 $1], [$0 $2], . . . [$7 $8], [$8 $9]. Moreover, some of those samples produce the same means. For example, [$0 $6], [$1 $5], and [$2 $4] all produce means of $3. In Figure 7-5, the three dots shown above the $3 mean represent those three samples.

The 45 sample means are not evenly distributed, as you can see. Rather, they are somewhat clustered around the true value of $4.50. Only two samples deviate by as much as four dollars from the true value ([$0 $1] and [$8 $9]), whereas five of the samples would give the true estimate of $4.50; another eight samples miss the mark by only 50 cents (plus or minus).

Now suppose we select even larger samples. What do you suppose that will do to our estimates of the mean? Figure 7-6 presents the sampling distributions of samples of 3, 4, 5, and 6.

The progression of sampling distributions is clear. Every increase in sample size improves the distribution of estimates of the mean. The limiting case in this procedure, of course, is to select a sample of ten. There would be only one possible sample (everyone), and it would give us the true mean of $4.50.

Binomial Sampling Distribution

Let's turn now to a more realistic sampling situation and see how the notion of sampling distribution applies, using a simple example involving a population much larger than ten. Let's assume for the moment that we wish to study the student population of State University (SU) to

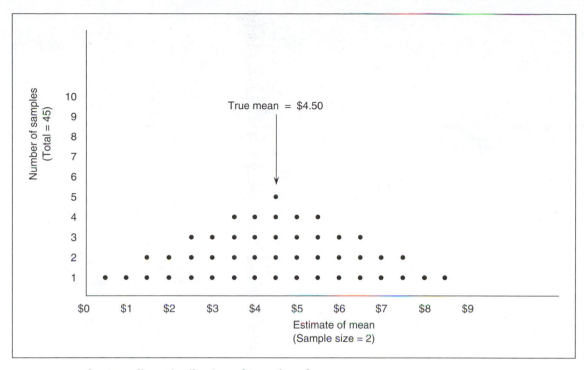

FIGURE 7-5   **The Sampling Distribution of Samples of 2**

determine approval or disapproval of a proposed computer literacy graduation requirement. The study population will be that aggregation of, say, 20,000 students contained in a student roster: the sampling frame. The elements will be the individual students at SU. The variable under consideration will be *attitudes toward the proposed requirement,* a binomial variable: *approve* and *disapprove.* We'll select a random sample of, say, 100 students for the purposes of estimating the entire student body.

The horizontal axis of Figure 7-7 presents all *possible* values of this parameter in the population—from 0-percent to 100-percent approval. The midpoint of the axis—50 percent—represents half the students approving of the proposed requirement and the other half disapproving.

To choose our sample, we give each student on the student roster a number and select 100 random numbers from a table of random numbers. Then we interview the 100 students whose numbers have been selected and ask for their attitudes toward the proposed requirement: whether they approve or disapprove. Suppose this operation gives us 48 students who approve of the requirement and 52 who disapprove. We present this statistic by placing a dot on the *x* axis at the point representing 48 percent.

Now let's suppose we select another sample of 100 students in exactly the same fashion and measure their approval or disapproval of the requirement. Perhaps 51 students in the second sample approve of the requirement. We place another dot in the appropriate place on the *x* axis. Repeating this process once more, we may discover that 52 students in the third sample approve of the proposed requirement.

Figure 7-8 presents the three different sample statistics representing the percentages of students in each of the three random samples who approved of the proposed requirement. The basic rule of random sampling is that such samples drawn from a population give estimates of the parameter that pertains in the total population. Each of the random samples, then, gives us an estimate of the percentage of students in the total student body who approve of the computer literacy requirement. Unhappily, however, we have selected three samples and now have three separate estimates.

To retrieve ourselves from this problem, let's draw more and more samples of 100 students each, question each of the samples concerning their approval or disapproval of the requirement, and plot the new sample statistics on our summary graph. In drawing many such samples, we discover that some of the new samples

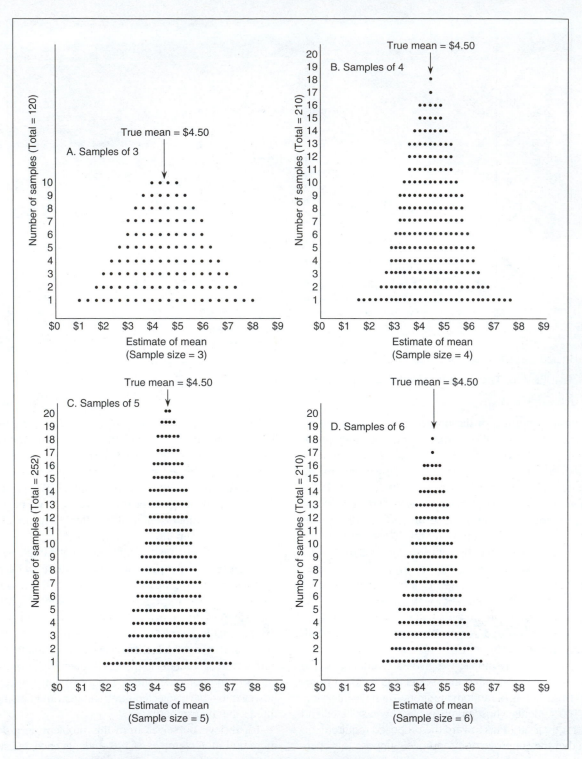

FIGURE 7-6 **The Sampling Distribution of Samples of 3, 4, 5, and 6**

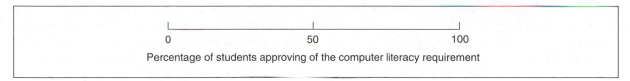

FIGURE 7-7   **Range of Possible Sample Study Results**

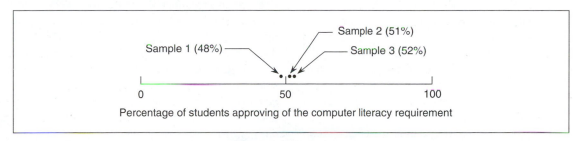

FIGURE 7-8   **Results Produced by Three Hypothetical Studies**

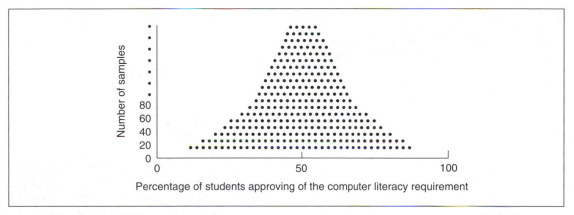

FIGURE 7-9   **The Sampling Distribution**

provide duplicate estimates, as in the illustration of ten cases. Figure 7-9 shows the sampling distribution of, say, hundreds of samples. This is often referred to as a *normal curve*.

Note that by increasing the number of samples selected and interviewed, we have also increased the range of estimates provided by the sampling operation. In one sense, we have increased our dilemma in attempting to guess the parameter in the population. However, probability theory provides certain important rules regarding the sampling distribution presented in Figure 7-9.

First, if many independent random samples are selected from a population, the sample statistics provided by those samples will be *distributed around the population parameter* in a known way. Thus, although Figure 7-9 shows a wide range of estimates, more of them are in the vicinity of 50 percent than elsewhere in the graph. Probability theory tells us, then, that the true value is in the vicinity of 50 percent.

Second, probability theory gives us a formula for estimating *how closely* the sample statistics are clustered around the true value. This formula contains three factors: the parameter, the sample size, and the *standard error* (a measure of sampling error):

$$s = \sqrt{\frac{P \times Q}{n}}$$

The symbols P and Q in the formula equal the population parameters for the binomial: If 60 percent of the student body approve of the code and 40 percent disapprove, P and Q are 60 percent and 40 percent, respectively, or .6 and .4. Note that $Q = (1 - P)$ and $P = (1 - Q)$.

The symbol n equals the number of cases in each sample, and s is the standard error.

Let's assume that the population parameter in the student example is 50 percent approving of the computer literacy requirement and 50 percent disapproving. Recall that we've been selecting samples of 100 cases each. When these numbers are put into the formula, we find that the standard error equals .05, or 5 percent.

In probability theory, the standard error is a valuable piece of information because it indicates the extent to which the sample estimates will be distributed around the population parameter. If you are familiar with the *standard deviation* in statistics, you may recognize that the standard error, in this case, is the standard deviation of the sampling distribution.

Specifically, probability theory indicates that certain proportions of the sample estimates will fall within specified increments—each equal to one standard error—from the population parameter. Approximately 34 percent (.3413) of the sample estimates will fall within one standard error increment above the population parameter, and another 34 percent will fall within one standard error below the parameter. In our example, the standard error increment is 5 percent, so we know that 34 percent of our samples will give estimates of student approval between 50 percent (the parameter) and 55 percent (one standard error above); another 34 percent of the samples will give estimates between 50 percent and 45 percent (one standard error below). Taken together, then, we know that roughly two-thirds (68 percent) of the samples will give estimates within plus or minus 5 percent of the parameter.

Moreover, probability theory dictates that roughly 95 percent of the samples will fall within plus or minus two standard errors of the true value, and 99.9 percent of the samples will fall within plus or minus three standard errors. In our present example, then, we know that only one sample out of a thousand would give an estimate lower than 35 percent approval or higher than 65 percent.

The proportion of samples falling within one, two, or three standard errors of the parameter is constant for any random sampling procedure such as the one just described, providing that a large number of samples are selected. However, the size of the standard error in any given case is a function of the population parameter and the sample size. If we return to the formula for a moment, we note that the standard error will increase as a function of an increase in the quantity P times Q. Note further that this quantity reaches its maximum in the situation of an even split in the population. If $P = .5$, $PQ = .25$; if

$P = .6$, $PQ = .24$; if $P = .8$, $PQ = .16$; if $P = .99$, $PQ = .0099$. By extension, if P is either 0.0 or 1.0 (either 0 percent or 100 percent approve of the computer literacy requirement), the standard error will be 0. If everyone in the population has the same attitude (no variation), then every sample will give exactly that estimate.

The standard error is also a function of the sample size—an *inverse* function. As the sample size increases, the standard error decreases. As the sample size increases, the several samples will be clustered nearer to the true value. Another general guideline is evident in the formula: Because of the square root formula, the standard error is reduced by half if the sample size is *quadrupled*. In our present example, samples of 100 produce a standard error of 5 percent; to reduce the standard error to 2.5 percent, we must increase the sample size to 400.

All of this information is provided by established probability theory in reference to the selection of large numbers of random samples. (If you've taken a statistics course, you may know this as the "Central Tendency Theorem.") If the population parameter is known and many random samples are selected, we can predict how many of the samples will fall within specified intervals from the parameter.

Be aware that this discussion illustrates only the *logic* of probability sampling; it does not describe the way research is actually conducted. Usually, we don't know the parameter: We conduct a sample survey to estimate that value. Moreover, we don't actually select large numbers of samples: We select only one sample. Nevertheless, the preceding discussion of probability theory provides the basis for inferences about the typical research situation. Knowing what it would be like to select thousands of samples allows us to make assumptions about the one sample we do select and study.

Whereas probability theory specifies that 68 percent of that fictitious large number of samples would produce estimates falling within one standard error of the parameter, we turn the logic around and infer that any single random sample has a 68-percent chance of falling within that range. In this regard, we speak of *confidence levels:* We are 68-percent confident that our sample estimate is within one standard error of the parameter. Or we may say that we are 95-percent confident that the sample statistic is within two standard errors of the parameter, and so forth. Quite reasonably, our confidence increases as the margin for error is extended. We are virtually positive (99.9 percent) that we are within three standard errors of the true value.

Although we may be confident (at some level) of being within a certain range of the parameter, we've already noted that we seldom know what the parameter is. To resolve this problem, we substitute our sample estimate for the parameter in the formula; that is, lacking the true value, we substitute the best available guess.

The result of these inferences and estimations is that we can estimate a population parameter and also the expected degree of error on the basis of one sample drawn from a population. Beginning with the question "What percentage of the student body approves of the proposed computer literacy requirement?" you could select a random sample of 100 students and interview them. You might then report that your best estimate is that 50 percent of the student body approve of the requirement and that you are 95-percent confident that between 40 and 60 percent (plus or minus two standard errors) approve. The range from 40 to 60 percent is called the *confidence interval.* (At the 68-percent confidence level, the confidence interval would be 45–55 percent.)

The logic of confidence levels and confidence intervals also provides the basis for determining the appropriate sample size for a study. Once you've decided on the degree of sampling error you can tolerate, you'll be able to calculate the number of cases needed in your sample. Thus, for example, if you want to be 95-percent confident that your study findings are accurate within plus or minus 5 percentage points of the population parameters, you should select a sample of at least 400. (Appendix F is a convenient guide in this regard.)

This, then, is the basic logic of probability sampling. Random selection permits the researcher to link findings from a sample to the body of probability theory in order to estimate the accuracy of those findings. All statements of accuracy in sampling must specify both a confidence level and a confidence interval. The researcher must report that he or she is *x*-percent confident that the population parameter is between two specific values.

Here's how George Gallup (1984, p. 7) described his sampling error in a newspaper report of a Gallup Poll regarding attitudes of children and parents:

> The adult findings are based on in-person interviews with 1520 adults, 18 and older, conducted in more than 300 scientifically selected localities across the nation during the period October 26–29. For results based on samples of this size, one can say with 95 percent confidence that the error attributable to sampling and other random effects could be three percentage points in either direction.

Or hear what the *New York Times* ("How the Poll Was Conducted," 1995, p. 15) had to say about a poll it conducted:

> In theory, in 19 cases out of 20 the results based on such samples will differ by no more than three percentage points in either direction, from what would have been obtained by seeking out all American adults.

The next time you read statements like these in the newspaper, they should make more sense to you. However, be aware that such statements are sometimes made when they are not warranted, but you can now make that determination. The box "How to Interpret a Public Opinion Poll Reported in the News" elaborates on this point.

The foregoing discussion has considered only one type of statistic: the percentages produced by a *binomial* or dichotomous variable. However, the same logic would apply to the examination of other statistics, such as the mean number of hours of television viewing per week. Because the computations are somewhat more complicated in such a case, we've chosen to consider only binomials in this introduction.

You should be cautioned that the survey uses of probability theory as discussed previously are technically not wholly justified. The theory of sampling distribution makes assumptions that almost never apply in research conditions. The number of samples contained within specified increments of standard errors, for example, assumes an infinitely large population, an infinite number of samples, and sampling with replacement. Moreover, the inferential jump from the distribution of several samples to the probable characteristics of one sample has been grossly oversimplified here.

These cautions are offered to give you perspective. Researchers often appear to overestimate the precision of estimates produced by using probability theory in connection with quantitative research. As we'll mention elsewhere in this chapter, variations in sampling techniques and nonsampling factors may further reduce the legitimacy of such estimates. Nevertheless, the calculations discussed in this section can be extremely valuable to you in understanding and evaluating your data. Although the calculations do not provide as precise estimates as some researchers might assume, they can be quite valid for practical purposes. Most important, you should be familiar with the basic *logic* underlying the calculations. Thus informed, you'll be able to react sensibly to your own data and to those reported by others.

HOW TO INTERPRET A PUBLIC OPINION POLL REPORTED IN THE NEWS

It is difficult to listen to a news broadcast or to read a newspaper these days without encountering a public opinion poll that is regarded as newsworthy. As you decide whether or not the results of the poll should be believed, here are some basic questions to keep in mind:

1. **Was the sample of respondents selected through probability sampling methods?** Probability sampling always works with a sampling error, and this should always be reported, because it provides you with information about the confidence interval for the poll's results. This sampling error informs you about how many percentage points equal a sampling error. Without probability sampling, you have no estimate of the poll's accuracy, and the representativeness of the sample is suspect. But representativeness of what population group? What is the population that the poll is supposed to represent?

2. **What is the confidence level used in reporting the poll's confidence interval?** The norm is for a confidence interval to be based on the 95-percent confidence level. What this means is that the pollster is 95-percent confident that the sample statistics (for example, 48 percent of voters favor candidate X) are within plus or minus 1.96 sampling errors of the true population parameter (for example, the actual percentage who favor candidate X if we were able to ask all voters). Sometimes, news reporting tells you about something called a margin of error, which may be the 95-percent confidence interval of plus or minus 1.96 sampling errors. When you are given information about "plus or minus Y percentage points," make sure you know the confidence level associated with this error margin.

3. **Are any breakout analyses reported?** Often, the reporting of polls provides results for subgroups of the sample. For example, in addition to being told that 48 percent of sampled persons favor candidate X, the news reporter might tell you about the percentage of males and the percentage of females who favor candidate X, or the percentage of older adult voters as opposed to younger adult voters who favor candidate X. These breakout analyses can shed important insight into systematic variations in opinion in a sample, but as a reader, you need to be especially cautious in interpreting such results. Remember that sampling error is inversely related to sample size. When sampling errors are reported, they are generally based on the entire sample of 500 or 1,200 people, or however many people were included in the whole sample. But when breakout analyses are provided, they are based on much smaller subgroups. For example, if we have a sample of 1,000 with a sampling error of plus or minus 3 percentage points, then any statement about the male subsample might have a larger sampling error because the number of males is less than 1,000 (probably it would be around 500 if males and females were equally represented in the sample). However, offsetting the problem of a smaller size is the possibility that the breakout group will have greater homogeneity. Ask yourself whether the reporter provides you with the sampling error information relevant to each subgroup analysis.

4. **Was there any bias in the questions posed to respondents?** In addition to questions 1 through 3, which are based on sampling issues, we face the matter of measurement reliability and validity. We'll spend a lot of time in Chapter 8 talking about what makes a good question, but we want to highlight this question here as part of the general process of evaluating the reporting of a public opinion poll.

POPULATIONS AND SAMPLING FRAMES

The preceding section deals with the theoretical model for quantitative research sampling. Although the research consumer, student, and researcher need to understand that theory, it is no less important that they appreciate the less-than-perfect conditions that exist in the field. The present section discusses one aspect of field conditions that requires a compromise with regard to theoretical conditions and assumptions. Here we'll consider the congruence of or disparity between populations of sampling frames.

Simply put, a sampling frame is the list or quasi-list of elements from which a probability sample is selected. Here are some reports of sampling frames appearing in some communication research journals:

Telephone interviews were conducted with a sample of adult residents (N = 559) of Columbus, Ohio (Franklin County). . . . In order to insure a representative sample of the population, respondents were selected by means of a systematic probability sample. Telephone call sheets were generated from the telephone directory for Franklin County using a computerized sampling procedure. A phone number is chosen by randomly selecting a page, a column, and a number on the page. The exchange and the first two digits (working block) of the telephone number is recorded (e.g., 442-01). Finally, a two-digit randomly generated suffix is added to the stem to produce the sampled telephone number (e.g., 442-0129). In this way, all telephone numbers, including unlisted numbers, in the specified geographical location are given an equal chance of inclusion in the sample. (Dimmick, Patterson, & Sikand, 1996, p. 51)

Counseling psychologists from a large, Southwestern city served as participants for this study. Therapists who worked with couples (as opposed to those who worked with children, or who only conducted individual therapy) were identified using a local telephone directory. Sixty counselors were randomly selected from the directory, telephoned, and asked if they were willing to be interviewed. Those who gave their consent served as participants. Of the therapists telephoned, one declined to participate, one had a disconnected phone number, and eight failed to return messages left by the researcher. The final group of respondents, therefore consisted of 50 counselors. (Vangelisti, 1994, p. 111)

The hypothesized model was tested with data gathered from nurses employed at an acute care medical/surgical hospital in a medium-sized city in the midwest. This hospital is a 529-bed, not for profit acute care facility and referral center, serving a 13 county area. The hospital consists of 25 patient care units and employs 3,500 staff members and 400 physicians. The single largest employee group at the hospital is the 1,356 part-time and full-time registered nurses and licensed practical nurses. . . . From a list of all nurses employed at the hospital, 100 names were randomly selected for possible inclusion in the focus groups. (Ellis & Miller, 1993, p. 333)

Properly drawn samples provide information appropriate for describing the population of elements composing the sampling frame—nothing more. We emphasize this point in view of the all-too-common tendency for researchers to select samples from a given sampling frame and then make assertions about a population similar to, but not identical to, the population defined by the sampling frame. For example, take a look at this report, which discusses the drugs most frequently prescribed by U.S. physicians:

Information on prescription drug sales is not easy to obtain. But Rinaldo V. DeNuzzo, a professor of pharmacy at the Albany College of Pharmacy, Union University, Albany, NY, has been tracking prescription drug sales for 25 years by polling nearby drugstores. He publishes the results in an industry trade magazine, MM&M.

DeNuzzo's latest survey, covering 1980, is based on reports from 66 pharmacies in 48 communities in New York and New Jersey. Unless there is something peculiar about that part of the country, his findings can be taken as representative of what happens across the country. (Moskowitz, 1981, p. 33)

The main thing that should strike you is the casual comment about whether there is anything peculiar about New York and New Jersey. There is. The lifestyle in these two states hardly typifies the other 48. We cannot assume that residents in these large, urbanized, eastern seaboard states necessarily have the same drug-use patterns as residents of Mississippi, Nebraska, or Vermont.

Does the survey even represent prescription patterns in New York and New Jersey? To determine that, we would have to know something about the way the 48 communities and the 66 pharmacies were selected. We should be wary in this regard, in view of the reference to "polling nearby drugstores." As we'll see, several methods for selecting samples ensure representativeness, and unless they're used, we shouldn't generalize from the study findings.

Studies of organizations are often the simplest from a sampling standpoint because organizations typically have membership lists. In such cases, the list of members constitutes an excellent sampling frame. If a random sample is selected from a membership list, the data collected from that sample may be taken as representative of all members—if all members are included in the list.

Populations that can be sampled from good organizational lists include elementary school, high school, and university students and faculty; church members; factory workers; fraternity or sorority members; members of social, service, or political clubs; and members of professional associations.

The preceding comments apply primarily to local organizations. Often, statewide or national organizations do not have a single membership list. For example, there is no single list of communication studies majors in the United States. However, a slightly more complex sample design could take advantage of universities' membership lists of declared communication studies majors by first sampling universities and then subsampling the declared-major membership lists of those universities selected.

Other lists of individuals may be especially relevant to the research needs of a particular study. Government agencies maintain lists of registered voters, for example, that might be used if you wanted to conduct a pre-election poll or an in-depth examination of voting behavior—but you would have to ensure that the list is up to date. Similar lists contain the names of automobile owners, welfare recipients, taxpayers, business permit holders, licensed professionals, and so forth. Although it may be difficult to gain access to some of these lists, they provide excellent sampling frames for specialized research purposes.

Realizing that the sampling elements in a study need not be individual persons, we may note that lists of other types of elements are also available: universities, businesses of various types, cities, academic journals, newspapers, unions, political clubs, professional associations, and so forth.

Telephone directories are frequently used for "quick and dirty" public opinion polls. Undeniably, they're easy and inexpensive to use—no doubt the reason for their popularity. And if you want to make assertions about telephone subscribers, the directory is a fairly good sampling frame. (Realize, of course, that a given directory will not include new subscribers or those who have requested unlisted numbers. Sampling is further complicated by the directories' inclusion of nonresidential listings.) Unfortunately, telephone directories are all too often used as a listing of a city's population or of its voters. Of the many defects in this reasoning, the chief one involves a social-class bias. Poor people are less likely to have telephones; rich people may have more than one line. Therefore, a telephone directory sample is likely to have a middle- or upper-class bias.

The class bias inherent in telephone directory samples is often hidden. Pre-election polls conducted in this fashion are sometimes quite accurate, perhaps because of the class bias evident in voting itself: Poor people are less likely to vote. Frequently, then, these two biases nearly coincide so that the results of a telephone poll may come very close to the final election outcome. Unhappily, you never know for sure until after the election. And sometimes, as in the case of the 1936 *Literary Digest* poll, you may discover that the voters have not acted according to their expected class biases. The ultimate disadvantage of this method, then, is the researcher's inability to estimate the degree of error to be expected in the sample findings. Street directories and tax maps are often used for easy samples of households, but they may also suffer from incompleteness and possible bias. For example, in strictly zoned urban regions, illegal housing units are unlikely to appear on official records. As a result, such units could not be selected, and sample findings could not be representative of those units, which are often poorer and more overcrowded than the average.

Though most of these comments apply to the United States, the situation is different in some other countries. In Japan, for example, the government maintains quite accurate population registration lists. Moreover, citizens are required by law to keep their information up to date, such as changes in residence or births and deaths in the household. As a consequence, you can select simple random samples of the Japanese population more easily. Such a registration list in the United States would conflict directly with this country's norms regarding individual privacy.

TYPES OF SAMPLING DESIGNS

Up to this point, we've focused on **simple random sampling** (SRS). And, indeed, the body of statistics typically used by communication researchers assumes such a sample. As you'll see shortly, however, you have several options in choosing your sampling method, and you'll seldom if ever choose simple random sampling. There are two reasons for this. First, with all but the simplest sampling frame, simple random sampling is not feasible. Second, and probably surprisingly, simple random sampling may not be the most accurate method available. Let's turn now to a discussion of simple random sampling and the other options available.

Simple Random Sampling

As noted, simple random sampling is the basic sampling method assumed in the statistical computations of quantitative communication research. Because the mathematics of random sampling are especially complex, we'll detour around them in favor of describing the ways of employing this method in the field.

Once a sampling frame has been properly established, to use simple random sampling the researcher assigns a single number to each element in the list, not skipping any number in the process. A table of random numbers (see Appendix G) is then used to select elements for the sample. The box titled "Using a Table of Random Numbers" explains its use.

If your sampling frame is in a machine-readable form, such as computer disk or magnetic tape, a simple random sample can be selected automatically by computer. (In effect, the computer program numbers the elements in the sampling frame, generates its own series of random numbers, and prints out the list of elements selected.)

Figure 7-10 offers a graphic illustration of simple random sampling. Note that the members of our hypothetical micropopulation have been numbered from 1 to 100. Moving to Appendix G, we decide to use the last two digits of the first column and to begin with the third number from the top. This yields person number 30 as the first one selected into the sample. Number 67 is next, and so forth. (Person 100 would have been selected if "00" had come up in the list.)

Pamela Kalbfleisch and Andrea Davies (1993) employed simple random sampling in their study of the communication variables that predict participation in a mentor–protégé relationship in a university setting. On the assumption that a faculty member could be either a mentor or a protégé, the researchers drew a random sample from all of the faculty members listed at

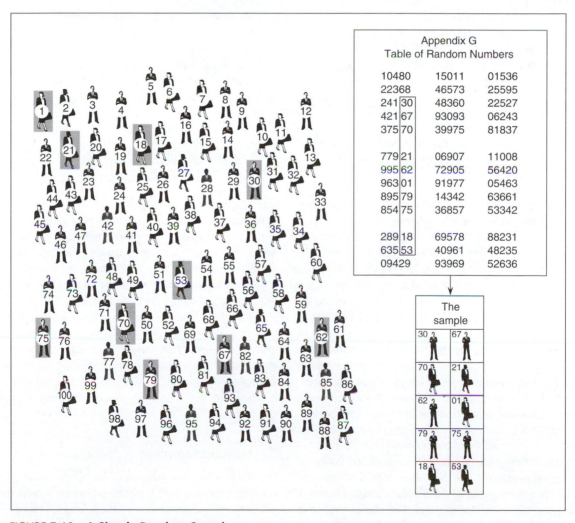

FIGURE 7-10   **A Simple Random Sample**

USING A TABLE OF RANDOM NUMBERS

In communication research, it's often appropriate to select a set of random numbers from a table such as the one in Appendix G. Here's how to do it.

Suppose you want to select a simple random sample of 100 people (or other units) out of a population totaling 980.

1. To begin, number the members of the population: in this case, from 1 to 980. Now the problem is to select 100 random numbers. Once you've done that, your sample will consist of the people having the numbers you've selected. (*Note:* It's not essential to actually number them, as long as you're sure of the total. If you have them in a list, for example, you can always count through the list after you've selected the numbers.)

2. The next step is to determine the number of digits you'll need in the random numbers you select. In our example, there are 980 members of the population, so you'll need three-digit numbers to give everyone a chance of selection. (If there were 11,825 members of the population, you'd need to select five-digit num-

bers.) Thus, we want to select 100 random numbers in the range from 001 to 980.

3. Now turn to the first page of Appendix G. Notice there are several rows and columns of five-digit numbers, and there are several pages. The table represents a series of random numbers in the range from 00001 to 99999. To use the table for your hypothetical sample, you have to answer these questions:
    a. How will you create three-digit numbers out of five-digit numbers?
    b. What pattern will you follow in moving through the table to select your numbers?
    c. Where will you start?
    Each of these questions has several satisfactory answers. The key is to create a plan and follow it. Here's an example.

4. To create three-digit numbers from five-digit numbers, let's agree to select five-digit numbers from the table but consider only the left-most three digits in each case. If we picked the first number on the first page—10480—we would only consider the 104. (We could agree to take the digits furthest to the right, 480, or the middle

a particular university. Selected faculty members were asked to complete an anonymous survey.

Random digit dialing (RDD) is a variation of simple random sampling. A computer is used to derive a telephone number through the random selection of digits. RDD sampling has become the standard method of interviewing by the national pollsters. The standard method of interviewing from the mid-1930s to the mid-1980s was face to face. Although a generally reliable method, it is very costly to execute. By the mid-1980s, a sufficiently high proportion of U.S. households had at least one telephone to make telephone interviewing a viable alternative, at much less cost per interview. Today, approximately 95 percent of all households have a telephone, and telephone interviews are now dominant in national polling.

Gallup, for example, starts with a computerized list of all telephone exchanges in the United States, along with estimates of the number of residential households those exchanges have attached to them. The computer, using RDD, creates telephone numbers from those exchanges, then pulls a random sample of them. Why not simply

use telephone directories, you might ask? An estimated 30 percent of American residential phones are unlisted. If a random sample of phone numbers were pulled from telephone directories, many unlisted households would be left out, creating a possible bias in the sample.

Robert Wyatt, Elihu Katz, and Joohan Kim (2000) used RDD sampling to conduct a nationwide survey study of 1,029 adults to discover how often people discussed a variety of topics in the conduct of their everyday lives. Contrary to the distinction between public life and private life that is drawn by many social commentators, Wyatt and his colleagues found that talk about public issues such as politics and the economy occurs with reasonable frequency in private life.

Systematic Sampling

Simple random sampling may not be the most efficient sampling method, and it can be laborious if done manually. SRS typically requires a list of elements. When such a list is available, researchers often employ **systematic sampling** rather than simple random sampling.

three digits, 048, and any of these plans would work.) The key is to make a plan and stick with it. For convenience, let's use the left-most three digits.

5. We can also choose to progress through the tables any way we want: down the columns, up them, across to the right or to the left, or diagonally. Again, any of these plans will work just fine as long as we stick to it. For convenience, let's agree to move down the columns. When we get to the bottom of one column, we'll go to the top of the next; when we exhaust a given page, we'll start at the top of the first column of the next page.

6. Now, where do we start? You can close your eyes and stick a pencil into the table and start wherever the pencil point lands. (We know it doesn't sound scientific, but it works.) Or, if you're afraid you'll hurt the book or miss it altogether, close your eyes and make up a column number and a row number. ("I'll pick the number in the fifth row of column 2.") Start with that number.

7. Let's suppose we decide to start with the fifth number in column 2. If you look on the first page of Appendix G, you'll see that the starting number is 39975. We've selected 399 as our first random number, and we have 99 more to go. Moving down the second column, we select 069, 729, 919, 143, 368, 695, 409, 939, and so forth. At the bottom of column 2, we select number 104 and continue to the top of column 3: 015, 255, and so on.

8. See how easy it is? But trouble lies ahead. When we reach column 5, we're speeding along, selecting 816, 309, 763, 078, 061, 277, 988. . . . Wait a minute! There are only 980 people in the population. How can we pick number 988? The solution is simple: ignore it. Anytime you come across a number that lies outside your range, skip it and continue on your way: 188, 174, and so forth. The same solution applies if the same number comes up more than once. If you select 399 again, for example, just ignore it the second time.

9. That's it. You keep up the procedure until you've selected 100 random numbers. Returning to your list, your sample consists of person number 399, person number 69, person number 729, and so forth.

In systematic sampling, every kth element in the total list is chosen (systematically) for inclusion in the sample. If the list contains 10,000 elements and you want a sample of 1,000, you select every tenth element for your sample. To guard against any possible human bias in using this method, you should select the first element at random. Thus, in the preceding example, you would begin by selecting a random number between one and ten. The element having that number is included in the sample, plus every tenth element following it. This method is technically referred to as a *systematic sample with a random start*. Two terms are frequently used in connection with systematic sampling. The *sampling interval* is the standard distance between elements selected in the sample: ten in the preceding sample. The *sampling ratio* is the proportion of elements in the population that are selected: $1/10$ in the example.

$$\text{sampling interval} = \frac{\text{population size}}{\text{sample size}}$$

$$\text{sampling ratio} = \frac{\text{sample size}}{\text{population size}}$$

In practice, systematic sampling is virtually identical to simple random sampling. If the list of elements is indeed randomized before sampling, one might argue that a systematic sample drawn from that list is in fact a simple random sample. By now, debates over the relative merits of simple random sampling and systematic sampling have been resolved largely in favor of the latter method. Empirically, the results are virtually identical. And, as you'll see in a later section, systematic sampling, in some instances, is slightly more accurate than simple random sampling.

There is one danger involved in systematic sampling. The arrangement of elements in the list can make systematic sampling unwise. Such an arrangement is usually called *periodicity*. If the list of elements is arranged in a cyclical pattern that coincides with the sampling interval, a grossly biased sample may be drawn. Two examples will illustrate this.

In a classic study of soldiers during World War II, the researchers selected a systematic sample from unit rosters. Every tenth soldier on the roster was selected for the study. However, the rosters were arranged in a table of organizations: sergeants first, then corporals and privates, squad by squad. Each squad had ten members. As a result, every tenth person on the roster was a squad sergeant. The systematic sample selected contained only sergeants. It could, of course, have been the case that no sergeants were selected for the same reason.

As another example, suppose we select a sample of apartments in an apartment building. If the sample is drawn from a list of apartments arranged in numerical order (for example, 101, 102, 103, 104, 201, 202, and so on), there is a danger of the sampling interval coinciding with the number of apartments on a floor or some multiple thereof. Then the samples might include only northwest-corner apartments or only apartments near the elevator. If these types of apartments have some other particular characteristic in common (for example, higher rent), the sample will be biased. The same danger would appear in a systematic sample of houses in a subdivision arranged with the same number of houses on a block.

In considering a systematic sample from a list, then, you should carefully examine the nature of that list. If the elements are arranged in any particular order, you should figure out whether that order will bias the sample to be selected and take steps to counteract any possible bias (for example, take a simple random sample from cyclical portions).

In summary, however, systematic sampling is usually superior to simple random sampling. Problems in the ordering of elements in the sampling frame can usually be remedied quite easily.

Stratified Sampling

In the two preceding sections, we discussed two methods of sample selection from a list: random and systematic. **Stratification** is not an alternative to these methods; rather, it represents a possible modification of their use.

Simple random sampling and systematic sampling both ensure a degree of representativeness and permit an estimate of the error present. Stratified sampling is a method for obtaining a greater degree of representativeness—decreasing the probable sampling error. To understand this method, we must return briefly to the basic theory of sampling distribution.

Recall that sampling error is reduced by two factors in the sample design. First, a large sample produces a smaller sampling error than a small sample does. Second, a homogeneous population produces samples with smaller sampling errors than does a heterogeneous population. If 99 percent of the population agrees with a certain statement, it's extremely unlikely that any probability sample will greatly misrepresent the extent of agreement. If the population is split 50–50 on the statement, then the sampling error will be much greater.

Stratified sampling is based on this second factor in sampling theory. Rather than selecting your sample from the total population at large, you ensure that appropriate numbers of elements are drawn from homogeneous subsets of that population. To get a stratified sample of university students, for example, you would first organize your population by college class and then draw appropriate numbers of freshmen, sophomores, juniors, and seniors. In a nonstratified sample, representation by class would be subjected to the same sampling error as other variables. In a sample stratified by class, the sampling error on this variable is reduced to zero.

Even more complex stratification methods are possible. In addition to stratifying by class, you might also stratify by sex, by GPA, and so forth. In this fashion you might be able to ensure that your sample would contain the proper numbers of male sophomores with a 4.0 average, of female sophomores with a 4.0 average, and so forth.

The ultimate function of stratification, then, is to organize the population into homogeneous subsets (with heterogeneity between subsets) and to select the appropriate number of elements from each. To the extent that the subsets are homogeneous on the stratification variables, they may be homogeneous on other variables as well. Because *age* is related to *college class,* a sample stratified by class will be more representative in terms of age as well. Because occupational aspirations still seem to be related to sex, a sample stratified by sex will be more representative in terms of occupational aspirations.

The choice of stratification variables typically depends on what variables are available. Sex can often be determined in a list of names. University lists are typically arranged by class. Lists of faculty members may indicate their departmental affiliation. Government agency files may be arranged by geographical region. Voter registration lists are arranged according to precinct.

In selecting stratification variables from among those available, however, you should be concerned primarily with those that are presumably related to variables you want to represent accurately. Because sex is related to many variables and is often available for stratification, it is often used. Education is related to many variables, but it is often not available for stratification. Geographical location within a city, state, or nation is related to many things. Within a city, stratification by geographical location usually increases representativeness in social class, ethnic group, and so forth. Within a nation, it increases

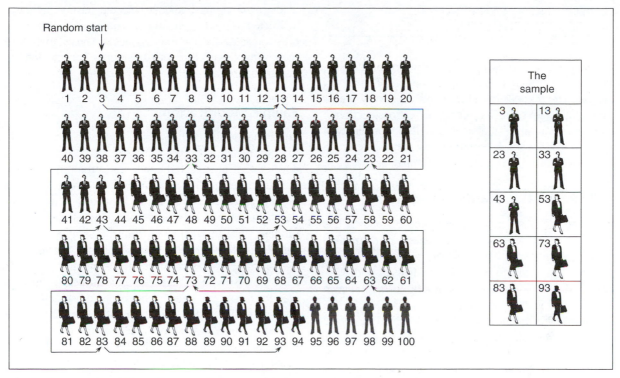

FIGURE 7-11   **A Stratified, Systematic Sample with a Random Start**

representativeness in a broad range of attitudes as well as in social class and ethnicity.

When you're working with a simple list of all elements in the population, two methods of stratification predominate. In one method, you sort the population elements into discrete groups based on whatever stratification variables are being used. On the basis of the relative proportion of the population represented by a given group, you select—randomly or systematically—several elements from that group constituting the same proportion of your desired sample size. For example, if sophomore men with a 4.0 average compose 1 percent of the student population and you desire a sample of 1,000 students, you would select 10 sophomore men with a 4.0 average.

The other method is to group students as described and then put those groups together in a continuous list, beginning with all male freshmen with a 4.0 average and ending with all senior women with a 1.0 or below. You would then select a systematic sample, with a random start, from the entire list. Given the arrangement of the list, a systematic sample would select proper numbers (within an error range of 1 or 2) from each subgroup. (*Note:* A simple random sample drawn from such a composite list would cancel out the stratification.)

Figure 7-11 offers a graphic illustration of stratified, systematic sampling. As you can see, we lined up our micropopulation according to sex and race. Then, beginning with a random start of "3," we've taken every tenth person thereafter: 3, 13, 23, . . . , 93.

Stratified sampling ensures the proper representation of the stratification variables in order to enhance representation of other variables related to them. Taken as a whole, then, a stratified sample is likely to be more representative on several variables than a simple random sample. Although the simple random sample is still regarded as somewhat sacred, it should now be clear that you can often do better.

Glenn Sparks and Robert Ogles (1990) employed stratified sampling in their study of whether TV viewing is correlated with fear of becoming a victim of crime. Because fear of victimization could result from the crime rate of the city in which one lives, they decided to stratify their sample into two lists: a high-crime city and a low-crime city (based on known crime rates). Within each city, participants were recruited for a telephone interview using random digit dialing. The researchers concluded that the relationship between television viewing and fear of victimization was quite modest.

ILLUSTRATION: SAMPLING UNIVERSITY STUDENTS

Let's put these principles into practice by looking at an actual sampling design used to select a sample of university students. The purpose of the study was to survey, with a mail-out questionnaire, a representative cross-section of students attending the main campus of the University of Hawaii. The following sections will describe the steps and decisions involved in selecting that sample.

Study Population and Sampling Frame

The obvious sampling frame available for use in this sample selection was the computerized file maintained by the university administration. The tape contained students' names, local and permanent addresses, Social Security numbers, and a variety of other information such as field of study, class, age, and sex.

However, the computer database contained files on all people who could, by any conceivable definition, be called students, many of whom seemed inappropriate for the purposes of the study. As a result, it was necessary to define the *study population* in a somewhat more restricted fashion. The final definition included those 15,225 day-program degree candidates registered for the fall semester on the Manoa campus of the university, including all colleges and departments, both undergraduate and graduate students, and both U.S. and foreign students. Therefore, the computer program used for sampling limited consideration to students fitting this definition.

Stratification

The sampling program also permitted stratification of students before sample selection. The researchers decided that stratification by college class would be sufficient, although the students might have been further stratified within class, if desired, by sex, college, major, and so forth.

Sample Selection

Once the students had been arranged by class, a systematic sample was selected across the entire rearranged list. The sample size for the study was initially set at 1,100. To achieve this sample, the sampling program was set for a 1:14 sampling ratio. The program generated a random number between 1 and 14; the student having that number and every fourteenth student thereafter was selected in the sample.

Once the sample had been selected, the computer was instructed to print each student's name and mailing address on self-adhesive mailing labels. These labels were then simply transferred to envelopes for mailing the questionnaires.

Sample Modification

This initial design of the sample had to be modified. Before the mailing of questionnaires, the researchers discovered that unexpected expenses in the production of the questionnaires made it impossible to cover the costs of mailing to all 1,100 students. As a result, one-third of the mailing labels were systematically selected (with a random start) for exclusion from the sample. The final sample for the study was thereby reduced to about 770.

This modification of the sample is mentioned here to illustrate the frequent need to change aspects of the study plan in midstream. Because the excluded students were systematically omitted from the initial systematic sample, the remaining 770 students could still be taken as reasonably representing the study population. The reduction in sample size did, of course, increase the range of sampling error.

MULTISTAGE CLUSTER SAMPLING

The preceding sections have dealt with reasonably simple procedures for sampling from lists of elements. Such a situation is ideal. Unfortunately, however, much interesting research requires the selection of samples from populations that cannot be easily listed for sampling purposes. Examples would be the population of a city, state, or nation; all university students in the United States; and so forth. In such cases, the sample design must be much more complex. Such a design typically involves the initial sampling of groups of elements—*clusters*—followed by the selection of elements within each of the selected clusters.

Cluster sampling may be used when it's either impossible or impractical to compile an exhaustive list of the elements composing the target population. All declared communication studies majors enrolled in colleges or universities in the United States would be an example of such a population. Often, however, the population elements are already grouped into subpopulations, and a list of those subpopulations either exists or can be created practically. In our example, communication studies majors in the United States belong to discrete colleges

SAMPLING SANTA'S FANS

With the approach of Christmas 1985, the *New York Times* thought it would be interesting to survey the nation's children regarding their beliefs in Santa Claus. There being no national registry of those who've been naughty and nice, the *Times* had to use some ingenuity. Here's their description of what they did:

> The latest New York Times Poll is based on telephone interviews conducted Dec. 14–18 with 261 children ages 3 through 10 around the United States, excluding Alaska and Hawaii.
>
> The sample of telephone exchanges called was selected by a computer from a complete list of exchanges in the country. The exchanges were chosen to ensure that each region of the country was represented in proportion to its population. For each exchange, the telephone numbers were formed by random digits, thus permitting access to both listed and unlisted residential numbers.
>
> After interviews with 1,358 adults were completed, parents were asked if their children could be interviewed on the subject of Christmas. The results have been weighted to take account of household size and number of residential telephones and to adjust for variations in the sample relation to region, race, sex, age and education.

By the way, 87 percent of the children said they believed in Santa Claus: ranging from 96 percent among those 3–5 down to 69 percent among the 9–10-year-olds.

Source: Sara Rimer, "Poll Sees Landslide for Santa: Of U.S. Children, 87% Believe," *New York Times,* December 24, 1985.

and universities, which are either listed or could be. Following a cluster sample format, then, you could sample the list of universities in some manner (for example, a stratified, systematic sample). Next, you would obtain lists of members from each of the selected colleges and universities. Each of the lists would then be sampled to provide samples of students whose declared major is communication studies.

Another typical situation concerns sampling among population areas such as a city. Although there is no single list of a city's population, citizens reside on discrete city blocks or census blocks. Therefore, you can select a sample of blocks initially, create a list of persons living on each of the selected blocks, and subsample persons on each block.

In a more complex design, you might sample blocks, list the households on each selected block, sample the households, list the persons residing in each household, and, finally, sample persons within each selected household. This multistage sample design would lead to the ultimate selection of a sample of individuals but would not require the initial listing of all individuals in the city's population.

Multistage cluster sampling, then, involves the repetition of two basic steps: listing and sampling. The list of primary sampling units (colleges/universities, blocks) is compiled and, perhaps, stratified for sampling. Then a sample of those units is selected. The selected primary sampling units are then listed and perhaps stratified. The list of secondary sampling units is then sampled, and so forth.

Multistage cluster sampling makes possible those studies that are otherwise impossible. Consider, for example, the "Santa Claus" survey described in the box titled "Sampling Santa's Fans."

Although cluster sampling is highly efficient, the price of that efficiency is a less accurate sample. A simple random sample drawn from a population list is subject to a single sampling error, but a two-stage cluster sample is subject to two sampling errors. First, the initial sample of clusters will represent the population of clusters only within a range of sampling error. Second, the sample of elements selected within a given cluster will represent all the elements in that cluster only within a range of sampling error. Thus, for example, you run a certain risk of selecting a sample of disproportionately wealthy city blocks, plus a sample of disproportionately wealthy households within those blocks. The best solution to this problem lies in the number of clusters selected initially and the number of elements selected within each.

Typically, you'll be restricted to a total sample size; for example, you may be limited to conducting 2,000 interviews in a city. Given this broad limitation, however, you have several options in designing your cluster sample. At the extremes you might choose one cluster and select 2,000 elements within that cluster, or else select 2,000 clusters with one element selected within each. Of course, neither is advisable, but a broad range of choices lies between them. Fortunately, the logic of sampling distributions provides a general guideline for this task.

Recall that sampling error is reduced by two factors: an increase in the sample size and increased homogeneity of the elements being sampled. These factors operate at each level of a multistage sample design. A sample of clusters will best represent all clusters if a large number are selected and if all clusters are very much alike. A sample of elements will best represent all elements in a given cluster if a large number are selected from the cluster and if all the elements in the cluster are very much alike.

With a given total sample size, however, if the number of clusters is increased, the number of elements within a cluster must be decreased. In this respect, the representativeness of the clusters is increased at the expense of more poorly representing the elements composing each cluster, or vice versa. Fortunately, homogeneity can ease this dilemma.

Typically, the elements composing a given natural cluster within a population are more homogeneous than are all elements composing the total population. The students of a given university are more alike than all university students are; the residents of a given city block are more alike than the residents of a whole city are. As a result, relatively fewer elements may be needed to represent a given natural cluster adequately, although a larger number of clusters may be needed to represent adequately the diversity found among the clusters. This fact is most clearly seen in the extreme case of very different clusters composed of identical elements within each. In such a situation, a large number of clusters would adequately represent all the members. Although this extreme situation never exists in reality, it's closer to the truth in most cases than its opposite: identical clusters composed of grossly divergent elements.

The general guideline for cluster design, then, is to maximize the number of clusters selected while decreasing the number of elements within each cluster. However, this scientific guideline must be balanced against an administrative constraint. The efficiency of cluster sampling is based on the ability to minimize the listing of population elements. By initially selecting clusters, you need list only the elements composing the selected clusters, not all elements in the entire population. However, increasing the number of clusters goes directly against this efficiency factor in cluster sampling. A small number of clusters may be listed more quickly and more cheaply than a large number. (Remember that all the elements in a selected cluster must be listed even if only a few are to be chosen in the sample.)

The final sample design will reflect these two constraints. In effect, you'll probably select as many clusters as you can afford. Lest this issue be left too open ended at this point, here's a general guideline. Population researchers conventionally aim at the selection of 5 households per census block. If a total of 2,000 households are to be interviewed, you would aim at 400 blocks with 5 household interviews on each. Figure 7-12 presents a graphic overview of this process.

Before turning to other, more detailed procedures available in cluster sampling, we'll repeat that this method almost inevitably involves a loss of accuracy. However, the manner in which this loss of accuracy appears is somewhat complex. First, as noted earlier, a multistage sample design is subject to a sampling error at each stage. Because the sample size is necessarily smaller at each stage than the total sample size, the sampling error at each stage will be greater than would be the case for a single-stage random sample of elements. Second, sampling error is estimated on the basis of observed variance among the sample elements. When those elements are drawn from among relatively homogeneous clusters, the estimated sampling error will be too optimistic and must be corrected in the light of the cluster sample design.

Multistage Cluster Sampling, Stratification

Thus far, we've looked at cluster sampling as though a simple random sample were selected at each stage of the design. In fact, stratification techniques can be used to refine and improve the sample being selected.

The basic options here are essentially the same as those in single-stage sampling from a list. In selecting a national sample of universities, for example, you might initially stratify your list of universities by their public or private status, geographical region, size, rural or urban location, and perhaps by some measure of institutional type—research universities, comprehensive universities, and so forth.

Once the primary sampling units (universities, blocks) have been grouped according to the relevant, available stratification variables, either simple random or systematic sampling techniques can be used to select the sample. You might select a specified number of units from each group, or *stratum,* or you might arrange the stratified clusters in a continuous list and systematically sample that list.

To the extent that clusters are combined into homogeneous strata, the sampling error at this stage will be

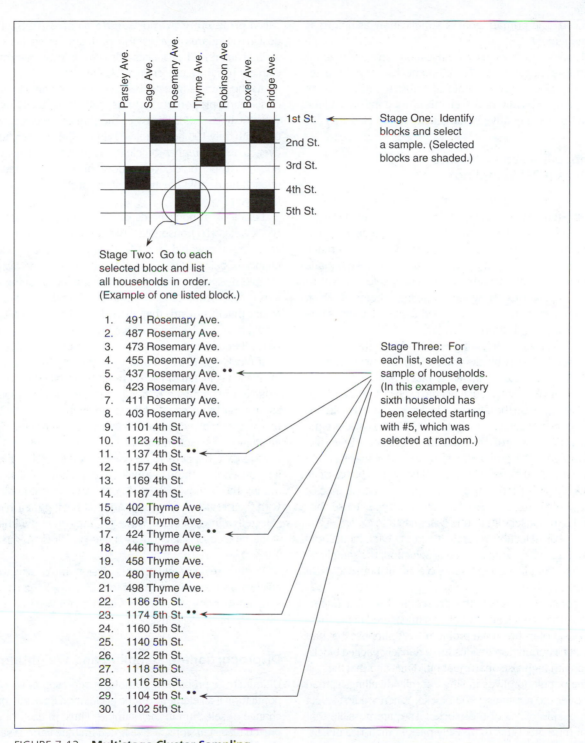

FIGURE 7-12 **Multistage Cluster Sampling**

reduced. The primary goal of stratification, as before, is homogeneity.

There's no reason why stratification can't take place at each level of sampling. The elements listed within a selected cluster might be stratified before the next stage of sampling. Typically, however, this is not done. (Recall the assumption of relative homogeneity within clusters.)

Probability Proportionate to Size (PPS) Sampling

In this section, we want to introduce you to a more sophisticated form of cluster sampling, used in many large-scale survey sampling projects. In the preceding discussion, we talked about selecting a random or systematic sample of clusters and then a random or systematic sample of elements within each cluster selected. Notice that this produces an overall sampling scheme in which every element in the whole population has the same probability of selection.

Let's say we're selecting households within a city. If there are 1,000 city blocks and we initially select a sample of 100, that means that each block has a $^{100}/_{1,000}$ (.1) chance of being selected. If we next select 1 household in 10 from those on the selected blocks, each household has a .1 chance of selection within its block. To calculate the overall probability of a household being selected, we simply multiply the probabilities at the individual steps in sampling. That is, each household has a $^1/_{10}$ chance of its block being selected and a $^1/_{10}$ chance of that specific household being selected if the block is one of those chosen. Each household, in this case, has a $^1/_{10} \times ^1/_{10} = ^1/_{100}$ chance of selection overall. Because each household would have the same chance of selection, the sample so selected should be representative of all households in the city.

There are dangers in this procedure, however. In particular, the varying sizes of blocks (measured in numbers of households) present a problem. Let's suppose that half the city's population resides in 10 densely packed blocks filled with high-rise apartment buildings and that the rest of the population lives in single-family dwellings spread out over the remaining 900 blocks. When we first select our sample of $^1/_{10}$ of the blocks, it's quite possible that we'll miss all of the 10 densely packed high-rise blocks. No matter what happens in the second stage of sampling, our final sample of households will be grossly unrepresentative of the city, comprising only single-family dwellings.

Whenever the clusters sampled are of greatly differing sizes, it's appropriate to use a modified sampling design called **probability proportionate to size (PPS).** This design (1) guards against the problem we've just described and (2) still produces a final sample in which each element has the same chance of selection.

As the name suggests, each cluster is given a chance of selection proportionate to its size. Thus, a city block with 200 households has twice the chance of selection as one with only 100 households. Within each cluster, however, a fixed *number* of elements is selected—say, 5 households per block. Notice how this procedure results in each household having the same probability of selection overall.

Let's look at households of two different city blocks. Block A has 100 households; Block B has only 10. In PPS sampling, we would give Block A ten times as good a chance of being selected as Block B. So if, in the overall sample design, Block A has a $^1/_{20}$ chance of being selected, that means Block B would only have a $^1/_{200}$ chance. Notice that this means that all the households on Block A would have a $^1/_{20}$ chance of having their block selected; Block B households have only a $^1/_{200}$ chance.

If Block A is selected and we're taking 5 households from each selected block, then the households on Block A have a $^5/_{100}$ chance of being selected into the block's sample. Since we can multiply probabilities in a case like this, we see that every household on Block A has an overall chance of selection equal to $^1/_{20} \times ^5/_{100} = ^5/_{2,000} = ^1/_{400}$.

If Block B happens to be selected, on the other hand, its households stand a much better chance of being among the 5 chosen there: $^5/_{10}$. When this is combined with their relatively poorer chance of having their block selected in the first place, however, they end up with the same chance of selection as those on Block A: $^1/_{200} \times ^5/_{10} = ^5/_{2,000} = ^1/_{400}$.

Further refinements to this design make it a very efficient and effective method for selecting large cluster samples. For now, however, it's enough for you to understand the basic logic involved.

Disproportionate Sampling and Weighting

Ultimately, a probability sample is representative of a population if all elements in the population have an equal chance of selection in that sample. Thus, in each of the preceding discussions, we've noted that the various sampling procedures result in an equal chance of selection—even though the ultimate selection probability is the product of several partial probabilities.

More generally, however, a probability sample is one in which each population element has a *known nonzero* probability of selection—even though different elements may have different probabilities. If controlled probability sampling procedures have been used, any such sample may be representative of the population from which it is drawn if each sample element is assigned a weight equal to the inverse of its probability of selection. Thus, where all sample elements have had the same chance of selection, each is given the same weight: 1. This is called a *self-weighting sample.*

Disproportionate sampling and weighting come into play in two basic ways. First, you may sample subpopulations disproportionately to ensure sufficient numbers of cases from each for analysis. For example, a given city may have a suburban area containing one-fourth of its total population. Yet you might be especially interested in a detailed analysis of households in that area and may feel that one-fourth of this total sample size would be too few. As a result, you might decide to select the same number of households from the suburban area as from the remainder of the city. Households in the suburban area, then, are given a disproportionately better chance of selection than are those located elsewhere in the city.

As long as you analyze the two area samples separately or comparatively, you need not worry about the differential sampling. If you want to combine the two samples to create a composite picture of the entire city, however, you must take the disproportionate sampling into account. If n is the number of households selected from each area, then the households in the suburban area have a chance of selection equal to n divided by one-fourth of the total city population. Because the total city population and the sample size are the same for both areas, the suburban-area households should be given a weight of $\frac{1}{4}n$, and the remaining households should be given a weight of $\frac{3}{4}n$. This weighting procedure could be simplified by merely giving a weight of 3 to each of the households selected outside the suburban area. (This procedure gives a proportionate representation to each sample element. The population figure would have to be included in the weighting if population estimates were desired.)

Here's an example of the problems that can be created when disproportionate sampling is not accompanied by a weighting scheme. When the *Harvard Business Review* decided to survey its subscribers on the issue of sexual harassment at work, it seemed appropriate to oversample women. Here's how G. C. Collins and Timothy Blodgett (1981) explained the matter:

> We also skewed the sample another way: to insure a representative response from women, we mailed a questionnaire to virtually every female subscriber, for a male/female ratio of 68% to 32%. This bias resulted in a response of 52% male and 44% female (and 4% who gave no indication of gender)—compared to HBR's U.S. subscriber proportion of 93% male and 7% female. (p. 78)

You should have noticed a couple of things in this passage. First, it would be nice to know a little more about what "virtually every female" means. Evidently, they didn't send questionnaires to all female subscribers, but there's no indication of who was omitted and why. Second, they didn't use the term *representative* in its normal social science usage. What they mean, of course, is that they want to get a substantial or "large enough" response from women, and oversampling is a perfectly acceptable way of accomplishing that.

By sampling more women than a straightforward probability sample would have produced, they've gotten enough women (812) to compare with the men (960). Thus, when the authors report, for example, that 32 percent of the women and 66 percent of the men agree that "the amount of sexual harassment at work is greatly exaggerated," we know that the female response is based on a substantial number of cases. That's good. There are problems, however.

To begin, subscriber surveys are always problematic. In this case, the best the researchers can hope to talk about is "what subscribers to *Harvard Business Review* think." In a loose way, it might make sense to think of that population as representing the more sophisticated portion of corporate management. Unfortunately, the overall response rate was 25 percent. Although that's quite good for subscriber surveys, it's a low response rate in terms of generalizing from probability samples.

Beyond that, however, the disproportionate sample design creates a further problem. When the authors state that 73 percent favor company policies against harassment (Collins & Blodgett, 1981, p. 78), that figure is undoubtedly too high, since the sample contains a disproportionately high percentage of women—who are more likely to favor such policies. And when the researchers report that top managers are more likely to feel that claims of sexual harassment are exaggerated than are middle- and lower-level managers (1981, p. 81), that finding is also suspect. As the researchers report, women are disproportionately represented in lower management. That alone might account for the apparent differences in different levels of management. In short, the failure to take account of the oversampling of women confounds all survey results that don't separate findings by sex.

PROBABILITY SAMPLING OF MESSAGES: SOME EXAMPLES

We have relied heavily in this chapter on examples linked to public opinion polling and efforts to sample individuals from larger populations. But probability sampling is used to sample more than individuals in communication research. Often, communication researchers want to study communicative messages of a certain kind—advertisements on Saturday morning cartoons, magazine ads targeted at adolescent girls, interactions between family members—but they can't study the entire population of messages. The same sampling methods we have discussed in this chapter are used by researchers in deriving a smaller, representative sample of messages from the larger population of all relevant messages. Let's turn to some examples in which messages, rather than individuals, are sampled.

Many researchers sample time as a way to select a representative sample of messages from a larger population of messages. For example, Reed Larson and Maryse Richards (1994) wanted to examine the kinds of interactions among mothers, fathers, and adolescents in U.S. families. Family members engage in many interactions over the course of a week—too many to study exhaustively. So Larson and Richards employed a probability sampling strategy called the *experience sampling method* (ESM). ESM is based on simple random sampling. Family members were provided with electronic pagers that beeped about eight randomly selected times between 7:30 A.M. and 9:30 P.M. for a seven-day period. Whenever the pager beeped, the family member was asked to complete a one-page diary report providing information on what he or she was doing, thinking, and feeling just prior to the beep. Larson and Richards estimated that study participants responded to about 90 percent of the beeping signals that were sent to them. By randomly sampling time, these researchers were able to gain a sense how family members interacted in their everyday lives.

Time also features prominently in the sampling of mass media messages. For example, Kathy McKee and Carol Pardun (1996) were interested in comparing the sexual and religious imagery of three kinds of music videos—rock (MTV), country (TNN), and contemporary Christian (Z music). Because it was not feasible to study all of the music videos shown on these music networks, the researchers taped randomly selected hours during a two-week period. Hour of day was thus sampled using simple random sampling. All of the music videos taped during a selected hour were subsequently analyzed for their imagery.

Time can feature in the selection of printed messages as well. For example, if you were interested in studying the body-weight images of female models in women's magazines over the last 20 years, you would be overwhelmed by the sheer quantity of images to analyze. You might want to narrow down your study by focusing only on those magazines that have been in continuous publication for the past two decades. But you will still have too many images to consider. You might want to stratify by year and by magazine. For each year's worth of a given magazine, you might want to randomly select an issue of the magazine. You might want to engage in further sampling, selecting page numbers at random and examining all female models shown on selected pages.

Or suppose you wanted to study personal ads in newspapers. You might want to use multistage cluster analysis to help you out. You could use newspapers as your cluster unit at stage 1, perhaps weighting the likelihood of a newspaper's selection by its circulation in order to increase the odds that you would sample the nation's largest-circulation newspapers. If personal ads typically run for a week, you might want to sample some subset of weeks from the 52 possible in a given year. If the personal ads are very numerous in a given edition of a selected newspaper, you might need a sampling plan to select which ads you would analyze if you decided you could not examine them all.

Our point here is that you can use probability sampling methods to derive a representative sample of anything so long as you can define your population and can ensure that all elements have a known, nonzero probability of selection.

A HYPOTHETICAL STUDY: SAMPLING GRAFFITI ON CAMPUS

Let's suppose you want to do a study of the content themes of graffiti on your campus. How might you go about doing this? The first task you face is defining your population. There are several different kinds of graffiti, and it appears in lots of different kinds of places. So, to simplify things, let's say you're interested in verbal graffiti (as opposed to visual graffiti) that appears in public restrooms. The next question you need to ask yourself is whether you need to sample the graffiti or whether you can access and study all of the graffiti. We're guessing that it would be too overwhelming to locate and study all of the verbal graffiti in public restrooms on your campus, so you decide to sample.

If you want to make claims about the representativeness of your sample of graffiti, you will want to use probability sampling methods to help you out. Our guess is that nobody at your campus has a master list of all of the graffiti on your campus, which means that you need to use some form of cluster sampling plan.

There are many ways you could perform cluster sampling. Here's one. Most campuses have published maps of where buildings are located. From this map, you could develop a master list of all of the public buildings on campus. From this list, you could employ a simple random sampling technique using a table of random numbers to derive a subset of buildings. Alternatively, you might want to stratify your list of buildings—maybe all of your university's professional programs (law, business, medicine) are located on one side of a river and the rest of campus is located on the other side of the river. You might want to stratify buildings by their locations to permit you to sample from buildings frequented by students enrolled in professional programs as opposed to buildings frequented by other students. Once you have a sample of buildings, you're ready for stage 2 of your multistage sampling.

For each of your sampled buildings, generate a list of all of its public restrooms. Maybe one large classroom and faculty office building has 5 floors, with a men's bathroom and a women's on each floor, for a total of 10. Maybe another sampled building is the library, with 2 men's bathrooms and 2 women's bathrooms on the first floor and 1 bathroom for each sex on each of the remaining 7 floors, for a total of 18 bathrooms. You might want to stratify your list of public restrooms by sex so that you have two lists for each of your sampled buildings: a list of men's restrooms and a list of women's restrooms. From each list, you would then randomly select a certain number of restrooms.

You're all ready to analyze the graffiti, and you walk into the public restrooms you have selected, and you are overwhelmed—there's simply too much of it on the walls to study it all. So you need stage 3 sampling so that you can figure out how to draw a representative sample of the graffiti from your randomly selected public restrooms. You could use a grid system, dividing each selected public restroom into north, south, east, and west walls, and for each wall, partitioning it off in your mind into quadrants, which you then would randomly sample. For each sampled quadrant of wall space, you would analyze

some specific number of graffiti texts—say, 5. Or you could have other decision rules: to use 5 graffiti texts that are written on the back of stall doors for randomly selected stalls. There are many ways you could draw a random sample of graffiti in a given restroom. The key is to have some systematic, consistent, and random method for selecting your graffiti texts once you are in your selected restrooms. You want to make sure that the graffiti you select in each restroom is representative of all of the graffiti that appears in that space.

Once you have identified the particular graffiti texts that will be included in your sample, you can then turn to the task of analyzing their content for recurring themes. For this particular task, the method of quantitative text analysis would best suit your purposes, a topic we will take up in Chapter 10.

PROBABILITY SAMPLING IN REVIEW

Probability sampling is the primary method available to communication researchers when they want to ensure the representativeness of their sampled phenomena—whether individuals or messages. In each of the variations examined, we've seen that elements are chosen for study from a population on a basis of random selection with known nonzero probabilities.

Depending on the field situation, probability sampling can be either very simple or extremely difficult, time consuming, and expensive. Whatever the situation, however, it remains an effective method for the representative selection of study elements. There are two reasons for this.

First, probability sampling avoids researchers' conscious or unconscious biases in element selection. If all elements in the population have an equal (or unequal and subsequently weighted) chance of selection, there is an excellent chance that the sample so selected will closely represent the population of all elements.

Second, probability sampling permits estimates of sampling error. Although no probability sample will be perfectly representative in all respects, controlled selection methods permit the researcher to estimate the degree of expected error in that regard.

In this lengthy chapter, we've taken on a basic issue in quantitative communication research: selecting observations that will tell us something more general than the specifics we've actually observed. Social scientists have devoted a good deal of attention to and have developed several techniques for dealing with this issue.

Main Points

❏ It's rarely possible to observe all the actions and actors relevant to the communication phenomenon under study.

❏ Communication researchers must select observations that will allow them to generalize to people and events not observed. Often, this involves a selection of people to observe.

❏ A sample is a special subset of a population observed in order to make inferences about the nature of the total population itself.

❏ Sampling has often centered on the ability of researchers to gauge public opinion, such as voting intentions. Despite a history of errors, current techniques are quite accurate.

❏ Social scientists have developed several sampling techniques appropriate to different research situations.

❏ Sometimes, you can and should select probability samples using precise statistical techniques, but at other times, nonprobability techniques are more appropriate.

❏ Sometimes, you must rely on available participants, or on an accidental sample, but it's difficult to know how representative such participants are.

❏ Purposive sampling is a type of nonprobability sampling in which the researcher uses his or her own judgment in the selection of sample members. It's sometimes called a judgmental sample.

❏ Quota sampling is another nonprobability sampling method. You begin with a detailed description of the characteristics of the total population (quota matrix) and then select your sample members so that they include different composite profiles that exist in the population. The representativeness of a quota sampling depends in large part on how accurately the quota matrix reflects the characteristics of the population.

❏ Snowball sampling is a technique often used in communication research; each participant is asked to identify others.

❏ Probability sampling methods provide an excellent way of selecting representative samples from large, known populations.

❏ The most carefully selected sample will never provide a perfect representation of the population from which it was selected. There will always be some degree of sampling error.

❏ Probability sampling methods make it possible to estimate the amount of sampling error expected in a given sample.

❏ The chief principle of probability sampling is that every member of the total population must have some known nonzero probability of being selected into the sample.

❏ An EPSEM sample is one in which every member of a population has the same probability of being selected.

❏ A sampling frame is a list or quasi-list of the members of a population. It is the resource used in the selection of a sample. A sample's representativeness depends directly on the extent to which a sampling frame contains all the members of the total population that the sample is intended to represent.

❏ Simple random sampling is logically the most fundamental technique in probability sampling.

❏ Systematic sampling involves the selection of every kth member from a sampling frame. This method is functionally equivalent to simple random sampling, with a few exceptions; systematic sampling is often more practical, however.

❏ Stratification is the process of grouping the members of a population into relatively homogeneous strata before sampling. This practice improves the representativeness of a sample by reducing the degree of sampling error.

❏ Multistage cluster sampling is a relatively complex sampling technique frequently used when a list of all the members of a population does not exist. An initial sample of groups of members (clusters) is selected first. Then all the members of each cluster are listed. Finally, the members listed in each of the selected clusters are subsampled, thereby providing the final sample of members.

❏ Probability proportionate to size (PPS) is a special, efficient method for multistage cluster sampling.

❏ If the members of a population have unequal probabilities of selection into the sample, researchers must assign weights to the different observations made in order to provide a representative picture of the total population. Basically, the weight assigned to a particular sample member should be the inverse of its probability of selection.

Key Terms

nonprobability sampling
probability sampling
purposive (judgmental)
   sampling
snowball sampling
quota sampling
convenience sampling
representativeness

EPSEM samples
sampling error
simple random sampling
systematic sampling
stratification
cluster sampling
probability proportionate
   to size (PPS)

Review Questions and Exercises

1. Put to the test our claim that sampling error is a function of homogeneity in the population and sample size, using the computation formula that we provided for the sampling error for the binomial. First, plug in different values for P and Q to reflect different degrees of homogeneity—.50 and .50, .10 and .90, .30 and .70—while holding the sample size constant. Notice what happens to the size of the sampling error with different numbers. Next, hold homogeneity constant and vary the sample size: 100, 500, 1,000, 5,000. Notice what happens to the size of the sampling error with different sample sizes.

2. Using Appendix G of this book, select a simple random sample of 10 numbers in the range from 1 to 9,876. Describe each step in the process.

3. In a paragraph or two, describe the steps involved in selecting a multistage cluster sample of students taking an introductory first-year course in journalism in the nation's colleges and universities.

4. Visit the web page of the Gallup Organization: http://www.gallup.com. Read about how Gallup conducts its public opinion polls. Select a topic and read the polling results on that topic.

5. Peruse several issues of the communication journals listed in Appendix A. Try to find examples of at least three kinds of sampling (probability or nonprobability) discussed in this chapter.

Continuity Project

Describe the method by which you might select a sample of your college's student body to study perceptions of how males and females communicate. Be sure to stratify on variables relevant to the topic and to defend your choices.

Additional Readings

Frankfort-Nachmias, C., & Leon-Guerrero, A. (1997). *Social statistics for a diverse society.* Thousand Oaks, CA: Pine Forge. See Chapter 11 especially. This statistics textbook covers many of the topics we've discussed in this chapter but in a more statistical context. It demonstrates the links between probability sampling and statistical analyses.

Kalton, G. (1983). *Introduction to survey sampling.* Newbury Park, CA: Sage. Kalton goes into more of the mathematical details of sampling than the present chapter without attempting to be as definitive as Kish, described next.

Kish, L. (1965). *Survey sampling.* New York: Wiley. Unquestionably the definitive work on sampling in social scientific research. Kish's coverage ranges from the simplest matters to the most complex and mathematical, both highly theoretical and downright practical. Easily readable and difficult passages intermingle as Kish exhausts everything you could want or need to know about each aspect of sampling.

Sudman, S. (1983). Applied sampling. In P. H. Rossi, J. D. Wright, & A. B. Anderson (Eds.), *Handbook of survey research* (pp. 145–194). New York: Academic Press. An excellent, practical guide to probability sampling in survey research.

InfoTrac College Edition
http://www.infotrac-college.com/
wadsworth/access.html

Access the latest news and journal articles with InfoTrac College Edition, an easy-to-use online database of reliable, full-length articles from hundreds of top academic journals. Conduct an electronic search using the following search terms:

- probability sample
- purposive sample
- convenience sample
- sampling error
- snowball sample
- stratification
- multistage cluster sampling
- random sample

CHAPTER 8

Survey Research

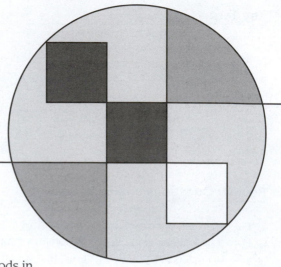

What You'll Learn in This Chapter

Here you'll learn about one of the most frequently used methods in quantitative communication research—the survey. A survey is a questionnaire given to respondents in self-administered or interviewer-administered forms.

INTRODUCTION

In quantitatively oriented communication research, researchers often operationalize variables by asking people structured questions. Survey research is the name of this method, and it involves three steps: (1) development of a questionnaire or survey, (2) selection of a sample of participants (referred to as respondents), and (3) administration of the questionnaire through any of several modes, including self-administration, face-to-face interviews, telephone interviews, and use of new technologies. Because (2) was addressed in our discussion of sampling in Chapter 7, we're going to emphasize (1) and (3) in this chapter.

Actually, questionnaires are often used as an integral part of other research methods, particularly experiments and evaluation research. In fact, questionnaires are perhaps the most frequently used form of measurement throughout the social sciences, including communication. We're certain that you've been a respondent to a survey more than once; you may have even done a survey of your own. So learning how to construct and administer a questionnaire is an important skill to have in your researcher's tool kit.

What kinds of questions do communication researchers ask of respondents? Here's a list of some of the primary kinds of data that researchers gather through structured question asking:

- Levels and kinds of *factual knowledge* held by respondents. As a student, this kind of survey is probably one you're very familiar with: The midterm and final exams that you take throughout your educational career are a form of knowledge survey. Communication researchers also use factual knowledge questions. For example, Michael Slater and his colleagues (2002) showed several different types of alcohol-warning messages to participants in order to determine which type of message was most effective. In part, they determined which type of message resulted in the greatest knowledge about alcohol risks.

- *Cognitive beliefs or perceptions* about some phenomenon. Sometimes, communication researchers are interested in gathering information about people's perceptions and beliefs about something. They may ask respondents the extent to which they believe certain claims to be true or accurate, or they may ask respondents the extent to which they agree with certain statements about some

phenomenon. For example, the Mean World Index (Gerbner & Gross, 1976) assesses whether respondents believe that people will try to take advantage of them, are untrustworthy, and are self-serving. The measure was developed in the context of TV violence research on the theoretical argument that watching a great deal of violence on TV will increase a person's beliefs that the world is populated with "mean" people.

- *Affective feelings or emotional responses* to some phenomenon. For example, respondents are asked to indicate whether they feel that something is positive or negative, liked or disliked, favorably or unfavorably evaluated, and so forth. Robert Norton (1983), for example, developed the Quality Marriage Index, which asks people to self-report on their feelings about their marriage by soliciting the extent of agreement with statements such as "We have a good marriage" and "Our marriage is strong."

- Reports on *behaviors.* Respondents can be asked to recall their past behaviors, their present behaviors, or their intended behaviors for the future. For example, the Revised Self-Disclosure Scale (RSDS; Wheeless & Grotz, 1976) asks respondents to indicate the extent to which they agree with statements such as the following: "I do not often talk about myself" and "Once I get started, my self-disclosures last a long time."

- *Trait or state orientations or dispositions.* A trait measure assesses a stable disposition or orientation of a person—for example, personality or style. By contrast, a state measure assesses a dispositional state or orientation that is specific to the moment or context at hand—for example, a person's level of stress when he or she is delivered bad news. Some variables can exist as both traits and states. For example, you can have a baseline, or trait, level of communication anxiety, which is your day-to-day general degree of anxiety in communicating with others. Your anxiety level could ebb and flow upwards or downwards, however, depending on the particular situation in which you find yourself. The Communicator Style Measure (Norton, 1978), for example, asks people to indicate their trait-like style of interacting with others through such items as "I am comfortable with all varieties of people" and "I readily express admiration for others." Although presented as a trait measure, it could easily be used as a state measure by asking people to indicate their communication style in a given situation in which they found themselves.

- *Networks of communication.* Organizational communication scholars are frequently interested in "mapping" the communication structure of a group or organization—who communicates with whom about what through which modalities. Typically, group/organizational members are asked in a survey to self-report their communication activities with other members. Based on these data, researchers can derive maps of how information and influence flow in the group or organization. For example, J. David Johnson and his colleagues (Johnson, Meyer, Berkowitz, Ethington, & Miller, 1997) performed a network analysis of a geographically dispersed government health information agency, the Cancer Information Service (CIS). They asked organizational members to keep logs of their communication activity for a three-day period, evaluating the role of formal and informal communication structures in organizational innovativeness.

- *Demographic features,* such as respondent age, years of education, socioeconomic status, race, and ethnicity.

In this chapter, we're going to address several aspects of survey research that extend the issues of operationalization and sampling discussed in Chapters 6 and 7. The chapter is organized in three general parts. The heart of trustworthy survey research rests with the reliability and validity of the questions asked. Thus, we open with a discussion of how to develop good questions. Next, we'll turn to issues of questionnaire organization—having good questions is only part of what makes a questionnaire trustworthy. Last, we'll examine a variety of different modes of questionnaire administration: self-administered surveys, face-to-face interviews, telephone interviews, and the role of new technologies in survey administration.

THE CHALLENGE OF ASKING GOOD QUESTIONS

Asking questions should be the easiest method around, right? After all, we ask and answer questions many times in the everyday conduct of our lives. Although asking questions is a common enough practice, it is very challenging to ask questions that will be reliable and valid. William Foddy (1993, pp. 2–9) has usefully pointed to several of these challenges:

1. *Factual questions sometimes elicit questionable answers.* You might think that if people are asked to report objective matters of fact, they can do so accurately. But it isn't as easy as this. For example, Foddy (1993, p. 3) cited an analysis of several health surveys in which it was found that at least 50 percent of the medical conditions listed in respondents' medical records were not reported by them in their questionnaire answers (Marquis, 1970). Maybe respondents were engaged in active concealment of their medical history, or maybe they simply forgot details about their medical history while filling out the survey.

People's memories of past events or practices can be biased in any of several ways. For example, people tend to recall events as taking place either more recently than they actually occurred or more in the past than the time of their actual occurrence (Weisberg, Krosnick, & Bowen, 1996). In general, the accuracy of people's reflections is worse the more distant the event. Details can be forgotten, particularly surrounding events or actions that were not important.

People's memories are also affected by their current emotional states. John Gottman (1994), for example, has found that dissatisfied marital pairs who are cascading toward divorce tend to reframe their past history together, putting a "negative spin" on events that at the time may have been regarded as positive. The opposite can happen, as well: People can disregard or downplay negative events under the halo of positive feelings in the present.

2. *What people say they do, or will do, and what they actually do are not always related.* As early as 1934, the discrepancy between actions and verbal reports of actions was noted by social scientists. In the 1930s, discrimination against members of the Chinese race was common. Richard LaPiere (1934) traveled around the United States in the 1930s with a Chinese couple, keeping records of how he was treated at restaurants, hotels, and motels. Only one establishment refused service. Six months later, LaPiere sent a survey to the places he had visited, asking them if they would accept members of the Chinese race as guests. LaPiere received a response rate of 50 percent, and 90 percent of those responses said "No!" Attitudes toward members of the Chinese race are not the same as they were in the 1930s, but the broader problem

of mismatch between people's actions and their reports about their actions can still pose a real threat to survey researchers.

Sometimes, people may feel that there is a preferred or socially desirable answer, and their answer might reflect this feeling. This *social desirability effect* can produce a gap between people's survey responses and their actual behaviors.

Some respondents have what is called an *acquiescence response bias,* which means that they have a tendency to say "yes" and display agreement in their answers. (The opposite bias can happen as well. A respondent can have a tendency to say "no" or be a naysayer.)

3. *Respondents' attitudes, beliefs, habits, and interests can appear highly unstable.* For example, Foddy (1993, p. 4) cited Gritching's (1986) research, in which respondents were asked the same question (their feelings about a gambling casino in their community) at the start and at the end of a structured interview. It seems that 18 percent of the respondents changed their position during the course of the interview! It might well be that these respondents in fact changed their mind as a result of participating in the interview—they might have been introduced to new ideas posed by the interviewer's questions. However, it just might be that respondents' answers reflect more than their attitudes—they may be responses to slight nuances in how the question was asked, tiredness or boredom at the end of the interview process, and so forth.

4. *Small changes in wording sometimes result in dramatically different responses.* Foddy (1993, p. 6) cited Peterson's (1984) study, in which only 3.2 percent of respondents failed to answer the question "What is your age?" But when the question "How old are you?" was posed to a similar sample, 9.7 percent of respondents failed to answer. It's disconcerting when a change this modest may be responsible for a threefold increase in the number of people who apparently can't report their age. Obviously, what a researcher regards as a modest change in wording can function as a major change from the perspective of respondents.

5. *Respondents can misinterpret what questions are asking.* For example, several researchers have found that respondents' interpretations of words commonly used in survey research, including *usually, generally, people,* and *weekday,* can be subject to a wide range of interpretations by respondents. Researchers need to make certain that their questions are clearly understood in the manner they intend them.

6. *The order in which questions are asked can affect respondents' answers.* Prior questions provide a context or frame in which respondents interpret later questions. Such a framing effect can affect the meaning of a given question. For example, Foddy (1993, p. 6) shared the results of a study by Noelle-Neumann (1970), in which German respondents were asked to rate several foods in terms of how "German" they were. "Potatoes" was regarded as more "German" if it followed rather than preceded "rice" in the list of foods.

The impact of item order is not uniform, however. When J. Edwin Benton and John Daly (1991) conducted a local government survey, they found that the less educated respondents were more influenced by the order of questionnaire items than were those with more education.

Other kinds of order effects can also occur. Respondents can grow fatigued or bored, especially with lengthy questionnaires or long interviews. The answers they provide to later questions may be a marker of their exhaustion or boredom rather than an accurate response.

Respondents might also display what is called a *response set,* characterized by the tendency to respond the same way without really thinking about each individual question. For example, if all of the questions in a survey are worded such that a positive response is always indicated by circling the right-most option, a respondent can simply go through the questionnaire in haste, choosing all of the options on the right (or, if he or she has a negative response, all of the options on the left).

7. *Changes in question format can affect respondent answers.* For example, *open-ended questions* (i.e., those that do not structure respondent answers) can produce different answers than *closed-ended questions* (i.e., those that present respondents with response options from which to choose). In citing Schuman and Presser (1981), Foddy (1993, p. 8) reported about a 20-percentage-point difference in the rate of respondents in a study who reported that the energy shortage was the most important problem facing the country when the question was posed in open-ended versus closed-ended fashion. Is it that people simply forgot about problems without the prompt of having options placed in front of them? Or did the prompt function as a source of bias in affecting people's answers? Unfortunately, we don't know the answers to these questions.

8. *Respondents often answer questions when they know little about the topic.* For instance, Foddy (1993, p. 8)

reported research suggesting that up to 25 percent of respondents will check substantive options in the absence of a "Don't know" option but will check a "Don't know" option when it is available. Foddy cited research indicating that when respondents are asked to respond to fictitious or obscure topics, upwards of 30 percent of them provide answers anyway. This point is illustrated occasionally when researchers ask for responses relating to fictitious people and issues. In a political poll one of us conducted, respondents were asked whether they were familiar with each of 15 political figures in the community. As a methodological exercise, one name was made up: Tom Sakumoto. In response, 9 percent of the respondents said they were familiar with him. Of those respondents familiar with him, about half reported seeing him on television and reading about him in the newspapers.

You can disregard responses to fictitious issues. But when the issue is real, you may have no way of telling which responses genuinely reflect attitudes and which reflect meaningless answers to an irrelevant question.

9. *Questions can have cultural bias that can result in different responses from people of varying cultural backgrounds.* Charles Briggs (1986) reported a vivid example of this problem. Respondents were asked to respond to how a certain neighborhood facility could best meet the demands of the local residents. Navajo respondents reported a much lower demand for services than did Zuni, Mexican American, or Anglo American respondents. Briggs discovered that the reason for this discrepancy had little to do with actual needs and more to do with cultural codes of rudeness. Among Navajo, it was apparently regarded as rude to make inquiries about the perceived needs of one's spouse and children. Yet the interviewer's questions asked respondents to answer how their families would use the services. As a way to deflect the rudeness of the interviewer's query, a Navajo would refrain from commenting.

After reading this long list of potential problems with question asking, we hope you appreciate just how challenging it can be for a survey researcher to produce good questions. Lest you are ready to throw in the towel and give up completely on survey research, we want to give you some assurances that these problems can be managed quite well through careful and thoughtful questionnaire construction. Let's turn to some general guidelines that are useful to keep in mind when constructing surveys or when evaluating the questions included in someone else's survey.

GUIDELINES FOR ASKING QUESTIONS

Although this section is about asking questions, an examination of a typical **questionnaire** or **interview protocol** will probably reveal as many statements as questions. This is not without reason. Often, the researcher is interested in determining the extent to which respondents hold a particular attitude or perspective. If you can summarize the attitude in a fairly brief statement, you can present that statement and ask respondents whether they agree or disagree with it. Rensis Likert has greatly formalized this procedure through the creation of the Likert scale, a format in which respondents are asked to strongly agree, agree, disagree, or strongly disagree, or perhaps strongly approve, approve, and so forth (we'll come back to Likert items a bit later).

Both questions and statements can be profitably used. Using both in a given questionnaire or interview gives you more flexibility in the design of items and can make the questionnaire more interesting as well. Whenever we use the term *question,* our intent is to refer as well to survey statements.

Several general guidelines can help you frame and ask questions that serve as excellent operationalizations of variables. These guidelines aren't foolproof, but they will help a survey researcher develop questions that can minimize many of the challenges we just discussed, thereby producing a measure that maximizes the likelihood of adequate measurement reliability and validity.

Appropriately Open-Ended and Closed-Ended Questions

In asking questions, researchers have two options: open ended and closed ended. Closed-ended questions are popular because they provide a greater uniformity of responses and are more easily processed than open-ended responses, which generally need to be coded before they can be processed for computer analysis, as will be discussed in Chapter 11. This coding process often requires that the researcher interpret the meaning of responses, opening the possibility of misunderstanding and researcher bias. There is also a danger that some respondents will give answers that are essentially irrelevant to the researcher's intent. Closed-ended responses, on the other hand, can often be transferred directly into a computer format. On the plus side, open-ended questions provide respondents with an opportunity to express themselves in their own words without the imposition of the researcher's framework. For example, if you wanted to know what characterized people's most satisfying communication encounters, you might want to phrase your question in an open-ended manner in order to find out about all of the different kinds of interactions that people find satisfying.

The chief shortcoming of closed-ended questions lies in the researcher's structuring of responses. When the relevant answers to a given question are relatively clear, there should be no problem. In other cases, however, the researcher's structuring of responses may overlook some important responses. In asking about "satisfying communication encounters," for example, your checklist of issues might omit certain features that respondents would have provided.

In the construction of closed-ended questions, you should be guided by two structural requirements. The response categories provided should be *exhaustive:* They should include all the possible responses that might be expected. Often, researchers ensure this by adding a category labeled something like "Other (Please specify: _____)."

Second, the answer categories must be *mutually exclusive:* The respondent should not feel compelled to select more than one. (In some cases, you may wish to solicit multiple answers, but these may create difficulties in data processing and analysis later on.) To ensure that your categories are mutually exclusive, carefully consider each combination of categories, asking yourself whether a person could reasonably choose more than one answer. In addition, it's useful to add an instruction to the question, asking the respondent to select the one best answer, but this technique is not a satisfactory substitute for a carefully constructed set of responses.

The response options in closed-ended questions should match the question asked. For example, if you're asking people the extent to which they enjoy talking to strangers at social gatherings, the response options should probably reflect degree of enjoyment (e.g., "A great deal" to "Not at all") rather than other kinds of dimensions of response (e.g., frequency, low to high). The box "Some Common Response Options" lists a number of frequently employed response dimensions employed in survey research. When choosing a response option, ask yourself what is best suited to the question asked and to your research purposes. Notice that the response options in this box are listed in a logical order along some implicit continuum of more–less agreement, positivity, satisfaction, approval. Such an ordering makes it easier for respondents to locate where their answer best fits.

Note that some of the response options in this box are anchored by endpoints of "Always" and "Never." Although some survey researchers recommend that such absolute categories be avoided because they are extremes, we think that there are questions for which it is useful to distinguish a response of "always" from a response of "almost always." For example, if you asked people how often they used condoms when having sex, this distinction might be an important one.

Closed-ended questions are used so frequently in communication research that several standard formats have been developed. We'll discuss these in greater detail later in the chapter when we discuss commonly used indexes and scales.

Question Clarity

It should go without saying that questions should be clear and unambiguous, but the broad proliferation of unclear and ambiguous questions in surveys makes the point worth stressing here. Often, you can become so deeply involved in the topic under examination that opinions and perspectives are clear to you but not to your respondents—many of whom have paid little or no attention to the topic. Or, if you have only a superficial understanding of the topic, you may fail to specify the intent of your question sufficiently. The question "What do you think about the new wireless Internet technology?" may evoke in the respondent a counterquestion: "*Which* new wireless Internet technology?" Questionnaire items should be precise so that the respondent knows exactly what the researcher is asking.

The possibilities for misunderstanding are endless, and no researcher is immune. Floyd Fowler (1995, p. 222) examined the questions used in national health surveys and found that several of them contained one or more terms lacking clarity. Here are some examples, along with Fowler's queries and rewordings:

Original Question	Problem	Reworded Question
1. What is the average number of days each week you have butter?	Does margarine count as butter?	Not including margarine, what is the average number of days each week you have butter?
2. What is your number of servings of eggs in a typical day?	How many eggs constitute a serving? What does "a typical day" mean?	On days when you eat eggs, how many eggs do you usually have?

SOME COMMON RESPONSE OPTIONS

Often, survey researchers wish to use closed-ended questions to measure the frequency with which something happens, the quantity of some phenomenon, the valence of feelings, favorableness of evaluation, and so forth. Here are some commonly employed standard response options to consider (Fowler, 1995; Sheatsley, 1983). The choice of which response format to use depends on your purpose and the kind of information you wish to collect from your respondent.

Frequency

Response Set 1	*Response Set 2*	*Response Set 3*	*Response Set 4*
More than once a day	Very often	Often	Always
Almost every day	Fairly often	Sometimes	Usually
A few times a week	Occasionally	Rarely	A good bit of the time
About once a month	Rarely	Never	Some of the time
Two or three times a month	Never		Rarely
About once a month			Never
Less than once a month			
A few times a year			
Once a year or less			

Response Set 5	*Response Set 6*	*Response Set 7*	*Response Set 8*
Almost always	Always	Regularly	Always
More than half the time	Usually	Often	Most of the time
About half the time	Sometimes	Seldom	Some of the time
Less than half the time	Rarely	Never	Rarely or never
Rarely	Never		
Never			

Quantity

Response Set 1	*Response Set 2*
A great deal	Big
Some	Medium
Only a little	Small
Not at all	None at all

In general, survey researchers are well advised to phrase questions with as much precision as possible. If you're inquiring about the frequency of some communicative behavior, be sure to specify a time period. For example, if you want to know how often people use e-mail, you should provide them with a specific time period: in the last 24 hours, during the past 7 days, and so forth. Surveys should also be free of overly technical language, abbreviations, acronyms, jargon, and slang. Although such terms might be very clear to the researcher, they could be a basis of misunderstanding for the respondent.

Avoiding Double-Barreled Questions

Frequently, researchers ask respondents for a single answer to a combination of questions. This seems to happen most often when the researcher has personally identified with a complex question. For example, you might ask respondents to agree or disagree with the statement "The FCC should mandate a violence code on television programming and eliminate violence on programs targeted to children." Although many people would unequivocally agree with the statement and others would unequivocally disagree, still others would be unable to answer this question as worded. Some would

Measuring Satisfaction

Response Set 1	*Response Set 2*	*Response Set 3*
Very satisfied	Completely satisfied	Perfectly satisfied
Generally satisfied	Mostly satisfied	Slightly dissatisfied
Somewhat dissatisfied	Mixed	Somewhat dissatisfied
Very dissatisfied	Mostly dissatisfied	Very dissatisfied
	Completely dissatisfied	

Measuring Perceived Importance

Response Set 1	*Response Set 2*
Very important	Very important
Fairly important	Somewhat important
Not at all important	Slightly important
	Not at all important

Evaluative Judgments

Response Set 1	*Response Set 2*	*Response Set 3*	*Response Set 4*	*Response Set 5*
Excellent	Excellent	Too many	Very much better	Choose a number from
Very good	Good	About right	Slightly better	0 to 10, where 10 is as
Good	Fair	Not enough	About the same	good as it can be and
Fair	Poor		Slightly worse	0 is as bad as it can be.
Poor			Very much worse	

Agreement

Response Set 1	*Response Set 2*	*Response Set 3*
Completely agree	Strongly agree	Strongly approve
Generally agree	Somewhat agree	Somewhat approve
Generally disagree	Neither agree nor disagree	Somewhat disapprove
Completely disagree	Somewhat disagree	Strongly disapprove
	Strongly disagree	

favor a mandatory FCC violence code yet disagree with limiting the ban to just children's programs. Others might reject any government action to limit freedom of speech and thus disagree with the idea of a mandatory FCC violence code, yet they might strongly support voluntary efforts by the television networks to eliminate violence in children's programming. These latter respondents could neither agree nor disagree without misleading you.

As a general rule, whenever the word *and* appears in a question or statement, you should check whether you are asking a *double-barreled* question. See the box titled "Double-Barreled and Beyond" for some imaginative variations on this theme. The solution to double-barreled questions is to develop separate items for each portion of the double-barreled item.

Respondent Competence to Answer

In asking respondents to provide information, you should continually ask yourself whether they are able to do so reliably. In a study of self-reported nonverbal behavior, for example, you might ask people to indicate on a scale from "Not at all" to "All the time" how often they establish eye contact with others during conversation. The problem with this question is that our eye-contact patterns are often habituated behaviors that we enact outside of

DOUBLE-BARRELED AND BEYOND

Even established, professional researchers have sometimes created double-barreled questions and worse. Consider this question, asked of U.S. citizens in April 1986, at a time when the country's relationship with Libya was at an especially low point. Some observers suggested the United States might end up in a shooting war with the small North African nation. The Harris Poll sought to find out what U.S. public opinion was:

> If Libya now increases its terrorist acts against the U.S. and we keep inflicting more damage on Libya, then inevitably it will all end in the U.S. going to war and finally invading that country which would be wrong.

Respondents were given the opportunity of answering "Agree," "Disagree," or "Not sure." Notice the elements contained in the complex statement:

1. Will Libya increase its terrorist acts against the U.S.?
2. Will the U.S. inflict more damage on Libya?
3. Will the U.S. inevitably or otherwise go to war against Libya?
4. Would the U.S. invade Libya?
5. Would that be right or wrong?

These several elements offer the possibility of numerous points of view—far more than the three alternatives offered to respondents to the survey. Even if we were to assume hypothetically that Libya would "increase its terrorist attacks" and the U.S. would "keep inflicting more damage" in return, you might have any one of at least seven distinct expectations about the outcome:

	U.S. will not go to war.	War is probable but not inevitable.	War is inevitable.
U.S. will not invade Libya.	1	2	3
U.S. will invade Libya, but it would be wrong.		4	5
U.S. will invade Libya, and it would be right.		6	7

The examination of prognoses about the Libyan situation is not the only example of double-barreled questions sneaking into public opinion research. Here are some statements the Harris Poll asked in an attempt to gauge U.S. public opinion about then Soviet General Secretary Gorbachev:

> He looks like the kind of Russian leader who will recognize that both the Soviets and the Americans can destroy each other with nuclear missiles so it is better to come to verifiable arms control agreements.
>
> He seems to be more modern, enlightened, and attractive, which is a good sign for the peace of the world.
>
> Even though he looks much more modern and attractive, it would be a mistake to think he will be much different from other Russian leaders.

How many elements can you identify in each of the statements? How many possible opinions could people have in each case? What does a simple "agree" or "disagree" really mean in such cases?

Source: Reported in *World Opinion Update,* October 1985 and May 1986, respectively.

conscious awareness. People would probably give you an answer to this question, but their answers would most likely reflect their views of themselves as honest, friendly, outgoing, and competent communicators; after all, in this culture we tend to think of someone who looks us in the eye and who doesn't look down while speaking as characterized by these qualities. If we want to measure eye contact, perhaps a better way would be through direct observation.

In general, people's ability to answer questions lessens as the time frame is removed from the present. Thus,

the more distant the behavior or event in the past, the more difficult it will be for people to provide an accurate answer. For example, if you ask people to tell you the extent to which their parents were responsive to them during infancy, the answers you receive will probably be much more revealing about their current attitudes toward their parents than their memories of their infancy.

Similarly, respondents are not very well positioned to tell you what they will do in the future. In the absence of crystal balls, none of us can say with accuracy what we will say or do at some future point.

Some researchers advise against "why" questions because of the complexity involved in causation. Why people think the way they do or behave the way they do can be a very complicated matter. People may not be positioned to provide a complete explanation of the causes for their actions. Nonetheless, several surveys do include "why" questions, less with the goal of gaining a comprehensive explanation of causality and more with the goal of gaining insight into people's account-making practices.

Respondent Willingness to Answer

Often, we would like to learn things from people that they are unwilling to share with us. This is especially likely when the topic is controversial, when people believe that they occupy a minority view, or when the topic has *social desirability* implications. For example, people who test positive for HIV often regard themselves as socially stigmatized (Dindia, 1998). If a researcher conducts a survey and asks people their HIV status, they may not answer the question or may provide a false answer. Researchers with an interest in how victims of sexual abuse tell their stories of survival may face similar difficulty with respondent unwillingness to discuss their experiences.

Researchers have devised measures of an individual's inclination to describe himself or herself in ways that he or she thinks are acceptable or desirable to others. For example, the Social Desirability Scale (Crowne & Marlowe, 1960) contains 33 items designed to measure a tendency to respond in socially desirable ways. Items from this measure could be interspersed with survey items for purposes of detecting responses biased toward social desirability.

Sometimes, researchers can minimize unwillingness to respond by giving assurance of anonymity. For example, the Gallup Organization has used a "secret ballot" format, which simulates actual election conditions in that the "voter" enjoys complete anonymity. In an analysis of the Gallup Poll election data from 1944 to 1988, Andrew Smith and G. F. Bishop (1992) have found that this technique substantially reduced the percentage saying they were undecided about how they would vote.

Researchers can sometimes increase people's willingness to respond by displaying sensitivity to the needs of their respondents. For example, questions should be worded in ways that reduce the likelihood that respondents will feel embarrassed, be angered, or have their self-esteem lessened. For example, a question about racial background with the response options "Black," "White," and "Other" glosses over racial differences grouped together as "Other"—Asians and Native Americans, among others, might be offended. Furthermore, multiracial persons might be offended in the question's bias toward single-race people.

Question Relevance

Questions asked in a questionnaire should be relevant to most respondents. When attitudes are requested on a topic that few respondents have thought about or really care about, the results are not likely to be very useful. Of course, because the respondents may express attitudes even though they've never given any thought to the issue, you run the risk of being misled.

It is helpful in closed-ended questions to provide respondents with a "Don't know" option. The respondent should be signaled that such a response is on equal terms with other response options. Respondents who truly don't know how to respond won't feel forced into giving an answer about which they are unsure.

Simplicity of Question Wording

In the interest of being unambiguous, precise, and concerned about the relevance of an issue, the researcher is often led into long and complicated items. This practice should be avoided. Respondents are often unwilling to study an item in order to understand it. The respondent should be able to read an item quickly, understand its intent, and select or provide an answer without difficulty. In general, you should assume that respondents *will* read items quickly and give quick answers; therefore, you should provide clear, short items that will not be misinterpreted under those conditions.

One check you can perform on question wording is to assess its *readability*. Fortunately, most computerized word processing software these days comes with built-in options, such as the Flesch Reading Score and the Flesch–Kincaid Grade Level, to measure the readability of any sample of prose. The Flesch Reading score is a number from 1 to 100, with higher numbers indicating greater reading ease (try to achieve a score in the 60–70 range if questioning adults). You can also determine a question's Flesch–Kincaid grade level, which tells you the grade level of your prose (try for a 7th–8th grade level when questioning adults).

Avoiding Negative Wording

The appearance of a negation in a questionnaire item paves the way for easy misinterpretation. Asked to agree or disagree with the statement "The United States should *not* recognize Cuba," a sizable portion of the respondents will read over the word *not* and answer on that basis. Thus, some will agree with the statement when they are in favor of recognition, and others will agree when they oppose it. And you may never know which is which. As a general rule, questions should be worded without negatives. Thus, the question would be better if asked this way: "The United States should recognize Cuba," with response options that allow for a range of agreement from strongly agree to strongly disagree.

Avoiding Biased Wording

Recall from the earlier discussion of conceptualization and operationalization that there are no ultimately true meanings for any of the concepts we typically study in communication. *Communication competence* has no ultimately correct definition, and whether a given person is *competent* in his or her communication depends on our definition of that term. This same general principle applies to the responses we get from people completing a questionnaire.

The meaning of someone's response to a question depends in large part on its wording. This is true of every question and answer. Some questions seem to encourage particular responses more than do other questions. Questions that encourage respondents to answer in a particular way are **biased.**

Most researchers recognize the likely effect of a question that begins, "Don't you agree with most people that. . . ." No reputable researcher would use such an item. Unhappily, the biasing effect of items and terms is far subtler than this example suggests.

The mere identification of an attitude or position with a prestigious person or agency can bias responses. The item "Do you agree or disagree with the recent Supreme Court decision that . . . " would have a similar effect. However, we're not suggesting that such wording will necessarily produce consensus or even a majority in support of the position identified with the prestigious person or agency, only that support would likely be increased over what would have been obtained without such identification.

Sometimes, the effect of different forms of question wording is relatively subtle. For example, when Kenneth Rasinski (1989) analyzed the results of several General Social Survey studies of attitudes toward government spending, he found that the way programs were identified had an impact on the amount of public support they received. Here are some comparisons:

More Support	Less Support
"Assistance to the poor"	"Welfare"
"Halting rising crime rate"	"Law enforcement"
"Dealing with drug addiction"	"Drug rehabilitation"
"Solving problems of big cities"	"Assistance to big cities"
"Improving conditions of blacks"	"Assistance to blacks"
"Protecting Social Security"	"Social Security"

In 1986, for example, 62.8 percent of the respondents said too little money was being spent on "assistance to the poor," while in a matched survey that year, only 23.1 percent said we were spending too little on "welfare."

The biasing effect of particular wording is often difficult to anticipate. In surveys, it's sometimes useful to ask respondents to consider hypothetical situations and say how they think they would behave. Because those situations often involve other people, the names used can affect responses. For example, researchers have long known that male names for the hypothetical people may produce different responses than female names would. Research by Joseph Kasof (1993) points to the importance of what the specific names are—whether they generally evoke positive or negative images in terms of attractiveness, age, intelligence, and so forth. Kasof's review of past research suggests there has been a tendency to use more positively valued names for men than for women.

As in all other examples, you must carefully examine the purpose of your inquiry and construct items that will be most useful to it. You should never be misled into thinking that there are ultimately "right" and "wrong" ways of asking the questions. When in doubt about the best question to ask, remember that you should ask more than one.

USING COMPOSITE MEASURES

Although you can sometimes construct a single questionnaire/interview question that captures the variable of interest—"Sex: _____ Male _____ Female" is a simple example—other variables are less straightforward and may require you to use several questions to measure them adequately. For example, if you wanted to measure someone's attitude toward the complex phenomenon of "freedom of speech," you'd probably need several questions to tease out all of the facets of your respondent's beliefs and attitudes. Many communication concepts have complex and varied meanings. Making measurements that capture such concepts can be a challenge. In particular, we'd like you to recall the discussion of content validity in Chapter 6, which concerns whether we've captured all the different dimensions of a concept. A **composite measure** is the use of several questions to measure a given variable.

Composite measures are frequently used in survey research, for several reasons. First, despite the care taken in designing studies to provide valid and reliable measurements of variables, the researcher can seldom develop in advance single indicators of complex concepts. This is especially true with regard to attitudes and orientations. More likely, researchers will devise several items, each of which provides some indication of the variables. However, each of these is likely to prove invalid or unreliable for many respondents.

Second, you may wish to employ a rather refined measure of your variable, arranging cases in several ordinal categories from, for example, very low to very high on a variable such as *communication apprehension*. A single data item might not have enough categories to provide the desired range of variation, but a composite measure formed from several items could.

Third, composite measures are efficient devices for data analysis. If considering a single data item gives us only a rough indication of a given variable, considering several data items may give us a more comprehensive and more accurate indication. For example, a single newspaper editorial may give us some indication of the political orientations of that newspaper. Examining several editorials would probably give us a better assessment, but the manipulation of several data items simultaneously could be very complicated. Composite measures are efficient *data-reduction devices:* Several indicators may be summarized in a single numerical score while sometimes nearly maintaining the specific details of all the individual indicators.

Composite measures can be organized according to two basic features: (1) whether they are unidimensional or multidimensional and (2) whether they are indexes or scales. Let's briefly discuss each of these features before turning to a discussion of some commonly used composite measures in communication research.

Unidimensional versus Multidimensional Composite Measures

When a variable has a single facet, it is *unidimensional,* and all of the questions asked will focus on this single facet. By contrast, when a variable has several facets, or components, it is known as *multidimensional.* Multi-dimensional measures have a set of questions focused around each underlying facet or dimension. When a measure is unidimensional, a respondent's answers to all of the questions can simply be added up or averaged. By contrast, when a measure is multidimensional, a separate score (whether a sum or an average) must be derived for each dimension.

Often, survey researchers assess the dimensionality of a given composite measure by employing statistical procedures such as factor analysis, cluster analysis, or multidimensional scaling. These statistical procedures basically examine the patterning of respondents' answers, determining if all answers "hang together" or if they appear to form several discrete clusters or factors of answers.

Let's consider the variable of source credibility, or how believable a message source is perceived to be by respondents. Many researchers have assessed the dimensionality of the credibility variable, and they have identified several underlying dimensions, including competence or expertise, character or trustworthiness, and dynamism (how sociable, extroverted, and composed a source is) (Berlo, Lemert, & Mertz, 1970; McCroskey, Hamilton, & Weiner, 1974). A given source—say, the anchor on the evening local news—could be high or low on each dimension. For example, one anchor could be perceived as a highly dynamic speaker but relatively low in expertise and trustworthiness. In order to measure a source's perceived credibility, three scores would be needed—one for the questions focusing on competence, one for the questions focusing on trustworthiness, and one for the questions focusing on dynamism.

Indexes versus Scales

The terms *index* and *scale* are typically used imprecisely and interchangeably in communication literature. Before considering the distinction between indexes and scales, let's first see what they have in common.

Both scales and indexes are *composite measures of variables:* measurements based on more than one data item. Thus, a survey respondent's score on an index or scale of communication anxiety would be determined by the specific responses given to several questionnaire items, each of which would provide some indication of his or her anxiety. Similarly, a person's IQ score is based on answers to a large number of test questions. The political orientation of a newspaper might be represented by an index or scale score reflecting its editorial policy on various political issues.

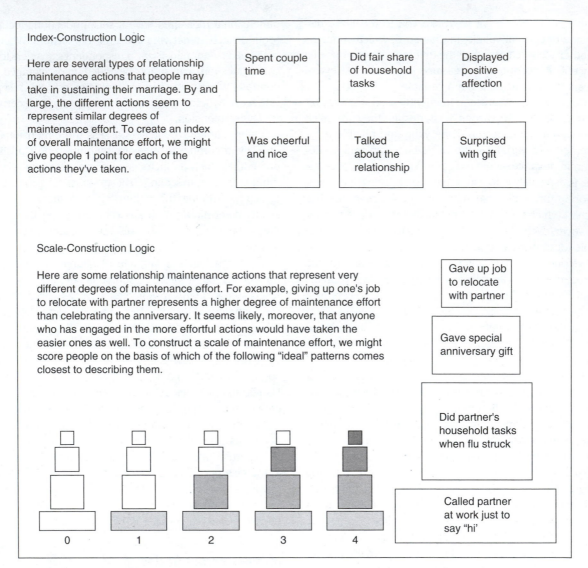

Index-Construction Logic

Here are several types of relationship maintenance actions that people may take in sustaining their marriage. By and large, the different actions seem to represent similar degrees of maintenance effort. To create an index of overall maintenance effort, we might give people 1 point for each of the actions they've taken.

Spent couple time	Did fair share of household tasks	Displayed positive affection
Was cheerful and nice	Talked about the relationship	Surprised with gift

Scale-Construction Logic

Here are some relationship maintenance actions that represent very different degrees of maintenance effort. For example, giving up one's job to relocate with partner represents a higher degree of maintenance effort than celebrating the anniversary. It seems likely, moreover, that anyone who has engaged in the more effortful actions would have taken the easier ones as well. To construct a scale of maintenance effort, we might score people on the basis of which of the following "ideal" patterns comes closest to describing them.

Gave up job to relocate with partner

Gave special anniversary gift

Did partner's household tasks when flu struck

Called partner at work just to say "hi'

0   1   2   3   4

FIGURE 8-1 **Indexes versus Scales**

We distinguish indexes and scales through the manner in which scores are assigned. An **index** is constructed through the simple accumulation of scores assigned to individual attributes. We might measure relationship closeness, for example, by adding up the circled numbers in response to several closeness statements, with various numbers representing the degree of agreement. A **scale** is constructed through the assignment of scores to *patterns* of responses, recognizing that some items reflect a relatively weak degree of the variable while others reflect something stronger. Agreeing that "Women are different from men" is certainly weak evidence of sexism compared with agreeing that "Women should not be allowed to vote." Thus, a scale takes advantage of any *intensity structure* that may exist among attributes. Another simple example should clarify this distinction.

Figure 8-1 provides a graphic illustration of the difference between indexes and scales. Let's assume we want to develop a measure of relationship maintenance effort, distinguishing those relationship parties who actively work to sustain their relationship's satisfaction level, those who aren't very active in sustaining their relationship, and those who are somewhere in between.

The first part of Figure 8-1 illustrates the logic of indexes. We've represented six different relationship maintenance actions. Although we might disagree on some specifics, we could probably agree that the six actions represent roughly the same degree of relationship maintenance activity. Although some people might feel less comfortable engaging in a talk about the state of their relationship than in surprising the partner with a gift—or vice versa—the six actions are probably more or less equal if we consider the population as a whole.

We could construct an index of relationship maintenance effort, using the six items, by giving each person 1 point for each of the actions he or she has taken. So if you spent couple time with your partner (say, going out to dinner and then to a movie) and if you performed your fair share of household tasks, you'd get a total of 2 points. If someone else displayed positive affection for his or her partner and bought a surprise gift, this person would get the same score as you. Using this approach, we'd conclude that the two of you had the same degree of relationship maintenance effort, even though different actions were taken.

The second part of Figure 8-1 describes the logic of scale construction. In this case, the actions clearly represent *different* degrees of relationship maintenance effort—ranging from simply calling the partner at work to say "hi" to displaying a willingness to give up one's job in order to relocate with the partner's new employment opportunity. Moreover, it seems safe to assume a pattern of actions in this case. For example, all those who were willing to relocate with the partner were also willing to buy a special anniversary gift for the partner. Those who celebrated special occasions were probably also willing to help out more around the house when the partner was ill. This suggests that most people will fall into only one of five "ideal" action patterns, represented by the small illustrations at the bottom of the figure.

Scales are generally superior to indexes because scales take into consideration the intensity with which different items reflect the variable being measured. Also, as the example in Figure 8-1 shows, scale scores convey more information than do index scores.

You should be cautioned against two common misconceptions about scaling. First, be wary of the common misuse of the term *scale;* merely calling a given measure a scale rather than an index does not make it so. Second, whether the combination of several data items results in a scale almost always depends on the particular sample of observations under study. Because certain items may form a scale among one sample but not among another, you should not assume that a given set of items is a scale because it has formed a scale among a given sample.

An examination of the communication literature will show that indexes are used much more frequently than scales. Indexes are more frequently used because scales are often difficult or impossible to construct from the data

at hand. Index construction is not a simple undertaking, however. In Appendix H we provide a detailed discussion of index construction. Once you fully understand the logic of index construction, you'll be better equipped to attempt the construction of scales, which we also discuss in Appendix H. Indeed, a carefully constructed index may turn out to be a scale.

Some Standard Indexes and Scales

Although questions can be asked in any of several ways, survey researchers tend to rely on a few basic types of index and scale formats in communication.

Likert-Type Indexes   You may sometimes hear people refer to a questionnaire item containing response categories of "strongly agree," "agree," "neither agree nor disagree," "disagree," and "strongly disagree" as a *Likert scale.* This is technically a misnomer (see our discussion above of indexes versus scales), although Rensis Likert (pronounced LICK-ert) did create this commonly used question form.

Communication researchers often use response options other than the agree–disagree continuum (for example, many of the response dimensions in the box "Some Common Response Options"), and they may use a 7-point or even a 9-point continuum instead of the 5-point continuum. Variations from the original format employed by Likert are referred to as a **Likert-type index.**

Sometimes when Likert-type items are used in a questionnaire, the numbers are presented; other times, word descriptions alone are used, and the researcher assigns the numbers 1–5 or 1–7 to the various response options.

In order to prevent a response set from taking place, researchers often word some statements to reflect a positive attitude and other statements to reflect a negative attitude. For example, if we were using Likert items to measure attitudes toward e-mail, we might include these two items in our composite measure:

E-mail has positively transformed communication between people.

1	2	3	4	5
Strongly Agree	Agree	Neither Agree nor Disagree	Disagree	Strongly Disagree

E-mail has increased misunderstandings between people.

1	2	3	4	5
Strongly Agree	Agree	Neither Agree nor Disagree	Disagree	Strongly Disagree

Notice that a response of "1" to the first statement would reflect a very positive attitude toward e-mail, whereas a response of "1" to the second item would reflect a very negative attitude toward e-mail. A person who holds a very positive attitude toward e-mail would likely circle the numbers "1" and "5" to these two questions, respectively.

Assuming that these two items represent the same underlying dimension, we could sum a respondent's answers to derive an index score of his or her attitude. But if we summarized our respondent's "1" and "5," we

would be making a big mistake because the questions are reverse-worded. In order to derive a valid sum, we would first need to do *reverse scoring,* a procedure in which all respondents' answers to negative statements are reversed: A "1" is re-scored a "7," a "2" is re-scored a "6," and so on. In the e-mail index above, we would take our respondent's answer of "5" to the second question and reverse score it as a "1" before summing the scores or averaging them.

Likert-type indexes are used very frequently in quantitative communication research. Table 8-1 provides a

TABLE 8-1 **A Sample of Likert-Type Measures in Communication Research**

Index	Description	Response Format	Sample Items
Communication Competence Scale	An index designed to measure a person's ability to choose appropriate behaviors and accomplish interpersonal goals while sensitive to the other's face needs and situational constraints (Wiemann, 1977)	36 statements to which respondent indicates extent of agreement on 7-point strongly agree–strongly disagree continuum. The instrument can be used to self-report on own communication behavior or to assess another's behavior.	"[I/my partner/my boss] treats people as individuals."
International Communication Association Audit	A package of paper-and-pencil survey instruments designed to assess employee perceptions of communication in their organization (Downs, 1988)	120 questions divided into 8 major sections: amount of information desired and received on work-related topics; amount of information sent on work-related topics; amount of follow-up; amount of information received from various sources; timeliness of information; organizational communication relationships; satisfaction with outcomes; amount of information received from various channels	"This is the amount of information I receive now on . . . —How well I am doing my job. —My job duties." 1 = very little 2 = little 3 = some 4 = great 5 = very great
Parasocial Interaction Scale	An index of the extent to which a media consumer perceives friendship or intimacy with a remote media persona (Rubin, Perse, & Powell, 1985)	20 statements about feelings toward a media persona such as a TV newscaster, to which respondents indicate extent of agreement: 1 = strongly disagree; 2 = disagree; 3 = disagree some and agree some; 4 = agree; 5 = strongly agree	"My favorite newscaster keeps me company when the news is on TV."
Teacher Nonverbal Immediacy Behaviors Instrument	An index of the extent to which a teacher is perceived to engage in a series of behaviors to increase physical and psychological closeness to students (Richmond, Gorham, & McCroskey, 1987)	The respondent rates each of 14 teacher immediacy behaviors using a 0–4 response continuum: 0 = never; 1 = rarely; 2 = occasionally; 3 = often; 4 = very often	[My teacher . . .] —"smiles at the class while talking." —"sits behind desk while teaching."
Verbal Aggressiveness Scale	A personality trait that predisposes people to attack the self-concepts of other people rather than their arguments (Infante & Wigley, 1986)	20 statements about behaviors to which the respondent indicates how often each statement is true for himself or herself: 1 = almost never true; 2 = rarely true; 3 = occasionally true; 4 = often true; 5 = almost always true	"When individuals are very stubborn, I use insults to soften the stubbornness."

TABLE 8-2   **A Sample of Semantic Differential Measures in Communication Research**

Index	Description	Sample Items
Individualized Trust Scale	An index to gauge the extent to which a person is regarded as trustworthy (Wheeless & Grotz, 1977)	15 bipolar adjective pairs, including confidential–divulging; safe–dangerous; honest–dishonest; insincere–sincere. 7 spaces separate the paired opposites.
News Credibility Scale	An index of the extent to which news coverage is regarded as credible (Gaziano & McGrath, 1986)	12 bipolar adjective pairs, including tells the whole story–doesn't tell the whole story; is concerned about the public interest–is concerned about profits; has well-trained reporters–has poorly trained reporters. 5 spaces separate the paired opposites.
Personal Involvement Inventory	An index to determine the extent to which a given mediated message (such as a PSA or an advertisement) is perceived as relevant to the respondent (Zaichkowsky, 1985)	20 bipolar adjective pairs, including important–unimportant; of no concern to me–of concern to me; means a lot to me–means nothing to me; boring–interesting. 7 spaces separate opposed anchors.
Student Motivation Scale	An index of the extent to which students self-report interest and involvement in a specific course or college in general (Christophel, 1990)	16 bipolar adjective pairs, including motivated–unmotivated; interested–uninterested; don't want to study–want to study; inspired–uninspired. 7 spaces separate the opposing terms.

sample of some of the many questionnaire measures that rely on Likert-type measures.

Semantic Differential Indexes Like the Likert-type format, the **semantic differential** asks respondents to choose between two opposite positions. Here's how it works.

Suppose you want to assess attitudes toward e-mail using a semantic differential format. To begin, you need to figure out what the underlying dimensions of respondent attitudes are. The originators of the semantic differential suggest that three underlying dimensions will be present for most attitudes: evaluation (e.g., good–bad), potency (e.g., strong–weak), and activity (e.g., fast–slow) (Osgood, Suci, & Tannenbaum, 1957). But a survey researcher who uses a semantic differential would want to perform careful pretesting work to identify the dimensions for the population of respondents to be studied. Then you need to find two opposite terms representing the polar extremes along each dimension. For evaluation, you might choose the bipolar pairs of good–bad and enjoyable–unenjoyable, for instance. Once you have determined the relevant dimensions and have identified pairs of bipolar adjectives to represent the extremes of each, you would lay them out something like the following, making certain to randomly position some positive adjectives on the right side and other positive adjectives on the left side (to offset a response set, as with Likert-type items):

```
                    E-mail
good      ___ : ___ : ___ : ___ : ___ : ___ : ___  bad
unenjoyable ___ : ___ : ___ : ___ : ___ : ___ : ___  enjoyable
                  [and so on]
```

For each pair of bipolar adjectives, respondents are asked to place an *X* on the space that comes closest to representing how they feel about the object under study, in this instance e-mail. Someone with a very favorable attitude toward e-mail might place his or her *X* in the space right next to "good" on the first line and in the space right next to "enjoyable" in the second line. The researcher assigns numbers to the blank spaces, typically 1 through 7, but researchers have been known to use 5, 9, or even 11 spaces between bipolar terms. The researcher determines that a "1" indicates the most favorable attitude and reverse-scores *X*'s accordingly.

Table 8-2 provides a sample of some semantic differential measures in communication research.

Thurstone Equal-Appearing Interval Scales Although Likert-type items and semantic differential items are technically ordinal-level data, many communication researchers use them as if they provided interval-level data. That is, many researchers assume that the interval between numbers is uniform: The distance between a 3 and a 4, for example, is the same as the distance between a

5 and a 6. **Thurstone equal-appearing interval scales** (Thurstone, 1931) are an attempt to develop items that are empirically demonstrated to be equally distant from one another. It's hard to develop Thurstone equal-appearing interval items, but here's how it's done, in a nutshell.

A group of judges is given perhaps a hundred items felt to be indicators of a given variable. Each judge is then asked to estimate how strong an indicator of a variable each item is—by assigning scores of perhaps 1 to 13 or some larger number. If the variable were attitudes toward e-mail, for example, the judges would be asked to assign the score of 1 to the least positive indicators and the score of 13 to the most positive indicators, and intermediate scores to those felt to be somewhere in between. Once the judges have completed this task, the researcher examines the scores assigned to each item by all of the judges to determine which items produced the greatest agreement among the judges. Among those items producing general agreement in scoring, one or more would be selected to represent each scale score from 1 to 13.

Selected items would then be included in a questionnaire (without their scale values showing), and respondents would be asked to mark those statements with which they agreed. Presumably, a respondent who agrees with a statement scored as, say, 5 would also agree with statements scored as 2, 3, and 4.

If the Thurstone scale items were adequately developed and scored, economy and effectiveness of data reduction would result. A single score might be assigned to each respondent (the strength of the hardest item accepted), and that score would adequately represent the responses to several questionnaire items. Thus, Thurstone items can meaningfully be labeled scales.

If we wanted to develop a Thurstone scale on attitudes toward e-mail communication, we would need a group of judges to evaluate about a hundred statements we would generate to capture a range of sentiments toward e-mail. We would winnow down this group of statements to a much smaller set—say, 20—selected to represent equal intervals of intensity along some continuum of favorability. Respondents would check those statements with which they agreed, and we could score a respondent with the most favorable statement that he or she would endorse.

Unfortunately, because of the tremendous expenditure of energy and time required to develop a Thurstone scale, this procedure is not used very much anymore. We introduce it here because of its historical significance and because it illustrates the logic of a scale. However, Guttman scaling is more commonly used these days.

Guttman Scalograms Guttman scaling, named after Louis Guttman, who originated the procedure, is based on the fact that some items under consideration may prove to be more extreme indicators of the variable than others. Appendix H discusses in detail how to construct a **Guttman scalogram.** For our purposes, the important point to remember in a Guttman scalogram is that the items included in the questionnaire have a definite order of intensity to them: If a respondent accepts a more intense statement, then he or she would presumably also accept a less intense statement as well. As a result, respondents can be scored with a single number which captures the highest-order, or most intense, item that they will endorse.

Illustrative of a Guttman scalogram is the Relationship Events Scale developed by Charles King and Andrew Christensen (1983). Respondents were presented with 19 statements about events that may or may not have occurred in their own romantic relationship. They were asked to place a check mark by those events that had occurred. Based on the pattern of responses provided by respondents, King and Christensen argued that the measure formed a scalogram of 6 levels of closeness. The highest level of closeness, level 6, was scored for respondents who agreed with at least one of these statements: "We are or have been engaged to be married" and "We have lived together or we live together now." The next lower level of closeness, level 5, was scored if respondents marked none of the level 6 items and marked at least two of these items: "I have lent my partner more than $20 for more than a week," "My partner has lent me more than $20 for more than a week," and "We have spent a vacation together that lasted longer than three days." Levels 4, 3, and 2 of closeness were scored when respondents endorsed none of the higher-order statements yet checked statements appropriate to these intermediate degrees of closeness, respectively. The lowest possible closeness score, level 1, was scored if none of the higher-order items were endorsed yet at least two of these items were checked: "My partner has called me an affectionate name (sweetheart, darling, etc.)," "I have called my partner an affectionate name (sweetheart, darling, etc.)," "We have spent a whole day with just each other," "We have arranged to spend time together without planning any activity," and "We have felt comfortable enough with each other so that we could be together without talking or doing an activity together." The researchers demonstrated that their 19 event statements formed a scale, in that there was a clear hierarchy of closeness captured in the various statements.

Comparative Judgments So far, we've been talking about standard index and scale formats to measure knowledge, feelings, beliefs, or actions surrounding a single phenomenon. Sometimes, however, communication researchers are interested in deriving **comparative judgments** from respondents, judgments in which people are asked to evaluate two or more phenomena in a direct comparison of some kind.

Many comparative judgments can be solicited from respondents, but the degree to which phenomena are judged to be similar is frequently of interest to communication researchers. When researchers are interested in perceptions of the extent to which phenomena are similar, they pose three kinds of research questions:

(1) Which phenomena are perceived to be in close proximity to each other? In this context, proximity refers to the psychological distance among phenomena. For example, if we were interested in people's perceptions of kinds of talk events, we might want to know whether people perceive "conflict" closer to "lying" or to "open disclosure."

(2) Do the psychological distances among phenomena converge into meaningful clusters? For example, if we were interested in perceptions of similarities among TV programs, would we find a cluster of programs that were all talk shows? A cluster of sitcoms? And so forth.

(3) What are the dimensions of judgment that underlie respondents' similarity perceptions? For example, in our analysis of TV programs, we might find that serious–light is an underlying dimension used by respondents to sort out similarities and differences among our phenomena of TV programs.

When respondents are asked to judge the similarity of phenomena, various formats can be employed. Often, researchers ask respondents for direct ratings on semantic differential items anchored by such endpoints as "exactly the same" and "completely different." For example, suppose we wanted to know people's perceptions of e-mail compared to other media of communication. We might ask respondents to make pairwise judgments of similarity among e-mail, postal-service mail, the telephone, and face to face. We could use direct rating items such as this:

How similar is e-mail communication to communication through postal-service mail?

Exactly the same 1 2 3 4 5 6 7 8 9 Completely different

Such rating items would be repeated for every pairwise combination of phenomena included in our study: e-mail and the telephone, e-mail and face to face, postal-service mail and the telephone, postal-service mail and face to face, and the telephone and face to face.

Judgments of similarity can also be solicited by giving people an unbroken, horizontal line in which people are asked to place a slash mark (/) on the line to capture their perceptions of how similar two phenomena are. This is simply a variation of the semantic differential item we discussed above:

Exactly the same ———————————— Completely different

If there are many phenomena to be compared, researchers sometimes use a *sorting task* instead of direct ratings. Each phenomena is written on a separate 3×5 card, and a respondent is handed a card deck containing all of the phenomena to be compared. The respondent is told to place cards in the same pile if they are the same and to place them in different piles if they are different. When this procedure is used with many respondents, the researcher can calculate the proportion of times that any two phenomena were placed in the same pile.

In a study designed to understand people's perceptions of deception, Robert Hopper and Robert Bell (1984) asked 180 university students to sort 46 different terms for deception into similar piles using a sorting task. Results indicated that respondents perceived six different clusters of deception: fictions (including such terms as *make-believe, tall tale, myth*), playings (including such terms as *joke, tease, kidding, trick*), lies (including such terms as *dishonesty, fib, lie*), crimes (including such terms as *con, counterfeit, forgery*), masks (including such terms as *hypocrisy, back-stabbing, two-faced*), and unlies (including such terms as *distortion, false implication*). The underlying dimensions used by the sorters to differentiate kinds of deception included evaluation (to what extent was the deception bad?), detectability (to what extent was the act of deception difficult to detect?), and premeditation (to what extent was the act of deception planned?).

Another popular comparative judgment is the ranking task, in which respondents are presented with a number of phenomena and asked to rank them in ascending or descending order according to some standard of judgment—the perceived importance of the phenomena or which phenomena are more and less preferred by the respondent. One way to obtain ranking information is a *paired-comparison* process, in which each phenomenon is paired with each other phenomenon and the respondent is asked to indicate which is preferred for each pair.

For example, in the e-mail study, we might present respondents with this paired-comparison set:

Do you prefer to communicate through e-mail or face to face?

Do you prefer to communicate through e-mail or through postal-service mail?

Do you prefer to communicate through e-mail or telephone?

Do you prefer to communicate through postal-service mail or face to face?

Do you prefer to communicate through postal-service mail or telephone?

Do you prefer to communicate through telephone or face to face?

Other item formats can be identified in communication research, but the Likert-type index, the semantic differential index, Thurstone scales, the Guttman scalogram, and comparative-judgment index procedures are more or less the standard types.

ORGANIZATION OF THE QUESTIONNAIRE

Once you have questions that are reliable and valid indicators of the variable you seek to measure, you need to figure out how to organize and present them in a questionnaire format. Three issues are of particular importance: the order of your questions, the layout of the questions, and instructions for responding.

Question Order

As we noted above in our "Challenge" section, the order in which questions are presented can affect the answers provided by respondents. Some researchers attempt to overcome an order effect by randomizing the order of items. This is usually a futile effort. To begin, a randomized set of items will probably strike respondents as chaotic and worthless. It will be difficult to answer, moreover, since respondents must continually switch their attention from one topic to another. Finally, even a randomized ordering of items will have the effect discussed previously—except that you'll have no control over the effect.

The safest solution is sensitivity to the problem. Although you cannot avoid the effect of item order, try to estimate what that effect will be so you can interpret results meaningfully. If the order of items seems an especially important issue in a given study, you might construct more than one version of the questionnaire containing different possible ordering of items. For example, researchers sometimes use a strategy of *counter-balancing,* in which a given question appears early to half of the respondents and later to the other half of the respondents. The researcher can then determine whether order made a difference for the question. At the very least, you should pretest your questionnaire in the different forms, a point we return to in a bit.

Researchers often strategically order their questions with a goal of making it easier for respondents to provide answers. Sometimes, they employ what is called a *funnel format,* in which broad, open questions appear first, followed by more narrow, closed questions. This order is helpful when people find it difficult to focus precisely on details without first reflecting in broader terms about a given topic area. At other times, researchers employ the opposite strategy, using a *reverse funnel format.* This format involves opening with narrowly focused or even closed questions, then moving to broader, more open questions. This order is helpful for topics on which people find it difficult to reflect on the "big picture" without first reflecting on smaller aspects or facets of the topic. Researchers also use what is known as a *coherence order,* simply grouping together questions that are similarly focused in order to provide a coherent packaging of items upon which a respondent can reflect.

One last form of question ordering is what we shall call *contingency ordering.* When the relevance of some questions is contingent on how respondents answered earlier questions, we face the need for a contingency ordering of questions. Quite often in questionnaires, certain questions will be relevant to some of the respondents and irrelevant to others. For example, you may want to ask whether your respondents use e-mail and, if so, how often they use it, for what purposes, and so forth. Questions about frequency of use and purpose are irrelevant for the respondents who indicated that they don't use e-mail.

The subsequent questions in series such as this are called **contingency questions:** Whether they are to be asked and answered is contingent on responses to the first question in the series. The proper use of contingency questions can aid the respondents' task in completing the questionnaire because they're not faced with trying to answer questions irrelevant to them.

There are several formats for contingency questions. The one shown in Figure 8-2 is probably the clearest and most effective. Note two key elements in this format. First, the contingency question is isolated from the other questions by being set off to the side and enclosed in a box. Second, an arrow connects the contingency question to the answer on which it is contingent. In the illus-

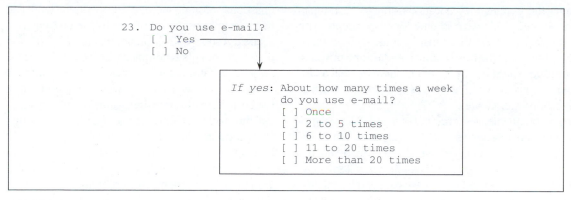

FIGURE 8-2   **Contingency Question Format**

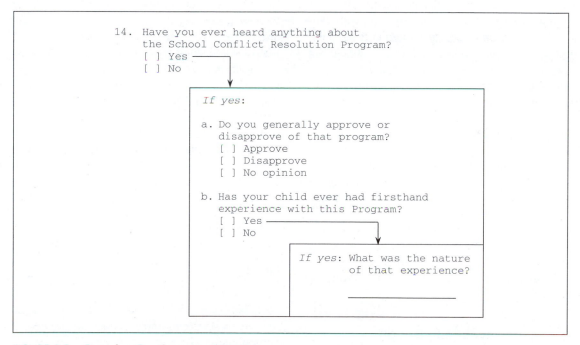

FIGURE 8-3   **Complex Contingency Question**

tration, only those respondents answering yes are expected to answer the contingency question. The rest of the respondents should simply skip it.

Note that the questions shown in Figure 8-2 could have been dealt with in a single question. The question might have read, "How many times, if any, do you use e-mail per week?" The response categories, then, might have read: "None," "Once," "2 to 5 times," and so forth. Such a single question would apply to all respondents, and each would find an appropriate answer category. However, such a question might put some pressure on respondents to report using e-mail, since the main question asks how many times they use it per week, even though it allows for those *exceptional cases who don't use e-mail*

even once. (The emphases used in the previous sentence give a fair indication of how respondents might read the question.) The contingency question format illustrated in Figure 8-2 should reduce the subtle pressure on respondents to report using e-mail. The foregoing discussion should show how seemingly theoretical issues of *validity* and *reliability* are involved in so mundane a matter as how to put questions on a piece of paper.

Used properly, even rather complex sets of contingency questions can be constructed without confusing the respondent. Figure 8-3 illustrates a more complicated example.

In addition to these instructions, it would be worthwhile to place an instruction at the top of each page that contains the contingency questions only. For example, you might say, "This page is only for respondents who have Internet access." Clear instructions such as these spare respondents the frustration of reading and puzzling over questions that are irrelevant to them as well as increasing the likelihood of responses from those for whom the questions are relevant.

In general, the desired ordering of items differs somewhat between interviews and self-administered questionnaires. In the latter, it's usually best to begin the questionnaire with the most interesting set of items. The potential respondents who glance casually over the first few items should *want* to answer them. Perhaps the items will ask for attitudes they're aching to express. At the same time, however, the initial items should not be threatening. (It might be a bad idea to begin with items about sexual behavior or drug use.) Requests for duller, demographic data (age, gender, and the like) should generally be placed at the end of a self-administered questionnaire. Placing these items at the beginning, as many inexperienced researchers are tempted to do, gives the questionnaire the initial appearance of a routine form, and the person receiving it may not be motivated to complete it.

Just the opposite is generally true for interview surveys. When the potential respondent's door first opens, the interviewer must gain rapport quickly. After a short introduction to the study, the interviewer can best begin by getting demographic data about the respondent. Such items are easily answered and generally nonthreatening. Once the initial rapport has been established, the interviewer can then move into the area of attitudes and more sensitive matters.

Questionnaire Layout and Design

The format of a questionnaire is just as important as the wording and ordering of the questions asked. An improperly laid out questionnaire can lead respondents to miss questions, confuse them about the nature of the data desired, and even lead them to throw the questionnaire away.

As a general rule, the questionnaire should be spread out and uncluttered. Inexperienced researchers tend to fear that their questionnaire will look too long; as a result, they squeeze several questions onto a single line, abbreviate questions, and try to use as few pages as possible. All these efforts are ill-advised and even dangerous. Putting more than one question on a line will cause some respondents to miss the second question altogether. Some respondents will misinterpret abbreviated

questions. More generally, respondents who find they have spent considerable time on the first page of what seemed a short questionnaire will be more demoralized than respondents who quickly complete the first several pages of what initially seems a rather long form. Moreover, the latter will make fewer errors and will not be forced to reread confusing, abbreviated questions. Nor will they be forced to write a long answer in a tiny space.

The desirability of spreading out questions cannot be overemphasized. Squeezed-together questionnaires are disastrous, whether they are to be completed by the respondents themselves or administered by trained interviewers.

Quite often, you'll want to ask several questions that have the same set of answer categories. This is typically the case whenever the Likert-type response categories are used. In such cases, it's often possible to construct a matrix of items and answers as illustrated in Figure 8-4.

This format offers several advantages over other formats. First, it uses space efficiently. Second, respondents will probably find it faster to complete a set of questions presented in this fashion. In addition, this format may increase the comparability of responses given to different questions for the respondent as well as for the researcher. Because respondents can quickly review their answers to earlier items in the set, they might choose between "strongly agree" and "agree" on a given statement by comparing the strength of their agreement with their earlier responses in the set.

Giving Instructions

Every questionnaire, whether to be completed by respondents or administered by interviewers, should contain clear instructions and introductory comments where appropriate.

It's useful to begin every questionnaire with basic instructions for completing it. Although many people these days are pretty familiar with forms and questionnaires, you should begin by telling them exactly what you want: that they are to indicate their answers to certain questions by placing a check mark or an *X* in the box beside the appropriate answer or by writing in their answer when asked to do so. If many open-ended questions are used, respondents should receive some guidelines about whether brief or lengthy answers are expected. If you wish to encourage your respondents to elaborate on their responses to closed-ended questions, that should be noted.

If a questionnaire is arranged into subsections, introduce each section with a short statement concerning

17. Beside *each* of the statements presented below, please indicate whether you Strongly
Agree (SA), Agree (A), Disagree (D), Strongly Disagree (SD), or are Undecided (U).

	SA	A	D	SD	U
a. What families need is more time together	[ ]	[ ]	[ ]	[ ]	[ ]
b. Parents should be allowed to take off more time from work to spend with their children	[ ]	[ ]	[ ]	[ ]	[ ]
c. Children should never come home to an empty house	[ ]	[ ]	[ ]	[ ]	[ ]

FIGURE 8-4   **Matrix Question Format**

its content and purpose—for example, "In this section, we'd like to know what people around here consider the most important communication problems." Demographic items at the end of a self-administered questionnaire might be introduced thus: "Finally, we'd like to know just a little about you so we can see how different types of people feel about the issues we've been examining."

Short introductions such as these help the respondent make sense of the questionnaire. They make the questionnaire seem less chaotic, especially when it taps a variety of data. And they help put the respondent in the proper frame of mind for answering the questions.

These, then, are some of the primary guidelines that survey researchers use in developing and organizing reliable and valid questionnaires, and that are helpful in assessing the surveys designed by others. But in the end, a researcher really can't have full confidence in his or her questionnaire without conducting some **pretesting** or pilot work with the questions.

PRETESTING THE QUESTIONNAIRE

No matter how carefully you design a data-collection instrument such as a questionnaire, there is always the possibility—indeed the certainty—of error. You are certain to make some mistake: an ambiguous question, one that people cannot answer, or some other violation of the guidelines just discussed.

The surest protection against such errors is to *pretest* the questionnaire in full and/or in part. Give the questionnaire to ten people in your office or on your dormitory floor, for example. Or conduct a "trial run" with a few folks from the population in which the actual study will be done. It's not usually essential that the pretest partici-

pants constitute a representative sample, although you should use people to whom the questionnaire is at least relevant.

By and large, you'll do better asking people to complete the questionnaire rather than asking them to reflect on whether the questions are good or bad.

Stanley Presser and Johnny Blair (1994) describe several different pretesting strategies and report on the effectiveness of each technique. They also provide data on the cost of the various methods. But whatever the costs, they pale in comparison to the risk that you run in implementing a study without first pretesting its adequacy.

MODES OF QUESTIONNAIRE ADMINISTRATION

This section will deal with the ways in which respondents are asked to complete the questionnaires themselves. We'll start with self-administered questionnaires, then turn to interviewer-administered surveys, telephone surveys, and surveys administered with new technologies (e.g., online surveys).

Self-Administered Questionnaires

Although the mailed questionnaire is the typical method used in self-administered surveys and thus the method we shall discuss most, there are several other common methods of self-administration. At times, it may be appropriate to administer the questionnaire to a group of respondents gathered at the same place at the same time. A survey of students taking introductory communication might be conducted in this manner during class. High school students might be surveyed during homeroom period.

Sometimes, a survey can be distributed in person to respondents, who then take the survey home to complete and return to the researcher. Such a strategy is used when a *diary study* is conducted. In a diary study, the researcher asks the respondents to complete a diary record (usually some combination of open-ended and closed-ended questions) about their communication encounters. For example, one of us recently completed a study about how people's friends and family members communicate guidelines for the conduct of personal relationships (Baxter, Dun, & Sahlstein, 2001). Respondents were asked to complete a diary record each time they were involved in a communication encounter in which someone communicated a guideline for how to conduct a relationship. The diary form contained both open-ended and closed-ended questions. At the end of the diary collection period, respondents turned in their packet of completed diary records to us for analysis.

Researchers sometimes distribute questionnaires through home delivery. A research worker delivers the questionnaire to the home of sample respondents and explains the study. Then the questionnaire is left for the respondent to complete, and the researcher picks it up later.

Home delivery and the mail can be used in combination as well. Questionnaires are mailed to families, and then research workers visit homes to pick up the questionnaires and check them for completeness. In just the opposite method, questionnaires can be hand delivered by research workers with a request that the respondents mail the completed questionnaires to the research office.

On the whole, when a research worker either delivers the questionnaire, picks it up, or both, the completion rate seems higher than for straightforward mail surveys. Mail surveys are the typical form of self-administered survey, however, and the remainder of this section is devoted specifically to that type of study.

Mail Distribution and Return The basic method for data collection through the mail has been transmittal of a questionnaire, accompanied by a letter of explanation and a self-addressed, stamped envelope for returning the questionnaire. You've doubtless received one or two in your lifetime. As a respondent, you're expected to complete the questionnaire, put it in the envelope, and return it. If, by any chance, you've received such a questionnaire and failed to return it, it would be extremely valuable for you to recall the reasons you had for not returning it— and keep them in mind anytime you plan to send questionnaires to others.

One big reason for not returning questionnaires is that it's too much trouble. To overcome this problem, researchers have developed several ways to make returning them easier. For instance, the *self-mailing* questionnaire requires no return envelope: When the questionnaire is folded a particular way, the return address appears on the outside; the respondent doesn't have to worry about losing the envelope. Anything you can do to make the job of completing and returning the questionnaire easier will improve your study. Imagine receiving a questionnaire that made no provisions for its return to the researcher. Suppose you had to (1) find an envelope, (2) write the address on it, (3) figure out how much postage it required, and (4) put the stamps on it. How likely would you be to return the questionnaire?

A few brief comments on postal options are in order. You have options for mailing questionnaires out and for getting them returned. On outgoing mail, your choices are essentially between first-class postage and bulk rate. First class is more certain, but bulk rate is far cheaper. (Check your local post office for rates and procedures.) On return mail, your choice is between postage stamps and business-reply permits. Here, the cost differential is more complicated. If you use stamps, you pay for them whether people return their questionnaires or not. With the business-reply permit, you pay for only those that are used, but you pay an additional surcharge of about a nickel. This means that stamps are cheaper if a lot of questionnaires are returned, but business-reply permits are cheaper if fewer are returned (and you won't know in advance how many will be returned).

There are many other considerations involved in choosing among the several postal options. For example, some researchers feel that the use of postage stamps communicates more "humanness" and sincerity than bulk-rate and business-reply permits. Others worry that respondents will steam off the stamps and use them for some purpose other than returning the questionnaires. Because both bulk-rate and business-reply permits require establishing accounts at the post office, you'll probably find stamps much easier in small surveys.

Monitoring Returns The mailing of questionnaires sets up a new research question that may prove valuable to a study. As questionnaires are returned, you should not sit back idly but should undertake a careful recording of the varying rates of return among respondents.

An invaluable tool in this activity will be a *return rate graph*. The day on which questionnaires were mailed should be labeled Day 1 on the graph, and every day thereafter the number of returned questionnaires should be logged on the graph. Because this is a minor activity, it's usually best to compile two graphs. One should show the number returned each day—rising, then dropping. Another should report the cumulative number or percentage. In part, this activity provides you with gratification, for you get to draw a picture of your successful data collection. More important, however, it's your guide to how the data collection is going. If you plan follow-up mailings, the graph provides a clue about when such mailings should be launched. (The dates of subsequent mailings should be noted on the graph.)

As completed questionnaires are returned, each should be opened, scanned, and assigned an identification number. These numbers should be assigned serially as the questionnaires are returned—even if other identification (ID) numbers have already been assigned. Two examples should illustrate the important advantages of this procedure.

Let's assume that you're studying attitudes toward a political figure as part of a political campaign. In the middle of the data collection, let's say that a natural disaster takes place that could affect voters' perceptions of the candidate's ability to perform the job. By knowing the date of that disaster and the dates when questionnaires were received, you'll be in a position to determine the effects of the disaster.

In a less sensational way, serialized ID numbers can be valuable in estimating nonresponse biases in the survey. Barring more direct tests of bias, you may wish to assume that those who failed to answer the questionnaire will be more like respondents who delayed answering than like those who answered right away. An analysis of questionnaires received at different points in the data collection might then be used for estimates of sampling bias. For example, if the grade point averages (GPAs) reported by student respondents decrease steadily through the data collection, with those replying right away having higher GPAs and those replying later having lower GPAs, then you might tentatively conclude that those who failed to answer at all have lower GPAs yet. Although it would not be advisable to make statistical estimates of bias in this fashion, you could take advantage of approximate estimates.

If respondents have been identified for purposes of follow-up mailings, then preparations for those mailings should be made as the questionnaires are returned.

Follow-up Mailings Follow-up mailings can be administered in several ways. In the simplest, nonrespondents are simply sent a letter of additional encouragement to participate. However, a better method is to send a new copy of the survey questionnaire with the follow-up letter. If potential respondents have not returned their questionnaires after two or three weeks, the questionnaires probably have been lost or misplaced. Receiving a follow-up letter might encourage them to look for the original questionnaire, but if they can't find it easily, the letter may go for naught.

The methodological literature on follow-up mailings strongly suggests that this is an effective method for increasing return rates in mail surveys. In general, the longer a potential respondent delays replying, the less likely he or she will answer at all. Properly timed follow-up mailings, then, provide additional stimuli to respond.

The effects of follow-up mailings will be seen in the response rate curves recorded during data collection. The initial mailings will be followed by a rise and then a subsiding of returns, the follow-up mailings will spur a resurgence of returns, and more follow-ups will do the same. In practice, three mailings (an original and two follow-ups) seem the most efficient.

The timing of follow-up mailings is also important. Here the methodological literature offers less precise guides, but it has been our experience that two or three weeks is a reasonable space between mailings. (This period might be increased by a few days if the mailing time—out and in—is more than two or three days.)

When researchers conduct several surveys of the same population over time, they can develop more specific guidelines in this regard. The Survey Research Office at the University of Hawaii conducts frequent student surveys and has been able to refine the mailing and remailing procedure considerably. Indeed, a consistent pattern of returns has been found that appears to transcend differences of survey content, quality of instrument, and so forth. Within two weeks of the first mailing, approximately 40 percent of the questionnaires are returned; within two weeks of the first follow-up, an additional 20 percent are received; and within two weeks of the final follow-up, an additional 10 percent are received. (These response rates all involved the sending of additional questionnaires, not just letters.) There are no grounds for assuming that a similar pattern would appear in surveys of different populations, but this illustration should indicate the value of carefully tabulating return rates for every survey conducted.

If the individuals in the survey sample are not identified on the questionnaires, it may not be possible to remail only to nonrespondents. In such a case, you should send your follow-up mailing to all members of the sample, thanking those who may have already participated and encouraging those who haven't to do so.

Acceptable Response Rates A question that new survey researchers frequently ask concerns the percentage return rate that should be achieved in a mail survey. The body of inferential statistics used in connection with survey analysis assumes that *all* members of the initial sample complete and return their questionnaires. Since this almost never happens, nonresponse bias becomes a concern, with the researcher testing (and hoping for) the possibility that the respondents look essentially like a random sample of the initial sample, and thus a somewhat smaller random sample of the total population. (For more detailed discussions of nonresponse bias, you might want to read Donald [1960] and Brownlee [1975].)

Nevertheless, overall **response rate** is one guide to the representativeness of the sample respondents. If a high response rate is achieved, there's less chance of significant problem with a biased sample than in a low rate. Conversely, a low response rate is a danger signal because the nonrespondents are likely to differ from the respondents in ways other than just their willingness to participate in your survey. Richard Bolstein (1991), for example, found that those who did not respond to a pre-election political poll were less likely to vote than those who did participate. Estimating the turnout rate from the survey respondents, then, would have overestimated the number who would show up at the polls.

A quick review of the survey literature uncovers a wide range of response rates. Each of these may be accompanied by a statement like "This is regarded as a relatively high response rate for a survey of this type." Even so, it's possible to state some rules of thumb about return rates. We feel that a response rate of 50 percent is *adequate* for analysis and reporting. A response of 60 percent is *good.* And a response rate of 70 percent is *very good.* However, you should bear in mind that these are only rough guides; they have no statistical basis, and a demonstrated lack of bias in a sample is far more important than a high response rate. If you want to pursue this matter further, Delbert Miller (1991, pp. 145–155) has reviewed several specific surveys to offer a better sense of the variability of response rates.

As you can imagine, one of the more persistent discussions among survey researchers is on ways of increasing response rates. You'll recall that this was a chief concern in terms of options for mailing out and receiving questionnaires. Survey researchers have developed a number of ingenious techniques to address this problem. Some have experimented with novel formats. Others have tried paying respondents to participate. The problem with paying, of course, is that it's expensive to make meaningfully high payments to hundreds or thousands of respondents, but some imaginative alternatives have been used. Some researchers have said, "We want to get your two-cents' worth on some issues, and we're willing to pay"—enclosing two pennies. Another enclosed a quarter, suggesting that the respondent make some little child happy. Still others have enclosed paper money.

Don Dillman (1978) provides an excellent review of the various techniques that survey researchers have used to increase return rates on mail surveys, and he evaluates the impact of each. More important, Dillman stresses the necessity of paying attention to *all* aspects of the study— what he calls the "Total Design Method"—rather than one or two special gimmicks.

More recently, Francis Yammarino, Steven Skinner, and Terry Childers (1991) have undertaken an in-depth analysis of the response rates achieved in many studies using different techniques. Their findings are too complex to summarize easily, but you might find some guidance there for effective survey design.

This has been a quick overview of some of the issues involved in self-administered questionnaires. Our goal has been to sensitize you to the fact that you can't take questionnaire administration for granted. It needs to be thought through as carefully as the construction of questions and their layout in the written questionnaire. Let's turn now to another method of conducting survey research—the standardized interview.

Standardized Interview Surveys

The **standardized interview** is an alternative method of collecting survey data. Rather than asking respondents to read questionnaires and enter their own answers, researchers send interviewers to ask the questions orally and record respondents' answers. Interviewing is typically done in a face-to-face encounter, but telephone interviewing, as you'll see next, follows most of the same guidelines. Also, most interview survey projects require more than one interviewer, although you might undertake a small-scale interview survey yourself. Portions of this section will discuss methods for training and supervising a staff of interviewers to assist you in the survey.

This section deals specifically with standardized interviewing used in survey research. In Chapter 14, we'll talk about the less structured, in-depth interviews often conducted in qualitative research.

The Role of the Survey Interviewer There are several advantages to having a survey administered by an interviewer rather than by the respondent. To begin, interview surveys typically attain higher response rates than do self-administered surveys. A properly designed and executed interview survey ought to achieve a completion rate of at least 80 to 85 percent. (Federally funded surveys often require one of these response rates.) Respondents seem more reluctant to turn down an interviewer who stands before them than to throw away a mailed questionnaire.

The presence of an interviewer also generally decreases the number of "don't knows" and "no answers." If minimizing such responses is important to the study, the interviewer can be instructed to probe for answers. ("If you had to pick one of the answers, which do you think would come closest to your feelings?")

Interviewers can also serve as a guard against confusing or complicated questions. If the respondent clearly misunderstands the intent of a question or indicates that he or she does not understand, the interviewer can clarify matters, thereby obtaining relevant responses. (However, such clarifications must be strictly controlled through formal *specifications,* as you'll soon see.)

Finally, the interviewer can observe respondents as well as ask questions. For example, the interviewer can note the respondent's race if this is considered too delicate a question to ask. Similar observations can be made regarding the respondent's ability to speak English, the respondent's general reactions to the study, and so forth. In one survey of students, respondents were given a short, self-administered questionnaire to complete— concerning sexual attitudes and behavior—during the course of the interview. While a student completed the questionnaire, the interviewer made detailed notes regarding the dress and grooming of the respondent.

This raises an ethical issue. Some researchers have objected that such practices violate the spirit of the agreement by which the respondent has allowed the interview. Although ethical issues are seldom open and shut in communication research, you need to be sensitive to that aspect of research.

Survey research is of necessity based on an unrealistic *stimulus–response* theory of cognition and behavior. It must be assumed that a questionnaire item will mean the same thing to every respondent and that every given response must mean the same when given by different respondents. Although this is an impossible goal, survey questions are drafted to approximate the ideal as closely as possible.

The interviewer must also fit into this ideal situation. The interviewer's presence should not affect a respondent's perception of a question or the answer given. The interviewer, then, should be a neutral medium through which questions and answers are transmitted.

If this goal is successfully accomplished, different interviewers will obtain exactly the same responses from a given respondent. (Recall earlier discussions of reliability.)

General Rules for Survey Interviewing The manner in which interviews ought to be conducted will vary somewhat by survey population and will be affected somewhat by the nature of the survey content as well. Nevertheless, some general guidelines apply to most if not all interviewing situations:

Appearance and Demeanor As a general rule, the interviewer should dress in a fashion similar to that of the people he or she will be interviewing. A richly dressed interviewer will probably have difficulty getting good cooperation and responses from poorer respondents. And a poorly dressed interviewer will have similar difficulties with richer respondents.

To the extent that the interviewer's dress and grooming differ from those of the respondents, it should be in the direction of cleanliness and neatness in modest apparel. If cleanliness is not next to godliness, it appears to be next to neutrality. Although middle-class neatness and cleanliness may not be accepted by all sectors of U.S. society, they remain the primary norm and are the most likely to be acceptable to the largest number of respondents. Rightly or wrongly, dress and grooming are typically regarded as signs of a person's attitudes and orientations.

In demeanor, interviewers should be pleasant if nothing else. Because they'll be prying into the respondent's personal life and attitudes, they must communicate a genuine interest in getting to know the respondent without appearing to spy. They must be relaxed and friendly without being too casual or clinging. Good interviewers also have the ability to determine very quickly the kind of person the respondent will feel most comfortable with, the kind of person the respondent would most enjoy talking to. Clearly, the interview will be more successful if the interviewer can become that kind of person. Further, because respondents are asked to volunteer a portion of their time and to divulge personal information, they deserve the most enjoyable experience that the researcher and interviewer can provide.

Familiarity with Survey Protocol If an interviewer is unfamiliar with the questions to be asked, known as the interview *protocol* or schedule, the study suffers, and an unfair burden is placed on the respondent. The interview is likely to take more time than necessary and be unpleasant. Moreover, the interviewer cannot acquire familiarity by skimming through the protocol two or three times. It must be studied carefully, question by question, and the interviewer must practice reading it aloud.

Ultimately, the interviewer must be able to read the questions to respondents without error, without stumbling over words and phrases. A good model for interviewers is the actor reading lines in a play or motion picture. The lines must be read as though they constituted a natural conversation, but that conversation must follow exactly the language set down in the protocol.

By the same token, the interviewer must be familiar with the **specifications** prepared in conjunction with the protocol. Specifications are explanatory and clarifying comments about handling difficult or confusing situations that may occur with regard to specific questions. Inevitably, some questions will not exactly fit a given respondent's situation, and the interviewer must determine how a question should be interpreted in that situation. The specifications provided to the interviewer should give adequate guidance in such cases, but the interviewer must know the organization and content of the specifications well enough to refer to them efficiently. It would be better for the interviewer to leave a given question unanswered than to spend five minutes searching through the specifications for clarification or trying to interpret the relevant instructions.

Following Question Wording Exactly Earlier in this chapter, we discussed the significance of question wording for the responses obtained. A slight change in the wording of a given question may lead a respondent to answer yes rather than no.

Even though you've very carefully phrased your questions to obtain the information you need and to ensure that respondents will interpret items precisely as you intend, all this effort will be wasted if interviewers rephrase questions in their own words.

Recording Responses Exactly Whenever the interview protocol contains open-ended questions, those soliciting the respondent's own answer, the interviewer must record that answer exactly as given. No attempt should be made to summarize, paraphrase, or correct bad grammar.

This exactness is especially important because the interviewer won't know how the responses are to be coded before processing. Indeed, the researchers may not know the coding until they've read a hundred or so responses. For example, the protocol might ask respondents how they feel about their primary health care provider. One re-

spondent might answer that there are too few doctors for the number of patients, which results in long periods of waiting in waiting rooms. Another might say that there are too few general practitioners and too many specialists. If the interviewer recorded these two responses with the same summary—"doctor shortage"—the researchers would not be able to take advantage of the important differences in the original responses.

Sometimes, the respondent may be so inarticulate that the verbal response is too ambiguous to permit interpretation. However, the interviewer may be able to understand the intent of the response through the respondent's gestures or tone. In such a situation, the exact verbal response should still be recorded, but the interviewer should add marginal comments giving both the interpretation and the reasons for arriving at it.

More generally, researchers can use any marginal comments explaining aspects of the response not conveyed in the verbal recording, such as the respondent's apparent uncertainty in answering, anger, embarrassment, and so forth. In each case, however, the exact verbal response should also be recorded.

Probing for Responses Sometimes, respondents will give an inappropriate or incomplete answer. For example, a question may present an attitudinal statement and ask the respondent to strongly agree, agree somewhat, disagree somewhat, or strongly disagree. However, the respondent may reply "I think that's true." The interviewer should follow this reply with "Would you say you strongly agree or agree somewhat?" If necessary, interviewers can explain that they must check one or the other of the categories provided. If the respondent adamantly refuses to choose, the interviewer should write in the exact response given by the respondent.

Probes are more frequently required in eliciting responses to open-ended questions. For example, in response to a question about health care providers, the respondent might simply reply "Pretty bad." The interviewer could obtain an elaboration on this response through a variety of probes. Sometimes, the best probe is silence; if the interviewer sits quietly with pencil poised, the respondent will probably fill the pause with additional comments. (This technique is used effectively by newspaper reporters.) Appropriate verbal probes might be "How is that?" or "In what ways?" Perhaps the most generally useful probe is "Anything else?"

Often, interviewers need to probe for answers that will be sufficiently informative for analytical purposes. In every case, however, it is imperative that such probes be completely *neutral.* The probe must not in any way affect the nature of the subsequent response. Whenever you anticipate that a given question may require probing for appropriate responses, you should present one or more useful probes next to the question in the interview protocol. This practice has two important advantages. First, you'll have more time to devise the best, most neutral probes. Second, all interviewers will use the same probes whenever they're needed. Thus, even if the probe isn't perfectly neutral, all respondents will be presented with the same stimulus. This is the same logical guideline discussed for question wording. Although a question shouldn't be loaded or biased, it's essential that every respondent be presented with the same question, even a biased one.

Coordination and Control   Most interview surveys require the assistance of several interviewers. In large-scale surveys, of course, such interviewers are hired and paid for their work. As a student researcher, you might find yourself recruiting friends to help you interview. Whenever more than one interviewer is involved in a survey, efforts must be carefully controlled. There are two aspects of this control: training interviewers and supervising them after they begin work.

The interviewers' training session should begin with the description of what the study is all about. Even though the interviewers may be involved only in the data-collection phase of the project, it will be useful to them to understand what will be done with the interviews they conduct and what purpose will be served. Morale and motivation are usually low when interviewers don't know what's going on.

The training on how to interview should begin with a discussion of general guidelines and procedures, such as those discussed earlier in this chapter. Then the whole group should go through the interview protocol together —question by question. Don't simply ask if anyone has any questions about the first page of the protocol. Read the first question aloud, explain its purpose, and then entertain any questions or comments the interviewers may have. Once all their questions and comments have been handled, go on to the next question in the protocol.

It's always a good idea to prepare specifications to accompany an interview protocol. When drafting the protocol, you should try to think of all the problem cases that might arise—the bizarre circumstances that might make a question difficult to answer. The survey specifications should provide detailed guidelines on how to handle such situations. For example, even as simple a matter as age might present problems. Suppose a respondent says he or she will be 25 next week. The interviewer might not be

sure whether to take the respondent's current age or the nearest one. The specifications for that question should explain what should be done. (Probably, you'd specify that "age as of last birthday" should be recorded in all cases.)

If you've prepared a set of specifications, you should go over them with the interviewers when you go over the individual questions in the protocol. Make sure your interviewers fully understand the specifications as well as the questions themselves and the reasons for them.

This portion of the interviewer training is likely to generate many troublesome questions from your interviewers. They'll ask, "What should I do if . . . ?" In such cases, you should never give a quick answer. If you have specifications, be sure to show how the solution to the problem could be determined from the specifications. If you don't have specifications prepared, show how the preferred handling of the situation fits within the general logic of the question and the purpose of the study. Giving offhand, unexplained answers to such questions will only confuse the interviewers, and they probably won't take their work seriously. If you don't know the answer to such a question, admit it and ask for some time to decide on the best answer. Then think out the situation carefully and be sure to give all the interviewers your answer, explaining your reasons.

Once you've gone through the whole questionnaire, you should conduct one or two demonstration interviews in front of everyone. Preferably, you should interview someone else. Realize that your interview will be a model for those you're training, so make it good. Moreover, it would be best if the demonstration interview were done as realistically as possible. Don't pause during the demonstration to point out how you've handled a complicated situation: Handle it, and then explain later. It's irrelevant if the person you are interviewing gives real answers or takes on some hypothetical identity for the purpose, just as long as the answers are consistent.

After the demonstration interviews, you should pair off your interviewers and have them practice on each other. When they've completed the questionnaire, have them reverse roles and do it over again. Interviewing is the best training for interviewing. As your interviewers are practicing on each other, you should wander around, listening in on the practice so you'll know how well they're doing. Once the practice is completed, the whole group should discuss their experiences and ask any other questions they may have.

The final stage of the training for interviewers should involve some "real" interviews. Have them conduct some interviews under the conditions that approximate those of the final survey. You may want to assign them people to interview, or perhaps you will want to allow them to pick people themselves. Don't have them practice on people you've selected for your sample, however. After each interviewer has completed three to five interviews, have him or her check back with you. Look over the completed interviews for any evidence of misunderstanding. Again, answer any questions that the interviewers may have. Once you're convinced that a given interviewer knows what to do, assign some actual interviews—using the sample you've selected for the study.

It's essential that you continue supervising the work of interviewers over the course of the study. It's probably unwise to let them conduct more than 20 or 30 interviews without seeing you. You might assign 20 interviews, have the interviewer bring back those interviews when completed, look them over, and assign another 20 or so. Although this may seem overly cautious, you must continually protect yourself against misunderstandings that may not be evident early in the study.

If you're the only interviewer in your study, these comments may not seem relevant to you. However, you would be advised, for example, to prepare specifications for potentially troublesome questions in your protocol. Otherwise, you run the risk of making ad hoc decisions during the course of the study that you'll later regret or forget. Also, the emphasis on practice applies equally to the one-person project and to the complex funded survey with a large interviewing staff.

Telephone Surveys

Throughout the early history of survey research, interview surveys were always conducted face to face, typically in the respondent's household. As the telephone became more omnipresent in U.S. society, however, researchers began experimenting with it for survey interviewing.

For years, telephone surveys had a rather bad reputation among professional researchers. Telephone surveys are limited by definition to people who have telephones. Years ago, then, this method produced a substantial social-class bias by excluding poor people from the surveys. Recall that this was vividly demonstrated by the *Literary Digest* fiasco of 1936. Even though voters were contacted by mail, the sample was partially selected from telephone subscribers—who were hardly typical in a nation in the midst of the Great Depression.

Over time, however, the telephone has become a standard fixture in almost all U.S. homes. A related sampling problem involved unlisted numbers. This potential bias has been erased through a technique that has advanced telephone sampling substantially: random-digit dialing, which we discussed in Chapter 7.

Telephone surveys have many advantages that underlie the growing popularity of this method. Probably the greatest are money and time, in that order. In a face-to-face, household interview, you may drive several miles to a respondent's home, find no one there, return to the research office, and drive back the next day—possibly finding no one there again. It's cheaper and quicker to let your fingers make the trips.

When interviewing by telephone, you can dress any way you please without affecting the answers that respondents give. And respondents will sometimes be more honest in giving socially disapproved answers if they don't have to look you in the eye. Similarly, it may be possible to probe into more sensitive areas, though this isn't necessarily the case. (People are, to some extent, more suspicious when they can't see the person asking them questions—perhaps a consequence of "surveys" aimed at selling magazine subscriptions and time-share condominiums.)

However, you should realize that people can communicate a lot about themselves over the phone, even though they can't be seen, as indicated in the box "Subtle Telephone Cues." For example, researchers worry about the impact of an interviewer's name (particularly if ethnicity is relevant to the study) and debate the ethics of having all interviewers use bland "stage names" such as Smith or Jones. (Female interviewers sometimes ask permission to do this, to avoid subsequent harassment from men they interview.)

Telephone surveys can give you greater control over data collection if several interviewers are engaged in the project. If all the interviewers are calling from the research office, they can get clarification from the person in charge whenever problems occur, as they inevitably do. Alone in the boondocks, an interviewer may have to wing it between weekly visits with the interviewing supervisor.

Finally, another important factor involved in the growing use of telephone surveys has to do with personal safety. Don Dillman (1978, p. 4) describes the situation this way:

> Interviewers must be able to operate comfortably in a climate in which strangers are viewed with distrust and must successfully counter respondents' objections to being interviewed. Increasingly, interviewers must be willing to work at night to contact residents in many households. In some cases, this necessitates providing protection for interviewers working in areas of a city in which a definite threat to the safety of individuals exists.

SUBTLE TELEPHONE CUES

The telephone does not eliminate all interviewer effects, because you can often tell something about the person you're talking to just by the sound of his or her voice. You can usually tell gender and perhaps age—and sometimes you can tell more.

In 1989, Douglas Wilder, an African American, was running for governor of Virginia (a race he won) against a white opponent. We might well imagine that the race of interviewers in face-to-face pre-election polls might have influenced the responses of voters when asked about their voting intentions.

In one pre-election poll, for example, the stated voting intentions of white voters interviewed by white interviewers were about evenly divided between the two candidates. White voters interviewed by African American interviewers, however, appeared much more supportive of Wilder: 52 percent, versus 33 percent for his white opponent.

What makes this particularly interesting is that the survey was conducted over the telephone! It gives powerful evidence of the extent to which we reveal ourselves in the ways we talk.

Source: Steven E. Finkel, Thomas M. Guterbok, and Marian J. Borg, "Race-of-Interviewer Effects in a Preelection Poll: Virginia 1989," *Public Opinion Quarterly,* Fall 1991, pp. 313–30.

Thus, concerns for safety work two ways to hamper face-to-face interviews. Potential respondents may refuse to be interviewed, fearing the stranger/interviewer. And the interviewers themselves may be in danger. All this is made even worse by the possibility of the researchers being sued for huge sums if anything goes wrong.

There are still problems involved in telephone interviewing. The method is hampered by the proliferation of bogus "surveys," which are actually sales campaigns disguised as research. If you have any questions about any such call you receive, by the way, ask the interviewer directly whether you've been selected for a survey only or if a sales "opportunity" is involved. It's also a good idea, if you have any doubts, to get the interviewer's name, phone number, and company. Hang up if they refuse to provide any of these.

The ease with which people can hang up is, of course, another shortcoming of telephone surveys. Once you've been let inside someone's home for an interview, he or she is unlikely to order you out of the house in mid-interview. It's much easier to terminate a telephone interview abruptly, saying something like "Whoops! Someone's at the door. I gotta go" or "Omigod! The pigs are eating my Volvo!" (That sort of thing is much harder to fake when you're sitting in someone's living room.)

Another potential problem for telephone interviewing is the continuing spread of telephone answering machines. Answering machines have not yet had a significant effect on the ability of telephone researchers to contact prospective respondents (Tuckel & Feinberg, 1991), but things could change as people become increasingly reliant on this technology.

New Technologies and Survey Research

A variety of new technologies are increasingly in use in survey research. For example, Jeffery Walker (1994) has explored the possibility of conducting surveys by fax machine. Questionnaires are faxed to respondents, who are asked to fax their answers back. Of course, such surveys can represent only that part of the population that has fax machines. Walker reports that fax surveys don't achieve as high response rates as face-to-face interviews do, but because of the perceived urgency, they do produce higher response rates than do mail or telephone surveys. In one test case, all those who had ignored a mail questionnaire were sent a fax follow-up, and 83 percent responded.

As a consumer of research, you should be wary of "surveys" whose apparent purpose is to raise money for the sponsor. This practice has already invaded the realm of "fax surveys," evidenced by a fax titled "Should Hand Guns Be Outlawed?" Two fax numbers were provided for expressing either a "yes" or "no" opinion. As the smaller print noted, "Calls to these numbers cost $2.95 per minute, a small price for greater democracy. Calls take approximately 1 or 2 minutes." You can imagine where the $2.95 went.

Many of the newest innovations in questionnaire administration make use of the computer. Several techniques have emerged and are being tested (Nicholls, Baker, & Martin, 1997):

- *CATI* (computer-assisted telephone interviewing): A telephone survey interviewer reads questions as they appear on a computer screen and types in the respondent's answers.
- *CAPI* (computer-assisted personal interviewing): Similar to CATI but used in face-to-face interviews rather than over the phone.

- *CASI* (computer-assisted self-interviewing): A research worker brings a computer to the respondent's home, and the respondent reads questions on the computer screen and enters his or her own answers.
- *CSAQ* (computerized self-administered questionnaire): The respondent receives the questionnaire via floppy disk, bulletin board, or other means and runs the software, which asks questions and accepts the respondent's answers. Then the respondent returns the data file.
- *TDE* (touchtone data entry): The respondent initiates the process by calling a number at the research organization. This prompts a series of computerized questions, which the respondent answers by pressing keys on the telephone keypad.
- *VR* (voice recognition): Instead of asking the respondent to use the telephone keypad as in TDE, this system accepts spoken responses.

Nicholls and colleagues report that such techniques are more efficient than conventional techniques, and they do not appear to result in a reduction of data quality. We'll go into greater detail about two of these computer-related ways of conducting surveys: CATI and one form of CSAQ, the online survey.

Computer-Assisted Telephone Interviewing (CATI)
In the years to come, you'll hear a great deal about CATI. Although there are variations in practice, here's what it can look like.

Imagine an interviewer wearing a telephone-operator headset, sitting in front of a computer terminal and its video screen. The central computer, programmed to select a telephone number at random, dials it. On the video screen is an introduction ("Hello, my name is . . . ") and the first question to be asked ("Could you tell me how many people live at this address?").

When the respondent answers the phone, the interviewer says hello, introduces the study, and asks the first question displayed on the screen. When the respondent answers the question, the interviewer types that answer into the computer terminal—either the verbatim response to an open-ended question or the code category for the appropriate answer to a closed-ended question. The answer is immediately stored in the central computer. The second question appears on the video screen, it is asked, and the answer is entered into the computer. Thus, the interview continues.

This is a method used increasingly by academic, government, and commercial survey researchers. Much of the development work for this technique has occurred at the University of California's Survey Research Center in Berkeley, sometimes in collaboration with the U.S. Department of Agriculture and other governmental agencies.

In addition to the obvious advantages in terms of data collection, CATI automatically prepares the data for analysis; in fact, the researcher can begin analyzing the data before the interviewing is complete, thereby gaining an advanced view of how the analysis will turn out. Alternatively, responses to a CATI interview can be recorded for later analysis, as the box "Voice Capture™" illustrates.

Online Surveys
The new technology of survey research includes the use of the Internet and the World Wide Web—two of the most far-reaching developments of the late 20th century. Some researchers feel that the Internet can be used to conduct meaningful survey research.

An immediate objection that many researchers make to online surveys concerns representativeness: Will the people who can be surveyed online be representative of meaningful populations, such as all U.S. adults, all voters, and so on? This is the criticism raised with regard to surveys via fax and, earlier, with regard to telephone surveys.

Camilo Wilson (personal communication, September 8, 1999), the founder of Cogix (http://www.cogix.com), points out that some populations are ideally suited to online surveys: specifically, those who visit a particular web site. For example, Wilson indicates that market research for online companies *should* be conducted online, and his firm has developed software, ViewsFlash, for precisely that purpose. Although web site surveys could easily collect data from all who visit a particular site, Wilson suggests that survey sampling techniques can provide sufficient consumer data without irritating thousands or millions of potential customers.

But how about general population surveys? As we write this, a debate is taking place within the survey research community. Humphrey Taylor and George Terhanian prompted part of the debate with an article titled "Heady Days Are Here Again." Acknowledging the need for caution, they urged that online polling be given a fair hearing:

> One test of the credibility of any new data collection method hinges on its ability to reliably and accurately forecast voting behavior. For this reason, last fall we attempted to estimate the 1998 election outcomes for governor and US Senate in 14 states on four separate occasions using internet surveys. (1999, p. 20)

The researchers compared their results with 52 telephone polls that addressed the same races. Online polling

VOICE CAPTURE™

by James E. Dannemiller
SMS Research, Honolulu

The development of various CATI techniques has been a boon to survey and marketing research, though mostly it has supported the collection, coding, and analysis of "data as usual." The Voice Capture™ technique developed by Survey Systems, however, offers quite unusual possibilities, which we are only beginning to explore.

In the course of a CATI-based telephone interview, the interviewer can trigger the computer to begin digitally recording the conversation with the respondent. Having determined that the respondent has recently changed his or her favorite TV news show, for example, the interviewer can ask, "Why did you change?" and begin recording the verbatim response. (Early in the interview, the interviewer has asked permission to record parts of the interview.)

Later on, coders can play back the responses and code them—much as they would do with the interviewer's typescript of the responses. This offers an easier and more accurate way of accomplishing a conventional task. But that's a tame use of the new capability.

It is also possible to incorporate such oral data as parts of a cross-tabulation during analysis. We may create a table of gender by age by reasons for switching TV news shows. Thus, we can hear, in turn, the responses of the young men, young women, middle-aged men, and so forth. In one such study we found the younger and older men tending to watch one TV news show, while the middle-aged men watched something else. Listening to the responses of the middle-aged men, one after another, we heard a common comment: "Well, now that I'm older . . ." This kind of aside might have been lost in the notes hastily typed by interviewers, but such comments stood out dramatically in the oral data. The middle-aged men seemed to be telling us they felt "maturity" required them to watch a particular show, while more years under their belts let them drift back to what they liked in the first place.

These kinds of data are especially compelling to clients, particularly in customer satisfaction studies. Rather than summarize what we feel a client's customers like and don't like, we can let the respondents speak directly to the client in their own words. It's like a focus group on demand. Going one step further, we have found that letting line employees (bank tellers, for example) listen to the responses has more impact than having their supervisors tell them what they are doing right or wrong.

As exciting as these experiences are, I have the strong feeling that we have scarcely begun to tap into the possibilities for such unconventional forms of data.

---

correctly picked 21 of the 22 winners, or 95 percent. However, simply picking the winner is not a sufficient test of effectiveness: How close did the polls come to the actual percentages received by the various candidates? Taylor and Terhanian report their online polls missed the actual vote by an average of 6.8 percentage points. The 52 telephone polls missed the same votes by an average of 6.2 percentage points.

Warren Mitofsky (1999) is a critic of online polling. In addition to disagreeing with the way Taylor and Terhanian calculated the ranges of error just reported, he has called for a sounder, theoretical basis on which to ground the new technique.

One key to online polling is the proper assessment and use of weights for different kinds of respondents—as was discussed in the context of quota sampling in Chapter 7. Taylor and Terhanian are aware of the criticisms of quota sampling, but their initial experiences with online polling suggest to them that the technique should be pursued. Indeed, they conclude by saying "This is an unstoppable train, and it is accelerating. Those who don't get on board run the risk of being left far behind" (1999, p. 23).

Whether online surveys will gain the respect and extensive use enjoyed by telephone surveys today remains to be seen. Students who consider using this technique should do so in full recognition of its potential shortcomings.

Researchers are amassing a body of experience with online surveying, yielding lessons for increasing success. For example, Survey Sampling, Inc. (2000) suggests the following do's and don'ts for conducting online surveys:

Do use consistent wording between the invitation and the survey.

Don't use terms such as "unique ID number" in the invitation, then ask respondents to type their "password" when they get to the survey. Changing terminology can be confusing.

Do use plain, simple language.

Don't force the respondent to scroll down the screen for the URL for the study location.

Do offer to share selected results from the study with everyone who completes the survey. Respondents will often welcome information as a reward for taking the study, especially when they are young adults and teens.

Do plan the time of day and day of week to mail, depending on the subject of the study and type of respondent. Send the invitation late afternoon, evening, or weekend, when respondents are most likely to be reading mail at home, especially if the study requests respondents to check an item in the kitchen or other area in the home. If a parent–child questionnaire is planned, send the invitation late afternoon when children are home, not early in the day, when respondents can't complete the study because children are at school.

Do be aware of technical limitations. For example, WebTV users currently cannot access surveys using Java. If respondents' systems need to be Java-enabled or require access to streaming video, alert panelists at the beginning of the study, not midway through.

Do test incentives, rewards, and prize drawings to determine the optimal offer for best response. Longer surveys usually require larger incentives.

Do limit studies to 15 minutes or less. (Reprinted with permission.)

COMPARISON OF THE DIFFERENT SURVEY ADMINISTRATION MODES

We've now seen several ways to collect survey data. Although we've touched on some of the relative advantages and disadvantages of each, let's take a minute to compare them more directly. Self-administered questionnaires are generally cheaper and quicker than face-to-face interview surveys. These considerations are likely to be important for an unfunded student wishing to undertake a survey for a term paper or a thesis. Moreover, if you use the self-administered mail format, it costs no more to conduct a national survey than a local one; a national interview survey (either face to face or by telephone) would cost far more than a local one. Also, mail surveys typically require a small staff: One person can conduct a reasonable mail survey alone, although you shouldn't underestimate the work involved.

Further, respondents are sometimes reluctant to report controversial or deviant attitudes or behaviors in interviews but are willing to respond to an anonymous self-administered questionnaire.

Interview surveys also offer many advantages. For example, they generally produce fewer incomplete surveys. Although respondents may skip questions in a self-administered questionnaire, interviewers are trained not to do so. The computer offers a further check on this in CATI surveys. Moreover, interview surveys have typically achieved higher completion rates than have self-administered ones.

Although self-administered questionnaires may be more effective for sensitive issues, interview surveys are definitely more effective for complicated ones. This advantage of interview surveys pertains generally to all complicated contingency questions.

With interviews, you can conduct a survey based on a sample of addresses or phone numbers rather than on names. An interviewer can arrive at an assigned address or call the assigned number, introduce the survey, and even—following instructions—choose the appropriate person at that address to respond to the survey. By contrast, self-administered questionnaires addressed to "occupant" receive a notoriously low response.

Finally, as we've seen, interviewers questioning respondents face to face can make important observations aside from responses to questions asked in the interview. In a household interview, they may note the characteristics of the neighborhood, the dwelling unit, and so forth. They may also note characteristics of the respondents or the quality of their interaction with the respondents—whether the respondent had difficulty communicating, was hostile, seemed to be lying, and so forth.

The chief advantages of telephone surveys over those conducted face to face center primarily on time and money. Telephone interviews are much cheaper and can be mounted and executed quickly. Also, interviewers are safer when interviewing in high-crime areas. Moreover, we've seen that the impact of the interviewers on responses is somewhat lessened when interviewers can't be seen by respondents. As only one indicator of the popularity of telephone interviewing, when Johnny Blair and his colleagues (1995) compiled a bibliography on sample designs for telephone interviews, they listed more than 200 items.

Online surveys have many of the strengths and weaknesses of mail surveys. Once the available software has been further developed, they are likely to be substantially cheaper. However, an important weakness lies in the difficulty of ensuring that respondents to an online survey will be representative of some more general population.

Clearly, each survey method has its place in communication research. Ultimately, you must balance all these advantages and disadvantages of the various modes of administration in relation to your research needs and your resources.

STRENGTHS AND WEAKNESSES OF SURVEY RESEARCH

Like other methods in communication research, surveys have special strengths and weaknesses. You should keep these in mind when determining whether the survey format is appropriate for your research goals.

Surveys are particularly useful in describing the characteristics of a large population. A carefully selected probability sample in combination with a standardized questionnaire or interview offers the possibility of making refined descriptive assertions about a student body, a city, a nation, or any other large population.

Surveys—especially self-administered ones—make large samples feasible. Surveys of 2,000 respondents are not unusual. A large number of cases is important for both descriptive and explanatory analyses, especially wherever several variables are to be analyzed simultaneously.

In one sense, surveys are flexible. Many questions may be asked on a given topic, giving you considerable flexibility in your analyses. Although experimental design (addressed in the next chapter) may require you to commit yourself in advance to a particular operational definition of a concept, surveys let you develop operational definitions from actual responses.

Finally, standardized questionnaires or interviews have an important strength in regard to measurement. Earlier chapters have discussed the ambiguous nature of most concepts: They have no ultimately *real* meanings. Although you must be able to define concepts in those ways most relevant to your research goals, you may not find it easy to apply the same definitions uniformly to all participants. The survey researcher is bound to this requirement by having to ask exactly the same questions of all respondents and having to impute the same intent to all respondents giving a particular response.

Survey research also has several weaknesses. First, the requirement for standardization just mentioned often seems to result in the fitting of round pegs into square holes. Standardized items often represent the least common denominator in assessing people's attitudes, orientations, circumstances, and experiences. By designing questions that will be at least minimally appropriate to all respondents, you may miss what is most appropriate to many respondents. In this sense, surveys often appear superficial in their coverage of complex topics. Although

this problem can be partly offset through sophisticated analyses, it's inherent in survey research.

Similarly, survey research can seldom deal with the context of social life. The survey researcher rarely develops the feel for the total life situation in which respondents are thinking and acting that, say, the participant observer can (see Part 3).

In many ways, surveys are inflexible. Studies involving direct observation can be modified as field conditions warrant, but surveys typically require that an initial study design remain unchanged throughout. As a field researcher, for example, you can become aware of an important new complexity operating in the phenomenon you're studying and begin making careful observations of it. The survey researcher would probably be unaware of the emergent complexities of a phenomenon and could do nothing about it in any event.

Finally, surveys are subject to artificiality (a weakness shared with experiments, as the next chapter will discuss). This shortcoming is especially salient in the realm of actions and behaviors. Surveys cannot measure communicative action; they can only collect self-reports of recalled past action or of prospective or hypothetical action.

This problem has two aspects. First, the topic of study may not be amenable to measurement through surveys. Second, the act of studying that topic—an attitude, for example—may affect it. A survey respondent may have given no thought to whether the governor should be impeached until asked for his or her opinion by an interviewer. He or she may, at that point, form an opinion on the matter.

As with all methods of research, a full awareness of the inherent or probable weaknesses of survey research can partially resolve them in some cases. Ultimately, though, you're on the safest ground when you can employ several research methods in studying a given topic.

SECONDARY ANALYSIS OF SURVEY DATA

We have seen that survey research involves the following steps: (1) question construction, (2) sample selection, and (3) data collection, through either interviewer- or self-administered questionnaires. As you will have gathered, surveys are usually major undertakings. Through **secondary analysis,** however, you can pursue your particular communication research interests—analyzing survey data from, say, a national sample of 2,000 respondents—while avoiding the enormous expenditure of time and money that such a survey entails.

The development of computer-based analyses in social science research has made it easy for researchers to share their data with one another. A network of data archives has been created in which survey data files (magnetic disks or tapes) are collected and distributed the way books are handled in a conventional library. Whereas library books are loaned, however, the data sets are reproduced and sold. You get to keep your copy and use it again and again for as long as you find new things to study.

E. Jill Kiecolt and Laura Nathan (1985) have compiled an annotated listing of the several U.S. and international archives available to social science researchers. It provides data on a wide variety of topics. Within the United States, for example, are a number of archives, such as the Inter-university Consortium for Political and Social Research (University of Michigan), the Roper Center for Public Opinion Research (University of Connecticut), and the National Opinion Research Center (University of Chicago). In these and other archives across the country, you can access a wide variety of data sets, including the wealth of data available from decades of Gallup, Harris, Roper, and Yankelovich polls.

For example, Moshe Engelberg, June Flora, and Clifford Nass (1995) used 17,696 surveys on AIDS gathered by the Centers for Disease Control's National Center for Health Statistics to examine the relationship between a person's knowledge about AIDS and the channels of communication that he or she used for AIDS information.

The advantages of secondary analysis are obvious and enormous: It's cheaper and faster than doing original surveys, and, depending on who did the original survey, you may benefit from the work of top-flight professionals. There are disadvantages, however. The key problem involves the recurrent question of validity. When one researcher collects data for one particular purpose, you have no assurance that those data will be appropriate for *your* research interests. Typically, you'll find that the original researcher asked a question that "comes close" to measuring what you're interested in, but you'll wish the question had been asked just a little differently—or that another, related question had also been asked.

Main Points

□ Survey research, a popular communication research method, is the administration of questionnaires to a sample of respondents selected from some population.

□ Survey research is especially appropriate for making descriptive studies of large populations. Communication researchers use surveys to measure knowledge, perceptions, feelings, self-reported behaviors, dispositional states and traits, and communication networks.

□ Surveys provide a method of collecting data by (1) asking people questions or (2) asking them to agree or disagree with statements representing different points of view.

□ Questions may be open ended (respondents supply their own answers) or closed ended (they select from a list of provided answers).

□ Question wording, question order, and question layout can influence the quality of data collected.

□ In general, avoid items that lack clarity, feature double-barreled questions, or ask questions that the respondent is unable or unwilling to answer.

□ Usually, short items in a questionnaire are better than long ones.

□ In questionnaires, negative items and terms should be avoided because they may confuse respondents.

□ Bias is the quality in questionnaire items that encourages respondents to answer in a particular way or to support a particular point of view. Avoid it.

□ Single indicators of variables seldom have sufficiently clear validity to warrant their use. Composite measures, such as scales and indexes, solve this problem by including several indicators of a variable in one summary measure.

□ Indexes are based on the simple cumulation of indicators of a variable.

□ Scales take advantage of any logical or empirical intensity structures that exist among a variable's indicators.

□ Likert items are measures based on the use of standardized response categories (for example, "strongly agree," "agree," "disagree," "strongly disagree") for several questionnaire statements.

□ The semantic differential is a question format that asks respondents to make ratings that lie between two bipolar extremes, such as "positive" and "negative."

□ Thurstone scaling is a technique for creating indicators of variables that have a clear intensity structure among them. Judges determine the intensities of different indicators.

- Guttman scaling is a method of discovering and using the empirical intensity structure among several indicators of a given variable.

- Comparative judgments ask respondents to evaluate at least two phenomena at once—for example, evaluate their degree of similarity, rank-order them according to some criterion, or indicate preference.

- The order of items in a questionnaire can influence the responses given.

- Contingency questions are those to be answered only by some respondents, based on answers to previous questions.

- The matrix question is an efficient format for presenting several items sharing the same response categories.

- Clear instructions are important for getting appropriate responses in a questionnaire.

- It's generally best to plan follow-up mailings in the case of self-administered questionnaires, sending new questionnaires to those respondents who fail to respond to the initial appeal.

- Properly monitoring questionnaire returns will provide a good guide to when a follow-up mailing is appropriate.

- The essential characteristic of interviewers is that they be neutral; their presence in the data-collection process must not have any effect on the responses given to survey items.

- Interviewers must be carefully trained to be familiar with the interview protocol, to follow the question wording and question order exactly, and to record responses exactly as they are given.

- A probe is a neutral, nondirective question designed to elicit an elaboration on an incomplete or ambiguous response given in an interview in response to an open-ended question. Examples include "Anything else?" "How is that?" "In what ways?"

- Surveys conducted over the telephone have become more common and more effective in recent years, and computer-assisted telephone interviewing (CATI) techniques are especially promising.

- Surveys conducted online are becoming increasingly popular in survey research. Concerns with sample representativeness have been expressed, however.

- The advantages of a self-administered questionnaire over an interview survey are economy, speed, lack of interviewer bias, and the possibility of anonymity and privacy to encourage candid responses on sensitive issues.

- The advantages of an interview survey over a self-administered questionnaire are fewer incomplete questionnaires and fewer misunderstood questions, generally higher return rates, and greater flexibility in terms of sampling and special observations.

- Survey research in general offers advantages in terms of economy and the amount of data that can be collected. The standardization of the data collected represents another special strength of survey research.

- Survey research has the weaknesses of being somewhat artificial and potentially superficial. It's difficult to gain a full sense of communication processes in their natural settings through the use of surveys.

- Secondary analysis refers to the analysis of data collected earlier by another researcher for some purpose other than the topic of the current study.

Key Terms

questionnaire	Guttman scalogram
interview protocol	comparative judgments
bias	contingency questions
composite measure	pretesting
index	response rate
scale	standardized interview
Likert-type index	specifications
semantic differential	probes
Thurstone equal-appearing interval scales	secondary analysis

Review Questions and Exercises

1. Find a questionnaire printed in a magazine or newspaper (a reader survey, for example). Bring the questionnaire to class and critique its strengths and weaknesses.

2. Find a questionnaire on the Web (hint: search for "questionnaire"). Critique at least five of the questions for their strengths and weaknesses. Be sure to give the Web address (URL) for the questionnaire and the exact wording of the questions you critique.

3. For each of the following open-ended questions, construct a closed-ended question that could be used in a questionnaire:

   a. Can you describe how members of your family typically communicate with one another?

   b. How do you feel about television programming targeted to children?

c. How important are computers in your life?

d. What was your main reason for having an e-mail account?

4. Construct a set of contingency questions for use in a self-administered questionnaire that would solicit the following information:

a. Is the respondent employed?

b. If unemployed, is the respondent looking for work?

c. If the unemployed respondent is not looking for work, is he or she retired, a student, or a home-maker?

d. If the respondent is looking for work, how long has he or she been looking?

5. Make up several questionnaire items that measure attitudes toward cell phones using each of the following question formats: Likert-type, semantic differential, Guttman scalogram, comparative judgment.

6. Suppose you've been asked to conduct a survey to determine public opinion regarding the Internet. Discuss the relative merits and demerits of doing the survey by mail, telephone, face-to-face interview, and online.

7. Visit the General Social Survey on the Web (http://www.icpsr.umich.edu/gss/subject/s-index.htm). Identify at least three questions contained in the codebook that might be useful in the pursuit of an applied purpose. Discuss how a business, government, or nonprofit client might use each of the questions.

Continuity Project

Write ten questions that would tap perceptions of gender differences in communication. Format the questions as they would appear in a questionnaire, using any of the formats illustrated in this chapter. For example, a sample Likert item might be "A masculine style of communication is more direct than a feminine style" (with a 5-point strongly agree–strongly disagree response).

Additional Readings

Anderson, A. B., Basilevsky, A., & Hum, D. (1983). Measurement: Theory and techniques. In P. H. Rossi, J. D. Wright, & A. B. Anderson (Eds.), *Handbook of survey research* (pp. 231–287). New York: Academic Press. The logic of measurement is analyzed in the context of composite measures.

Converse, J. M. (1987). *Survey research in the United States: Roots and emergence, 1890–1960*. Berkeley: University of Califor-nia Press. Here's a history of the several faces of survey research: academic, commercial, and governmental. You'll meet the major players involved and see the unfolding of this research specialty over the course of seven decades.

Converse, J. M., & Presser, S. (1986). *Survey questions: Hand-crafting the standardized questionnaire*. Newbury Park, CA: Sage. This is a useful book for the questionnaire designer. It's very readable and contains many helpful tips.

Dillman, D. A. (1978). *Mail and telephone surveys: The total design method*. New York: Wiley. An excellent review of the methodological literature on mail and telephone surveys. Dillman makes many good suggestions for improving response rates.

Elder, G. H., Jr., Pavalko, E. K., & Clipp, E. C. (1993). *Working with archival data: Studying lives*. Newbury Park, CA: Sage. This book discusses the possibilities and techniques for using existing data archives in the United States, especially those providing longitudinal data.

Feick, L. F. (1989). Latent class analysis of survey questions that include don't know responses. *Public Opinion Quarterly, 53*, 525–547. *Don't know* can mean a variety of things, as this analysis indicates.

Foddy, W. (1993). *Constructing questions for interviews and questionnaires*. New York: Cambridge University Press. An excellent treatment of the challenges in constructing valid questions and concrete suggestions for asking good questions.

Fowler, F. J., Jr. (1995). *Improving survey questions: Design and evaluation*. Thousand Oaks, CA: Sage. A comprehensive discussion of questionnaire construction, including a number of suggestions for pretesting questions.

Gubrium, J. F., & Holstein, J. A. (Eds.) (2002). *Handbook of interview research*. Thousand Oaks, CA: Sage. An excellent handbook relevant to both quantitatively oriented and qualitatively oriented interviewing. Chapters 3, 26, 27, 28, and 29 are especially relevant to the issues examined in this chapter, especially the role of new technologies in survey research.

Kiecolt, E. J., & Nathan, L. E. (1985). *Secondary analysis of survey data*. Beverly Hills, CA: Sage. An excellent overview of the major sources of data for secondary analysis and guidelines for taking advantage of them.

McIver, J. P., & Carmines, E. G. (1981). *Unidimensional scaling*. Newbury Park, CA: Sage. Here's an excellent way to pursue Thurstone, Likert, and Guttman scaling in further depth.

Miller, D. (1991). *Handbook of research design and social measurement*. Newbury Park, CA: Sage. An excellent compilation of frequently used and semistandardized scales. The many illustrations reported in Part 4 of this resource may be directly adaptable to studies or at least suggestive of modified measures. Moreover, studying the several different scales may also give you a better understanding of the logic of composite measures in general.

Rubin, R. B., Palmgreen, P., & Sypher, H. E. (Eds.) (1994). *Communication research methods: A sourcebook*. New York: Guilford. An excellent collection of frequently used questionnaire measures in communication research.

Schwarz, N., & Sudman, S. (Eds.) (1996). *Answering questions: Methodology for determining cognitive and communicative processes in survey research.* San Francisco: Jossey-Bass. An overview of how social scientists can pretest survey questions by gaining insights into the meaning-making process of respondents.

Sheatsley, P. F. (1983). Questionnaire construction and item writing. In P. H. Rossi, J. D. Wright, & A. B. Anderson (Eds.), *Handbook of survey research* (pp. 195–230). New York: Academic Press. An excellent examination of the topic by an expert in the field.

Smith, E. R. A. N., & Squire, P. (1990). The effects of prestige names in question wording. *Public Opinion Quarterly, 54,* 97–116. Not only do prestigious names affect the overall responses given to survey questionnaires, but they also affect such things as the correlation between education and the number of "don't know" answers.

InfoTrac College Edition
http://www.infotrac-college.com/
wadsworth/access.html

Access the latest news and journal articles with InfoTrac College Edition, an easy-to-use online database of reliable, full-length articles from hundreds of top academic journals. Conduct an electronic search using the following search terms:

- questionnaire
- structured interview (standardized interview)
- index
- scale
- Likert items
- semantic differential items
- comparative judgment
- response rate
- pretesting
- secondary analysis

CHAPTER 9

Experiments

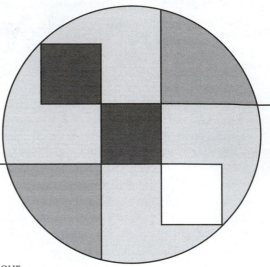

What You'll Learn in This Chapter

This chapter examines the experimental method. We also use our discussion of this method as a way to elaborate on issues of internal validity and external validity.

INTRODUCTION

This chapter addresses the research method most frequently associated with structured science in general, the experiment. Here we'll discuss the experiment as a mode of scientific observation. Most basically, experiments involve (1) taking action and (2) observing the consequences of that action. Communication researchers typically select a group of participants, do something to them, and observe the effect of what was done. In this chapter, we'll examine both the logic and the various techniques of communication experiments.

It's worth noting that experiments also are used often in nonscientific human inquiry. In preparing a stew, for example, we add salt, taste, add more salt, and taste again. In defusing a bomb, we clip a wire, observe whether the bomb explodes, clip another, and. . . .

We also experiment copiously in our attempts to develop generalized understandings about the world we live in. All skills are learned through experimentation: eating, walking, riding a bicycle, and so forth. This chapter will discuss some ways that communication researchers use experiments to develop generalized understandings. We'll see that, like other methods available, experimenting has its special strengths and weaknesses.

TOPICS APPROPRIATE TO EXPERIMENTS

Experiments are especially well suited to research projects involving relatively limited and well-defined concepts and propositions. The positivist image of science, discussed earlier in this book, and the experimental model are closely related to each other. Experimentation, then, is especially appropriate for hypothesis testing. It's also better suited to cause–effect explanation than to descriptive purposes.

Three basic kinds of communication experiments can be identified in the research literature. First, we can identify experiments in which some communication-related variable serves as the independent variable in affecting some attitude, perception, or behavior, known as the dependent variable. For example, researchers who study the persuasion process typically employ this kind of experiment. They examine some feature of a communicative message—its level of fear appeal or its emotional appeals, for instance—to determine whether it produces a change in experimental participants' attitudes, beliefs, or behaviors toward the topic of the message. This is exactly the kind of experiment conducted by Mark Mor-

man (2000). In part, Morman was interested in determining whether messages about testicular cancer presented in a factual manner were more or less effective than messages presented in narrative, or storytelling, form in changing males' attitudes and behavioral intentions toward testicular self-exams.

This first kind of communication experiment could deal with some feature of the message's delivery or transmission, not just the message's content. For example, Matthew Lombard and his colleagues (2000) conducted an experiment to determine whether the size of a TV screen affected viewers' TV viewing experiences. Experimental participants watched the same videotape on a 12-inch screen or on a 46-inch screen. The dependent variable was a physiological measure of arousal, electrodermal activity. Participants who watched on the large screen experienced the TV program as more exciting and experienced a greater sense of physical movement than did participants who watched on the small screen.

In contrast to the first kind of experiment, in which a communication variable serves as the independent variable for some noncommunication dependent variable, the second kind of communication experiment features just the opposite: Some noncommunication variable serves as the independent variable in affecting some communication-related dependent variable. Whereas the first kind of experiment asks "How does communication affect people's attitudes, beliefs, or behaviors?" the second kind of experiment asks "How is communication affected by some phenomenon or factor?" For example, Tim Kuhn and Marshall Scott Poole (2000) examined, in part, the effects of a task's complexity on the effectiveness of decision-making communication. They found that tasks high in complexity (that is, tasks in which the group has a large number of goals, a large number of paths that could be taken to achieve those goals, and the need for cooperation among group members) needed an integrative conflict management style among group members in order to produce effective decisions.

The third kind of experiment found in communication research involves communication-related variables as both the independent variable and the dependent variable. This kind of experiment addresses the general question "How does some aspect of communication affect another aspect of communication?" Cindy White and Judee Burgoon (2001) conducted a study that illustrates this third kind of experiment. The researchers randomly assigned participants to either tell the truth or engage in deception during a conversation with another—thus, the truthfulness of the talk (truthful–not truthful) served as the independent variable. In part, they were interested in whether the participant's truthfulness affected the amount of nonverbal involvement that he or she displayed while talking—that is, how detached, expressive, and attentive the participant was during the conversation. Nonverbal involvement, then, was the dependent variable.

We typically think experiments are conducted in laboratories, and they are known as *laboratory experiments.* Indeed, most of the examples in this chapter will involve such a setting. This need not be the case, however. As you'll see, communication researchers often study *field experiments:* "experiments" that occur in the regular course of social events. For example, the study of task complexity, conflict management style, and decision-making effectiveness in task-oriented groups by Kuhn and Poole (2000) studied naturally occurring groups as they went about their business of reaching real-life decisions.

Experiments, then, examine the cause-and-effect relation between independent variables and dependent variables. The three kinds of experiments summarized here vary in how communication is positioned: as the independent variable, as the dependent variable, and as both the independent variable and the dependent variable.

You may remember from Chapter 3 that cause–effect explanation hinges on three issues: (1) time order (the independent variable must precede the dependent variable), (2) evidence of correlation between the independent and the dependent variable, and (3) the elimination of other factors, or rival explanations to causation, that could explain the relationship between the independent and the dependent variable.

In experimental design, the first two of these three conditions are generally quite easy to demonstrate. The third criterion of causality is often challenging to researchers, however. Several kinds of rival explanations can account for the findings in a study; these *rival explanations* involve third variables in some way. These threats to internal validity are discussed in a classic 1963 book by Donald Campbell and Julian Stanley and expanded in a follow-up book by Thomas Cook and Donald Campbell (1979). Having examined these sources of internal invalidity, we'll be in a position to appreciate the advantages of some of the more sophisticated experimental designs that communication researchers sometimes use.

THREATS TO INTERNAL VALIDITY

The problem of internal invalidity refers to the possibility that the conclusions drawn from experimental results may not accurately reflect what has gone on in the experiment itself. The threat of internal invalidity is present whenever anything other than the experimental stimulus can affect the dependent variable. Here's a list of the most common types of problems that can stand in the way of making internally valid causal claims (Campbell & Stanley, 1963; Cook & Campbell, 1979; Huck & Sandler, 1979; Katzer, Cook, & Crouch, 1991), grouped for convenience into three basic categories: researcher-related threats, participant-related threats, and procedure-related threats.

Researcher-Related Threats

These threats to internal validity result from something the researcher does that affects the research participants in some way related to the dependent variable.

1. *Experimenter effect* (also known as the Rosenthal effect or the Pygmalion effect). If the experiment involves a researcher or a *confederate* (someone who assists the researcher in some way) who is aware of the study's purpose, variables, and hypotheses, this individual could unconsciously treat participants differently in the various conditions of the study, thereby affecting how those participants behave. Robert Rosenthal (1966) discusses the many ways the experimenter (or his or her confederate) can influence the results of a study. A researcher could unintentionally relax his or her body posture or establish eye contact with the participants who behave in ways that support the hypothesis, for example. In Chapter 8, we discussed a variation of this problem for survey research when we talked about appropriate and inappropriate interviewer conduct.

2. *Observer bias.* This threat can occur when the researchers' knowledge of the research study's purpose, variables, and hypotheses biases their observations of the dependent variable in some way. For example, if a researcher hypothesized that satisfied couples would engage in more smiling than dissatisfied couples, he or she might observe more smiles among satisfied couples than are actually there. If this bias was intentional, it would be an ethical breach of conduct. Usually, this problem refers to unconscious bias on the observer's part.

3. *Researcher attribute effect.* This threat takes place when some characteristic or feature of the researcher (or the confederates) systematically affects participant responses in a study. For example, if participants exposed to one experimental treatment were met at the laboratory by a male assistant and participants exposed to another experimental treatment were met at the laboratory by a female assistant, then the participants' responses in the

two treatments might have been the result of the sex of the person who greeted them. In Chapter 8, we discussed a similar problem for survey research when we discussed the appearance of the interviewer.

Participant-Related Threats

This category of threats to internal validity includes problems related to the study's participants.

4. *The Hawthorne effect.* This threat occurs when participants' responses are influenced by the fact that they are aware of being observed. In Chapter 8, we discussed a similar problem for survey research when we mentioned the problem of a social desirability effect. This effect derives its name from a famous series of studies of employee satisfaction conducted by F. J. Roethlisberger and W. J. Dickson (1939) in the late 1920s and early 1930s. These two researchers studied working conditions in the telephone "bank wiring room" of the Western Electric Works in the Chicago suburb of Hawthorne, Illinois, attempting to discover what changes in working conditions would improve employee satisfaction and productivity. To the researchers' great satisfaction, they discovered that making working conditions better consistently increased satisfaction and productivity. As the workroom was brightened up through better lighting, for example, productivity went up. Lighting was further improved, and productivity went up again. To further substantiate their scientific conclusion, the researchers then dimmed the lights: *Productivity again improved!*

It then became evident that the wiring room workers were responding more to the attention given them by the researchers than to improved working conditions. As a result of this phenomenon, often called the Hawthorne effect, communication researchers have become more sensitive to and cautious about participant awareness of being observed.

5. *Testing effect.* Often, the process of measuring (frequently referred to as *testing* in experiments) and re-measuring (*retesting*) will influence people's behavior, thereby confounding the experimental results. You probably counted on such a testing effect if you sat for your SAT or ACT tests as a junior and again as a senior in high school, hoping that your score would improve the second time simply as a result of your taking the exam once as a warm-up exercise.

Researchers do not welcome testing effects because they can interfere with their ability to claim that the change from test 1 to test 2 is the result of the independent variable. Suppose we administer a questionnaire to

a group as a way of measuring their attitudes toward using sun screen. Then we administer an experimental stimulus, a message about skin cancer, and re-measure their attitudes toward using sun screen. By the time we conduct the second measure, known as the posttest, the participants may have gotten more sensitive to the issue of skin cancer and sun screen simply as a result of responding to the questionnaire the first time around. Thus, any changes we noted could have resulted from the testing effect rather than the experimental stimulus. In Chapter 8, our discussion of question order examined a problem similar to the testing effect that faces survey researchers—how respondents answer earlier questions can affect how they answer later questions.

6. *Maturation.* People are continually growing and changing, whether in an experiment or not, and such changes can affect the results of the experiment. The maturation effect doesn't necessarily mean that participants grow more mature. The effect refers to any systematic change in an experiment's participants during the course of the experiment that is related to how they score on the dependent variable. In a long-term experiment, for example, the fact that the participants grow older (and wiser?) may have an effect. In shorter experiments, they may grow tired, sleepy, bored, or hungry, or change in other ways that may affect their behavior in the experiment. In Chapter 8, we discussed a similar problem with survey research related to question order—if a questionnaire is too long, respondents can grow weary or bored and lose interest in the questions.

7. *Experimental mortality.* Although some experiments could, we suppose, kill participants, this problem refers to a more general and less extreme form of mortality. Often, experimental participants will drop out of the experiment before it's completed, which can affect statistical comparisons and conclusions. In Chapter 8, we discussed a similar challenge facing survey researchers when respondents fail to return mailed surveys.

Let's suppose we're testing the effects of a series of public service announcements (PSAs) against smoking among adolescents. We ask a group of adolescents to watch the message series and then provide us with data on attitudes toward smoking at the conclusion of the study. If adolescents who already smoke or who are inclined to smoke find the PSA series offensive or stupid and they leave before the study's over, we would be left with only those participants who were nonsmokers to begin with. The PSAs were not responsible for the anti-smoking attitude at the conclusion of the study—the results were an indicator of who was left behind in the study.

8. *Selection biases.* Comparisons between groups of participants don't have any meaning unless the groups are *comparable.* A selection bias results when the groups being compared in an experiment are not the same at the beginning of the study. One of the most common ways that a selection bias occurs is through self-selection, in which the participants have determined for themselves which experimental treatment they are going to receive. Any comparison between groups may be the result of factors other than the experimental variable under examination. For example, let's suppose we are interested in whether exposure to PBS science programming for children increases kids' grades in science courses. We compare children who watch these programs regularly to those who don't, and we measure their grades in science courses for one year following the viewing period. The problem with this study is that the children self-selected into viewer and nonviewer groups. Other factors could be systematically related to this self-selection—academic motivation, curiosity about the world, and so forth. And these factors could be the ones responsible for grades in science courses, not viewing the PBS programs per se (excellent though they may be).

9. *Intersubject biases.* These biases result when the participants in different experimental groups have an opportunity to influence one another in some way. The most common form of this bias is the *diffusion or imitation of treatments.* When participants in different experimental groups can communicate with one another, participants in one group could pass on some elements of the experimental stimulus to participants in the other group. In that case, the second group becomes affected by the same stimulus as the first group, and the researcher has lost the ability to compare the two groups meaningfully. Sometimes, we speak of the second group as having been "contaminated."

10. *Compensatory rivalry.* In real-life experiments, the participants deprived of the experimental stimulus (known as the *control group*) may try to compensate for the missing stimulus by working harder. They may perceive themselves as the "underdog" and thus try harder, undermining a meaningful comparison by the researcher. Suppose a researcher has devised a form of intervention treatment to help people who are fearful of speaking in public overcome their anxiety. She assigns some anxious participants to receive the treatment, and she assigns other anxious participants to the control group. If the participants in the control group perceive that they are being denied something of potential benefit to them, they may work harder to overcome their anxiety and thereby show up the other group. This would be compensatory rivalry.

11. *Demoralization.* On the other hand, feelings of deprivation within the control group may result in their giving up. This is known as a demoralization effect. In some studies, demoralized control group participants may act up, get angry, or grow depressed. The researcher's ability to meaningfully compare the experimental and the control group has been compromised.

Procedure-Related Threats

This third category of threats to internal validity is related to the procedures associated with the conduct of the study itself.

12. *History.* The results of an experimental study could be the result of current events that take place while the experiment is being conducted. These outside events are known as a history effect. For example, an exposé uncovering shady financial dealings of a political candidate, released during a field experiment to determine the effects of political campaign ads on voter decisions, would be an example. We would be unable to determine whether the dependent variable—voter decision—was the result of the political campaign ads, the exposé, or a combination of both.

13. *Instrumentation.* This problem occurs if the instrument we are using to measure the dependent variable changes from the first measurement (known in experiments as the *pretest*) to the second measurement (known as the *posttest*). If we use different measures of the dependent variable (say, different questions), how can we be sure they're comparable to one another? Perhaps our dependent variable will seem to have decreased simply because the pretest measure was more sensitive than the posttest measure. Or, if the measurements are being made by the experimenters, their standards or their abilities may change over the course of the experiment.

Of course, instrumentation is simply another way of flagging measurement reliability issues—if the measure, or instrument, does not perform consistently (that is, it lacks adequate measurement reliability), then we have an instrumentation effect.

14. *Treatment confound.* When researchers conduct experiments, they examine how an independent variable affects a dependent variable. Sometimes, however, the independent variable is woven together with another variable, and it is this other variable that produces the effect on the dependent variable. That is, the effect of the independent variable (the treatment) is confounded by another variable. For example, suppose a researcher wants to examine the effects of a social-skills program on

kids who get in trouble on the playground. In order for kids to be enrolled in the program, their parents have to pay a $25 enrollment fee. The researcher wants to see if kids who go through the program are involved in fewer playground fights than kids who do not go through the program. But notice that the variable of parental investment (on the order of $25) was packaged with participation in the social-skills program. Maybe any observed improvement in playground behavior among participating kids was the result of the fact that their parents made an investment at the beginning of the study. In paying $25, the parents may have behaved in ways at home to get their money's worth—for example, emphasizing the importance of getting along. Thus, the effects of the program were confounded with parental investment.

A treatment confound is a problem of measurement validity: The operationalization is of a variable other than what the researcher claims.

15. *Statistical regression.* This problem refers to the tendency for people who score at the extremes (extremely high or extremely low) during the pretest to produce posttest scores that have regressed toward the middle, or the mean: Extremely high scorers regress downward, and extremely low scorers regress upward.

Sometimes, it's appropriate to conduct experiments on participants who start out with extreme scores on the dependent variable. If you were testing a new method for reducing speech anxiety among hard-core apprehensives, you'd want to conduct your experiment on people who score very high in communication apprehension. But consider for a minute what's likely to happen to the anxiety scores of such people over time, without any experimental interference. They're starting out so high that they can only stay at the top or decrease: They can't get any more apprehensive. Even without any experimental stimulus, then, the group as a whole is likely to show some improvement over time. Referring to a *regression to the mean,* statisticians often point out that extremely tall people as a group are likely to have children shorter than themselves, and extremely short people as a group are likely to have children taller than themselves. There's a danger, then, that changes occurring by virtue of participants starting out in extreme positions will be attributed erroneously to the effects of the experimental stimulus.

16. *Compensation.* In experiments in real-life situations —such as a special educational program—participants in the control group are often deprived of something considered to be of value. In such cases, there may be pressures to offer some form of compensation. For example, hospital staff might feel sorry for medical control group patients and give them extra "tender loving care." In such a situation, the control group is no longer a genuine control group.

These, then, are some of the primary threats to internal validity. Aware of these, experimenters have devised designs aimed at handling them. However, some designs are more effective than others in eliminating threats to internal validity when researchers want to make cause–effect claims.

PRE-, QUASI-, CLASSICAL, AND FACTORIAL EXPERIMENTAL DESIGNS

Researchers have devised several basic kinds of experimental designs to examine cause-and-effect relations between independent and dependent variables. Essentially, all experimental designs examine the effect of an independent variable on a dependent variable. Typically, the independent variable takes the form of an experimental stimulus, which is either present or absent—that is, a *dichotomous variable,* having two attributes. (This need not be the case, however, as later sections of this chapter will show.) The independent and dependent variables appropriate to experimentation are nearly limitless. Moreover, a given variable might serve as an independent variable in one experiment and as a dependent variable in another.

In other terms, the independent variable is the cause and the dependent variable is the effect. Thus, for example, we might say that watching a PSA against smoking caused a change in smoking behavior among adolescents or that reduced smoking was an effect of watching the PSA.

Both independent and dependent variables must be operationally defined for purposes of experimentation. Such operational definitions might involve a variety of observation methods. Conventionally, in the experimental model, dependent and independent variables must be operationally defined before the experiment begins. Ultimately, however, experimentation, like other quantitative methods, requires specific and standardized measurements and observations.

Donald Campbell and Julian Stanley (1963), in an excellent little book on research design, describe several different experimental designs. In this section, we're going to describe some of these briefly to give you a broader view of the potential for experimentation in communication research. The various kinds of experimental designs can usefully be grouped into four basic categories: pre-experiments, quasi-experiments, classical or "true" experiments, and factorial experiments. Experimental designs have different strengths and weaknesses, as we shall see. But before we turn to each design, we want to introduce you to the scientific notation that is often used in mapping the particulars of a given experimental design.

The Scientific Notation of Various Experimental Designs

Shortly, we will present a dazzling array of experimental designs: a grand total of nine different designs, to be exact. In order to help you digest the differences among these various design options, we present Figure 9-1 as a preview, derived from similar charts by Campbell and Stanley (1963).

We have a second goal in this figure—to introduce you to the scientific symbols or notations commonly used by social scientists to describe these designs in "shorthand." In this figure, "X" stands for the independent variable, or the experimental treatment. A blank space indicates a control group, a group not exposed to the independent variable. "O" stands for the observation of the dependent variable. If the "O" appears before the "X," it is a pretest, and if it appears after the "X," it's a posttest. If there are multiple observations of the dependent variable, or multiple attributes of the independent variable, these are indicated by numerical subscripts. An "R" by a group symbolizes random assignment, and the absence of random assignment is symbolized by a dotted line (--------) separating groups. We'll make more sense of these symbols as we proceed through each of the design options.

We have found a summary chart such as Figure 9-1 to be a very helpful tool in remembering the various designs discussed in this chapter. When we read a study in which a causal claim is being made, this notation system is a useful shorthand tool to sketch the overall design employed by the researcher.

Pre-Experimental Designs

To begin, Campbell and Stanley discuss three so-called **pre-experimental designs.** In the first such design—

Pre-Experimental Designs							
1. One-Shot Case Study			X	O			
2. One-Group Pretest–Posttest Design	O_1		X	O_2			
3. Static-Group Comparison			X	O_1			
				O_2			
Quasi-Experimental Designs							
4. Time-Series Design	O_1	O_2	O_3 X	O_4	O_5	O_6	
5. Nonequivalent Control Group Design	O_1		X	O_2			
	O_3			O_4			
6. Multiple-Time-Series Design	O_1	O_2	O_3 X	O_4	O_5	O_6	
	O_7	O_8	O_9	O_{10}	O_{11}	O_{12}	
True Experimental Designs							
7. Pretest–Posttest Control Group Design	R	O_1	X	O_2			
	R	O_3		O_4			
8. Posttest-Only Control Group Design	R		X	O_1			
	R			O_2			
9. Solomon Four-Group Design	R	O_1	X	O_2			
	R	O_3		O_4			
	R		X	O_5			
	R			O_6			

Note: "X" stands for independent variable; "O" stands for observation of dependent variable; "R" stands for random assignment of subjects to the group; "--------" stands for the absence of random assignment.

Source: From Campbell, D. T., & Stanley, J. C. (1963). *Experimental and Quasi-Experimental Designs for Research.* Boston: Houghton Mifflin. Adapted with permission.

FIGURE 9-1   **Summary of Experimental Designs and Their Scientific Notations**

the *one-shot case study*—a single group of participants is measured on a dependent variable (O) following the administration of some experimental stimulus (X). Design 1 in Figure 9-1 shows this design in scientific notation form. Suppose, for example, that we show the anti-smoking PSA mentioned earlier to a group of adolescents for a two-week period and then administer a questionnaire that seems to measure attitudes toward smoking. Suppose further that the answers given to the questionnaire seem to represent a negative attitude toward smoking. We might be tempted to conclude that the PSA message produced negative attitudes toward smoking.

But we would be mistaken in drawing this conclusion. Perhaps the questionnaire doesn't really represent a very good measure of attitudes toward smoking (a problem with measurement reliability or validity), or perhaps the group we're studying was negative toward smoking to begin with (a selection bias). Maybe one of the participant's parents, a lifelong smoker, was diagnosed with lung cancer at the time of the experiment, and word of this spread among the students (a history effect and an intersubject bias). Maybe the pro-smokers in the group dropped out and failed to attend the PSA showings, leaving us with only adolescents whose attitudes were unfavorable toward smoking (a mortality effect). Maybe the adolescents knew they were participating in an experiment and wanted to please the experimenter by giving the socially desirable answer (a Hawthorne effect). Maybe the research assistant who introduced the PSA messages was dressed to look "cool," and the adolescents wanted to impress her by giving the most positive answers they could think of (a researcher-attribute effect). Maybe the adolescents grew restless and bored by the end of the two-week period, and they provided socially desirable answers in the hope that the experiment would end (a maturation effect). And so on. In short, the PSA message might have made no difference, though our experimental results might have misled us into thinking it did. The one-shot case study is the weakest of all of the experimental designs with respect to trustworthy causal claims because it does the poorest job in eliminating the threats to internal validity discussed above.

If it's so poor, why bother to discuss it then? We include it because it is a frequent kind of argument to which we are exposed on a daily basis, particularly in advertising messages. We are shown a product and the good outcomes that presumably ensue for customers who purchase the product: Clothes come out whiter if detergent X is used, happiness swells upon the purchase of a certain make of automobile, and so forth. However, the problem with this form of argumentative claim is that it

is very weak in internal validity: We cannot attribute the outcome, the dependent variable, to the claimed independent variable.

The second pre-experimental design discussed by Campbell and Stanley adds a pretest for the experimental group. This design—which the authors call the *one-group pretest–posttest design*—might appear better than the one-shot case study because it adds a pretest baseline against which to assess change at the second testing, or posttest. In this design, then, participants are measured in terms of a dependent variable (pretested), exposed to a stimulus representing an independent variable, and then re-measured in terms of the dependent variable (posttested). The second design in Figure 9-1 shows this design in scientific-notation form. Differences noted between the first and last measurements on the dependent variable are then attributed to the independent variable.

However, this design suffers from many of the same threats to internal validity as the first pre-experimental design, and then some. Because participants are being measured twice, possibilities exist for a testing effect, an instrumentation effect, and, if the group of participants were extreme scorers to begin with (for example, a group of students identified by teachers as smokers), statistical regression toward the mean. About the only thing we can determine with this second design is whether we started with a group of adolescents whose attitudes were already unfavorable toward smoking—that is, we can address the selection bias threat.

If this design is still a weak one when it comes to making cause–effect claims, why bother with it? Again, we would point to its frequency in everyday argument claims, especially in advertising. We are shown a person on the TV screen against a backdrop of a modest house and an old car, told that this person enrolled in a ten-week program in how to make money fast, and then shown the "after" shot in which the person is shown lounging beside the pool on his or her mansion estate. Although this before-and-after design allows us to determine that the person did not start out wealthy and merely maintain that status, we still can't conclude that the ten-week program was the cause of the change in financial status. See if you can think of all the rival explanations that might have produced the same outcome and identify which threats to internal validity are at play.

To round out the possibilities for pre-experimental designs, Campbell and Stanley point out that some research is based on a comparison of two groups but has no pretests. One of the groups is exposed to the independent variable, and the other group is not exposed to it. Campbell and Stanley call this design the *static-group comparison,* and it is the third design shown in scientific-notation form in Figure 9-1. In the case of the anti-smoking PSA message, we might show the message to one group but not to another, and then measure attitudes toward smoking in both groups. We would attribute any difference in the scores of the two groups to the presence of the PSA message.

Again, however, we would be wrong in reaching this conclusion. And, again, the problem rests with those threats to internal validity. The addition of a comparison group helps us out in some respects but adds to our woes in other respects. The addition of a second group, one denied the viewing opportunity of the experimental group, might set us up for problems with intersubject biases, compensatory rivalry, demoralization, or compensation effects. If the researcher knows which group was exposed to the PSAs and which group was not, and then interacts with the groups of adolescents, we may find ourselves with an experimenter effect. At least we don't have the possible problems with pretests and posttests identified above for the one-group pretest–posttest design. And if the experiences of the two groups are comparable, we can probably eliminate a history effect because it has been neutralized—if some external incident occurs that could affect the outcome, at least participants in both groups would be similarly exposed to the incident, and any difference between the groups would not be the result of a history effect. But what if the two groups were not comparable at the outset of the study? We'd lose any ability to make a meaningful comparison between them.

The logic of this third pre-experimental design also appears frequently in advertising venues where causal claims are made. We're shown two piles of white laundry: One glistens brightly with no stains, and the other has lingering stains and is no longer sparkling white. A voice-over tells us that the glistening clothes were washed in detergent Z, whereas the dull, stained clothes were washed in some other laundry detergent. The argumentative claim of the commercial is that detergent Z causes clothes to become sparkling clean. But does it? Not according to our understanding of rival explanations. Maybe the two piles of clothes were not equally soiled prior to washing.

Figure 9-2 graphically illustrates these three pre-experimental research designs, using a different research question: *Does exercise cause weight reduction?* To make the several designs clearer, we've used individuals rather than groups, but you should realize that the same logic pertains to group comparisons. Let's review the three pre-experimental designs with this new example.

The one-shot study design represents a common form of logical reasoning. Asked whether exercise causes weight reduction, we may bring to mind an example that would seem to support the proposition: someone who exercises and is thin. There are problems with this reasoning, however. Perhaps the person was thin long before beginning to exercise. Or perhaps he became thin for some other reason, like eating less or getting sick. The observations shown in the diagram do not guard against these other possibilities. Moreover, the observation that the man in the diagram is in trim shape depends on our intuitive idea of what constitutes trim and overweight body shapes. All told, this is very weak evidence for testing the relationship between exercise and weight loss.

The one-group pretest–posttest design offers somewhat better evidence that exercise produces weight loss. Specifically, we've ruled out the possibility that the man was thin before beginning to exercise. However, we still have no assurance that it was his exercising that caused him to lose weight.

Finally, the static-group comparison eliminates the problem of our questionable definition of what constitutes trim or overweight body shapes. In this case, we can compare the shapes of the man who exercises and the one who does not. However, this design reopens the possibility that the man who exercises was thin to begin with.

Fortunately, researchers who want to make confident claims about cause-and-effect relations between variables have some better designs to use. We'll turn to the quasi-experimental designs next. These designs, as a group, do not eliminate all the threats to internal validity, but they are an improvement over the pre-experimental designs.

Quasi-Experimental Designs

Pre-experiments and quasi-experiments are alike in that they both involve the observation of a naturally occurring independent variable or the manipulation of an independent variable by the researcher. However, **quasi-experimental designs** use pretests and posttests in more complicated ways than do pre-experiments, and this contributes to the greater trustworthiness that generally characterizes the quasi-experiment. Three basic designs are used in quasi-experimental research.

The first quasi-experimental design is the *time-series design*—studies of processes occurring over time. The fourth design in Figure 9-1 displays its scientific notation. To illustrate this design, we'll begin by asking you to assess the meaning of some hypothetical data. Suppose we come to you with what we say is an effective technique for getting students to participate in classroom discussion. To prove our assertion, we tell you that on Monday, only four students asked questions or made a comment in class; on Wednesday, the class time was devoted to an

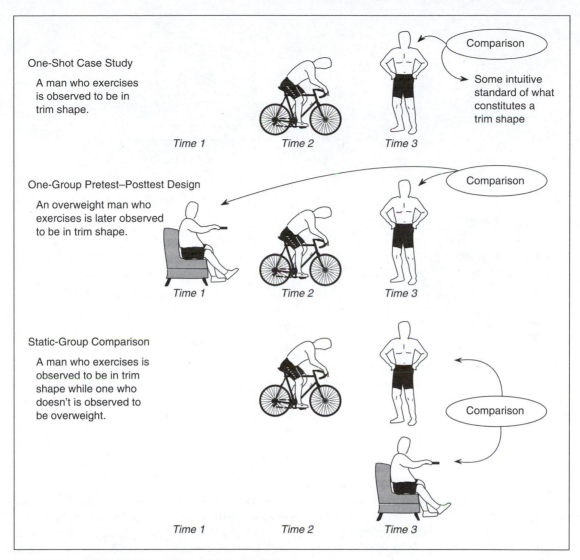

One-Shot Case Study

A man who exercises is observed to be in trim shape.

Time 1   *Time 2*   *Time 3*

Comparison

Some intuitive standard of what constitutes a trim shape

One-Group Pretest–Posttest Design

An overweight man who exercises is later observed to be in trim shape.

Time 1   *Time 2*   *Time 3*

Comparison

Static-Group Comparison

A man who exercises is observed to be in trim shape while one who doesn't is observed to be overweight.

Time 1   *Time 2*   *Time 3*

Comparison

FIGURE 9-2   **Three Pre-experimental Research Designs**

open discussion of a controversial issue raging on campus; and on Friday, when the subject matter of the course was returned to, eight students asked questions or made comments. In other words, we contend, the discussion of a controversial issue on Wednesday doubled classroom participation. This simple set of data is presented graphically in Figure 9-3.

Have we persuaded you that the open discussion on Wednesday has had the consequence we say it has? Probably you'd object that our data don't prove the case. Two observations (Monday and Friday) aren't really enough to prove anything. Instead, we've been keeping a record of class participation throughout the semester for the one class. This record would allow us to conduct a time-series evaluation.

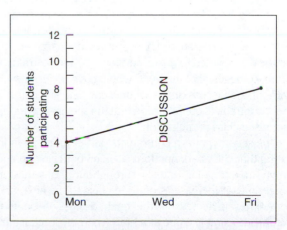

FIGURE 9-3   **Two Observations of Class Participation: Before and After an Open Discussion**

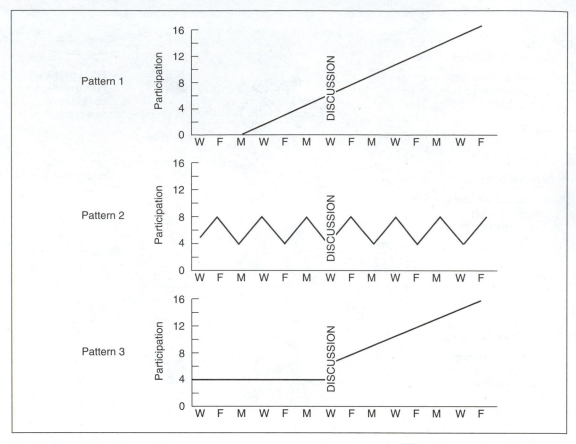

FIGURE 9-4   **Three Patterns of Class Participation in a Longer Historical Perspective**

Figure 9-4 presents three possible patterns of class participation over time—both before and after the open discussion on Wednesday. Which of these patterns would give you some confidence that the discussion had the impact we contend it had?

If the time-series results looked like the first pattern in Figure 9-4, you'd probably conclude that the process of greater class participation had begun on the Wednesday before the discussion and had continued, unaffected, after the day devoted to the discussion. The long-term data seem to suggest that the trend would have occurred even without the discussion on Wednesday. The first pattern, then, contradicts our assertion that the special discussion increased class participation.

The second pattern contradicts our assertion by indicating that class participation has been bouncing up and down in a regular pattern throughout the semester. Sometimes it increases from one class to the next, and sometimes it decreases; the open discussion on that Wednesday simply came at a time when the level of participation was about to increase. More to the point, we note that class participation decreased again at the class following the alleged post-discussion increase.

Only the third pattern in Figure 9-4 supports our contention that the open discussion mattered. As we see, the level of discussion before that Wednesday had been a steady four students per class. Not only did the level of participation double following the day of discussion, but it continued to increase further afterward. Although these data do not protect us against the possible influence of some extraneous factor (it might also have been mentioned that participation would figure into students' grades), they do exclude the possibility that the increase resulted from a process of maturation (indicated in the first pattern) or from regular fluctuations (indicated in the second).

In the context of the scientific notation we are using, the number of students who participated is our dependent or O variable. If we gathered this datum at three points prior to the discussion on a controversial topic (X), we have O_1, O_2, and O_3 pretest data. The posttest data collections (O_4, O_5, and O_6) give us information about the number of students who participated at three time points after X. Of course, the time-series design could involve more time points than three before and three after X. Central to a time-series design is having enough pretest and posttest data points to determine patterns and trends in our dependent variable over a length of time. The time-series design takes the one-group pretest–posttest pre-experimental design and simply builds time into the design.

The time-series design just described involves only an experimental or treatment group—a group exposed to the independent variable. You'll recall from our discussion of the static-group comparison design the value to be gained from having a comparison group. In the second quasi-experimental design, the *nonequivalent control group design,* you create a comparison group that is as similar as it can be to the experimental or treatment group, only it is not exposed to the independent variable. If you try to choose a similar comparison group, why is the design called "nonequivalent control group"? Good question. As we shall see below when we come to classical experimental designs, the best kind of a comparison involves randomly assigning some participants to the experimental group and some participants to the control group. Without random assignment, we can't be as confident as we'd like that the two groups are the same. This lack of confidence is flagged in the term "nonequivalent control group." The scientific notation for this design is shown as design 5 in Figure 9-1; the dotted line that separates our two groups signifies that participants have not been randomly assigned to the two groups. It is evident from this figure that the nonequivalent control group design is simply a static-group-comparison pre-experiment to which pretests have been added for both groups.

If an innovative foreign language program (X) is being tried in one class in a large high school, for example, you may be able to find another foreign language class in the same school that has a very similar student population: one that has about the same composition in terms of grade in school, gender, ethnicity, IQ, and so forth. The second class, then, could provide a point of comparison. At the beginning and end of the semester, both classes could be given the same foreign language test (O), and you could compare the improvements of both classes.

Here's how two junior high schools were selected for purposes of evaluating a program aimed at discouraging tobacco, alcohol, and drug use:

The pairing of the two schools and their assignment to "experimental" and "control" conditions was not ran-

dom. The local Lung Association had identified the school where we delivered the program as one in which administrators were seeking a solution to admitted problems of smoking, alcohol, and drug abuse. The "control" school was chosen as a convenient and nearby demographic match where administrators were willing to allow our surveying and breath-testing procedures. The principal of that school considered the existing program of health education to be effective and believed that the onset of smoking was relatively uncommon among his students. The communities served by the two schools were very similar. The rate of parental smoking reported by the students was just above 40 percent in both schools. (McAlister et al., 1980, p. 720)

In the initial set of observations, the two groups reported virtually the same (low) frequency of smoking. Over the 21 months of the study, smoking increased in both groups, but it increased less in the experimental group than in the control group, suggesting that the program had an effect on students' behavior.

The nonequivalent control group design is reliant on a procedure known as **matching,** instead of random assignment, to provide two comparable groups at the outset of a study. In matching, a researcher tries to determine in advance the variables that might relate systematically to the dependent variable as measured through a posttest. Obviously, included in this list of variables is the pretest score on the dependent variable, because a participant's posttest score might be directly related to his or her pretest score. The researcher then identifies a control group that is comparable to the experimental group on all of the identified variables.

Note that we haven't said clearly what those important matching variables are. Of course, we can't give a definite answer to this question; the answer ultimately depends on the nature and purpose of the particular study. But here's the rub—you may not be in a position to know in advance what the relevant variables are for the matching process.

As we shall see below, random assignment is preferable to matching for two reasons. First, random assignment produces comparable groups on all possible variables, including those not explicitly identified by the researcher. Second, most of the statistics used to evaluate the results of experiments assume randomization. Failure to design your experiment that way, then, makes your later use of those statistics less meaningful. However, if you can't conduct a classical experiment with random assignment, matching is the next best thing.

The third quasi-experimental design—the *multiple-time-series design*—is basically a combination of the two quasi-experimental designs we have just discussed. That is, we can collect time-series data on two or more matched comparison groups. The scientific notation for this one appears as design 6 in Figure 9-1. This design is an improved version of both the time-series design and the nonequivalent control group design just described. Carol Weiss has presented a useful example of this design:

> An interesting example of multiple time series was the evaluation of the Connecticut crackdown on highway speeding. Evaluators collected reports of traffic fatalities for several periods before and after the new program went into effect. They found that fatalities went down after the crackdown, but since the series had had an unstable up-and-down pattern for many years, it was not certain that the drop was due to the program. They then compared the statistics with time-series data from four neighboring states where there had been no changes in traffic enforcement. Those states registered no equivalent drop in fatalities. The comparison lent credence to the conclusion that the crackdown had had some effect. (1972, p. 69)

Although this type of study design is not as good as one in which participants are assigned randomly—that is, a classical experiment—it's nonetheless an improvement over assessing the experimental group's performance without any comparison except that provided by multiple data points through time from the experimental group alone. The key in making trustworthy claims is comparability.

You may have gotten the impression that quasi-experiments are better than pre-experiments with respect to internal validity, but not as strong as another kind of experimental design that uses something called random assignment to treatment and control groups. We turn next to the classical experimental designs, which generally make claim to having the strongest internal validity.

The Classical or "True" Experiment

The **classical** or **"true" experiments** involve the **random assignment** of participants to **experimental groups** and **control groups.** Using a randomly assigned control group allows the researcher to detect any effects of the treatment itself.

The need for control groups in experimentation has been nowhere more evident than in medical research. Time and again, patients who participate in medical experiments have appeared to improve, and it has been un-

clear how much of the improvement has come from the experimental treatment and how much from the experiment. In testing the effects of new drugs, then, medical researchers frequently administer a *placebo* (for example, sugar pills) to a control group. Thus, the control group patients believe they, like the experimental group, are receiving an experimental drug. Often, they improve. If the new drug is effective, however, those receiving that drug will improve more than those receiving the placebo.

Use of a control group, with a placebo, effectively neutralizes a number of possible threats to internal validity. The Hawthorne effect could occur equally in both experimental and control groups; thus, this potential problem has been neutralized as a possible rival explanation of any difference observed between the experimental and control groups. Similarly, the placebo effectively handles possible problems with compensatory rivalry, demoralization, and compensation. If participants are affected by some attribute or feature of the researcher (or his or her confederates), such an effect is equally likely to occur in the experimental group and in the control group, thereby neutralizing a researcher attribute effect as a rival explanation of any difference noted between the two groups.

Other participant-related threats are similarly neutralized. Maturation and mortality could happen to participants in both groups, but because they are equally likely for experimental and control participants, these two threats have been neutralized as rival explanations of any difference noted between the two groups.

If the true experiment employs both a pretest and a posttest, possible problems associated with re-measuring participants are again neutralized because they are equally likely to appear in experimental and control groups. Thus, testing and instrumentation effects are neutralized as possible explanations of any difference noted between the experimental and control groups. If extreme groups of scorers are used in both groups, regression toward the mean is equally likely to happen in both experimental and control groups, thereby neutralizing this as a possible rival explanation of any differences observed between the two groups.

In classical experiments, control groups provide an important guard against not only the effects of the experiments themselves but also the effects of any events outside the laboratory during the experiments. Because any such history effect should happen about equally for members of the control and experimental groups, history has been neutralized as an explanation of any difference between the two groups.

Sometimes, an experimental design will require more than one experimental or control group. In the case of the anti-smoking PSA study we discussed earlier, you might also want to examine the effect of reading the text of the PSA versus seeing the PSA on a videotape. In that case, you might have one experimental group see the PSA, another experimental group read the text of the PSA, and the control group do neither, instead being exposed to messages whose content was unrelated to smoking (a message placebo, in other words). The two experimental groups are randomly assigned comparison groups.

In experimental research, you need either a randomly assigned comparison group(s) or a randomly assigned control group. Sometimes, researchers want both, as in this example. However, if you weren't interested in the question of whether a PSA works but only which form of a PSA works better, you wouldn't need a control group, only a comparison group.

Notice that we have emphasized random assignment in our discussion of comparison and control groups. What's so powerful about random assignment anyway?

Random Assignment The cardinal rule of participant selection in experimentation concerns the comparability of experimental and control groups. Ideally, the control group represents what the experimental group would have been like had it not been exposed to the experimental stimulus. Therefore, it's essential that experimental and control groups be as similar as possible.

The earlier discussions of the logic and techniques of probability sampling (Chapter 7) provide the best method for selecting two groups of people similar to each other. Having recruited, by whatever means, a total group of participants, the experimenter may randomly assign those participants to either the experimental group or the control group. Such randomization might be accomplished by numbering all of the participants serially and selecting numbers by means of a random numbers table, or the experimenter might assign the odd-numbered participants to the experimental group and the even-numbered participants to the control group.

Let's return again to the basic concept of probability sampling. If the experimenter has recruited 40 participants altogether, in response to a newspaper advertisement, for example, we may have reasonable confidence that the 20 participants randomly assigned to the experimental group will be reasonably similar to the 20 assigned to the control group. Reasonable confidence is not a guarantee, however. Although random assignment cannot guarantee that two groups are truly equivalent, it is, within the laws of probability sampling, the best method available to us. It is better than the next best alternative, matching, which we described earlier for the nonequivalent control group quasi-experimental design.

Within the logic of our earlier discussions of sampling, it's as though the 40 participants in this instance are a population from which we select two probability samples—each consisting of half the population. Because each sample will reflect the characteristics of the total population, the two samples will mirror each other. And, as we saw in Chapter 7, the number of participants involved is important. In the extreme, if we recruited only two participants and designated, by the flip of a coin, one as the experimental participant and one as the control, there would be no reason to assume that the two participants are similar to each other. With larger numbers of participants, however, randomization makes good sense.

Thus, random assignment gives us reasonable assurance that our experimental and control groups are equivalent groups of participants on any and all characteristics upon which they could be compared. Within the laws of probability sampling, we will end up with as many males in the experimental group as in the control group. As many lovers of novels in one group as in the other. As many people of average intelligence in one group as in the other. As many people likely to grow tired in one group as in the other. As many people who drop out because of sickness in one group as in the other. As many people who have testing effects from pretest to posttest occasions. And so forth.

In short, random assignment eliminates the threat of selection biases. Because the researcher uses probability sampling to determine who is in the experimental group and who is in the control group, the participants themselves do not self-select exposure to the independent variable. And, given our understanding of probability sampling, we have two groups comparable in every way we can imagine them to be.

If you're keeping track of that rather lengthy list of possible threats to internal validity, you realize that the true experiment neutralizes, within the laws of probability, almost everything from the list. Random assignment to experimental and control groups is a very powerful device in the logic of experimentation. But we're still left with a few niggling threats: observer bias, experimenter effect, compensation, compensatory rivalry, demoralization, intersubject bias between groups, and treatment confound. The first five of these remaining possible threats to internal validity are handled through a procedural solution known as the double-blind experiment.

The Double-Blind Experiment A **double-blind experiment** is one in which neither the participants nor anyone who comes in contact with the participants has knowledge of the group to which a given participant has been assigned. Like patients who improve when they merely *think* they're receiving a new drug, experimenters sometimes tend to prejudge results. In medical research, the experimenters may be more likely to "observe" improvements among patients receiving the experimental drug than among those receiving the placebo. (This would be most likely, perhaps, for the researcher who had developed the drug.) A double-blind experiment eliminates this possibility of observer bias because neither the participants nor the experimenters know which is the experimental group and which is the control.

Similarly, because the researcher's assistants lack knowledge of the group to which a given participant has been randomly assigned, they are not positioned to produce an experimenter effect. In the medical case, those researchers responsible for administering the drug and for noting improvements would not be told which participants were receiving the drug and which the placebo. Conversely, the researcher who knew which participants were in which group would not administer the experiment.

In fact, no one who comes in contact with the study participants knows "who's who." Thus, no group members are positioned to receive special compensation because of the particular conditions to which they have been assigned.

The double-blind experiment also means that the participant doesn't know whether he or she is in the experimental group or the control group. This lack of awareness works against compensatory rivalry and demoralization effects, which we have already discussed earlier in conjunction with the concept of a placebo.

The double-blind procedure still leaves us with two threats to internal validity—intersubject bias and treatment confound. The solution to a possible problem with intersubject bias between experimental and control participants is fairly easy to solve procedurally—the researcher should plan the experiment in such a way that the two groups do not have opportunity to interact with each other throughout the period of the study. The remedy for a problem with treatment confound sits in the researcher's operationalization of the independent variable; the researcher needs to take great care to ensure that the operationalization procedures separate the independent variable of interest from other variables with which it might be "packaged." Operationalization of the independent variable brings us to a discussion of manipulation checks.

Manipulation Checks We have now addressed all of the possible threats to internal validity that could stand in the way of a causal claim that our independent variable produced an effect on our dependent variable. Of course, this presumes that the first two criteria of causality have been met—appropriate time order and a correlation between our variables. But there's one more matter we need to discuss before we can make our claim of causation, and it brings us back to measurement reliability and validity, discussed in Chapter 6. Before we can say that "X causes Y," we need to make certain that we have operationalized our independent and dependent variables in a trustworthy manner.

We're not going to repeat ourselves here by restating material from Chapter 6, but we want to supplement that discussion by addressing a particular kind of validity check appropriate to experiments—the **manipulation check.** To make certain that the operationalization of the independent variable was what the researcher intended, experimental participants are often asked their perceptions of the conditions to which they were exposed. In the anti-smoking PSA message discussed earlier, for example, experimental participants would typically be given a manipulation check in the form of a survey designed to measure whether in fact they perceived the PSA as anti-smoking in nature. Such a check ensures that the independent variable that the researcher is operationalizing is the one to which the participants are responding, by their own report. Often, such a manipulation check is camouflaged when presented to the experimental participant. Thus, our anti-smoking PSA message would probably be assessed by our experimental participants on a wide range of features—estimated length, volume level, pace of motion, and position on smoking.

With this general discussion as a backdrop, let's turn to the three designs that are known as classical or "true" experiments.

Three True Experimental Designs Campbell and Stanley (1963) discuss three basic true experimental designs: the pretest–posttest control group design, the posttest-only control group design, and the Solomon four-group design. All three of these designs are characterized by the random assignment of participants to experimental and control groups.

The pretest–posttest control group design is depicted in scientific-notation form as design 7 in Figure 9-1. Participants are randomly assigned to experimental and control groups, symbolized by the "R" that precedes each group. All participants are measured on the dependent variable in the form of a pretest administered before introduction of the independent variable. After the independent variable has been introduced, all participants are measured again, in a posttest of the dependent variable.

Pursuing our example with the anti-smoking PSA message to adolescents, we would locate a pool of participants—perhaps by posting advertisements in high school newspapers or by visiting homerooms. We would then randomly assign half of our adolescents to view the PSA message and half to view alternative programming, unrelated to smoking, as our control. Before exposure to any programming, we would measure all of our participants on a reliable and valid measure of attitudes toward smoking—perhaps through a Likert-type questionnaire instrument (see Chapter 8). Then experimental and control groups would view the videotapes to which they had been randomly assigned. At the conclusion of the viewing, we would reassess attitudes toward smoking in a posttest administration of our Likert-type questionnaire.

What would we expect to find? Well, for starters, we would expect that experimental and control participants had comparable attitudes toward smoking at the pretest measure. That is, O_1 and O_3 would not differ significantly from each other in a statistical test. We would expect this because we employed random assignment. Additionally, if our PSA message worked as we would hypothesize, we should find two substantive findings. We should find more negative attitudes toward smoking in the posttest scores of our experimental participants than in the posttest scores of our control participants. That is, the difference between O_2 and O_4 should be statistically significant in the direction of a more negative average score in the experimental group than the control group. Further, we should find that the change from pretest to posttest was significantly greater for experimental participants than for control participants. That is, $(O_1 - O_2) > (O_3 - O_4)$.

This kind of true experiment is frequently conducted by communication researchers. For example, Roxanne Parrott and Ashley Duggan (1999) used a pretest–posttest design in assessing the value of using soccer coaches as role models of sun protection for youth. Soccer-playing youth filled out questionnaires at both pretest and posttest occasions on their knowledge, attitudes, and behaviors surrounding sun protection and skin cancer. Teams were randomly assigned to one of three conditions: coach modeling, in which the soccer coach actively taught the team players about sun protection and the dangers of skin cancer; parent mailing, in which parents were sent a pamphlet containing the same information as what coaches presented to their teams; and the control group.

The posttest-only control group design is depicted in scientific-notation form as design 8 in Figure 9-1. This design is simpler than the pretest–posttest control group design because no pretests are involved prior to the introduction of the independent variable. To continue with our example of the anti-smoking PSA, we would randomly assign our pool of adolescent participants to either the control group or the experimental group. Each group would be exposed to a videotaped message—the experimental group seeing the anti-smoking PSA and the control group seeing some alternative programming irrelevant to the issue of smoking. At the conclusion of the viewing, all participants would complete the Likert-type questionnaire designed to measure attitudes toward smoking. If our independent variable functioned as hypothesized, we would expect to find more negative attitudes toward smoking among experimental participants than among control participants. That is, O_1 would be significantly more negative than O_2.

The posttest-only control group design is also employed frequently in communication research. For example, this design was used by Patrick Rossler and Hans-Bernd Brosius (2001) in their study of the effects of talk shows on German adolescents' views about real life. Adolescents were randomly assigned to either an experimental group (which watched a week's worth of talk shows discussing, in a favorable light, relationships and actions that were viewed as morally controversial in German society at large—gay and lesbian relationships, transsexuality, and tattooing) or a control group (which watched a week's worth of talk shows on more neutral topics, such as celebrities and fashion). At the conclusion of the viewing exposure, participants were given questionnaires to solicit their perceptions of the estimates of how many homosexuals, transsexuals, and tattooed persons were in the society, and their attitudes toward people with these characteristics. Obviously, the researchers were interested in putting to the test a version of the well-known cultivation thesis that mass media content shapes viewers' perceptions of social reality (Morgan & Shanahan, 1997).

Given the greater simplicity that accompanies the posttest-only control group design, why would researchers ever choose the more complex pretest–posttest control group design to begin with? Three reasons often lead researchers to opt for the pretest–posttest control group design over the posttest-only control group design. First, a researcher might want to double-check that experimental and control participants are comparable on the dependent variable prior to introduction of the independent variable. Although random assignment is likely to result in this equivalence between groups, researchers sometimes work with small participant pools; random assignment works better when we are dealing with a larger pool of participants to be assigned. Second, the researcher's dependent variable might be conceived as a change score—how much participants changed over time in their attitudes, beliefs, or behaviors. If we used the posttest-only control group design, we could not measure the extent of change in our participants. Third, the independent variable might work only if participants have been "primed" first by taking a pretest. Perhaps the anti-smoking PSA message works only if adolescents have first responded to a questionnaire that started them thinking seriously about their bodies, health, and smoking. Such a "priming effect" is impossible in the posttest-only control group design. But how can researchers know for certain whether a "priming effect" is present with their independent variables? This brings us to the third true experimental design.

The third true experimental design is known as the *Solomon four-group design.* Its scientific notation is given in design 9 in Figure 9-1. This design addresses the problem of a "priming effect," whose technical name is *a testing interaction with the stimulus.* If you look closely at this design, it is nothing more than a combination of the pretest–posttest control group design and the posttest-only control group design.

This latest experimental design permits four meaningful comparisons. If the anti-smoking PSA message really works in making attitudes more negative toward smoking, we should expect four findings:

1. In Group 1, posttest attitudes (O_2) toward smoking should be more negative than pretest attitudes (O_1).
2. There should be more negative attitudes toward smoking evident in the Group 1 posttest (O_2) than in the Group 2 posttest (O_4).
3. The Group 3 posttest (O_5) should show more negative attitudes toward smoking than the Group 2 pretest (O_3).
4. The Group 3 posttest (O_5) should show more negative attitudes toward smoking than the Group 4 posttest (O_6).

Notice that findings (3) and (4) rule out any interaction between the testing and the stimulus. And remember that these comparisons are meaningful only if participants have been assigned randomly to the different groups, thereby giving us reasonable confidence of comparable attitudes initially, even though their pre-experiment attitude is measured only in groups 1 and 2.

There is a side benefit to this research design, as Campbell and Stanley (1963) point out. Not only does the Solomon four-group design rule out interactions between testing and the stimulus; it also provides data for comparisons that will reveal the amount of such interaction that occurs in the classical experimental design.

This knowledge would allow a researcher to review and evaluate the value of any prior research that used the simpler design.

Thus far, we've been discussing the true experimental designs with only a single independent variable under study by the researcher. This independent variable could be examined with dichotomous presence-absence attributes, in which case we're talking about a true experiment of two groups: the experimental treatment group and the control group. Alternatively, as we noted earlier, we could have multiple attributes within our independent variable. Thus, we could have multiple comparison groups and a control group. But communication researchers who conduct experiments are often interested in studying multiple independent variables at once. These are known as **factorial designs.**

Factorial Experiments

Why would a researcher be interested in studying more than one independent variable at the same time? Put simply, to see how the independent variables function separately and together. Sometimes, how a single independent variable works is affected by other independent variables with which it is interdependent. How each independent variable functions in isolation of other independent variables is known as a *main effect.* How independent variables function in combination is known as an *interaction effect.*

Let's look in detail at one particular factorial experiment in order to better understand the logic of main effects and interaction effects. Valerie Smith, Susan Siltanen, and Lawrence Hosman (1998) were interested in examining how the language use of jury witnesses affected the judgments of juries. Because they could not conduct an experiment with real juries, they used mock juries. In particular, they were interested in whether witness hesitations (for example, "uh's") and witness hedges (for example, "kind of," "sometimes") affected mock jurists' perceptions of witness culpability (guilt and blameworthiness). They were interested in each of these independent variables, separately and together. In addition, the researchers recognized that when a witness takes the stand, he or she has an initial level of expertise or credibility, and they were interested in finding out how hedges and hesitations affected the perceptions of culpability of witnesses who had different levels of initial expertise. Their experiment thus had three independent variables: *hedges* (high and low), *hesitations* (high and low), and *initial speaker expertise* (high, moderate, low). Their dependent variable was *perceived culpability of the witness,* which they measured in both a pretest (perceptions of the witness's guilt based on a presentation of the apparent facts of the case) and a posttest (perceptions of the witness's guilt after reading mock testimony by the witness).

The researchers devised hypothetical transcripts of a trial. Experimental participants (the mock jurists) were randomly assigned to read one transcript. In a third of the transcripts, the witness was described with high initial expertise (holding a Ph.D. degree); in another third of the transcripts, the witness was described with moderate expertise (holding a B.A. or B.S. degree); the final third of transcripts described the witness as low in initial expertise (holding a high school degree). (The researchers included some questions in the posttest designed to perform a manipulation check on initial expertise, making sure that variations in education level were sufficient to affect participant perceptions of initial expertise. They were.)

Although the content of the witness testimony was the same, half of the transcripts had hesitations inserted into the text, and half did not; further, half of the transcripts had hedges inserted into the text, and half did not. Here are some samples from the transcripts to describe the four possible combinations of hedges and hesitations (Smith, Siltanen, & Hosman, 1998, p. 30):

Low hedges/Low hesitations: "I was feeling intense sharp pain as soon as I landed on the floor. I had some sharp pains in my lower back. It wasn't just a muscle spasm."

Low hedges/High hesitations: "Um, I was feeling intense sharp pains as soon as I landed on the floor. I had er . . . some sharp pains in my lower back. It wasn't just a muscle spasm."

High hedges/Low hesitations: "I was sort of feeling sharp pain as soon as I landed on the floor. I had some sharp pains in my back. I don't think it was just a muscle spasm."

High hedges/High hesitations: "Um, I was feeling sharp pain as soon as I landed on the floor. I had some sharp pains in my back. I don't think it was just a muscle spasm."

Throughout the transcripts, the "high" conditions featured 12–15 occurrences of hedges and/or hesitations. Each of these four possible combinations of language features was associated with a witness described with one of three levels of initial expertise, producing a total of twelve different transcripts to which participants were randomly assigned. The researchers found a significant main effect for the *hedges* independent variable: Witness testimony containing a low number of hedges was perceived as more authoritative than testimony containing a high number of hedges.

The researchers found a significant main effect for initial speaker expertise: In contrast to the moderate and low levels of initial expertise, witnesses initially described as high in expertise produced a pretest–posttest change of lessened culpability. But this finding was qualified once the researchers examined how initial expertise interacted with the language-use independent variables. High-expertise witnesses who had a high level of hesitations produced a judgment of greater, not lesser, culpability, when compared to high-expertise witnesses who spoke with a low level of hesitations. When speakers were low to moderate in initial expertise, hesitations did not affect participants' judgments of culpability. Hedges didn't produce any effect—maybe because in a court of a law, everyone expects witnesses to be cautious and qualify their claims to some extent.

The researchers found, then, that the effects of initial witness expertise on perceptions of culpability interacted with hesitations. Witnesses high in initial expertise produced judgments of less culpability, so long as they spoke without hesitations. However, if they hesitated in their testimony, they were found more guilty. If we were consultants in the business of preparing witnesses for testimony, we would work very hard to make sure that witnesses with initially high expertise spoke in a manner free of hesitations, based on the findings of this study! However, if our witnesses had less initial expertise, we wouldn't worry so much about whether they hesitated when they spoke.

This study is very characteristic of factorial experiments in communication research. First, notice that it is nothing more than a variation of the pretest–posttest control group design we described above, only now we have three independent variables instead of one. The researchers have a total of twelve different experimental treatment groups, instead of one experimental group and one control group, reflecting all of the possible combinations of the attributes of the independent variables. Factorial experiments are always variations of one of the true experimental designs we presented above.

When researchers describe their factorial experiments, they usually have a shorthand *factorial design statement* that captures the number of independent variables in the experiment and the number of attributes associated with each independent variable. For the mock jury study, the factorial design statement would be "a 3 × 2 × 2 factorial design." Notice that there are three terms that are multiplied, one term for each independent variable. The "3" refers to the three levels of initial witness expertise, the "2" refers to the two levels of hesitations (high and low), and the second "2" refers to the two levels of hedges (high and low). We could just as well describe this design as a "$2 \times 2 \times 3$" or a "$2 \times 3 \times 2$" factorial design— the order in which the independent variables are presented in the design statement is immaterial. Notice further that if we multiply the terms of a factorial design statement, we have the total number of experimental treatment groups, or comparison groups, in the experiment: $3 \times 2 \times 2 = 12$. This will always be the case in factorial design statements.

Let's suppose that instead of doing the factorial experiment we just described, we did an alternative experiment, one in which we threw into the mix the sex of the witness. So we would keep everything the same except that in half of the transcripts we would describe the witness as a male, and in half of the transcripts the witness would be described as female. Our new factorial design statement would thus be $3 \times 2 \times 2 \times 2$, for a total of 24 different experimental treatment, or comparison, groups. You can see that each time you add a new independent variable to the experiment, the result is dramatic in terms of the total number of groups to which you must randomly assign participants. Generally, experiments in communication rarely exceed four independent variables, and most are conducted with two or three independent variables.

Researchers often provide a display of the results of their study in a manner that reflects all of the possible combinations of the independent variables. This display usually takes the form of a *design diagram,* whose cells represent all of the comparison groups. For the Smith and colleagues (1998) study, the table would look like Figure 9-5.

When researchers conduct experiments with multiple independent variables, there are several possible main effects and several possible interaction effects to be ex- amined. For each independent variable, there is a possible main effect, and there is an interaction effect possible for each combination of independent variables. Let's assign the letter A to represent the *witness expertise* variable in the Smith and colleagues study (1998), the letter B to represent the *hesitation* variable, and the letter C to represent the *hedges* variable. There are three possible main effects in their experiment: the A main effect, the B main effect, and the C main effect. The researchers found a significant main effect for the A variable. In addition, there were several possible interaction effects: the AB interaction, the AC interaction, the BC interaction, and the ABC interaction. Of these possible interaction effects, the researchers found evidence for only one significant combination effect: the AB interaction. When researchers examine their data from factorial experiments, they always perform analyses to see which main effects and which interaction effects are evident.

As independent variables are added to the study, the number of main effects and interaction effects increases multiplicatively. If we label our *sex* variable from above as D, then our factorial experiment would have four possible main effects (A, B, C, and D), and the following possible interaction effects: AB, AC, AD, BC, BD, CD, ABC, ABD, ACD, BCD, and ABCD. Whew! Interaction effects get very complicated very quickly in factorial experiments!

Blocking Variables   Often, communication researchers are interested in examining how an independent variable to which participants are randomly assigned works in combination with another independent variable to which participants are not randomly assigned. This second kind of variable is known as a *blocking variable* (it is also known as a stratifying variable or a leveling variable— Campbell and Stanley [1963]). For example, in the mock jury study by Smith and colleagues (1998), we might have been interested in finding out whether male and female participants respond differently to the *expertise, hesitation,* and *hedges* independent variables. Short of sex-change operations to which our participant pool is randomly assigned, we can't randomly assign participants to their sex. But we could add this variable to our design as a blocking variable and analyze it the way we would any other independent variable. If we took the $3 \times 2 \times 2$ study conducted by Smith and colleagues and replicated it by adding *sex of participant* to the design, we would have a $3 \times 2 \times 2 \times 2$ factorial design. Such blocking would allow us to determine whether the original three independent variables, separately and in combination, produce the same effects for male participants as for female participants.

	High Hesitations		Low Hesitations	
	High Hedges	Low Hedges	High Hedges	Low Hedges
High Initial Expertise	1	2	3	4
Moderate Initial Expertise	5	6	7	8
Low Initial Expertise	9	10	11	12

FIGURE 9-5   **Sample Factorial Design Diagram**

Between-Subjects versus Within-Subjects Designs
There are many different types of factorial experiments that can be conducted, but we will mention only one because of the frequency with which it is encountered in the communication research literature: *between-subject* versus *within-subject* factorial designs. In a between-subjects factorial design, a given participant is assigned to one and only one experimental, or comparison, group. By contrast, in a within-subjects design, a given participant is tested two or more times. Although within-subjects designs require fewer participants than between-subjects designs, they are more complicated to execute. Let's see why.

Let's return to the mock jury study by Smith and colleagues (1998). We could replicate this study as a within-subjects design by exposing all participants to all twelve possible combinations of *witness expertise* (high, moderate, low), *hesitations* (high, low), and *hedges* (high, low), but we'd face some additional challenges. First, because the order in which participants are exposed to stimuli can affect their responses (recall our discussion of order effects with survey questions in Chapter 8), we would need to conduct our replication as a *counterbalanced design*, making certain that the transcripts were "packaged" in all possible orders across our sample as a whole and that a given participant was randomly assigned to a given order. Second, our participants would probably grow very bored, and likely suspicious, if we repeated the same scenario twelve times, changing words here and there to reflect the particular manipulations of the independent variables. In order to conduct this study in a manner that would not arouse suspicion and that would sustain participant interest, we'd probably need many different hypothetical trials in which the content of transcripts would vary. But in order to do this, we would need to add these factors systematically into our design.

Up to this point in the chapter, our discussion of experimental designs has been oriented to issues of internal validity: the extent to which the researcher can attribute the outcome of the study to the independent variable under examination. Now we're going to turn our attention to external validity—generalizability—and in so doing, we'll examine field experiments and evaluation research.

EXTERNAL VALIDITY AND EXPERIMENTS

Internal invalidity accounts for only some of the complications faced by experimenters. In addition, there are problems of what Campbell and Stanley (1963) call external invalidity, which relates to the *generalizability* of experimental findings to the "real" world. Even if the results of an experiment are an accurate gauge of what happened during that experiment, do they really tell us anything about life in the wilds of society?

Cook and Campbell (1979) highlight four primary threats to external validity. First, the generalizability of experimental findings is jeopardized, as the authors point out, if there is an *interaction between the testing setting and the treatment.* Here's an example of what they mean.

Let's return to our prior example of the anti-smoking PSA shown to adolescents. Let's suppose that we've conducted a perfectly adequate true experiment, maybe even a factorial experiment, and in fact found that adolescents exposed to the anti-smoking PSA developed more negative attitudes toward smoking. But would we get the same finding if we showed the PSA on television instead of in the classroom under artificially controlled circumstances? When adolescents are watching PSAs on television in their homes, they may be engaged in any of several parallel activities, such as eating, reading, and talking on the phone. The effects of the PSA might not be the same in a different testing situation.

Second, Cook and Campbell discuss an *interaction of selection and treatment*. Basically, the issue here is whether the findings of a particular experiment, conducted on a specific group of participants, generalize to other people who did not participate in the study.

Many beginning researchers confuse random assignment of participants with random selection of participants from a larger population. Random assignment relies on the logic and techniques of probability sampling once a pool of participants has been recruited to participate in a study. We discussed this procedure earlier in this chapter. Often, however, the initial pool of participants is *not* selected using probability sampling. Many laboratory experiments are conducted with college undergraduates as participants. Typically, the experimenter asks students enrolled in his or her classes to participate in experiments or advertises for participants in a college newspaper.

In relation to the criterion of *generalizability* in quantitatively oriented science, this tendency clearly represents a potential defect in experimental research. Simply put, college undergraduates do not typify the public at large. Therefore, we may learn much about the communication of college undergraduates but not about communication in general.

However, this potential defect is thought by some to be less significant in explanatory research than it would be in descriptive research. True, having noted the attitudes toward smoking among a group of adolescents, we would have little confidence that the same attitude existed among adolescents at large. If a PSA, on the other hand, were found to produce more negative attitudes toward smoking among those adolescents, we could have a bit more confidence—without being certain—that it would have a similar effect for adolescents at large. Social processes and patterns of causal relationships appear to be more generalizable and more stable than are specific characteristics.

Of course, this presumption that causal relations work the same way regardless of the particular people involved can be problematic. Many experiments conducted in the United States are criticized by scholars of cultural communication, who emphasize differences between cultures. U.S. adolescents might respond very differently to a persuasive message presented in a PSA than would, say, Colombian adolescents exposed to the same message.

The third threat to internal validity discussed by Cook and Campbell (1979) is an *interaction of history and the treatment.* The issue with this third threat is generalizability across time: Can the causal relationship demonstrated in a particular laboratory experiment generalize to different periods in the past and in the future?

For example, in the past 50 years, there has been significant change in U.S. society in knowledge about and attitudes toward smoking. Medical research has uncovered the link between smoking and cancer. In many communities, it is against the law to smoke in public locations such as restaurants. A PSA designed today to change adolescents' attitudes toward smoking might not have worked the same way with adolescents of 20 or 30 years ago, and the same PSA may have very different effects 20 years from now.

The fourth, and final, threat to external validity is one we have already discussed in introducing the Solomon four-group design—an interaction between testing and treatment. If the experimental treatment produces an effect only if there is a prior "priming effect" that comes through pretesting, findings may not generalize to different conditions that lack a pretest.

External validity, then, addresses the issue of generalizability: generalizability to different settings, to different participants, to different times, and to different testing conditions. In general, we will find that the strength of experimental research is internal validity, not external validity. However, experimental researchers have identified some designs that offer greater external validity than do other designs.

Laboratory Experiments versus Field Experiments

Although we tend to equate the terms *experiment* and *laboratory experiment,* many important communication experiments occur outside settings created by the researcher for the purpose of the study, often in the course of normal social events. Sometimes, nature designs and executes experiments that we can observe and analyze; sometimes, social and political decision makers serve this natural function.

Let's imagine that a hurricane has struck a particular town. Some residents of the town suffer severe financial damages, while others escape relatively lightly. What, we might ask, are the consequences for communication of experiencing a natural disaster? Are those who suffer the most more likely to reach out to others communicatively, asking for and giving verbal and nonverbal social support? To answer this question, we might interview residents of the town at some time after the hurricane. We might question them regarding their usual patterns of communication before the hurricane and their current communication practices, comparing those who suffered greatly from the hurricane with those who suffered relatively little. In this fashion, we might take advantage of a **field experiment,** which we could not have arranged even if perversely willing to do so.

A natural disaster provides an extreme example of a field experiment. But many field experiments in communication research take advantage of natural events and settings a bit closer to everyday life experiences. For instance, Barbara Wilson and her colleagues (1992) conducted a field experiment on the impact of a television movie about acquaintance rape on viewers' subsequent attitudes about rape.

The sample for the study was selected through probability-based sampling. Here's how it was done. A survey research organization that regularly conducts studies for the television networks randomly selected over 13,000 telephone numbers from lists of cable TV subscribers in four geographic regions in the United States: a mid-sized Delaware town, a small town in Indiana, a large city in Oklahoma, and a medium-sized town in northern California. Of these selected telephone numbers, 57 percent resulted in no contact. Of the remaining 5,924 active numbers (i.e., someone was home), 1,038 adults were able and willing to participate in the viewing of a two-hour movie, *She Said No.* This movie was to be shown on network television, and contacted participants were invited to view the program three days prior to its national broadcast, without commercial interruption. The survey research organization said that it was doing audience research on the movie and was interested in soliciting viewers' honest opinions.

Of those willing to view the movie on an advance basis, half were randomly assigned to view the movie and half were assigned to the control group. The viewers saw the movie through closed-circuit cable, in their homes. The following night, a telephone interviewer from the survey research organization called the viewers (and participants in the control group) to ask their opinions about many topics; embedded in these questions were some designed to measure attitudes toward rape, the dependent variable.

The design of the true experiment, then, was a posttest-only control group design. In fact, the experiment was a factorial design, because the researchers used three blocking variables: the sex of the participant, the age of the participant (18–34 years, 35–49 years, 50 years and older), and whether or not the participant had personal knowledge of a rape victim (determined at the time of the posttest survey). Among other findings, results of the experiment indicated that the movie increased awareness of date rape as a social problem for all demographic groups.

This field experiment was strong with respect to generalizability of the sample and generalizability of the setting. Within the designated geographic regions, potential participants were randomly selected for inclusion in the study. In addition, participants viewed a real movie that was subsequently broadcast on national television, and they did so under natural circumstances—in their living rooms.

Field experiments that use classical or true designs are not too common in communication research because researchers don't have sufficient control over circumstances to randomly assign participants to experimental groups. But they are hesitant to resort to the pre-experimental designs we discussed previously. Instead, they often take the middle ground and use quasi-experimental designs, designs that we saw as stronger than pre-experimental designs although not as good as classical experiments with respect to internal validity. However, quasi-experiments often have reasonably strong external validity, given that they usually are conducted under natural conditions. They are commonly used in evaluation research.

EVALUATION RESEARCH

You may not be familiar with *Twende na Wakati (Let's Go with the Times),* but it's the most popular radio show in Tanzania. It's a soap opera. The main character, Mkwaju, is a truck driver with some pretty traditional ideas about gender roles and sex. By contrast, Fundi Mitindo, a tailor, and his wife, Mama Waridi, have more modern ideas regarding the roles of men and women and, particularly, on the issues of overpopulation and family planning.

Twende na Wakati was the creation of Population Communications International (PCI) and other organizations working in conjunction with the Tanzanian government in response to two problems facing that country today: (1) a population growth rate over twice that of the rest of the world and (2) an AIDS epidemic particularly heavy along the international truck route, where more than a fourth of the truck drivers and over half the commercial sex workers were found to be HIV positive in 1991. The prevalence of contraceptive use was 11 percent (Rogers et al., 1996, pp. 5–6).

The purpose of the soap opera was to bring about a change in knowledge, attitudes, and practices (KAP) relating to contraception and family planning. Rather than instituting a conventional educational campaign, PCI felt it would be more effective to illustrate the message through entertainment.

Between 1993 and 1995, 108 episodes of *Twende na Wakati* were aired, aiming at the 67 percent of Tanzanians who listen to the radio. Eighty-four percent of the radio listeners reported listening to the PCI soap opera, making it the most popular show in the country. Ninety percent of the show's listeners recognized Mkwaju, the sexist truck driver, and only 3 percent regarded him as a positive role model. Over two-thirds identified Mama Waridi, a businesswoman, and her tailor husband as positive role models.

Surveys conducted to measure the impact of the show indicated it had affected knowledge, attitudes, and behavior. For example, 49 percent of the married women who listened to the show said they now practiced family planning, compared with only 19 percent of the nonlisteners. There were other effects:

> Some 72 percent of the listeners in 1994 said that they adopted an HIV/AIDS prevention behavior because of listening to "Twende na Wakati," and this percentage increased to 82 percent in our 1995 survey. Seventy-seven percent of these individuals adopted monogamy, 16 percent began using condoms, and 6 percent

stopped sharing razors and/or needles. (Rogers et al., 1996, p. 21)

Evaluating the effectiveness of the soap opera illustrates a particular kind of research activity known as **evaluation research**—sometimes called *program evaluation.* This kind of research is characterized by its research purpose rather than a specific research method. This purpose is to evaluate the effect of social interventions such as new training programs, the introduction of innovations such as new ways of farming, and so forth. Many methods can be used in evaluation research, but the most frequently used method is the quasi-experiment.

Evaluation research is probably as old as general social scientific research itself. Whenever people have instituted a social reform for a specific purpose, they've paid attention to its actual consequences, even if they haven't always done so in a conscious, deliberate, or sophisticated fashion. In recent years, however, the field of evaluation research has become an increasingly popular and active research specialty, as reflected in textbooks, courses, and projects. In part, the growth of evaluation research no doubt reflects researchers' increasing desire to make an actual difference in the world. At the same time, we can't discount the influence of (1) increased federal requirements for program evaluations to accompany the implementation of new programs and (2) the availability of research funds to fulfill that requirement. Whatever the mixture of these influences, it seems clear that researchers will be bringing their skills into the real world more than ever before.

Communication researchers have joined other social scientists in their increasing interest in evaluation research. Many of the research articles that you find in such journals as the *Journal of Applied Communication Research* and *Health Communication,* for instance, illustrate evaluation research in one form or another.

Most fundamentally, evaluation research is appropriate whenever some social intervention occurs or is planned. A *social intervention* is an action taken within a social context for the purpose of producing some intended result. In its simplest sense, evaluation research is a process of determining whether the intended result was produced.

Because evaluation research is conducted in "real-world" situations, classical experiments are often not possible. Quasi-experiments become the fall-back method of choice.

Evaluation research presents a host of challenges to researchers precisely because of its "real-world" nature. We will mention three.

The first challenge is the need to specify outcomes clearly in advance of the study. Clearly, a key variable for evaluation researchers to measure is the outcome or response variable. If a given program or intervention is intended to accomplish something, we must be able to measure that something. Sometimes, the definitions of a problem and a sufficient solution are defined by law or agency regulations; the evaluation researcher must be aware of such specifications and accommodate them.

Often, however, there are no clear guidelines or standards by which to determine a program's success or failure. As you may anticipate, there are almost never clear-cut answers to questions like these. This dilemma has surely been the source of what is generally called cost/benefit analysis. How much does the program cost in relation to what it returns in benefits? If the benefits outweigh the cost, keep the program going. If the reverse, junk it. That's simple enough, and it seems to apply in straightforward economic situations. Unfortunately, the situations usually faced by evaluation researchers are seldom amenable to straightforward economic accounting. Ultimately, the criteria of success and failure are often a matter of agreement. The people responsible for the program may commit themselves in advance to a particular outcome that will be regarded as an indication of success. If not, it is important before the evaluation study is conducted to have agreement on what the outcome variable will be. Evaluation researchers often collect data on several different outcomes in an effort to provide as complete a picture as possible of a program's effects.

In the case of the Tanzanian soap opera, there were several outcome measures. In part, PCI wanted to improve knowledge about both family planning and AIDS. Thus, for example, one show debunked the belief that the AIDS virus was spread by mosquitoes and could be avoided by the use of insect repellent. Studies of listeners showed a reduction in that belief (Rogers et al., 1996, p. 21).

PCI also wanted to change Tanzanian attitudes toward family size, gender roles, HIV/AIDS, and other related topics; the research indicated that the show had affected these as well. Finally, the program aimed at affecting behavior. We've already seen that radio listeners reported changing their behavior with regard to AIDS prevention. They reported a greater use of family planning as well. However, because there's always the possibility of a gap between what people say they do and what they actually do, the researchers sought independent, confirming data. Tanzania's national AIDS-control program had been offering condoms free of charge to citizens. In the areas covered by the soap opera, the number of condoms given

TESTING SOAP OPERAS IN TANZANIA

by William N. Ryerson
Executive Vice-President
Population Communications International

Twende na Wakati ("Let's Go With the Times") has been broadcast on Radio Tanzania since mid-1993 with support from the United Nations Population Fund. The program was designed to encourage family planning use and AIDS prevention measures.

There were many different elements to the research. One was a nationwide, random-sample survey given prior to the first airing of the soap opera in June 1993 and then annually after that. Many interviewers faced particularly interesting challenges. For example, one interviewer, Fridolan Banzi, had never been in or on water in his life and couldn't swim. He arranged for a small boat to take him through the rough waters of Lake Victoria so he could carry out his interviews at a village that had no access by road. He repeated this nerve-wracking trip each year afterward in order to measure the change in that village.

Another interviewer, Mr. Tende, was invited to participate in a village feast that the villagers held to welcome him and to indicate their enthusiasm about having been selected for the study. They served him barbequed rats. Though they weren't part of his normal diet, he ate them anyway to be polite and to ensure that the research interviews could be carried out in that village.

Still another interviewer, Mrs. Masanja, was working in a village in the Pwani region along the coast of the Indian Ocean when cholera broke out in that village. She wisely chose to abandon the interviews there, which reduced the 1993 sample size by one ward.

The unsung heroes of this research, the Tanzanian interviewers, deserve a great deal of credit for carrying out this important work under difficult circumstances.

---

out increased sixfold between 1992 and 1994. This far exceeded the increase of 1.4 times in the comparison group, where broadcasters did not carry the soap opera.

The second challenge is the need for flexibility and adaptability in response to unforeseen circumstances. Of course, all forms of research can run into problems, but evaluation research has a special propensity for it. Logistical problems can be especially plaguing to evaluation researchers.

In a military context, *logistics* refers to moving supplies around—making sure that people have food, guns, and tent pegs when they need them. Here, we use it to refer to getting participants to do what they're supposed to do, getting research instruments distributed and returned, and other seemingly unchallenging tasks. These tasks are more challenging than you might guess! The accompanying box, "Testing Soap Operas in Tanzania," describes some of the logistical problems involved in the research discussed at the outset of this section.

Third, evaluation research can pose ethical challenges. Ethics and evaluation are intertwined in many ways. Sometimes, the social interventions being evaluated raise ethical issues. For example, if we were to evaluate the effectiveness of a safe sex campaign among middle-school students, it would be impossible to avoid involvement in the often heated political, ideological, and ethical issues surrounding sex education more generally.

The designs employed in evaluation research often require that some participants (the controls) will be deprived of some intervention thought desirable. Perhaps one of the most problematic examples of this ethical problem is the infamous Tuskegee syphilis study. In 1932, researchers in Tuskegee, Alabama, began a program of providing free treatment for syphilis to poor, black men suffering from the disease. Over the years that followed, several hundred men participated in the program. What they didn't know was that they were not actually receiving any treatment at all; the physicians conducting the study merely wanted to observe the natural progress of the disease. Even after penicillin was found to be an effective cure, the researchers still withheld the treatment. While there is, no doubt, unanimous agreement today as to the unethical nature of the study, such was not the case at the time. Even when the study began being reported in research publications, the researchers refused to acknowledge they had done anything wrong. When professional complaints were finally lodged with the U.S. Center for Disease Control in 1965, there was no reply (Jones, 1981).

Our purpose in mentioning some of the challenges that face evaluation researchers has not been to cast a shadow on evaluation research. Rather, we want to bring home the real-life issues that face evaluation researchers and the real-life consequences of evaluation researchers' actions. Evaluation research gives us a concrete example of experimental research that is high in external validity.

STRENGTHS AND WEAKNESSES OF THE EXPERIMENTAL METHOD

The chief advantage of an experiment lies in the isolation of the experimental variable and its effect over time. This is seen most clearly in terms of the basic experimental model. A group of experimental participants are found, at the outset of the experiment, to have a certain characteristic; following the administration of an experimental stimulus, they're found to have a different characteristic. To the extent that participants have experienced no other stimuli, we may conclude that the change of characteristics is attributable to the experimental stimulus.

Further, since individual experiments are often rather limited in scope, requiring relatively little time and money and relatively few participants, we often can replicate a given experiment several times using many different groups of participants. (This isn't always the case, of course, but it's usually easier to repeat experiments than, say, surveys.) As in all other forms of scientific research, the replication of research findings strengthens our confidence in the validity and generalizability of those findings.

The greatest weakness of laboratory experiments lies in their artificiality. Communication processes that occur in a laboratory setting might not necessarily occur in more natural social settings. Artificiality is not as much of a problem, of course, for field experiments or evaluation research studies.

In discussing several of the sources of internal and external invalidity mentioned by Campbell, Stanley, and Cook, among others, we saw that we can create experimental designs that logically control such problems. This possibility points to one of the great advantages of experiments: They can have a logical rigor that is often much more difficult to achieve in other methods.

Main Points

- There are 16 threats to internal validity that can function as rival explanations of the dependent-variable outcome. These threats to internal validity are researcher related, participant related, or procedure related in their origin.

- There are three forms of pre-experiments: the one-shot case study, the one-group pretest–posttest design, and the static-group comparison. These designs, although frequently used, are weak in internal validity.

- There are three kinds of quasi-experimental designs: the time-series design, the nonequivalent control group design, and the multiple time-series design. These designs are intermediate in their internal validity.

- The classical or true experiment tests the effect of an experimental stimulus on some dependent variable through the random assignment of participants to experimental and control groups.

- There are three basic forms of the classical experiment: the pretest–posttest control group design, the posttest-only control group design, and the Solomon four-group design.

- The classical experiment with random assignment of participants guards against most of the sources of internal invalidity, especially if it features a double-blind procedure.

- For purposes of internal validity, it's not important that a group of experimental participants be representative of some larger population, but it is important that experimental and control groups be similar to each other.

- When a true experiment has multiple independent variables, it is known as a factorial design. Factorial experiments allow researchers to identify main effects and interaction effects in the findings.

- There are four primary threats to external validity that can limit the generalizability of an experiment's findings.

- Classical experiments often face problems of external invalidity: Experimental findings may not reflect real life.

- The Solomon four-group design, field experiments, and quasi-experiments generally have greater external validity than do the other types of experimental designs.

- Evaluation research is a specific type of research designed to evaluate the outcomes of some social intervention or program. It is often based on quasi-experimental designs.

Key Terms

pre-experimental designs
quasi-experimental designs
matching
classical ("true") experiments
random assignment
experimental groups

control groups
double-blind experiment
manipulation check
factorial designs
field experiment
evaluation research

Review Questions and Exercises

1. Read an article or an editorial in a newspaper or magazine in which a causal claim is made: X caused Y. What kind of research evidence would you need in order to be convinced that this claim is trustworthy? Design an experiment that would examine whether X causes Y.

2. Watch some commercials on television, and identify argument claims based on the logic of the one-shot case study, the one-group pretest–posttest design, and the static-group comparison.

3. Consult the communication journals in Appendix A, and locate an example of evaluation research. Describe the kind of design employed in the study.

4. Internal validity and external validity are both important in making causal claims. Yet they are often in a trade-off relationship: Actions to increase internal validity often reduce external validity, and vice versa. If you had to make a choice in a given study, which would you rather sacrifice, and why: internal validity or external validity?

Continuity Project

Suppose you are interested in determining whether messages characterized by a masculine style are more persuasive than messages characterized by a feminine style. Develop a pre-experimental design, a quasi-experimental design, and a classical experimental design responsive to this research purpose. Discuss your designs in detail, addressing how each is responsive (or not) to the threats to internal validity and the threats to external validity.

Additional Readings

Campbell, D., & Stanley, J. (1963). *Experimental and quasi-experimental designs for research.* Chicago: Rand McNally. An excellent analysis of the logic and methods of experi-mentation in social scientific research. Though fairly old, this book has attained the status of a classic and is still frequently cited.

Cook, T. D., & Campbell, D. (1979). *Quasi-experimentation: Design and analysis issues for field settings.* Chicago: Rand McNally. An expanded and updated version of Campbell and Stanley.

Hedrick, T. E., Bickman, L., & Rog, D. J. (1993). *Applied research design: A practical guide.* Newbury Park, CA: Sage. This introduction to evaluation research is, as its subtitle claims, a practical guide, dealing straight-on with the compromises that must usually be made in research design and execution.

Jones, S. R. G. (1990). Worker independence and output: The Hawthorne studies reevaluated. *American Sociological Review, 55,* 176–190. This article reviews these classical studies and questions the traditional interpretation (which was presented in this chapter).

Ray, W., & Ravizza R. (2000). *Methods toward a science of behavior and experience* (6th ed.). Belmont, CA: Wadsworth. A comprehensive examination of social science research methods, with a special emphasis on experimentation. This book is especially strong in the philosophy of science.

Rossi, P. H., & Freeman, H. E. (1993). *Evaluation: A systematic approach.* Newbury Park, CA: Sage. This thorough examination of evaluation research is an excellent resource. In addition to discussing the key concepts of evaluation research, the authors provide numerous examples that might be useful in guiding your own designs.

InfoTrac College Edition
http://www.infotrac-college.com/wadsworth/access.html

Access the latest news and journal articles with Info-Trac College Edition, an easy-to-use online database of reliable, full-length articles from hundreds of top academic journals. Conduct an electronic search using the following search terms:

- quasi-experimental design
- factorial design
- control group
- double-blind experiment
- manipulation check
- evaluation research
- matching
- random assignment
- experimental group (also treatment group)

CHAPTER **10**

Quantitative Text Analysis

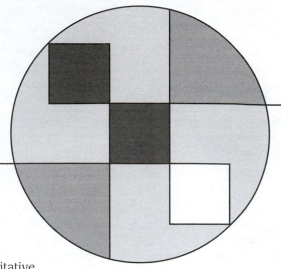

What You'll Learn in This Chapter

This chapter will present overviews of two methods of quantitative text analysis: content analysis and interaction analysis. Each of these methods focuses on the analysis of actual communication messages.

INTRODUCTION

Let's suppose you're interested in what people write in their e-mail messages to others. One way you could go about finding out would be survey research (remember Chapter 8?), asking people to provide a self-report of their e-mail practices through either a questionnaire or a standardized interview. Another way would be to gather a sample of actual e-mail messages and systematically analyze their content. This chapter discusses this second way—the analysis of communication messages through **content analysis.**

Or suppose you're interested in how team meetings in a particular organization are conducted—you want to try to figure out what goes on in the interaction among team members that leads to more, as opposed to less, effective decision making. One way you try to find an answer to your research question is to use survey research. You might interview team members, or provide them with a paper-and-pencil questionnaire, about their perceptions of what goes on in the meetings that they experience as effective versus what goes on in the meetings that they experience as ineffective. Another way you could go after this research question would be to analyze audiotapes or videotapes of actual team meetings systematically, looking for patterns in who said what to whom. This second method is known as **interaction analysis,** and we will also discuss it in this chapter.

Content analysis and interaction analysis are the primary methods that quantitative communication researchers employ when they want to enumerate the details of communicative messages—their content, their function, their form or structure. Taken together, these methods are known as *quantitative text analysis.*

Why would a researcher be attracted to quantitative text analysis instead of survey research? At least four circumstances come to mind in which a researcher might find quantitative text analysis a better choice than survey research. First, participants may be unable to report on the details of messages. Memories of communication can be retrieved for purposes of answering a survey question, but communication researchers have found that the type of information recalled from conversations tends to be (1) the "gist" of the conversation rather than a verbatim reconstruction, (2) biased toward recollection of linguistic or verbal information to the relative neglect of nonverbal information, and (3) biased toward presence–absence information rather than informative of the frequencies with which behaviors of certain types occur (Benoit & Benoit, 1988). Immediately after participating in a conversation, participants recall approximately 10 percent of its content (Stafford, Burggraf, & Sharkey, 1987; Stafford & Daly, 1984). Laura Stafford and her colleagues (Stafford, Burggraf, & Sharkey, 1987) found that people could recall only about 4 percent of a conversation after the passage of one month. When quantitative text analysis is performed, researchers usually have written transcripts of audio/videotapes of the messages, allowing them to examine details of talk without the problems of recall that often characterize participants' survey answers. So if a researcher is interested in studying the microscopic details of communication, quantitative text analysis might serve this goal better than survey research would.

Second, participants in a conversation appear to display limited agreement on what happened during the conversation (Sillars & Scott, 1983). Thus, if a researcher relies on participant reports of messages, a problem arises with respect to whose report should be used. Although one could average reports, such a solution is based on a faulty assumption that the "truth" of what actually transpired lies somewhere in the middle between the parties' individual reports. Communication researchers are concerned about the reliability of their observations about communication messages, and they normally conduct quantitative text analysis by asking two coders to make independent observations of messages; a study's findings are based on observations about which the coders agree. You may recall this as an instance of intercoder reliability from our discussion in Chapter 6.

Outsider-researcher observations of messages often differ from the perceptions provided by the insider-participants themselves (Surra and Ridley [1991] provide a useful summary of the substantial research literature on this matter). Researchers and participants appear to be tapping into different communication realities. Who is right, and who is wrong? In light of our discussion about reality in Chapter 1, it should come as no surprise that we don't find this a very helpful question.

Neither the outsider-researcher nor the insider-participant has a monopoly on the "truth" of what actually happens during communication. Communicative messages are meaningful actions, and meaning making is an inherently subjective process, whether it is done by researchers or by participants. In general, outsider-researchers and insider-participants tend to display greater agreement on the description of behaviors and less agreement on the valenced (positive–negative) meaning of behaviors (Surra & Ridley, 1991).

Insider-participants in established relationships have greater access to the private code of communication that they have developed in their history together, and such knowledge can shed insight into the positive or negative nature of a message; an outsider-researcher, oblivious to such private meanings, can misunderstand the positive or negative nature of a given utterance in a conversation. For example, an outsider-researcher might interpret a given utterance as an insult, whereas the insider-participants to the relationship have a history together such that the utterance is not meant, or taken, as an insult at all.

However, the down side of having a history together is that insider-participants carry subjective "baggage" about their relationship, their partner, and themselves, and such subjectivity can bias perceptions. For example, dissatisfied relational partners often "see" more negativity than an outsider sees, and the reason for this discrepancy may reside in their general level of dissatisfaction rather than the display of negatively valenced behavior per se (e.g., Gottman, 1994). The opposite holds true as well. When people have on their "rose-colored glasses," they tend to perceive more positivity in communication than an outsider sees.

To this point, our discussion of the accuracy of insider versus outsider observations has drawn upon research in face-to-face communication. But the same points could be made in considering mass-mediated messages (Bandura, 1994; Fiske, 1995). Individuals routinely direct attention to some message stimuli and away from others, categorize information in different ways depending on their backgrounds and dispositions, "fill in" missing information in biased ways, and recall information in ways not unlike what happens in the recollection of conversations.

For example, Mary Beth Oliver (1999) examined the extent to which Caucasian viewers could accurately recall the race of a suspected murderer shown on a wanted poster in a newscast, both immediately after viewing and after a three-month delay. Over time, participants in the study displayed a tendency to misremember the suspect as African American when he was Caucasian, and this effect was intensified among participants who held an anti-black attitude. By contrast, a communication researcher could overcome such problems of recall by relying on the systematic observation of race based on videotaped newscast archives.

A third reason that a researcher might find quantitative text analysis an attractive option is an interest in historical texts. If your interest is in existing records kept in archives of one kind or another, survey research obviously isn't an option. Webb and his colleagues (1981) discuss a variety of archival records, both public and private, of potential interest to communication researchers. With respect to public archives, four kinds of archival records exist: (1) actuarial records, such as births, deaths, mar-

riage licenses, and divorces; (2) political/judicial records, such as the *Congressional Record,* in which speeches by members of Congress are recorded; (3) other government records, such as city strategic planning documents; and (4) existing mass media texts, including television programs, films, and newspapers.

Webb and his colleagues (1981) also suggest a variety of private records that hold potential for research. They describe three classes of private archival records—that is, records that are not available in the public domain: (1) sales records; (2) industrial and institutional records, such as in-house memos; and (3) private written documents, such as private letters and diaries. Whether public or private, archival records give researchers access to historical texts. If, for example, you wanted to compare presidential inaugural addresses throughout U.S. history, you would be reliant on archival records.

A fourth, and final, reason that a researcher might be attracted to quantitative text analysis instead of survey research is its relative unobtrusiveness. In Chapter 2, we introduced you to the notion of unobtrusive or nonreactive measures, suggesting that they were useful when individuals might alter their behavior or provide false accounts of their attitudes, beliefs, and actions if they knew they were being observed. Often, researchers can conduct content analysis or interaction analysis without participant awareness of the observation.

Suppose for a moment that you're interested in violence on television. Maybe you suspect that the manufacturers of men's products are more likely to sponsor violent TV shows than other kinds of sponsors are. If you conducted a survey of these manufacturers, they might deny such a manipulative and sexist goal. Content analysis would be the best way of finding out if it's nonetheless true. You could tape some commercials and systematically analyze the content of the programming in which the ads were embedded.

In sum, the reports about communication messages that are elicited in survey research are different from the kinds of observations made in quantitative text analysis. Reports of your own or another's communication in survey research lack detailed recollection, and they are affected by the subjective perceptions and motivations of the participant-respondent. Observations by outsider-researchers often afford a more detailed description of communicative messages. In addition, researchers who code communication attempt to control the subjective biases of the observers. However, observations by outsider-researchers may provide more limited insight into highly contextualized meanings of messages.

We have falsely "pitted" survey research against quantitative text analysis, when in practice the two methods are often integrally linked. For example, whenever researchers use open-ended questions, either in an interview or in a written questionnaire, they may find it useful to perform a quantitative text analysis of the respondents' unstructured answers in order to identify content themes that can be summarized for the sample as a whole. Thus, open-ended answers are a specific kind of communication message that can be analyzed with quantitative text analysis.

For example, one of us recently conducted an interview of stepfamily members on the turning-point events in the development of their stepfamily—events that retrospectively were seen by the participants as important milestones or critical incidents that functioned either to increase a sense of family-ness or to decrease a sense of family-ness (Baxter, Braithwaite, & Nicholson, 1999). The 53 respondents in the study generated a total of 980 single-spaced pages of interview transcript, identifying a total of 566 turning points. We needed some way to reduce this massive quantity of information, so we conducted a content analysis of recurrent themes in the respondents' talk about their turning points. We developed a list of 15 different types of turning-point events from this data set, enumerating the frequencies with which the different turning-point event types were reported.

Quantitative text analysis is often used in tandem with experimental research. When the dependent, or outcome, variable is some message-related behavior by the participant, quantitative text analysis can be employed to enumerate patterns of response across participants. For example, Kory Floyd and Michael Voloudakis (1999) were interested in what happened in platonic friendships when one friend unexpectedly changed his or her level of expressed affection. The researchers were interested in observing how the participants responded to their friends' changed behavior. They coded a number of nonverbal communicative behaviors in the participants, including expressiveness and positive affection displays.

Sometimes, a communication researcher is interested in examining a hypothesized causal relationship between some characteristic of communication messages and a specific effect of the message. Quantitative data about messages need to be linked to data gathered from receivers of the message. For example, researchers interested in studying the agenda-setting function of mass media argue that the salience of issues in media coverage affects the salience of these issues in viewers' minds (McCombs & Bell, 1996). In order to examine this matter empirically, researchers need to gather data on the content of media coverage (through quantitative text analysis) and data on media audiences (through surveys or through experiments).

In short, quantitative text analysis can be employed either as a "stand-alone" method, or it can be used in conjunction with either survey or experimental research. Whether used alone or together with another method, quantitative text analysis enumerates the content, functions, and/or structures of communicative messages.

THE "TEXTS" IN QUANTITATIVE TEXT ANALYSIS

What counts as a "text" to communication researchers? Basically, a **text** is any kind of communication message in which symbols are used. The possibilities are endless.

Communication messages can be *public* in nature—that is, messages whose intended audience is a large group of individuals. For instance, John Ballotti and Lynda Lee Kaid (2000) performed a content analysis of the 1,267 presidential spots from 1952 through 1996 that are archived at the Political Commercial Archive at the University of Oklahoma. They coded for content themes and analyzed differences among the presidential candidates, the political parties, winners versus losers, and trends across time.

Communication messages can also be *private* in nature—that is, messages targeted at one or a few individuals. For instance, Carol Bruess and Judy Pearson (1997) performed a content analysis of open-ended interviews and questionnaires in which married couples reported on the kinds of interaction rituals they enacted.

Communication messages can be *mediated* in some fashion—for example, telephone conversations over cell phones, e-mail messages, televised news, and radio talk shows. Thomas Skill and Sam Wallace (1990) performed a content analysis of portrayed family interaction in prime-time television. They were particularly interested in the extent to which characters occupying different family roles displayed different amounts of assertive power.

Communication messages can be *nonmediated,* or face to face—for example, greetings exchanged by strangers at bus stops, dinner conversations among family members, and public speeches to "live" audiences. Abran Salazar (1997) conducted an interaction analysis of the face-to-face talk among members of decision-making groups that varied in the kind of task they faced and the extent of member agreement about the task at the outset of the study. He coded member interaction by its function—whether a given utterance was concerned with group management, problem identification and analysis, criteria for the evaluation of solutions, the suggestion of solutions, the evaluation of solutions, or some other miscellaneous function.

Communication messages can be *scripted*—that is, planned, or "canned." Wayne Wanta and Joe Foote (1994) examined a highly scripted form of communication message—newscasts of the (then) three national networks. In particular, they sought to assess the extent to which the President functioned as an agenda setter, influencing the issues that received coverage in network news.

Or communication messages can be *spontaneous*—for example, informal conversations between friends or acquaintances. Sally Planalp (1993) provides an interesting example of this kind of study. She had coders systematically observe friends' conversations and acquaintances' conversations. Her goal was to determine which communicative behaviors differentiated acquaintance talk from friendship talk.

Planalp's study also illustrates the two kinds of symbol systems examined by communication researchers—linguistic and nonverbal. Her analysis of communication messages focused on *linguistic* symbols as well as *nonverbal* symbols of various kinds. With respect to linguistic, or verbal, message behavior, her research assistants coded such behaviors as profanity, slang, expression of disagreement, reference to mutual acquaintances, and expression of opinions or advice. In terms of nonverbal behavior, her research assistants coded a wide range of phenomena, including laughter, degree of body relaxation, degree of involvement in the conversation, and interaction smoothness.

In sum, a wide variety of message phenomena—public–private, mediated–nonmediated, scripted–spontaneous, linguistic–nonverbal—hold potential interest for communication researchers. A "text" is simply a term to refer to any unit of symbol use.

THE KINDS OF QUESTIONS ANSWERED WITH QUANTITATIVE TEXT ANALYSIS

Communication researchers who employ quantitative text analysis are generally interested in three kinds of questions about texts: questions about **distributional structure,** questions about **interactive structure,** and questions about **sequential structure.**

First, they are interested in analyzing a sample of texts by enumerating the frequencies with which certain message features are present. Content analysis provides this description through an analysis of what is called the *distributional structure*—that is, a profile of the frequencies

of the categories used to represent message features (Hirokawa, 1988). The researcher seeks to determine how many instances are coded for each of the available categories.

Anita Vangelisti (1994) conducted a distributional-structure analysis of interviews she conducted with marital counselors on their perceptions of couples' communication problems. Her description took the form of a frequency count of the kinds of problems identified by the counselors (clients blaming their partner for negative occurrences, the failure to take the other's perspective when listening, and putting the other down were at the top of the list). In this example, the coding categories for this analysis were the various problems identified by the counselors; the distribution structure was how frequently each problem category appeared in the data set. The variable studied by Vangelisti was *reported problem type.*

Sometimes, communication researchers are interested in examining the relationship between some text feature and another variable. Often, this takes the form of a research question or hypothesis of relationship in which some quantitative indicator is derived from a distributional structure and correlated with another variable. For example, John Gottman and his colleagues (2001) coded the facial expression of emotions in husbands and in wives who were engaged in a 15-minute videotaped conversation. They counted the number of times given emotions were expressed through facial expressions—for example, the number of times "disgust," "anger," "fear," and "sadness" were coded. These couples were approached four years later and were asked the number of months they had been separated since their conversations had been videotaped—this value could range from "0" for pairs that were still together to "48" for pairs on the brink of break-up at the time their conversation had been recorded. The researchers found that expressed disgust in wives correlated positively with the number of months of reported marital separation.

Issues of distributional structure can also appear in research questions or hypotheses of difference. For example, at the four-year follow-up, Gottman and his colleagues could have divided their sample into two groups: those who were still together and those who were separated/divorced. The two groups could have been compared on the prevalence of expressed disgust, sadness, and so forth.

While the method of content analysis allows a researcher to make claims only about distributional structure, interaction analysis lends itself to two additional kinds of insight: *interactive structure* and *sequential structure* (Hirokawa, 1988). Interaction analysis codes interaction between individuals. In paying attention to who says what to whom, these additional structures become evident.

Suppose we had a small group of five members (A, B, C, D, and E). In conducting an interaction analysis, we would have a running record of how many times A talked to B, A to C, A to D, A to E, B to A, B to C, and so forth. These who-to-whom data inform us about the interaction network that emerged among the group members, and this network is known as the group's interactive structure.

The sequential structure of interaction results when coders pay attention to the sequencing of the coded utterances—what kind of utterance follows what kind of utterance. For example, to what extent are questions followed by answers, as opposed to topic shifts, put-downs, and so forth?

When researchers conduct interaction-analysis research, they also gather the information that would allow them to examine the distributional structure of interaction. Thus, interaction analysis positions researchers to describe three kinds of issues related to interaction—distributional, interactive, and sequential—whereas content analysis is limited to a single feature of interaction—its distributional structure.

Researchers who are interested in interaction analysis can also use this method to examine research hypotheses or questions of difference. For example, groups who are coping with complex tasks can be compared to groups who are facing simpler tasks with respect to distributional structure. For example, do various kinds of communicative acts occur with similar frequencies in the two kinds of groups? In this question of difference, *type of interaction* (assessed through the distributional structure of act types) and *task complexity* (complex and simple) are the two variables of interest.

We could just as easily examine a question or hypothesis of relationship. For example, we could determine what proportion of a group's total utterances were coded as information gathering and then correlate this with another variable—say, average group satisfaction with the group's process, perhaps measured in a survey.

Interactive-structure questions could also be posed. For example, to what extent is interaction centralized in both kinds of task groups? This question of difference could be tackled by determining the proportion of a group's total utterances that were associated with its most talkative member: the larger this proportion, the more centralized the group's interaction. This centralization score could then be compared for groups with complex tasks versus groups with simple tasks.

We could also examine questions and hypotheses of relationship. For example, we could take this same centralization score and correlate it with a second variable, say, the group's cohesiveness level. We would be determining whether there is a relationship between the two variables of *interaction centralization* and *group cohesiveness*.

Finally, interaction analysis is useful in addressing research questions and hypotheses about sequential structure. For example, we could ask "To what extent are disagreements followed by topic shifts in effective versus ineffective groups?" This question might interest us because we think that ineffective groups manage differences of opinion by simply changing the topic rather than dealing with the expressed disagreement. We could code group interaction, locating all disagreements and topic shifts. We could then calculate the proportion of a group's total expressed disagreements that were met with topic shifts. We could then compare this score for groups judged effective or ineffective (perhaps judges evaluated group decisions as high or low in quality), thereby addressing a question of difference. Or we might examine the relationship between our topic-shift score and the average satisfaction that group members felt with their decision-making process, thereby examining a question of relationship between the two variables of *prevalence of topic shift* and *member satisfaction*.

None of these examples is better or worse than the others. They simply represent different ways that communication researchers can study message features, depending on their interests. Sometimes, researchers are interested in descriptive questions that profile distributional structure, interactive structure, or sequential structure. Other times, they are interested in linking text features (whether distributional, interactive, or sequential) to other variables.

SAMPLING IN QUANTITATIVE TEXT ANALYSIS

In the study of communication texts, you often can't observe directly all of the texts you're interested in. In the hypothetical study of TV violence and sponsorship discussed earlier, we'd advise against attempting to watch everything that's broadcast. It wouldn't be possible, and your brain would probably short-circuit before you got close to discovering that fact for yourself. Usually, then, it's appropriate to sample. Let's begin by looking again at units of analysis and then review some of the sampling techniques that might be applied to them in quantitative text analysis.

Units of Analysis

You'll recall from Chapter 2 that determining appropriate units of analysis, the individual units about which or whom descriptive and explanatory statements are to be made, can be a complicated task. For example, if we wished to compute the average family's TV consumption, the individual family would be the unit of analysis. But we would have to ask individual members of families how much TV they watch. Thus, individuals would be the units of observation, and the individual family would be the unit of analysis. Similarly, we may wish to compare rates of talk of different cities in terms of their sizes, geographical regions, racial composition, and other differences. Even though the characteristics of these cities are partly a function of the behaviors and characteristics of their individual residents, the cities would ultimately be the units of analysis.

The complexity of this issue is often more apparent in quantitative text analysis than in other research methods, especially when the units of observation differ from the units of analysis. A few examples should clarify this distinction.

Let's suppose we want to find out which kind of message is characterized by greater verbal immediacy or closeness (Wiener & Mehrabian, 1968)—e-mail messages or face-to-face messages. We ask each participant to bring a friend to our laboratory, and then we ask each participant to communicate a message on a designated topic to his or her friend. Half of our participants communicate the message via e-mail to the friend (who is sitting at a computer terminal in an adjoining room, logged onto an e-mail account set up especially for our study), and half communicate the message face to face with the friend. We then compare the messages on their immediacy—for example, counting references to "us" or "we" rather than "you and I," or references to "these things" rather than "those things." In this instance, individual messages—the texts—would be both the units of observation and the units of analysis. In this fashion, we would be able to determine which kind of message features more verbal immediacy. We could count up the number of verbally immediate words (e.g., "we," "our," "these") per 100 words of text and compare face-to-face and e-mail messages on this score.

Somewhat differently, we might wish to determine whether friends and romantic partners display different degrees of verbal immediacy in their communication. Al-though the examination of this question would also involve the coding of communication messages, the unit of analysis in this case is the relationship type, not the message.

Or, changing topics radically, let's suppose we're interested in representationalism in painting. If we wish to compare the relative popularity of representational and nonrepresentational paintings, the individual paintings would be our units of analysis. If, on the other hand, we wish to discover whether representationalism in painting is more characteristic of wealthy or impoverished painters, of educated or uneducated painters, or of capitalist or socialist painters, the individual painters would be our units of analysis.

It's essential that this issue be clear, because sample selection depends largely on what the unit of analysis is. If individual writers are the units of analysis, the sample design should select all or a sample of the writers appropriate to the research question. If books are the units of analysis, we should select a sample of books, regardless of their authors.

We're not suggesting that sampling should be based solely on the units of analysis. Indeed, we may often *subsample*—select samples of subcategories—for each individual unit of analysis. Thus, if writers are the units of analysis, we might (1) select a sample of writers from the total population of writers, (2) select a sample of books written by each writer selected, and (3) select portions of each selected book for observation and coding.

Let's work through a concrete example we mentioned earlier—televised advertising for men's products and violent programming. You could approach this general topic in any of several ways, depending on your specific research question or hypothesis. For example, we might want to frame a research hypothesis as follows: Violent TV programs will have a higher proportion of commercials for men's products than will nonviolent programs. Our unit of analysis would be the TV program. For each program, we would need to code it as either "violent" or "nonviolent" based on some operationalization—maybe a TV program receives a code of "violent" if it contains at least one threatened or enacted act of physical harm directed at someone. Thus, we would need to observe actions, looking for the presence of at least one instance of violence. We would also code all of the commercials shown during this program, making a decision about whether the product was targeted at men. The commercial is thus an observation unit. We could then derive a score for each program of the proportion of commercials for men's products and compare our two program groups

TV Program	Length of Program	At Least One Violent Act?	Commercial Product	Men's Product?
Superhero Sam	30 minutes	Yes	Grunt Aftershave	Yes
			Brute Jock Strap	Yes
			Buttercup Bras	No
			Big Thumb Hammers	?
			Beard Trimmer	Yes

FIGURE 10-1   **Example of Coding Sheet for Study One**

TV Program	Length of Program	Counter #	Violent Act Description	Commercial Product	Men's Product?
Superhero Sam	30 minutes	:45	Villain explodes train	Grunt Aftershave	Yes
		10:15	SS punches villain	Brute Jock Strap	Yes
		12:20	Villain takes hostage and threatens	Buttercup Bras	No
		17:35	SS punches villain out	Big Thumb Hammers	?
				Beard Trimmer	Yes

FIGURE 10-2   **Example of Coding Sheet for Study Two**

(violent and nonviolent) to determine if our hypothesis was supported. Our coding sheet for this study might look like Figure 10-1. For our hypothetical program, *Superhero Sam,* we would have a score of .60 (three of the five commercials were for men's products).

Maybe you'd rather approach this as a hypothesis of relationship: There will be a positive correlation between the number of violent acts portrayed on a program and the proportion of its commercials that feature men's products. Your unit of analysis would still be the TV program, but now you'd need to code every instance of violence on the program in addition to coding each commercial associated with the program. You would thus have two observation units—violent acts and commercials. Your coding sheet might look something like Figure 10-2. ("Counter #" refers to when the violent act took place in order to allow comparisons between coders for purposes of assessing inter-coder reliability, and the description column allows the researcher to determine whether coders were focusing on the same act, again for purposes of assessing inter-coder reliability.) Because programs could vary in length, the number of violent acts would probably need to be calibrated against the same time interval, say, the number of violent acts per half-hour of program length. Our first unit of analysis— the TV program *Superhero Sam*—would have scores of 4

(number of violent acts per half hour) and .60 (proportion of commercials featuring men's products).

In both of these hypothetical studies, our unit of analysis is the TV program. But let's suppose that you have reason to believe that commercials are placed strategically within a program, and you think that men's products are likely to be placed adjacent to the segments within a TV program that are most likely to be violent. Thus, you might have this hypothesis: Commercials for men's products will have more instances of violence in the surrounding program segments than will commercials for women's products. Using the TV program as your unit of analysis no longer seems fruitful, given this thinking. Your unit of analysis here is not the TV program but the commercial. Your observation unit would be violent acts in the preceding and following program segments. Your coding sheet might look like Figure 10-3. In this figure we have three products, one for men and two for women. The men's product would have a combined score of 7 violent acts (4 in the preceding program segment and 3 in the subsequent program segment), whereas each commercial for a woman's product would have a score of 1. We would compare the mean score for all men's product commercials with the mean score for all women's product commercials to determine whether our hypothesis was supported.

Commercial Product	Target of Product		Violent Acts in Prior Segment	Counter #	Violent Acts in Subsequent Segment	Counter #
	M	F				
Grunt Aftershave	X		Gunman shoots first victim	:10	Gunman shoots third victim	10:15
			Victim returns fire	:12	Gunman sets explosive in doorway	11:05
			Gunman's pal robs bank	3:14	Gunman's pal shot by police	12:16
			Gunman shoots second victim	4:20		
Buttercup Bras		X	Boy threatens to wreck neighbor's car	6:23		
Stretch Panty Hose		X			Girl stabs attacker	8:45

FIGURE 10-3   **Example of Coding Sheet for Study Three**

The point of this illustration is to demonstrate how units of analysis and units of observation figure into data collection and analysis. There are no right or wrong units here—simply different units depending on the particular research question or hypothesis you have in mind.

You need to be clear about your unit of analysis before planning your sampling strategy. In this illustration, our first two hypothetical studies would develop a sampling plan designed to draw a representative sample of TV programs. In the third hypothetical study, we would want a sampling plan that would produce a representative sample of commercials.

Let's consider how you might go about sampling for TV programs. In designing the sample, you would need to establish the universe to be sampled from. In this case, what channels will you observe? Broadcast and/or cable? What will be the period of the study—do you want to sample programs from a whole season or some shorter time period? And what hours of each day will you observe—prime time only or daytime as well? Although you could probably get your hands on a list of programs for your specified universe, it would be easier if you used cluster sampling to sample days, channels, and times, and then observed whatever programs were on during the sampled programming slots. Your final sampling frame, from which a sample would be selected and watched, might look something like this:

Jan. 7, Channel 2, 7–8 P.M.
Jan. 7, Channel 2, 8–9 P.M.
Jan. 7, Channel 2, 9–10 P.M.
Jan. 7, Channel 4, 7–8 P.M.
Jan. 7, Channel 4, 8–9 P.M.
Jan. 7, Channel 4, 9–10 P.M.
Jan. 7, Channel 8, 7–8 P.M.
Jan. 7, Channel 8, 8–9 P.M.
Jan. 7, Channel 8, 9–10 P.M.

Jan. 8, Channel 2, 7–8 P.M.
Jan. 8, Channel 2, 8–9 P.M.
Jan. 8, Channel 2, 9–10 P.M.
Jan. 8, Channel 4, 7–8 P.M.
Jan. 8, Channel 4, 8–9 P.M.
etc.

Notice that we've made several decisions for you in the illustration. First, we've assumed that channels 2, 4, and 9 are the ones appropriate to your study. We've assumed that you found the 7 to 10 P.M. prime-time hours to be the most relevant and that one-hour periods would do the job. We picked January 7 out of the hat for a starting date. In practice, of course, all these decisions should be based on your careful consideration of what would be appropriate for your particular study. You might randomly select days within randomly selected weeks within randomly selected months.

Unless you have access to a TV station's program logs, you don't know what commercials will be aired when. You might want to sample days, channels, and times, as above. Once you have selected a given hour, however, you will need some way to randomly select a commercial. After watching some TV, you might have a sense of how many commercial interruptions there are per hour of programming. You could number these 1 through n and use a random numbers table to pick a commercial break. You could have a decision rule to code, say, the first commercial that is aired during this selected commercial break. Obviously, you would need to observe the program segments that surround the selected commercial.

Once you have become clear about your units of analysis and the observations appropriate to those units and have created a sampling frame like the one we've illustrated, sampling is simple and straightforward. The alternative procedures available to you are the same ones described in Chapter 7.

Sampling Techniques

As you've seen, in the quantitative analysis of communication texts, sampling may occur at any or all of several levels, including the contexts relevant to the works. We could employ any of the conventional, probability-based sampling techniques discussed in Chapter 7. We might select a *random* or *systematic* sample of all of the speeches recorded in the *Congressional Record* for a given year, for example. We might select (with a random start) every third front-page headline in the *New York Times* for a given year. Or we might number all of the songs recorded by the Beatles and select a random sample of 25.

Stratified sampling is also appropriate to quantitative text analysis. To analyze the editorial policies of U.S. newspapers, for example, we might first group all newspapers by region of the country, size of the community in which they are published, frequency of publication, or average circulation. We might then select a stratified random or systematic sample of newspapers for analysis. Having done so, we might select a sample of editorials from each selected newspaper, perhaps stratified chronologically.

Cluster sampling is equally appropriate to quantitative text analysis. Indeed, if individual editorials were to be the unit of analysis in the previous example, then the selection of newspapers at the first stage of sampling would be a cluster sample. In an analysis of political speeches, we might begin by selecting a sample of politicians; each politician would represent a cluster of political speeches.

Nonprobability-based sampling is also employed in quantitative text analysis, particularly in behavioral observation research in which the researcher is interested in studying face-to-face interaction between people (Sillars, 1991). For example, suppose you are interested in coding the topics of conversation during family dinners. Although you could attempt a probability-based sampling of all households, asking selected households if they would permit you into their homes to observe them eating dinner together, our guess is that this method might not work so well for you due to the obtrusiveness of your observations. You might need to rely on a convenience sample of people who volunteer their families for observation.

Or suppose you're interested in studying marital communication. Many researchers have studied marital interaction, but their samples of married couples have often been biased in their reliance on married university pairs or couples seeking counseling (Krokoff, 1987). Of course, this isn't always the case, and some researchers go to great effort to rely on probability-based sampling in deriving an initial sample of people whose interaction will be observed. For example, Lowell Krokoff (1987) described a three-stage recruitment process designed to draw a more representative sample of married couples to observe. During stage one, a random sample of telephone numbers was drawn from the Urbana–Champaign, Illinois, telephone directory. Wives were sampled during this stage and given a brief telephone survey about demographic features of their marriages (e.g., length, number of children). During stage 2, these wives were sent recruitment letters. During stage 3, a home visit took place in which the researcher described the details of the study and signed up couples in exchange for the promise of $100 at the study's completion. Couples had to agree to an oral history interview in their home, videotaping in a university laboratory, audiotaping at home, and completion of questionnaires. Krokoff found little evidence of a differential drop-out of couples after the telephone survey with respect to marital happiness, socioeconomic status, age, premarital acquaintance length, length of marriage, family size, and age of children. Krokoff's experience suggests that representative samples of people can be obtained for purposes of observing face-to-face communication, yet considerable effort is needed to accomplish this feat.

Let's return to our family dinner talk study. Once you have some families lined up to participate, you might determine through probability sampling which nights to visit and observe dinner talk, but again, this might prove challenging—maybe on Mondays and Wednesdays one family doesn't eat together because the kids have practice, lessons, and so forth. Maybe Tuesdays and Thursdays are out for another family because Mom is enrolled in an evening class. Maybe Fridays are bad for some families because they celebrate the end of the week by eating out. Maybe some of the dinners you would like to record and analyze are atypical in that the kids bring home friends as guests. In short, you might need to take what you can get—another instance of availability or convenience sampling—and observe whatever dinnertimes are possible in your selected families.

Sometimes, researchers interested in behavioral observation find that it is difficult to locate naturally occurring interactions to observe. Often, the topics of interest to researchers are regarded as private by the participants. For example, intimates might not welcome an outside observer eavesdropping on their conflicts. You might hang out in a shopping mall, waiting to stumble on couples who walk by arguing about something, but such instances are not regular enough for your purposes, and ethical problems can present themselves in accessing personal conversations within your earshot. You might need to do what many researchers do—simulate interaction (Sillars, 1991).

In simulated interaction, people are usually brought into a laboratory environment so that their interaction can be videotaped for future analysis. People are provided with instructions by the researcher. Sometimes, these instructions are very general, such as "Have a normal conversation." Other times, people are provided with a task to complete, and their interaction during the task is recorded and observed. For example, each member of a married pair might be asked prior to the interaction to list five topics about which they have conflict, and then the pair is asked to talk through these topics together while being videotaped. Couples or families might be given games to play, and the interaction that transpires during the game playing is videotaped for subsequent analysis. Sometimes, couples or families are asked to role-play a hypothetical, but typical, scenario. For example, a husband and wife might be asked to role-play a scenario in which he has invested time and effort in making plans to spend the evening out together, while she has invested similar time and effort in preparing a special meal at home. Pairs might be asked to role-play a reenactment of some event from their past—for example, their most recent argument or their "end of the day" chat the prior evening.

Once a communication researcher has a sample of messages to work with, further subsamples might be drawn. You could be overwhelmed by the sheer quantity of text in need of analysis. For example, John Gottman (1979) estimates that every hour of husband–wife interaction requires approximately 28 hours to transcribe and code. As a matter of feasibility, then, you might randomly select a segment of interaction to analyze in depth.

Alternatively, you might employ a purposive sampling decision. For example, on the reasonable assumption that conversational openers are likely to be highly scripted from one interaction to another, you might decide to begin your analysis after the initial two minutes of interaction in order to capture interaction that is uniquely enacted by a given interacting pair. Or you might suspect that people have some initial self-consciousness about being audiotaped or videotaped, and thus start your analysis five or ten minutes into a given tape of an interaction after people cease to be aware of, or concerned about, being taped.

Whether you use probability-based or nonprobability-based sampling, you will end up with a corpus of communication messages, or texts, that require analysis. How exactly is this analysis done? Researchers employ either content analysis or interaction analysis, depending on their specific purpose.

CONTENT ANALYSIS

Content analysis is a method that has been around for quite some time. Klaus Krippendorff (1980) dates the systematic use of content analysis back to the 18th century, when Swedish scholars and clergy analyzed a collection of nonorthodox hymns called the "Songs of Zion" to determine whether the songs blasphemed the doctrines of the Swedish state church.

However, most modern social scientists associate the origins of the method with the analyses of propaganda messages during the Second World War and the publication in 1952 of a now classic book on the subject (Berelson, 1952). In that book, content analysis was defined as "a research technique for the objective, systematic, and quantitative description of the manifest content of communication" (Berelson, 1952, p. 18). Central to this definition was a focus on the manifest, or surface features, of content—content features that could be categorized with little or no interpretation by the coder, such as word counts.

Although this definition of content analysis is still widely accepted, a broader definition has been provided by Klauss Krippendorff (1980). Krippendorff (1980, p. 21) conceived of content analysis as "a technique for making replicable and valid inferences from data to their context." Among other points, Krippendorff argued that content analysts should not limit themselves to summarizing the surface features of messages but instead should interpret the deeper meanings of messages. Often, this requires an analyst to pay attention to latent textual features.

Our definition encompasses both manifest and latent forms of content analysis: *Content analysis is a research technique for the systematic, replicable, and quantitative description of the manifest or latent features of communication texts.* Let's see how content analysis is done.

Coding in Content Analysis

Content analysis is essentially a coding operation. Communication texts—oral, written, or other—are coded or classified according to some conceptual framework. Thus, for example, newspaper editorials may be coded as liberal or conservative. Radio talk show calls might be coded as racist or not, novels as romantic or not, paintings as representational or not, and political speeches as containing character assassinations or not. Recall that terms such as these are subject to many interpretations, and the researcher must specify definitions clearly.

CALCULATING UNITIZING RELIABILITY

For purposes of determining unitizing reliability, researchers often use the coefficient of reliability. Basically, it reflects the ratio of coder agreed-upon decisions to the total number of unitizing decisions made by the two coders. Its formula is as follows:

$$\frac{2A}{(U_1 + U_2)},$$

where

A = the number of units agreed upon by the two coders

U_1 = the number of units identified by coder 1

U_2 = the number of units identified by coder 2

Let's suppose we conducted a study in which we asked coders to identify the themes that were present in interview transcripts of participants talking about communication in their family. Every time a new theme is identified, it is counted as a unit of observation. For 50 transcripts, let's suppose that coder 1 identified a total of 495 themes and coder 2 identified a total of 510 themes. In comparing the coders' decisions transcript by transcript, the researcher found that 450 themes were agreed upon by both coders. What's the coefficient of unitizing reliability for our two coders?

$$\frac{2(450)}{(495 + 510)} = \frac{900}{1005} = .8955 \text{ or } 89.6\%$$

Because this coefficient value is larger than the minimum acceptable standard of .70, we would conclude that our two coders unitized the texts in a reliable manner.

Coding in content analysis involves the logic of conceptualization and operationalization, as discussed in Chapter 6. In content analysis, as in other research methods, you must refine your conceptual framework and develop specific methods for observing in relation to that framework.

Coding Units   When a content analyst undertakes a coding project, he or she needs to decide on the *coding unit*—the "chunk" of text to be coded in some way. The process of segmenting a text into its "chunks" for coding purposes is known as parsing or **unitizing.** Generally, researchers need to demonstrate that their unitizing activity is done in a reliable and valid manner. To demonstrate unitizing reliability, a researcher often asks two coders to independently segment the texts to be analyzed, comparing the extent to which they agree on the various coding units of a text. The "Calculating Unitizing Reliability" box provides you with an example of how unitizing reliability can be determined.

For example, one of us once conducted a study on people's metaphors of romantic relationship development that were evident in unstructured interviews about their current relationship (Baxter, 1992). Metaphors can be challenging to isolate in a stream of text. Here's an excerpt from one person's interview, in which the metaphorical units have been underlined: "We experienced a lot of potholes along the way that took time and effort to get over but, looking back, I guess we really moved fast from the time we first met to get to this chapter" (p. 259). This person told the interviewer that relationship development was like potholes, something effortful to get over, motion whose speed can be gauged in moving toward some destination, and chapters in a book. In order to determine whether the metaphors were unitized reliably by the researcher, a second independent coder independently read a 25-percent random sample of the transcripts and underlined metaphors that she could identify. The researcher and the independent coder agreed in the identification of 80 percent of the metaphorical images in the text, an adequate level for unitizing reliability.

Crucial to valid unitizing is the selection of a unit appropriate to the research purpose at hand. There is no right or wrong unit of text—you need to ask what is the most valid unit of meaning in a particular research context. The answer to this question is rarely obvious. Ideally, this decision is based on theoretical arguments about semantics and pragmatics—how symbols come to mean and how symbols are used—in addition to the researcher's purpose.

Krippendorff (1980) has identified five different types of coding units often found in content analysis research. First, researchers code *physical units.* Usually, this involves counting the amount of space or time devoted to content. For example, Leslie Dinauer and Kristine Ondeck (1999) counted the number of articles published in a leading communication journal authored by women as opposed to men. In this study, the physical object that was counted was the journal article, regardless of its length or subject matter.

The second type of coding unit is the *syntactical unit.* This involves a discrete unit of language such as the word, sentence, or paragraph. Many content analysts employ word-counting computer software to assist them in syntactical word counts. One of these programs is named DICTION (Hart, 1984, 1985). Rod Hart (1984, 1987, 2000) has developed this program to assist him in identifying the political themes of presidential candidates. Like all computer word-search programs, DICTION involves the development of word lists, or dictionaries, for targeted themes. In particular, DICTION relies on 28 word lists, or subdictionaries, that comprise the more than 3,000 search words included in the counting program. For example, the "Rigidity" word list notes all forms of the verb *to be* as indicators of complete certainty. The "Praise" list contains verbal affirmations of a particular person or concept. The "Adversity" subdictionary consists of words that give reference to negative feelings or dangerous events. And so forth.

Once the words of a given political text have been sorted, counted, and placed in a particular subdictionary, the major dictionary variables are created by Hart through a series of mathematical calculations. For example, a given political text would receive an *Optimism* score, calculated as follows:

$$\text{Optimism} = [\text{Praise} + \text{Satisfaction} + \text{Inspiration}] - [\text{Adversity} + \text{Negation}]$$

Hart (1984) used DICTION to analyze the middle 500 words of presidential speeches. In his analysis of the 1996 presidential campaign (Hart, 2000; Hart & Jarvis, 1997), he used the complete texts of political campaign spots, along with news broadcasts, editorial letters of varying lengths, and 500-word speech excerpts.

John Ballotti and Lynda Lee Kaid (2000) employed a similar computer program, WORD CRUNCHER, in counting words in more than 1,200 presidential candidate campaign spots from 1952 through 1996 contained in the Political Commercial Archive at the University of Oklahoma.

DICTION and WORD CRUNCHER are examples of a growing number of computerized content analysis software packages (Roberts, 1997). Many of these software packages work with syntactic units—often the word or phrase.

The third coding unit described by Krippendorff (1980) is the *referential unit.* A referential unit is a reference to events, people, objects, or issues in the content of a text. For example, Wayne Wanta and Joe Foote (1994) were interested in the influence of presidential addresses on news coverage on the (then) three national networks. They counted the frequencies with which various is-

sues were covered, including such topics as international crises, unemployment, homelessness, and abortion. Each topic was a referential unit.

The fourth coding unit is the *propositional unit.* This unit codes the content for each thought unit—for example, assertions about a given object or topic. A single thought unit could be expressed in a clause, in a sentence, or in several sentences. For example, Tamara Golish and John Caughlin (2002) recently examined topic avoidance in stepfamilies. Among other things, they performed a content analysis of the reasons that participants gave for why they avoided a given topic. Each reason— which could be expressed in one or several sentences— counted as one propositional unit.

The fifth coding unit mentioned by Krippendorff (1980) is the *thematic unit.* A thematic unit can be highly variable in length, but it is generally applied to a larger segment of text involving multiple sentences or utterances. For example, John Gottman and his colleagues (2001) had coders rate on several dimensions husband-and-wife oral history narratives about their marriage. After listening to a couple describe the history of their relationship, the good and the bad times in their marriage, their philosophy of marriage, and so on, coders rated each spouse's narrative on several dimensions, including their fondness for each other, their negativity toward the spouse, and the extent to which they identified with being part of a couple as opposed to emphasizing individuality. Each of these dimensions—fondness, negativity, coupleness— illustrates a theme. These themes were undercurrents of meaning that surfaced in multiple ways throughout a couple's narrative.

Why is it important to distinguish units in this way? Put simply, the quantitative findings are a reflection of the coding unit employed in the study. Let's work through a sample text to illustrate this point. Consider this textual excerpt from an interviewee who is discussing her relationship with her stepparent:

> He comes between me and my mom. My mom and I were really close and now she sides with him all the time. He tries to act like my father, but he's not. I resent that my mom makes me call my stepparent "dad." I feel like they're trying to take me away from my real dad. I mean, sometimes he's OK and stuff—don't get me wrong—he's done some favors for me over the years, like he's always there with money when I need it.

Let's approach this sample text with different coding units in mind. First, let's use the syntactic unit of the sentence. Let's suppose we are trying to measure the interviewee's attitude toward her stepparent as the proportion of sentences that are positive about the stepparent. We would go through the text and identify all sentences that reflect a positive attitude toward the stepparent. There's only one: sentence 6. Now let's do the same with negative sentences. We come up with a count of five—sentences 1 through 5. We could say that positivity is present in $\frac{1}{6}$, or .17, of all coded units. But the meaning of this interviewee's feelings might not be captured well at the sentence level, because successive sentences are often elaborations of the same theme. So let's shift to the thematic unit. There are three themes expressed in this excerpt: (1) the stepfather as wedge between the interviewee and her mom (sentences 1 and 2); (2) the stepfather as wedge between the interviewee and her "real" dad (sentences 3–5); and (3) the stepfather as a source of instrumental reward (sentence 6). Using this unit of analysis, positivity is represented in $\frac{1}{3}$, or .33, of all coded units. This coding exercise makes the point that our reported findings are very much affected by the unit we choose to work with. A researcher needs to have a good reason that the textual data are unitized with one unit instead of another. Select the unit that offers the most valid categorization of meaning.

Krippendorff (1980) envisioned his coding units as nominal-level data. That is, mutually exclusive and exhaustive coding categories are developed, and a given unit of data is placed by a coder into a single category. The researcher then tallies up the frequencies with which the categories appeared in the texts under study.

However, as we mentioned above for thematic units, it is possible for coders to provide ratings. For example, Judee Burgoon and her colleagues (1995) have used seven-point bipolar adjective items, wherein higher rating scores indicate a greater presence, frequency, or intensity of behavior. Coders observe interaction between people and then rate each participant on the overall thematic nature of his or her nonverbal communication on such bipolar items as direct body orientation–indirect body orientation, sat close–sat far, very expressive facially–very inexpressive facially, matched partner's gestures–did not match partner's gestures. Such thematic ratings are useful when there are many, continuous behaviors and when segmentation into smaller, discreet behaviors would be meaningless or impossible to accomplish. On the assumption that the two coders reasonably agree in their ratings, a person's coding score on a given nonverbal theme is simply the average of the two coders' ratings (for example, if one coder rated a participant a 5 on sitting close to the partner, and the second coder rated the same participant with a 6, the partner's score on seating proximity would be 5.5).

No coding unit is inherently better or worse than the others—the issue is one of suitability to the research question and theory of meaning that motivates the researcher. One important issue is whether the researcher is interested in manifest or latent meanings.

Manifest and Latent Meanings   The two strands in the content analysis tradition are a focus on manifest meanings (the Berelson tradition, articulated in 1952) and a focus on latent meanings (the Krippendorff tradition, articulated in 1980). At issue here is the kind of meanings the researcher is interested in: meanings as they "sit on the surface" of a text or meanings as they "lie deeply embedded" in a text.

Coding the **manifest content**—the visible, surface content—of a text is analogous to using a standardized questionnaire. The researcher doesn't have to engage in any interpretive work in analyzing a given response: A 5 is a 5 is a 5 in participant responses to a given questionnaire item. Similarly, manifest content analysis requires no interpretive work on the part of the coders. For example, word counts afford us understanding about manifest meaning. Because no interpretive work is needed, a computer software program can perform as well as a human coder. Because little interpretive work is needed by coders of manifest content, manifest content analyses tend to be very high in coder reliability—not only unitizing reliability as discussed earlier but content reliability as well—that is, the extent to which the two coders categorize a given unit of data similarly.

Alternatively, the researcher may be interested in the **latent content** of the text: its underlying meaning. For example, suppose you were interested in measuring how erotic the films are by a certain director. If you were approaching this as a problem of manifest meaning, you might develop a list of words and a list of nonverbal behaviors that you regard as high in eroticism and count every time a listed word or listed nonverbal behavior is displayed. On the other hand, you might feel that eroticism is not easily measured at the surface level of discrete words and behaviors. Instead, you might have to view an entire film and make an overall thematic assessment of how erotic it is. Although your total assessment might very well be influenced by the appearance of certain words and nonverbal behaviors, it would not depend fully on their frequency.

Clearly, this second method seems better designed for tapping the underlying meaning of texts, but its advantage comes at a cost of reliability and specificity. Especially if more than one person is coding the films, somewhat different definitions or standards may be employed.

A film that one coder regards as very erotic may not seem as erotic to another. Even if you do all the coding yourself, there's no guarantee that your definitions and standards will remain constant throughout the enterprise. Moreover, the reader of your research report would be generally uncertain about the definitions you've employed.

Generally, the selection of meaning units is closely related to whether a researcher is interested in manifest or latent meanings. Syntactical and referential units are usually employed in research focused on the manifest meanings of texts. By contrast, propositional and thematic units are usually employed by researchers interested in latent meanings.

Conceptualization and the Creation of Code Categories For all research methods, conceptualization and operationalization typically involve the interaction of theoretical concerns and empirical observations. If, for example, you believe some newspaper editorials to be liberal and others to be conservative, ask yourself why you think so. Read some editorials, asking yourself which ones are liberal and which ones are conservative. Was the political orientation of a particular editorial most clearly indicated by its manifest content or by its latent content—for example, its tone? Was your decision based on the use of certain terms (for example, *pinko* or *fascist*) or on the support or opposition given to a particular issue or political personality?

Both inductive and deductive methods can be used in this activity. If you're testing theoretical propositions, your theories should suggest empirical indicators of concepts. For example, if you have a theory of political orientation, the propositions of this theory should provide guidance in what to look for in developing a coding scheme. If you are trying to develop a theory of political orientation, you will start at the opposite end of the ladder of abstraction, locating patterns in content that appear to differentiate newspapers commonly identified by their readers as "liberal" or "conservative." If you begin with specific empirical observations, you should attempt to derive general principles relating to them and then apply those principles to the other empirical observations by developing a set of coding categories.

Communication researchers employ both deductive and inductive methods in deriving their coding schemes. Thomas Skill and Sam Wallace (1990) functioned deductively in their study of assertive power interactions among family members portrayed on prime-time television. The researchers selected a sample of television programs in which family interaction was portrayed. They coded each utterance as assertive, conforming, rejecting, or neutral based on existing research and theory on the assertion of power in talk. The researchers found that mothers engaged most often in assertive interaction.

An example of inductive content analysis is found in a study of the criteria that people use in deciding whether or not to reveal family secrets to outsiders (Vangelisti, Caughlin, & Timmerman, 2001). The researchers asked people to indicate in open-ended surveys the factors they would use in deciding whether or not to reveal a family secret to someone outside the family. The researchers looked for commonalities in the criteria that emerged in these surveys, developing 12 different categories for their sample as a whole, including whether the other person disclosed an equivalent secret, the need to confide in and talk about the secret, and whether the secret would assist the other person in some way.

Throughout this activity of developing a coding scheme, you should remember that the operational definition of any variable is composed of the attributes included in it. Moreover, such attributes should be mutually exclusive and exhaustive. For example, a newspaper editorial should not be described as both liberal and conservative, though you should probably allow for some to be middle-of-the-road. It may be sufficient for your purposes to code films as erotic or nonerotic, but you may also want to consider that some could be antierotic. Paintings might be classified as representational or not, if that satisfied your research purpose, or you might wish to further classify them as impressionistic, abstract, allegorical, and so forth.

Realize further that different levels of measurement may be used in content analysis. You may, for example, use the *nominal* categories of liberal and conservative for characterizing newspaper editorials, or you might wish to use a more refined ordinal ranking, ranging from extremely liberal to extremely conservative. However, bear in mind that the level of measurement implicit in your coding methods—nominal, ordinal, interval, or ratio—does not necessarily reflect the nature of your variables. If a kiss appears 100 times in film A and 50 times in film B, you would be justified in saying that the behavior of kissing appears twice as often in film A but not that film A is twice as erotic as film B. Similarly, agreeing with twice as many anti-Semitic statements in a questionnaire does not make one twice as anti-Semitic, necessarily.

Counting and Record Keeping

Most content analysis work involves a minimum of two coders to allow determination of inter-coder reliability. Two coders are reliable if they independently code a given unit of data into the same category with a reliability coefficient at least equal to .70. Usually, a researcher trains both coders to use the coding scheme. This is a lengthy process that often takes many hours. The researcher reviews the coding scheme in detail, and the coders undertake some sample coding. Once coders have achieved an adequate level of reliability in their training session, the actual data coding process can begin.

Sometimes, both coders code all of the texts, and their agreement is based on all of the data in the set. However, to save time and resources, researchers often ask each coder to code both unique and overlapping portions of the data. For example, two coders might code the same 25 percent of the texts, with the remaining 75 percent of the data equally divided between the two coders. Inter-coder reliability would be determined based on the 25-percent sample independently coded by each coder.

Researchers are often concerned about a problem with *coder drift*. In coder drift, two coders start out as high in their reliability, but over time, each coder drifts from the training process and interprets texts slightly differently as he or she gains more experience in doing coding work. One check against coder drift is to periodically check inter-coder reliability at various stages in the coding process. If coders have drifted, a researcher can stop the coding process midstream in order to "recalibrate" the coders before they undertake further coding activity.

Since content analysis data are analyzed quantitatively, any coding operation must be amenable to enumeration and data processing.

First, the end product of coding must be *numerical*. If you're counting the frequency of certain words, phrases, or other manifest content, this will necessarily be the case. Even if you're coding latent content on the basis of overall judgments, it will be necessary to represent your coding decision numerically: 4 "very liberal" editorials, 10 "moderately liberal" editorials, 6 "moderately conservative" editorials, and so forth.

Second, record keeping must clearly distinguish between the units of analysis and the units of observation, especially if the two differ. The initial coding, of course, must relate to the units of observation—physical, syntactic, referential, propositional, or thematic units. If film directors are your units of analysis and you wish to characterize them through a content analysis of their films, your primary records will represent films. You might decide to unitize each film holistically in coding its (non)erotic content theme, or you might unitize each film into smaller text segments, particularly if you were adopting a manifest content approach. You would then combine your numerical scoring of individual films to characterize each director.

Third, when counting, it will normally be important to record the *base* from which the counting is done. It would probably be useless to know the number of realist paintings produced by a given painter without knowing the number he or she had painted all together; the painter would be regarded as *realistic* if a high percentage of paintings were of that genre. Similarly, it would tell us little that kissing scenes appear six times in a film if we didn't know how many scenes there are in the film altogether. The issue of observational base is most easily resolved if every observation is coded in terms of one of the attributes making up a variable. Rather than simply counting the number of liberal editorials in a given collection, for example, code each editorial by its political orientation, even if it must be coded "no apparent orientation."

An Illustration of Content Analysis

A growing number of communication researchers are interested in the role of communication in affecting people's health practices. Eric Hoffman and Gary Heald (2000) were interested in whether magazines that targeted African American readers differed from general readership magazines in the frequency with which tobacco and alcohol use were featured in advertisements. They chose a content analysis method to answer their question.

The researchers analyzed magazines for the year 1998. In order to select magazines that had the greatest minority audience advertising coverage, the African American oriented magazines with the largest paid circulation (at least 15,000) were identified by using the *Gale Directory of Publications and Broadcast Media* (1999) as well as the *Standard Periodical Directory* (1999). Seven magazines were chosen and categorized as to type: general editorial, women's interest, music and art, business and finance, lifestyle and culture, and news. The researchers then chose a matched sample of general readership magazines with comparably high circulation and type. One issue for each magazine was selected for each month of 1998; the selection was random for magazines publishing multiple issues per month.

The sample issues were then coded for a variety of variables: number of pages, number of articles, number of tobacco product ads, number of alcoholic beverage ads, and total number of product and service advertisements. Ads were counted in the study if they were paid commercial ads at least one-third of a page in size.

Because these variables are at the manifest content level, inter-coder reliabilities were uniformly high.

The researchers found that the magazines targeted at African American readers had an average of 1.99 tobacco and 3.65 alcohol ads per issue; the corresponding values for the general readership magazines were 1.89 and 2.39, respectively. However, the researchers felt uncomfortable using these values because the magazine issues were not of comparable length—larger magazines had more ads. So they adjusted their figures to take into account the baseline of the number of pages in the issue.

The adjusted frequencies indicated that African American magazines carried significantly more tobacco and alcohol ads than did corresponding general readership magazines. Adjusting for magazine size, African American magazines carried an average of 1.34 tobacco ads per 100 pages and 2.33 alcohol ads per 100 pages. General audience magazines carried 1.19 tobacco ads per 100 pages and 1.45 alcohol ads per 100 pages. Converting these data to percentages, the researchers reported that tobacco-related ads represented an average of 3.6 percent of the total ads in African American magazines versus 3.3 percent of the ads in general readership magazines. For alcohol products, an average of 5.8 percent of the total ads in the African American magazines featured alcoholic beverages, compared to 4.4 percent of the ads in the general readership magazines.

In sum, report the researchers, "Compared to the advertisements in general audience magazines, the average adjusted frequency of tobacco and alcohol ads was about 40 percent higher and the average density of these ads was about 24 percent higher in African-American periodicals" (2000, p. 421). Although the researchers noted that the presence of such ads does not demonstrate a causal link to tobacco and alcohol use among readers, they expressed concern that minority readers were exposed to more advertisements promoting unhealthy practices when compared to the general population.

Although this study dealt with manifest content, it is possible to imagine several related studies that could be undertaken with a focus on latent meaning instead. For example, coders might code the extent to which tobacco and/or alcohol use was symbolically associated with positive outcomes such as romance, popularity, and status.

INTERACTION ANALYSIS

Interaction analysis is a "close cousin" to content analysis. In fact, everything we have written about content analysis applies as well to interaction analysis. Definitionally, we can describe interaction analysis as *a research technique for the systematic, replicable, and quantitative description of the content, functions, and structures of interaction between people*. Three features about this definition help us distinguish between content analysis and interaction. First, interaction analysis is focused on only one kind of text—interaction between people—whereas content analysis can be applied to any kind of text. Second, interaction analysis informs us about the interactive and sequential structure of interaction, in addition to the distributional structure; by contrast, content analysis addresses only issues of distributional structure. Third, and last, interaction analysis can be used to address not only manifest and latent content of messages but also to examine the functions of messages.

Interaction analysis is an especially important method in the study of the process of communication. In examining who talks to whom (interactive structure) and how utterances are linked sequentially (sequential structure), interaction analysts gain insight into how communication unfolds across time.

Interaction analysis is the primary quantitative method used in observation studies of communication. It is often employed by researchers who seek to understand the communication process of decision-making small groups and the process of interaction in marital and family systems.

The mechanics of performing an interaction analysis are very similar to the procedures of content analysis. There are some unique features of interaction analysis, however.

Coding in Interaction Analysis

Interaction analysis, like content analysis, involves a process of unitizing a text into its coding units, then having at least two coders categorize each coding unit against a coding scheme that has been deductively or inductively developed by the researcher.

Coding Units Because interaction analysis focuses exclusively on face-to-face interaction between people, the coding unit tends to be some unit of talk. Randy Hirokawa (1988, pp. 233–234) identifies four coding units that are commonly employed in interaction analysis:

1. *The thought unit.* A thought unit is a verbal and/or nonverbal act that expresses a single complete thought or idea. A single utterance by a person can consist of one or multiple thought units. For example, if a husband says "I think we should hire the landscape specialist to remake the backyard," a coder would regard this as a

single thought unit. If, however, his utterance were more complex, like "I think we should hire the landscape specialist to remake the backyard, because it will increase the value of the property when it comes time to sell the house next spring," we would have two thought units: "I think we should hire the landscape specialist to remake the backyard" and "It will increase the value of the property when it comes time to sell the house next spring."

2. *The theme.* Similar to our discussion of the theme unit in content analysis, a theme is a conversational motif. A theme can include a single utterance or a series of utterances all focused on the same underlying theme.

3. *The time interval.* Sometimes, interaction analysts segment interaction into time units—for example, ten-second intervals—and then code each time period into the categories of analysis.

4. *The speech act.* A speech act is an uninterrupted utterance that is perceived to perform a specific function. What distinguishes the speech-act coding unit is its emphasis on the function, rather than the content, of interaction. Obviously, coders must take an utterance's content into account in making a coding decision, but the focus of the categorization is not on content per se but rather on what the utterance does in the context of the interaction event. For example, in studying interaction between friends, you might identify the speech act of compliance seeking and then code instances of when one friend tries to get the other to do something that he or she might otherwise not do. Hirokawa (1988) argues that this unit is probably the most frequently employed in the small-group communication research literature. It also appears frequently in the marital communication research literature.

Selection of a coding unit is based on the researcher's purpose. For example, if your purpose is to track how ideas emerge and develop in conversation, the thought unit might best serve your interests. However, if you are interested in how interactants influence one another, manage conflict, or coordinate their talk into a "seamless conversation," you are asking questions about function; thus, the speech act would better serve your purposes. If you want to trace how emotional tones shift over the course of a conversation, the theme might be your best bet. And if you wonder how verbal and nonverbal behaviors of a speaker are synchronized, then time interval would probably be your preferred coding unit.

Coding Schemes As in content analysis, the researcher who uses interaction analysis must employ a coding scheme to categorize the units of interaction. A researcher can develop a coding scheme inductively, observing patterns in the talk and then formalizing those into a set of categories that coders subsequently use in coding all of the interaction. Alternatively, a researcher can rely on a pre-existing coding scheme.

Many different coding schemes have been developed in the contexts of dyadic interaction (that is, interaction between two persons), marital interaction, and group communication. Table 10-1 lists some of the coding schemes that are frequently employed by communication researchers. We're going to discuss one of these in some detail in the next section in order to provide a concrete illustration of how interaction analysis is done.

In general, coding schemes emphasize either content or function of interaction. Further, they can be distinguished in terms of their scope: Some coding schemes focus microscopically on interaction behavior, whereas other coding schemes categorize larger, more macroscopic segments of interaction.

With respect to content, interaction analysts often distinguish between *report* and *command* levels of meaning, following the classic work by Paul Watzlawick, Janet Beavin, and Don Jackson (1967). Report-level meaning is generally what is said, whereas command-level meaning "refers to what sort of a message it is to be taken as, and therefore, ultimately to the relationship between the communicants" (Watzlawick et al., p. 52). For example, the utterances "Open the window" and "Please open the window if it's no trouble" basically contain the same content meaning—a request to have someone open a window. However, the two utterances have very different command, or relational, meanings. The first statement is a command, with an implicit relationship of dominance between the speaker and the addressed person. By contrast, the second statement is a request, and one conveyed with deference, instead of dominance, by the speaker.

Inter-Coder Reliability Inter-coder reliability needs to be demonstrated in interaction analysis, just as it does in content analysis. Two kinds of reliability are often reported in interaction analysis, and we have discussed both kinds earlier in the section on content analysis. First, coders need to agree on identifying the coding units, known as *unitizing reliability.* Unlike content analysis, in which a single text can function as the coding unit (e.g., the advertisement, the editorial, the film), interaction analysis tends to be more complicated. As the discussion of coding units makes clear, there is often no necessary one-to-one correspondence between a speaker's utterance and a coding unit—a given utterance can

TABLE 10-1   **A Sample of Some Coding Schemes Used in Interaction Analysis Research**

Coding Scheme	Citation	Description
Conversational Argument Coding Scheme	Canary, Brossmann, & Seibold (1987); Meyers, Seibold, & Brashers (1991)	A coding scheme to track how group members present logical arguments to one another.
Couples Interaction Scoring System (CISS)	Gottman (1979)	Verbal acts are coded into 28 content categories, which are reduced to eight summary codes such as "mindreading," "agreement," "summarizing other." The nonverbal behaviors of both speaker and listener that accompany each coded verbal act are coded for affect (positive, negative, neutral). The CISS is designed to analyze conflict management behaviors in married couples.
Function-Oriented Interaction Analysis System	Hirokawa (1982)	A coding scheme for examining communication in task-oriented groups. Acts are coded by function (e.g., establishes operating procedures, analyzes the problem) and by form (assertions and requests).
Marital Interaction Coding Scheme (MICS)	Weiss & Summers (1983)	A set of 30 coding categories to code problem-solving attempts in married couples. Sample categories include "agree," "approve," "mindread."
Nonverbal Conversational Involvement	Coker & Burgoon (1987)	Burgoon and her colleagues have developed a set of bipolar rating scales that coders use in evaluating interactants' nonverbal communication. This source provides a detailed presentation of the scales for one facet of nonverbal behavior—conversational involvement. For a broader perspective on how rating scales can be used in coder judgments of nonverbal relational communication more generally, see Burgoon and LePoire (1999).
Relational Coding Schemes	Rogers & Farace (1975)	Several coding systems have been derived from the work of Watzlawick and associates (1967) on command, or relational, communication. These coding systems focus on relational control—dominance and submission in interaction in marriages, families, and groups.

conceivably contain multiple coding units. This complexity makes unitizing a complex operation.

Second, coders need to agree in categorizing the coding units, known as *categorizing reliability.* This is complicated as well. Because messages are complex actions, they often convey multiple meanings and functions simultaneously. Sometimes, researchers allow their coders to categorize a given coding unit into multiple categories to capture this complexity. Usually, however, they develop detailed coding rules that guide coders in making the single best choice among categories.

In calculating a reliability index between coders, it is important to take into account the extent to which coders would agree by chance alone. Factoring chance expectations into the calculation of a reliability index applies both to interaction analysis and content analysis. If acts are disproportionately of one or a few types, then agreement between coders will be artificially inflated because of the unequal distribution of act types that happened to exist in a given data set. If 90 percent of the acts in an interaction text are of type A, then our two coders

will agree a lot in identifying A acts, not because they are making the same nuanced distinctions between coding categories but because the data set happened not to require coders to make many distinctions among act types. To correct for this problem, researchers often report a reliability coefficient that takes the distribution of coding units in the data into account in the calculation of the agreement index. Two such reliability coefficients to use, and watch for in reading interaction analysis research, are Scott's pi (1955) and Cohen's kappa (1960). You want to find coefficient values larger than .70, as a general rule of thumb. In the "Calculating Categorizing Reliability" box, we show you how to calculate Cohen's kappa, which is appropriate for both content analysis and interaction analysis.

What's done when coders do not agree? Coders will rarely agree 100 percent of the time, even though they have an acceptably high reliability coefficient. Researchers solve coder discrepancies in any of several ways. Sometimes, the researcher or some other third party "breaks ties" between the two coders, and the coding

There are many ways that categorizing reliability can be calculated. Cohen's (1960) kappa is one of these. Cohen's kappa has the advantage of taking into account the agreement between coders that would be expected by chance alone. Here's the formula:

$$\kappa = \frac{P_{obs} - P_{exp}}{1 - P_{exp}}$$

where

P_{obs} = the proportion of agreement observed between two coders

P_{exp} = the proportion of agreement expected by chance alone

Let's suppose we asked two coders to code the body weight of female characters in TV soaps using this coding scheme:

Code	Label
1	Greatly overweight (e.g., fat, obese)
2	Slightly overweight (e.g., plump, pudgy)
3	Normal for height and build
4	Slightly underweight (e.g., skinny)
5	Greatly underweight (e.g., anorexic)

Suppose that our two coders produced the following decisions for 181 female characters. In this matrix, the diagonal cells represent instances of coding agreement; off-diagonal cells represent instances of coder disagreements. That is, the two coders agreed in coding "1" 10 times, "2" 20 times, "3" 45 times, and so on. In one instance, coder 1 judged a person's body as a "1" while coder 2 judged it as "2," and so on.

Were our two coders reliable at an acceptable level? Let's find out!

Step 1. Calculate P_{obs}. Sum up the diagonal cells and divide this value by the total number of units coded:

$$P_{obs} = \frac{(10 + 20 + 45 + 58 + 14)}{181} = \frac{147}{181} = .81$$

Step 2. Calculate P_{exp} by summing up the chance agreement probabilities for each category. Multiply the first-column total by the first-row total, add this to the second-column total multiplied by the second-row total, and so on; then divide the sum of what are known as the column-row products by the square of the total number of observed units.

$$P_{exp} = \frac{(16 \cdot 14) + (28 \cdot 28) + (52 \cdot 54) + (65 \cdot 65) + (20 \cdot 20)}{(181 \cdot 181)}$$

$$= \frac{8441}{32761} = .26$$

Step 3. Now compute kappa.

$$\kappa = \frac{.81 - .26}{1 - .26}$$

$$= \frac{.55}{.74} = .74$$

As you can see, the amount of coder agreement corrected for chance (.74) is less than the uncorrected value of .81. This will usually be the case when there are a few coding categories that are disproportionate to the others. In this example, there were many normal and slightly underweight female characters on TV soaps relative to the other body-weight categories.

		Coding Decisions by Coder 2					
		1	2	3	4	5	Totals
	1	10	1	2	1	0	14
	2	3	20	2	2	1	28
Coding Decisions by Coder 1	3	1	2	45	2	4	54
	4	1	3	2	58	1	65
	5	1	2	1	2	14	20
	Totals	16	28	52	65	20	181

decision made by this third party is how a given coding unit is categorized. Another strategy for resolving discrepancies is for the two coders to meet, discuss, and resolve their discrepancies once they have completed independent coding. Such a meeting may or may not involve a researcher/third party as a participant. When the coding takes the form of counting up some phenomenon or rating some phenomenon on, say, a seven-point rating item, a researcher can "split the difference" and derive an average between the two coders' judgments. A researcher could also decide to throw out the discrepant data and analyze only the coding units agreed upon by the coders; this is a radical move, however, and researchers generally try to salvage as much of their data as possible in interaction analysis.

Analyzing Interaction Structures

Although Chapters 11 and 12 of the book are devoted to quantitative data analysis, we want to discuss here the logic of interaction analysis. As discussed above, interaction analysis, like content analysis, provides a distributional structure of the coding units. That is, we are given a frequency distribution of how often each category is coded in the data set. But interaction analysis sheds insight into two additional kinds of information: interactive structure and sequential structure.

When coders assess a given communicative act, they record who the speaker is. When you look at this record of speakers across time, you get a sense of the interaction network among speakers. The interactive structure basically is a matrix of how frequently speakers address one another. Let's imagine that we have a management team of four members: Joanne, Judd, Tamar, and Bill. Their interactive structure might look like Figure 10-4. From this sample matrix, it is clear that Joanne spoke more frequently than any other member and that she replied to

others' utterances more often than any other member. From what we know about group leadership, Joanne might be a candidate for who functioned as a leader in the group. Beyond this insight, the matrix reveals information about the configuration or network of utterances among team members. Judd appeared almost "out of the loop" of interaction—he spoke relatively infrequently, and few members directed comments to him. The Joanne–Tamar dyad had more exchanges between them than any other combination of speakers. We might conclude from this pattern that Joanne and Tamar form an interactional coalition. From this hypothetical example, it's possible to see how interaction coding can shed insight into the network of communicative acts among group members—its interactive structure.

Sequential structure addresses the question of what follows what in the unfolding process of communication across time. Sequential structure is also captured in a matrix, this time a matrix in which all possible coding categories are listed as the antecedent, or prior, acts and again as the consequent, or following, acts. From such a matrix, we can determine the frequencies and proportions of acts of a given type that follow different kinds of antecedent acts.

Let's consider an interaction coding scheme that focuses on the affective meaning of utterances. For the sake of ease, let's imagine that our coders make a simple coding decision for each utterance: positive, negative, or neutral. Let's imagine that our coders analyzed a conversation 25 utterances long between a married couple, producing the sequential structure matrix in Figure 10-5. In sequential analysis, each act is positioned as both an antecedent and a consequent act, with the exceptions of the first and last acts: With these exceptions, each act is responded to by the following act and is a response to a prior act.

Figure 10-5 indicates that when the prior act is positive in tone, such positivity is most frequently met with a neutral response: Of the 3 positive acts, 3 (100 percent)

			Respondent			
		Bill	Joanne	Judd	Tamar	TOTAL
	Bill	—	11	6	7	24
	Joanne	13	—	5	16	34
Speaker	Judd	2	4	—	1	7
	Tamar	3	10	1	—	14
	TOTAL	18	25	12	24	

FIGURE 10-4 **Sample Interactive Structure Matrix**

		Consequent Act		
		Positive	Negative	Neutral
	Positive	0	0	3
Antecedent Act	Negative	0	8	3
	Neutral	2	4	4

FIGURE 10-5 **Sample Sequential Structure Matrix**

were responded to with emotional neutrality. By contrast, when negative acts were engaged in, they were reciprocated with negative responses: Of the 11 negative acts in this marital exchange, 8 (73 percent) were met with a negative response. When an act was emotionally neutral, it tended to be responded to negatively or neutrally: Of the 10 emotionally neutral utterances, 40 percent were met with a negative response and 40 percent with a neutral response. If this exchange were typical of the marital pair's communication, we might have reason to worry based on what we know about marital communication (Gottman, 1994). About the only departure this pair has from emotional neutrality comes from negativity—negative utterances tend to be reciprocated with negative responses, and even neutral utterances stand a good chance of being responded to negatively. This pair is having trouble constructing a positive interaction experience.

Note that Figure 10-5 ignores whether the wife is responding to the husband's utterances or whether the husband is responding to the wife's utterances. If this were a real interaction analysis study, we would probably want to examine two sequential structure matrices: one with the husband's acts as antecedents and one with the wife's acts as antecedents. In comparing these two matrices, we would get a sense of whether the husband and the wife respond similarly to each other.

When researchers employ the method of interaction analysis, they rarely examine a single group or a single married couple. In the interests of generalizability, interaction analysts study several social groupings: task groups, married couples, families, friendship pairs, and so on. They generally ask whether patterns in the distributional, interactive, and sequential structures of interaction are related to other variables, such as satisfaction, effectiveness, and relationship closeness.

We've worked through a couple of hypothetical examples. Now let's turn to an actual interaction analysis coding system to give you a "feel" for interaction coding.

An Illustration of Interaction Analysis

Randy Hirokawa is one of the leading scholars of group decision making, and he takes a functional perspective to the question of how communication among group members is related to the quality of their group decisions. In 1982 he presented the Function-Oriented Analysis System for coding group interaction. Figure 10-6 presents that coding system. This coding scheme uses the speech act as its coding unit. A speech act is defined as "an un-

interrupted utterance of a single group member, which appears to perform a specific function within the group interaction process" (p. 139). Based on this definition of his coding unit, segmenting between two coding units could occur in one of two ways: "(1) the interruption of one individual's contribution by the functional utterance of another group member, or (2) the crossing of functions within a single contribution of a group member" (p. 139). Thus, a group member's turn-at-talk or utterance could be coded into more than one functional act if it enacted multiple functions.

Each functional act is coded according to one of four functions performed by the act: establishing operating procedures for the group, analyzing the problem facing the group, generating solutions for the group to consider, and evaluating proposed solutions. These four functional codes serve as "anchors" for the rest of the interaction analysis system.

Each functional act is then coded into one of twelve behavioral types, eight of which take the form of assertions and four of which take the form of requests. These twelve behaviors capture the class of behaviors that hold the potential to enact any (or all) of the four functions.

Hirokawa (1982, p. 139) presented an excerpt from a group discussion with his coders' decisions recorded for each act. The problem presented to the group required them to find a way to control speeding on the streets of their city. Here's a portion of that conversation:

Code:
301 Jack: I think they should, you know, like put those speed bumps on the road . . .
306 Dave: Yeah . . . that's a thought . . .
409 Ron: Yeah, but wouldn't that kinda' wreck the cars? I mean . . .
401 Jan: Yeah, I think they would really, you know, wreck the bottoms of the cars, the shocks and stuff like that . . .

In this excerpt, Jack's utterance functioned to generate a solution—he proposed the solution of speed bumps to solve the speeding problem. This function was an assertion of introduction, because it was the first time such an idea had been introduced to the group discussion. Dave's response was coded "306." He was simply agreeing with Jack's suggestion. Notice that he didn't evaluate the solution ("that's a thought"), but uttered a more neutral statement in support of Jack's putting an idea before the group. However, Ron moved into evaluation; thus, it was given a function code of "4." The behavioral form of his act was that of asking for ideas—he was inquiring of his fellow

I. TASK FUNCTIONS:

    1 = ESTABLISH OPERATING PROCEDURES (The group must establish a set of operating procedures. They need to decide what needs to be done to solve the problem, and, more importantly, how they should go about doing it.)

    2 = ANALYSIS OF PROBLEM (The group must understand and analyze the problem. They must (a) identify the nature of the problem, (b) determine the extent of the problem, (c) identify the possible causes of the problem, and (d) identify the symptoms of the problem.)

    3 = GENERATION OF SOLUTIONS (They must consider as many feasible alternatives as possible before deciding on a final decision or solution.)

    4 = EVALUATION OF SOLUTIONS (They must carefully evaluate all alternative solutions, making certain that all important implications and consequences of accepting such a solution have been considered, and the one finally selected meets the criteria for a "good" solution.)

II. BEHAVIORAL TYPES:

  A. ASSERTIONS

    1 = Introduction. Any statement which introduces a fact, opinion, belief, idea, or judgment into the group discussion.

    2 = Restatement. Any statement which repeats an earlier statement of fact, opinion, belief, or judgment in the same or similar terms.

    3 = Development. Any statement which seeks to develop or expand upon an earlier statement of fact, opinion, belief, or judgment; or to make that earlier statement more understandable through elaboration, example, illustration, or explanation.

    4 = Substantiation. Any statement which attempts to provide proof, support, or evidence which establishes the correctness, truth, or validity of an earlier statement of act, opinion, belief, or judgment.

    5 = Modification. Any statement which reflects an attempt to alter or change an idea presented earlier in the discussion.

    6 = Agreement. Any statement which reflects direct agreement, approval, or consent with a fact, idea, opinion, or judgment under consideration by the group.

    7 = Disagreement. Any statement which reflects direct disapproval or disagreement with a fact, idea, opinion, or judgment under consideration by the group.

    8 = Summarization/synthesis. Any statement which reflects an attempt to summarize, bring together, narrow, or add emphasis to elements (e.g., facts, ideas, etc.) introduced, substantiated, developed, or modified in previous lines of discussion.

  B. REQUESTS

    9 = Asks for ideas. Any question which seeks facts, ideas, opinions, beliefs, or judgments from some member(s) of the group.

    10 = Asks for approval. Any question which seeks consent or approval from group members regarding a specific fact, idea, opinion, belief, or judgment previously brought before the group.

    11 = Asks for clarification. Any question which seeks to have a particular statement of fact, idea, opinion, belief, or judgment made more understandable or precise.

    12 = Asks for summary/synthesis. Any question which seeks to have some member(s) bring together, narrow, or add emphasis to facts, ideas, opinions, or judgments introduced in earlier portions of the discussion.

FIGURE 10-6   **Hirokawa's Function-Oriented Analysis System**

Source: Hirokawa, R. Y. (1982). Group communication and problem-solving effectiveness I: A critical review of inconsistent findings. *Communication Quarterly, 30,* 134–141. Used by permission.

group members whether speed bumps would damage the cars as they drive over the bumps. Jan continued in the evaluative mode, so her act also received a function code of "4." In contrast to Ron, however, Jan made an assertion. She introduced an opinion or belief that the bottoms of cars would receive damage in driving over the bumps.

This coding system, or variations of it, has been used in a number of studies in group communication.

STRENGTHS AND WEAKNESSES OF QUANTITATIVE TEXT ANALYSIS

Quantitative text analysis, like any method, has strengths as well as limitations. Quantitative text analysis affords you a more detailed examination of actual communicative messages than what you could obtain through other quantitative methods such as survey research. People have difficulty remembering the details of messages, and they tend to remember in biased ways. Further, if you are interested in analyzing historical documents, the people associated with those texts may no longer be available to share their recollections.

Also important, quantitative text analysis permits you to study processes occurring over time. In a content analysis, you might focus on the imagery of African Americans conveyed in U.S. novels from 1850 to 1860, for example, or you might examine changing imagery from 1850 to the present. In an interaction analysis, you might focus on how a group's dynamics change over the course of its history together.

Quantitative text analysis also has the advantage, mentioned at the outset of this chapter, of being *unobtrusive*. That is, the content analyst or interaction analyst seldom has any effect on the participant being studied. Because the TV programs have already been shown, the diaries already written, and the speeches already presented, quantitative text analyses can have no effect on them. Even when simulated interaction is used, the participants lack knowledge of what it is in their communication that is being analyzed.

Finally, safety is also an advantage of quantitative text analysis. If you discover you've botched a survey or an experiment, you may be forced to repeat the whole research project with all the attendant costs in time and money. In content analysis and interaction analysis, it's usually easier to repeat a portion of the study than in other research methods. Moreover, you might be required to recode only a portion of your data rather than all of it. But even if you have to recode everything, you don't have to start over in the selection of your texts.

Content analysis and interaction analysis have disadvantages as well. For one thing, they are limited to the examination of *recorded* communication. Such texts may be oral, written, or graphic, but they must be recorded in some fashion to permit analysis. It is a labor-intensive activity to produce written transcriptions of talk. In addition, recorded communication may miss some important features that were present in the "real time" of the interaction event.

As we've seen, quantitative text analysis has both advantages and disadvantages in terms of validity and reliability. Problems of validity are possible unless you happen to be studying communication processes per se. For example, if you wanted to study the kinds of music presented on radio stations in your community, keeping a record of the pieces presented by the various stations over some period of time would be a perfectly valid measurement technique. Notice that it would not be as valid a measure of community musical tastes, but it would measure radio station programming perfectly. Notice that you might have a validity problem regarding how you coded various pieces of music: as jazz, classical, rock, and so on.

Critics of quantitative text analysis argue that the procedure of coding content and function is inherently too simplistic, losing detail and richness in the very act of fitting a textual segment to a category and then counting up the frequencies of the various categories. We'll have more to say about this issue when we discuss qualitative text analysis in Chapters 15 and 16.

Quantitative text analysis is based on the assumption that there is a uniform relationship between symbols and meanings. Such an assumption ignores connotative meanings and cultural (or subcultural) differences in meaning making. Further, content analysis and interaction analysis assume that the construction of meaning in the minds of receivers of the message matches the coding scheme used by the researcher. These assumptions argue for the particular importance of representational validity in quantitative text analysis (recall Chapter 6).

On the other side of the ledger, the concreteness of materials studied in quantitative text analysis strengthens the likelihood of reliability. You can always code and recode and even recode again if you want, making certain that the coding is consistent.

Main Points

- Coding is the process of transforming raw textual data into categories.
- Quantitative text analysis is a systematic method of coding textual segments into nominal or ordinal categories for their enumeration.

- Any kind of text is appropriate for quantitative text analysis. A text is any behavior, object, or artifact that involves symbol use.
- The selection of texts for quantitative analysis is based on either probability sampling or nonprobability sampling.
- Content analysis and interaction analysis are the two

forms of quantitative text analysis. Content analysis is the systematic coding of the manifest or latent meanings of texts. Interaction analysis is the systematic coding of the content, structures, and functions of face-to-face interactions between people.

❑ Manifest content refers to the directly visible, objectively identifiable characteristics of a text, such as the specific words in a book or the specific colors used in a painting.

❑ Latent content refers to the underlying meanings contained within texts. The determination of latent content requires judgments on the part of the coders.

❑ Content analysis and interaction analysis provide information on a text's distributional structure. In addition, interaction analysis provides information about interactive structure and sequential structure.

Key Terms

content analysis
interaction analysis
text
distributional structure
interactive structure

sequential structure
unitizing
manifest content
latent content

Review Questions and Exercises

1. Locate some political texts generated by Republicans and Democrats. If it's an election year, you might locate political campaign materials produced by two competing candidates. Or you might locate all of the Republican and Democratic speeches that appear in an issue of the *Congressional Record*. Or you might examine the inaugural addresses of Republican and Democratic presidents for the past 25 years. Formulate a research question appropriate to content analysis. Design a research plan for your study, paying particular attention to defining your unit of analysis and your units of observation (your coding units). Formulate a possible coding scheme that would be responsive to your research question.

2. Create a quantitative text analysis design to study the host–guest interaction on TV talk shows. Determine what variables interest you in the interaction; then address sampling methods, coding units, and measurements of your variables.

3. Develop a quantitative text analysis design to study the portrayal of parent–child interaction on TV sit-

coms. Determine what variables interest you in the interaction; then address sampling methods, coding units, and measurements of your variables.

4. Develop a quantitative text analysis design to study the personal dating ads in your local newspaper. Develop a coding scheme inductively. Figure out how you could select a sample of ads. Code a few ads to see how well your coding scheme works.

Continuity Project

Examine how men and women are portrayed in the mass media. Develop a research study in which you select some mass communication medium (popular music, network television, popular magazines) of interest to you. Develop a sampling plan for selecting a sample of texts in that medium. Narrow down the portrayal concept by conceptualizing and operationalizing variables in a manner appropriate to a quantitative text analysis. Develop a coding sheet that could be used in the study.

Additional Readings

Bakeman, R., & Gottman, J. M. (1997). *Observing interaction: An introduction to sequential analysis* (2nd ed.). New York: Cambridge University Press. An outstanding book on interaction analysis in general and sequential structure in particular.

Berelson, B. (1952). *Content analysis in communication research.* New York: Free Press. A classic book on manifest content analysis, with an emphasis on mass media texts.

Evans, W. (1996). Computer-supported content analysis: Trends, tools, and techniques. *Social Science Computer Review, 14,* 269–279. Here's a review of some current computer software for content analysis, such as CETA, DICTION, INTEXT, MCCA, MECA, TEXTPACK, VBPro, and WORDLINK.

Krippendorff, K. (1980). *Content analysis: An introduction to its methodology.* Beverly Hills, CA: Sage. Along with the Berelson book cited above, a classic in the theory and method of content analysis for communication researchers.

Montgomery, B. M., & Duck, S. (Eds.) (1991). *Studying interpersonal interaction.* New York: Guilford. Like the Tardy book, this edited collection contains some very helpful chapters on content analysis and interaction analysis.

Riffe, D., Lacy, S., & Fico, F. G. (1998). *Analyzing media messages: Using quantitative content analysis in research.* Mahweh, NJ: Erlbaum. An excellent book on how to use content analysis in analyzing mass-media texts.

Tardy, C. (Ed.) (1988). *A handbook for the study of human communication: Methods and instruments for observing, measuring, and assessing communication processes.* Norwood, NJ:

Ablex. This edited book contains very useful chapters on how to do interaction analysis.

Webb, E. T., Campbell, D. T., Schwartz, R. D., Sechrest, L., & Grove, J. B. (1981). *Nonreactive measures in the social sciences*. Boston: Houghton Mifflin. A compendium of unobtrusive measures. Includes physical traces, a variety of archival sources, and observation. Good discussion of the ethics involved and the limitations of such measures.

Weber, R. P. (1990). *Basic content analysis*. Newbury Park, CA: Sage. Here's an excellent beginner's book for the design and execution of content analysis. Both general issues and specific techniques are presented.

InfoTrac College Edition
http://www.infotrac-college.com/
wadsworth/access.html

Access the latest news and journal articles with InfoTrac College Edition, an easy-to-use online database of reliable, full-length articles from hundreds of top academic journals. Conduct an electronic search using the following search terms:

- content analysis
- interaction analysis
- unitizing
- manifest content
- latent content
- interaction sequence

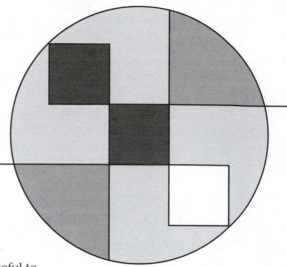

CHAPTER **11**

The Basics of Quantitative Data Analysis

What You'll Learn in This Chapter

Having amassed a volume of observations, you may find it useful to transform them into a form appropriate to computerized statistical analysis. We'll discuss how to do this. Then we'll discuss ways to generate summary descriptions of quantified variables.

INTRODUCTION

For the last several chapters, our attention has been focused on how to gather quantitative data. In this chapter, we discuss the basics of quantitative data analysis. To begin, we'll look at quantification—the process of converting data into a numerical format. This involves converting data into a case X variable matrix that can be read and manipulated by computers through statistical software packages. The rest of the chapter will present a discussion of basic descriptive statistics that are commonly used in quantitative communication research.

Before we can do any sort of analysis, we need to quantify our data. Let's turn now to the basic steps involved in converting data amenable to computer processing and analysis.

QUANTIFICATION OF DATA

Today, quantitative analysis is almost always done by computer programs such as SPSS and MicroCase. For those programs to work their magic, they must be able to read the data you've collected in your research. If you've conducted a survey, for example, some of the data are inherently numerical: age or income, for instance. While the writing and check marks on a questionnaire are qualitative in nature, a scribbled age is easily converted to quantitative data.

Other data are also easily quantified: Transforming "male" and "female" into "1" and "2" is hardly rocket science. Researchers can also easily assign numerical representations to such variables as region of the country ("1" = North, "2" = South, and so on). The structured response options to standard questionnaire formats—such as Likert-type and semantic differential—can also be assigned numbers from "1" to "5" (or "7," or however many response options are possible). We discussed the specifics of this in Chapter 8.

Some data are more challenging, however. If a survey respondent tells you that he or she thinks the biggest problem facing children is how to say "no" to drugs, the computer can't understand that response. You must translate these data through *coding*. The discussion of content analysis in Chapter 10 dealt with the coding process in a manner close to our present concern. Recall that the content analyst must develop methods of assigning individual paragraphs, editorials, books, songs, and so forth with specific classifications or attributes. In content analysis, the coding process is inherent in data collection or observation.

To conduct a quantitative analysis when other research methods are employed, you often must engage in a coding process after the data have been collected. For example, open-ended questionnaire items result in nonnumerical responses, which must be coded before analysis. Or, in an experiment, participants' nonverbal or verbal responses may be the outcome variable—a stream of nonverbal behaviors or words needs translation into quantitative form.

As with content analysis, the task here is to reduce a wide variety of idiosyncratic items of information to a more limited set of attributes composing a variable. Suppose that a survey researcher has asked respondents, "What are your favorite TV programs?" The responses to such a question would vary considerably. Although it would be possible to assign each separate TV program reported a separate numerical code, this procedure would not help in analysis, which typically depends on several participants having the same attribute. You might want to differentiate daytime talk shows from daytime soap operas, prime-time dramas, prime-time sitcoms, news programs, and "reality TV" programs. The coding scheme chosen should be appropriate to the theoretical concepts being examined in the study. Each of these coding categories would be represented with a nominal-level number, "1" through "*n*."

Although the coding scheme ought to be tailored to meet particular requirements of the analysis, one general guideline should be kept in mind. If the data are coded to maintain a great deal of detail, code categories can always be combined during analysis that does not require such detail. If the data are coded into relatively few, gross categories, however, there's no way during analysis to recreate the original detail. Thus, you would be well advised to code your data in somewhat more detail than you plan to use in your analysis.

Researchers use the same basic approaches to the development of code categories that we discussed in Chapter 10: inductive and deductive. In inductive approaches, researchers examine the range and patterning of nonnumerical data in order to develop the set of categories that best fits the data. In deductive approaches, researchers code nonnumerical data into preexisting code categories.

CODEBOOK CONSTRUCTION

The end product of the coding process is the conversion of data items into numerical codes. These codes represent attributes composing variables, which, in turn, are assigned names and locations within a data file. A **codebook** is a document that describes the locations of

Column 4: NARR

Kind of narrative told by the informant.

1 = A first-hand narrative in which the story is based on the informant's personal experience or personal observation; this kind of narrative represents knowledge known by the informant, or personal knowledge.

2 = A second-hand narrative in which the informant recounts a story told to him or her by someone else; this kind of narrative is knowledge known of by the informant. This is second-hand knowledge.

3 = Narrative form unclear from the interview transcript. Use this category sparingly—only in those instances in which there is a story but it is not clearly first-hand or second-hand in nature.

0 = Missing data. We will not code interviews in which a "0" appears in this column. Use this option sparingly to mark interviews in which no narrative appears—e.g., a persistent "I don't know" response by the informant or something like "I saw this movie where somebody got busted."

FIGURE 11-1 **A Partial Codebook: Drug Narrative Study**

variables and lists the code assignments to the attributes composing those variables. A codebook serves two essential functions. First, it's the primary guide used in the coding process. Second, it's your guide for locating variables and interpreting codes in your data file during analysis. If you decide to correlate two variables as part of your analysis of your data, the codebook tells you where to find the variables and what the codes represent.

Figure 11-1 is a partial codebook for one variable in a data set dealing with adolescent narratives about drugs (Baxter, 1999). We had transcripts from semistructured interviews in which adolescent informants were asked to tell a story about drugs. We coded more than 100 variables from these interviews, including the type of narrative story that an informant told us. There is no one right format for a codebook, so we've presented some of the common elements in this example.

There are several elements worth noting in the partial codebook illustrated in this figure. First, the variable is identified by an abbreviated variable name: *NARR*. We could determine, for example, whether male or female informants told different kinds of narratives by referencing *NARR*. You must have *some* identifier that will allow you to locate and use the variable in question, although the specific format for this identification may vary depending on the statistical software package you are employing for data-analysis purposes (SPSS was used in this study).

Next, every codebook should contain the full definition of the variable. In the case of a questionnaire, this would be the exact wording of the questions asked because, as we've seen, the wording of questions strongly influences the answers returned. In the case of *NARR,* the full definition of the variable was "kind of narrative told by the informant."

Your codebook will also indicate the attributes composing each variable. For the *NARR* variable, basically two forms of narratives could be told by informants: first-hand and second-hand. For example, if an informant told a story that involved him or her personally, a "1" would be coded to indicate a first-hand narrative. If, by contrast, an informant told a story about a friend, family member, or stranger, this was coded as a second-hand story, "2." Notice that we allow for two additional possibilities—an interview in which the form of the narrative was not clear (coded with a "3"), and a missing values code ("0") to allow for interviews in which the informant, for whatever reason, failed to tell a story.

The numerical codes for attributes are subject to a variety of statistical calculations. Later in this chapter, we'll discuss several descriptive summary statistics. For *NARR,* we could summarize this variable by counting the frequencies with which "1," "2," "3," and "4" appeared in the data set.

DATA ENTRY

There are many ways of entering data for computer analysis, depending on the original form of your data and also the computer program you will use for analyzing the data. We'll simply introduce you to the process here. If you find yourself undertaking this task, you should be able to tailor your work to the particular data source and program you are using.

If your data have been collected by questionnaire, you might do your coding on the questionnaire itself. Then data entry specialists (including yourself) could enter the data into, say, an SPSS data matrix or into an Excel spreadsheet and later imported into SPSS. Sometimes, communication researchers use optical scan sheets for data collection. These sheets can be fed into machines that will convert the black marks into data, which can be imported into the computer analysis program. This procedure will work only with participants who are comfortable using such sheets, and it will usually be limited to closed-ended questions. Sometimes, data entry occurs in the process of data collection. In computer-assisted telephone interviewing, for example, the interviewer keys responses directly into the computer, where the data are compiled for analysis (see Chapter 8). Even more effortlessly, online surveys can be constructed so that the

Int#	School	Ethnic	Narr
1	1	1	1
2	1	2	2
3	1	3	1
4	2	1	2
5	1	2	2
6	1	1	2
7	2	2	1
8	1	1	2
9	2	3	1

FIGURE 11-2   **Partial Data Entry File: Drug Narrative Study**

respondents enter their own answers directly into the accumulating database, without the need for an intervening interviewer or data entry person.

Different computer programs structure data sets in different ways. In most cases, you'll probably use your data-analysis program for data entry. SPSS, for example, will present you with a blank matrix of rows and columns. You can assign variable names to the columns and enter data for each case (such as a survey respondent, experimental participant, or communication text) on a separate line. Once you're finished, your data will be ready for analysis.

As an alternative, you can often create your data set using some other means (such as a spreadsheet or a word processor) and then import the data into the analysis program. In the case of SPSS, for example, a text file with data items separated by tabs (such as *datafile.dat*) can be imported and then can be saved in the SPSS format (such as *datafile.sav*). Subsequently, you can load the data file as though it had been initially created through SPSS. Most data-analysis programs have similar options.

In general, statistical analysis programs share a common case X variable format: The cases are your rows, and the variables measured are each captured in a column. Figure 11-2 provides a partial data entry file for the drug narratives study discussed above; this file was analyzed using SPSS. Each respondent represented a case, or row, and the columns represent each of the variables measured in the interview, including *NARR*, described above. The interview number (Int#), the participant's school (School), and the participant's ethnicity (Ethnic) were also coded.

DATA CLEANING

Once you have created a data file suitable for statistical analysis, you need to check for data-entry errors and eliminate them—a process known as **cleaning** the data.

No matter how, or how carefully, the data have been entered, some errors are inevitable. Depending on the data-processing method, these errors may result from incorrect coding, incorrect reading of written codes, incorrect sensing of blackened marks, and so forth. Two types of cleaning should be done: *possible-code cleaning* and *contingency cleaning*.

Possible-Code Cleaning

Any given variable has a specified set of legitimate attributes, translated into a set of possible codes. In the variable *gender*, there will be perhaps three possible codes: 1 for masculine, 2 for feminine, and 0 for no answer. If a case has been coded 5, say, in the column assigned to the gender variable, it's clear that an error has been made.

Possible-code cleaning can be accomplished in two different ways. First, many of the computer programs available for data entry today can check for errors as the data are being entered. If you tried to enter a 5 for gender in such programs, for example, the computer might "beep" and refuse the erroneous code. Other computer programs are designed to test for illegitimate codes in data files that weren't checked during data entry.

If you don't have access to these kinds of computer programs, you can achieve a possible-code cleaning by examining the distribution of responses to each item in your data set. Thus, if you find that your data set contains 350 people coded 1 on gender (for masculine), 400 people coded 2 (for feminine), and one person coded 5, you'll probably suspect the 5 is an error.

Whenever you discover errors, the next step is to locate the appropriate source document (for example, the questionnaire), determine what code should have been entered, and make the necessary correction.

Contingency Cleaning

Contingency cleaning is more complicated. The logical structure of the data may place special limits on the responses of certain participants. For example, a questionnaire may ask for the number of children that women have given birth to. All female respondents, then, should have a response recorded (from 0 to *n*, or a special code for failure to answer), but no male respondent should have an answer recorded (or should have only a special code indicating the question is inappropriate to him). If a given male respondent is coded as having borne three children, either an error has been made and should be corrected or your study is about to become more famous than you ever dreamed.

Although data cleaning is an essential step in data processing, you can safely avoid it in certain cases. Perhaps you'll feel you can safely exclude the very few errors that appear in a given item—if the exclusion of those cases will not significantly affect your results. Or some inappropriate contingency responses may be safely ignored. If some men have received motherhood status, you can limit your analysis of this variable to women. However, you should not use these comments as rationalizations for sloppy research. "Dirty" data will almost always produce misleading research findings.

Once you have your quantified data entered into a computer and cleaned, you will need to perform some basic descriptive statistical analyses of each variable. These basic descriptive statistics tell you about the basic patterns for each of your variables. Before you advance to more complex statistics, addressed in the next chapter, you need to determine the basic overall profile of your data for each variable.

These basic descriptive statistical analyses can be executed by your statistical analysis software, such as SPSS. However, we're going to show you how to calculate them by hand so that you can gain some understanding of what each descriptive statistic is all about.

DESCRIPTIVE STATISTICS

When you have a large number of cases, you need a way to summarize them concisely, and that's where **descriptive statistics** come into play. We'll discuss three types of summary descriptions: distributions, central tendency, and dispersion.

These descriptive statistics are usually accompanied by shorthand symbol notations. As discussed in Chapter 2, most communication journals follow the publication guidelines that appear in the *Publication Manual of the American Psychological Association* (5th edition). Table 11-1 summarizes the symbol notations used in the APA style so that you'll know what they mean when you encounter them while reading published research articles.

Distributions

The most basic format for presenting data about a given variable is to report all individual cases: that is, to list the attribute for each case under study in terms of the variable in question.

TABLE 11-1 Summary of Symbols for Various Descriptive Statistics

Symbol	Meaning
f	Frequency
M	Arithmetic mean
Mdn	Median
mode	Mode
n	Number in a subsample
N	Total number in a sample
SD	Standard deviation

Source: American Psychological Association (2001). *Publication Manual of the American Psychological Association* (5th ed.). Washington, DC: Author.

Let's consider the 1998 General Social Survey (GSS) data on TV viewing hours per day. In Chapter 8 we discussed the secondary analysis of data, and the GSS contains data often used by social scientists for secondary-data-analysis purposes. The GSS is an annual national probability-based interview conducted by the National Opinion Research Center (NORC). Since 1972, more than 38,000 households have been involved in the survey on a variety of social issues. Not all survey questions are asked each year. The most recent survey in which adults were asked to report on their TV viewing is 1998. Table 11-2 presents the frequency distribution of the variable TVHOURS ("On the average day, about how many hours do you personally watch television?"). A **frequency distribution** is simply a summary of the frequencies with which each reported value appeared in the sample. (Go to www.icpsr.umich.edu/gss for more details on the wealth of data you can download and analyze from the GSS.)

Let's examine the table, piece by piece. First, if you look at the note at the bottom of the table, you'll see that the sample being analyzed has a total of 2,337 valid cases. You'll also see that an additional 495 respondents said they didn't know, gave no answer in response to this question, or found the question not applicable to their life circumstance. It's important to know what the baseline number is for the table.

Go back to the top of the table now. You'll see that 119 people said they do not watch TV. This number in and of itself tells us nothing about TV viewing practices. If the data we're examining were based on 4,674 respondents instead of 2,337, we could assume that about 238 people would have said they do not watch TV. Neither the 119 nor the 238 gives us an idea of whether the "average adult American" watches TV a little or a lot.

By analogy, suppose your best friend tells you that he or she drank a six-pack of beer. Notice that your reaction

TABLE 11-2   **1998 GSS TVHOURS**
(Average Hours per Day Watching TV)

TVHOURS ("On the average day, about how many hours do you personally watch television?")

Response	Frequency	Percent	Cumulative Frequency	Cumulative Percent
0 hours	119	5.1	119	5.1
1 hour	499	21.4	618	26.5
2 hours	642	27.5	1,260	54.0
3 hours	399	17.1	1,659	71.1
4 hours	318	13.6	1,977	84.7
5 hours	157	6.7	2,134	91.4
6 hours	89	3.8	2,223	95.2
7 hours	18	.8	2,241	96.0
8 hours	47	2.0	2,288	98.0
9 hours	7	.3	2,295	98.3
10 hours	17	.7	2,312	99.0
11 hours	3	.1	2,315	99.1
12 hours	6	.3	2,321	99.4
13 hours	1	.0	2,322	99.4
14 hours	1	.0	2,323	99.4
15 hours	7	.3	2,330	99.7
16 hours	0	0	2,330	99.7
17 hours	0	0	2,330	99.7
18 hours	2	.1	2,332	99.8
19 hours	0	0	2,332	99.8
20 hours	4	.2	2,336	100.0
21 hours	1	.0	2,337	100.0

Note: Percentages based on 2,337 valid responses. A total of 495 respondents had invalid responses to this question ("Don't know"; "No answer"; "Not applicable").

Source: National Opinion Research Center, 1998. Used by permission.

to that statement would depend on whether the beer had been consumed in a month, a week, a day, or an hour. In the case of TV viewing, similarly, we need some basis for assessing the 119 people who do not view TV.

If you were to divide 119 by the 2,337 who gave some answer, you would get 5.1 percent, which appears in the table in the "percent" column. So we see that 5.1 percent, or roughly one U.S. adult in twenty, reports not viewing TV. Actually, this is referred to as the *valid percent* because it is the percentage of valid cases, excluding those who provided a "don't know" or other invalid response.

Sometimes, it's useful to get a sense of the "running tally" of your frequency-distribution data. The "cumulative frequency" column in this table tells you total frequency as you move down the various response options; by the time you reach the last option, you should reach your grand total, in this case 2,337. The "cumulative percent" column provides you with "running tally" information in percentage form; by the time you reach the last option, you have 100 percent of your cases accounted for. (Notice that you have two "100.0" values in this table—that's because of rounding error when you work with percentage values.)

Sometimes, it's easier to see a frequency distribution graphically, as in Figure 11-3. This graph is known as a *polygon.* The *y*-axis plots the frequencies with which values were reported, and the *x*-axis plots the different reported values, in this instance number of reported hours spent daily in viewing TV, from 0 to 21.

It is always advisable as a first step in summarizing a data set to derive a frequency distribution of each variable and a polygon graph of this frequency distribution. This way, you can assess the extent to which the distribution of your sample approximates a **normal curve.**

We were introduced to the logic of a normal curve in Chapter 7, where we discussed probability-based sampling. Over time, scientists have discovered that frequency distributions for a wide range of variables tend to take the shape of a normal curve.

As you may recall from Chapter 7, a normal, or bell-shaped curve tends to look like a bell: Its two halves are

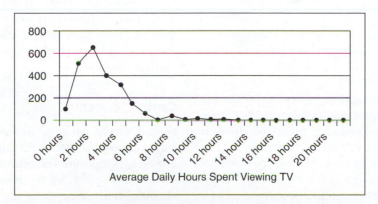

FIGURE 11-3   **Polygon of 1998 GSS TVHOURS**
Source: National Opinion Research Center, 1998. Used by permission.

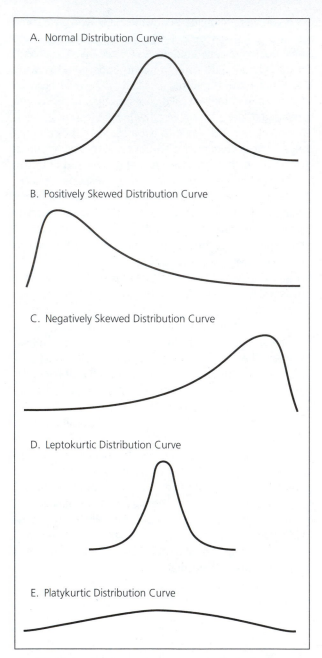

FIGURE 11-4 **Normal, Skewed, and Kurtic Distribution Curves**

shows a *positively skewed distribution,* one in which the most positive, or highest, values tend to appear with less frequency than would be the case with a normal distribution. In a positively skewed distribution, the curve has a long tail trailing to the right. The opposite is the case for a *negatively skewed distribution,* shown in Figure 11-4C. There are fewer negative, or low, values in the distribution, which produces a long tail trailing to the left. Most of the common statistical software packages can calculate a formula that provides a measure of the degree to which a frequency distribution is skewed. Let's return to Figure 11-3 in light of our discussion of the normal curve and skewness. It is apparent that the frequency distribution of TVHOURS in the 1998 GSS sample is positively skewed.

Another feature of a distribution curve is its **kurtosis,** the height of its middle "peak." A normal curve has a peak as high as 3 standard deviations are wide (we'll discuss standard deviations below, but you've already been introduced to their logic in Chapter 7, where we discussed the standard sampling error). It has a kurtosis of 3, in other words. Another name for this shape is *mesokurtic,* which means middle ("meso") peakness ("kurtic"). There are mathematical formulas for determining the kurtosis of a distribution. Generally, anything larger than 3 will have a rather tall and thin "peak" in the middle; this kind of distribution is known as *leptokurtic,* and an example is shown in Figure 11-4D. A kurtosis value less than 3 indicates fatter, flatter "peaks." Figure 11-4E shows one of these *platykurtic* distributions. (If we apply the kurtosis concept to geography, we might say that the mild, rolling hills of the Midwest would be platykurtic, in contrast to the leptokurtic quality of the Rocky Mountains!)

Why is it important to determine whether a frequency distribution approximates a normal curve? The most frequently employed family of inferential statistics—*parametric statistics*—assumes that the variables' distributions are normally distributed. If the departure is too great from a normal distribution, researchers need to shift to a different family of inferential statistics, known as *nonparametric statistics.* We'll discuss this issue a bit more in the next chapter.

Central Tendency

Beyond simply reporting frequencies, you will probably want to present your data in the form of summary averages, or measures of **central tendency.** Your options in this regard are the **mode** (the most frequent attribute, either grouped or ungrouped), the arithmetic **mean,** and the **median** (the middle attribute in the

symmetrically opposite each other, and the cases are distributed in known ways around the sample's central tendency. Figure 11-4A shows a normal distribution curve. The normal curve is a theoretical model only; in real life, sampled variables only approximate a normal curve.

There are several ways a distribution could depart from a normal curve. One of these is **skew.** Figure 11-4B

ranked distribution of observed attributes). Here's how the three averages would be calculated.

Suppose you're conducting an experiment that involves teenagers as participants. They range in age from 13 to 19, as indicated in the following frequency distribution table:

Age	f	Cumulative f
13	3	3
14	4	7
15	6	13
16	8	21
17	4	25
18	3	28
19	3	31

Now that you've seen the actual ages of the 31 participants, how old would you say they are in general, or on the average? Let's look at three different ways you might answer that question.

The easiest average to calculate is the *mode,* the most frequent value. As you can see, there were more 16-year-olds (8 of them) than any other age, so the modal age is 16.

Doubtless the most commonly calculated average is the *mean.* The mean score is derived by taking the sum of the scores in a distribution and dividing this value by the number of scores. For our example, this calculation could be accomplished in three steps: (1) multiply each age by the number of participants who have that age, (2) total the results of all those multiplications, and (3) divide that total by the number of participants. In Figure 11-5, we work through this calculation for you, producing the mean age score of 15.87.

The *median* represents the "middle" value: Half of the scores are above it, half below. When we are working with grouped data in which multiple participants share a common value, the median is simply the grouped score in which the middle score would fall. Based on the cumulative frequencies for our sample distribution of ages, we would say that the median age is 16 because our middle case (#16 in a sample of 31) would fall in the group whose value is 16.

When you are working with ungrouped data, the median is simply the middle score if the total number of scores is odd. When the total number of scores is even, you take the mean of the two middle scores, and this value serves as the median score. Figure 11-6 provides some examples of ungrouped data.

In the research literature, you will find both means and medians presented. Whenever means are presented, you should be aware that they are susceptible to extreme

$$M = \sum \frac{X}{n}$$ The mean is the sum (Σ) of scores (X) divided by the number of scores (n)

Step 1. Sum all of the age scores:

$3 \times 13 = 39$
$4 \times 14 = 56$
$6 \times 15 = 90$
$8 \times 16 = 128$
$4 \times 17 = 68$
$3 \times 18 = 54$
$3 \times 19 = 57$

$39 + 56 + 90 + 128 + 68 + 54 + 57 = 492$

Step 2. Determine the total number of scores:

$3 + 4 + 6 + 8 + 4 + 3 + 3 = 31$

Step 3. Divide the sum by the total number of scores:

$\frac{492}{31} = 15.87$

FIGURE 11-5   **Calculating a Mean Score: Sample Distribution of Ages**

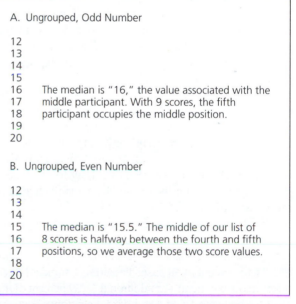

A. Ungrouped, Odd Number

12
13
14
15
16   The median is "16," the value associated with the
17   middle participant. With 9 scores, the fifth
18   participant occupies the middle position.
19
20

B. Ungrouped, Even Number

12
13
14
15   The median is "15.5." The middle of our list of
16   8 scores is halfway between the fourth and fifth
17   positions, so we average those two score values.
18
20

FIGURE 11-6   **Calculating a Median Score: Some Examples of Ungrouped Age Distributions**

values: a few very large or very small numbers. These are known as *outliers.* If a sample has outliers, a median should probably be reported.

When a frequency distribution is a normal curve, the mean, median, and mode are identical. When working with actual data sets, these three indicators of central tendency are often close but not identical to one another. That's because data sets at best approximate a normal distribution curve.

Dispersion

Averages offer readers the special advantage of reducing the raw data to the most manageable form: A single number (or attribute) can represent all the detailed data collected in regard to the variable. This advantage comes at a cost, of course, because the reader can't reconstruct the original data from an average. Summaries of the **dispersion** of responses can somewhat alleviate this disadvantage. Dispersion tells you something about the spread of score values from lowest to highest. The simplest measure of dispersion is the **range:** the distance separating the highest from the lowest value. Thus, besides reporting that our participants have a mean age of 15.87, we might also indicate that their ages ranged from 13 to 19.

There are many other measures of dispersion. One of these is the interquartile range, the range of scores for the middle 50 percent of participants. Let's suppose you wanted to use this measure of dispersion for a sample of scores reflecting speaking rate—that is, words uttered per minute. If the highest one-fourth had scores ranging from 320 to 350 and if the lowest one-fourth had scores ranging from 60 to 90, you could report that the interquartile range was 90–320.

A more sophisticated measure of dispersion is the **standard deviation.** This is probably the most frequently calculated measure of dispersion reported in communication research. The logic of this measure was discussed in Chapter 7 as the standard error of a sampling distribution. Figure 11-7 shows you how to calculate a standard deviation for the grouped age distribution data presented earlier.

The standard deviation is an important descriptor of dispersion. In a normal curve, 34.13 percent of all of the cases lie within 1 standard deviation above the mean, and 34.13 percent of all cases lie within 1 standard deviation below the mean. An additional 13.59 percent of the cases lie between 1 and 2 standard deviations above the mean, and an equivalent percentage of cases lie between 1 and 2 standard deviations below the mean. In the range 2–3 standard deviations above the mean, 2.14 percent of cases are located, and 2.14 percent of cases lie in the range 2–3 standard deviations below the mean.

Essentially, the standard deviation is an index of the amount of variability in a set of data. A higher standard deviation means that the data are more dispersed; a lower standard deviation means that they are more bunched together. Figure 11-8 illustrates the basic idea. In Figure 11-8A, we have represented the distribution of scores for an amateur golfer across many rounds of golf. Figure 11-8B provides the comparable information for a professional golfer. Notice that the professional golfer not only has a lower mean score (70) but is also more consistent—represented by the smaller standard deviation. The duffer, on the other hand, has a higher average but is also less consistent: sometimes doing much better, sometimes much worse.

The standard deviation also provides us with an additional tool of description: the **standard score.** Basically, a standard score tells us how many standard deviations a given score is above or below the mean of a distribution.

The mathematical formula for the standard deviation is as follows:

$$SD = \sqrt{\frac{\Sigma X^2 - (\Sigma X)^2/N}{N-1}}$$

where ΣX^2 = the sum of the squared score values
$(\Sigma X)^2$ = the square of the sum of all of the scores
N = the total number of scores used in the calculation

Step 1. Square all of the scores and add the squared values:

$$13^2 + 13^2 + 13^2 + 14^2 + \ldots + 19^2 + 19^2 + 19^2 = 7900$$

Step 2. Add up all of the scores:

13 + 13 + 13 + 14 + 14 + 14 + 14 + 15 + 15 + 15 + 15 + 15 + 15 + 16 + 16 + 16 + 16 + 16 + 16 + 16 + 16 + 17 + 17 + 17 + 17 + 18 + 18 + 18 + 19 + 19 + 19 = 492

Step 3. Square the sum derived in step 2 and divide by the number of total scores:

$$\frac{492 \cdot 492}{31} = \frac{242064}{31} = 7808.52$$

Step 4. Subtract the value derived in step 3 from the sum derived in step 1:

7900 − 7808.52 = 91.48

Step 5. Divide the value derived in step 4 by $(N-1)$:

$$\frac{91.48}{30} = 3.049$$

Step 6. Take the square root of the value derived in step 5. This is the standard deviation:

$$\sqrt{3.049} = 1.75$$

FIGURE 11-7 **Calculating a Standard Deviation: Sample Distribution of Ages**

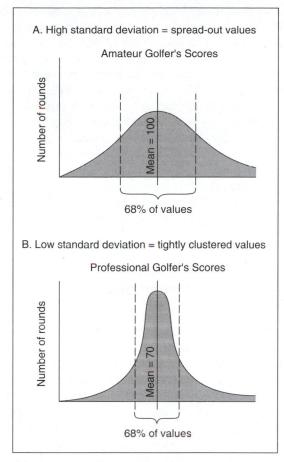

A. High standard deviation = spread-out values

Amateur Golfer's Scores

Number of rounds

Mean = 100

68% of values

B. Low standard deviation = tightly clustered values

Professional Golfer's Scores

Number of rounds

Mean = 70

68% of values

FIGURE 11-8 **High and Low Standard Deviations**

There are several types of standard scores, but probably the most frequently used in communication research is the *z-score*. If you calculate the mean of a set of *z*-scores, it equals zero.

Figure 11-9 demonstrates how to calculate the *z*-scores for a hypothetical set of data from five participants on the number of filled pauses they utter per minute of talk—that is, the number of times per minute they say "uh," "um," and so forth. Basically, you take a person's score, subtract the mean from it, and then divide this value by the standard deviation.

Why go to the trouble of calculating *z*-scores? First of all, a *z*-score gives us a handy summary of where a given participant's score is positioned in the data set—we can say, for example, that the score of the first participant in Figure 11-9 is 1 standard deviation below the sample's mean, whereas the score of the fifth participant is 1.38 standard deviations above the sample's mean.

Z-scores are also helpful when we have multiple indicators available for a given unit of analysis and wish

Suppose we had scores on the number of times a speaker uttered a filled pause ("uh," "um," and so forth) per minute of talk:

Participant #	Score
1	2
2	3
3	5
4	9
5	12

The formula for *z*-scores is as follows:

$$Z = \frac{(X - M)}{SD}, \text{ where}$$

X is a given score
M is the sample mean
SD is the sample's standard deviation

Step 1. Determine the sample mean:

$$M = \frac{(2 + 3 + 5 + 9 + 12)}{5} = \frac{31}{5} = 6.20$$

Step 2. Determine the standard deviation:

$$\Sigma X^2 = 4 + 9 + 25 + 81 + 124 = 263$$

$$\frac{(\Sigma X)^2}{N} = \frac{(2 + 3 + 5 + 9 + 12)^2}{5} = \frac{961}{5} = 192.2$$

$$SD = \sqrt{\frac{(263 - 192.2)}{4}} = \sqrt{17.7} = 4.21$$

Step 3. Derive the $(X - M)$ value for each score and divide each by the *SD*:

X	(X − M)	z
2	−4.2	−1.00
3	−3.2	−.76
4	−1.2	−.29
9	2.8	.67
12	5.8	1.38

FIGURE 11-9 **Calculating *Z*-Scores: An Example**

to compare them. The rub comes if those various indicators are calibrated differently. Suppose we had two measures of something, one a 5-point Likert item and another a 9-point semantic differential item. How can we compare these two items and use them together in understanding the phenomenon that they measure, since they aren't calibrated alike? It would be like comparing apples to oranges. A solution to this problem is to convert each score to its standardized form. We would calculate a standard score for the sample of Likert-type scores and a standard score for the sample of semantic differential scores. Then we would be in business to make a comparison between them.

Sometimes, z-scores are helpful even when the same measure is used. For example, suppose we were interested in rating how outgoing participants were in their nonverbal behaviors, on a 9-point rating scale from "not at all" to "very." We asked two judges to watch videotapes of participants' nonverbal behaviors during a conversation and then rate them. Suppose one rater is very conservative in what she judges to be outgoing—her ratings will be biased toward the lower end of the rating continuum. Suppose our second rater is very liberal in what he judges to be outgoing—his ratings will be biased toward the higher end of the rating continuum. How can the two raters' judgments possibly be compared? On the reasonable assumption that both judges engaged in a relative judgment task, judging each participant against other participants, we could convert both judges' scores to z-scores; then we'd be able to compare their judgments in evaluating participants. Each participant would be described by two scores: the z-score from rater 1 and the z-score from rater 2. If we wanted, we could take the mean between those two z-scores to derive an overall rating.

Level of Measurement and Descriptive Statistics

The preceding calculations of central tendency and dispersion are not appropriate for all levels of measurement used with variables. When you are using numbers at the nominal level, your index of central tendency should be the mode. No dispersion index is very meaningful with nominal-level data because your numbers do not even vary on a high-to-low continuum. With ordinal-level measures, you can use the mode or the median for your index of central tendency and the range or interquartile range as your index of dispersion. Interval- and ratio-level measures can use the mode, the median, or the mean. Although you could use the range or interquartile range as an index of dispersion, the standard deviation is the preferred dispersion index for interval- or ratio-level data.

The level of measurement of your numbers affects more than the kind of descriptive statistics that can be used. When numbers are interval or ratio in nature, then parametric inferential statistics can be used. However, when numbers are nominal or ordinal in nature, nonparametric inferential statistics are appropriate. This is a topic for Chapter 12.

Detail versus Manageability

In presenting data, you'll be constrained by two often conflicting goals. On the one hand, you should attempt to provide your reader with the fullest degree of detail regarding those data. On the other hand, the data should be presented in a manageable form. Because these two goals often directly counter each other, you'll find yourself continually seeking the best compromise between them. One useful solution is to report a given set of data in more than one form. In the case of age, for example, you might report all three measures of central tendency (mode, median, and mean) and all three measures of dispersion (range, interquartile range, and standard deviation).

As you can see from this introductory discussion of descriptive statistics, this seemingly simple matter can be rather complex. The lessons of this section, in any event, will be important as we move now to a consideration of subgroup comparisons.

SUBGROUP COMPARISONS

Often, it's appropriate to describe subsets of cases, participants, or respondents. Table 11-3, for example, presents 1998 GSS frequency data on hours of TV viewing per day for males and females separately. In some situations, the researcher presents subgroup comparisons purely for descriptive purposes. More often, the purpose of subgroup descriptions is comparative: Do males or females watch more TV per day? To make comparative statements, you probably need inferential statistics, which we address in the next chapter. For now, let's focus only on the descriptive goal of presenting subgroup data.

Notice that this table also reports values in parentheses after each frequency value is reported. These parenthetical numbers represent the percentages of column totals. Thus, for example, the modal value of 2 hours of viewing time was reported by 304 males, or 29.8 percent of all males included in the table. It would be meaningless to compare the male number of 304 with the 2-hour viewing number of 338 for females, because the numbers of males and females in the sample were not equal. We need to convert our numbers to percentages.

One of the chief bugaboos for new data analysts is deciding on the appropriate "direction of percentaging" for any given table. In Table 11-3, for example, we've divided the group of participants into two subgroups—men and women—and then described the behavior of each subgroup. That's the correct method for constructing this table.

But notice that we could—however inappropriately— construct the table differently. We could first divide the participants into different degrees of TV viewing and

TABLE 11-3   **1998 GSS TVHOURS by Sex of Viewer**

Reported Hours per Day	Sex of Viewer	
	Males	*Females*
0 hours	52 (5.1)	67 (5.1)
1 hour	212 (20.8)	287 (21.8)
2 hours	304 (29.8)	338 (25.6)
3 hours	173 (17.0)	226 (17.1)
4 hours	136 (13.3)	182 (13.8)
5 hours	61 (6.0)	96 (7.3)
6 hours	32 (3.1)	57 (4.3)
7 hours	10 (1.0)	8 (.6)
8 hours	18 (1.8)	29 (2.2)
9 hours	4 (.4)	3 (.2)
10 hours	8 (.8)	9 (.7)
11 hours	0 (0)	3 (.2)
12 hours	2 (.2)	4 (.3)
13 hours	0 (0)	1 (.1)
14 hours	0 (0)	1 (.1)
15 hours	2 (.2)	5 (.4)
16 hours	0 (0)	0 (0)
17 hours	0 (0)	0 (0)
18 hours	2 (.2)	0 (0)
19 hours	0 (0)	0 (0)
20 hours	2 (.2)	2 (.2)
21 hours	1 (.1)	0 (0)

Note: Male subsample $n = 1,019$; female subsample $n = 1,318$. A total of 495 respondents had invalid responses ("Don't know"; "No answer"; "Not applicable"). Values in parentheses represent percentages of column totals—"percentage down."

Source: National Opinion Research Center, 1998. Used by permission.

then describe each of those subgroups in terms of the percentage of men and women in each. This method would make no sense, however.

In constructing and presenting Table 11-3, we have used a convention called *percentage down.* This term means that you can add the percentages down each column to total 100 percent (within rounding error). You read this form of table across a row. For the row labeled "0 hours," what percentage of the men do not report watching any TV? What percentage of the women report no TV viewing?

The direction of percentaging in tables is arbitrary, and some researchers prefer to percentage across. They would organize Table 11-3 so that "men" and "women" were shown on the left side of the table, identifying the two rows, and viewing hours (0, 1, 2, and so forth) would appear at the top to identify the columns. The actual numbers in the table would be moved around accordingly, and each *row* of percentages would total 100 per-

cent. In that case, you would read the table down a column, still asking what percentage of men and women watch TV with specified frequencies. The logic and the conclusion would be the same in either case; only the form would differ.

Therefore, in reading a table that someone else has constructed, you need to find out in which direction it has been percentaged. Usually, this will be labeled or be clear from the logic of the variables being analyzed. As a last resort, however, you should add the percentages in each column and each row. If each of the columns totals 100 percent, the table has been percentaged down. If the rows total 100 percent each, the table has been percentaged across. The rule, then, is as follows:

1. If the table is percentaged down, read across.
2. If the table is percentaged across, read down.

Subgroup comparisons typically have an explanatory causal purpose. We would be framing sex of viewer as the independent variable, asking whether males and females differ in their TV viewing practices. Hours of daily TV viewing is thus framed as the dependent variable. In this example, it would make no sense to frame TV viewing as the independent variable with sex as the dependent variable—watching TV cannot change a participant's sex.

Tables such as 11-3 are commonly called **contingency tables:** Values of the dependent variable, reported as frequencies, are contingent on values of the independent variable. Although contingency tables are common in quantitative communication research, their format has never been standardized. As a result, you'll find a variety of formats in research literature. As long as a table is easy to read and interpret, there's probably no reason to strive for standardization. The key is making certain that you know how percentaging was done.

Our subgroup comparison of TVHOURS by sex of viewer has been presented in terms of frequencies. However, because viewing hours is technically a ratio-level variable (a viewer could report 0 hours of viewing), we could just as well use other descriptive statistics to summarize each subgroup—in particular, the mean and the standard deviation. Based on the results of the 1998 GSS as reported in Table 11-3, we would probably conclude that males and females watch a comparable number of hours of TV daily. The mean number of viewing hours for males is 2.81 (with a standard deviation of 2.26 hours), compared to the mean of 2.90 hours (with a standard deviation of 2.24 hours) for females. These values are not identical, but appropriate inferential statistics (discussed in the next chapter) indicate that the difference between these values is insignificant.

This chapter has provided us with the basics of quantitative data analysis—how to produce quantified data organized into case X variable matrix form suitable for computer analysis using statistical software packages, and how to derive basic descriptive summaries of variables. In the next chapter, we address the second part of quantitative data analysis—the use of inferential statistics to study differences and relationships among variables.

Main Points

- The quantification of data is necessary when statistical analyses are desired.

- The observations describing each unit of analysis must be transformed into standardized, numerical codes for retrieval and manipulation by computer.

- A given variable is assigned a specific identifier in the data file, such as an abbreviated name.

- The attributes of a given variable are represented by numerical codes.

- A codebook is the document that describes the identifiers assigned to different variables and the codes assigned to represent different attributes.

- Possible-code cleaning refers to the process of checking to see that only those codes assigned to particular attributes—possible codes—appear in the data files. This process guards against one class of data-processing error.

- Contingency cleaning is the process of checking to see that only those cases that *should* have data on a particular variable do in fact have such data. This process guards against another class of data-processing error.

- The full, original data collected with regard to a single variable are, in that form, usually impossible to interpret. Data reduction is the process of summarizing the original data to make them more manageable, all the while maintaining as much of the original detail as possible.

- Descriptive statistics provide a summary of a variable.

- A frequency distribution shows the number of cases having each of the attributes of a given variable.

- Frequency distributions should approximate a normal curve; to the extent that they depart from a normal curve, they are positively or negatively skewed, and/or have kurtosis values that depart from 3.

- Grouped data are created through the combination of attributes of a variable.

- Measures of central tendency (the mean, median, and mode) reduce data to an easily manageable form, but they do not convey the detail of the original data.

- Measures of dispersion (range, interquartile range, and standard deviation) give a summary indication of the distribution of cases around an average value.

- The most frequently reported indicator of dispersion is the standard deviation. The standard deviation fits a normal curve in known ways.

- The standard deviation and the mean allow us to derive standard scores, useful when we have multiple measures of a variable that are not calibrated alike or different applications of a single measure.

- Subgroup comparisons involve (1) dividing cases into subgroups in terms of their attributes on some independent variable, (2) describing each subgroup in terms of some dependent variable, and (3) comparing the dependent-variable descriptions of the subgroups.

- To interpret subgroup percentage tables properly, (1) "percentage down" and "read across" or (2) "percentage across" and "read down" in making subgroup comparisons.

Key Terms

codebook	mode
cleaning data	mean
descriptive statistics	median
frequency distribution	dispersion
normal curve	range
skew	standard deviation
kurtosis	standard score
central tendency	contingency tables

Review Questions and Exercises

1. Suppose you have the following questionnaire instrument. Develop a codebook for the instrument that

would enable you to produce a quantitative data file appropriate for statistical analysis on the computer:

1. Sex: M   F

2. Age: _____ years

3. Formal education completed:
   Less than 12 years
   High school completed
   B.A./B.S. degree earned
   Graduate degree earned

4. How often do you use e-mail?
   Several times a day
   About once a day
   A couple of times a week
   Once a week
   A couple of times a month
   Once a month
   Less than once a month

5. What do you use e-mail for? List in the space below all of the ways you use e-mail: [Let's suppose your data indicated the following categories of response: "for school-related purposes," "for work-related purposes," "to communicate with family," "to communicate with friends," and "other uses."]

6. What type of computer do you own?
   I don't own a computer
   An IBM-compatible PC
   An IBM-compatible notebook
   A Macintosh desk computer
   A Mac notebook
   Other (specify: _____)

2. Go to the web site of the National Communication Association (www.natcom.org). Hit the "Research" button to access the 1998 Roper–Starch national probability-based interview survey on "How Americans Communicate." Locate one variable of interest in the survey results. Gather appropriate descriptive statistics for central tendency and dispersion on the variable you have selected.

3. Suppose that you were interested in studying the narrative stories of organizational employees as an indicator of organizational loyalty. You tape-record employees telling stories about work in the organization and then ask two judges to evaluate the loyalty evidenced in each story on a 7-point scale, where "1" indicates "betrayal" and "7" indicates "loyalty." Your coders base their ratings on such things as inclusive language (e.g., "we") and the extent to which the organization is portrayed in a positive light. Here are the results from your two judges:

Judge 1	Judge 2
2	5
1	3
5	7
3	4
4	6
3	5
2	4
4	6
3	5
1	3

After examining these two sets of ratings for ten stories, you see a definite difference in how the two judges appear to be executing their judgments: The evaluations from Judge 2 are consistently higher. You decide that the best way to proceed is to calculate z-scores separately for each judge and then take the mean of the two judges' z-scores as a way to determine the loyalty index of each story. How would you do that?

4. Suppose that you were interested in studying portrayals of the family on prime-time TV. You conduct a content analysis and produce the following data— the frequencies of various family forms broken out by type of TV program (sitcom versus drama):

	Sitcom	Drama
Nuclear family	24	15
Single parent (mother)	15	14
Single parent (father)	18	20
Stepfamily	10	16

Suppose that the research question you were answering with your data was this: "Does the portrayal of the family differ depending on the type of program?" How will you percentage this table in order to provide the best answer—by row or by column?

5. Suppose that you have data on communication satisfaction with romantic partner, which you have collected through a questionnaire Likert-type 1–5 rating scale, with "5" indicating high satisfaction and "1" indicating low satisfaction. Here is a distribution of your data:

Rating	f
1	3
2	5
3	7
4	20
5	15

Describe the central tendency of this data set, reporting the mode, the median, and the mean. Describe the dispersion of this data set, using the range and the standard deviation.

Continuity Project

Suppose that you were interested in the portrayal of occupations of men and women on prime-time TV on the major broadcast networks (ABC, CBS, Fox, NBC). In particular, you are interested in whether men are shown in stereotypical "male occupations" (e.g., business executive, construction worker) and women are shown in stereotypical "female occupations" (e.g., secretary, homemaker). Watch a sample of TV programs, and keep track of the frequencies with which men and women are shown in stereotypical gendered occupations or in occupations that are nonstereotypical (e.g., a male homemaker or a female construction worker). Derive appropriate descriptive statistics for your data set.

Additional Readings

Babbie, E., Halley, F., & Zaino, J. (2000). *Adventures in social research.* Newbury Park, CA: Pine Forge. This book introduces you to the analysis of social research data through SPSS for Windows.

Weisberg, H. F. (1992). *Central tendency and variability.* Newbury Park, CA: Sage. Provides a more in-depth examination of levels of measurement and measures of central tendency.

Williams, F. (1992). *Reasoning with statistics: How to read quantitative research* (4th ed.). New York: Holt, Rinehart & Winston. A very user-friendly introduction to statistics, both descriptive and inferential.

Ziesel, H. (1957). *Say it with figures.* New York: Harper & Row. An excellent discussion of table construction and other elementary analyses. Though many years old, this is still perhaps the best available presentation of that specific topic. It is eminently readable and understandable and has many concrete examples.

InfoTrac College Edition
http://www.infotrac-college.com/
wadsworth/access.html

Access the latest news and journal articles with InfoTrac College Edition, an easy-to-use online database of reliable, full-length articles from hundreds of top academic journals. Conduct an electronic search using the following search terms:

- descriptive statistics
- mode
- median
- mean
- skew
- kurtosis
- normally distributed
- range
- standard deviation
- standard score (z-score)
- contingency table

CHAPTER 12

Inferential Statistics in Quantitative Data Analysis

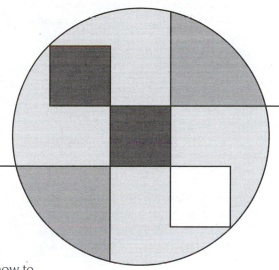

What You'll Learn in This Chapter

Here you'll learn about the logic of inferential statistics and how to calculate a few simple statistics frequently used in quantitative communication research.

INTRODUCTION

It has been our experience over the years that many students are intimidated by statistics. Sometimes, statistics makes them feel they're a few feathers short of a duck or missing a few buttons on their remote control.

Many people are intimidated by quantitative research because they feel uncomfortable with mathematics and statistics. Indeed, many research reports are filled with unspecified computations. The role of statistics in quantitative communication research is quite important, but it's equally important that you see this role in its proper perspective.

Quantitative communication research is first and foremost a logical rather than a mathematical operation. Mathematics is merely a convenient and efficient language for accomplishing the logical operations inherent in good data analysis. Statistics is the applied branch of mathematics especially appropriate to a variety of research analyses.

In this chapter, we'll be looking at **inferential statistics.** In the last chapter, we examined descriptive statistics, useful in providing a numerical summary of data with respect to a given variable. However, researchers are rarely interested only in summarizing their sample with respect to each variable considered separately. In addition, quantitative researchers are interested in how variables relate to one another; thus, they are interested in examining the patterning of at least two variables at a time. Further, quantitative researchers are usually interested in making claims of difference or relationship beyond the immediate sample included in their study—they seek to make broader claims of how the variables under study function. Inferential statistics assist you in drawing conclusions about a population from the study of a sample drawn from it.

Our primary goals in this chapter are to help you understand the logic of inferential statistics and to teach you how to calculate a few basic inferential statistics. Although computerized statistical packages such as SPSS can perform these and many other statistical tests, we think it's helpful for you to get some "hands-on" experience with a few simple statistics.

THE LOGIC OF INFERENTIAL STATISTICS

Many, if not most, quantitative communication research projects involve the examination of data collected from a sample drawn from a larger population. A sample of people may be interviewed in a survey, or a sample of TV programs may be coded and analyzed. Researchers seldom if ever study samples just to describe the samples per se; in most instances, their ultimate purpose is to make assertions about the larger population from which the sample has been selected. Frequently, then, you'll wish to interpret your sample findings as the basis for *inferences* about some population.

This section will examine the logical basis for such inferences. We'll begin by establishing the link between inferential statistics and a topic you have already studied—probability sampling.

The Link Between Probability Sampling and Inferential Statistics

Because communication researchers are usually interested in understanding the pattern between two or more variables, you might wonder why we are starting with the discussion of single variables. We want to build a conceptual bridge back to Chapter 7, where we discussed probability-based sampling, because the logic of statistical inference is the same as the one we discussed in that chapter.

Chapter 11 dealt with methods of summarizing data through descriptive statistics. Each summary measure was intended as a method of describing the sample studied. Now we'll use such measures to make broader assertions about the population. This section uses as its example one possible summary measure: percentages. But the logic of this section applies to all summary measures, including the mean and the median.

If 50 percent of a sample of people say they've had colds during the past year, 50 percent is also our best estimate of the proportion of colds in the total population from which the sample was drawn. (This estimate assumes a simple random sample, of course.) However, it's rather unlikely that *precisely* 50 percent of the population have had colds during the year. Yet if a rigorous sampling design for random selection has been followed, we will be able to estimate the expected range of error when the sample finding is applied to the population.

Chapter 7, on sampling theory, covered the procedures for making such estimates, so we'll only review them here. In the case of a percentage, the quantity

$$\sqrt{\frac{p \times q}{n}}$$

where p is a percentage, q equals $(1 - p)$, and n is the sample size, is called the **standard error.** As noted in Chapter 7, this quantity is very important in the estimation of sampling error. We may be 68-percent confident that the population figure falls within plus or minus one standard error of the sample figure, we may be 95-percent confident that it falls within plus or minus two standard errors, and we may be 99.9-percent confident that it falls within plus or minus three standard errors.

Any statement of sampling error, then, must contain two essential components: the *confidence level* and the *confidence interval*. If 50 percent of a sample of 1,600 people say they've had colds during the year, we might say we're 95-percent confident that the population figure is between 47.5 percent and 52.5 percent.

Recognize in this example that we've moved beyond simply describing the sample into the realm of making estimates (inferences) about the larger population. In doing so, we must take care in several ways.

First, the sample must be drawn from the population about which inferences are being made. A sample taken from a telephone directory cannot legitimately be the basis for statistical inferences about the population of a city.

Second, the inferential statistics assume simple random sampling, which is often not the case in research. The statistics assume sampling with replacement, which is almost never done—but this is probably not a serious problem. Although systematic sampling is used more frequently than random sampling, it, too, probably presents no serious problem if done correctly. Stratified sampling, because it improves representativeness, clearly presents no problem. Cluster sampling does present a problem, however, as the estimates of sampling error may be too small. Quite clearly, street-corner sampling does not warrant the use of inferential statistics. This standard error sampling technique also assumes a 100-percent completion rate. This problem increases in seriousness as the completion rate decreases.

Third, inferential statistics are addressed to sampling error only, not **nonsampling errors.** Thus, although we might state with 95-percent confidence that between 47.5 and 52.5 percent of the population would *report* having colds during the previous year, we couldn't so confidently guess the percentage who had actually *had* them. Because nonsampling errors are probably larger than sampling errors in a respectable sample design, we need to be especially cautious in generalizing from our sample findings to the population.

Tests of Statistical Significance

There is no scientific answer to the question of whether a given association between two variables is significant, meaning strong, important, interesting, or worth reporting. Perhaps the ultimate test of significance rests with your ability to persuade your audience (present and future) of the association's significance. At the same time,

tests of statistical significance can assist you in arguing that a given association is not a fluke finding.

Although **tests of statistical significance** are widely reported in communication research literature, the logic underlying them is rather subtle and often misunderstood. Tests of significance are based on the logic of probability sampling, which we have just been reviewing.

Recall that a sample statistic normally provides the best single estimate of the corresponding population parameter but that the statistic and the parameter seldom correspond precisely. Thus, we report the probability that the parameter falls within a certain range (confidence interval). The degree of uncertainty within that range is due to normal sampling error. The corollary of such a statement is, of course, that it is *improbable* that the parameter would fall outside the specified range only as a result of sampling error. Thus, if we estimate that a parameter (99.9-percent confidence) lies between 45 percent and 55 percent, we say by implication that it is *extremely improbable* that the parameter is actually, say, 90 percent if our only error of estimation is due to normal sampling. This is the basic logic behind all tests of significance.

The Logic of Statistical Significance

We think we can illustrate this logic of statistical significance best in a series of diagrams representing the selection of samples from a population. Here are the elements in the logic we'll illustrate:

1. Assumptions regarding the independence of two variables in the population study
2. Assumptions regarding the representativeness of samples selected through conventional probability sampling procedures
3. The observed joint distribution of sample elements in terms of the two variables

Figure 12-1 represents a hypothetical population of 256 people; half are women, and half are men. The diagram also indicates how comfortable each person feels about making purchases over the Internet.

The question we'll be investigating is whether there is any relationship between sex and feelings of comfort in using the Internet for making purchases. More specifically, we'll see if women are more likely to feel comfortable than men. Take a moment to look at Figure 12-1 and see what the answer to this question is.

The illustration in the figure indicates there is no relationship between sex and comfort using the Internet for making purchases. Exactly half of each group feels comfortable, and half feels uncomfortable. Knowing a person's sex would not reduce the errors we'd make in

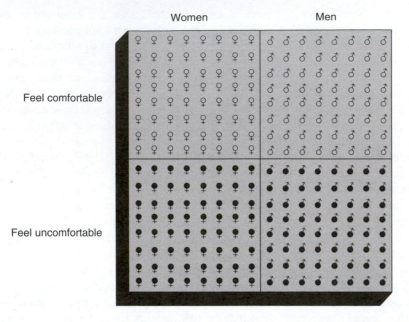

FIGURE 12-1 **A Hypothetical Population of Women and Men Who Feel Comfortable Using the Internet for Making Purchases**

guessing his or her comfort level. The table at the bottom of Figure 12-1 provides a tabular view of what you can observe in the graphic diagram.

Figure 12-2 represents the selection of a one-fourth sample from the hypothetical population. In terms of the graphic illustration, a "square" selection from the center of the population provides a representative sample. Notice that our sample contains 16 of each type of person: Half are men, and half are women. Half of each sex feels comfortable using the Internet for purchasing items, and the other half feels uncomfortable.

The sample selected in Figure 12-2 would allow us to draw accurate conclusions about the relationship between sex and comfort in using the Internet for purchasing in the larger population. Following the sampling logic we saw in Chapter 7, we'd note there was no relationship between sex and comfort in the sample; thus, we'd

conclude there was similarly no relationship in the larger population—since we've presumably selected a sample in accord with the conventional rules of probability-based sampling.

Of course, real-life samples are seldom such perfect reflections of the populations from which they're drawn. It would not be unusual for us to have selected, say, one or two extra men who felt uncomfortable using the Internet for purchasing goods and a couple of extra women who felt comfortable using it—even if there was no relationship between the two variables in the population. Such minor variations are part and parcel of probability sampling, as we saw in Chapter 7.

Figure 12-3, however, represents a sample that falls far short of the mark in reflecting the larger population. Notice it has selected far too many comfortable women and too many uncomfortable men. As the table shows,

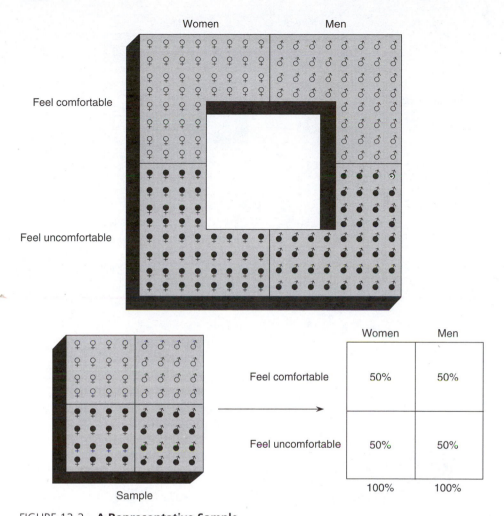

FIGURE 12-2 **A Representative Sample**

three-fourths of the women in the sample feel comfortable using the Internet for making purchases, but only one-fourth of the men feel such comfort. If we had selected this sample from a population in which the two variables were unrelated to each other, we'd be sorely misled by the analysis of our sample.

As you'll recall, it's unlikely that a properly drawn probability sample would ever be as inaccurate as the one shown in Figure 12-3. In fact, if we had actually selected a sample that gave us the results this one does, we'd look for a different explanation. Figure 12-4 illustrates.

Notice that the sample selected in Figure 12-4 also shows a strong relationship between sex and comfort level. However, the reason is quite different this time. We've selected a perfectly representative sample, but we see that there is actually a strong relationship between the two variables in the population at large. In this latest

figure, women are more likely than men to feel comfortable using the Internet: That's the case in the population, and the sample reflects it.

In practice, of course, we never know what's so for the total population; that's why we select samples. So if we selected a sample and found the strong relationship presented in Figures 12-3 and 12-4, we'd need to decide whether that finding accurately reflected the population or was simply a product of sampling error.

The fundamental logic of tests of statistical significance, then, is this: Faced with any discrepancy between the assumed independence of variables in a population and the observed distribution of sample elements, we may explain that discrepancy in either of two ways: (1) we may attribute it to an unrepresentative sample, or (2) we may reject the assumption of independence. The logic and statistics associated with probability sampling

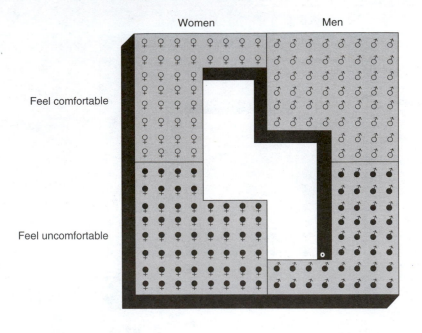

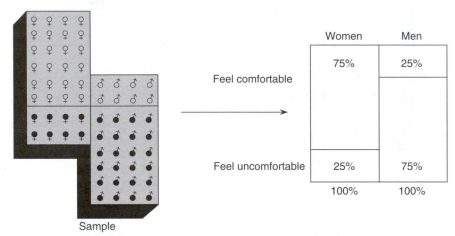

FIGURE 12-3 **An Unrepresentative Sample**

methods offer guidance about the varying probabilities of varying degrees of unrepresentativeness (expressed as sampling error). Most simply put, there is a *high* probability of a *small* degree of unrepresentativeness and a *low* probability of a *large* degree of unrepresentativeness.

The **statistical significance** of a relationship observed in a set of sample data, then, is always expressed in terms of probabilities. Significance at the .05 level (*p* < .05) simply means that the probability of a relationship as strong as the observed one being attributable to sampling error alone is no more than 5 in 100. Put somewhat differently, if two variables are independent of each other in the population, and if 100 probability samples were selected from that population, no more than 5 of those samples should provide through chance alone a relationship as strong as the one that has been observed.

There is, then, a corollary to confidence intervals in tests of significance, which represents the probability of the measured associations being due *only* to *sampling error*. This is called the **level of significance.** Like confidence intervals, levels of significance are derived from a logical model in which several samples are drawn from a given population. In the present case, we assume that there is no association between the variables in the population and then ask what proportion of the samples drawn from that population would produce associations

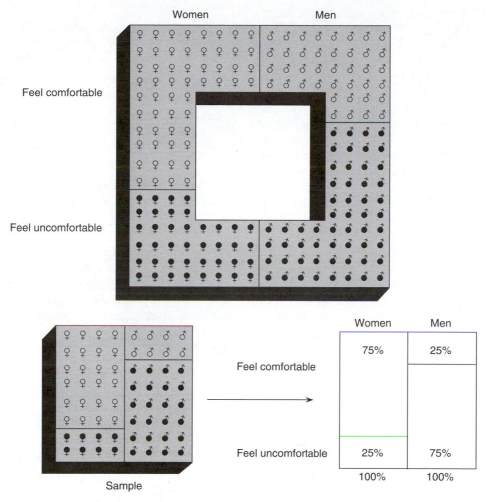

FIGURE 12-4   **A Representative Sample from a Population in Which the Variables Are Related**

at least as great as those measured in the empirical data. Three levels of significance are frequently used in research reports: .05, .01, and .001. These mean, respectively, that the chances of obtaining the measured association as a result of sampling error are $^5/_{100}$, $^1/_{100}$, and $^1/_{1,000}$.

Researchers who use tests of significance normally follow one of two patterns. Some specify in advance the level of significance they will regard as sufficient. If any measured association is statistically significant at that level, they will regard it as representing a genuine association between the two variables. In other words, they're willing to discount the possibility of its resulting from sampling error only.

Other researchers prefer to report the specific level of significance for each association, disregarding the con-

ventions of .05, .01, and .001. Rather than reporting that a given association is significant at the .05 level, they might report significance at the .023 level, indicating the chances of its having resulted from sampling error as 23 out of 1,000.

Type I and Type II Statistical Decision Errors

Now that we've captured the logic of statistical inference by a detailed example of sex and comfort level in using the Internet for making purchases, let's move the discussion to a more abstract level.

The assumption that the variables are independent of each other in the population—represented in our example by a 50–50 split for each sex in their comfort level in using the Internet—is known as the **null hypothesis** (and is usually symbolized as H_0). By contrast, the researcher's prediction—in our example the expectation that women would feel greater comfort than men—is known as the *research hypothesis* (and is usually symbolized as H_1). We introduced these concepts in Chapter 4.

All statistical tests have a presumption in favor of the null hypothesis. Think of the U.S. court system, with its presumption of defendant innocence until the burden of proof is met to demonstrate guilt. The evidence must overcome the presumption for a verdict of guilty to be rendered. In the "court system" of quantitative research, the presumption of statistics is that two variables are independent of each other unless there is reasonable evidence to suggest that the variables are actually related in the population. The "reasonable evidence" demanded by statistical tests is achieving the acceptable level of significance, usually set at .05 in most quantitative communication research. If this level of statistical significance is found in a statistical test applied to the sample's data, the null hypothesis is said to be *rejected* in favor of the research hypothesis. If, on the other hand, the significance level of .05 is not achieved, the statistic concludes that the null hypothesis is *not rejected.*

The level of significance established at the outset of a study—usually .05—is a sizable hurdle for any set of data to overcome. Why not loosen the standard a bit and establish the significance level at, say, .10 or even .20? With less stringent standards for the level of significance, it would be easier for a researcher to reject the null hypothesis in favor of his or her research hypothesis. But there are problems with this solution.

The level of significance that you establish as your standard for rejecting the null hypothesis is known by several names—the alpha level (symbolized α) and the *p* value are two you will frequently encounter in the communication research literature. It's also known as the Type I error level. To label something as a "I" implies that there is a "II" lurking out there somewhere, and this is certainly the case when it comes to statistical decision making.

Figure 12-5 presents a statistical decision table of the two kinds of errors that are possible—**Type I errors** and **Type II errors.** The two columns in the decision table capture the "true state of affairs" for the population—unknown to mere mortals like us, because we don't work with entire populations, just samples drawn from those populations. However, if we were omniscient, we would know whether two variables are independent (null hypothesis is true) or related (null hypothesis is false) in the population.

Because we're not omniscient, we can only make a guess about the population based on our study's sample.

FIGURE 12-5 **Type I and Type II Errors in Statistical Decision Making**

The decision we reach in a given study—either to reject the null hypothesis or not to reject the null hypothesis—could implicate us in two kinds of errors. If the true state of affairs in the population is that the null hypothesis is true—the two variables are independent of each other—yet we conclude that they are related in our decision to reject the null hypothesis, we have committed a Type I error, or an alpha (α) error. The standard you set for your level of significance to achieve is your protection against making a Type I error. The more stringent your standard for significance (.001, for example, is more stringent than .01, which in turn is more stringent than the commonly accepted standard of .05), the greater your protection from Type I errors. Well, that's easy enough.

The rub comes in the understanding that Type I and Type II errors are interrelated: The more you protect yourself against committing a Type I error, the greater your likelihood of committing a Type II error, all other things being equal. What's a Type II error, anyway? As Figure 12-5 suggests, you make a Type II error when the true state of affairs in the population is that the two variables are related (i.e., the null hypothesis is false), yet you fail to reject the null hypothesis. Anytime you become more stringent in establishing the threshold for your level of significance, you make it more difficult for your evidence to meet the burden of proof needed to reject the null hypothesis. Think of the standard you set for your level of significance as the height you place your bar in the high jump. The higher the "bar" (the more stringent your established level of significance), the more powerful your "jumper" (the evidence of your data) needs to be to overcome it.

Precautions against committing a Type II error (also known as a beta [β] error), apart from lowering the threshold for your level of significance, are too complicated to discuss here. In general, you want your statistical test to be as powerful as it can possibly be to find a relationship between variables if one is there to be found. **Statistical power** refers to the likelihood of rejecting the null hypothesis when it is false. We'll return to statistical power in the next section, but in general, the larger your sample size, the greater your statistical power and the less your likelihood of committing a Type II error.

The goal of statistical decision making is to end up with the "happy faces" in the decision table shown in Figure 12-5: to decide to reject the null hypothesis when it is false and to decide not to reject the null hypothesis when it is true. Of course, you never know in a given study whether you've committed a Type I or Type II error. All you can do is to take precautionary measures.

If you make a Type I error and falsely conclude that two variables are related when in fact they are not, your finding will not stand much chance of gaining replication in subsequent research—conducted by yourself or by others. If you make a Type II error, subsequent researchers are likely to find a statistically significant relationship between the variables, whereas you did not.

THE PROCESS OF MAKING A STATISTICAL DECISION

The process of making a statistical decision is a process that involves five steps. We'll discuss each one in turn, starting with the step we've already discussed—establishing your Type I and Type II error risks.

Step 1: Establishing Type I and Type II Error Risk Levels

Before you begin to collect your data, you need to decide your risk levels for Type I and Type II errors.

Usually, researchers adopt the conventional .05 level as the threshold for rejecting the null hypothesis. If your observed findings could be the result of chance no more than 5 times out of 100, you will reject the null hypothesis. This means that you are running a 5-percent risk that you are making a Type I error. The implication of this risk factor is that about 1 in 20 studies where the null has been rejected have committed a Type I error. Unfortunately, you don't know which study this is!

Sometimes, researchers adopt a more conservative alpha level than .05—for example, .01 or even .001. One circumstance in which they take this action is when they are making several statistical comparisons to test the same research hypothesis. For example, suppose you had three experimental groups and wanted to know if they were different on the dependent variable. If you answered this question by using three statistical tests (com-

paring groups 1 and 2, groups 2 and 3, and groups 1 and 3), you would have an inflated alpha error. In fact, your *familywise error* would be approximately .15 (.05 + .05 + .05). To correct this problem, you would adjust your alpha threshold at the outset by dividing .05 by the number of statistical tests you would be using. In this case, the adjusted alpha level you would establish would be $.05/3$, or .02. You would not reject the null hypothesis unless you achieved a level of statistical significance of .02 or less with your statistical tests. (Actually, in this example of a three-group comparison, you would probably use one statistical test first: a one-way analysis of variance, or one-way ANOVA as it is commonly called.)

Establishing your Type II error risk is a more complicated enterprise and well beyond the scope of this book. You could reduce your risk of a Type II error by opting for a less conservative alpha level (say, .10), but this would increase your risk of a Type I error, as we noted above. Generally, if it comes to a choice between making a Type I error and a Type II error, most researchers would rather make a Type II error than a Type I error. So using a less conservative alpha level probably isn't the best solution when trying to lower your Type II error risk.

The best action you can take to reduce your Type II error risk is to have sufficiently high statistical power. The statistical power of a test is found by subtracting the likelihood of a beta error from one: $1 - \beta$. Jacob Cohen (1988) recommends that researchers work with statistical powers equal to .80 (with a range of .00 to 1.00).

There are three ways to increase the power of your statistical test (Levy & Steelman, 1996). First, the family of parametric statistics generally has greater statistical power than the family of nonparametric statistics. This means that whenever you have the choice, you should use interval-level or ratio-level measures, because parametric statistical tests are inappropriate with nominal or ordinal levels of measurement.

Second, statistics are generally more powerful when they are testing directional as opposed to nondirectional hypotheses (remember our discussion of this in Chapter 4). The reason is that directional research hypotheses enable you to use what are called one-tailed statistical tests rather than two-tailed tests. Thus, when it is warranted, you should always work with directional hypotheses rather than nondirectional ones.

Third, you can increase your sample size. By how much? This is a complicated question, and it depends on several factors, the most important of which is a factor over which you have no control: the **effect size,** or the degree to which your variables are interdependent in the population. Two variables could be related to each other beyond chance levels, but the magnitude of that relationship might not be large. Beginning students sometimes confuse the statistical significance level with the effect size, yet the two concepts are distinct. Two variables can be related at the .05 level of significance or at the .001 level of significance; however, significance at the .001 level doesn't necessarily mean a "bigger" or "stronger" relationship between the two variables. Effect size refers to the strength of the interdependency between variables.

Earlier in the book, we shared the thoughts of several scholars who argue that there are persistent, but small, differences between males and females on a variety of communication-related behaviors. These scholars would probably say that the sex variable has a small effect size on communication behavior. How large do you think the effect size is between studying for an exam and the grade earned on the exam? If you believe that the effect size is large, you'll probably be a person who spends many hours preparing for each of your midterm and final exams! If, on the other hand, you believe that the effect size is small, you will probably be a person who invests some—but not a lot—of time in studying for your exams. Before researchers begin to collect data, they make an estimate about the effect size of the variables under study. The estimate of effect size affects your decision about sample size.

Jacob Cohen (1988) distinguishes three types of effect sizes: small, medium, and large. In his 1992 "power primer" article, Cohen estimates that for a recommended level of statistical power of .80 and the .05 level of significance for a nondirectional hypothesis, the necessary sample sizes for small, medium, and large effects are, respectively, 393, 64, and 26. The differences in these sample sizes are dramatic evidence of the fact that it is more difficult to study small-effect relationships between variables than it is to study large-effect relationships between variables. Cohen's (1988) classic book on statistical power provides page after page of tables of recommended sample sizes for various statistical tests and assumptions.

After you've made basic decisions about your error risk levels, and thus your desired sample size, you can go ahead and gather your data and then convert it to a form appropriate for statistical analysis. But what statistics are appropriate for your analysis?

Step 2: Selecting the Appropriate Statistical Test

You need several statistics courses to have a comprehensive understanding of all the available statistical tests.

Obviously, in this brief section, we can't possibly give you that level of mastery. What we can do is provide you with a general sense of the "map of the territory."

Parametric and Nonparametric Families of Statistics

Generally speaking, statistical tests belong to one of two families: the family of **parametric statistics** and the family of **nonparametric statistics.** Parametric statistics make more assumptions about the data:

- The assumption that the sample was selected using probability-based sampling methods. Implicated in this assumption is the independence of observations—the selection of any one case for inclusion in the sample won't bias the chances of any other case being included.
- The assumption that the observations were drawn from normally distributed populations—in other words, populations that fit a normal curve.
- The assumption that the groups being compared reflect populations with the same variance or variation.
- The assumption that dependent variables are measured with interval-level or ratio-level measures.

When a researcher's data violate these assumptions, he or she can use the alternative family of statistical tests known as nonparametric statistics. Sometimes, researchers employ parametric statistical tests even though they have not met the first three assumptions. Interpretations should always be more cautious when the assumptions of a statistical test have been violated in some way.

Nonparametric tests generally make fewer assumptions (Siegel & Castellan, 1988). Although nonparametric statistics usually presume independence of observations, they do not presume a normally distributed curve with equal variances for the variables under study. Nonparametric tests are also appropriate when the dependent variable is measured at the nominal or ordinal level of measurement.

Statistics of Difference and Statistics of Association

Both parametric and nonparametric statistical families have statistics designed to gauge the extent to which two (or more) variables are associated with, or related to, one another. These are known as statistics of association. For example, if you hypothesized that study time is positively correlated with exam grade, you would be positing an association between two variables—amount of study and exam grade. A statistic of association would be appropriate—probably the Pearson correlation in this instance.

Alternatively, you could hypothesize that persons who study a lot (high preparers) will earn higher exam grades than persons who study less (low preparers). You could divide your sample into two groups divided at the median (known as a *median split procedure*)—high versus low preparers—and then examine whether these two groups differed, on average, in their earned exam scores. When the hypothesis is worded this way—in terms of difference—it requires statistics of difference. (In this instance, a t-test would be appropriate.)

Within this simplified organizing framework (parametric or nonparametric, difference or association), we could locate a myriad of individual statistical tests. Gopal Kanji (1993), for example, lists 100 parametric and nonparametric tests for which there is a single dependent variable. We can't possibly survey these statistics here. However, in the final section of this chapter, we show you when to use and how to calculate five statistics frequently encountered in communication research: a nonparametric test of difference (chi square), a parametric test of difference between two groups (t-test), a parametric test of difference for three or more groups that vary on one independent variable (one-way ANOVA), a factorial ANOVA, and a parametric test of association (Pearson correlation).

Step 3: Computing the Test Statistic

Each statistical test has its own computation formula. The formula calculates one value, which is the value you will use in the next step, when you consult a statistical table of critical values. This isn't a statistics book, so we won't pursue computation in any detail. We do give you some exposure to computations in the next section, however, where we discuss our "sampler" of five simple statistical tests.

Step 4: Consulting the Appropriate Statistical Table

Each statistical test is accompanied by a *table of critical values*. This table is a numerical rendering of the sampling distribution of the statistic you are using. It tells you the likelihood that your computed statistical value could be the result of sampling error, at some specified level of confidence (usually 95 percent). Your computed statistical value needs to be at least as large as the critical value for you to reject the null hypothesis.

Most critical-value tables require you to have two pieces of information in hand—the alpha level you have established and information about your degrees of freedom. These two pieces of information are the rows and columns of the critical-value table. The cell where the appropriate row and column intersect is the critical value that your computed statistic must exceed. We've already discussed how you establish your alpha level (see Step 1, above). But what are degrees of freedom?

Degrees of freedom is a term that refers to the possibilities for variation within a statistical model. Suppose we challenge you to find three numbers whose mean is 11. There is an infinite number of solutions to this problem: (11, 11, 11), (10, 11, 12), (21, 1, 11), etc. Now suppose we require that one of the numbers be 7. There would still be an infinite number of possibilities for the other two numbers.

If we told you one number had to be 7 and another 10, there would be only one possible value for the third. If the average of three numbers is 11, their sum must be 33. If two total 17, the third must be 16. In this situation, we say there are two degrees of freedom. Two of the numbers could have any values we choose, but once they are specified, the third number is determined.

More generally, whenever we're examining the mean of N values, we can see that the degrees of freedom are represented by $(N - 1)$. Thus, in the case of the mean of 23 values, we could make 22 of them anything we liked, but the 23rd would then be determined.

A similar logic applies to contingency tables with two variables. Consider a table reporting the relationship between two dichotomous variables: *age* (older and younger) and *confidence in televised news* (high/low). Notice that the table provides the marginal frequencies of both variables:

Confidence Level	Younger	Older	Total
High			500
Low			500
Total	500	500	1,000

Despite the conveniently round numbers in this hypothetical example, notice there are numerous possibilities for the cell frequencies. For example, it could be the case that all 500 younger viewers have high confidence and all 500 older viewers lack confidence, or it could be just the reverse. Or there could be 250 cases in each cell, and so forth.

Now the question is this: How many cells could we fill in pretty much as we choose before the remainder are determined by the marginal frequencies? The answer is only one. If we know that 300 younger viewers have high confidence in televised news, for example, then 200 younger viewers would have low confidence, and the distribution would need to be just the opposite for the older viewers.

In this instance, then, we say the table has *one degree of freedom*. Take a few minutes to construct a three-by-three table. Assume you know the marginal frequencies for each variable, and see if you can determine how many degrees of freedom it has.

Each statistical test has a formula for determining the degrees of freedom. We've just illustrated two examples of this concept. In general, however, degrees of freedom are closely linked to sample size and the number of groups being compared.

Step 5: Deciding to Reject or Not Reject the Null Hypothesis

If the computed statistical value is at least as large as the critical value in the table of critical values, the null hypothesis can be rejected at *x* level of significance, usually .05. This means that you are 95-percent confident that the results of your study are not attributable to sampling error. At the same time, you are running a 5-percent risk of an alpha (Type I) error. That is, there is a 5-percent chance that you are deciding to reject the null hypothesis even though it might be true.

If the computed statistical value is smaller than the critical value in the table of critical values, the null hypothesis cannot be rejected at the .05 level of significance. This means that you think your study's findings were within sampling error at the 95-percent confidence level. However, you are running a risk of a beta (Type II) error—the null hypothesis might be false.

A SAMPLER OF SOME COMMONLY USED STATISTICS

In this section, we're going to discuss five statistics in some detail. You'll get several opportunities to see the logic of inferential statistics in action.

Chi Square

Chi square (x^2) is a frequently used nonparametric test of significance to identify differences in frequency data. Actually, there are several chi square statistics, depending on the specifics of your data. We'll illustrate two common variations of chi square. All of the variations are based on a comparison of observed frequencies to the frequencies that would be expected by chance alone (i.e., if the null hypothesis were true).

One-Sample Chi Square This statistic is used when you are interested in the number of participants, objects, responses, or other units that fall into two or more categories. For example, suppose you are interested in finding out whether getting an *A* in a large lecture class of 500 students varies by the row in which a student typically sits. Suppose you have the following data, indicating the number of *A* grades for three row positions: rows in the front third, rows in the middle third, and rows in the back third of available rows:

Front	Middle	Back	Total
30	15	5	50

If seat position were totally unrelated to earning an *A*, you would expect an equal number of students with *A*s in the front, middle, and back rows. The one-sample chi square test basically compares the frequency distribution you observed to what you would expect by chance alone (that is, if seat position were unrelated to earning an *A*) to assess the magnitude of the gap between observed and expected frequencies. In particular, here's the formula for the one-group chi square test:

$$x^2 = \sum \frac{(O - E)^2}{E}$$

where
O = the observed frequency for a given category
E = the expected frequency for a given category
Σ = the sum of $(O - E)^2/E$ calculations for all categories

In our example, the expected frequency, by chance alone, would be $^{50}/_3$, or 16.67 for each of our categories. For the "front" category, $(O - E)^2/E$ equals $(30 - 16.67)^2/16.67$, or 10.66. For the "middle" category, we have $(15 - 16.67)^2/16.67$, or .17. For the "back" category, we have $(5 - 16.67)^2/16.67$, or 8.17. Taking the sum of these three values $(10.66 + .17 + 8.17)$, we produce a x^2 value of 19.0.

For this statistical test, the degrees of freedom are calculated by subtracting 1 from the number of categories; in this case, df = 3 − 1 = 2. From the table of critical values for chi square (found in Appendix I), we know that our x^2 value must be at least equal to 5.991 to reject the null hypothesis of no difference at the .05 level of significance (5.991 is the critical value where row 2, representing 2 degrees of freedom, intersects with the column header ".05").

Because our calculated value exceeds the minimum critical value, we would reject the null hypothesis in this hypothetical example, concluding that *A* grades are not equally distributed among row positions. (Of course, we wouldn't know why this is the case—maybe it has something to do with interaction patterns between instructors and students. But that's a different study.)

Chi Square for Contingency Tables   The logic of the one-sample chi square can simply be extended for a larger number of samples. Basically, we're still going to compare observed frequencies for each cell against the frequencies we would expect by chance alone, just as we did for the one-sample chi square. Let's suppose we're interested in finding out whether a persuasive campaign affects the likelihood that pregnant women will stop drinking alcohol. We design a quasi-experiment with three matched communities serving as the three comparison groups: a control group, a group exposed to 15-second PSAs on fetal alcohol syndrome shown on local television, and a group exposed to the PSAs plus a 15-minute video on fetal alcohol syndrome shown in the waiting rooms of all local health care clinics. Our two variables are the persuasive campaign (with three attributes or groups: control, PSAs only, PSAs + video) and whether or not our participants drank any alcoholic beverages in the month following the campaign. Our data are frequencies.

Let's suppose that our hypothetical data at the conclusion of the campaign were as follows: A total of 20 percent ($^{10}/_{50}$) of the pregnant women in the control condition reported abstaining from alcohol consumption (versus 80 percent of controls who reported drinking), 40 percent ($^{20}/_{50}$) of the women in the PSA-only group reported abstaining (versus 60 percent who reported drinking), and 80 percent ($^{40}/_{50}$) of the women in the PSA + video group reported abstaining (versus 20 percent of the women in this group who reported drinking). But do these observations depart from the frequencies we would expect as the result of sampling error alone? We need to calculate a chi square test for contingency tables to get the answer.

Figure 12-6 shows you how to calculate a chi square for contingency tables. As was the case for the one-sample chi square, we will assess the size of the "gap" between what was observed and compare this to what would be expected to occur by sampling error alone.

In our example, our χ^2 value of 37.51 certainly exceeds the critical value—in fact, it exceeds the critical value needed for significance at the .001 level (13.82). Check it yourself in Appendix I. If we were writing up these results in a report, we might report this finding by saying that the "null hypothesis was rejected at beyond the .05 level." We might also say "Persuasive campaign affected alcohol use in our sample at beyond the .05 level of significance." Alternatively, we could express the same finding by saying

"The obtained χ^2 value of 37.51 exceeded significance at the .001 level."

Although the three groups in our example (control, PSA only, PSA + video) contained an equal number of participants, this is not a requirement of chi square. However, for chi square to perform a valid statistical test, the rule of thumb is that no more than 20 percent of the cells can have expected values of less than 5 and no cell can have an expected frequency of less than 1 (Siegel & Castellan, 1988).

T-Test

The parametric **t-test** is used when we wish to determine whether two groups, representing nominal-level attributes of an independent variable, differ on some dependent variable, measured at the interval or ratio level of measurement. There are two variations of the t-test: the independent-sample t-test, which compares two different groups, and the paired-sample t-test, which compares two related groups. We'll illustrate how to calculate both types.

The Independent-Samples T-Test   Let's imagine that we have developed a communication training program to train medical students to be more effective in communicating with patients. We run a small experiment to gauge the effectiveness of our training program. Ten medical school students are randomly assigned to one of two groups: our training program or a control group. Thus, the two groups are independent of each other—different groups of medical students. The medical students are observed interacting with patients and given an effectiveness score from 1 to 10, where 10 means maximum effectiveness. The 5 students in the training program produced a mean effectiveness score of 7.4, and the 5 students in the control group produced a mean effectiveness score of 4.4. On its face, the training program appears to have produced its desired outcome. But is this difference greater than what we could expect once sampling error was taken into account?

That's where the t-test for independent samples comes into play. Figure 12-7 takes you through the calculation steps to determine whether the observed difference in means (7.4 − 4.4 = 3.0) produces a t value sufficient for us to reject the null hypothesis at the .05 alpha level. Because our research hypothesis is directional, we work with the critical value of t for a one-tailed test. Because our obtained t value exceeds the critical value shown in Appendix J, we decide to reject the null hypothesis of no difference between the two groups. We conclude,

Our hypothetical data:

	Reported Use of Alcohol		
Campaign Group	*Abstained*	*Drank*	*Totals*
Control	10	40	50
PSA only	20	30	50
PSA + video	40	10	50
Totals	70	80	150

The formula for chi square is the same as in the one-sample example:

$$\chi^2 = \sum \frac{(O - E)^2}{E}$$

where
O is the observed frequency for a given cell
E is the expected frequency for a given cell
Σ is the sum of $\frac{(O - E)^2}{E}$ calculations across all cells

Step 1. Identify the O values for each cell and place them in the O column of the calculation table below. These values are simply the observed frequencies found in the study.

Step 2. Calculate E, the expected frequency, for each cell in the contingency table. The expected frequency for a given cell in the contingency table is the product of the column total (known as a column marginal) and the row total (known as the row marginal), divided by the grand total.

For controls who abstained, the column total is 70 and the row total is 50. The grand total of women in the study was 150. Thus, the E for this cell is (70 · 50)/150 = 23.33.

For controls who drank, the column total is 80; the row total is 50; the grand total is 150. Thus, the E for this cell is (80 · 50)/150 = 26.67.

For PSA-only women who abstained, the column, row, and grand total values are, respectively, 70, 50, and 150. Thus, the E for this cell is (70 · 50)/150, or 23.33.

And so on. Enter your calculated E values into the calculation table below.

Step 3. Calculate (O − E) values for each cell, and enter those values in the calculation table.

Step 4. Square all (O − E) values, and enter those into the calculation table.

Step 5. Divide the values derived in step 4 by the appropriate E value and enter those calculations into the last column of the calculation table.

Step 6. Derive the sum of all values in the last column of the calculation table:

$$\chi^2 = 7.62 + 6.66 + .48 + .42 + 11.91 + 10.42 = 37.51$$

Step 7. Determine the degrees of freedom. For contingency tables, df = the number of rows minus 1 multiplied by the number of columns minus 1. Our contingency table has 3 rows and 2 columns. Thus,

$$df = (r - 1)(c - 1) = (3 - 1)(2 - 1) = (2)(1) = 2$$

Step 8. Determine the minimum value our χ^2 value must hold in order to reject the null hypothesis of no difference at the .05 level. In consulting Appendix I, we see that the critical value is 5.991. Our chi square value of 37.51 exceeds the minimum value. Therefore, we would conclude that the quasi-experimental groups are significantly different at the .05 level of significance. Stated another way, we rejected the null hypothesis of no difference at the .05 level.

Cell	*O*	*E*	*(O − E)*	*(O − E)²*	*(O − E)²/E*
Control—abstained	10	23.33	−13.33	177.69	7.62
Control—drank	40	26.67	13.33	177.69	6.66
PSA only—abstained	20	23.33	−3.33	11.09	.48
PSA only—drank	30	26.67	3.33	11.09	.42
PSA + video—abstained	40	23.33	16.67	277.89	11.91
PSA + video—drank	10	26.67	−16.67	277.89	10.42

FIGURE 12-6 **Calculating Chi Square for Contingency Tables**

then, that the difference in effectiveness scores between the two groups is statistically significant at beyond the .05 level.

The Paired-Samples T-Test The paired-samples t-test is used when you compare two related groups on a dependent variable measured at the interval or ratio level. Sometimes, the two groups are related because they are the same group of participants measured twice: for ex-

ample, pretest scores and posttest scores. Other times, you wish to compare matched, or paired, groups of participants. Let's suppose you wanted to determine whether husbands and wives hold different beliefs about communication. Each marital pair represents a matched pair; thus, you would want to use the paired-samples t-test rather than the independent-samples t-test to determine whether their beliefs are different. Let's suppose you have 5 marital pairs willing to provide you with questionnaire

Example: Control group and training-program group of medical students. Dependent variable is judged effectiveness, on a 1–10 scale, where 10 = maximum effectiveness.

Training Group (Group 1)	Control Group (Group 2)
8	3
9	4
7	5
7	4
6	6

Here's the formula for a t-test:

$$t = \frac{M_1 - M_2}{\sqrt{((SS_1 + SS_2)/(N - 2)) \cdot (N/n_1 \cdot n_2)}}$$

where
M_1 = the mean score for group 1
M_2 = the mean score for group 2
SS_1 = the sum of squares for group 1
SS_2 = the sum of squares for group 2
N = the total number of participants in the study
n_1 = the number of observations in group 1
n_2 = the number of observations in group 2

Step 1. Calculate the mean for each group by summing up the values and dividing each sum by the number of participants in the group:

$$M_1 = \frac{(8 + 9 + 7 + 7 + 6)}{5} = 7.40$$

$$M_2 = \frac{(3 + 4 + 5 + 4 + 6)}{5} = 4.40$$

Step 2. For the first group, calculate deviation scores by subtracting the group's mean from each score $(X - M)$. Enter these values in the deviation column below for group 1. Calculate the deviation scores for group 2 and enter them in the deviation column for group 2 below.

Step 3. Square each deviation score and enter it in the appropriate column below.

Step 4. Sum the squared deviations for each group. These are known as the sums of squares (SS).

$$SS_1 = (.36 + 2.56 + .16 + .16 + 1.96) = 5.20$$
$$SS_2 = (1.96 + .16 + .36 + .16 + 2.56) = 5.20$$

Step 5. Total the two SS values and divide this by the total number of participants minus 2:

$$\frac{(5.20 + 5.20)}{10 - 2} = \frac{10.40}{8} = 1.30$$

Step 6. Divide the total number of participants by the product of the number of participants in each group:

$$\frac{10}{(5 \cdot 5)} = \frac{10}{25} = .40$$

Step 7. Multiply the answer in step 5 by the answer in step 6, and then take the square root:

$$\sqrt{(1.30)(.40)} = .72$$

Step 8. Calculate the numerator of the formula for the t-test by subtracting the mean of group 2 from the mean of group 1:

$$(7.4 - 4.4) = 3.0$$

Step 9. To calculate the t value, divide the answer in step 8 by the answer in step 7:

$$t = \frac{3.0}{.72} = 4.17$$

Step 10. Determine the degrees of freedom: $(N - 2) = 8$

Step 11. Determine whether the t value exceeds the critical value at the .05 level of significance. Consult the table of critical t values, found in Appendix J. This appendix gives you critical t values for two-tailed (nondirectional) t-tests at various significance levels (the column values). Because we had a directional hypothesis (those who received training would be more effective than those without training), our t-test was one-tailed. In order to use this table for one-tailed t-tests, simply take your desired alpha level (.05 in this case) and double it: .10. At the .05 level of significance for a one-tailed test with 8 df, the minimum critical value we need would be 1.86 (1.86 is the value in the cell where the row value of 8 intersects with the column value of .10). Because $4.17 > 1.86$, we would reject the null hypothesis and accept the research hypothesis that those who received training were more effective than those who did not.

	Training Group				**Control Group**		
Score	Deviation $(X - M)$	Squared Deviation $(X - M)^2$		Score	Deviation $(X - M)$	Squared Deviation $(X - M)^2$
8	.60	.36		3	−1.40	1.96
9	1.60	2.56		4	−.40	.16
7	−.40	.16		5	.6	.36
7	−.40	.16		4	−.40	.16
6	−1.40	1.96		6	1.60	2.56

FIGURE 12-7   **Calculating an Independent-Samples T-Test**

Example: Paired data from husbands and wives on beliefs about communication.

Couple #	Husband's Score	Wife's Score
1	2	5
2	3	5
3	3	6
4	4	5
5	2	4

The formula for calculating a paired t-test:

$$t = \frac{\Sigma D/N}{\sqrt{\dfrac{\Sigma D^2 - (\Sigma D)^2/N}{N(N-1)}}}$$

where
M_1 = mean of group 1
M_2 = mean of group 2
D = difference score between each matched pair
N = total number of pairs

Step 1. Calculate the difference (D) between each pair of scores and enter it into the calculation table below.

Step 2. Square the difference scores (D^2) and enter them into the calculation table below.

Step 3. Add up the squared difference scores:

$\Sigma D^2 = 9 + 4 + 9 + 1 + 4 = 27$

Step 4. Sum up the difference scores (ΣD) obtained in step 1, then square this value (($\Sigma D)^2$):

$(-3) + (-2) + (-3) + (-1) + (-2) = -11.0$
$(-11)^2 = 121$

Step 5. Divide the answer in step 4 by N:

$\dfrac{121}{5} = 24.2$

Step 6. Subtract the answer to step 5 from the answer to step 3:

$27 - 24.2 = 2.8$

Step 7. Divide the answer in step 6 by N(N − 1):

$\dfrac{2.8}{20} = .14$

Step 8. Take the square root of the answer in step 7:

$.37$

Step 9. Derive the mean of the difference scores:

$\dfrac{\Sigma D}{N} = \dfrac{-11}{5} = -2.20$

Step 10. Calculate your t value by dividing the answer in step 9 by the answer in step 8:

$\dfrac{-2.20}{.37} = -5.95$

Step 11. Determine the degrees of freedom (N − 1):

$5 - 1 = 4$

Step 12. Consult the table for critical values of t. Because the research question was nondirectional, we work with the column values as provided in the table. For significance at the .05 level for a two-tailed test with 4 df with a two-tailed t, we need a minimum value of 2.776. This is the value in the cell where the row value of 4 intersects with the column value of .05. Because our obtained t value of 5.95 (ignore the minus) is larger than our critical value, we would conclude that the difference between husband and wife pairs is significant at the .05 level. We can ignore the difference because it simply reflects that husband scores were less than wife scores. If, for a given pair, the scores had been reversed so that the wives had the smaller score, we would still end up with a t value of 5.95, but it would be positive in value because we subtract group 2 (wife score) from group 1 (husband score).

Pair	H's Score	W's Score	D	D^2
1	2	5	−3	9
2	3	5	−2	4
3	3	6	−3	9
4	4	5	−1	1
5	2	4	−2	4

FIGURE 12-8   **Calculating a Paired-Samples T-Test**

data on their beliefs about communication. The mean score for husbands was 2.8, compared to the mean score of 5.0 for wives. The higher score represents a belief in total openness, whereas a lower score represents a belief in discretion over candor. Is the difference between these mean scores sufficiently large that it is beyond what you would expect by sampling error alone? That's where the paired-samples t-test comes in.

Figure 12-8 shows you how to calculate a paired-samples t-test in order to determine whether husbands and wives differ—a nondirectional research question. As it turns out, the answer to our question is "yes." The observed difference is larger than what we would expect by sampling error alone. We would say that we reject the null hypothesis of no difference and conclude that there is a difference between husbands and wives. Specifically, women in our sample endorsed greater openness than did their husbands.

If we simply had a group of married men and a group of married women, but our participants were not married to one another, we would have two independent groups and would have used the independent-samples t-test.

One-Way ANOVA

Sometimes, researchers want to compare more than two groups representing the nominal-level attributes of an independent variable on some dependent variable measured at the interval or ratio level. Instead of using multiple t-tests to conduct the comparison (group 1 versus group 2, group 2 versus group 3, and group 1 versus group 3), researchers use instead a parametric statistical test known as analysis of variance (ANOVA). ANOVA tells us whether the several groups differ significantly on the dependent variable.

Let's suppose we have data from an experiment in which we have three randomly assigned groups:

- Treatment group 1, which was exposed to a high-fear-appeal persuasive message on skin cancer and the need to use a sun screen. Viewers were exposed to graphic visual images of what skin cancer looks like.
- Treatment group 2, which was exposed to a low-fear-appeal persuasive message on the need to use a sun screen. Skin cancer was talked about but not shown.
- The third group, a control group, which was exposed to a videotape with a different message entirely.

Our dependent measure is attitude toward using sun screen, where "7" represents a very positive attitude and "1" represents a very negative attitude. Suppose that the mean attitude for group 1 was 3.4, the mean for group 2 was 6.2, and the mean for group 3 was 3.2. Are these three groups significantly different beyond what you could expect through sampling error? We need a **one-way ANOVA** to help us get the answer.

Figure 12-9 shows you how to calculate a one-way ANOVA. After calculating our F ratio and consulting the table of critical F values (Appendix K), we can reject the null hypothesis of no difference at beyond the .05 level. But an F ratio is what is known as an *omnibus test*—while it can tell us that significant difference sits somewhere in the results, it cannot tell us exactly where. Maybe all three groups are significantly different from one another. Maybe one group is significantly different from the other two, and these two do not differ significantly. In order to determine where the significant difference is located, researchers need to perform follow-up statistical tests, also known as *post hoc comparisons*. There are many possible statistics used for post hoc comparisons. We used one of the most popular, the Bonferroni technique, concluding that group 2 (the low-fear-appeal group) had significantly more positive attitudes than did

either of the other two groups, which did not differ significantly from each other. It's beyond the scope of this book to introduce you to post hoc comparisons. We raised the issue so that you can appreciate that the F ratio gives us a general, or omnibus, answer to the question of statistical significance between more than two groups on a single independent variable.

Factorial ANOVA

Sometimes, researchers are interested in examining more than one independent variable against a dependent variable measured at the interval or ratio level. When there are two or more independent variables, and the attributes of each are nominal groups, we need to use a **factorial ANOVA,** a parametric test. This statistical procedure is the one most likely to be used when we have a factorial experiment (see Chapter 9). There are many different kinds of factorial ANOVAs that can be performed, depending on the details of the design used by the researcher. We'll illustrate a very simple factorial ANOVA.

Suppose we wanted to know the effects of a message designed to improve people's knowledge of the relationship between nutrition and heart disease. Our dependent variable is a factual knowledge test of what is known about the link between nutritional habits and heart disease. We conduct an experiment in which participants are randomly assigned to one of four groups in a 2 × 2 factorial design. We have two independent variables: message medium (video message or printed brochure) and presentation style (a factual style or a narrative style in which a person's story is told). After exposure to the message in one of four conditions, all participants are given the measure of knowledge, which could range from a low of 0 to a high of 10. Suppose we obtained the results shown in Figure 12-10: The highest knowledge score was obtained with the video in narrative style (M = 6.6), and the lowest knowledge score was produced with the factual brochure (M = 2.8). How can we sort out whether there is any significant difference among these groups? How can we sort out the separate, and combined, effects of each independent variable? Sounds like a summons for factorial ANOVA to us.

Figure 12-10 shows how to calculate this simple factorial ANOVA. Basically, we are going to build on the logic of the one-way ANOVA. However, we will have three F ratios: one for the *message medium* variable, one for the *presentation style* variable, and one for the interaction between medium and presentation style. As Figure 12-10 indicates, both main effects are significant at beyond the .05 level. Participants exposed to the video message

Group 1 (High Fear)	Group 2 (Low Fear)	Group 3 (Control)
3	6	3
4	7	4
3	7	3
4	6	3
3	5	3

ANOVA produces an F ratio. Here's how to calculate it, using our hypothetical data:

Step 1. Add the scores in each group to get the sum of each group:

Group 1: 3 + 4 + 3 + 4 + 3 = 17
Group 2: 6 + 7 + 7 + 6 + 5 = 31
Group 3: 3 + 4 + 3 + 3 + 3 = 16

Step 2. Square all of the scores and add these squared scores together:

$3^2 + 4^2 + 3^2 + 4^2 + 3^2 + 6^2 + 7^2 + 7^2 + 6^2 + 5^2 + 3^2 + 4^2 + 3^2 + 3^2 + 3^2 = 306$

Step 3. Add the group sums from step 1 together to obtain a grand sum:

17 + 31 + 16 = 64

Step 4. Square the answer to step 3 and divide by N, the total number of scores:

$$\frac{(64 \cdot 64)}{15} = 273.07$$

Step 5. Subtract the value derived in step 4 from the value derived in step 2. This is known as the sum of squares total, or SS_t:

$SS_t = 306 - 273.07 = 32.93$

Step 6. Square the sum of each of the groups (step 1), divide each value by the number of scores in a given group, and add these values together:

$$\frac{17^2}{5} + \frac{31^2}{5} + \frac{16^2}{5} = 57.8 + 192.2 + 51.2 = 301.2$$

Step 7. Subtract the answer in step 4 from the value derived in step 6. This value is known as the sum of squares between groups, or SS_b.

$SS_b = 301.2 - 273.07 = 28.13$

Step 8. Subtract the value derived in step 7 from the value derived in step 5. This value is known as the sum of squares within groups, SS_w.

$SS_w = SS_t - SS_b = 32.93 - 28.13 = 4.8$

Step 9. Compute the appropriate degrees of freedom:

df for $SS_t = N - 1 = 15 - 1 = 14$
df for SS_b = the number of groups minus 1 = 3 − 1 = 2
df for SS_w = the total df minus the between df = 14 − 2 = 12

Step 10. Calculate what are known as the mean square (ms) values:

$$ms_t = \frac{SS_t}{df_t} = \frac{32.93}{14} = 2.35$$

$$ms_b = \frac{SS_b}{df_b} = \frac{28.13}{2} = 14.07$$

$$ms_w = \frac{SS_w}{df_w} = \frac{4.8}{12} = .40$$

Step 11. You are now ready to calculate the F ratio:

$$F = \frac{ms_b}{ms_w} = \frac{14.07}{.40} = 35.18$$

Step 12. F ratios are often presented in tabular form, like the following:

Source	SS	df	ms	F	p
Total	32.93	14			
Between groups	28.13	2	14.07	35.18	< .05
Within groups	4.80	12	.40		

Step 13. Check the table for critical F values. Appendix K provides you with tabled critical values of F for two levels of significance: .05 ("Upper 5% points") and .01 ("Upper 1% points"). If your threshold of statistical significance is .05, use the tabled values for "Upper 5% points"; if your threshold of statistical significance is .01, use the tabled values for "Upper 1% points." We need to enter the table using two df values—the df value for the numerator in the F ratio (i.e., the df for the Between groups), symbolized by the column values v_1 in the table; and the df value for the denominator in the F ratio (i.e., the df for the Within groups), symbolized by the row values of v_2 in the table. For our example, these values are 2 and 12, respectively. For significance at the .05 level, we need an F ratio at least equal to 3.89. This is the critical value where the numerator (column) value is 2 and the denominator (row) value is 12. Because our obtained F ratio is greater than the minimum critical value, we reject the null hypothesis and conclude that the groups are significantly different.

FIGURE 12-9 **Calculating a One-Way ANOVA**

Message Medium	Style of Presentation	
	Factual Style	Narrative Style
Video	5	6
	3	7
	3 M = 4.2	8 M = 6.6
	4	4
	6	8
ΣX	21	33
Print	3	5
	4	4
	3 M = 2.8	6 M = 5.0
	2	5
	2	5
ΣX	14	25

Step 1. Add the scores (X) for each group to produce its sum (ΣX).

Step 2. Square each score in the table and add these squared values:

$$5^2 + 3^2 + 3^2 + 4^2 + 6^2 + \cdots + 5^2 + 4^2 + 6^2 + 5^2 + 5^2 = 493$$

Step 3. Add the sums of all of the groups (step 1) to produce a grand sum:

$$21 + 33 + 14 + 25 = 93$$

Step 4. Square the value derived in step 3 and then divide it by N:

$$\frac{(93 \cdot 93)}{20} = 432.45$$

Step 5. Compute the total sum of squares (SS_t) by subtracting the answer in step 4 from the answer derived in step 2:

$$SS_t = 493 - 432.45 = 60.55$$

Step 6. Compute the effects of the first independent variable—message medium (video or print). First, add the sums of each attribute:

21 + 33 = 54 (sum of the video groups)
14 + 25 = 39 (sum of the print groups)

Then square these two sums and divide each by the number of scores upon which each was based, and add the two quotients together:

$$\frac{54^2}{10} + \frac{39^2}{10} = 291.6 + 152.1 = 443.7$$

Finally, subtract the value derived in step 4 from this value to produce the SS for the message medium variable, SS_m:

$$443.7 - 432.45 = 11.25 = SS_m$$

Step 7. Compute the effects of the second factor, presentation style. First, add the sums of each attribute:

21 + 14 = 35 (sum of the factual-style groups)
33 + 25 = 58 (sum of the narrative-style groups)

Then square these two sums and divide each by the number of scores upon which each was based, and add the two quotients together:

$$\frac{35^2}{10} + \frac{58^2}{10} = 122.5 + 336.4 = 458.90$$

Finally, subtract the value derived in step 4 from this value to produce the SS for the presentation-style variable, SS_p:

$$458.90 - 432.45 = 26.45 = SS_p$$

Step 8. Compute the interaction effect of message medium with presentation style. First, square the sum of each of the

groups, divide each by the number of scores upon which the sum was based, and add the quotients:

$$\frac{21^2}{5} + \frac{14^2}{5} + \frac{33^2}{5} + \frac{25^2}{5} = 88.2 + 39.2 + 217.8 + 125.0$$
$$= 470.2$$

From this value, subtract the answer from step 4, SS_m, and SS_p:

$$470.2 - 432.45 - 11.25 - 26.45 = .05 = SS_{mp}$$

Step 9. Compute the error-term sum of squares, SS_{error}, by subtracting all three SS terms from the SS_t:

$$SS_{error} = SS_t - SS_m - SS_p - SS_{mp} = 60.55 - 11.25 - 26.45 - .05 = 22.8$$

Step 10. Calculate the degrees of freedom for each F ratio in the analysis:

df for SS_t = N − 1 = 20 − 1 = 19
df for SS_m = the number of medium attributes minus 1 = 2 − 1 = 1
df for SS_p = the number of presentation-style attributes minus 1 = 2 − 1 = 1
df for SS_{mp} = the product of the df for SS_m and the df for SS_p = 1 · 1 = 1
df for SS_{error} = the df for SS_t minus the dfs for SS_m, SS_p, and SS_{mp} = 19 − 1 − 1 − 1 = 16

Step 11. Calculate the mean squares SS/df:

$$ms_m = \frac{11.25}{1} = 11.25$$

$$ms_p = \frac{26.45}{1} = 26.45$$

$$ms_{mp} = \frac{.05}{1} = .05$$

$$ms_{error} = \frac{22.8}{16} = 1.43$$

Step 12. Calculate the several F ratios by dividing the appropriate ms value by the ms_{error} value:

$$F_m = \frac{ms_m}{ms_{error}} = \frac{11.25}{1.43} = 7.87$$

$$F_p = \frac{ms_p}{ms_{error}} = \frac{26.45}{1.43} = 18.50$$

$$F_{mp} = \frac{.05}{1.43} = .03$$

Step 13. Summarize the analysis in a table:

Source	SS	df	ms	F	p
Total	60.55	19			
Message medium	11.25	1	11.25	7.87	p < .05
Presentation style	26.45	1	26.45	18.50	p < .05
M × P	.05	1	.05	.03	NS
Error	22.80	16	1.43		

Step 14. Determine the critical values for each F value, based on its df for the numerator and its df for the denominator. For all three of our F values, the df for the numerator is the same: 1. The df for the denominator is the same for all three as well: 16. At the .05 level, with 1 and 16 df, the critical value is 4.49 (consult Appendix K—this value lies in the cell where column 1 and row 16 intersect in the "Upper 5% points" set of critical values). The interaction effect is not significant, but both of the main effects are significant. Viewing the video message increased knowledge more so than reading the print message. The narrative style resulted in higher knowledge scores than did the factual style.

FIGURE 12-10   Calculating a Factorial ANOVA

produced higher knowledge scores (M = 5.4) than did participants exposed to the brochure (M = 3.9). Participants exposed to the narrative presentation style had higher knowledge scores (M = 5.8) than did participants exposed to the factual style (M = 3.5). However, there was no significant combined, or interaction, effect between medium and presentation style.

If we had a factorial design larger than a 2 × 2 (say, a 3 × 2, 4 × 3, and so forth), we would simply extend the computation logic of Figure 12-10. Because each of our independent variables had only two groups, there was no need for follow-up post hoc comparisons. However, if we were working with a larger number of groups for each independent variable, we would need follow-up tests to help us determine exactly where a significant difference was located, more or less as we did for the one-way ANOVA.

Pearson Product-Moment Correlation

The **Pearson product-moment correlation** coefficient (r) is one of the most frequently used parametric statistics in communication research. The correlation coefficient is a value that captures the extent to which two variables, both measured at the interval or ratio level, are linearly related to each other. To use the correlation statistic, you need to have measures of your two variables for each of your units of analysis.

Your two variables are related to the extent that they covary—they increase and decrease in value in a predictable way. A correlation coefficient can range from −1.00 (which would indicate that two variables are perfectly, yet inversely, related to each other), through 0 (which would indicate that two variables are independent of each other), to +1.00 (which would indicate that two variables are perfectly, and positively, related to each other). Rarely do you encounter perfect 1.00 correlations, either positive or negative. More typical in communication research are values somewhere between zero and 1. Here are some common meanings for intermediate values (we have not distinguished positive correlation values from negative correlation values here because whether two variables are related positively or negatively is a separate matter from the strength of the correlation) (Cohen, 1988):

r = .10: small effect size
r = .30: medium effect size
r = .50: large effect size

Figure 12-11 provides a visual sense of what various correlation values would look like. These charts are known as **scattergrams**—they give us a plot of {X,Y} values on each unit for which we have measures of both variables, X and Y. Figure 12-11A shows the scattergram of a perfect +1.00 correlation, whereas Figure 12-11B shows the scattergram of a perfect −1.00 correlation. Notice that in both of these diagrams the various {X,Y} points fit a line exactly; the only difference between the two scattergrams is whether the line is positively or negatively sloped.

Figure 12-11C shows a positive correlation somewhere between 0 and +1.00, and Figure 12-11D shows a negative correlation somewhere between 0 and −1.00. In both of these diagrams, we can imagine a line projected through the center of the points, approximating their coherence. However, the points do not fit perfectly on our imaginary line, which means that the correlation is not 1.00. The only difference between scattergrams C and D is the slope of the imaginary line that we could fit to the point patterns.

If X and Y variables had a correlation value of zero, it would be impossible to fit an imaginary line to the plotted {X,Y} points.

Some students falsely interpret a correlation coefficient as the percentage of overlap between the two sets of scores. If you want to think in terms of percentage overlap, you need to take the square of r (r^2), which gives you the **coefficient of determination.** The coefficient of determination tells you the percentage of variation in one variable that can be predicted by a knowledge of the second variable. For example, a correlation of .70 means that 49 percent of the variation in one variable can be predicted from knowledge of the other variable.

Let's imagine that we have collected data from hospital nurses. "Burnout" of nurses is a common experience, and we want to determine its communication correlates. We hypothesize that feeling burned out correlates negatively with feeling listened to by physicians and hospital administrators. So we collect information from a sample of 10 nurses, soliciting their feelings of "burnout" and our communication variable—the extent to which they feel listened to by physicians and hospital administrators. Figure 12-12 provides our hypothetical data and shows you how to calculate a correlation. The obtained r value of −.56 means that there is a fairly strong, negative relationship between our two variables: As feelings of "burnout" increase, feelings of being listened to decrease, and vice versa. In consulting the table of critical values for r, we conclude that this correlation value is statistically significant at the .05 level. Thus, we are 95-percent confident that our negative correlation is not the result of sampling error.

A. r = +1.00

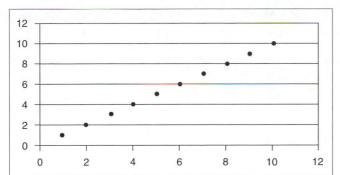

C. 0 < r < +1.00

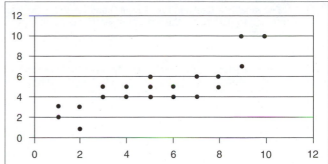

B. r = −1.00

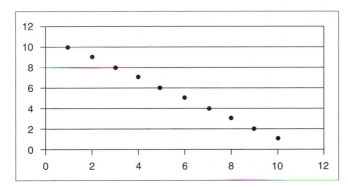

D. −1.00 < r < 0.00

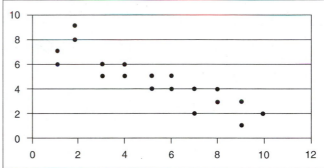

FIGURE 12-11 **Scattergrams of Some Possible Correlation Values**

SOME SUMMARY THOUGHTS

If you are math phobic, you've probably had more than your share of equations and computations in this chapter. But we thought it was important to give you a feel for inferential statistics by discussing in greater detail some basic statistics from the inferential statistics family. The inferential statistics family is a large one, mastery of which will require several statistics courses. We hope this brief treatment has enhanced your understanding of the logic of inferential statistics as well as provided you with some further understanding of five statistical procedures commonly encountered in communication research.

If you read the communication research journals, you will be overwhelmed by the variety of statistical procedures used—multiple regression analysis, discriminant analysis, canonical correlation analysis, MANOVA, factor analysis, structural equation modeling, time-series analysis, multidimensional scaling analysis—the list is a long

one. Try to keep your eye on the prize—what's the "bottom-line" statistical finding reported by the researcher? Was the obtained statistical value at least as large as the critical value, allowing the researcher to reject the null hypothesis at some predetermined alpha level (commonly .05)? If no, you can conclude that the study's findings were probably the result of sampling error. If yes, you can probably leave the study with some confidence in the researcher's substantive claims.

Tests of significance provide an objective yardstick against which to estimate the significance of patterns between variables. They help us rule out patterns that may not represent genuine relationships in the population under study. The researcher who uses or reads reports of significance tests should remain wary of several dangers in their interpretation, however.

First, we've been discussing tests of *statistical significance*; there are no objective tests of substantive significance. Thus, we may be legitimately convinced that a given association is not due to sampling error, but we

Suppose we have gathered data from 10 nurses on two variables: variable X (feeling "burned out") and variable Y (feeling "listened to"). Here are the scores for the 10 nurses on both variables:

X Feeling "burned out" (1–7, with 7 high)		Y Feeling "listened to" (1–7, with 7 high)	
1		7	
4		2	
6		3	
5		3	
7	$M_x = 3.8$	4	$M_y = 4.1$
2	$SD_x = 2.15$	5	$SD_y = 1.37$
6		4	
3		5	
1		4	
3		4	

X	$(X - M_x)$	Y	$(Y - M_y)$	$(X - M_x) \cdot (Y - M_y)$
1	−2.8	7	2.9	−8.12
4	0.2	2	−2.1	−0.42
6	2.2	3	−1.1	−2.42
5	1.2	3	−1.1	−1.32
7	3.2	4	−0.1	−0.32
2	−1.8	5	0.9	−1.62
6	2.2	4	−0.1	−0.22
3	−0.8	5	0.9	−0.72
1	−2.8	4	−0.1	0.28
3	−0.8	4	−0.1	0.08
				−14.8

Step 1. Make sure you know how the mean (M) and standard deviation (SD) values were derived for each group—if you're unsure, review Chapter 11.

Step 2. For each variable, subtract the mean score for the group from each individual score. This gives you two deviation scores, one for variable X $(X - M_x)$ and one for variable Y $(Y - M_y)$. Enter these values in the calculation table below.

Step 3. Multiple the two values together and enter these values in the right-most column in the calculation table below.

Step 4. Calculate covariance of X and Y using this formula:

$$\text{Cov}(X,Y) = \frac{\Sigma(X - M_x) \cdot (Y - M_y)}{N - 1}$$

$$= \frac{-14.8}{9} = -1.64$$

Step 5. Substitute values into the formula for r:

$$r = \frac{\text{cov}(X, Y)}{SD_x \cdot SD_y} = \frac{-1.64}{(2.15)(1.37)} = \frac{-1.64}{2.94} = -.56$$

Step 6. Determine the statistical significance of this correlation value. In order to do this, you need to know the degrees of freedom: N − 2 = 10 − 2 = 8. We also need to know whether we should use the one-tailed or the two-tailed critical r. Because we were hypothesizing a positive relationship between burnout and being listened to, our hypothesis is directional, or one-tailed. The critical two-tailed r values at various levels of significance are shown in Appendix L. In order to use this table for one-tailed critical r values, simply take the desired significance level for the one-tailed test (.05 in this instance) and double it. In consulting the table, we discover that the critical value of a one-tailed r with 8 df at the .05 level of significance is .549. This is the cell value where a row value of 8 intersects with the column value of .1 (.05 × 2). Because our obtained r value is larger than this critical value, we reject the null hypothesis at the .05 level of significance. Burnout and being listened to are correlated negatively.

FIGURE 12-12   A Hypothetical Illustration of Pearson Product-Moment Correlation

may be in the position of asserting without fear of contradiction that two variables are only slightly related to each other. Recall that sampling error is an inverse function of sample size—the larger the sample, the smaller the expected error. Thus, a correlation of, say, .1 might very well be significant (at a given level) if discovered in a large sample, whereas the same correlation between the same two variables would not be significant if found in a smaller sample. Of course, this makes perfectly good sense if one understands the basic logic of tests of significance: In the larger sample, there is less chance that the correlation could be simply the product of sampling error. In both samples, however, it might represent an essentially trivial correlation.

The distinction between statistical and substantive significance is perhaps best illustrated by those cases where there is *absolute certainty* that observed differences cannot be a result of sampling error. This would be the case when we observe an entire population. Suppose we were able to learn the ages of every public official in the United States and also the ages of every public official in Russia. For argument's sake, let's assume further that the average age of U.S. officials is 45.2 years compared to, say, 45.5 years for the Russian officials. Because we would have the ages of all officials, there would be no question of sampling error. We know with certainty that the Russian officials are older than their U.S. counterparts. At the same time, we would say that the difference is of no substantive significance. We'd conclude, in fact, that they are essentially the same age.

Second, lest you be misled by this hypothetical example, you should not calculate statistical significance on relationships observed in data collected from whole populations. Remember, tests of statistical significance measure the likelihood of relationships between variables being only a product of sampling error; if there's no sampling, there's no sampling error.

Third, tests of significance are based on the same sampling assumptions we used in computing confidence intervals. To the extent that these assumptions are not met by the actual sampling design, the tests of significance should be interpreted with caution.

This may sound like a negative note upon which to conclude our discussion of inferential statistics. We don't intend it this way. Inferential statistics have given quantitative communication researchers a powerful analytic tool in their research methods tool kit. But all tools need to be used appropriately. Virtually all of the statistical tests available to communication researchers can be calculated fairly easily with any number of statistical software packages. Most of the statistics we have discussed in this chapter can even be obtained with spreadsheet software such as Excel. However, we caution you with the old adage: "Garbage in, garbage out." If you don't understand the assumptions of statistics, it is all too easy to plug in some numerical data and derive a statistical value and pretend that it is meaningful. If you understand what you are doing, however, inferential statistics are invaluable.

Main Points

- Inferential statistics are used to estimate the generalizability of findings arrived at through the analysis of a sample to the larger population from which the sample has been selected.

- Inferences about some characteristic of a population—such as the percentage of voters favoring Candidate A—must contain an indication of a confidence interval (the range within which the value is expected to be: for example, between 45 and 55 percent favor Candidate A) and an indication of the confidence level (the likelihood the value does fall within that range: for example, 95-percent confidence). Computations of confidence levels and intervals are based on probability theory and assume that conventional probability sampling techniques have been employed in the study.

- Inferences about the generalizability to a population of the relationships between variables in a sample involve tests of statistical significance. Most simply put, these tests estimate the likelihood that a relationship as large as the observed one could result from normal sampling error if no such relationship exists between the variables in the larger population. Tests of statistical significance, then, are also based on probability theory and assume that conventional probability sampling techniques have been employed in the study.

- Statistical significance must not be confused with substantive significance, the latter meaning that an observed relationship is strong, important, meaningful, or worth writing home about.

- The level of significance of an observed relationship is reported in the form of the probability that the relationship could have been produced merely by sampling error. To say that a relationship is significant at the .05 level is to say that a relationship as large as the observed one could not be expected to result from sampling error more than 5 times out of 100.

- Communication researchers tend to use a particular set of levels of significance in connection with tests of statistical significance: .05, .01, and .001. The .05 is the usual convention.

- The particular level of significance you establish at the outset of your study is your risk of making a Type I error—rejecting the null hypothesis when it is true.

- A Type II error results when you decide not to reject the null hypothesis when it is, in fact, false.

- Type I and Type II errors are inversely related to each other. The more stringent your significance level, the lower your risk of a Type I error but the higher your risk of making a Type II error, all other things being equal.

- Inferential statistics come in many different forms, each appropriate under certain circumstances.

Statistics can be parametric or nonparametric, and designed to locate differences or associations between variables.

❑ Tests of statistical significance, strictly speaking, make assumptions about data and methods that are almost never completely satisfied by communication research. Despite this, the tests can serve a useful function in the analysis and interpretation of data. You should be wary of interpreting the "significance" of the test results too precisely, however.

Key Terms

inferential statistics	effect size
standard error	parametric statistics
nonsampling errors	nonparametric statistics
tests of statistical significance	chi square
statistical significance	t-test
level of significance	one-way ANOVA
null hypothesis	factorial ANOVA
Type I errors	Pearson product-moment correlation
Type II errors	scattergram
statistical power	coefficient of determination

Review Questions and Exercises

1. This chapter has discussed the concept of statistical significance. Use one of the Web search engines to search for "statistical significance," using quotation marks around the phrase. Write up a report on what you discovered in your Web surfing.

2. Suppose we had the following hypothetical set of frequency data, reporting the number of respondents who reported rejecting an offer of drugs from a stranger, an acquaintance, and a friend during the prior month. Identify the appropriate inferential statistic to apply to these data, given the study's purpose to determine whether people's decision to reject drugs is affected by the relationship they have with the person making the offer. Calculate the statistical value and reach a decision to reject or not reject the null hypothesis, using the conventional alpha level of .05.

	Strangers	Acquaintances	Friends
Reject offer	72	48	39
Do not reject offer	28	52	61

3. Gather anonymous information from a sample of your classmates on two variables: height (in inches) and amount of cash they have on them that day. Is there a statistical association between these two variables? Perform a correlation test to reject or not reject the null hypothesis of independence between these two variables. Then divide your classmates into two nominal groups: taller and shorter. Perform a t-test to see if your groups differ in the amount of cash they have on them that day.

4. Consult the communication journals listed in Appendix A, locating at least one instance of each of the following statistics: chi square, t-test, ANOVA (either a one-way or a factorial), and correlation.

5. Some critics of the Food and Drug Administration have argued that the FDA is overly cautious in approving drugs for prescription. As a result of such caution, they argue, Americans are denied quick access to drugs that could possibly improve their health. The rejoinder by FDA officials is that their mission is to do their utmost to protect the U.S. populace from bogus prescription drugs. Recast this controversy in terms of Type I and Type II error risks.

Continuity Project

Search the communication journals listed in Appendix A for a quantitatively oriented journal about gender/sex. What statistic was employed in the analysis? Discuss the substantive significance and the statistical significance of the researcher's findings.

Additional Readings

Babbie, E., Halley, F., & Zaino, J. (2000). *Adventures in social research*. Newbury Park, CA: Pine Forge. This book introduces you to the analysis of social research data through SPSS for Windows.

Blalock, H. M., Jr. (1979). *Social statistics*. New York: McGraw-Hill. Blalock's textbook has been a standard for social science students (and faculty) for decades. Tad Blalock's death was a loss to all social science.

Mohr, L. B. (1990). *Understanding significance testing*. Newbury Park, CA: Sage. Here's an excellent and comprehensive examination of the topic: both the technical details of testing statistical significance and the meaning of such tests.

Williams, F. (1992). *Reasoning with statistics: How to read quantitative research* (4th ed.). New York: Harcourt. If Blalock's book is a bit much, try Williams's text for a user-friendly introduction to the logic of statistics and an overview of some commonly used statistics in communication research.

InfoTrac College Edition
http://www.infotrac-college.com/
wadsworth/access.html
Access the latest news and journal articles with Info-Trac College Edition, an easy-to-use online database of reliable, full-length articles from hundreds of top academic journals. Conduct an electronic search using the following search terms:

- chi square
- t-test
- ANOVA
- Pearson correlation
- significance level
- null hypothesis

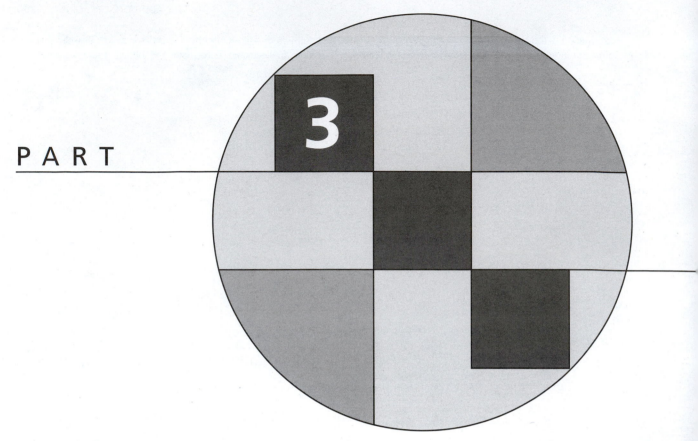

PART 3

Qualitative
Communication
Research

In this third part of the book, we're going to take a close look at three methods—participant observation, qualitative interviewing, and social text analysis—that form the triad of methods known as *qualitative research*. You'll probably discover that you've been using these three methods casually in your daily life for as long as you can remember. You do participant observation every time you enter a new scene and try to make sense of it. You engage in qualitative interviewing every time you have a conversation with someone. You employ a crude form of text analysis every time you watch TV. The chapters in Part 3 will show you how to improve your use of these methods in order to avoid the pitfalls of casual, uncontrolled observation.

In Chapter 13, we'll discuss the process of engaging in field research using the method known as participant observation. A researcher can conduct field research in several ways, and we'll discuss the main ones. In field research, the researcher is the primary instrument or method. In Chapter 14, we'll discuss qualitative interviewing. Think of this chapter as the qualitative counterpart of Chapter 8, where we discussed survey research. In Chapter 15, we'll discuss the analysis of social texts. Think of this chapter as the qualitative equivalent of Chapter 10, where we discussed quantitative text analysis. Last, Chapter 16 discusses the nitty-gritty details of how to process qualitative data analytically. Think of it as the qualitative counterpart of Chapters 11 and 12, where we discussed quantitative data analysis.

These methods are often used together in a single study. Thus, our decision to discuss them in separate chapters is a matter of convenience rather than a comment about their independence from one another. The analysis of qualitative data occurs while data are being gathered; thus, our decision to devote a separate chapter to some of the details of how to analyze qualitative data is also a matter of convenience.

The three methods addressed in this part of the book yield *qualitative* data: observations not easily reduced to numbers. Thus, for example, a field researcher may note the "paternalistic demeanor" of a manager at a staff meeting or the "defensive evasions" of a public official at a public hearing without trying to express either the paternalism or the defensiveness as numerical quantities or degrees.

Our experience is that people who are reticent to embrace quantitative data are initially attracted to qualitative data because they perceive it to be somehow easier to gather and analyze. Each of us has conducted both quantitative and qualitative research, and we can assure you that qualitative data are at least as challenging as quantitative data, maybe even more so. Certainly, qualitative data can often be gathered with lower "start-up" costs than quantitative data—a notepad and tape recorder will usually be sufficient. However, the construction of qualitative data texts tends to be a more labor-intensive undertaking than the collection of quantitative data.

However, if you recall our discussions of qualitative research from Chapters 2, 3, and 4, you appreciate that the differences between quantitative and qualitative research are often greater than the form of the data that the researcher is analyzing. Qualitative research methods are often employed by interpretive researchers and critical researchers. From our discussion of paradigms of knowing in Chapter 3, you may recall that the purpose of qualitative research is the understanding of meaning from the participant's point of view and the rules that organize the meaning-making process. The qualitative research process can be described as inductive (rather than deductive) and idiographic (rather than nomothetic).

Qualitative research, like quantitative research, is evaluated for its trustworthiness. But the specific criteria by which trustworthiness is demonstrated are not the same as those applied to the conduct of quantitative research. You may recall that the trustworthiness of quantitative research is assessed by applying the criteria of internal validity, measurement reliability, measurement validity, and external validity.

Yvonna Lincoln and Egon Guba (1985) have provided us with this classic list of criteria by which the trustworthiness of qualitative research is established: credibility, dependability, confirmability, and transferability. We'll provide an overview of these criteria in this introduction and then return to them in the chapters to follow.

CREDIBILITY

As we discussed in Chapter 3, researchers who align with the interpretive tradition are interested in reason explanations, or understanding, instead of causal or functional explanations. Thus, to qualitative researchers, the criterion of internal validity isn't very helpful in figuring out whether a qualitative study is trustworthy. Instead, they ask whether a given study is credible. Credibility basically asks whether the study's conclusions "ring true" for the people studied. Qualitative researchers hope that the "natives," the people studied, will react something like this to the study's findings: "Yeah, that's right, but I hadn't thought of it that way."

DEPENDABILITY

To qualitative researchers, the criterion of measurement reliability employed by quantitative researchers presupposes a single, objective reality: There must be something tangible and stable "out there" to function as a benchmark for the notion of replication, or repeatability, to make any sense. Because researchers who adopt interpretive and critical paradigms believe in multiple realities and believe that those realities are always under construction by social actors, and thus changeable, the concept of measurement reliability isn't a useful criterion by which to evaluate the trustworthiness of qualitative research. To qualitative researchers, observed instability may be attributed to shifts in reality (as actors construct it or as researchers gain better insights into it). Instead of judging observations by their consistency, qualitative researchers evaluate whether the observations are dependable.

To demonstrate that his or her interpretations are dependable, a qualitative researcher must make it possible for an external check to be conducted on the process by which the study was done. This external check should make the researcher's process *trackable*—an outsider must be able to see how a researcher went from point A to point B to point C in his or her interpretive process. Often, this means that the researcher's observations will not be stable. After all, if the researcher is learning more about a given field setting or social group, his or her analysis should be changing over time toward increased understanding. And with increased sensitivity to the group or setting under study comes an increased ability to detect changes in that social world as it constantly evolves and adapts. Thus, dependable qualitative research is based on trackable research, not the consistency of the researcher's observations.

CONFIRMABILITY

Instead of evaluating measurement validity, qualitative researchers talk in terms of confirmability. To interpretivists, the concept of measurement validity presupposes a single, objective reality that can be measured. The criterion of measurement validity is thus not very useful to qualitative researchers who believe in multiple, subjective realities. Instead, qualitative researchers judge whether the researcher's conclusions are the result of the phenomenon under study rather than the biases of the researcher. Qualitative observations must be confirmable. Data must be traceable to their sources. In addition, the logic used by the researcher in moving from the particular data to the conclusions drawn from those data must be systematic, coherent, and explicit.

You may find the distinction between dependability and confirmability somewhat confusing. Dependability tracks the researcher's flow of understanding to ensure that changes across time make sense. Confirmability traces a researcher's conclusions back to his or her data to ensure that they are well reasoned.

TRANSFERABILITY

Qualitative researchers do not find the criterion of external validity to be very useful. As you may recall from Chapter 3, the interpretive research tradition tends to favor idiographic over nomothetic research. That is, qualitative researchers seek in-depth understanding of a single setting or social group rather than generalized laws of explanation. Given their idiographic focus, qualitative researchers do not seek generalized claims.

Qualitative researchers substitute the criterion of transferability for external validity. The obligation of the qualitative researcher is to provide a detailed description of the setting or group under study—what some researchers call a "thick description" (Geertz, 1973). If the researcher has successfully provided a thick description, then readers can judge for themselves whether and how the researcher's analysis is relevant to them. To meet the criterion of external validity, it is the quantitative researcher's obligation to demonstrate that findings are generalizable. By contrast, to meet the criterion of transferability, a qualitative researcher needs to provide sufficient details so that a reader can make the decision about whether to apply the findings elsewhere to a different context or group.

Qualitative research will always be found wanting when the criteria applied to quantitative research are brought to bear, just as quantitative research always suffers against the criteria of trustworthy qualitative research. Each general approach to research has its strengths as well as its limitations. As we have noted throughout this book, we encourage you to become familiar with the whole research methods tool kit—both quantitative methods and qualitative methods. Let's now turn to the qualitative tools in the communication research kit.

CHAPTER 13

Participant Observation

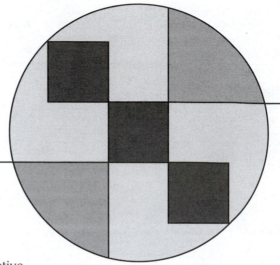

What You'll Learn in This Chapter

You'll learn about one of the primary methods used in qualitative research: participant observation. This method involves observing communication in its natural habitat: going where the action is, watching it, and participating in it. You'll learn how to prepare for the field, observe, record field notes, and exit the field.

INTRODUCTION

Several chapters ago, we said that you've been doing communication research all your life. This should become even clearer to you as we turn now to what probably seems like the most obvious method of making observations: participant observation. If you want to know about something related to communication, why not just go where it's happening and watch it happen, experience it, perhaps even participate in it? While these are "natural" activities, you'll see that they're also skills to be learned and honed. That's what this chapter is all about. We've used the term *participant observation* to include methods of research sometimes referred to as *field research, naturalistic inquiry, naturalism,* and *field studies.*

Participant observation is a qualitative method in which the researcher participates as an actor in the events under study. To study the TV viewing experiences of children, the researcher hangs out with some children while they watch TV, watching what they watch, engaging to the extent possible in the parallel activities they engage in while watching, eating the foods they eat while watching, and so forth. In participant-observation research, the people you observe and interact with are often known as "natives."

One of the key strengths of this method is the comprehensiveness of perspective it gives researchers. By going directly to the communication phenomenon under study and observing it as completely as possible, they can develop a deeper and fuller understanding of it. This mode of observation, then, is especially, though not exclusively, appropriate to research topics that appear to defy simple quantification. Field researchers may recognize several nuances of attitude and behavior that might escape researchers using other methods.

Participant observation is especially appropriate to the study of those attitudes and behaviors best understood within their natural setting, as opposed to the somewhat artificial settings of experiments and surveys. If, for example, you are interested in studying those synergistic moments in a group discussion when everything seems to "click" and group members seem to just take off in an eruption of creative problem solving, participant observation would probably be more useful to you than an experiment or a quantitative survey.

Finally, participant observation is well suited to the study of communication processes over time. Thus, the field researcher might be in a position to examine the rumblings and final explosion of a conflict as events actually occur rather than afterward, in a reconstruction of the same event.

TOPICS APPROPRIATE FOR PARTICIPANT-OBSERVATION RESEARCH

We've introduced you in a general way to the sorts of issues that are especially appropriate to participant-observation research. Now we want to flesh that subject out in greater detail.

Some Thinking Topics

In their *Analyzing Social Settings* (1995, pp. 101–113), John and Lyn Lofland discuss several elements of social life appropriate for participant-observation research. They call them *thinking topics.* Thinking topics can focus our attention on various facets of the communication process:

1. *Practices.* This refers to various kinds of socially recognized talk or action. With respect to communication, we could study the communicative practices involved in delivering bad news, gossiping, self-presentation to a prospective dating partner, identity management in a chat room, and so forth. The list of communication practices to study is seemingly endless.

2. *Episodes.* Here the Loflands include a variety of dramatic events such as divorce, the experience of natural disasters, and illness. A communication researcher might be interested in communication during such extraordinary episodes, perhaps with an eye toward understanding how communication is used to construct the meaning of these episodes or how communication is used by people to cope with such episodes.

3. *Encounters.* This involves two or more people meeting and interacting in immediate proximity with one another. Idle small talk while waiting for a bus, job interviews between prospective employers and applicants, or the end-of-day conversation between spouses might be of interest to the communication researcher.

4. *Roles.* Participant-observation research is also appropriate to the analysis of the positions that people occupy and the communication behavior associated with those positions. Some roles are ascribed—for example, a person's role as a "man" or a "woman" in a given society. Other roles are formalized, as in the role of teacher in a kindergarten classroom. Sometimes, roles are informal, such as the role of "good ol' boy" in an organizational department. Some roles are associated with various social types—for example, the role

of "bully" on a children's playground. A communication researcher might be interested in studying the communication behaviors associated with a given role, or how a given role is constituted in the verbal and nonverbal communicative actions of the role occupant.

5. *Relationships.* Much social life can be examined in terms of the kinds of communicative behavior appropriate to pairs or sets of roles: mother–son relationships, friendships, and the like. Much of the research in the area of interpersonal communication is devoted to understanding the enactment of communication in a variety of kinds of personal relationships.

6. *Groups.* Moving beyond relationships, participant-observation research can also be used to study the communication that is enacted in small groups, such as friendship cliques, athletic teams, families, and work groups.

7. *Organizations.* Beyond small groups, field researchers also study communication in formal organizations, such as hospitals, corporations, and service agencies.

8. *Settlements.* It's difficult to study large societies such as nations, but field researchers often study communication that is enacted in smaller-scale "societies" such as villages, ghettos, and neighborhoods.

9. *Social worlds.* Ambiguous social entities with vague boundaries and populations can nonetheless be proper subjects for social scientific study: "communication in the sports world," "the communicative dynamics of Wall Street," and the like.

10. *Lifestyles or subcultures.* Finally, communication researchers sometimes focus on how large numbers of people conduct their communicative life: groups such as a "ruling class" or an "urban underclass."

Thomas Lindlof (1995) provides an alternative way to organize thinking topics relevant to communication. He suggests that participant observation generally revolves around these four areas of inquiry:

- "Communication as a substantive act" (Lindlof, 1995, p. 92). You might study communication acts or events that are recognized in common by natives, such as the employment interview or the President's State of the Union address.

- "Communication as an explicit or implicit referent" (Lindlof, 1995, p. 93). You might study references to communication that appear in discourse.

For example, you might study how people talk about the evening news to fellow family members, or how family members talk about how they communicate with one another.

- "Communication as a constitutive component of social action" (Lindlof, 1995, p. 93). You might be interested in how various social or cultural forms are constructed or accomplished through communication. For instance, you might be interested in how "popularity" among adolescents is accomplished through studying the communicative actions of "popular" and "unpopular" adolescents in a school setting.

- "Communication as a regulatory component of social action" (Lindlof, 1995, p. 93). You might be interested in seeing how communication is used to regulate, control, or evaluate. For example, you might be interested in how co-workers regulate one another's work habits day to day through such communicative practices as teasing and gossip.

Obviously, there's substantial overlap between Lindlof's list of thinking topics and the list provided by the Loflands. Our point in sharing these two lists is to suggest to you that there are many possible topic areas usefully addressed through participant observation.

Participant observation is particularly popular among communication researchers who are interested in the ethnography of communication. We were briefly introduced to this perspective in our discussion of inductive logic systems in Chapter 4. We're going to elaborate a bit more here on that approach because of the particular topics of interest to participant observers who adopt an ethnography-of-communication perspective.

The Ethnography of Communication

The anthropologist Dell Hymes (1962) is responsible for coining the phrase *ethnography of speaking,* from which the broader **ethnography of communication** has evolved. According to Hymes (1962), "The ethnography of speaking is concerned with all the situations and uses, the patterns and functions, of speaking as an activity in its own right" (p. 16). *Communication* is a broader term than *speaking* and includes the ethnographic focus on all facets of communication.

Researchers who take an ethnography-of-communication perspective focus on the *speech community* as their primary unit of analysis. A speech community is "a universe of discourse with a finely organized, distinctive pattern of meaning and action" (Philipsen, 1992, p. 4).

Although some ethnographers operationalize a speech community as a nationality (e.g., Israeli, U.S.), more common is the recognition that a given nation or culture consists of many speech communities. Everywhere there is a coherent universe of discourse, there is a speech community. Thus, for example, many of the groups in which you hold membership may be distinct speech communities—your family, your co-workers, your soccer club, and so forth.

Gerry Philipsen (1992) has described three key assumptions of research from the ethnography-of-communication tradition:

- "Speaking is structured" (Philipsen, 1992, p. 9). Everywhere that communication is used, it is structured in some way—structured in who speaks to whom, where, about what. The rules that guide the enactment and interpretation of communication can be summarized in the speech community's code of communication, which consists of "a socially constructed and historically transmitted system of symbols and meanings pertaining to communication" (Philipsen, 1992, p. 8).

Hymes's SPEAKING acronym (1972, pp. 59–65), mentioned in Chapter 4, is a useful heuristic framework for identifying the code of communication in a given speech community. The acronym basically orients the researcher to a set of thinking topics to guide his or her field observations:

S: *Situation.* What is the setting or scene of the communicative action?

P: *Participants.* Who are the participants in a given communication event, and what is their relationship to one another?

E: *Ends.* What are the goals, purposes, and outcomes, or ends, of the communicative action?

A: *Act Characteristics.* What is the form and content of what is said?

K: *Key.* What is the tone or manner in which a communicative act is enacted? For example, is it serious? Teasing? And so forth.

I: *Instrumentalities.* What is the channel of communication? What language or dialect is being used?

N: *Norms of Interaction.* What are the norms for enacting and interpreting communication?

G: *Genres.* What is the recognized category or type of communicative action being enacted?

- "Speaking is distinctive" (Philipsen, 1992, p. 10). Speech communities differ in their codes of communication, which is to say that communication is not

everywhere the same. It can perform different functions, be directed at different goals, and take different forms of enactment. Thus, we can never fully understand communication without recognizing that it is a deeply cultured act.

- "Speaking is social" (Philipsen, 1992, p. 13). Communication is not merely a medium for accomplishing some individual purpose or social function. Communication also constitutes social life. Thus, whenever we are communicating, we are also in the process of "doing" social life, including the construction of our identities as male, female, midwestern, and so on.

Illustrative of an ethnography-of-communication study is one undertaken by Charles Braithwaite (1997b) of Navajo educational communication practices. He engaged in participant observation research during his eight-month stay at a Navajo community college, a bilingual/bicultural college. During this period of time, he used the resources of the college (such as the library), attended faculty meetings, lived with students in a dormitory, ate in the cafeteria, attended celebrations and ceremonies, and participated in several off-campus activities (e.g., Pow Wows sponsored by the Navajo Nation). All in all, Braithwaite observed over 100 hours of classroom interaction; in addition, he taught a course at the college. His goal was to describe the communication code of this speech community.

Some ethnographers on communication believe that research should function to enhance social justice, emancipating oppressed people. Researchers who subscribe to this belief are engaged in what is known as *critical ethnography.* A critical ethnography is often characterized by its analysis of power relations in the speech community, and it gives voice to groups or individuals who have been silenced in one way or another by their relative powerlessness. A critical ethnographer has a goal of using ethnography as a tool of social change.

An example of critical ethnography is an ethnographic study of how traditional gender roles are reproduced and resisted in academic discourse by Victoria Bergvall and Kathryn Remlinger (1996). These researchers engaged in a five-year study of classroom talk in a mid-sized technological university. Although the female students appeared to have gained equal access to the public floor in classroom contexts by traditional quantitative measures of the number of turns and word counts, the researchers' qualitative data indicated "complex struggles for control of the conversational floor" (p. 452). In their effort to examine power relations in classroom discourse, these researchers clearly positioned themselves within the critical ethnographic tradition.

Actually, in its consideration of a particular "case" known as a speech community, the ethnography-of-communication approach is a specific form of a more general kind of research that uses participant observation—the case study.

Case-Study Research

A **case study** is an investigation of a "specific, unique, bounded system" (Stake, 1994, p. 237). Stake (1994, p. 236) elaborates on what is and is not a "case":

> Custom has it that not everything is a case. . . . An agency may be a case. The reasons for child neglect or the policies of dealing with neglectful parents would seldom be considered a case. Those topics are generalities rather than specificities. The case is a specific. Even more, the case is a functioning specific. . . . [I]t has working parts, it probably is purposive, even having a self. It is an integrated system. The parts do not have to be working well, the purposes may be irrational, but it is a system.

Thus, a group, an organization, a family, a given speech community—all of these would "count" as cases. Any abstraction would not be considered a case.

Stake (1994) distinguishes *single-case studies,* in which a single case is examined in depth, from what he calls *collective-case studies,* in which a number of cases are studied for the insights they provide into the broader category of similar cases. In a collective-case study, the researcher typically presents a detailed description of each case separately (known as a within-case analysis), followed by a thematic analysis across cases (known as a cross-case analysis).

The case-study tradition is popular among scholars of organizational communication. Researchers select a single organization and analyze its communication. For example, Katherine Miller, Lori Joseph, and Julie Apker (2000) conducted a case-study analysis of a care coordinator program at a specific hospital. Their analysis centered on the ambiguity they observed in defining the role of the "care coordinator"—the nurse who coordinated patient care "from admission to discharge" (p. 200).

Although a researcher may have a particular thinking topic in mind when he or she enters the field, the general question that guides all participant observation during its initial stages is much broader: "What is going on here?" Through participant-observation data gathering, the re-

searcher gradually narrows down this question using the iterative reasoning process discussed in Chapter 4. Often, these thinking topics become salient to the researcher as he or she conducts fieldwork and gradually focuses on what is most significant or interesting in the field site. So let's turn to the process of participant observation in order to better understand this research process.

THE CHOREOGRAPHY OF PARTICIPANT OBSERVATION

Valerie Janesick (1994) has an elegant metaphor for the participant-observation method: a dance choreography. Like a choreography, a participant-observation study has three stages: the warm-up stage, the floor exercise stage, and the cool-down stage:

> Just as the dancer begins with a warm-up of the body, follows through with floor exercises, and then moves to a cool-down period, I like to think of qualitative design as made up of three stages. First there is the warm-up stage, or design decisions made at the beginning of the study; second is the total workout stage, during which design decisions are made throughout the study; and third is the cool-down stage, when design decisions are made at the end of the study. (p. 211)

Janesick is quick to point out that participant observation, like choreographed dance, is an elastic process; important to both dynamics is an ability to adapt and adjust as the enactment unfolds. Without this commitment to elasticity, participant observation, like dance, can easily become a mechanical, stilted enterprise. Let's take apart each of the three stages that Janesick identifies.

THE "WARM-UP" PERIOD

Janesick (1994, pp. 211–212) identifies eight important activities that need to take place during this phase of the participant-observation research process.

Questions to Guide the Study

First, the researcher needs to determine the general questions that will guide the research. Our discussion of thinking topics is relevant here. We underscore that the research questions that characterize participant observation are usually different from the research questions and research hypotheses characteristic of quantitative research. In contrast to the mandate in quantitative research to develop narrowly focused, clear questions or hypotheses about possible relationships between variables, the research questions that guide qualitative researchers are much more general in nature, and they change and evolve as the study progresses. The initial expression of a general, guiding question is simply a starting point.

One of us once held a half-time administrative position in a provost's office while simultaneously occupying a faculty position at the same institution. At this time in the institution's history, the faculty and the administration were at odds about the governance system that should organize decision making—who was authorized to make what kinds of decisions with or without prior consultation with appropriate constituencies. The position of having one foot in a faculty role and one foot in an administrative role was an ideal one for conducting participant-observation research about the conflict. The general, guiding question of the study was to find out how faculty members and administrators were making sense of the conflict (Baxter, 1993).

This guiding question would probably be classified as an episode-based topic using the Loflands' (1995) list: The focus was on understanding the meaning making that surrounded a particularly dramatic moment in the institution's history. Using Lindlof's (1995) list, the study's guiding question illustrates the second topic area—a study of participants' explicit or implicit references to a particular communication episode, the governance conflict. From an ethnography-of-communication perspective, the focus was initially about norms—natives' understandings of how decision making should take place.

However, as with all participant-observation research, the initial question displayed elasticity—it changed as the study unfolded. During the two-year period of fieldwork, the guiding question actually ended up addressing Lindlof's (1995) third and fourth topic areas as well. In reacting to the governance conflict the way they did, faculty members constituted what it meant to be a faculty member, just as administrators constituted what it meant to be an administrator, through their reactions to the conflict event. Whenever faculty members and administrators talked about one another in the context of the conflict, their communication also functioned to evaluate the other and to attempt to control their subsequent actions. In the ethnography-of-communication framework, the study evolved from a focus on norms to include, as

well, analytic attention to participants, ends, keys, and instrumentalities.

The Literature Review

Related to the selection of a guiding question is the matter of reading relevant research literature before undertaking fieldwork—the second activity of the "warm-up" phase. Because we discussed this topic at length in Chapter 2, we won't say anything further about how to do this at this point.

Although some might think that inductive research frees the researcher from the obligation to conduct a literature review in advance of the study, we and many others think this is misguided advice. The more informed you are, the more astute your observations are likely to be in the field. This quality is what Anselm Strauss and Juliet Corbin (1990, p. 41) refer to as **theoretical sensitivity.** By doing adequate background reading, you are sensitizing yourself to what might be going on with the phenomenon under study.

Of course, elasticity is the key here. You don't want to let your background reading bias what you see in the field, and you need to be ready to challenge existing literature if your observations do not match what others have found. The point is to enter the field open-minded but not empty-headed (Erlandson et al., 1993).

Self-Reflection

A third important activity for you to undertake during this period is to try to identify your own biases and ideologies. This reflexive process is a conscious one, and this should be used as a reason to initiate a **reflexive journal,** or diary of the entire research process. Participant observation involves two kinds of note taking: **field notes,** in which the researcher records his or her observations of the phenomenon under study, and the reflexive journal. The reflexive journal is a chronological record of the process of conducting the research study. The researcher should record factually what was done: when and how. In addition, because the researcher is the instrument in qualitative research, the reflexive journal is a record of the researcher's thoughts and feelings during the process. The reflexive journal for the warm-up stage should contain a discussion of the researcher's biases and, in addition, a record of the thoughts and feelings surrounding each of the activities of this period. Throughout the study, the researcher revisits the reflexive journal, rereading its entries and adding additional ones. We'll return to this topic below when we describe in detail the process of recording field notes.

At the conclusion of the study, the reflexive journal provides an *audit trail* of the research process (Lincoln & Guba, 1985). Just as a fiscal audit checks the books to ensure their integrity, the audit trail afforded by the reflexive journal provides the best single evidence the researcher has to demonstrate his or her dependability. From the introduction to Part 3, you know that a qualitative researcher needs to demonstrate that his or her work is trackable: that the researcher moved analytically from point A to point B to point C in a logical manner. The reflexive journal is a trackability log of the researcher's analysis.

Site Selection

The selection of a site for your study is a very important decision. Sometimes, researchers opt for convenience sampling, using whatever sites happen to be available— groups to which you already belong, places you ordinarily hang out, and so on. Once you are in the field, conducting participation-observation research at your site, the expectation is that something interesting will surface as a question for research. Certainly, much research has been done this way, sometimes with a positive end result. But this strikes us as a very risky way to go about the siteselection process. It is heavily reliant on luck to produce a "data-rich" site. Unless you are highly sensitized to observing communicative life, it might be a challenge to uncover a significant or interesting phenomenon upon which to focus your energies.

One of us recently taught a research methods class for which the assignment was to undertake a group research project on some communication phenomenon. One group selected a bowling team to observe because one of the class members happened to be a member of the team and the research team could get easy access to the site of study—the weekly bowling match at a local bowling alley. Sounds good. The only problem was that the group was hard-pressed to find anything interesting that they could focus on—unfortunately, this team didn't do much talking while engaged in bowling, nor did members really interact much outside of the weekly bowling match. After many weeks of agonizing, the research team brought in an audiotape of talk during one of the weekly bowling matches, and we were able to glean a possible topic from their talk—how members engaged in face-saving when a fellow bowling teammate failed to get a good score. Our point here is that the site selected for its convenience just

might turn out to present a real observational and analytic challenge. Choose a site carefully.

The selection of a site (or sites) for participant-observation work should be guided by a general stance of purposive sampling. Remember from Chapter 7 that researchers can use either probability-based sampling or nonprobability-based sampling. We've just been discussing the limitations of a convenience sample in site selection. A more helpful sampling approach is purposive sampling. In general, a researcher should choose a site that is intentionally biased toward "information-rich cases" (Patton, 1990, p. 169). Remember that the goal of qualitative research is not generalizability but detailed or "thick" description and interpretation. Thus, the site should be selected strategically to provide rich opportunities to gather data relevant to the guiding question. For example, Kristine Fitch (1994) was interested in the general question of how Colombians enact directives— attempts to compel the actions of others. So she selected sites for her participant observation in which people would likely be using a lot of directives—what she called "directive-intensive environments" (p. 190). Sites included day-care centers and preschools, instructional settings, manufacturing firms, and service encounters.

Lindlof (1995, p. 83) recommends that researchers conduct a reconnaissance mission to check out prospective sites before making a selection. For example, just how common are directives in day-care centers? Reconnaissance work can also shed insight into whether you will be able to gain access to the site.

Just because you would like to conduct your research in a given site doesn't necessarily mean that you will be able to gain access to it. Some sites are permeable to researcher access, whereas other sites pose greater access challenges. There are a variety of ways to establish your initial contact with the people you plan to study. How you do it will depend, in part, on the role you intend to play.

The Various Roles of the Researcher

To this point in the chapter, we have used the term *participant observation* as if the researcher always participates in the process or phenomenon being studied. Actually, it's more complicated than that. **Participation observation** refers to a family of observation strategies, or roles that can be assumed by the researcher. As Catherine Marshall and Gretchen Rossman (1995) point out,

The researcher may plan a role that entails varying degrees of "participantness"—that is, the degree of actual participation in daily life. At one extreme is the full participant, who goes about ordinary life in a role or set of roles constructed in the setting. At the other extreme is the complete observer, who engages not at all in social interaction and may even shun involvement in the world being studied. And, of course, all possible complementary mixes along the continuum are available to the researcher. (p. 60)

Raymond Gold (1958) has organized a typology of four different participant-observation roles. Figure 13-1A provides a visual display of these four roles, organized according to their two underlying dimensions: whether the participants are aware that the researcher is conducting research and whether the researcher interacts with participants. Of course, each of these dimensions is oversimplified by dichotomizing them into presence/absence or yes/no options. Nonetheless, Gold's typology is helpful in pointing out that participant observation can be done in several ways.

The **complete-participant role** is characterized by participants' lack of awareness that they are being observed. In addition, the researcher is involved in the setting as actively as he or she can be, attempting to behave like the "natives." The researcher may be a genuine participant in what he or she is studying (for example, a study of a speech community of which the researcher is an actual member) or may pretend to be a genuine participant. In any event, if you act as the complete participant, you let people see you *only* as a participant, not as a researcher. For instance, if you're studying a group made up of uneducated and inarticulate people, it wouldn't be appropriate for you to talk and act like a university professor or student. (Not to imply that all professors are always articulate!)

Let us draw your attention to an ethical issue here, one on which researchers themselves are divided. Is it ethical to deceive the people you're studying in the hope that they will confide in you as they will not confide in an identified researcher? Do the interests of science—the scientific values of the research—offset such considerations? Although many professional associations have addressed this issue, the norms to be followed remain somewhat ambiguous when applied to specific situations.

Related to this ethical consideration is a scientific one. No researcher deceives his or her study participants solely for the purpose of deception. Rather, it's done in the belief that the data will be more trustworthy, that the participants will be more natural and honest if they don't know the researcher is doing a research project. If the

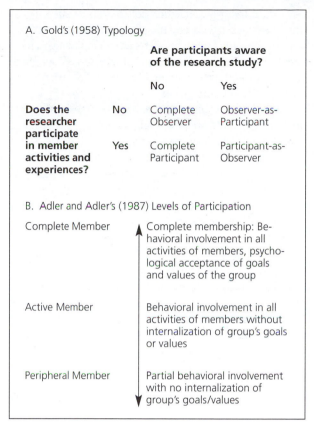

FIGURE 13-1   **Participant-Observation Roles**

people being studied know they're being studied, they might modify their behavior in a variety of ways. First, they might expel the researcher. Second, they might modify their speech and behavior to appear more "respectable" than would otherwise be the case. Third, the social process itself might be radically changed. For example, students making plans to burn down the university administration building might give up the plan altogether once they learn that one of their group members is a communication researcher conducting a research project on group communication.

On the other side of the coin, if you're a complete participant, you may affect what you're studying. To play the role of participant, you must *participate*. Yet your participation may importantly affect the very process you're studying. Suppose that you're asked for your ideas about what the group should do next. No matter what you say, you will affect the process in some fashion. If the group follows your suggestion, your influence on the process is obvious. If the group decides not to follow your suggestion, the process whereby the suggestion is rejected may importantly affect what happens next. Finally, if you indicate that you just don't know what should be done next, you may be adding to a general feeling of uncertainty and indecisiveness in the group.

Ultimately, *anything* a field researcher does or does not do will have some effect on what is being observed; it is simply inevitable. More seriously, what you do or do not do may have an *important* effect on what happens. There is no complete protection against this effect, though sensitivity to the issue may provide a partial protection.

The complete-participant role allows a researcher to gain a total immersion in the experiences of the field site. It thus is a useful tool for the subjective understanding of communication.

But such an immersion experience also has its down side. The researcher could over-identify with the participants, "going native." This could complicate leaving the field, and it could compromise the insights the researcher could have garnered about the site by stepping back and gaining a bit of perspective on it. Furthermore, in performing the role of a member, the researcher's attitudes and actions are constrained. If you're a regular member, then you can do only what regular members are allowed to do, and nothing beyond this. Such constraints could hamper researcher efforts to gain a more comprehensive understanding of all of the facets of the phenomenon or site of study.

Sometimes, the complete-participant role isn't an option because of the guiding question that interests the researcher. If you're interested in preschoolers' sense making of Saturday-morning TV cartoons as they watch in their homes, there's no way for you to become a child again (despite the magic fortune-telling machine in the movie *Big*).

Because of these several ethical and scientific considerations, the field researcher frequently chooses a different role from that of complete participant. However, sometimes a communication researcher does choose the complete-participant role. For example, Charles Braithwaite (1997a) undertook a participant-observation study of the interactions that took place at a plasma donation center, where people sold their blood plasma. Braithwaite became known as a "regular" among the technicians, which is not surprising given that he donated plasma 16 times over a 2-month period. Braithwaite thus functioned as a complete participant, selling blood like his fellow participants and interacting with them while the plasma was removed from his blood. Fifteen to 25 people were donating their plasma at a time, a procedure that

took anywhere from 2 to 3.5 hours to complete. Braithwaite took detailed notes during his donation visits, but such behavior was quite consistent with the behavior of fellow donors, many of whom were students who brought along material to read or write.

You could participate fully with the group under study but make it clear that you were also undertaking research; that is, you could adopt the **participant-as-observer role.** The participant-as-observer role has the ethical advantage of awareness by the natives that they are being observed. In this role, you reap the advantages of involvement, yet you have more freedom of movement than as a complete participant because the natives understand that you are a researcher. Your involvement is understood as part time, voluntary, and temporary. As a participant-as-observer, you have license to participate in a wide range of experiences, perhaps more than might be possible if you were an actual member fulfilling only a single position.

There are disadvantages in this role, however. The people being studied may shift much of their attention to the research project rather than focus on the natural social process, making the process being observed no longer typical. Although you may experience more freedom to engage in a full range of perspectives, activities, and actions, your experience may be more superficial than what could be experienced by a complete participant.

Despite its possible disadvantages, the participant-as-observer role is a popular one in participant-observation research in communication. Illustrative of this role is a study undertaken by Mary McComb (1995) about becoming a travelers aid volunteer. Washington, D.C.'s National Airport has a volunteer agency, the Travelers Aid Society (TAS), to assist travelers in a variety of capacities. To understand how newcomers are socialized to an organization, McComb assumed the participant-as-observer role, entering the training program in how to become a TAS volunteer. McComb conducted interviews with fellow organizational members, and they cooperated with her goal of acting like a newcomer in order to understand what the experience was like. Here's what McComb had to say about her participant-as-observer role:

> TAS cooperated completely with the study. . . . During the investigation, I attended 13 hours of classroom training over a period of three months, and observed a veteran volunteer at the desk for $4\frac{1}{2}$ hours. Then, in one month, with 19 different veteran partners, I worked 28 shifts (110.5 hours) as a trainee at the National Airport desks. Near the end of my study, I worked one $4\frac{1}{2}$ hour shift by myself. The typical volunteer would

have taken 28 weeks to work the same amount I did in a little over one month. During this field experience, I took notes, kept a diary and an activity log, and conducted formal and informal interviews with organizational members. (1995, p. 301)

McComb participated like a trainee, but her experience was not that of a complete participant. She conducted formal interviews with fellow organizational members, in which her identity as a researcher was known. In addition, the training she received was a highly condensed process, in which she completed the work in one month that a "typical volunteer" would complete in 28 weeks.

The third of Gold's roles is that of the **observer-as-participant.** In contrast to the participant-as-observer role, in which participation is primary and observation is secondary, the observer-as-participant features just the opposite mix—observation is primary, and participation is secondary. Participation tends to be more fleeting and superficial than with the participant-as-observer role. An example of this role is provided in a study of how first-year teachers achieved classroom discipline published by Kimberly Barquist Hogelucht and Patricia Geist (1997). The researchers report that they observed classroom interaction for 40 hours and, in addition, conducted interviews with the teacher and students. The teacher and the students had full knowledge that they were part of a research study. However, the researchers did not participate in the classroom sessions themselves—they did not try to function, in even a limited way, as a teacher or as a student.

Lindlof (1995) argues that the observer-as-participant role does allow the researcher to reach conclusions that emerge over time. Further, because interviewing is often a common practice in the observer-as-participant role, the researcher gains the native's view on the phenomenon under study. Finally, the role meets ethical standards of conduct because participants are aware that they are being observed as part of a research project. However, Lindlof suggests that the limited first-hand participation with the phenomenon may result in findings that are biased due to the researcher's own conceptions.

The **complete observer,** the fourth of Gold's roles, observes a social process without becoming a part of it in any way. Quite possibly, the participants of the study might not realize they're being studied, because of the researcher's unobtrusiveness. Sitting at a bus stop to observe jaywalking at a nearby intersection would be an example. Although the complete observer is less likely to affect what's being studied and less likely to "go native" than the complete participant, she or he is also less likely

to develop a full appreciation of what's being studied. Observations may be more sketchy and transitory.

Kristine Fitch (1994) conducted a participant-observation study of directives—verbal attempts to compel action from others—in both the United States and Colombia. She used a variety of Gold's participant-observation roles, including the role of complete observer, fully cognizant that each role has strengths and limitations. The complete-observer role involved having field researchers "shadow" a person for a day, recording all instances in which a directive was given or received. In addition, audiotapes were made of approximately ten hours of conversation among friends, co-workers, or family members. Researchers were not present during these tapings, or their participation in the conversations was curtailed.

An alternative way to describe the variety of participation-observation roles is by their degree of involvement (Adler & Adler, 1987). We can recast the participation side of the participant-observation method in terms of three roles: the **complete member,** the **active member,** and the **peripheral member** (Adler & Adler, 1987). This alternative organizing framework for participation-observation roles is summarized in Figure 13-1B. These three types of participation vary in the social function of the researcher—how integrated he or she is into the scene. Basically, the Adler and Adler typology of three participant roles is a different way to slice Gold's two roles of complete participant and participant-as-observer, the roles in which participation features prominently.

The complete-member form of participation involves the researcher as an actual member of the group under study. The researcher selects a group in which he or she held prior membership, currently holds membership, or becomes a member. It is closely aligned with Gold's complete-participant role.

The active-member form of participation involves the researcher in the central or core activities of the group, much like a member, but he or she refrains from adopting the group's goals and values. Active-member participation is feigned membership, not "real" membership.

Peripheral membership involves participation in some of the group's activities, but the researcher refrains from participating in the most central activities of the group, unlike "real" or "feigned" members. The term *peripheral* says it all—this is a limited kind of participation, one that is partial with clear boundaries against "over-involvement."

Suppose you've decided to study the communicative practices of a religious cult that has enrolled many people in your neighborhood. You might study the group by joining it or pretending to join it. Take a moment to ask yourself what the difference is between "really" joining and "pretending" to join. The main difference is whether you actually take on the beliefs, attitudes, and other points of view shared by the "real" members. If the cult members believe that Jesus will come next Thursday night to destroy the world and save the members of the cult, do you believe it, or do you simply pretend to believe it? If you really believe it, your role is closer to that of a complete member. If you merely pretend to believe it, your role is closer to that of an active member. If you don't even pretend to believe it, your role is closer to that of a peripheral member.

Traditionally, researchers have tended to emphasize the importance of "objectivity" in such matters. In this example, that injunction would be to avoid getting swept up in the beliefs of the group. Without denying the advantages of objectivity, researchers today also recognize the benefits gained by immersing themselves in the points of view they're studying, what Lofland and Lofland (1995, p. 61) refer to as "insider understanding." Ultimately, you won't be able to understand the thoughts and actions of the cult members unless you can *adopt their points of view as true*—even if only temporarily. To fully appreciate the phenomenon you've set out to study, you need to *believe* that Jesus is coming Thursday night.

Adopting an alien point of view is an uncomfortable prospect for most people. It's one thing to learn about the strange views that others may hold. Sometimes, you probably find it hard just to tolerate certain views. But to take them as your own is ten times worse. Robert Bellah (1970) has offered the term *symbolic realism* in this regard, indicating the need for researchers to treat the beliefs they study as worthy of respect rather than as objects of ridicule. If you seriously entertain this prospect, you may appreciate why William Shaffir and Robert Stebbins (1991, p. 1) conclude that "fieldwork must certainly rank with the more disagreeable activities that humanity has fashioned for itself."

There is, of course, a danger in adopting the points of view of the people you're studying. When you abandon your objectivity in favor of adopting such views, you lose the possibility of seeing and understanding the phenomenon within frames of reference unavailable to the natives. On the one hand, accepting the belief that the world will end Thursday night allows you to appreciate aspects of that belief available only to believers; however, stepping outside that view makes it possible for you to consider some reasons why people might adopt such a view. You may discover some did so as a consequence of personal traumas (such as unemployment or divorce) while others were brought into the fold through their participation in particular social networks (for example, their

whole soccer team joined the cult). Notice that the cult members might disagree with those "objective" explanations, and you might not have come up with them if you had operated legitimately within the group's views.

There is, of course, an apparent dilemma here: There are important advantages in both postures, even though they seem mutually exclusive. It is, in fact, possible to assume both postures. Sometimes, you can simply shift viewpoints at will. When appropriate, you can fully assume the beliefs of the cult; later, you can step outside those beliefs. As you become more adept at this kind of research, you may come to hold contradictory viewpoints simultaneously, rather than switch back and forth.

The issue we've just been discussing could be seen as psychological, occurring mostly inside the researcher's head. There is a corresponding problem at a social level, however. When you become deeply involved in the lives of the people you're studying, you're likely to be moved by their personal problems and crises. Imagine, for example, that one of the cult members becomes ill and needs a ride to the hospital. Should you provide transportation? Sure. Suppose someone wants to borrow money to buy a stereo. Should you lend it? Probably not. Suppose they need the money for food?

There are no black-and-white rules for resolving situations such as these. However, you should be warned that such problems can arise and that you'll need to deal with them, regardless of whether you've revealed yourself to be a researcher or not. Such problems do not tend to arise in other types of research—surveys and experiments, for example—but they are part and parcel of participant observation. Although participant observation is often a fluid and changing process once you are in the field, it all starts in the "warm-up" period, when you decide what your initial role will be in the field.

Different situations and different research goals ultimately require different roles for the researcher. Unfortunately, there are no clear guidelines for making this choice—you must rely on your understanding of the situation and your own good judgment. In making your decision, however, you must be guided by both methodological and ethical considerations. Because these considerations often conflict, your decision will frequently be difficult, and you may find sometimes that your role limits your study.

Informed Consent Procedures

In order to gain permission to conduct a participant-observation study from your local IRB, you will need to submit a detailed proposal, or plan, for the study, as we discussed in Chapters 2 and 5. Because the job of the institutional review board is to oversee the ethical conduct of research, you will need to address the matter of informed consent from your prospective participants. In order to complete an IRB application, you need to have worked through in your mind the anticipated participant-observer roles we have just discussed. Central to this decision is the extent to which members have knowledge of your status as a researcher during your proposed time in the field. If you do not propose to gain prior informed consent from anyone affiliated with your field site, you need to have good reasons for this omission. It might be that your field site is a public location where people engage in public behavior—for example, engaging in idle chitchat while waiting for a bus. Or it might be that people's awareness of your researcher role could severely compromise the quality of the data you could gather.

If informed consent is necessary, the question arises as to whose consent is needed. Do you need to gain the prior permission of everybody you interact with in the field, or will it suffice to gain permission of certain specific persons? As a general rule, it is often sufficient to gain the prior consent of a few key people who grant permission on behalf of everyone in a given organization or group. These people are often known as the **gatekeepers** (Lindlof, 1995, p. 106) because they control the "access gate" that determines whether or not you are allowed to "pass through."

Sometimes, gatekeepers can be readily identified because of the role they occupy. In the study one of us conducted about a faculty–administration conflict in an academic institution (Baxter, 1993), the gatekeepers were clear: the person occupying the position of provost, the chief officer of the day-to-day internal operations of the institution, and the person occupying the position of president, the officer in overall charge of the institution, who represented the institution to its several constituencies. These two individuals were approached and informed of the general goals and the participation-observation process to be employed, and the study commenced only after they had given it the go-ahead.

At other times, however, it isn't so easy to determine who the gatekeepers are. Let's suppose you want to conduct a field study on how family members have incorporated the computer into their daily lives. You want to conduct observer-as-participant research, observing family members and talking with them in their home. Whose permission do you need to enter the home? The children's permission? The mother's? The father's? Generally, you are going to need the permission of adults, not minors. And in order to have good rapport with the family as a whole, you'd probably be better served by gaining the permission of both parents, not just one. Moreover, it

would probably be a good idea to discuss the study's purpose with the children, simply to ensure that they felt comfortable with your presence. Often, it is necessary to do some informal "reconnaissance work" at a potential field site in order to identify the gatekeepers whose informed consent you will need to obtain.

Although participant observation is always conducted in specific settings with specific natives, it is important to protect the confidentiality of participants from the very outset of the study. In order to accomplish this, researchers use pseudonyms instead of real names in recording their participation-observation data. For example, when Gerry Philipsen (1975) studied "talking like a man" in a southside Chicago neighborhood, he protected the identity of the neighborhood by naming it "Teamsterville." A bit later in his report, he describes an interaction with someone he has named "John," whom he describes as "a long-time resident of the neighborhood" (pp. 16–17). "John" is a pseudonym, not the person's actual name.

Any IRB application form will ask the researcher to address the possible risks and benefits to the research participant. Related to this assessment is a discussion of what rewards, if any, participants will receive for their involvement in the study. Some researchers pay participants a small gratuity for their time, say, if you were planning to interview them for a couple of hours. Often, however, it is impossible to know in advance of the study what kinds of reciprocal exchanges will unfold once a researcher is in the field. In general, however, the kind of participant-observer role assumed by the researcher sets some guidelines for expected behavior on the part of the researcher.

Of course, given the emergent and dynamic nature of participation-observation fieldwork, it is never possible to foresee all of the possible ethical issues that will arise in the course of conducting a study. During the "warm-up" period, however, it is necessary to anticipate as many issues as you can and act accordingly in proposing the study for IRB approval.

Sustaining Access

Selecting your initial participant-observer role and obtaining informed consent from appropriate gatekeepers are integral steps in the broader task of building and sustaining access to your field site and its members. But other steps are involved, as well.

For starters, you need to exert a great deal of time and energy building trust and rapport with participants so that they will feel comfortable interacting with you. There is no quick-and-easy set of steps to instant rapport—rapport is an ongoing relationship between the researcher and the participants that needs to be nurtured throughout the entire period of conducting a study. But the rapport process needs to start at the very beginning, as the study "warms up." The researcher needs to be fully mindful that today's actions may come back to help or haunt tomorrow.

Important to this rapport-building process is building a sponsorship relationship with key group members. A **sponsor** is a group member who takes an interest in you and your project (Lindlof, 1995, p. 109). Sponsors help open doors for you, perhaps introducing you around and legitimating you and your study to others in the group. A sponsor can lead you to **informants,** people who are positioned to provide you with quality information about the setting or the group.

As a researcher "warms up" to the field site, he or she is basically gaining initial familiarity with its physical and social contours—what's the lay of the land? Each additional day that the researcher spends in the field, the answer to this question grows increasingly more sophisticated. At first, however, the researcher is simply trying to get his or her initial bearings. Many field researchers have described this warming up to the field site as one of the most exhausting and emotionally draining stages of the entire study. Things get easier after the initial entry phase has taken place.

Development of a Timeline

When you submit an IRB application, you are usually asked to present an approximate timeline for the conduct of the study in the field. Although it is necessary to make a tentative plan, it is virtually impossible to predict how much time will need to be spent in the field. Unlike survey research or an experiment, in which the entire research study is planned at the outset and executed precisely, the very nature of participant-observation research is uncertain at the outset—it is an emergent enterprise.

As a guideline, however, more time in the field is generally recommended over less time. One of the foremost ways that a researcher establishes the credibility of his or her study is by informing the reader how much time was spent in the field. Remember from our introduction to Part 3 that qualitative research is, in part, assessed against the criterion of credibility—the extent to which the study's findings "ring true" to natives. Most published participant-observation studies present explicitly to the reader evidence of *prolonged engagement* (Lincoln & Guba, 1985). Readers are often told the number of months in the field, the number of hours of involvement, the number of participants who were interviewed and for how

long, and the number of transcript pages of field notes taken by the researcher. All of this is designed to demonstrate that the researcher spent a sufficiently long period of time in the field to understand the native's experience.

Prolonged engagement is also important in order to fulfill the criterion of transferability, discussed in the introduction to Part 3. A participant-observation study needs to be rich in detail so that readers can judge for themselves where and how the study's findings are transferable to other contexts. In general, the more time a researcher spends in the field, the greater the capacity to describe it in a detailed manner.

The "warm-up" period often segues seamlessly into the next period of the choreography of participation observation: the "floor exercise" period, in which the researcher is fully immersed in the business of gathering field data. In fact, many of the activities of the "floor exercise" overlap activities already initiated during the "warm-up."

THE "FLOOR EXERCISE" PERIOD

The second of Janesick's (1994) stages is that of gathering data in the field. We will describe six components of this period of the study: sampling, constructing field notes, constructing visual records, making ethical decisions, triangulating sources of data, and sustaining elasticity. Our treatment of the process of fieldwork implies that it is a tidy and orderly process, when in fact it is much more unpredictable and dynamic.

Sampling Participants, Activities, Scenes

Just as settings are sampled purposively, so is the sampling of participants, activities, or scenes in your setting or site. In particular, sampling should seek out "information-rich cases" (Patton, 1990, p. 169)—participants, activities, or scenes that will increase the researcher's understanding of the field setting in some way. A variety of specific nonprobability-based sampling techniques can be identified in participant-observation research.

First, you can use what is called **maximum-variation sampling** (Lincoln & Guba, 1985; Patton, 1990). In this form of sampling, the researcher is interested in intentionally seeking out people, activities, or scenes that will add a different, contrasting perspective on the phenomenon. In general, qualitative researchers are as interested in describing the variations within a population as they are in identifying commonalities across population members.

For example, suppose you were interested in doing a participant-observation study of how people communicatively cope with unethical workplace conduct by their co-workers. In order to maximize the variation of your sample, you would probably want to talk with people who are in management positions as well as people who are in nonmanagement positions—their roles might expose them to different kinds of ethical challenges, and they might have different resources available to them in terms of their responses. You might want to seek out people who willingly admit that they have been known to take home the occasional pen or pad of paper in order to increase your chances of talking to people who have engaged in behaviors that others might frame as unethical. And, of course, you would be interested in the opposite sort of person—the one who adamantly refuses to walk out of the office with so much as a paper clip that belongs to the organization. You might want to talk to someone in human resources about the organization's formalized code of ethical conduct, should one exist. And so forth. In short, you would be trying to engage as many different perspectives as you could in your study of the communication responses to unethical workplace conduct.

Second, you could use **typical case sampling** (Lindlof, 1995). You seek out a scene or a participant that you think is typical and provide an in-depth description of that case. The goal in typical case sampling is to provide an illustration of the phenomenon of interest, with no statistical claims to the representativeness of the selected case.

For example, in the workplace ethics study, you might discover in your early interactions with workers that a certain kind of behavior is frequently nominated as unethical—let's say drinking coffee from the communal pot without contributing the expected $1.00 per week to the "coffee fund." You might want to pursue this one ethical violation in greater depth, given the frequency with which it is mentioned, because you think it is typical of the kind of everyday workplace ethical matters encountered by co-workers. You might want to hang out around the coffee pot, observing how people give excuses for never seeming to have their dollar handy. You might want to actively violate the ethic of coffee-fund contributions in order to see how fellow organizational members bring the violation to your attention and seek corrective action from you. You might talk to people who are known violators to gain their perspective. In short, you may end up analyzing the ethics of the coffee pot as your typical case, based on your early fieldwork data.

Third, you could use **snowball sampling.** You might ask a current informant to refer you to other people with whom you could or should interact. Snowball sampling is generally a quick and efficient way to identify people regarded by fellow natives as relevant to the researcher's study. In the workplace ethics study, you might ask your current informants to refer you to other co-workers who have had to deal with unethical workplace conduct in one way or another. You could then track down these referrals, talk to them, and then ask them for other referrals.

Generally, informants who are nominated through referral are connected in some way to the person making the referral; usually, they are members of the nominator's social network. In order to make sure that your contacts are not limited to the members of a single social network, you can choose your "starter" informants through some other sampling strategy and then snowball off of each of your starter persons; with multiple starting points, you increase the likelihood that you will be referred to different social networks.

Theoretical construct sampling (Patton, 1990) is also a useful sampling strategy for participant-observation researchers. Basically, you select participants or cases based on their explicit relevance to the central phenomenon that interests you. This strategy often involves the articulation of criteria for inclusion in a study. For example, Dawn Braithwaite (1995) was interested in cross-sex embarrassment in the ritualized events of baby showers and wedding showers. In order to be eligible for her participant-observation study, a given shower had to be "co-ed" so that both males and females would be present. In the context of workplace ethics, you might want to find out how newcomers to the organization learn about the informal code of ethical conduct, so you might interact with employees who have been affiliated with the organization for a year or less.

You might also employ **critical case sampling** (Lindlof, 1995). A critical case is one that embodies in a dramatic way characteristics or features that are important in understanding the phenomenon under study. Critical cases may be quite rare, which is to say they aren't necessarily typical. Instead, critical cases provide a vivid, often intense, instance of features that can typically be found in less dramatic form. In the context of the workplace ethics study, your early fieldwork might stumble across a particularly dramatic incident that earned a lot of attention among workers because of its ethical implications. Maybe this incident was a one-time event, yet as you studied it, it became clear to you that this event involved all of the emergent characteristics that were surfacing in other instances of unethical conduct—ambiguity about whether the action was "allowed" in the organization, a self-serving motive by the person who engaged in the un-ethical act, and "slippery" accountability for the unethical act. You might purposively sample informants who had knowledge of or experience with this critical case so that you could provide a richly detailed description of it.

Last, there's **convenience sampling.** The researcher talks to people who are available and willing to interact, engages in activities because it is possible to do so, and visits particular scenes because he or she can. This is gen-erally the weakest form of nonprobability sampling, but it may prove helpful to a researcher, particularly in very early fieldwork, before other sampling strategies become possible.

Unlike survey and experimental research, in which a researcher identifies a sampling strategy in the planning stage of the study and then executes that single sampling plan, participant-observation research is often character-ized by an emergent sampling strategy in which multiple sampling techniques are used over the course of data gathering. The particular kind of sampling strategy de-pends on what is emerging as interesting and significant in the fieldwork to that point. Throughout data gathering, you use whatever sampling strategy seems appropriate at the time.

Central to data gathering is keeping a written record, also known as the researcher's field notes. It's vital to make full and accurate notes of what goes on in the field. Even tape recorders and cameras cannot capture all the relevant aspects of communication processes. The great-est advantage of the participant-observation method is the presence of an observing, thinking researcher on the scene of the action. In this sense, the researcher is the most important instrument or research tool.

Constructing Field Notes

Notice our word choice in the title to this section—we want to underscore that field notes are constructions of the researcher. Field notes are the researcher's texts of his or her observations and experiences in the field. Robert Emerson, Rachel Fretz, and Linda Shaw (1995) empha-size that taking field notes is not as straightforward as we might initially imagine:

> To view the writing of descriptions simply as a matter of producing texts that *correspond* accurately to what has been observed is to assume that there is but one "best" description of any particular event. But in fact, there is no one "natural" or "correct" way to write about what one observes. Rather, because descriptions involve issues of perception and interpretation, differ-ent descriptions of "the same" situations and events are possible. (p. 5)

Although a field researcher must be faithful to his or her observations and experiences, field notes necessarily reflect the researcher's subjectivity.

Field notes are thus a reductionist exercise—the "raw" experiences and observations of the researcher are re-duced to a written record. This writing-down process "freezes" the experience, providing an account that can be revisited time and again, unlike the experience itself, which is a fleeting moment in time. Of course, all quan-titative methods are also reductionist—people's per-ceptions and experiences are reduced to 1–7 Likert-type response options, quantitative indicators of the frequen-cies or intensities with which behaviors of a given type take place, and so forth. All research involves reduction. The reductionist exercise of taking field notes emerges in qualitative form—the researcher's written words on a page or in a computer file.

Some Guidelines for Taking Field Notes We know you're familiar with the process of taking notes. Every student is. And as we've said earlier, everybody is some-what familiar with participant-observation research in general. Like *good* field research, however, *good* note tak-ing requires careful and deliberate attention and involves some specific skills.

Researchers take field notes in different ways. In fact, one of the trademarks of field notes is that researchers de-velop unique ways of recording them—not unlike student variations in how class notes are taken. Some prefer to write in pencil only on a certain kind of paper; others pre-fer inks of varying colors, each color signifying something to the note taker. Nonetheless, there are some general guidelines that most qualitative researchers would agree upon. (You can learn more from John and Lyn Lofland's *Analyzing Social Settings* [1995, pp. 91–96].)

First, don't trust your memory any more than you have to; it's untrustworthy. If we're being too unkind to your mind, try this experiment. Recall the last few movies you saw that you really liked. Now name five of the actors or actresses. Who had the longest hair? Who was the most likely to start conversations? Who was the most likely to make suggestions that others followed? If you didn't have any trouble answering any of those questions, how *sure* are you of your answers? Would you be willing to bet a hundred dollars that a panel of impartial judges would observe what you recall?

Even if you pride yourself on having a photographic memory, it's a good idea to take notes either during the observation or as soon afterward as possible. If you take notes during the observation, do it unobtrusively, since people are likely to behave differently if they see you writing down everything they say or do.

Second, it's usually a good idea to take notes in stages. In the first stage, you may need to take sketchy notes (words and phrases) in order to keep abreast of what's happening. Then go off by yourself and rewrite your notes in more detail. If you do this soon after the events you've observed, the sketchy notes should allow you to recall most of the details. The longer you delay, the less likely you'll be able to recall things accurately and fully.

Emerson and his colleagues (1995) discuss *jotting* as a way to take quick field notes during observational work; this step helps with remembering later in the day, when a fuller-blown field note entry can be completed. Jottings are shorthand notes—words and phrases that "flag" important points you want to remember later. Here's a jotting one of us recorded in the field study of a faculty–administration conflict over governance issues at an academic institution (Baxter, 1993): "G.L. button test." This is a brief note made on a pocket-sized notepad, serving as a reminder of something that seemed important at the time. This jotting was recorded immediately after the interaction event had concluded, while waiting in a line to purchase a cup of coffee.

Should jottings be done openly, in the presence of natives, or should they be done in private? The answer depends on the kind of participant-observer role you are adopting and the particular circumstances of the event you are recording. In the governance-conflict field study, it was quite common for the researcher, who functioned as a complete participant given her membership in the groups she was observing, to be seen taking notes as part of her job; thus, note taking per se didn't appear strange. However, it might have appeared strange to whip out a notepad in the middle of the "G.L. button test" interaction

event, so the jotting was made immediately after the interaction event had concluded.

Hot on the trail of some communication phenomenon, you'll likely end a day of observations with a mass of scribbled notes. Depending on how late in the day or night you complete your observations, you may be tempted to set the notes aside and get some sleep. Don't! Field researchers can't work on a 9-to-5 schedule, and it's vital that you rewrite your notes as soon as possible after making a set of observations.

Use your jottings as a stimulus to re-create as many details of the day's experiences as possible. Your goal should be to produce typed notes as comprehensive and detailed as you would have made them in the first place if you could have recorded everything that seemed potentially relevant. If you regard your scribbled on-the-spot notes as a trigger for your memory, then you'll see the importance of retyping each night, and you'll have a clear sense of how to proceed.

Figure 13-2 shows a typed version of the field note entry that expanded on the "G.L. button test" jotting. Notice a few things about this field note entry. It has two columns. The left column is a description of the event—who the participants were, where the interaction took place, when it took place, what the event was about. The right column captures the researcher's reflections and analysis at the time the entry was created—preliminary thoughts on the meaning of the interaction event, feelings during the event, and so forth. This full-blown entry was typed in the evening of the day the "jotting" was made, while the event was still reasonably fresh in the researcher's mind.

We know this two-stage method sounds logical, and you've probably made a mental resolve to do it this way if you're ever involved in field research. However, let us warn you that you'll need some self-discipline to keep

---

[date]

I was walking across campus to get a morning cup of coffee at the canteen. As I walked into the main entrance, I ran into two colleagues (O and PS) who were each wearing a green button about 2 inches in diameter with the words "Governance Lite" on it. They had several extra buttons and asked me, with a smile, if I wanted one. I paused and then said "sure!" They laughed as they handed me my button. I quickly put it on my sweater, for all eyes to see. I laughed; so did they. I then told them I needed to get a cup of coffee to start the day, that it was a busy one with a lot of meetings. They asked me, as I turned to go, whether I wanted to take any spare buttons to the administration building to distribute them there. I said "pass," and we all laughed again.

These buttons, created by some faculty members, are a play on "lite beer"—low in calories. The faculty wanted a "lite" governance policy, with very little formalized into policy statements. The color green symbolized "healthy"? perhaps also "environmentally friendly"? I experienced this offering as a real test of my faculty loyalty—was I willing to wear a button endorsing a "lite" governance policy, even though I was currently working half-time in the administration building, where a different attitude was held about the governance policy. Because I personally did favor a "lite" policy statement, I had no problems accepting the button. It felt good to put it on, in fact.

FIGURE 13-2 **Sample Field Note Entry**

your resolution. Careful observation and note taking can be tiring, especially if it involves excitement or tension and if it extends over a long period. If you've just spent eight hours straight observing and making notes on how people have been coping with a disastrous flood, your first desire afterward will likely be getting some sleep, dry clothes, or a drink. You may need to take some inspiration from newspaper reporters who undergo the same sorts of hardships, then write their stories to meet their deadlines.

Third, you'll inevitably wonder *how much* you should record. Is it really worth the effort to write out all the details you can recall right after the observation session? The general guideline here is *yes*. In participant-observation research, frequently you can't be really sure of what's important and what's unimportant until you've had a chance to review and analyze a great volume of information, so you should even record things that don't seem important at the outset. They may turn out to be significant after all. Also, the act of recording the details of something "unimportant" may jog your memory of something that is important. Your ability to meet the criteria of confirmability, credibility, and transferability hinges, in the end, on the breadth and depth of your field notes. You can never have "too many" pages of field notes.

Field notes can be written from any of several perspectives. Emerson and colleagues (1995, pp. 52–60) mention three in particular: *first-person perspective, third-person perspective,* and *omniscient perspective.* First-person field notes are written as "I" statements—they capture the researcher's personal experience. The field note entry in Figure 13-2 illustrates a first-person point of view: The entry is written from the perspective of the researcher. This perspective is very useful when the researcher is actively participating, either as a complete participant or as a participant-as-observer.

By contrast, a third-person perspective primarily attempts to describe what others are saying and doing. Had the field note entry recorded in Figure 13-2 been written in the third person, it might read, in part, like this: "Two faculty members, standing by the entrance to the canteen, asked an approaching faculty member (the researcher) whether she wanted a green 2-inch button saying 'Governance lite' on it." Because fieldwork is supposed to understand how natives construct meaning, it is obviously important to record what they say and do.

The omniscient perspective involves writing in the third person, but, additionally, it writes with an all-knowing perspective on others' thoughts, motives, and feelings. Figure 13-2, as an omniscient point of view entry, might read, in part, as follows: "The two faculty members who offered the button to a third faculty member (the researcher) wondered whether the button would be accepted. To them, the button was a public declaration of where the wearer stood with respect to the faculty–administration governance conflict." The omniscient perspective is grounded in the researcher's experiences in the field; it does not use idle guesses about what informants are thinking or feeling. Omniscient field note entries emphasize the researcher's sense making of what certain actions mean to the natives, and this is an important goal of fieldwork.

Your field notes, as a whole, will probably move back and forth between first-person, third-person, and omniscient-third-person perspectives. This is because you are shifting back and forth between your participation experiences, your observations of others' actions, and your sense making of others' meanings.

Apart from the matter of perspective, what should a field note entry contain? This depends entirely on the purpose of the study. However, some good generic advice is to pay attention to the five *W*'s: *W*ho were the participants in the interaction event? *W*hat was said and done? *W*hen did the event take place? *W*here did the event take place? *W*hy did the interaction event happen the way it did? With respect to the fifth question—why—we suggest that you focus on functional explanations (how did actions function?) and reason explanations (what were the meanings of the actions to the participants?) because these are closer to the general goals and purposes of qualitative research.

Your notes should also include a reflexive record of your process, a continuation of the audit trail you began during the "warm-up" period, as described above. An important part of the reflexive journal is your emergent analysis of your observations. Unlike quantitative research, in which all of the data are collected prior to data analysis, participant observation is characterized by ongoing data analysis, which parallels data gathering.

Field notes change over the course of participant-observation work. Early in the process, you don't know the basic "lay of the land," or what is important. Your field notes will be about everything, because you don't know enough to make discriminating decisions about what to write about. Gradually, as your observations and experiences accumulate, certain analytic themes and patterns will become salient to you, and subsequent field note entries will reflect this emergent process. In Chapter 4, we discussed the iterative reasoning process that characterizes qualitative research in general. The researcher employs inductive reasoning to develop tentative, or working, hypotheses about meanings and rules, which are then checked against subsequent field observations and modified accordingly. Over time, field note entries reflect this iterative process between inductive and deductive reasoning.

Field notes should be recorded chronologically, from the first contact with the field site to the last contact with the field site. This way, the researcher is in a position to demonstrate the dependability of his or her field note data—observations and reflections can be tracked through time.

You should realize that most of your field notes will not be reflected in your final report on the project. Put more harshly, most of the notes you take will be "wasted." The field note entry in Figure 13-2 ended up being mentioned in a sentence or two in the final published article based on the field notes, but the mention was to the button itself rather than the loyalty test to see if the button would be accepted.

But take heart: Even the richest gold ore yields only about 30 grams of gold per metric ton, meaning that 99.997 percent of the ore is wasted. Yet that 30 grams of gold can be hammered out to cover an area 18 feet square—the equivalent of about 685 book pages. So take a ton of notes, and plan to select and use only the gold.

Your field notes are crucial to your ability to demonstrate that you have fulfilled the criteria of trustworthiness for qualitative research: dependability, confirmability, credibility, and transferability. As we discussed earlier, your reflexive note taking forms the basis of your audit trail, critical in establishing the dependability of your research process. The quantity of detailed information you are able to record in your field notes determines the extent to which you will meet the transferability and confirmability criteria. You cannot provide thick descriptions without detailed field notes. You will not have detailed evidence to support your analytical claims in the absence of detailed field notes. Prolonged engagement in the field means very little if you don't have detailed field notes to show for it.

Constructing Visual Records

To this point, we have exclusively focused on written field notes. However, communication researchers also construct visual records for analytic purposes—photographs, films, and videos. The construction of visual records has a long tradition in anthropology, where ethnographers have used the camera along with written field notes as basic tools of the trade for quite some time (Collier, 1967). The use of film and video for documenting a field setting has a natural home in the discipline of communication studies, where video and film production study has long held membership as one of the disciplinary sub-specialties. As Douglas Harper (1994, p. 411) suggests, "images allow us to make kinds of statements that cannot be made by words; thus images enlarge our consciousness."

The construction of visual records usually happens in two ways in communication research. First, the researcher can control the camera, determining what to record and how to frame the shot. Alternatively, the researcher can turn the camera over to the participants in the field, asking them to record what they choose. Common to both of these approaches is an appreciation of the subjective nature of the activity. The camera is not a "neutral vessel" for visually recording the facts of what is happening. Instead, the camera is a tool used by the holder to create a text—an interpretation of some phenomenon.

A communication researcher who has actively incorporated the camera into his participant-observation tool kit is Dwight Conquergood. In one ethnographic project, Conquergood studied immigrant Hmong who had relocated to the United States from their native homes in the hills of Southeast Asia. The result of his ethnographic work was a documentary film about their experience (Conquergood & Siegel, 1985). Conquergood also conducted ethnographic work in an urban street gang, involving gang members as camera operators in the production of a documentary film about communication in the gang (Conquergood & Siegel, 1990).

Another useful demonstration of the power of the visual image is an ethnographic video about a residential facility for people with AIDS (Adelman & Schultz, 1991). The visual tour of the facility helps the viewer to see the individuals behind the AIDS in a way difficult to achieve with words alone. And the images of rooms vacated because of the deaths of AIDS residents provide a kind of understanding of loss that goes beyond words.

Sometimes, **visual images** are incorporated into traditional written reports of research studies. For example, Leslie Jarmon (1996) provided photographs in her article on how conversation analysis researchers use performance to assist them in understanding a conversational sequence. The photos illustrate the performances enacted by the researchers. Given the ease with which digitized visual images (both still shots and motion) can be uploaded onto Web pages, we anticipate that qualitative researchers in communication will increasingly link traditional written reports of their research with these electronic outlets.

Research Ethics in the Field

When we discussed the topic of research ethics in Chapter 5, we pointed out that all forms of communication research raise a wide range of ethical issues. By bringing researchers into direct and often intimate contact with study participants, field research raises these concerns in a particularly dramatic way. Some of these ethical issues can be anticipated and thought through during the "warm-up," as discussed above. However, like other facets of participant observation, many ethical challenges seem to pop up unexpectedly while you're in the field.

As a reminder of the importance of ethical concerns in gathering field data, we've reported here some of the problems mentioned by John and Lyn Lofland (1995, p. 63):

- Is it ethical to talk to people when they do not know you will be recording their words?
- Is it ethical to get information for your own purposes from people you hate?
- Is it ethical to see a severe need for help and not respond to it directly?
- Is it ethical to be in a setting or situation but not commit yourself wholeheartedly to it?
- Is it ethical to develop a calculated stance toward other humans—that is, to be strategic in your relations?
- Is it ethical to take sides or to avoid taking sides in a factionalized situation?
- Is it ethical to "pay" people with trade-offs for access to their lives and minds?
- Is it ethical to "use" people as allies or informants in order to gain entrée to other people or to elusive understandings?

These questions are not easily handled. In the end, you need to make a judgment call "in the moment," keeping in mind your general ethical obligation to standards of voluntary participation, the absence of harm, the protections of confidentiality and anonymity, and the absence of deception.

Triangulation

Triangulation refers to the use of multiple kinds of data and/or multiple methods in studying a given phenomenon. Triangulation is useful to any researcher, including the participant-observer. Yvonna Lincoln and Egon Guba (1985) argue that triangulation is an important way in which a qualitative researcher establishes the *credibility* of his or her study. Norman Denzin (1978) has identified four different forms of triangulation:

- *The use of multiple and different sources of data.* You can accomplish this form of triangulation by comparing the experiences and perceptions of one informant with those of other informants, for example. You could also accomplish data-source triangulation by comparing the perceptions of the researcher against those of the natives. The researcher–native form of triangulation is often known as *member checking* (Lincoln & Guba, 1985). For example, a researcher could ask informants if the working hypothesis formulated after some time in the field "rings true" to them.

There are obviously many different ways to compare data sources to one another. Is agreement among data sources the goal? Not necessarily. When data sources are discrepant, it is important for the researcher to have an understanding of what accounts for this difference—it may reflect meaningful variation in the population being studied.

- *The use of multiple and different methods of research.* In the context of participation-observation research, method triangulation could take the form of moving from one participant-observation role to another. For example, you could triangulate your observations as a complete participant against those gathered while in the participant-as-observer role. Another common form of method triangulation is to triangulate observations gathered through participant observation against data gathered through qualitative interviewing (Chapter 14) or data gathered through the qualitative study of social texts (Chapter 15). In fact, most qualitative researchers argue that participant observation always uses interviewing in one form or another; even casual conversations with natives are a form of interviewing. Sometimes, participation observation is triangulated against quantitative methods such as survey research—the natives could be given a questionnaire, for example. Or a researcher could conduct a content analysis of written documents gathered from the field site.

- *The use of multiple researchers.* Sometimes, it makes sense to have a team of participant observers in the field, thereby allowing a comparison of their recorded observations. A variation of this kind of triangulation is the use of *peer debriefing* (Lincoln & Guba, 1985), in which the researcher engages in a data-analysis session with a disinterested peer. For example, you might ask a peer to read your field notes to find out if he or she sees what you see, or ask the peer to assess your field notes against your analysis of what you think is going on in the field site. Peer debriefing is a very helpful way for the researcher to gain external feedback, crucial to subsequent observational and analytic work.

- *The use of multiple theoretical perspectives.* As we discussed in Chapter 4, more than one theory can be brought to bear to help understand a given phenomenon. By bringing multiple theories into conversation with one another, the researcher could produce a richer, more sophisticated understanding of the phenomenon.

The emergent nature of participant-observation research makes it relatively easy for a researcher to add triangulation procedures throughout the "floor exercise" period. After all, the choreography of participant observation is not a rigidly scripted dance but a free-form dance whose elegance rests in its adaptation to the needs of the moment.

Elasticity

We want to end our discussion of the "floor exercise" period by underscoring its evolving, emergent, dynamic quality. This elasticity is often misunderstood and viewed as carelessness, sloppiness, and lack of rigor. Nothing could be further from the mark from the perspective of qualitative research. Participant observation is a rigorous and trustworthy method, but it is not a linear, mechanical, predetermined undertaking.

THE "COOL-DOWN" PERIOD

Janesick's (1994) third stage of participant observation is the period of cooling down and concluding the dance. How do you know when you're finished with data gathering? In the end, a researcher knows that he or she has been in the field long enough when **saturation** (Morse, 1994) has been achieved. As Janice Morse (1994, p. 230) indicates, saturation occurs when "variation is both accounted for and understood." This means that additional data do not add additional insights—the analysis to that point accounts for the observations. Saturation means you have reached the point where your data are repetitive.

Saturation hinges on analysis of your observations. Thus, you need to analyze your field notes as you gather data. Without a tentative analysis of your findings, it is impossible for you to determine if additional observations reap new insights or provide redundancy with what you already have concluded. If you wait to analyze your data until you leave the field, you will have no justifiable rea-

son beyond convenience to conclude the data-gathering phase of your study.

When you have decided that the point of saturation has been reached, it is important to figure out how to exit your field site in a way that is mutually acceptable to you and to the informants with whom you have by now come to know quite well. Janesick (1994) recommends a gradual withdrawal from the field rather than the abrupt disappearance of the researcher.

Once you have left the field, you analyze your data in a more comprehensive way than the ongoing analysis you engaged in during the "floor exercise" period. We'll have more to say on this topic in Chapter 16. You may discover that you haven't reached saturation after all and need to return to the field for a bit more observational work to fill gaps. Or you may wish to triangulate your more thorough analysis against native perceptions, returning to the field for purposes of member checking. In short, you might need to make an "encore appearance" in the field, even though you have withdrawn from the full-time gathering of data. It is in your interests to sustain viable, working relationships with your informants and to let them know when you leave the field that you might need to return at a later point.

SOME ILLUSTRATIONS OF PARTICIPANT-OBSERVATION RESEARCH

The creative, malleable, and open-ended nature of participant-observation research makes it harder to be as precise about how to gather and interpret data as quantitative research allows. In participant-observation research, there are fewer strict rules to determine whether it's being done appropriately or whether the data are being interpreted correctly. Books on qualitative methodology often refer to all forms of qualitative inquiry as a craft or a mindset, and suggest that the best way to learn about the many ways of doing it may be involvement in a qualitative study. Therefore, let's now examine a couple of lengthier illustrations of participant-observation inquiry in action. We hope these descriptions will give you a feel for what participant-observation research is all about.

Connie Kubo Della-Piana and James Anderson (1995) published a participant-observation study titled "Performing Community: Community Service as Cultural Conversation." The general question that guided their study was to understand how "community" is constructed and enacted in a particular group of people. They noted that references to "community" were widespread in the American culture, and they wanted to understand better what "community" meant and how it was constructed and sustained through talk among their natives. In particular, they sought to understand "how the organizational practices and discourse of a community service organization make meaningful and are made meaningful by the term 'community'" (p. 187).

Della-Piana was invited to the field site, a student-centered community service organization, as an "invited researcher" and then "stumbled into community" (p. 190). This is her description of her immersion in the mission of the organization:

> I joined the alumni group in cleaning a home for unwed mothers. I served, celebrated, and ate Thanksgiving dinner with urban-bound Native Americans and volunteers from the Rural Project. With the Center's summer leadership team, I painted a house for a senior citizen who had qualified for the Home Beautification Program. I attended a legislative session and committee hearing in support of the Public Interest Advocacy Project efforts to retain funding for an infant care program. (p. 190)

Della-Piana worked as a member of the community service center from November 1990 to October 1991 and "off and on for the remainder of the 1991–1992 academic year" (p. 190). The researcher had this to say about her role as a participant-as-observer:

> Through immersion in the activities of the public arena of community service, I came face-to-face with those who serve and those who are served, encountering and enacting their dilemmas. I came to experience, intensely, the ambiguous, though normative, significance of "community." (p. 191)

This role was not without its stresses. In particular, the researcher reports that she experienced ethical qualms about the irony of her status as a researcher studying "community":

> Questions about the ethics of the research strategy plagued me during service project activities when I suddenly and unexpectedly became aware that I was "doing social science research" disguised as "doing community service." . . . After working alongside volunteers and recipients who did not know (and would not know) I was doing research, I began to view my research disguised as community service as a form of exploitation—advancing my own agenda in the name of service to others. A Center norm and belief, articulated by Rick [an informant] . . . was that people who

used service as an item on their resume did not last. Community service was more than a line on one's resume; it was a way of life. (p. 192)

Despite these stresses (and perhaps because of them), Della-Piana was able to understand the construction of "community" by these community service volunteers.

A second, quite different participant-observation study was conducted by Kristine Fitch (1998). Fitch, an ethnographer of communication, was interested in the communicative practices through which urban Colombian professionals constructed and maintained their interpersonal relationships. Her speech community was defined as this segment of Colombian culture. Fitch's work also had a critical agenda—to present a different side of Colombian life from the image of violence and political upheaval often portrayed in American media. As she states,

> Although nearly every person in Colombia is affected to some degree by the pervasive violence and corresponding mistrust and fear it generates, there is a distinctive system of interpersonal relationships that centers around connectedness. Despite the effects of more than half a century of first political then social upheaval, that interpersonal ideology of connectedness generates a tremendous human warmth. A goal of this book . . . is to show another side of Colombia: an interpersonal system that counters, and acts as a way of dealing with, the harsh social, political and economic realities that are already quite well known. (p. 6)

Data were collected by Fitch in two phases. In 1987 she spent ten months in Colombia, and in 1992 she spent an additional three months. During these fieldwork periods, she lived in Bogotá with her in-laws, "a middle-class, middle-aged Colombian couple" (Fitch, 1998, p. 6). By being included in the daily life of a Colombian family, Fitch gained access to many possible informants. In addition, she was involved with a linguistics research and teaching institution, which provided her with an even wider network of Colombian contacts. We might refer to her in-laws and the officials at the research/teaching institution as her sponsors in the field.

Fitch triangulated several methods in her ethnography of communication. She engaged in ethnographic observation of interaction patterns, conducted individual and group interviews, tape-recorded and transcribed conversations, and analyzed written documents of various kinds. She studied a wide variety of interactional settings, including "schools, a printing plant, a free legal aid clinic, a family and couples counseling service, several business organizations, and numerous social functions" (p. 7).

Fitch also employed multiple researchers, achieving researcher triangulation. In particular, she used six Colombian student research assistants who provided her with greater access to naturally occurring interactions in their own respective networks of families and friends.

By her own admission, Fitch painted a thick, ethnographic description of Colombian life in which "the very real and pervasive influence of violence on the lives of the people I worked with there has largely disappeared" (p. 194). To correct that oversight, she ends her book with a powerful personal narrative of how violence takes a toll on the lives of Colombians. Her preview to that narrative displays self-reflexivity at work:

> For the most part, as is obvious from the rest of this book, I have listened to these discussions [about objectivity in how a culture is represented] from the sideline, generally choosing to follow the conventions of traditional ethnographic practice and writing. I have gotten less comfortable with those decisions during the process, seeing all too clearly the impact of my presence, my relationships with the people I "studied," and my inevitable value judgments on events and my interpretations of them. I have also become more uneasy with the absence, in virtually all of this discussion of "Colombian culture," of an all-too-pervasive aspect of everyday life and personal relationships in that speech communication. There is no question that public violence is an inescapable parameter for existence there; yet it is invisible in these pages because I have found it to be undefinable. A narrative that seeks to begin to address these issues thus seemed the most appropriate way to close. (p. 196)

In all communication research methods, a large gap lies between understanding the skills of data collection and actually using those skills effectively. Typically, experience is the only effective bridge across the gap. This situation certainly applies to qualitative research, including participant observation. It's worth recalling the parallel between the activities of the scientist and those of the investigative detective. Although fledgling detectives can be taught technical skills and can be given general guidelines, insight and experience separate good detectives from mediocre ones. The same is true of field researchers. You can understand the three stages of the choreography of participant observation, but what will make you an elegant and inspired participant-observer dancer is practice in the field.

STRENGTHS AND WEAKNESSES OF PARTICIPANT-OBSERVATION RESEARCH

It's time now to wrap up the discussion of participant observation and move on to the other qualitative methods available to communication researchers. We want to conclude this chapter by assessing the relative strengths and weaknesses of this particular method.

As we've already indicated, participant-observation research is especially effective for studying the subtle nuances of attitudes and behaviors and for examining communication processes over time. As such, the chief strength of this method lies in the depth of understanding it may permit. Although other research methods may be challenged as "superficial," this charge is seldom lodged against participant-observation research.

Flexibility is another advantage of participant observation. In this method, you may modify your research design at any time, as discussed earlier. Moreover, you're always prepared to engage in field research whenever the occasion should arise, whereas you could not as easily initiate a survey or an experiment.

Participant-observation research can be relatively inexpensive. Other research methods may require expensive equipment or an extensive research staff, but field research typically can be undertaken by one researcher with a notebook and a pencil. This is not to say that field research is never expensive. For example, the nature of the research project may require a large number of trained observers. Expensive recording equipment may be needed. Or you may wish to undertake participant observation of interactions in expensive Paris nightclubs.

Participant-observation research has some weaknesses as well. First, being qualitative rather than quantitative, it's not an appropriate means to use to arrive at statistical descriptions of a large population. For example, observing casual political discussions in laundromats would not yield trustworthy estimates of the future voting behavior of the total electorate. Nevertheless, the study could provide important, richly detailed insights into the process of political attitude formation.

Further, much of the field note (and visual) data collected by the researcher is not readily accessible to the reader of the published findings of the study—the reader must trust the integrity of the participant-observation process as described by the researcher.

Main Points

❑ Participant-observation research is a qualitative research method that involves the direct observation of communication phenomena in their natural settings. The researcher often participates as an actor in the events under study.

❑ Appropriate topics for participant-observation research include communication practices, episodes, and encounters, and the communication that is associated with given roles, relationships, groups, organizations, settlements, social worlds, lifestyles, and subcultures.

❑ The ethnography of communication involves naturalistic observations and holistic understandings of communication codes in cultures or subcultures.

❑ Participant observation is a choreography of three stages: the "warm-up" period, the "floor exercise" period, and the "cool-down" period. All three periods require data gathering, data analysis, and self-reflexivity by the researcher.

❑ The researcher can take a number of different roles in participation-observation research. These roles vary by the natives' awareness of the research study, the level of active participation in the activities of the natives, and the kind of membership adopted by the researcher.

❑ The field journal is the backbone of participant-observation research, for that is where the researcher records his or her observations.

❑ Taking field notes is a two-stage process: jottings in the field and full-blown notes.

❑ Field notes involve description, preliminary analysis, and reflexive notes on the research process.

❑ Field notes are taken from one or more perspectives: first-person, third-person, omniscient perspective.

❑ Field notes will change over the course of fieldwork but generally should attend to the five *W*'s: who, what, when, where, and why.

❑ Field notes should be chronological and detailed.

❑ Increasingly, written field notes are supplemented by visual records such as photographs, films, and videos.

❑ Participation observation requires a flexible and adaptive research design—elasticity.

Key Terms

ethnography of
  communication
case study
theoretical sensitivity
reflexive journal
field notes
participation observation
complete-participant role
participant-as-observer role
observer-as-participant
complete observer
complete member
active member
peripheral member

gatekeepers
sponsor
informants
maximum-variation
  sampling
typical case sampling
snowball sampling
theoretical construct
  sampling
critical case sampling
convenience sampling
visual images
triangulation
saturation

Review Questions and Exercises

1. Think of some group or activity you participate in or are very familiar with. Think through all of the steps needed for "warming up" to this field site.

2. Form a research team and identify a setting where you could conduct field observations (e.g., a public restaurant, a class session, a bench at the local shopping mall). Use complete observation simultaneously and independently, and then compare your respective field notes. How are they similar and different in describing the "same" phenomenon? What are the implications of these similarities and differences?

3. View one of the visual ethnographies mentioned in this chapter, or another you have located. Assess the ways in which "a picture speaks a thousand words"— the kinds of understandings difficult to accomplish with words alone.

4. Imagine that you've been asked to investigate allegations that local automobile dealerships treat male customers more seriously in their communication practices than female customers. Describe how you might go about studying this question through participant-observation techniques.

Continuity Project

In what ways is going to the movies a gendered activity? Choose a local movie theater as your field site, and conduct a small-scale participant-observation study to answer this research question.

Additional Readings

Collier, J., Jr. (1967). *Visual anthropology: Photography as a research method.* New York: Holt, Rinehart and Winston. A classic book on issues that face ethnographers in using photographs to document social life. The issues discussed hold relevance for all forms of visual imagery, including film and video.

Creswell, J. W. (1998). *Qualitative inquiry and research design: Choosing among five traditions.* Thousand Oaks, CA: Sage. An excellent book in its treatment of five primary traditions of qualitative research—phenomenology, case study, ethnography, biographical research, and grounded theory.

Emerson, R. M. (Ed.) (1988). *Contemporary field research.* Boston: Little, Brown. A diverse and interesting collection of articles on how field research contributes to understanding, the role of theory in such research, personal and relational issues that emerge, and ethical and political issues.

Emerson, R. M., Fretz, R. I., & Shaw, L. L. (1995). *Writing ethnographic fieldnotes.* Chicago: University of Chicago Press. An outstanding book on the process of constructing and analyzing field notes, and then writing up the results of the analysis.

Harper, D. (1994). On the authority of the image: Visual methods at the crossroads. In N. K. Denzin & Y. S. Lincoln (Eds.), *Handbook of qualitative research* (pp. 403–412). Thousand Oaks, CA: Sage. This chapter is an excellent overview of how qualitative researchers use the visual image—photographs, videos, films—in their research. It emphasizes the theory of the visual image in qualitative research, not practical "how-to" issues.

Johnson, J. C. (1990). *Selecting ethnographic informants.* Newbury Park, CA: Sage. The author discusses the various strategies that apply to the task of sampling in field research.

Lincoln, Y. S., & Guba, E. G. (1985). *Naturalistic inquiry.* Newbury Park, CA: Sage. An excellent book about the full range of qualitative methods. This book is especially strong in its treatment of the criteria by which we evaluate the trustworthiness of qualitative research.

Lindlof, T. R. (1995). *Qualitative communication research methods.* Thousand Oaks, CA: Sage. An outstanding book that discusses the full range of qualitative research methods. Lindlof is a mass media scholar, so many of his examples are drawn from qualitative research on various facets of the mass media.

Lofland, J., & Lofland, L. (1995). *Analyzing social settings* (3rd ed.). Belmont, CA: Wadsworth. An unexcelled presentation of field research methods from beginning to end. This eminently readable book manages to draw the links between the logic of scientific inquiry and the nitty-gritty practicalities of observing, communicating, recording, filing, reporting, and everything else involved in field research. In addition, the book contains a wealth of references to field research illustrations.

Shaffir, W. B., & Stebbins, R. A. (Eds.) (1991). *Experiencing fieldwork: An inside view of qualitative research.* Newbury Park, CA: Sage. Several field research practitioners discuss the nature of the craft and recall experiences in the field. Here's an opportunity to gain a "feel" for the method as well as learn some techniques.

InfoTrac College Edition
http://www.infotrac-college.com/wadsworth/access.html

Access the latest news and journal articles with InfoTrac College Edition, an easy-to-use online database of reliable, full-length articles from hundreds of top academic journals. Conduct an electronic search using the following search terms:

- participant observation
- field research
- field notes
- informants
- saturation
- theoretical sensitivity

CHAPTER **14**

Qualitative Interviewing

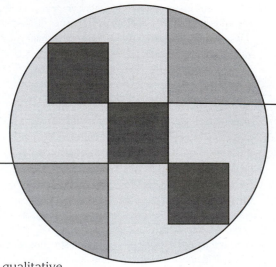

What You'll Learn in This Chapter

We'll discuss the second of the triad of qualitative methods—qualitative interviewing. You'll learn the purposes of qualitative interviewing, the importance of planning an interview, the kinds of questions asked, and how this kind of interviewing is done.

INTRODUCTION

In part, qualitative research is a matter of going where the action is and simply watching and listening. You can learn a lot merely by paying attention to what's going on. At the same time, as we've already indicated, qualitative research can involve more active inquiry. Often, it's appropriate to ask people questions and record their answers. Some scholars regard interviewing as inseparable from participant-observation research and don't differentiate the two as distinct methods. We can see their point: All participant observation involves interviewing of one kind or another. Every time a researcher talks to a native, an interview is taking place, even if it seems like just a casual, friendly conversation. In fact, qualitative interviewing has been described as a conversation with a purpose (Bingham & Moore, 1959). However, although all participant observation involves qualitative interviewing, not all qualitative interviewing involves participant observation. Many studies use qualitative interviewing without identifying a field site per se and without experiencing first-hand the lives of native participants. Thus, we've devoted separate chapters to participant observation and qualitative interviewing despite the many intersections and overlaps between them.

Like participant observation, qualitative interviewing focuses on understanding meanings and the rules of meaning-making. The selection of informants to interview is guided by the same sampling techniques that we discussed in Chapter 13. Qualitative interviewing is evaluated by the same criteria of trustworthiness that guide all qualitative research—dependability, confirmability, credibility, and transferability.

We've already discussed interviewing in Chapter 8, on survey research. However, the interviewing you'll do in connection with qualitative research is different enough to demand a separate treatment here. In survey research, questionnaires and interviews are standardized and structured. In qualitative interviewing, by contrast, the preference is for unstructured questioning or, at most, semistructured questioning.

Herbert and Riene Rubin (1995, p. 43) make this distinction: "Qualitative interviewing design is flexible, iterative, and continuous, rather than prepared in advance and locked in stone." They continue their discussion as follows:

> Design in qualitative interviewing is iterative. That means that each time you repeat the basic process of gathering information, analyzing it, winnowing it, and testing it, you come closer to a clear and convincing model of the phenomenon you are studying. . . .

> The continuous nature of qualitative interviewing means that the questioning is redesigned throughout the project. (Rubin & Rubin, 1995, pp. 46, 47)

A **qualitative interview** is an interaction between an interviewer and a participant in which the interviewer has a general plan of inquiry but not a specific set of questions that must be asked using particular words and in a particular order. It is essentially a conversation in which the interviewer establishes a general direction for the conversation and pursues specific topics raised by the respondent. Ideally the participant, often referred to as an *informant*, does most of the talking.

Steinar Kvale (1996, pp. 3–5) offers two metaphors for interviewing: The interviewer is a "miner" or a "traveler." The first model assumes that the participant possesses specific information and that the interviewer's job is to dig it out. By contrast, in the second model, the interviewer

> wanders through the landscape and enters into conversations with the people encountered. The traveler explores the many domains of the country, as unknown territory or with maps, roaming freely around the territory. . . . The interviewer wanders along with the local inhabitants, asks questions that lead the subjects to tell their own stories of their lived world.

Obviously, "mining" is the kind of interviewing we discussed in Chapter 8—it is survey research. By contrast, "traveling" is the kind of interviewing that we're discussing in this chapter. Although "mining" and "traveling" are different activities, they often complement each other. You could "travel" with informants, exploring their experiences in their own words, as well as asking them to complete questionnaires.

Asking questions and noting answers is a natural process for us all, and it seems simple enough to add it to your bag of tricks as a qualitative researcher. Be a little cautious, however. As we've already discussed in Chapter 8, wording questions is a tricky business. All too often, the way we ask questions subtly biases the answers we get. Sometimes, we put our informant under pressure to look good. Sometimes, we put the question in a particular context that omits the most relevant answers.

Suppose you want to find out why a group of students is engaged in a social protest at the central administration building. You might be tempted to focus your questions on how students feel about the dean's recent ruling that requires students always to carry *The Basics of Communication Research* with them on campus. (Makes sense to us.) Although you may collect a great deal of information about students' attitudes toward the infamous ruling, they may be protesting for some other reason. Or perhaps most are simply joining in for the excitement. Properly done, qualitative interviewing would enable you to find out.

Although you may set out to conduct interviews with a pretty clear idea of what you want to ask, one of the special strengths of qualitative research is its flexibility, or what we called elasticity in the previous chapter. The answers evoked by your initial questions should shape your subsequent questions. It doesn't work, in this situation, merely to ask pre-established questions and record the answers. You need to ask a question, hear the answer, interpret its meaning for your general inquiry, and frame another question either to dig into the earlier answer in more depth or to redirect the person's attention to an area more relevant to your inquiry. In short, you need to be able to listen, think, and talk almost at the same time. That's what qualitative interviewing is, in a nutshell.

But all methods have their complexities and variations, and qualitative interviewing is no exception. Let's begin with a general discussion of the topics that can usefully be examined with qualitative interviewing.

RESEARCH PURPOSES APPROPRIATE FOR QUALITATIVE INTERVIEWING

Qualitative interviewing is used for a variety of purposes by communication researchers. We'll mention five of the most common. First, it is used as a way to learn about phenomena that can't be directly observed. For example, qualitative interviewing is a useful tool for researchers who study communication in personal relationships. Often, relationship partners do not welcome the prospect of being "shadowed" by a third-party participant-observer as they conduct the private business of relating. Interviewing is a way to gain some understanding of how relationships are initiated, developed, sustained, and ended.

Elizabeth Graham (1997), for instance, was interested in understanding the post-divorce relationship between co-parents. She conducted an in-depth, semistructured interview with ex-spouses on turning points in the development of their relationship from the point of divorce until the time of the interview. Thirty-five divorced parents provided Graham with retrospective reports of the events that had made a difference (either positive or negative) in the development of the post-divorce, co-parenting relationship. Graham's results centered on commonly identified types of turning points across her sample of informants. Clearly, Graham could not have "shadowed" these individuals to understand how ex-spouses construct a new relationship after their divorce.

However, the researcher needs to understand that interviewees are not neutral reporters of the facts. Interviewees have biased memories. Further, what they say to an interviewer can be, in part, a communicative performance motivated by concerns about self-presentation.

Second, qualitative interviews are especially appropriate when the researcher wants to understand in a richly detailed manner what an interviewee thinks and feels about some phenomenon. Although thoughts and feelings can be assessed through structured questionnaires and surveys, survey research limits individuals' responses to a selection of a number or a phrase as defined by the researcher. When a researcher wants an in-depth understanding of the interviewee's perceptions and feelings in his or her own words, a qualitative interview is the method of choice.

Phenomenological research and interpretive research share in common the purpose of understanding what a given phenomenon or experience means to its participants, and qualitative interviewing is a primary method in this kind of research. **Phenomenology** is a philosophical term, mostly associated with Edmund Husserl, that refers to a consideration of all perceived phenomena, both the "objective" and the "subjective." A phenomenological study "describes the meaning of the lived experience for several individuals about a concept or the phenomenon" (Creswell, 1998, p. 51). Researchers who adopt this approach are interested in what a given experience is like for those who have experienced it. The goal of this kind of research is to position readers to come away feeling that they have a better understanding of what it is like for someone to have the given experience (Polkinghorne, 1983).

In phenomenological research, the researcher is careful to resist his or her own subjectivity. The researcher brackets this subjectivity—acknowledging it and temporarily setting it aside—in order to get inside the minds of the participants (Creswell, 1998). Central to phenomenological research is the belief that there is "an essential, invariant structure (or essence)" (Creswell, 1998, p. 52) to experiencing a given phenomenon, and the researcher's search is to uncover that essence, often through qualitative interviewing.

Akin to phenomenology, **interpretivism** also aims at discovering how the participants understand their lives. In contrast to phenomenological research, however, the interpretive researcher believes that his or her own interpretation of the situation cannot, and should not, be removed from the research process (Potter, 1996). The goal of interpretive research, then, is to weave together native and researcher subjectivities in an attempt to understand the life experience of the native.

An example of phenomenological/interpretive research is Hiram Sachs's (1995) study of how public opinion is formed through electronic conversations on a computer network, PeaceNet. Noting that most work on public opinion is concerned with measuring public opinions once they have formed, Sachs was curious about how public opinion is formed. PeaceNet is a public forum for electronic political discussion about alternative stories usually ignored by conventional media. Sachs conducted in-depth interviews with 15 heavy users of the forum. His purpose was to gain a detailed understanding of whether PeaceNet users perceived the network as an effective way to discuss issues that were excluded from conventional political dialogue. Given Sachs's interest in obtaining a deep understanding of users' perceptions, qualitative interviewing was a useful choice of method.

Third, qualitative interviewing is a very useful method when the researcher wants to study informants' language use—their vocabularies and idioms. Qualitative interviewers try very hard not to put words into the mouths of their informants, instead encouraging them to talk using their own words. Generally speaking, the more the interviewee talks, the better from the researcher's perspective, because this provides more natural talk for the researcher to analyze. Sometimes, the interview is used to ask informants explicitly about their native terms for things.

One of us once participated in a qualitative study of American middle-class high school students' cultural terms for talk (Baxter & Goldsmith, 1990). In particular, we were interested in finding out, from the students' perspective, all of the different kinds of communication events that made up their day and the terms they used to label these different events. We interviewed the students who were involved with a six-week residential summer program, and we identified many different kinds of talk, such as "B.S.ing," "small talk," and "having a heated argument." We asked each informant to walk us through the communication events that took place during a recent, typical day. We explicitly asked our informants to tell us how they would describe each event to someone else—what their label or term was for the event.

Fourth, qualitative interviewing is also used as a tool of triangulation. As we discussed in the previous chapter, researchers often use qualitative interviewing to conduct member checking, assessing the extent to which preliminary findings from one method will "ring true" for the natives. In the cultural terms for talk study, for example, later interviewees were explicitly asked about the cultural terms that had been identified in earlier interviews so that we could determine if terms were idiosyncratic or commonly used and understood across our sample (Baxter & Goldsmith, 1990).

Fifth, and last, a researcher can view the qualitative interview as a communicative performance jointly enacted with the interviewee. In studying how the interviewee performs the interview event, the researcher can gain insight into the interviewee's code of communication.

For example, Charles Briggs (1986) studied the interviewing "blunders" he engaged in while interviewing Mexicanos in northern New Mexico. Mexicanos are descendants of Spanish and Mexican citizens who settled in northern New Mexico and southern Colorado in the 17th century; they consider themselves culturally Hispanic. Briggs discovered that the traditional question-and-answer format of interviewing common to middle-class Caucasians in the United States was antithetical to norms of communicative competence among the Mexicanos. Briggs was having trouble getting answers, and then he began to reflect on why this was so. In framing the interview as a communicative performance, he was able to learn a great deal about the rules for talk that guided Mexicanos' communicative practices.

QUALITATIVE INTERVIEWS AS SPEECH EVENTS

Several scholars have noted that the qualitative interview is similar to, yet different from, the speech event of casual conversation (Mishler, 1986; Spradley, 1979). But what exactly is a speech event? A speech event, according to Dell Hymes (1962, p. 19), who originated the term, refers to "activities, or aspects of activities, that are directly governed by rules for the use of speech." Speech events are oriented toward specific goals, carry expectations of normal progression from beginning to end, and feature patterned interaction between the participants. By referring to interviews as speech events, we are emphasizing that they are jointly enacted in the communication between the interviewer and the informant. Thus, what the informant says is interdependent with what the interviewer says, and vice versa. The interviewer is more than a neutral conduit of questions, more than an oral version of a paper-and-pencil questionnaire.

The speech event of a casual conversation is one that most members of U.S. society can readily identify and enact. It takes place between two or a few people who attempt to sustain an easy familiarity and rapport with one another through talk. It opens with a greeting, terminates with some kind of leave taking, and features turn taking between participants between the bookends of its beginning and its ending. Participants ask and answer questions of one another, and they elaborate and extend on one another's remarks, all the while sustaining nonverbal involvement with one another. Although some casual conversations are utterly boring and predictable, most of the time participants learn something new. Although some casual conversations have a clear purpose, most of the time the purpose is nothing more than passing the time pleasurably with someone else.

This is sort of what a qualitative interview is like. It has a distinct beginning and endpoint, with turn taking between participants in the middle. When it is executed well, the interviewer and informant have created a positive relationship of easy familiarity and rapport with each other, and both have interacted with a high level of verbal and nonverbal involvement with each other's utterances. Both the interviewer and the informant learn something. Participants ask and answer questions, and provide elaborations and extensions of one another's comments. However, the interviewer probably asks most of the questions. Further, the interview, unlike a casual conversation, has a clear purpose, at least for the interviewer: to gather data that help him or her understand what or how something means to the informant.

Because qualitative interviewing is so much like normal conversation, you must keep reminding yourself that you are *not* having a normal conversation. In normal conversations, each of us wants to come across as an interesting, worthwhile person. If you watch yourself the next time you chat with someone you don't know too well, we think you'll find that much of your attention is spent on thinking up interesting things to *say*—contributions to the conversation that will make a good impression. Often, we don't really hear each other because we're too busy thinking of what we'll say next. As an interviewer, the desire to appear interesting is counterproductive to your job. You need to make the *other* person seem interesting, by being interested. (Do this in ordinary conversations, by the way, and people will actually regard you as a great conversationalist.)

John and Lyn Lofland (1995, pp. 56–57) suggest that investigators adopt the role of the "socially acceptable incompetent" when interviewing. You should offer yourself as someone who does not understand the situation you find yourself in and must be helped to grasp even the most basic and obvious aspects of that situation:

> A naturalistic investigator, almost by definition, is one who does not understand. She or he is "ignorant" and needs to be "taught." This role of watcher and asker of questions is the quintessential student role. (Lofland & Lofland, 1995, p. 56)

Interviewing, like participant observation, is an emergent process. The day's interviews are recorded, usually audiotaped for later transcription, and field notes about the process of interviewing are taken. You need to review your field notes every night—making sense out of what you've learned, getting a clearer feel for the phenomenon you're studying, and finding out what you should pay more attention to in future interviews. In detecting all those questions you should have asked but didn't, your interviewing design emerges as it goes. You start asking such questions the next time you interview either the same informant or a different person.

Steinar Kvale (1996, p. 88) details seven stages in a complete interviewing process, which we describe here:

1. *Thematizing:* clarifying the purpose of the interviews and the concepts to be explored
2. *Designing:* laying out the process through which you'll accomplish your purpose, including a consideration of the ethical dimension
3. *Interviewing:* doing the actual interviews
4. *Transcribing:* creating a written text of the interviews
5. *Analyzing:* determining the meaning of gathered materials in relation to the purpose of the study
6. *Verifying:* assessing the trustworthiness of the materials
7. *Reporting:* telling others what you've learned.

In this chapter, we're going to concentrate on stages 1, 2, 3, and 6 of Kvale's list. We'll address the issue of transcribing in Chapter 15 and analyzing in Chapter 16. We already talked about reporting as part of our general discussion on reading and writing research reports in Chapter 2.

PLANNING THE INTERVIEW

The discussion of probes in Chapter 8 provides a useful guide to getting answers in more depth without biasing later answers. In essence, doing good qualitative interviewing involves learning the skills of being a good listener. Be more interested than interesting. Learn to say things like "How is that?" "In what ways?" "How do you mean that?" "What would be an example of that?" Learn to look and listen expectantly, and let the person you're interviewing fill in the silence.

At the same time, you can't afford to be a totally passive receiver in the interaction. You need to go into your interviews with some general (or specific) questions you want answered and some topics you want addressed, and then you'll have to learn the skills of subtly directing the flow of conversation. It's a delicate dance that needs to take place between you and the informant. You don't want to be so directed and rigid in your planned questions that you constrain or extinguish the informant's line of conversation, yet you don't want to passively let the conversation go wherever the informant wants to take it.

There's something you can learn here from the martial arts. The aikido master never resists an opponent's blow but instead accepts it, joins with it, and then subtly redirects it in a more appropriate direction. You should master a similar sensibility for qualitative interviewing. Don't try to halt your informant's line of discussion, but learn to take what he or she has just said and branch that comment back in the direction appropriate to your purposes. Most people love to talk to anyone who's really interested. Your challenge is to direct the line of the conversation to your purposes while still signaling your interest in everything that the informant has to say. Stopping the line of conversation tells the informant that you aren't interested; asking him or her to elaborate in a particular direction indicates that you are.

This is hard work! If you don't have a clear purpose in mind when you plan the interview, it is very easy for it to wander off in directions that won't be productive to your research project. Consider this hypothetical example in which you're interested in why college students chose their majors:

1 YOU: What are you majoring in?
2 INFORMANT: Engineering.
3 YOU: I see. How did you come to choose engineering?
4 INFORMANT: I have an uncle who was voted the best engineer in Arizona in 1981.
5 YOU: Gee, that's great.
6 INFORMANT: Yeah. He was the engineer in charge of developing the new civic center in Tucson. It was written up in most of the engineering journals.
7 YOU: I see. Did you talk to him about your becoming an engineer?
8 INFORMANT: Yeah. He said that he got into engineering by accident. He needed a job when he graduated from high school, so he went to work as a laborer on a construction job. He spent eight years working his way up from the bottom, until he decided to go to college and come back nearer the top.
9 YOU: So is your main interest civil engineering, like your uncle, or are you more interested in some other branch of engineering?
10 INFORMANT: Actually, I'm leaning more toward electrical engineering—computers, in particular.

I started messing around with computers when I was in high school, and my long-term plan is . . .

Notice how the interview first begins to wander off in utterance #4 into a story about the informant's uncle. The first attempt to focus things back on the student's own choice of major (in utterance #7) failed. The second attempt (in utterance #9) succeeded. Now the student is providing the kind of information you're looking for. It's important for you to develop the ability to guide conversations in this fashion. Having an interview theme and design is crucial to your ability to keep a conversation "on track."

The Interview Protocol

Once you have figured out what your purpose is in conducting an interview, you need to develop a plan for how to conduct the interview. We'll call this your *interview protocol,* but other labels include your *interview guide* and your *interview schedule.* Basically, this is a guide to what you will say during the interview. Interview protocols come in three main types: *structured, semistructured,* and *unstructured.*

The **structured interview** protocol is the kind of interview we discussed in Chapter 8 as part of survey research. In a structured, or standardized interview, the interviewer "asks each respondent a series of preestablished questions with a limited set of response categories" (Fontana & Frey, 1994, p. 363). The interviewer has a standardized wording for all questions, which must be followed in all interviews. The order of the questions is the same in all the interviews. There is no latitude for improvisation or flexibility on the part of the interviewer. Except for an infrequent open-ended question, there is little room for the respondent to vary his or her response beyond the response options provided by the researcher. Basically, qualitative interviewing does not rely on a structured interview protocol. We are mentioning it here to underscore the point that the survey interview is different from qualitative interviewing in how it is conducted.

For the most part, qualitative interviewing relies on semistructured and unstructured protocols. A **semistructured** protocol generally consists of a list of questions that the interviewer wants answered by the informant. With the exception of an occasional closed-ended question, these questions are open-ended in nature. However, in contrast to structured interviewing, semistructured interviewing is characterized by substantial freedom on the part of the interviewer. The interviewer can pose the questions in whatever order makes greatest sense given the flow of the conversation with the informant. Further, the interviewer is free to use alternative language in paraphrasing the questions for the informant, if that is what is needed. The interviewer is trying to maximize in-depth talk by the informant, so the interviewer expends a lot of energy trying to probe for additional details. Some of these probes may be "boilerplate" (e.g., "Can you tell me more about that?"), but in general, semistructured probes emerge from what the informant says (e.g., "You mentioned that your stepmother is mean when she talks to you. Can you help me understand a bit more how she talks to you?").

Unstructured interviewing affords the greatest freedom to the interviewer. Basically, the interview protocol consists of a series of topic areas or "talking points" that the interviewer wants to cover at some point during the interview. The interviewer is free to create questions during the interview that touch on those talking points in a manner appropriate to the interview moment.

Structured, semistructured, and unstructured interview protocols have distinct advantages and disadvantages. Because qualitative researchers are interested in understanding a phenomenon from the informant's perspective, using the informant's language, structured interviewing has three key disadvantages. First, structured interviews reflect the researcher's point of view rather than the view of the informant: The questions are the researcher's, and the response options are in the words of the researcher. Second, structured interviews limit the depth of insight that can be gained from open-ended questions. Third, structured interviews do not display much adaptation to the particular informant and his or her circumstances. Sometimes, however, qualitative researchers use structured protocols when the information they are seeking is relatively straightforward and they wish to compare answers across informants. For example, questions about demographic background are often structured in qualitative research.

By contrast, unstructured interviews score well, by qualitative standards, on adaptation to the unique circumstances of the informant, depth of insight, and informant perspective. Semistructured interviews fall somewhere in the middle on these criteria.

A qualitative researcher might favor a semistructured interview over an unstructured one for two reasons. First, the researcher may have narrowed down his or her focus to the point of wanting information from an informant only on those specific questions. Perhaps the researcher is conducting verification interviews for purposes of member checking. Or perhaps the researcher is informed by an extensive body of existing research literature that allows him or her to focus on a narrow set of questions. It would be inefficient to use an unstructured protocol when the researcher has a set of clearly defined questions in need of responses.

A second reason that a researcher might prefer a semistructured protocol is if he or she wants to make explicit comparisons between informants. For example, if you want to identify commonalities in responses, perhaps summarizing the frequencies with which certain themes surface in informant remarks, it might be in your interests to work with questions that are worded the same for all informants.

Semistructured and unstructured interviewing often involve the same basic kinds of questions—the difference is whether the wording of these questions is done in the design for the study or on the spot during the interview.

But the questions are only part of what goes into an interview protocol. In addition, the protocol involves presenting the interview's purpose, presenting a preview of the interview's scope and format, and dealing with ethical issues. We'll call this the *tee-up* to the interview. Tee-ups can be structured, semistructured, or unstructured. In a structured tee-up, the interviewer basically has a written script, with no permissible deviations, which is memorized for standardized presentation to all respondents. In a semistructured tee-up, the protocol basically has suggested wording for the study's purpose, format, and ethical issues such as handling the informed consent form and letting the informant know about his or her human subjects rights; however, the interviewer is free to paraphrase this wording as appropriate. In the unstructured tee-up, the protocol would simply list the topic areas that needed to be discussed at the beginning of the interview, with no suggested wording.

Almost always, there is symmetry between the degree of structure in the tee-up and the degree of structure in the questions: Unstructured questions are accompanied by an unstructured tee-up, semistructured questions are prefaced by a semistructured tee-up, and structured questions are preceded by a structured tee-up.

To give you a concrete feel for what an interview protocol looks like, here's an excerpt from the interviewer protocol that one of us used in a qualitative interviewing study about communication in stepfamilies with college undergraduates who were members of stepfamilies (Baxter, Braithwaite, Bryant, & Wagner, 2001). It's semistructured in nature:

Tee-Up:

Introduce yourself to the informant—take a couple of minutes to engage in informal, casual "chitchat" about whatever subject matter seems timely and appropriate—the weather, the busy time of the semester, etc.

Next, provide a description of what the interview will be about. Here's some wording to help you—feel free to paraphrase as appropriate. Whatever you do, don't read this information or make it sound like a memorized script—you need to sound informal and conversational!

"This interview will take about one-and-a-half hours. The first thing I'm going to do is ask you to do is to help me fill out a family tree of who is in your blended family. Then I'm going to ask you to complete a brief questionnaire about life in your blended family. Then we'll turn to the actual interview—I have about ten questions about various facets of communication in your blended family that I'm interested in having you talk about. You've probably noticed that I'm using the term 'blended family' instead of 'stepfamily.' Actually, we think of these as meaning the same thing."

After previewing what the interview is about and how it will happen, ask the informant if he or she has any questions. Don't proceed until the informant feels comfortable.

Next, you need to have the informant sign an informed consent form. You need to be careful how you present this—we must not alarm our informant or apply pressure to him or her! Here's a suggested wording:

"If you are willing to participate, please read and sign two copies of this consent form required by the institution for all research that involves human beings. I will keep one copy, and you should keep the other one. Are you receiving extra credit for your participation? Let's make sure I have the information I need to ensure that you receive that from your instructor."

Please verify that you have all you need so that extra credit can be granted to the informant, if appropriate.

Next, a few housekeeping details need to be taken care of. Although we think that this informant has met all of our eligibility criteria, pause and verify that now! We don't want to waste his or her time and yours. Here's a suggested wording for that verification:

"Are you a part of a blended family right now? [Yes, No]

"To participate in this interview, you should have been part of a blended family for no less than four years and lived with basically the same residential parent for the majority of that time. Would this be true of your family situation?" [Yes, No]

If the informant says "No" to either question, he or she isn't eligible to participate in this study. Tell the informant that there are other studies for which extra credit is available, and indicate how he or she can go about finding out about those.

The last housekeeping detail is to remind the informant that the interview will be tape-recorded and what will be done with the tape. Here's suggested wording:

"In order for me to be able to pay careful attention to what you are saying, I will be tape-recording the interview. As the informed consent form indicates, your name and identity won't be linked in any way to any of the information you provide me today. Only the primary researchers and the research assistants will ever hear the tape for purposes of preparing a written transcript."

Check with the informant to make sure that this is OK before you set up the tape recorder.

Interview Questions:

Here are ten questions we want the informant to respond to during the interview. If the following wording and question order works, follow the "script" below. However, if the informant answers questions out of order, that's fine—whatever feels natural for the informant is what we want. Feel free to paraphrase question wording as you think needed. Also, *probe, probe, probe* for more details as you think necessary and appropriate:

1. Describe when and how your blended family started.
2. I am going to show you five different graphs or patterns we have identified in a prior study of how blended families develop in their first four years together. [Show the graphs and provide a verbal description of them.] Can you tell me which of these patterns best represents the way your blended family developed? Please explain why you selected this pattern.
3. I'd like you to tell me a story about an event that you feel best describes what communication in your blended family is typically like. In what ways is this story typical of how members in your blended family communicate?
4. Now, I'd like you to retell the story you just told me, only now, tell the story the way you think it would happen if your blended family had what you consider "ideal" communication. What about this retold story made it ideal in your opinion?
5. Describe the best or most positive aspects of your communication with your stepmother/stepfather. Now describe the most challenging or difficult aspects of your communication with your stepmother/stepfather.

6. Repeat #5 with the residential parent.
7. Repeat #5 with the nonresidential parent.
8. Repeat #5 with stepsiblings, if there are any.
9. Repeat #5 with siblings, if there are any.
10. Are there any other important aspects of your communication within your blended family that you believe I should know in order to understand your experience in your blended family?

Express thanks to the informant for taking the time to talk with you.

This interview protocol is semistructured in several ways. Although the interviewer is provided with suggested wordings of questions and statements, he or she is told that the exact wording does not need to be followed and that paraphrasing responsive to the interviewer's perceptions of the needs of the moment is appropriate. At several points, the interviewer isn't provided with wordings and is simply told what needs to happen.

Note that the protocol for the tee-up portion of the interview provides the informant with information about the interview's purpose and process. The tee-up also fulfills the study's ethical obligations to the informant, including an informed consent form that addresses all of the informant's ethical rights. One of the best ways to put informants at ease is to inform them about the purpose of the study and how the interview will be conducted—it reduces their uncertainty and thereby is the best single activity an interviewer can engage in for purposes of building rapport with them.

The interview questions are semistructured also, matching the semistructured nature of the tee-up portion of the protocol. All but one of the questions (#2) is open-ended, and even that question ends on an open-ended note by asking the informant to explain his or her selection of which graph best captures the development of the blended family. Questions encourage informants to use their own words in providing answers. Although the interviewer has suggested question wordings, he or she is encouraged to paraphrase as appropriate. Such paraphrasing would be critical for questions 6–9; the interviewer doesn't want the informant to grow weary or bored when basically the same question is being posed. Last, the interviewer is instructed to probe for additional details throughout the interview, reminding him or her to seek in-depth and clear responses from the informant.

To give you a feel for what an unstructured protocol is like, we'll turn to Julia Wood's (2001) interview with heterosexual women who had been in romantic relation-ships that included emotional and physical violence. Here's how Wood describes her protocol:

> The interview was minimally structured so that participants could present their experiences in their own words and follow the sequences that made sense to them. . . . [E]ach interviewee was asked: "To start us off, could you help me understand who you were when this relationship began? Can you tell me something about what you were like then—how you felt about yourself, your self-esteem, your friends, and activities, and how much dating experience you had had?" Each interviewee was then encouraged to tell the story of her relationship. . . . Prompting questions were used to encourage interviewees to elaborate and clarify their accounts, but were not used to direct or structure those accounts. (pp. 245–246)

The value of the opening question used by Wood was to present a relatively easy question, low in risk to the informant. Then the protocol basically asked the informant to tell her story, without the imposition of questions by the interviewer. Researcher prompts emerged out of the informant's talk, consistent with unstructured interviewing.

Common Types of Qualitative Interview Questions

Whether questions are worded in the protocol or emergent during the execution of the interview, qualitative interviewers fall back on a stockpile of basic types of questions. James Spradley (1979, p. 60) clusters these questions into three types: *descriptive, structural,* and *contrast.* We'll use the same grouping.

Descriptive Questions **Descriptive questions** ask the informant to describe some phenomenon using his or her own words. Spradley (1979, pp. 87–91) identifies five major types of descriptive questions. The first type, the *grand-tour question,* is very useful early in the research process because it basically asks the informant to provide a verbal "map" of some phenomenon or scene. There are several variations of the grand-tour question. The *typical-grand-tour question* asks the informant to construct a verbal map of what is typical. The interviewer could ask the informant to take him or her on a grand tour of almost anything: a group of people (e.g., "Describe for me all of the members of your blended family who are typically present in the household"), an activity (e.g., "Describe for me all the things you typically do when your family gathers together on Thanksgiving"), a domain of objects (e.g.,

"Tell me about all of the kinds of communication technology you use in a typical day"), a cultural scene (e.g., "Can you tell me about life in your academic department?"), or a time period (e.g., "Can you walk me through what a typical day is like for you?"). Whatever the phenomenon is that the interviewer is querying about, the goal is to get the informant's holistic perceptions of what something is typically like.

Specific-grand-tour questions ask about the most recent day, event, activity, and so forth. When an informant experiences difficulty in generalizing to the typical, the interviewer can ask about a recent situation. For example, instead of asking an informant to describe a typical day, we might ask the informant to describe a recent day—perhaps yesterday or another recent day that he or she can remember easily.

A *guided-grand-tour question* is involved when the informant is actually asked to take the interviewer on a physical tour of some kind (e.g., "Can you show me what your house is like?").

Similar to the guided grand-tour question is the *task-related-grand-tour question,* in which the informant is asked to perform some task and verbally explain it along the way. For example, you might ask an elementary school child to show you how to play hopscotch, asking the child to elaborate on the players, rules, and skills as he or she demonstrates the game.

The second of Spradley's (1979) types of descriptive questions is the *mini-tour question.* Basically, this type of question parallels the variations of the grand-tour question, except that it deals with a much smaller domain of experiences. Whereas a task-related grand-tour question might be "Tell me about how you go about playing hopscotch," the mini-task-related question might be "Tell me more about what makes a good hopscotch player" while the child is playing the game. Often, mini-tour questions emerge out of the interview, following up on grand-tour questions.

The third kind of Spradley's (1979) descriptive questions is the *example question.* As the label suggests, example questions ask informants to provide an example of something. For example, in a study on conflict in romantic relationships, we might ask our informant to give us an example of a kind of destructive conflict experienced with his or her romantic partner. Often, when an interviewer is asking a follow-up probe to a main question, it takes the form of an example question. For example, "A minute ago you mentioned hoppers and scotchers as two different kinds of players of hopscotch. Can you give me an example of what a hopper would do? An example of what a scotcher would do?"

The *experience question* is the fourth type of descriptive question. Basically, this type of question asks the informant to describe some experience that he or she has had—a typical experience, a recent experience, a memorable experience. For example, in a study of long-term marriages, we might ask husbands and wives to tell us about an experience in their marriage that they regarded as a turning point in some way, some experience that affected the subsequent course of the marriage.

Last, of particular interest to ethnographers of communication, is the *natural-language question.* This question asks informants to describe their terms of reference for various phenomena. Spradley (1979) identifies three types of natural-language questions. First is the *direct-language question,* which asks informants directly and explicitly what their labels are for something. In the study of conflict between romantic partners, we might ask "How do you refer to conflicts between the two of you? What are some labels you use in referring these to each other or to third parties outside the relationship?" Second is the *hypothetical-interaction question,* in which the informant is asked to imagine a scenario and then project into the scenario the talk that he or she thinks would actually happen. For example, in the conflict study, we might ask our informant this question: "If I were a friend of yours who asked about how things were going between the two of you, how would you refer to the conflict that had just taken place between you and your boy/girlfriend?" Third is the *typical-sentence question.* As the term suggests, the informant is asked to generate typical sentences in which the natural-language term might be used. To return to the hopscotch example, we might ask our child informant to tell us "If someone were to refer to a 'hopper,' how might they say it?"

Structural Questions   **Structural questions** ask about how informants structure different domains of knowledge or perceptions. For example, if we wanted to learn about all of the different kinds of games that can be played on a playground at an elementary school, we might ask our child informant "What are all the different kinds of games you can play at recess?" This question is asking the informant to share with us his or her perceptual domain of "games that can be played at recess." Spradley (1979, pp. 126–131) identifies five different kinds of structural questions.

The first kind of structural question is the *verification question.* Basically, this type of question is useful later in the research process, when the researcher has formulated a tentative hypothesis about the existence of some domain. The verification question asks the informant to confirm or disconfirm the domain in some way. In our conflict study, we might ask our romantic partners to answer the question "Are there different kinds of conflicts that the two of you have?" An affirmative answer verifies that informants perceive a domain—a grouping—of some phenomenon, *types of conflict* in this instance. An interviewer could present a single member of the domain and ask informants to confirm or disconfirm its membership. For example, in the interview of elementary school children, we might ask "Is 'monkey bars' a kind of game that can be played at recess?" If this is a legitimate member of the domain, we would receive an affirmative response. We might also receive a disconfirmation, like this one: "No, it's not a game because there aren't any rules and you play it alone." This type of answer is a joy to an interviewer's ears—although a candidate for membership was disconfirmed, the informant elaborated on criteria that are used to determine if some activity counts as a game.

Sometimes, a researcher has identified something of interest but doesn't know the kind of semantic relationship at stake for the informant. Remember semantic relationships from Chapter 3? A semantic relationship is a kind of meaning structure. To elementary school children, is "monkey bars" a kind of recess activity (a semantic relationship of strict inclusion) or a place to have fun on the playground (a semantic relationship of location)? The answer to this question would tell the researcher how "monkey bars" is meaningful to these children. A semantic-relationship verification question is helpful in determining the way a phenomenon is meaningful. In this instance, we might ask our child informants "Is 'monkey bars' something you do or a place to do something?"

Sometimes, a researcher wants to verify that the way something is said is representative of the population being studied. A natural-language verification question could do this nicely: "Would a kid ever say 'I did monkey bars today' in describing what they did with the monkey bars?"

The second kind of structural question presented by Spradley (1979) is the *cover-term question.* A cover term is a naturally occurring label for a given domain or grouping. For example, the six-year-old of one of us talks a lot about behaving "I Care." So do her friends, if you drop in and visit her school. This is obviously a domain of *ways of behaving.* A useful cover-term question to find out about this structural domain would be "Are there different kinds of 'I Care'?" Useful follow-up probes would be "Can you tell me what some of them are?" (In fact, the school song is the "I Care Song," a song about the ways that kids can be "super cool" at XXX School—showing respect, being polite, etc. Kids are socialized to the song, and its ways, starting in kindergarten, and it is a theme throughout their school years in the school.) Cover-term questions can shed insight into the various phenomena that occupy membership in the given domain.

Included-term questions also probe domain membership. But they go at it in the opposite way from cover-term questions. Cover-term questions start with the overarching term and inquire about the members of the group or domain. Included-term questions start with various members of the domain or group and ask the informant what the group is they all belong to. This third kind of structural question poses different candidates for membership and asks informants whether they belong in the same category or domain of meaning. For example, to continue with the "I Care" example, we might ask kids "Are 'showing respect,' 'taking responsibility,' and 'being nice' part of something else? Any well-socialized child enrolled in the school will quickly say "They are three of the points on the 'I Care' star."

The fourth kind of structural question is the *substitution-frame question.* This kind of question provides the framework for the domain or group and asks informants to reveal some of the other domain elements in the framework that is provided. For example, we might ask our elementary school children this substitution-frame question: "I heard a teacher say to a child 'You were I Care when you said you were sorry.' What are other ways this sentence could be completed: 'You were I Care when _____?'" Substitution-frame questions take a statement uttered by a native and ask fellow natives to substitute other meaningful phrases into the sentence. The substitutions inform the researcher about domain membership.

The fifth, and final, kind of structural question is actually a task for the informant to complete: the *card-sorting structural question.* The informant is handed a stack of cards with candidates for domain membership recorded on each card. For example, in studying the socialization of schoolchildren to the ways of "I Care" conduct, we might have 20 behaviors recorded on 20 cards. We might give this card deck to an informant and ask him or her to place all of the cards that are examples of "I Care" behavior in one stack.

Common to all structural questions is a researcher goal of finding out which things belong together in some way in the informant's mind. They are the key set of questions by which a researcher understands the informant's organization of meaning—the set of semantic relationships used by the informant in making sense of the world.

Contrast Questions **Contrast questions** are predicated on the assumption that no phenomenon is meaningful in isolation from other phenomena. In particular, the meaning of a given phenomenon rests, in part, on the web of related concepts to which it is similar and different. Contrast questions help you figure out the larger web of meanings that surround a given phenomenon. Spradley (1979, pp. 160–172) discusses seven different kinds of contrast questions helpful to the interviewer.

Contrast verification questions are helpful once a researcher has formulated a tentative hypothesis that two concepts or phenomena are similar or different. The interviewer presents the hypothesis for confirmation or disconfirmation by the informant. For example, let's suppose you have formulated the tentative hypothesis that "hoppers" are regarded as skilled players of hopscotch, whereas "scotchers" are regarded as relatively inept. You might present this hypothesis in the following contrast verification question: "I've heard various kids refer to 'hoppers' and 'scotchers.' Would you say that 'hoppers' are good at playing hopscotch, while 'scotchers' are not very good at playing hopscotch?"

The *directed contrast question* explicitly asks the informant to sort phenomena on some characteristic that you have identified from native talk. For example, in the "I Care" example above, you might have noticed that kids evaluate one another's behavior as "I Care" and "not I Care." So you might have a list of behaviors that kids enact and ask your informant to tell you which would be "I Care" and which would be "not I Care."

The interviewer can use *rating questions* to uncover contrasts. These questions try to discover the values placed on a set of phenomena. Informants are asked to rate a set of phenomena by some evaluative criterion—what is best, hardest, the most destructive, the most desirable, and so forth. For the study of conflict in romantic pairs, for instance, an informant might be presented with the list of different kinds of conflicts and asked "Which of these is the most destructive form of conflict? Next most destructive?" and so on.

Unlike the first three kinds of contrast questions, in which informants are presented with a characteristic, the remaining kinds of contrast questions do not identify an explicit characteristic for the informant. *Dyadic contrast questions* present an informant with two native terms that have already surfaced in your research, and the informant is asked to identify any differences between them. For example, suppose in your conflict study of romantic pairs you hear people talk about "having an argument" and "having a fight." You would probably want to know if these are synonyms or if they are referencing different kinds of conflict. You could pose the following dyadic contrast question to informants to find out: "Can you tell me any differences between 'having an argument' and 'having a fight?'"

Triadic contrast questions work with three native terms but are otherwise very similar to dyadic contrast questions. Let's suppose that our romantic pairs discussed their conflicts with three phrases: "having an argument," "having a fight," and "the silent treatment." Basically, the triadic contrast question asks the informant to decide which two are alike and which one is different: "Can you tell me which two of these descriptions of conflict are alike and which one is different from the others?" Obviously, you might find it useful to use follow-up questions to pursue the reasons that the informant sorted the terms as he or she did.

The fifth kind of contrast question, the *contrast set sorting question,* extends the logic of the triadic contrast question to the whole set of phenomena you are trying to understand. Let's suppose that when romantic pairs talk about their conflicts, eight different descriptive phrases are used by multiple informants: "having an argument," "having a fight," "having a little spat," "the silent treatment," "having a knock-down-drag-out," "having a quibble," "guerilla warfare," and "hit-and-run conflict." You want to know how these are similar to and different from one another. You could present them as a set to informants (often on 3 × 5 cards), and pose this contrast set sorting question: "Would you sort these into two or more piles in terms of how they are alike or different? Put similar things into the same pile." Follow-up probes could pursue why the informant sorted the phenomena the way she or he did.

The *twenty-questions game* is the sixth kind of contrast question discussed by Spradley (1979). You've probably played the game of Twenty Questions before: Someone thinks of an object (often identified as an animal, a vegetable, or a mineral), and the players have 20 yes–no questions to figure out what the object is. If nobody can guess the object, the person who thought of the object is declared the winner. A similar kind of logic is used in the twenty-questions question strategy. The interviewer lays out a set of phenomena for the informant and tells the informant to play Twenty Questions to try to guess the phenomenon that the interviewer is thinking of. The questions that the informant poses reveal his or her web of meanings. Although this is a useful strategy with young informants, because it can be presented as a game, it is actually very helpful regardless of the informant's age.

We bet you've never pondered the fact that there are so many different kinds of questions to ask of informants! Notice a few things about these questions as a set.

First, they are all focused on understanding meaning from the informant's point of view. In order to accomplish this task, the interviewer takes the informant's language use very seriously. Words and phrases used by the informant are not taken for granted but become objects of inquiry.

Second, these questions have a hierarchy to them. Descriptive questions are most useful early in a qualitative study, when the researcher is trying to get the basic "lay of the land." Once the researcher has identified several phenomena or concepts for a given sample of informants, he or she can turn to the more complicated tasks of determining how they fit together into groups, categories, or domains. And evaluations of sameness and difference are central to the judgments that people make when they are categorizing the world to render it meaningful.

For semistructured and unstructured interviewing, the interview protocol is a guide, not a script, for the interviewer. Grant McCracken (1988) describes the protocol in the following manner:

> With this [protocol] in hand, the investigator has a rough travel itinerary with which to negotiate the interview. It does not specify precisely what will happen at every stage of the journey, how long each lay-over will last, or where the investigator will be at any given moment, but it does establish a clear sense of the direction of the journey and the ground it will eventually cover. (p. 37)

The final issue that faces the qualitative interviewer in the planning stage is the selection of informants: Who should be interviewed? We have already discussed this topic in the previous chapter on participant-observation research, so we won't repeat ourselves here. Like participant observation, qualitative interviewing relies largely on nonprobability-based sampling that is purposive in nature.

An interview protocol is a planning device. Once an interviewer is conducting an interview, additional considerations need to be taken into account.

EXECUTING THE INTERVIEW: SOME DO'S AND DON'TS

Unlike casual conversations you enact many times in the course of a typical day, qualitative interviews—conversations with a purpose—are often challenging to pull off. It takes a lot of practice to become a good interviewer. Generally, before a researcher conducts actual interviews with informants, he or she needs to have several "practice interviews" with people to get the hang of interviewing. If a researcher is using a team of research assistants as interviewers, they need to undergo a period of *interview training*. Training involves careful study of the inter-

view protocol. Then the interviewers-in-training conduct multiple "mock interviews," which are usually observed or listened to by the researcher for purposes of providing feedback to the interviewer. Our experience is that the training process for qualitative interviewing takes 30–40 hours in a typical research project. What are the interviewing skills that the trainer is watching for during the training process? Let's turn to those now.

Creating and Sustaining Rapport

Webster's Ninth New Collegiate Dictionary (1987) defines *rapport* as a "relation marked by harmony, conformity, accord, or affinity" (p. 976). Easy to define, difficult to achieve. The cultural anthropologist Clifford Geertz (1973, p. 416) tells us that rapport is "that mysterious necessity of fieldwork." Like Jane Jorgenson (1995), we have difficulty thinking of rapport as a set of behaviors enacted by the interviewer for the instrumental purpose of eliciting good data from the informant. We also have difficulty thinking of rapport building as something confined to the opening moments of an interview, and once it is achieved, the interviewer can launch into question asking. We think rapport is a much more complex, and subtle, process that is accomplished throughout an interview.

The definition of *rapport* is illuminating to us because it suggests that rapport is a relationship between the interviewer and the informant, not something that the interviewer does to the informant. Given its relational quality, rapport is a relationship jointly constructed by the interviewer and the informant throughout the interview.

Like all relationships, the communication between interviewer and informant in an interview setting has two levels of communicative meaning: the report level and the command level (Watzlawick, Beavin, & Jackson, 1967). The report level is the content of the talk, whereas the command level addresses how that talk is to be taken with respect to its relationship implications for the interactants. We introduced this distinction in levels of meaning in the first part of this book. In the context of an interview, the report level is what we've been addressing so far with respect to development of the interview protocol—our focus has been on the research purpose and the desired content of the interview. But every time the interviewer opens his or her mouth to utter a content-based statement or question, a message is sent about the nature of the relationship between the interviewer and the informant. In addition, every time the informant provides a content-based statement, he or she is similarly making a command-level statement about the state of the relationship between the interviewer and the interviewee.

How can a relationship of harmony and affinity be crafted between the interviewer and the informant? If we had a clear answer to this question, we'd go into the counseling business, because we could help a lot of relationship pairs develop and sustain harmony in their relating practices! Jane Jorgenson (1995) has some initial suggestions, however. First, Jorgenson (1995) suggests that interviewers need to shift their priorities a bit, balancing a focus on interview content with a simultaneous focus on the interaction process of the interview.

Second, to the extent that it is possible, Jorgenson suggests that the interviewer needs to think of the interview as a dialogue between participants rather than a question-and-answer exchange. In a dialogue, both interactants are co-participants in the construction of meaning. The implications of this view are that the informant should feel free to ask questions, not just answer them. Further, the interviewer should feel comfortable answering questions, not just asking them. In general, this dialogue process is easier to accomplish when the interviewer is committed to an unstructured interview protocol.

Third, Jorgenson recommends that the interviewer and informant need to work to accomplish a relationship liberated from rigid role expectations of "interviewer" and "informant." Such rigid roles make it difficult for the interactants to get to know and respond to each other as persons rather than as occupants of roles. It is hard to build affinity with a role; it is possible to build affinity with a person. Rigid adherence to the interviewer–informant roles also implies a dominance relationship in which the interviewer is "in charge." To the extent possible, control should be shared by both people, who jointly construct the process of the interview.

A simple action that signals a relational message of joint control is to let the informant decide on the time and setting for the interview. Our experience is that informants will select locations comfortable to them, which is fine because this makes it easier for the two of you to build a relationship of rapport. So long as the setting affords reasonable privacy and adequate acoustics for tape-recording the interview, you should let the informant take charge of the time and location for the interview.

Fourth, Jorgenson suggests that rapport is built on the mutual perception of trust and respect. If an interviewer isn't open and honest with an informant, why should the informant be open and honest in return? If an interviewer's tone is patronizing or condescending, how can the informant feel respected?

One way that an interviewer signals respect for the informant is a clear statement of the purpose of the interview. The interviewer owes the informant a description of what the interview will be about, approximately how long it will take, and what topics will be addressed. The interviewee also needs to know what will be done with the interview data once they are collected. Such an introduction is not only ethical conduct; in addition, it signals a relational message to informants that you respect them.

Another way the interviewer signals respect for the informant is by doing adequate "homework" in advance of the interview. Show that you value the informant's time by not wasting it. Spend time thinking about your interview protocol.

Rapport is difficult to create, yet it is very easy to destroy. It is a fragile, emergent state of relating that takes a heavy dose of hard work, commitment, patience, and perseverance. Don't take it for granted, don't rush it, and nurture it once you think it is present.

Doing Questions and Answers

One of the greatest challenges in performing an interview is entering the dance of a guided conversation with the informant. In light of our discussion of rapport, the interviewer doesn't want to be "in control" of the interview. Yet the interviewer doesn't want to abdicate influence either, because the purposes of the interview might not be met. Here are some suggestions for how to proceed with the dance.

First, let informants talk using their words at their pace. Consistent with good survey interviewing practices, the qualitative interviewer doesn't want to bias the informant by asking leading questions or by putting words into his or her mouth. After all, you are trying to maximize informant talk in order to gather as much data as possible. Be patient and listen hard to what informants have to say, rather than thinking about what you are going to say next. Grant McCracken (1988) has this advice once informants "have been brought within sight of the topic":

> They must be allowed to "go" wherever they wish. It is impossible to tell, in advance of careful analysis, whether (and how) what they are saying bears on the topic. The objective here is to generate enough testimony around these key terms that there will be sufficient data for later analysis. (p. 40)

If the informant is encouraged to talk on his or her terms, it signals a relational message of respect for the informant and a willingness on the part of the interviewer to share control.

Second, probe, probe, probe for further details. One of the best ways to signal that you are listening carefully to the informant is to ask follow-up questions that emerge from what he or she has said. Grant McCracken (1988,

p. 35) writes about the use of **floating prompts** to accomplish this purpose. A floating prompt is a relational message to the informant to "tell me more," often tied in some way to something the informant has just said. Some floating prompts can be nonverbal—for example, raising an eyebrow at a strategic moment in the informant's utterance. Or perhaps the informant has used a term that ought not to be taken for granted. The interviewer can prompt the informant to elaborate on that term (e.g., "You described your computer as your 'greatest ally' at work. What do you mean by this?").

Some prompts can be more planned, or boilerplate, in nature. Some good boilerplate probes are "Can you tell me more about that?" and "Can you give me an example of that?" Although descriptive questions make for good boilerplate probes, so do structural and contrast questions. For example, a useful probe is always the contrast question "You mentioned X and Y just now. How are X and Y alike and different?" Even though the question form may be boilerplate, its use must not be mechanical in any way. Follow-up probes should emerge from the informant's utterances, signaling to the informant at the relational level that you are listening and are interested in what he or she has to say. You will also accomplish a content goal with probes: acquiring more information from the informant.

Third, use transitions between questions in a guiding but not a controlling way. Herbert and Riene Rubin offer this advice:

> If you can limit the number of main topics, it is easier to maintain a conversational flow from one topic to another. Transitions should be smooth and logical. "We have been talking about mothers, now let's talk about fathers," sounds abrupt. A smoother transition might be, "You mentioned your mother did not care how you performed in school—was your father more involved?" The more abrupt the transition, the more it sounds like the interviewer has an agenda that he or she wants to get through, rather than wanting to hear what the interviewee has to say. (1995, p. 123)

Again, the relational message with smooth transitions is one of respect for and interest in the informant. At a content level, the interviewer ensures that all of the topic areas will be addressed over the course of the interview.

Fourth, use paraphrasing often. Paraphrasing means restating the informant's utterance in what you think is alternative language. Because you are paying special attention to language use by the informant, it is important to be vigilant and never take the informant's language for granted. The way to check your understanding is to attempt a paraphrase and seek the informant's confirmation or disconfirmation of its adequacy. The relational meaning of the paraphrase is that you are genuinely interested in understanding what the informant has to say—another way to show respect.

Fifth, display supportiveness of the informant. Don't second-guess informants or somehow make them feel that they "got it wrong." You need to enter the interview on the assumption that the informant is the resident expert on the topic at hand (which is true—the informant knows more about his or her own experiences and perceptions than anyone else around!). Sometimes, a display of supportiveness can be as easy as a simple up-and-down head nod accompanied by an "Uh-huh." Other times, you'll need to be a bit more explicit in your display of support or encouragement: "That's really an interesting story! Can you tell me more about what happened?"

If an informant is inconsistent or contradictory in what he or she says, it is important not to evaluate this negatively and signal this evaluation to the informant. Our experience is that when informants are inconsistent or contradictory, it's rarely because they are irrational and more likely because the experience itself contains contradictory or ambivalent elements. Respect your informants enough to legitimate what they have to say.

Sixth, and perhaps most important, be flexible and adaptive. No matter how much time and effort you put into designing the interview protocol, be prepared to modify it once you're in the interview. Sometimes, you may need to abandon the protocol entirely and "fly by the seat of your pants," preferably in a way that still has your overall research purpose on your mind. For beginning interviewers, adapting the protocol can be difficult. The interview protocol is a kind of security blanket for the interviewer, after all. However, if the interviewer is to be true to a model of equal partnership with the informant, it is important not to display a rigid adherence to the list of questions prepared in advance of the interview. Our experience is that often the most interesting issues and questions emerge during the interview itself. Seize the moment, and adapt accordingly.

These suggestions may appear obvious, and on one level, they are. But they are difficult to achieve without practice. As with participant-observation research, interviewing improves with practice. Fortunately, it's something you can practice anytime you want. Practice on your friends.

Up to this point in the chapter, we have discussed qualitative interviews as if they were all alike. To some extent, this is true—all qualitative interviews face the same set of issues with respect to determining a purpose, designing a protocol, sampling informants, and executing the interview. But qualitative interviews also come in different stripes. We'll discuss these next.

GENRES OF QUALITATIVE INTERVIEWING

No two qualitative interviews are alike. However, it is possible to identify several basic types of qualitative interviewing. We'll discuss five: the ethnographic conversation, the depth interview, the group or focus interview, the narrative interview, and the postmodern interview.

The Ethnographic Conversation

This genre of qualitative interviewing is usually seen in participant-observation studies. Also referred to as a "situational conversation" (Schatzman & Strauss, 1973, p. 71), this form of interviewing is closely tied to the field site of the participant observer. The interview is often indistinguishable from a casual conversation. The informant rarely thinks of the interaction as an interview; in fact, he or she may not even be aware that the other person is a researcher.

Sheryl Lindsley (1999) conducted an ethnography of communication among Mexican workers employed at U.S.-owned assembly plants in Mexico. Her participant-observation work was accompanied by two kinds of interviews—the depth interview we will describe below and the **ethnographic conversation.** In contrast to the four-hour, formal depth interviews, ethnographic conversations were described as follows:

> I conducted informal interviews as conversations on the topics of cultural and intercultural communication in the maquiladoras [U.S.-owned plants]. These conversations emerged from interactions with participants in the formal interviews and with others who were knowledgeable about maquiladoras. These were unplanned conversations which occurred spontaneously during the time I was living in a U.S.-Mexican border-town. For example, I met one Mexican maquiladora line-worker at a local Denny's restaurant, and this acquaintance led to a discussion of his work and differences between U.S. American and Mexican cultures. . . . These interviews had no formal structure; they simply occupied portions of naturally occurring conversations. (Lindsley, 1999, p. 5)

Now that you have learned something about what a qualitative interview is, we hope you appreciate why the ethnographic conversation is inseparable from the method of participant observation. It is impossible for us to imagine a participant-observation study fully achieving its goal of understanding the native's point of view without talking with informant natives.

Kristine Fitch's (1998) ethnography of communication of urban Colombians illustrates the interdependence of participant-observation and qualitative-interviewing methods:

> Interviews are in a sense artificial: talk about an event or a relationship is clearly not the same as talk during an event or within a relationship. . . . Nonetheless, given that the meaning of communicative practice is generally left unsaid, particularly those aspects of meaning derived from taken-for-granted understandings, analysis of meaning necessarily goes outside of interaction itself to other locations of the knowledge brought to bear on it. . . . [T]hese interview data are presented as complementary to observational data presented earlier. (p. 8)

The Depth Interview

In contrast to the ethnographic interview, the **depth interview** (also referred to as a long interview; see McCracken, 1988) tends to be longer and more formalized. The informant and the researcher frame the interaction event as an interview. Depth interviewing can be used together with participant observation or as a stand-alone research method. In either instance, the goal of the depth interview is to understand the informant's point of view on some phenomenon or experience in as richly detailed a manner as possible.

Lindsley's (1999) ethnography of communication about U.S.-owned assembly plants in Mexico employed participant observation, ethnographic conversations, and depth interviews. Her depth interviews lasted, on average, four hours. Here's her description of the basic interview process she employed in conducting these depth interviews:

> These interviews began by informing the participants of the purpose of the study and assuring them [of their rights]. . . . Next, I obtained background information. . . . Subsequently, I posed a "grand tour" question in which I asked the participants to describe a typical work day. After this introductory sequence, the interviews became more focused; I began asking questions about actual interactions in the maquiladora context. In this part of the interviews, I asked open-ended questions designed to ascertain each participant's recall of both intercultural and cultural interaction situations. Finally,

I asked each participant what advice s/he would give others about how these situations should be handled. (p. 5)

An example of depth interviewing as a stand-alone method comes from a study conducted by Leigh Ford, Eileen Berlin Ray, and Beth Ellis (1999). They conducted depth interviews with adult survivors of incest, focusing in particular on how they disclosed their abuse to others. Interviews ranged from 45 to 90 minutes in length. Here's their description of their protocol:

The interview began with demographic information followed by a brief recounting of the abuse. Participants were encouraged to share only those aspects of their stories that they felt comfortable revealing. The primary questions of the interview focused on eliciting survivors' accounts of their disclosure experiences. Three specific accounts were requested: (1) a first experience with disclosure, (2) a disclosure experience that was met with support by the recipient, and (3) a disclosure experience that was met with disbelief and nonsupport by a recipient. For each retrospective account, the interviewer used follow-up questions when necessary to encourage the participant to elaborate on the circumstances. (pp. 141–142)

The Group or Focus Interview

So far, we've been discussing interviews that take place with a single informant at a time. An alternative kind of interview is the **group interview,** in which the researcher conducts an interview with two or more informants at once. Why would a researcher be interested in doing this? Communication is a collaborative, social process. In conducting an interview with two or more people at once, the interviewer gains the added insight that comes from observing the interaction that takes place between the informants themselves. You get to see how they jointly construct a response. The presence of fellow informants can spark thoughts that might not come to mind when there are only the interviewer and a single informant. The opportunity to observe interaction between the informants also brings the researcher one step closer to naturally occurring communication.

A particular kind of group interview that has gained popularity, particularly among multi-method researchers, is the **focus group.** A focus group interview is a face-to-face interview conducted with a group of persons, in contrast to interviewing individuals one at a time. Focus groups have a long legacy in social scientific research.

The method originated with the work of Robert Merton and his collaborators, who used focus groups to examine the persuasiveness of wartime propaganda efforts (Merton, 1987). Focus groups have been popular since the 1950s in marketing research (Morgan, 2002).

In a focus group, typically 7–12 people are brought together in a room to engage in a guided discussion of some topic. As Krueger (1988) advises, there's no "magic number" that captures the ideal size for a focus group. In general, the rule of thumb is that you want the group to be small enough so that everybody gets ample opportunity to talk yet large enough to ensure some diversity of opinion among participants.

Typically, more than one focus group is convened in a given study because there is a serious danger that a single group might be too atypical to offer insights. Because focus groups are used to provide an in-depth understanding of some phenomenon, the number of groups studied is less important than the quality of insight gained from the discussions. Generally, a focus group researcher knows he or she has enough groups when the saturation point is reached—no new insights are gained from additional group discussions. In focus group research, the unit of analysis is the group discussion, not the individual participant who is a member of a group.

The participants for focus group discussions are selected on the basis of relevance to the topic under study, although they are not likely to be chosen through probability sampling methods. However, the purpose of the focus group study is to explore rather than to develop causal explanations that generalize to a population. Krueger (1988, p. 28) suggests that the key question to answer in defining the population of participants for focus group participation is "Who do you want to hear from?" If you are a marketing researcher interested in testing out attitudes toward a new soft drink, then the target population is likely consumers of soft drinks.

In general, a focus group researcher is interested in constructing a focus group so that the participants are homogeneous with respect to background characteristics such as age, sex, and ethnicity, yet ideally hold different opinions about the phenomenon under study. As a general rule of thumb, participants in a given focus group should be strangers to one another. If the participants are acquainted, it may be more difficult for the moderator to guide the discussion. For example, participants may have shared knowledge that enables them to understand one another, yet they might not make this shared knowledge explicit so that the moderator can understand. In addition, if participants know one another, they might fall back on established patterns of interaction, which could present a challenge to the moderator interested in encouraging all participants to talk openly and freely.

David Morgan (2002) distinguishes more and less structured focus group interviewing. Both kinds of interviewing have a moderator ask questions of the assembled group, but the moderator's role differs depending on the amount of structure in the experience. The more structured approach, which is quite common in marketing research, according to Morgan (2002), tends to be characterized by a moderator who directs the discussion. The moderator's questions set the agenda for the group's discussion. Usually, a larger number of more narrowly focused questions are used, often with specific amounts of time devoted to each question. Participants direct their comments to and through the moderator. When a participant says something that is off the topic, the moderator brings the discussion back to the question at hand.

By contrast, Morgan (2002) suggests an alternative way to conduct a focus group, a less structured approach. In this alternative approach, the moderator facilitates the discussion but does not direct it. The moderator generally has a smaller number of questions, each quite general in nature. Participants talk to one another, and the moderator attends to the group's process to make certain that all participants have an opportunity to discuss and that the general questions get discussed, although the order and amount of time devoted to a given question topic are determined largely by the group's dynamic.

Richard Krueger (1988) points to five advantages of focus groups:

1. The technique is a socially oriented research method capturing real-life data in a social environment.
2. It has flexibility.
3. It has high face validity.
4. It has speedy results.
5. It is low in cost. (p. 47)

The group dynamics that occur in focus groups frequently bring out aspects of the topic that would not have been anticipated by the researcher and would not have emerged from interviews with individuals. In a side conversation, for example, a couple of the participants might start joking about the risk of leaving out one letter from a product's name, if the focus groups were convened to discuss a new consumer product. This realization might save great embarrassment later on. Similar research might have spared Chevrolet an unsuccessful attempt to sell its

Nova in Spanish-speaking countries, where the name translates roughly as "no go."

Krueger also notes some disadvantages of the method:

1. Focus groups afford the researcher less control than individual interviews.
2. Data are difficult to analyze.
3. Moderators require special skills.
4. Difference between groups can be troublesome.
5. Groups are difficult to assemble.
6. The discussion must be conducted in a conducive environment. (1988, pp. 44–45)

Focus group research is increasingly used by communication researchers. For example, Ernest Bormann and his colleagues (Bormann, Bormann, & Harty, 1995) used findings from six focus group discussions with junior and senior high school students to create recommendations for public service announcements on tobacco use. Patrick McLaurin (1995) used focus group discussions for a similar purpose. He conducted focus group interviews with African American youths to examine their world view and sense-making schemata as part of a larger project designed to develop effective, pro-social mediated messages targeted to this population.

In addition, David Morgan (1988) suggests that focus groups are an excellent device for generating questionnaire items for a subsequent survey. For example, Beth Ellis and Katherine Miller (1993) employed focus group interviews with a hospital's nursing staff to determine the salient issues related to nurse burnout and commitment. Based on the findings from these discussions, the researchers developed a questionnaire that they subsequently sent to the entire nursing staff of the hospital.

To give you a concrete feel for a focus group protocol, we'll share a protocol that one of us recently developed as part of a grant proposal to develop mediated messages designed to discourage pregnant women from drinking alcohol. We planned to conduct four to six focus groups with lower-income pregnant women. We decided to use a less structured question format. The group moderator, the interviewer, initially would "set the stage" by providing a welcome, providing an overview of the discussion's purpose and process, and starting off the discussion with an initial "icebreaker" question. Subsequent questions would be raised, as needed, when the moderator sensed a lull in the conversation. Here's the starter question that we planned to use: "What are your experiences with being pregnant?" This question would "get the ball rolling." The protocol included other questions, which are referred to as "talking points," to emphasize that the interviewer/moderator has substantial latitude in question wording and sequence:

- Who do you talk to about your pregnancy?
- One of the things we're especially interested in is drinking alcohol during pregnancy. What are your opinions about that?
- What are the barriers that make it hard to avoid drinking alcohol during pregnancy?
- What do others—family members, friends, your partner, your health-care providers—think about drinking alcohol while pregnant?

The Narrative Interview

The **narrative interview** often employs an unstructured or a semistructured protocol to elicit informant stories about some phenomenon of interest to the researcher. People use stories, or narratives, to make sense of their lives (Fisher, 1987). We learn to listen and to tell stories very early in our lives, and one of the most frequent ways we interact with others is by telling (and listening to) stories about various things. Narrative researchers use a variety of methods to locate stories, including the narrative interview.

Narratives are often used in biographical studies. A **biographical study** is "the study of an individual and his or her experiences as told to the researcher or found in documents and archival material" (Creswell, 1998, p. 47). Creswell (1998, p. 49) discusses several basic types of biographical research, including the two most common in communication research:

- *The life-history study:* Heavily reliant on the individual's own words, this is a chronological life story of an individual. The researcher attempts to link the individual's life story to larger societal and cultural themes.
- *The oral-history study:* This is a study in which the researcher gathers personal recollections of events of an individual's life, or the lives of several individuals. Usually, an oral history focuses more narrowly on some slice of life rather than focusing on the participant's chronological life history.

You might be wondering how biographical research holds relevance for communication researchers. A researcher might want to conduct a life-history study of someone who has been very influential in the development of the communication field. Or you might want to understand how scholars' research programs take shape by studying the research careers of prolific scholars from the time they were in graduate school up to the present.

A researcher might have an interest in the everyday person as well. For example, a researcher might be interested in telling the story of how communication technologies have entered and affected the life of a typical older person—memories of listening as a family to radio programs after dinner in the years before television, memories of the first TV their family owned, recollections of the shift from the typewriter to computerized word-processing software, and so forth. Basically, this would be an oral-history study anchored in the sea of technologies that a sample of older persons grew up with.

An actual example of oral-history narrative research comes from Catherine Sullivan Norton's (1989) study of people's stories of survival—how they coped with the challenges of everyday life. She conducted in-depth interviews with 46 people from a variety of walks of life. She describes her protocol as follows:

> The interview schedule was formulated to encourage people to talk about their lives. It specifies major questions and provides a repertoire of possible probes. The major questions were structured openly to permit sufficient freedom to elaborate. Because I needed to examine the individual's life orientation, the topics covered life issues and life experiences relating to the following ten dimensions: work, interest in work, survival strategies, other work, purposes of life, difficult times, personality, life metaphor, view of life, and core life issues. Each area was selected to provide evidence of how a person copes. (pp. 199–201)

The protocol did not explicitly ask for stories from her informants. But in asking informants to talk about their lives, Norton was confident that they would tell stories because of the prevalence of this communication form in everyday interaction. Her hunch was correct.

Sometimes, researchers are interested in hearing stories from a third-person perspective—that is, stories that participants tell about others. An example of a narrative study in which both first-person and third-person stories were collected is John Meyer's (1997) use of narrative interviews to elicit stories about the organization where informants worked. Like Norton, Meyer did not explicitly ask informants for stories. Instead, he asked informants to talk about work life in the organization, assuming that the telling of stories would be a common way in which workers talked about their organization. It was. Here are some of his questions from his interview protocol (p. 194):

- How would you describe a typical day at work for you?
- What is the best thing that typically happens in a day at work?
- What is the worst thing that typically happens in a day at work?
- How do you perceive the way decisions are made around here?
- Describe a recent work event that demonstrates to you an instance of poor communication.
- Describe a recent work event that demonstrates to you an instance of good communication.
- What is the funniest event to happen recently at work?

Sometimes, researchers explicitly ask informants to tell stories. Julia Wood's study (2001) of abusive relationships, described above, explicitly asked informants to tell the story of their relationships. The interview study of stepchildren (Baxter et al., 2001), whose protocol was presented earlier in the chapter, similarly included a question in which informants were explicitly asked to tell a story that was typical of how their stepfamily interacted.

Narrative interviews differ from in-depth interviews in their focus on a particular communicative form—the story or narrative. Otherwise, they are indistinguishable from each other.

The Postmodern Interview

Andrea Fontana and James Frey (1994) present a form of interviewing that they label the **postmodern interview.** Most researchers who subscribe to this form of interviewing align with the critical theory paradigm of knowing (see Chapter 3). Researchers committed to the postmodern interview are suspicious of the power relations and domination inherent in the interviewer role. Even if the interviewer strives for a relationship of equality with the informant, it is the interviewer's voice and perspective in the end that dominate the study—from planning, to execution, to analysis, to write-up of the results. Postmodern interviews attempt to achieve what's called polyphonic interviewing,

> in which the voices of the subjects are recorded with minimal influence from the researcher and are not collapsed together and reported as one, through the interpretation of the researcher. Instead, the multiple perspectives of the various subjects are reported and differences and problems encountered are discussed, rather than glossed over. (Fontana & Frey, 1994, pp. 368–369)

Postmodern interviewing is an explicitly self-reflexive process, one in which the interviewer goes beyond rapport as we have discussed it earlier to empower, or give voice, to the range and complexities of informant experiences. This is a tall order.

A study that comes close is Nikki Townsley and Patricia Geist's (2000) study of "unwanted sexual attention" in academic settings. The researchers tell us that "We attempted to 'give voice' to the victims' stories otherwise not heard or validated organizationally by conducting the interviews in a non-directional manner" (p. 198). They didn't have an interview protocol, choosing simply to ask informants to describe their experiences. Townsley and Geist were explicitly reflexive on the power relations of the interview situation in which they found themselves:

> We are cognizant of the obvious power differential between researchers and research "subjects" and the benefits that we gain from informant stories. To reconcile the discord at least minimally, we utilized feminist based, conversational interviewing techniques and discussed our vulnerabilities as researchers with each other and with our participants. (pp. 198–199)

In an attempt to "give voice" to their informants, the researchers did not gloss their individual experiences. Instead, they decided to focus on the experiences of a selected few of their informants to illuminate the broader experiences that the sample of informants shared in common. In this way, the reader is brought closer to the intact experiences of real people.

Researchers who endorse postmodern interviewing are profoundly rethinking what an interview is and how it ought to be conducted and reported.

We don't claim to have exhausted the full range of interview types in this section. But we think we have described some of the more common genres of qualitative interviewing that you will encounter in communication research.

TRUSTWORTHINESS AND QUALITATIVE INTERVIEWING

Let's end this chapter by returning to those four criteria by which the trustworthiness of all qualitative research is evaluated: dependability, confirmability, credibility, and transferability. How do qualitative interviewers meet these criteria?

The dependability criterion is met in the same way that participant observers go about documenting that their research process is trackable: field notes and a reflexive journal. In addition to having audiotapes and written transcripts of interviews, qualitative interviewers keep detailed notes about other relevant observations that could possibly inform them as they try to understand the interviews. They keep ongoing reflexive notes about their process and their emergent analysis. Like participant observation, qualitative interviewing is an iterative process, one in which the researcher is analyzing at the same time that data are being gathered. Subsequent data collection is informed by the analysis of prior collected data, with appropriate adaptations, changes, and so forth. Such emergent research is not stable, but its evolution is trackable. That's what the dependability criterion speaks to—whether the evolving nature of the research process is systematic and sensical.

The qualitative researcher achieves confirmability by gathering richly detailed data from a sufficient number of informants. Confirmability basically asks whether the conclusions reached by the researcher are warranted from the evidence. The qualitative interviewer gathers detailed informant talk sufficient to support his or her conclusions. Of course, the researcher has available the same confirmability tools as the participant-observer, including the full range of triangulation options.

Credibility asks whether the researcher's conclusions "ring true" to the native/informant. The easiest way for the qualitative interviewer to demonstrate this criterion is to loop back for another round of interviews with the same or similar informants when the analysis has crystallized. Verification questions feature prominently in these credibility-checking interviews.

Last, transferability: As with participant observation, qualitative interviewers are not attempting to make generalized claims about an entire population. They typically rely on a sample size that is small by quantitative standards, but sufficient to the task so long as saturation is achieved. The qualitative researcher, like the participant observer, is attempting to paint a detailed portrait of something. If the portrait has been painted with sufficient detail, then readers can judge for themselves how it holds relevance. With transferability, then, the researcher's burden is to render intelligible some specific phenomenon, setting, or group in a richly textured and detailed manner. An interview that allows an informant to talk in detailed ways, in his or her own words, is the best guarantee that the transferability criterion can be met.

Main Points

❏ Qualitative interviewing is the second in the triad of qualitative methods. Data are gathered by talking with informants in an open-ended manner.

❏ Qualitative interviewing is a speech event: an interaction with a beginning, middle, and end, in which participants interact according to their expectations for how they think an interview should be conducted. Qualitative interviewing is similar to, yet different from, a casual conversation. Qualitative interviewing is a conversation with a purpose.

❏ Qualitative interviewing requires the researcher to identify his or her purpose and design an interview plan, or protocol, for how to conduct the interview.

❏ Qualitative interviews are generally semistructured or unstructured, in contrast to quantitatively oriented structured or standardized interviews.

❏ Qualitative interviews generally rely on three basic types of open-ended questions, each with several variants: descriptive questions, structural questions, and contrast questions.

❏ Trustworthy qualitative interviewing involves the creation and nurturing of rapport between the interviewer and the informant.

❏ Trustworthy qualitative interviewing requires the interviewer to be flexible, adaptive, and responsive to the experiences and utterances of the informant.

❏ There are several genres of qualitative interviewing. We discussed five: the ethnographic conversation, the depth interview, the group or focus interview, the narrative interview, and the postmodern interview.

❏ Similar to other qualitative methods, qualitative interviewing is accountable to the criteria of dependability, confirmability, credibility, and transferability.

❏ Qualitative interviewing is often used in conjunction with the other two qualitative methods in the execution of a single research project.

❏ Qualitative interviewing, especially focus group interviewing, is a useful tool in combination with quantitatively oriented research.

Key Terms

qualitative interview
phenomenology
interpretivism
structured interview
semistructured interview
unstructured interviewing
descriptive questions
structural questions
contrast questions

floating prompts
ethnographic conversation
depth interview
group (focus) interview
focus group
narrative interview
biographical study
postmodern interview

Review Questions and Exercises

1. Identify a research question about communication that you think could be answered through the method of qualitative interviewing. Plan an interview protocol in which you illustrate at least two different kinds of questions.

2. Watch a televised talk show in which the host frequently interviews guests, or watch a news program in which individuals are frequently interviewed in depth. Evaluate the interviewer's performance in light of this chapter's discussion on how to execute a qualitative interview.

3. Identify a job or career in which you have a possible interest. Identify a person who holds this job or career. Plan and execute a qualitative interview with the person that is designed to inform you about this person's experience with the job/career. Reflect on the type of interview and questions you used.

4. Pick some topic of interest to students at your university. Gather a group of students and conduct a small focus group with them on the topic. Assess the ways in which the information you gathered was likely different from what could have been gathered by interviewing each participant separately—that is, reflect on what happened *between* the participants.

Continuity Project

Suppose you are interested in the question of how women experience "being female" in the culture and how men experience "being male" in the culture. Devise a qualitative interview protocol that would be responsive to this research purpose. Identify the various kinds of questions you would be using, and explain why you are using them.

Additional Readings

Briggs, C. L. (1986). *Learning how to ask: A sociolinguistic appraisal of the role of the interview in social science research.* New York: Cambridge University Press. A grounded argument for appreciating the interview as a culture-specific speech event.

Gubrium, J. F., & Holstein, J. A. (Eds.) (2002). *Handbook of interview research: Context & method.* Thousand Oaks, CA: Sage. A comprehensive volume on interviewing, both more structured and less structured. The treatment of qualitative interviewing genres is particularly strong.

Krueger, R. A. (1988). *Focus groups: A practical guide for applied research.* Newbury Park, CA: Sage. An excellent step-by-step book on how to conduct focus group interviews.

Kvale, S. (1996). *InterViews: An introduction to qualitative research interviewing.* Thousand Oaks, CA: Sage. An in-depth presentation on in-depth interviewing. Besides presenting techniques, Kvale places interviewing in the context of postmodernism and other philosophical systems.

Lindlof, T. R. (1995). *Qualitative communication research methods.* Thousand Oaks, CA: Sage. This book is outstanding in its treatment of qualitative interviewing, along with its treatment of other qualitative methods.

McCracken, G. (1988). *The long interview.* Newbury Park, CA: Sage. An excellent book that compares quantitative and qualitative forms of research as a backdrop to his discussion of depth interviewing.

Mishler, E. G. (1986). *Research interviewing: Context and narrative.* Cambridge, MA: Harvard University Press. A well-argued critique of traditional interviewing, in which the interviewer and informant occupy distinct roles with an unequal power relationship. Mishler emphasizes the interview as a collaborative speech event.

Morgan, D. L. (1988). *Focus groups as qualitative research.* Newbury Park, CA: Sage. A useful guide to the conduct of focus group interviews. Morgan emphasizes the focus group not as a "first step" that is preliminary to other methods but as a valid method in its own right. He also emphasizes unstructured focus group discussions to permit unstructured interaction among group participants.

Spradley, J. P. (1979). *The ethnographic interview.* New York: Holt, Rinehart and Winston. A classic book on how to conduct semistructured interviews. Although the book discusses interviewing in the context of ethnographic participant-observation research, Spradley's discussion of types of questions is relevant to any kind of interviewing.

Stewart, D. W., & Shamdasani, P. N. (1990). *Focus groups: Theory and practice.* Newbury Park, CA: Sage. A good introduction to focus group interviewing methods and techniques.

InfoTrac College Edition
http://www.infotrac-college.com/
wadsworth/access.html

Access the latest news and journal articles with Info-Trac College Edition, an easy-to-use online database of reliable, full-length articles from hundreds of top academic journals. Conduct an electronic search using the following search terms:

- semistructured interview
- unstructured interview
- focus group
- depth interview
- narrative
- interpretivism
- phenomenology

CHAPTER 15

Social Text Analysis

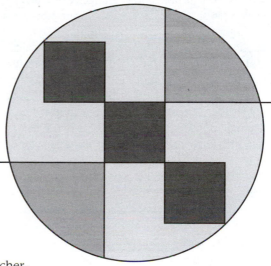

What You'll Learn in This Chapter

Thus far in Part 3, we've studied methods that produce researcher-generated texts in the form of field notes and interview transcripts. In this chapter, we'll discuss how qualitative researchers work with social texts—that is, naturally occurring "texts" such as conversations, communicative performances, and symbolic artifacts, including documents.

INTRODUCTION

The product of participant observation is a text—the researcher's field notes. The product of qualitative interviewing is also a text—a written transcript of a qualitative interview. In this chapter, we're going to be talking about another kind of text, what we'll be calling a **social text.** A social text is a naturally occurring text rather than a researcher-generated text. Social texts—symbols-in-use—are everywhere in the conduct of private and public life. Virtually anything can function as a social text, so long as it involves symbols and meaning: naturally occurring conversations at home or at work, letters and diaries, photographs, films, magazine articles, public speeches, news conferences, memorials, art exhibits, Web pages, and so forth.

The range of electronic, material, visual, and written social texts examined in communication research is staggering. Here's a sampler drawn from communication journals, intended to stretch your understanding of what can "count" as a "text" to communication researchers:

- Vietnam war films (*The Deer Hunter, Apocalypse Now, Platoon, Full Metal Jacket*) (Rasmussen & Downey, 1991)
- Israeli pioneering settlement museums (Katriel, 1994)
- The architecture of "Old Pasadena" (Dickinson, 1997)
- The names of sports stadiums (Boyd, 2000)
- Televised sports events (Brummett & Duncan, 1990)
- Televised soap opera episodes (Livingstone & Leibes, 1995)
- Chicano rap music (Delgado, 1998)
- Scrapbooks (Katriel & Farrell, 1991)
- The Vietnam Veterans Memorial (Blair, Jeppeson, & Pucci, 1991)

We've encountered social texts before—in Chapter 10, in our discussion of content analysis and interaction analysis. However, qualitative researchers and quantitative researchers don't approach these social texts in the same way. Whereas a quantitative researcher is interested in enumerating the frequencies with which coded variables appear in a sample of social texts and their statistical relationships with other variables, the qualitative researcher is interested in understanding the meanings and uses of such social texts. The enterprise is an interpretive one, not a numerical one. Of course, a given text could be analyzed using both quantitative and qualitative methods, thereby lending multi-method strength to your analysis.

RESEARCH USING SOCIAL TEXTS

The qualitative analysis of social texts generally takes two forms in communication research. First, researchers analyze social texts as a form of triangulation with participant observation and qualitative interviewing. Second, researchers analyze selected social texts in their own right.

Qualitative scholars often use social texts as a way to complement their participant-observer and interviewing methods. For example, one of us conducted a study on older married couples who had renewed their wedding vows (Braithwaite & Baxter, 1995). Our primary method was the qualitative interview—we conducted in-depth interviews with spouses about their vow renewal. As part of the interview process, however, we also relied on a variety of social texts as a form of triangulation—written copies of the actual wedding renewal vows, scrapbooks of pictures and other mementos from the ceremony and the reception, videotapes of the ceremony, displays of the wedding gowns used in the renewal ceremony, and so forth. These social texts were used in conjunction with interview transcripts to shed insight into what these renewal events meant to the couples who participated in them.

Communication researchers also analyze social texts in the absence of participant observation and interviewing methods. Social texts thus function as the primary data to be analyzed, not as complementary data to other qualitative methods. However, it would be misleading to imply that this approach is free of triangulation. When social texts are the primary form of data, they are corroborated with other social texts of relevance. Social texts contextualize one another, positioning the researcher to construct a mosaic of meaning from this "conversation between texts."

THE PROCESS OF WORKING WITH SOCIAL TEXTS

Malcolm Sillars and Bruce Gronbeck (2001, pp. 23–27) make the useful distinction between "a work" and "a text." "A work" is some communicative message—a speech, a TV program, a conversation. By contrast, "a text" is an interpretation of a work. A given work could contain multiple texts, or interpretations.

The first job of a qualitative researcher is to locate a work or sample of works—some public/private, mediated/nonmediated, scripted/spontaneous, linguistic/

nonlinguistic communicative message(s). How are messages sampled? Consistent with sampling designs in other kinds of qualitative research, purposive nonprobability sampling is the dominant strategy. Communicative works are usually selected because the researcher thinks that they are rich in information.

After sampling "works," the job of a qualitative researcher is to construct a text from that work—a process Sillars and Gronbeck (2001, p. 23) call **textualization.** Textualization recognizes the subjectivity of the researcher. Unlike the quantitative text analyst, who frames the message as an objective phenomenon, the qualitative text researcher assumes that many credible "texts" can be located in a single "work" or message. The analytic task of the qualitative researcher is not to persuade you that he or she has discovered the single "objective truth" of what a given message or "work" means. Instead, the task is to persuade the reader that the "text" identified by the researcher is reasonable and insightful. Here's what Sillars and Gronbeck (2001) have to say about the process of textualization: "The difficult-but-crucial point to understand about textualizations is that they are constructions made *from* the work yet, in an important sense, are grounded *in* that work" (p. 26). In other words, the researcher creates a sense making of a communicative act, message, or episode, but that sense making is constructed out of important features of that work. The researcher is obligated to stay grounded in the symbols-in-use—to remain faithful to the work—yet he or she engages in a subjective process of constructing an interpretation.

The very act of positing a "text" involves a researcher in analysis: It is through analysis that a researcher identifies a "text." Analysis by the qualitative researcher is built into the process of data gathering, unlike quantitative methods, where data gathering and data analysis are discrete steps in the research enterprise. Qualitative text analysis is evaluated by the same four criteria as other qualitative methods: dependability, confirmability, credibility, and transferability.

Although social texts can come in a variety of forms, we will discuss two in particular: documents (whether electronic, visual, or written) and enacted talk.

DOCUMENTS AS SOCIAL TEXTS

One kind of social text that holds particular relevance to qualitative researchers is the document. One powerful form of document is the written record. As Thomas Lindlof (1995, p. 208) indicates,

To the analyst, documents are very important because they are the "paper trail" left by events and processes. Documents indicate, among other things, what an organization *produces* and how it *certifies* certain kinds of activities (e.g., a license or a deed), *categorizes* events or people (e.g., a membership list), *codifies* procedures or policies (e.g., rules for using equipment), *instructs* a readership (e.g., an operating manual), *explains* past or future actions (e.g., memoranda), and *tracks* its own activities (e.g., minutes of meetings).

Sometimes, documents (whether electronic, visual, or written) are of interest to researchers because they are explicitly used as resources by participants as they conduct their everyday lives. For example, organizational members standing around the coffee pot may engage in a conversation about a recent e-mail memo sent from top management; the researcher obviously would need to consult the e-mail in order to more fully understand members' talk.

Documents (of any kind) are also helpful in providing information that is not easily obtained through direct observation or interviewing alone. This point is most obvious when the researcher is trying to understand a historical event or process, but it also applies to research about present events and processes.

A wide range of documents hold potential utility to qualitative researchers. These data vary, of course, according to the topic under study. When W. I. Thomas and Florian Znaniecki (1918) studied the adjustment process for Polish peasants coming to the United States early in the last century, they examined letters written by the immigrants to their families in Poland. (They obtained the letters through newspaper advertisements.) Other researchers have analyzed old diaries. Such personal documents only scratch the surface, however.

In discussing procedures for studying the history of family life, Ellen Rothman (1981) points to the following sources:

In addition to personal sources, there are public records which are also revealing of family history. Newspapers are especially rich in evidence on the educational, legal, and recreational aspects of family life in the past as seen from a local point of view. Magazines reflect more general patterns of family life; students often find them interesting to explore for data on perceptions and expectations of mainstream family values. Magazines offer several different kinds of sources at once: visual materials (illustrations and advertisements), commentary (editorial and advice columns), and fiction. Popular periodicals are particularly rich in the last two. Advice on many questions of concern to families—from the proper way to discipline children to the economics of wallpaper—fills magazine columns from the early nineteenth century to the present. Stories that suggest common experiences or perceptions of family life appear with the same continuity. (p. 53)

Organizations generally document themselves, so if you're studying some facet of organizational communication, you should examine the entity's official documents: charters, policy statements, speeches by leaders stored in written form or in a video library, and so on. Melissa Gibson and Michael Papa (2000), for example, conducted an ethnographic field study of how blue-collar workers at Industry International (a pseudonym for an international manufacturing organization) were assimilated to the organization's culture as newcomers. In order to understand the organization's culture, the researchers examined memos, brochures, organizational records and reports, newsletters, and books written about the organization's founders. The organization's culture emerged from its past and was reproduced in current organizational practices. The documents produced by the organization—in its past as well as during the period of the study—shed insight into salient organizational values and themes.

A couple of cautions are in order when using documents. Sometimes, you can't trust the accuracy of records—official or unofficial, primary or secondary. Your protection lies in replication: In the case of historical research, where triangulation through participant observation and interviewing isn't possible, it lies in corroboration. If several sources point to the same set of "facts," your confidence in them might reasonably increase.

You always need to be wary of bias in your data sources. If all of your data on the development of a political movement are taken from the movement itself, you may not gain a well-rounded view of it. Where possible, obtain data from a variety of sources, representing different points of view.

Documents, like all texts, are not transparent in their meaning. As Ian Hodder (1994, p. 394) reminds us,

Meaning does not reside in a text but in the writing and reading of it. As the text is reread in different contexts it is given new meanings, often contradictory and always socially embedded. Thus there is no "original" or "true" meaning of a text outside specific historical contexts.

Hodder's observation means that researchers need to fully contextualize documents in order to gain insight into their meanings. A document's origins and history need to be understood: Who wrote the document, when, under what circumstances, and for what purposes? A document's place in the present also needs to be understood: How and when is the document referenced in the everyday activity of natives in the field setting? The researcher also needs to reflexively position his or her reading of a document—the circumstances in which you read a document affect your interpretation of it. All of this is part of what we discussed above as triangulation.

The box "Reading and Evaluating Documents," by Ron Aminzade and Barbara Laslett, poses useful questions to ask of any document, whether its origins are in the past or in the present. Consider applying some of their questions to presidential press conferences, advertising, or (gasp) college textbooks. None of these offers a direct view of reality; all have human authors and human participants.

ENACTED TALK AS SOCIAL TEXTS

Researchers in the field often gather audiotapes of naturally occurring conversations among natives. We don't wish to suggest that participant-observers ignore conversations entirely in their field notes. Interaction events such as conversations are often the subject of field note entries. But field notes often provide a gloss of conversations, providing the researcher with only the gist of what was said along with an occasional quotation of a key word, phrase, or utterance.

For some research purposes, the gist of conversations (or interviews, for that matter) is sufficient. However, many qualitative researchers believe that it is important to pay attention to the details of talk. Thus, field notes are an insufficient tool, and written **transcripts** are necessary.

Qualitative interviewers also work with audiotapes. Although their conversations-with-a-purpose are not naturally occurring, the following discussion of how to transcribe applies to interview transcripts as well as transcripts of naturally occurring talk.

Constructing Written Transcriptions

Transcribing is not a transparent activity, but an activity in which a text is created out of the "raw material" of a face-to-face interaction event between people.

Transcribing uttered talk is a very time-consuming process. How long it takes depends on the quality of the tape, the number of participants to the interaction event, the pace of the conversation, the level of redundancy in the talk, access to a transcription machine with a foot

READING AND EVALUATING DOCUMENTS

by Ron Aminzade and Barbara Laslett
University of Minnesota

The purpose of the following comments is to give you some sense of the kind of interpretive work historians do and the critical approach they take toward their sources. It should help you to appreciate some of the skills historians develop in their efforts to reconstruct the past from residues, to assess the evidentiary status of different types of documents, and to determine the range of permissible inferences and interpretations. Here are some of the questions historians ask about documents:

1. Who composed the documents? Why were they written? Why have they survived all these years? What methods were used to acquire the information contained in the documents?

2. What are some of the biases in the documents and how might you go about checking or correcting them? How inclusive or representative is the sample of individuals, events, and so on, contained in the document? What were the institutional constraints and the general organizational routines under which the document was prepared? To what extent does the document provide more of an index of institutional activity than of the phenomenon being studied? What is the time lapse between the observation of the events documented and the witnesses' documentation of them? How confidential or public was the document meant to be? What role did etiquette, convention, and custom play in the presentation of the material contained within the document? If you relied solely upon the evidence contained in these documents, how might your vision of the past be distorted? What other kinds of documents might you look at for evidence on the same issues?

3. What are the key categories and concepts used by the writer of the document to organize the information presented? What selectivities or silences result from these categories of thought?

4. What sorts of theoretical issues and debates do these documents cast light on? What kinds of historical and/or sociological questions do they help to answer? What sorts of valid inferences can one make from the information contained in these documents? What sorts of generalizations can one make on the basis of the information contained in these documents?

---

petal control, the experience level of the transcriber, and the purpose of the study. Thomas Lindlof (1995) indicates that it takes him "four to five hours to transcribe a one-hour interview involving two voices" (p. 211). That matches very closely to our rule of thumb: no less than one hour of transcription time for every 15 minutes of audiotaped conversation between two people. Why does it take so long? For starters, the transcriber listens to a tape several times to hear all that is going on in the conversation. Then the transcriber needs to record that hearing using a variety of transcription codes and symbols.

Given the labor-intensive nature of transcription work, you might think that the efficient course of action (financial resources permitting) is to hire someone to derive transcripts from audiotapes of uttered talk. Although this is a common practice, many qualitative researchers believe that it is important for them to perform their own transcribing work. Two reasons support their view. First, transcribing is not a neutral activity, and the researcher needs to take control of it. Second, through transcription, the researcher becomes intimately familiar with the data, hearing things that might otherwise be missed.

A key question in all transcription work is the purpose of the researcher. Depending on the researcher's purpose, different features of uttered talk are important to transcribe. What the researcher decides to pay attention to (and ignore) is closely related to the researcher's goals and interests. As Jane Edwards (1993, p. 3) indicates, "no transcript is completely theory-neutral or without bias." A given interview or conversation thus could be the basis of multiple transcripts, or texts. Earlier, we referred to this as textualization.

Systems of Transcription

Edwards (1993) has discussed three general types of principles that guide the creation or selection of a transcription system: principles of category design, readability, and tractability. We'll discuss each of these types of principles in turn.

Principles of Category Design Edwards (1993, pp. 5–6) emphasizes that the design of a transcription system should be guided by three properties. First, the categories of the transcription system must be *systematically discriminable.* For example, if you are transcribing the length of pauses by discriminating "short" from "long" pauses, you need to have a clear basis for noting that a given pause is "short" or "long." Maybe you time pauses in tenths of seconds, and use the half-second cut-off as the boundary between "short" and "long" pauses.

Second, the notation system needs to have *exhaustive categories.* If you are transcribing pauses in uttered talk, you need to have a transcription system whose categories include all possible kinds of pauses. For example, pauses can be silent, or "unfilled," in which case measuring their length by tenths of seconds is useful. But there are also "filled pauses," where people fill the airwaves by uttering sounds such as "um." If you claim to study all kinds of pauses, then you need transcription categories that are appropriate to the full domain of phenomena at hand.

Third, the categories of notation in a transcription system should be *systematically contrastive.* How to develop transcriptions that maximize contrast features in talk is very much a function of the theoretical purpose of the researcher. If you're interested in how spoken language reflects information processing, maybe the upper threshold for a "short pause" is .2 seconds, whereas if you are interested in the flow of turn taking between speakers, maybe a "short pause" is .5 seconds or less. The contrast you are making—between short and long pauses—is very much a function of your purpose.

Principles of Readability Edwards (1993, p. 6) suggests that transcription systems should maximize readability. Generally, this is accomplished to the extent that the transcription system can rely on usual conventions of reading. Two cues used widely in print to guide reading habits are *visual prominence* (e.g., using boldface, underlining, or italics) and *spatial arrangement.* Visual prominence cues are used to signal to the reader that certain information should be read as particularly important, salient, or somehow different from other text. For example, if we write "No" versus "NO," our guess is that you interpreted the capitalized "no" as more emphatic.

Visual prominence is also useful in highlighting different orders of information. In a newspaper, for example, a large font means that we are reading a headline, whereas a smaller font means that we are reading the text of an article. In transcribing speakers, you might put speaker names (or pseudonyms) in all caps followed by a colon, then use lower-case letters to capture what they say:

SPEAKER A: Well, I think we should go.
SPEAKER B: I don't agree.

As another example, you might place transcriber comments in parentheses, perhaps in a smaller font, to somehow mark these comments off as different from words uttered by the speakers. For example,

SPEAKER A: Well, I think we should go. ((said emphatically))
SPEAKER B: I don't agree. ((slams fist on table))

The double parenthetical information in a smaller font is provided to the reader by the transcriber to provide understanding of how the words were uttered.

Spatial arrangement refers to what features are placed in proximity on the transcribed page and whether reading is organized left to right or top to bottom. Generally, transcription systems should place notation markers of related events next to each other. For example, when marking prominent syllable stress, transcribers place stress symbols immediately beside the relevant syllable.

If you were interested in transcribing interruptions and overlaps in speaker turns, you might want to spatially align the utterances in a way that uses the principle of spatial arrangement, such as the following format:

SPEAKER A: Well, I think uh that uh we should uh

                                        [   ]
SPEAKER B: not go?

The layout of these utterances makes it clear that Speaker B interrupted Speaker A's utterance at the point of the word "should."

Spatial arrangement is also important in how to present uttered talk on a transcribed page. If you are interested in the utterance-by-utterance flow of conversation *between* speakers, for example, it is important to have the utterances appear top to bottom on the page in the order in which they were uttered by the speakers. By contrast, if you are interested in studying the *internal coherence* of a speaker's talk across his or her own utterances, it might be better to arrange utterances in columns; a given column would contain all of the sequential utterances of a given speaker, and each speaker would have his or her own column of utterances. Spatial layout, then, could vary depending on your purpose. Figure 15-1 illustrates top-to-bottom sequential layout versus column layout.

Sometimes, readability and category design work at cross-purposes: What is "easy" to read often involves few notation marks, yet detailed notation marks may be necessary for the researcher's goal of capturing the details of the talk on paper. For example, the researcher may want to employ the International Phonetic Alphabet (IPA), a standardized set of notations to record pronunciations.

A. Sequential

   1 A: Well, where do you want to go for dinner tonight?
   2 B: How 'bout pizza? We could go to that new place that just opened up.
   3 A: Yeah. Or we could just go with the usual Italian.
   4 B: I have a coupon for the new pizza place—5 bucks off a large, with 3 toppings.
   5 A: Yeah, but I think I'm really in the mood for a full dinner. I skipped lunch.

B. Column

Speaker A	Speaker B
1 Well, where do you want to go for dinner tonight?	2 How 'bout pizza? We could go to that new place that just opened up.
3 Yeah. Or we could just go with the usual Italian.	4 I have a coupon for the new pizza place—5 bucks off a large, with 3 toppings.
5 Yeah, but I think I'm really in the mood for a full dinner. I skipped lunch.	

FIGURE 15-1   **Sequential versus Column Formats**

But without training in the IPA, a reader will likely find IPA transcriptions unintelligible. For example, "cuz" (because) would appear as "kʰʌz" in IPA transcription. As a general guideline, a transcription should tell the reader how to read the uttered talk without making the reading process overwhelming.

Principles of Tractability   Edwards (1993, pp. 9–10) suggests that transcription systems should be easy for the researcher to use. For example, if you are planning to use a computer to identify certain themes or words, you will need to have a system in place to deal with issues of literal pronunciation: A transcribed "y'know" or "didja" will likely pop up as a spelling error unless you have thought about how to deal with the "slippage" between how words are spelled on paper and how they are spoken. You may decide to transcribe by immediately converting all utterances to their written word equivalents—"you know" and "did you," for example. However, many researchers think that this loses much valuable information—pronunciation can often signal things like the level of informality or the status levels of speakers.

Tractability also involves the use of notational shorthands. Instead of writing "rising pitch," for example, use a "?" symbol or a "/" symbol. Such shorthands allow transcription work to proceed more quickly.

Tractability also includes the necessity of numbering utterance lines. Usually, transcribers number lines so that they can refer back to selected segments of text. Common word-processing software packages include the option to number lines automatically, and if you're performing transcription work, you ought to get into the habit of using this option.

Category design, readability, and tractability are all relative criteria, in the end guided by your research purpose.

Different kinds of qualitative research require different kinds of transcription systems. Discourse analysis and conversation analysis are two related kinds of communication research whose purposes require specialized transcription systems, and we will turn to these analytic approaches in the next section.

APPROACHES TO THE ANALYSIS OF SOCIAL TEXTS

There are many different approaches to the analysis of social texts. In this section, we will briefly describe five approaches that are frequently used by communication researchers: communication criticism, discourse and conversation analysis, the narrative approach, performative/dramatistic approaches, and the semiotic approach.

Communication Criticism

The family of approaches that studies public social texts (e.g., public speeches, television programs, films) is what Malcolm Sillars and Bruce Gronbeck (2001) refer to as **communication criticism.** If you are coming from a background in which there is a clear boundary between the social sciences and the humanities, it may strike you as peculiar to talk about communication criticism—usually identified with the humanities—in a book devoted to social scientific methods. From our perspective, there isn't a meaningful difference between qualitative approaches to communication and the more humanistically oriented approach found in communication criticism.

The enterprise of communication criticism minimally involves three related aspects, according to Sillars and Gronbeck (2001): textualization, analysis, and interpretation.

We discussed textualization earlier in this chapter—the process of constructing a "text" from a "work." Analysis involves the taking-apart process, breaking down a social text into its relevant units, dimensions, or themes. Using the vocabulary we first introduced in Chapter 4, analysis involves an identification of the relevant semantic relationships in the social text. Interpretation—the heart of social text analysis—is a putting-back-together process that culminates in an argument by the researcher about what the text means to him or to her.

In addition, Sillars and Gronbeck (2001, p. 32) argue that some communication criticism adds a fourth feature—judgment:

> For some, judgment is not an essential critical activity; criticism can end in interpretation. To others, judgment is the final activity that makes a critic a special observer and commentator on the world.

Judgment is not a simple subjective reaction to a social text ("I liked it," "I thought it was morally corrupt," and so on), but instead a reasoned argument in which an evaluation of some kind is rendered. Often, this judgment addresses the effect of the message and the communication competence of the speaker.

Communication criticism is an approach that fits within the case study tradition (Chapter 13) because communication critics usually seek to understand a single public message (e.g., a presidential address) or a cluster of specific messages (e.g., discourse surrounding airline [de]regulation).

Actually, communication criticism isn't a single framework but a family of perspectives that share in common the analytic task of communication criticism. Sillars and Gronbeck (2001) identify three broad families of communication criticism: the rhetorical tradition, the social tradition, and the cultural tradition. Each of these broad traditions can be further divided into subcategories, but that's a task beyond our scope (see Sillars & Gronbeck, 2001, for these details).

The Western roots of rhetorical criticism extend back to Plato and Aristotle. Central to rhetorical criticism is a view of communication as a persuasive process. The analytical task of the neo-Aristotelian critic is to evaluate whether the most effective and appropriate means of persuasion were used in the selected text(s). Usually, this analysis involves analytic attention to several features identified in Aristotle's *Rhetoric*. The critic examines the development of the text's persuasive elements. This involves, in turn, an analysis of the *ethos* (credibility appeals of the speaker), *pathos* (emotional appeals of the speaker), and *logos* (logical appeals of the speaker). Consider a TV commercial for a jazzy new car. The person who pitches the fine qualities of the car is a well-known athlete, who mentions in passing that he drives the car to the stadium so he'll be on time (ethos appeal). He talks about how driving the new car makes him feel, implying that anybody who drives this car will feel like they are admired by envious bystanders (a pathos appeal). Finally, the author talks about the safety record of the car—the odds of getting hurt in an accident are small in crash tests (a logos appeal). The organization of the text is also analyzed for its rhetorical effect. Which appeal is mentioned first? How are images and words used together in the ad? The speaker's style and delivery are examined as well. Scholars from the rhetorical tradition often approach a message text with the goal of determining its fidelity, form, structure, style, artistic merit, logical merit, and effects on intended audiences.

Herbert Simons (2000, p. 438) illustrated a classical approach to rhetorical criticism in his analysis of President Clinton's August 17, 1998, speech to the nation surrounding his infamous relationship with a White House intern. The analysis centered on the "pragmatic questions of strategic appropriateness: i.e., did Clinton do as well as could be expected given his very difficult rhetorical situation?" Simons assessed the rhetorical dilemmas that Clinton faced in the speech and how effectively Clinton's speech responded to those dilemmas. For example, he faced an ethical dilemma between truth telling and evasiveness to protect his image as president.

The social tradition replaces persuasion with a different assumption about communication. Instead of viewing communication as a message transmission designed to persuade, scholars from the social tradition view communication as a process of identification: "showing people what they share in common" (Sillars & Gronbeck, 2001, p. 139). From this perspective, analysis is organized around goals of understanding how rhetorical texts construct (or fail to construct) shared meaning between people.

An example of communication criticism from the social tradition is J. Michael Hogan and Glen Williams's (2000) analysis of Thomas Paine's famous pamphlet of the American Revolution, *Common Sense*. You may remember reading about this pamphlet in your high school U.S. history class. The authors argue that the powerful effect of that rhetorical work was the result of the new rhetorical style evidenced in it—a "republican charisma" (p. 1) in tune with the egalitarian ideology of revolutionary America. For example, Paine wrote it anonymously, thereby identifying with everyone, the common man, rather than relying on particular credibility associated with his reputation.

The third tradition identified by Sillars and Gronbeck (2001) is the cultural tradition. Often aligned with the critical theory paradigm (Chapter 3), scholars who employ this tradition view the homogeneous commonality of the social tradition as naive at best and, at worst, domination of the powerless by the powerful. The social world is a world of fragmented voices, cultures, and groups, according to this third tradition. The goal of communication criticism is to liberate voices from cultural domination and to understand how cooperation is possible under conditions of cultural diversity.

An example of the cultural approach is found in Lisa Gring-Pemble's (2001) critical analysis of congressional hearings leading up to the 1996 Personal Responsibility and Work Opportunity Reconciliation Act, which was designed to reform the welfare system in the United States. Although the hearings appeared to solicit a variety of opinions and perspectives from interested citizens, Gring-Pemble argues that they were elitist in nature. She argued that only the viewpoint compatible with the majority political party was given voice. Further, welfare recipients were relegated to "it" status—that is, they were spoken about, but they were never invited to speak for themselves. The rhetoric of the hearings, argued Gring-Pemble, portrayed "the feckless welfare recipient as immoral and incompetent and the young welfare recipient as immature and inexperienced," thereby creating "an image of welfare recipients as incapable of speaking wisely on the subject of welfare reform" (p. 360). Such rhetoric, argued the author, stripped welfare recipients of any voice, or influence, in welfare reform.

Although Sillars and Gronbeck (2001) present these three traditions in the context of the analysis of public communication, we think that communication criticism (and its three traditions) holds relevance to the analysis of nonpublic communication as well—communication between lovers, co-workers, and Internet chatroom buddies.

Discourse Analysis and Conversation Analysis

Sometimes, *discourse analysis* and *conversation analysis* are used interchangeably. Technically speaking, *conversation analysis* is a narrower term referring to a particular kind of discourse analysis.

Deborah Schiffrin (1994) summarizes two broad traditions of **discourse analysis,** and thus two conceptions of "discourse." From a structural perspective, *discourse* refers to language above the sentence level. With respect to spoken language, this language-above-the-sentence unit might refer to utterances (which can contain multiple sentences) or perhaps entire conversations. With respect to written discourse, we might be interested in such discourse units as newspaper articles or Web pages. From a structural perspective, discourse analysis is the qualitative study of constituent units of discourse and how they are arranged in a system, structure, or grammar.

For example, Richard Conville (1991) performed a structural discourse analysis of relationship partners' accounts of their personal relationships. He relied on a method known as structuralism, whose intellectual roots come from Ferdinand de Saussure in linguistics and Claude Levi-Strauss in anthropology. In a nutshell, structural analysis examines discourse for its underlying structure with respect to binary features. Just as we understand that the word "bat" is different from the word "pat" because of the presence/absence of a voiced plosive sound (the voiced plosive sound is "b," and the unvoiced plosive sound is "p"), we can similarly understand larger units of discourse based on the underlying structure of the binary features of which they are constituted. Conville identified a number of binary pairs that organized people's accounts of their relationship, including such binary features as integration and disintegration.

A second approach to discourse analysis, identified by Schiffrin (1994), is the functional tradition. From this perspective, discourse refers to any kind of language use, with the emphasis on "use." Researchers from this tradition believe that discourse can be understood only by taking into account its purposes and functions in human life. Functional discourse analysts believe that discourse is interdependent with social life, "such that its analysis necessarily intersects with meanings, activities, and systems outside of itself" (Schiffrin, 1994, p. 31). A functional approach, like a structural approach, seeks to understand patterns or regularities in discourse. However, unlike the structural approach, in which the analyst looks inside the discourse to locate regularity in its underlying structures, the functional approach views discourse as a socially and culturally organized way of speaking in which certain functions are enacted.

An example of a functional approach to discourse analysis is an analysis of intellectual discussion in a university setting by Karen Tracy and Sheryl Baratz (1993). These researchers studied the discourse of a weekly colloquium session in which academics presented their research for purposes of intellectual feedback and discussion. These researchers noted that much more than an intellectual presentation was getting done in these weekly sessions. For example, speakers were using their talk to affect their self-presentations and to sustain one another's face.

Let's contrast these two approaches to discourse analysis by using the same example. Jenny Mandelbaum (1989) analyzed a short conversation among five friends in which a story was told about one of the friends, who had ordered a huge lobster for lunch. The storyteller was trying to make the friend the butt of a joke—a pig who eats a lot of messy food. From a structural perspective, Mandelbaum was interested in analyzing the internal structure of how a storytelling episode is enacted—for example, the parts of a story (including story initiation, the story's punch line, and so forth). From a functional perspective, Mandelbaum was interested in analyzing how utterances, particularly those associated with listening to the story, functioned to help tell the story. In this particular instance, however, Mandelbaum found that listeners changed the story so that the original story line, in which the lobster eater was being set up as the butt of the story's joke, was derailed in favor of an alternative story line—the lobster eater was portrayed as someone who can find good deals (a lot of food for a cheap price).

Within these two broad traditions of discourse analysis, many different variations can be identified. For example, Schiffrin (1994) identifies six different approaches to discourse analysis, and Teun van Dijk (1997a, 1997b) edited two volumes to introduce approximately 20 different approaches to discourse analysis.

Transcription systems vary, depending on the approach to discourse analysis that is adopted by the researcher. However, for purposes of illustrating a transcription system, we will discuss in a bit more detail one particular kind of discourse analysis, known as **conversation analysis.**

Conversation analysis (CA) is an approach to discourse analysis whose origin is in ethnomethodology. *Ethno* refers to a group, and *methodology* refers to the methods those people use to construct ways of doing things that are sensible and orderly. Ethnomethodologists are interested in how everyday people create a sense of reality—a sense of its "objectivity, factuality, and orderliness" (Lindlof, 1995, p. 36). Ethnomethodology rejects a view that society exists "out there"; instead, ethnomethodologists are committed to the study of how members of a society produce a sense of social order or society through their everyday activities. Because conversation is a key way in which people construct a sense of social order in everyday life, conversation analysis became an important discourse analysis approach beginning in the 1960s with such scholars as Harvey Sacks, Emanuel Schegloff, and Gail Jefferson.

Conversation analysts study naturally occurring interaction, whether informal (e.g., conversations) or formal (e.g., doctor–patient interviews). They examine verbalized talk, including paralinguistic features (e.g., pauses, pitch, loudness) and nonverbal cues (e.g., posture, hand–arm gestures). Schiffrin (1994) categorizes CA as a structural approach, drawing attention to the body of CA work that examines how conversations are structured or organized by the speakers. Although many CA workers seek to understand the underlying structures or regularities of conversational talk, this is not the primary focus of conversation analysis. The central purpose of CA work, according to Anita Pomerantz and B. J. Fehr (1997), is "the organization of the meaningful conduct of people in society, that is, how people in society produce their activities and make sense of the world around them" (p. 65). Implicated in this goal is a functional perspective. Thus, we think that CA is an approach to discourse analysis that bridges both the structural and the functional approaches.

Unlike other discourse analysis approaches, in which social factors are recognized outside of talk (e.g., the gender of the speakers), CA gives no a priori status to any concepts or factors except as they are manifest in the interaction. A CA researcher would argue that, for example, gender may or may not be relevant to the speakers in a given interaction. If it holds relevance, the CA researcher will be able to point to how gender work is getting done in the careful study of the details of the talk. For example, Robert Hopper and Curtis LeBaron (1998), in an article titled "How Gender Creeps into Talk," argue that gender becomes relevant in some conversations through the discursive work of the interactants. In part, this is accomplished by a verbal noticing—an utterance in which gender is somehow introduced into the conversation as relevant. Here's an example of a noticing provided by Hopper and LeBaron (1998, p. 66):

1 BRANDON: And what's Shipe Park named after.
2   (0.4)
3   Some guy named Shipe?
4 KATE: (Or a lady) Or a lady named Shipe?
5 BRANDON: Yeah.
6   (0.5)
7   Or a dog named Shipe.

Hopper and LeBaron argue that gender is introduced in line 4, when Kate suggests that "Shipe" was "a lady." However, Brandon's response in line 7 functions to suggest the absurdity of Kate's claim. Line 4 is a gender noticing, one that Brandon doesn't seem to legitimate.

In this brief excerpt, we see some transcription notations based on a commonly used transcription system developed by Gail Jefferson. The underline in line 1 is used

These transcript techniques and symbols were devised by Gail Jefferson. They are designed to be used with audiotapes or videotapes of enacted talk.

Arrows. Up and down arrows mark points where there was a dramatic rise and fall, respectively, in intonation.

Brackets. Indicate that the bracketed portions of utterances were uttered simultaneously. The left-hand bracket marks the beginning of simultaneity, and the right-hand bracket indicates its end.

```
I don' know
    [       ]
    you    don't
```

Brackets doubled. Indicate that two utterances were said simultaneously.

```
John: No, I think it's ten.
      [[
Dave: No, it's ten.
```

Breathing indicators. A dot followed by hh marks an inhalation—e.g., a gasp. The hh alone stands for exhalation—e.g., a sigh.

```
·hh        hh
```

Capital letters. Represent increased loudness of the utterances (or parts of utterances).

```
CAPS
```

Colons. Indicate that the immediately prior syllable is prolonged or stretched out. The number of colons is an attempt to represent the length of the prolongation.

```
We:::ll now.
```

Dash. Used to indicate a short, untimed pause within an utterance.

```
He—no they—went to town.
```

Degree symbols. Represent softness, or decreased amplitude of the utterance portion enclosed by them.

```
°I did it° But it was an accident.
```

Equal signs. Used to indicate that a next speaker starts at precisely the end of a current speaker's utterance, with no pause or interval of silence.

```
'Swhat I said=
=But you didn't
```

Greater than/less than signs. Symbols pointing inward (> <) indicate that the enclosed utterance, or portion of an utterance, was said more quickly. Symbols pointing outward (< >) indicate that the enclosed utterance, or portion of an utterance, was said more slowly.

```
>  <   faster
<  >   slower
```

Hyphen. Represents a halting or cutting off of the immediately prior syllable.

```
But-
```

Italics and underscoring. Used to indicate increased emphasis

```
italics        underscoring
```

Parentheses containing a decimal value. Indicate the seconds and tenths of seconds of silence between speaker turns. These may also be used to indicate the duration of pauses internal to a speaker's turn.

```
(1.3)
```

Parentheses doubled. Enclose descriptions, not transcribed utterances. Generally, these descriptions are notes by the transcriber to assist the interpreter in understanding how something was said or some relevant background event.

```
((knock on door))
```

Parentheses (single) encasing words. Indicate that something was heard but that the transcriber is not sure what it was. These can serve as a warning that the transcript may be unreliable.

```
(to town yesterday)
```

Parentheses (single) left empty. Indicate that something was said but that the transcriber can't even venture a guess as to what.

```
(        )
```

Punctuation marks. Used to indicate intonation, not grammar. A period represents falling intonation; a question mark represents rising intonation; a comma represents a falling–rising contour; an exclamation point indicates an animated tone.

```
.     ?    ,    !
```

FIGURE 15-2   Commonly Used Transcription Conventions for Conversation Analysis

Source: Adapted from J. M. Atkinson & J. Heritage (Eds.) (1984). *Structure of social action: Studies in conversation analysis* (pp. ix–xvi). New York: Cambridge University Press.

to indicate a point of vocalic stress or emphasis. The period on lines 1, 5, and 7 is used to indicate falling vocal pitch or intonation. Lines 2 and 6 contain parenthetical information about the lengths (in tenths of seconds) of Brandon's pauses. The question mark at the end of line 3 indicates a rising vocal pitch or intonation. The parenthetical information in line 4 indicates that the transcriber

was in doubt about what was said but attempted to decipher it. It seems that Kate noticed gender twice—first in a quiet, somewhat muffled manner and then again, with greater clarity and volume.

In Figure 15-2, we have provided a summary of many of the important features of the transcription system developed by Gail Jefferson (Atkinson & Heritage, 1984).

This transcription notation system, or some close variant, is frequently employed in CA research conducted by communication researchers. To understand how difficult it can be to perform CA transcription work, try out this transcription system on some tape-recorded conversation. Because CA transcription work attends to the microlevel details of interaction, it is generally the most labor-intensive kind of transcription. Some CA researchers estimate that it can take 30–60 minutes to transcribe every minute of uttered talk (Patterson, Neupauer, Burant, Koehn, & Reed, 1996; Wrobbel, 1998). Because of the labor-intensive nature of CA transcription work, CA researchers generally work with only a few conversations, perhaps even one.

Pomerantz and Fehr (1997, pp. 71–75) suggest five issues to consider in conducting a CA study. We summarize these as a way of giving you a feel for the kinds of issues of interest to CA researchers:

1. *Select a sequence of talk for study.* In order to accomplish this, you will need to have a transcription of an audiotaped conversation. In order to study naturally occurring conversations, many CA researchers ask volunteers to simply tape-record conversations in their everyday life (following all of the guidelines for ethical conduct of research, of course!). After examining the transcript, locate something interesting that you think is going on in it—perhaps the way participants are "beating around the bush" and avoiding direct statements, or perhaps the telling of a story. This is your selected sequence. Sequences are jointly enacted by all of the speakers, so it is important not to examine just one utterance but the dance of utterances that is taking place between the speakers.

2. *Identify the actions in the sequence.* An "action" is a core analytic term among CA researchers. It is what you think is being done in a given turn at talk. For example, if you were to join us for lunch and one of us said to you "It's really drafty in this room," the action here might be a simple expression of a perception, or it might be an indirect request for someone to close a window or door. An action is what is done with words—making a request, greeting, expressing a complaint, giving an order, telling a story, and so forth. For each turn at talk, identify its action(s). Then look at the preceding and following turns at talk. As Pomerantz and Fehr (1997, p. 72) remind us, "Actions are not islands unto themselves." Your identification of the actions in a sequence may change in the process of your analysis work. But you have to start somewhere with your analysis.

3. *Identify how the actions are performed.* Here you are attending to the details of how a given action was accomplished. If the action you are examining is "disagreeing," notice how disagreement is packaged: How is it that fellow speakers will understand it as an act of disagreement? Important to this analytic step is a consideration of other possible ways that the action might have been performed, thereby drawing your attention to the particular work being done by the performance as it was enacted. For example, there are many ways to enact "disagreement"—directly, indirectly, with humor, with affront, and so forth. What is interesting about how the action was accomplished in this sequence?

4. *Identify how the timing and taking of turns construct certain understandings of the action.* As we noted above, actions do not take place in isolation of the chain of utterances in which they are embedded. In focusing on the turn taking between speakers, you are attempting to understand how the action of "disagreeing" was jointly constructed and understood as "disagreeing" by participants to the talk.

5. *Consider how the actions construct certain identities, roles, and relationships for the speakers.* As we commented above, CA researchers, unlike some other discourse analysts, do not "overlay" social factors on top of the talk; instead, they consider how the talk constructs social factors such as social class, gender, and friendship. Ask yourself how the actions function to implicate these social factors.

The Narrative Approach

We've already encountered the narrative approach in Chapter 14. When interviewers ask people to discuss their lives, it often takes the form of a story. But **narrative** approaches are adopted in the analysis of social texts, in addition to the researcher-generated texts of interview transcripts. Basically, the researcher is examining naturally occurring instances of storytelling. Stories can be told in any number of communicative events—from public speeches, to stand-up comedic monologues, to family reunions. Art Bochner stated well the central assumption of this analytic framework: "Narrative—the stories people tell about their lives—is both a means of 'knowing' and a way of 'telling' about the social world and communicative experience" (1994, p. 30).

People construct the meaning of their lives through the stories they tell. If researchers want to understand the life of a single person or the lives of a group of people, they must study their stories and the process of storytelling. In addition, many narrative researchers believe that if you want readers to understand people's life stories, you need to write up your interpretations in a narrative form.

According to Catherine Riessman (1993), a narrative is a form of discourse with a definite beginning, middle, and end in which a specific past event is recounted either chronologically or thematically. Narrative researchers who study social texts are interested in the process of *telling* a story, the *form* of a story, and the *content* of a story.

With respect to the storytelling process, researchers might be interested in such issues as the contexts in which stories are told, how stories are introduced into naturally occurring conversation, and how tellers and listeners jointly participate in accomplishing a storytelling. For example, Jenny Mandelbaum's (1989) study of the lobster-for-lunch story that we described earlier illustrates this focus. Mandelbaum examined how a story unfolded, arguing that stories are not occasions where one person "tells" others; rather, she found, storytelling is a joint undertaking in which all of the participants play an active role in how the story unfolds, and even which story gets told.

With respect to story form, researchers might be interested in such issues as how the story is structured and narrative voice. For example, Marjorie Goodwin (1990) examined a particular story form called "he-said-she-said" enacted among a group of African American girls she studied. This story form is basically a gossip dispute, in which one girl approaches a second girl, recounting a story of how the second girl talked about her behind her back. The offended girl's confrontation is for purposes of "getting something straight" (p. 190).

Researchers with an interest in content might be drawn to the story's themes and meanings. For example, Baxter and Pittman (2001) examined the extent to which the important turning points in the development of romantic relationships were remembered through couple reminiscing events and storytelling to third parties. For example, couples were particularly likely to reminisce about their "quality times" together—those romantic occasions when they could escape daily routines and retreat into their couple-ness for a weekend getaway or an evening on the town.

Performative/Dramatistic Approaches

Scholars from the performative/dramatistic tradition perform texts as a way to understand them. They also analyze a variety of communicative performances enacted by others.

All qualitative research is reliant on the researcher as the research instrument. Nowhere is this point more apparent than in the research tradition known as **performance studies.** Scholars who adopt a performative approach to communication take a dramaturgical view, a view in which communication is conceived as a performance (Jarmon, 1996). In performing a text, the researcher uses his or her embodied experience as a way to understand another's words. The researcher's voice and body are tools that assist the researcher in coming to understand what, and how, a given text means.

Leslie Jarmon (1996) provides us with an example of performative research in her discussion of a weekly data session held at her university. Researchers who attended the data session examined a brief segment of naturally occurring, videotaped interaction. In collaboratively analyzing the conversational segment, the researchers improvised performances of the videotaped interactions. The various performances, or reenactments, of the conversation helped the researchers understand the details of talk and the construction of meaning. As Jarmon (1996, p. 352) tells the reader, performing analysts "provided continuously what might be thought of as embodied virtual recordings. . . . Analysts used their bodies as synesthetic, multimedia playback instruments capable of producing details of sight, sound, and motion." Put simply, if a researcher can act like you—utter your words and mimic your mannerisms—he or she is better positioned to understand you.

Building on the theme of body as instrument, Robert DeChaine (2002) provides us with an alternative example of a performative approach. He posed the question of how we experience music as an embodied experience and then proceeded to conduct what is called an *autoethnography*—a participant-observation study of himself. His study is a detailed rendering of how a body (his) "performs" music in listening to it—his breathing rhythms and so forth.

Those who adopt a performative approach also analyze communicative performances of others. According to Richard Bauman (1977, p. 4), the term *performance* has been used in a dual sense to refer both to the artistic *action* (the act or process of performing) and to the artistic *event* (the artistic situation, including the performer, the art form, the audience, and the setting). A communication act or event is performative if it somehow transforms the basic referential uses of language in which words are used to represent ideas, objects, and so forth. As Bauman (1977, p. 9) tells us,

In other words, in artistic performance . . . there is something going on in the communicative interchange which says to the auditor, "interpret what I say in some special sense; do not take it to mean what the words alone, taken literally, would convey." . . . [P]erformance sets up . . . an interpretive frame within which the messages being communicated are to be understood, and that this frame contrasts with at least one other frame, the literal.

Performance researchers thus analyze a variety of performance events, including theatrical performances and rock concerts. Matthew Spangler (2002), for example, examined how Irish identity is performed in Dublin's annual Bloomsday festival, an event created to honor one of Ireland's greatest literary figures, James Joyce. By participating in the festival, participants enact what it means to be Irish.

In addition to formal performance events, it is possible to see a performative dimension in a wide variety of other kinds of communicative actions and events. For example, when intimate partners adopt the mannerisms and words of celebrities or people known to them, they are engaging in performative role-playing. When a politician speaks to his or her constituency, we might find it helpful to view the event through a performative lens. When attending a basketball game, the fans are enacting the role of "fan." And so forth.

Whenever a person has adopted a role or persona of any kind, it is possible to view the enactment as a performance intended for others' consumption. Erving Goffman (1959) argues that we are always engaged in the social drama of self-presentation. We are always engaged in the business of impression management, putting forth a certain image of ourselves that we want others to legitimate. Put simply, life is a stage.

A Semiotic Approach

Peter Manning (1987, pp. 25–26) defines **semiotics** as "primarily a mode of analysis that seeks to understand how signs perform or convey meaning in context. . . . The work of semiotics is . . . to uncover the rules that govern the conventions of signification." Semiotics, in short, is the science of signs.

Semiotics uses the model of language as the basis of understanding signification more generally. A semiotic analysis "pulls itself in two separate directions: one in the direction of the study of the rules themselves, or language, and the other, the relationships between the language and performance or the consequences of speech acts, pragmatics" (Manning, 1987, p. 29). In other words, if you're studying language, you can do it either by focus-

ing on the rules of grammar or on the uses of language as it is enacted. When you studied a foreign language, you probably studied it in both linguistic and pragmatic ways.

However, semiotics broadens its focus beyond spoken and written languages per se. Peter Manning and Betsy Cullum-Swan (1994) offer some sense of the applicability of semiotics: "Although semiotics is based on language, language is but one of the many sign systems of varying degrees of unity, applicability, and complexity. Morse code, etiquette, mathematics, music, and even highway signs are examples of semiotic systems" (p. 46).

There is no meaning inherent in any sign, however. Meanings reside in minds. So a particular sign means something to a particular person. However, the agreements we have about the meanings associated with particular signs make semiotics a *social* science. As Manning and Cullum-Swan point out,

For example, a lily is an expression linked conventionally to death, Easter, and resurrection as a content. Smoke is linked to cigarettes and to cancer, and Marilyn Monroe to sex. Each of these connections is social and arbitrary, so that many kinds of links exist between expression and content. (1994, p. 466)

To explore this contention, see if you can link the signs with their meanings in Figure 15-3. We're confident enough that you know all the "correct" associations that there's no need for us to give the answers. (OK, you should have said 1c, 2a, 3b, 4e, 5d.) The point is this: What do any of these signs have to do with their "meanings"? Draft an e-mail message to a Martian social scientist explaining the logic at work here. (You might want to include some "emoticons" like :)—another example of semiotics.)

While there is no doubt a story behind each of the linkages in Figure 15-3, the meanings that we "know" are socially constructed. Semiotic analysis involves a search for the meanings intentionally or unintentionally attached to signs.

SIGN	MEANING
1. Poinsettia	a. Good luck
2. Horseshoe	b. First prize
3. Blue ribbon	c. Christmas
4. "Say cheese"	d. Acting
5. "Break a leg"	e. Smile for a picture

FIGURE 15-3 **Matching Signs and Their Meanings**

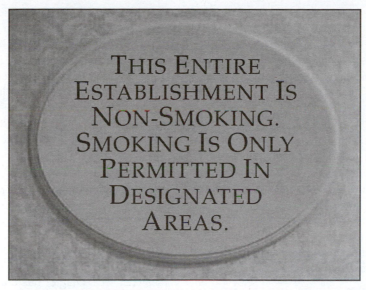

FIGURE 15-4   **Mixed Signals?**

Consider the sign shown in Figure 15-4, from a hotel lobby in Portland, Oregon. What's being communicated by this rather ambiguous sign? The first sentence seems to be saying that the hotel is up to date with the current move away from tobacco in the United States. Guests who want a smoke-free environment need look no further: This is a healthy place to stay. At the same time, says the second sentence, the hotel would not like to be seen as inhospitable to smokers. There's room for everyone under this roof. No one needs to feel excluded. This sign is more easily understood within a marketing paradigm than one of logic.

The "signs" examined in semiotics, of course, are not limited to this kind of sign. Most are quite different, in fact. *Signs* are any things that are assigned special meanings. They can include such things as logos, animals, people, and consumer products. Sometimes, the symbolism is a bit subtle. A classic analysis can be found in Erving Goffman's *Gender Advertisements* (1979). Goffman focused on advertising pictures found in magazines and newspapers. The overt purpose of the ads, of course, was to sell specific products. But what else was communicated? What in particular did the ads say about men and women?

Analyzing pictures containing both men and women, Goffman was struck by the fact that men were almost always bigger and taller than the women accompanying them. (In many cases, in fact, the picture managed to convey the distinct impression that the women were merely accompanying the men.) While the most obvious explanation is that men are, on average, heavier and taller than women, Goffman suggested the pattern had a different meaning: that size and placement implied *status*. Those larger and taller presumably had higher social standing— more power and authority (1979, p. 28). Goffman suggested that the ads communicated that men were more important than women.

In the spirit of Freud's comment that "sometimes a cigar is just a cigar" (he was a smoker), how would you decide whether the ads simply reflected the biological differences in the average sizes of men and women or whether they sent a message about social status? In part, Goffman's conclusion was based on an analysis of the exceptional cases: those in which the women appeared taller than the men. In these cases, the men were typically of a lower social status—the chef beside the society matron, for example. This confirmed Goffman's main point, that size and height indicate social status.

The same conclusion was to be drawn from pictures with men of different heights. Those of higher status were taller, whether it was the gentleman speaking to a waiter or the boss guiding the work of his younger assistants. Where actual height was unclear, Goffman noted the placement of heads in the picture. The assistants were crouching down while the boss leaned over them. The servant's head was bowed so it was lower than that of the master.

The latent message conveyed by the ads, then, was that the higher a person's head appeared in the ad, the more important that person was. And in the great majority of ads containing men and women, the former were clearly portrayed as more important. The subliminal message in the ads, whether intended or not, was that men are more powerful and enjoy a higher status than do women.

Goffman examined several differences in the portrayal of men and women besides physical size. As another example, men were typically portrayed in active roles, women in passive ones. The (male) doctor examined the child while the (female) nurse or mother looked on, often admiringly. A man guided a woman's tennis stroke (all the while keeping his head higher than hers). A man gripped the reins of his galloping horse, while a woman rode behind him with her arms wrapped around his waist. A woman held the football, while a man kicked it. A man took a photo, which contained only women.

Goffman suggested that such pictorial patterns subtly perpetuated a host of gender stereotypes. Even as people spoke publicly about gender equality, these advertising photos established a quiet backdrop of men and women in the "proper roles."

Some Final Comments about Analytic Approaches

There are many different kinds of analytic frameworks employed by qualitative communication researchers in the study of social texts. Most of these are tied to particular theoretical perspectives. This isn't a book about theory, so a comprehensive review of these approaches is beyond our scope. The goal of this section was to touch on some frequently encountered analytic frameworks in order to illustrate our basic methodological point. Analytic frameworks are intellectual scaffolding for the qualitative analysis of social texts, providing a lens through which to interpret what is going on in a text.

Analytic frameworks are guides, not blinders. A good qualitative researcher always remains open to emergent questions during the process of analyzing a social text, no matter how radically he or she may step outside the boundaries of a given analytic framework. Analyzing social texts is like a conversation between the researcher and the text. If the researcher is blind to what is going on in the text, his or her interpretation is a monologue, not a conversation. Similarly, if the researcher is a mere summarizer (rather than interpreter) of a text, we end up with a monologue of a different sort.

We have discussed these analytic frameworks separately from one another. In practice, communication researchers often combine them. For example, you could use conversation analysis to study how stories are told. Or you could examine the performance of professional storytellers, combining performative/dramatistic approaches with narrative approaches. Many communica-tion critics view public communication messages as narratives, thereby combining communication criticism with the narrative approach. The key here is to choose the analytic approach, or approaches, most appropriate to the social text that you want to understand.

In the next chapter, we are going to examine in a more detailed way how to process qualitative data. The nuts-and-bolts discussion of the next chapter fleshes out in greater detail how the qualitative analysis of data is done.

STRENGTHS AND WEAKNESSES OF SOCIAL TEXT ANALYSIS

Texts are the "meat and potatoes" of qualitative research —they are the data analyzed and interpreted by the researcher. This chapter has emphasized social texts—naturally occurring symbols-in-use—in contrast to the researcher-generated texts of field notes and interview transcripts of the prior two chapters.

Social texts can provide a useful source of triangulation, particularly for participant-observation researchers. Part of spending time "in the field" involves being surrounded by symbols-in-use—the conversations people have, the magazines they read, the stories they tell, the posters on their walls, and so forth. Part of understanding the natives' point of view involves close scrutiny of their social texts.

The detailed study of social texts gives a researcher a closer view than either participant observation or qualitative interviewing does alone. Although a researcher can write up a summary of a social text in field notes, this is always one step removed from the social text itself. Similarly, an informant's description of a social text in an interview is also one step removed from the social text itself.

There's a cautionary note about studying social texts, however: Meaning doesn't sit in the text per se. If you want to know what a text means, it is important to have a full understanding of the context that surrounds the text, the uses that are made of the text, and what natives think is going on in the text. If all you do is scrutinize a social text in isolation, you can end up with a myopic—and empty—analysis.

The analysis of social texts is a labor-intensive undertaking, particularly when you need to transcribe uttered talk, whether a public speech by a political figure, a TV talk show, or a conversation between friends. Although a researcher can "hire out" such tedious transcription work, it is often important for the researcher to do this work in order to gain a deep understanding of what is going on in the text.

The qualitative analysis of social texts is the counterpart to the quantitative analysis of social texts that we discussed in Chapter 10—content analysis and interaction analysis. Rather than favoring one method over the other, we think a better way to approach the analysis of social texts is to appreciate the strengths and limitations of each method. The qualitative analysis of social texts lacks the precision that comes from the numerical analysis of coded textual units. However, meaning cannot be adequately captured in frequency distributions alone, which makes the holistic, interpretive task of the qualitative researcher a valuable addition to the researcher's tool kit.

Main Points

- ❑ A social text is a naturally occurring text, in contrast to the researcher-generated texts of field notes and interview transcripts.
- ❑ Qualitative researchers study social texts as a form of triangulation with participant observation and qualitative interviewing, or in their own right.
- ❑ A variety of social texts are studied by communication researchers. Two of the most common kinds of social texts are documents and enacted talk.
- ❑ A "work" is a communication message of some sort, whereas a "text" is the researcher's "take" on that message.
- ❑ Transcription systems reflect the purposes of the researcher.
- ❑ In general, transcription systems should be developed with an eye toward principles of category design, readability, and researcher's ease of use.
- ❑ Communication criticism refers to the family of approaches that analyzes public communication texts such as public speeches and TV programs.
- ❑ Discourse analysis is a kind of qualitative research heavily reliant on transcription.
- ❑ Discourse analysis takes two basic approaches—structural and functional.
- ❑ Conversation analysis, the microscopic study of enacted formal and informal interaction between people, is a particular kind of discourse analysis encountered in communication research.
- ❑ In the narrative approach, researchers examine naturally occurring stories for their form, content, and function.
- ❑ When researchers study social texts from a performative/dramatistic framework, they may perform others' words and actions in order to better understand them. Alternatively, they may systematically analyze formal performance events such as plays and concerts as well as the informal performance of everyday communication.
- ❑ In using a semiotics framework, researchers are interested in understanding what signs mean through the grammar of their structure and the pragmatics of their use.

Key Terms

social text	conversation analysis
textualization	narrative
transcript	performance studies
communication criticism	semiotics
discourse analysis	

Review Questions and Exercises

1. Transcribe a minute of uttered talk from a TV talk show. Compare your transcription to someone else's of the same minute of talk. To what extent do these transcriptions illustrate the concept of textualization?

2. Take out a piece of paper and record all of the possible "social texts" that you see in your immediate surroundings—for example, a textbook, a newspaper, the televised TV programming guide. Don't limit yourself to the most obvious form of social text, the written word. Consider other kinds of symbols-in-use, as well. For example, to what extent is your choice of clothing a social text? Select one of these social texts and indicate how you might approach its analysis using one of the approaches discussed in this chapter.

3. Consult the communication journals described in Appendix A. Locate three different kinds of social texts employed by researchers.

4. Select a well-known social text, such as Lincoln's Gettysburg Address. How could you approach the analysis of this text using communication criticism,

discourse analysis, and narrative, performative/ dramatistic, and semiotic frameworks? Which would be more helpful? Less helpful? Why so?

Continuity Project

Review Goffman's examination of gender advertising, and collect and analyze a set of advertising photos from magazines or newspapers. What is the relationship between gender and status in the texts you analyzed?

Additional Readings

Edwards, J. A., & Lampert, M. D. (Eds.) (1993). *Talking data: Transcription and coding in discourse research.* Hillsdale, NJ: Erlbaum. A useful volume on various philosophies of, and approaches to, the transcription process in qualitative research.

Hodder, I. (1994). The interpretation of documents and material culture. In N. K. Denzin & Y. S. Lincoln (Eds.), *Handbook of qualitative research* (pp. 393–402). Thousand Oaks, CA: Sage. This chapter provides an excellent overview of how qualitative researchers approach social texts.

Riessman, C. K. (1993). *Narrative analysis.* Newbury Park, CA: Sage. A short and very readable introduction to the kinds of analyses that characterize the narrative approach.

Schiffrin, D. (1994). *Approaches to discourse.* Cambridge, MA: Blackwell. An excellent introduction to both structural and functional approaches to discourse analysis. Schiffrin presents several different transcription systems in Appendix 2, and sample discourse data in Appendix 3.

Sillars, M. O., & Gronbeck, B. E. (2001). *Communication criticism: Rhetoric, social codes, cultural studies.* Prospect Heights, IL: Waveland. An excellent book on the various genres of communication criticism employed by qualitative communication scholars.

Van Dijk, T. A. (Ed.) (1997a). *Discourse as structure and process.* Thousand Oaks, CA: Sage. Volume 1 of 2 in this outstanding multidisciplinary introduction to discourse analysis.

Van Dijk, T. A. (Ed.) (1997b). *Discourse as social interaction.* Thousand Oaks, CA: Sage. Volume 2 of 2 in this outstanding multidisciplinary introduction to discourse analysis.

InfoTrac College Edition
http://www.infotrac-college.com/ wadsworth/access.html

Access the latest news and journal articles with InfoTrac College Edition, an easy-to-use online database of reliable, full-length articles from hundreds of top academic journals. Conduct an electronic search using the following search terms:

- communication criticism
- discourse analysis
- conversation analysis
- narrative
- performance
- dramatistic
- semiotics

CHAPTER **16**

Qualitative Data Analysis

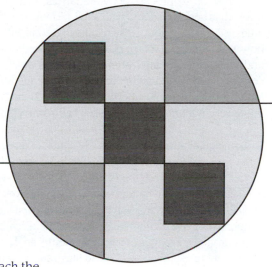

What You'll Learn in This Chapter

We'll examine some of the nitty-gritty details of how to approach the analysis of qualitative data.

INTRODUCTION

Readers have often criticized qualitative researchers for their "black box" process of data analysis. Too often, the reader has been presented with a full-blown analysis with little discussion of how those results materialized: Somehow, texts enter the "black box" of the researcher's mind, and what emerges after some mysterious analytic process is a finely honed set of interpretive findings. Matthew Miles and A. Michael Huberman (1994, p. 2), both qualitative researchers, have expressed the same complaint:

> Some qualitative researchers still consider analysis to be an art form and insist on intuitive approaches to it. We are left with the researcher's telling us of classifications and patterns drawn from the welter of field data, in ways that are irreducible or even incommunicable. We do not really see how the researcher got from 3,600 pages of field notes to the final conclusions, as sprinkled with vivid illustrations as they may be.

Although qualitative data analysis is a creative process, we agree with Miles and Huberman that there are explicit, systematic methods that qualitative researchers can employ, and report, as they interpret their textual data. The purpose of this chapter is to introduce you to what is systematic about qualitative data analysis.

We're going to start at a general level, providing a more-or-less generic description of how qualitative analysis is done. Then we're going to turn to two specific approaches to qualitative data analysis often found in communication research: the Developmental Research Sequence (DRS) and Grounded-Theory Development (GTD).

THE GENERAL PROCESS OF QUALITATIVE DATA ANALYSIS

Although each approach to qualitative analysis is characterized by its own unique features, the process of **coding** is common to most qualitative endeavors. As Kathy Charmaz (1983, p. 111) tells us, "Coding, the initial phase of the analytic method, is simply the process of *categorizing* and *sorting* data. Codes then serve as shorthand devices to *label, separate, compile,* and *organize* data" [emphasis in original]. The coding process involves seven basic steps.

Step 1: Determining Questions

Often, qualitative researchers begin their research with a general question like "What is going on here?" Other times, qualitative researchers have a slightly more focused question to guide their research (e.g., "How is identity work accomplished communicatively by members of this group?"). These "start-up" questions reflect the researcher's general framework or orientation to the data. An ethnographer of communication, for example, starts with general questions about what the code of communication is that guides members of a given cultural group. A conversation analyst starts with the general question of what is getting done by the utterances in a conversation. And so on. We've already talked about start-up questions in qualitative research in Chapters 3, 4, 13, 14, and 15, so we won't repeat ourselves again.

Regardless of the start-up question(s) of the researcher, additional questions surface as the mystery of the data begins to unfold. These emergent questions arise out of the data as the researcher attempts to make sense of them. Questions—start-up and emergent—help focus the analytic process for the qualitative researcher.

Step 2: Unitizing Textual Data

For purposes of analysis, a text (whether field notes, an interview transcript, or a social text) needs to be broken down, or unitized. Yvonna Lincoln and Egon Guba (1985, p. 345) tell us that a qualitative unit should have two characteristics:

> First, it should be heuristic, that is, aimed at some understanding or some action that the inquirer needs to have or to take. Unless it is heuristic it is useless, however intrinsically interesting. Second, it must be the smallest piece of information about something that can stand by itself, that is, it must be interpretable in the absence of any additional information other than a broad understanding of the context in which the inquiry is carried out.

The first characteristic—that a unit must be heuristic—links **unitizing** to question asking. A unit is heuristic if it provides an answer to a question posed by the researcher. If we're asking the most general question possible ("What is going on here?"), a unit is a segment of text that provides insight to this question. The same thing holds for a more focused question. If we are interested in how group members construct their identity as belonging to the group, a unit of textual data is a segment that helps us answer that question.

Another name for a unit of textual data is the concept. A concept is a segment of text that answers a question. John van Maanen (1979, pp. 540–541) distinguishes first-order from second-order concepts. *First-order concepts* are indigenous ways of understanding used by participants in rendering their social world meaningful. By contrast, *second-order concepts* are concepts used by the researcher to make sense of the field setting or the participants' actions. With respect to unitizing, some units might refer to first-order concepts, informing us about ways that participants understand their world. Other units might reflect second-order concepts, as the researcher attempts to make sense of the textual data. As we discussed in Chapters 3 and 4, qualitative researchers are often interested, at the second order, in identifying meanings and meaning making: what we call semantic relationships and rules, respectively.

For example, suppose you're doing an ethnography of communication of your friend's dorm floor. As part of your study, you want to identify all the different ways of talking among floor residents. Because you want to understand the perspective of the floor residents themselves, one first-order question you would be interested in answering is "What are the different ways of talking according to floor residents?" As a participant-observer, your observations might not match exactly those of the floor residents. In order to answer the question about the ways of talking that *you* can identity, you pose a second-order question. Any segment of text in your field notes or interview transcripts that tells you about different ways of talking is a unit because it is heuristic.

Obviously, qualitative units of data are rarely the same standardized size. A qualitative unit could be a word, a phrase, a sentence, a paragraph—length may vary. One person might take two minutes to express a single thought in an interview, whereas another participant can articulate a thought in one sentence. Or the same person can experience greater or lesser ease of expression within the same interview. The same point applies to field notes—a single unit could be a single sentence of textual entry, or it might be several pages of typed field notes.

In short, a unit is what gets categorized by the researcher, which brings us to our next element of the coding process.

Step 3: Developing Coding Categories

The coding categories developed by the researcher stand at the heart of qualitative data analysis. The process of developing coding categories is an iterative cycle that you engage in over and over, each time revising the coding categories until they capture all of your data units. The process of developing categories begins during data collection, guides subsequent data gathering, and continues after you have finished with data collection.

Categories go hand in hand with the creation of files (whether electronic or the old-fashioned manila folder). John and Lyn Lofland (1995, pp. 189–192) discuss three broad types of category coding: housekeeping coding, research-process coding, and analytic coding. *Housekeeping coding* involves attending to the sources of textual units (for example, keeping track of the participant, the transcript page and line number, the date and page from field notes, and so forth). Coding for purposes of housekeeping allows you ready access to your raw textual data. It also provides a convenient way to provide a general profile of your database (e.g., the total number of your transcript pages, the total number of your informants and their demographic description, the total time frame spent in the field, and so forth). For your study of communication among floor residents, your housekeeping coding would involve noting, for example, that you studied 8 first-year women, 7 first-year men, 5 second-year women, 5 second-year men, and 7 third-year women.

Research-process coding is an analysis of your reflexive journal—it involves the categorization of the process employed by you in collecting and analyzing your textual data. For example, you might read your field notes over and notice that you moved in and out of accepting the floor residents' values and beliefs. This would tell you something important about which participant-observation role you were employing, and at what times, during your fieldwork.

Analytic coding addresses the meanings and meaning making evident to the researcher in his or her textual data. The process of developing analytic categories goes by several names. Several researchers refer to the process as the **constant comparative method,** described initially by Barney Glaser and Anselm Strauss (1967). Although the constant comparative method is aligned with a very specific analytic framework known as grounded theory, the process of initial coding described in the method is shared by most qualitative researchers. Other researchers refer to the emergent coding process as **analytic induction** (Goetz & LeCompte, 1981), although analytic induction involves not only coding but also negative case analysis, a process we describe separately below.

Generally speaking, the process of categorizing involves these steps, which we have adapted from David Erlandson and his colleagues (1993, pp. 118–119):

- *Read all of your data through completely, in order to experience a total immersion in them.* This holistic reading can be overwhelming, but it is important to provide you with a broad sense of the whole of your textual data. If your textual data are five thick field notebooks, then sit down and read through all five, cover to cover.

- *Identify your first unit of data as we discussed above.* Locate a textual segment that answers a question for you. This automatically becomes your first entry in your first category. For example, in the floor residents study, your first unit in your field notes might be this, in response to the question of different ways of talking: "Two first-year female roommates, Sally and Jane, were having what they later described to me as 'a heart-to-heart talk.'"

- *Identify your second unit of data.* That is, locate another textual segment that also gives you an answer to a question. Again, in the context of the floor residents, the field notes might include this segment: "Joe and Dan were having an argument. It came to my attention because I heard someone yelling out 'Hey, our warring roomies are duking it out again in the bathroom. Stay clear!'"

- *Make a basic judgment of similarity–difference between these two units.* Overall, is this second unit similar to the first unit, or is it different? If your judgment is that it is similar, it is grouped with the first unit under the first category. If your judgment is that it is different, you have the first entry in your second category. What do you think about "having a heart-to-heart" and "duking it out"? Based on the limited information we have provided here, we'd probably place these two units in separate categories.

- *Proceed with the similarity-judgment task for all of your units of data.* Each time you come to a unit of text that is different from existing categories, make a new category. At the end of this process, you will probably have a large number of categories, including a "miscellaneous" category.

- *Develop category labels and descriptions for each of your categories.* This is also known as *memoing* (Lofland & Lofland, 1995, p. 193): writing memos to yourself about the characteristics that typify each category. For example, if we had a category labeled "arguments," we might write this description of the category that contained the "duking it out" unit as well as other similar units: "Arguments is a category to refer to any verbal or physical fight, disagreement, or conflict between people on the floor, whether residents or visitors to the floor."

Write your labels and descriptions in pencil, or if you're using a computer software package for qualitative analysis, be ever ready to hit the delete key. Your trail of memos is important to your research-process coding. Your memo trail is crucial to your ability to meet the dependability and confirmability criteria of qualitative research.

- *Start over.* You may be exhausted by this point in the process, but it is important to repeat the whole coding exercise again. This revisiting of your data allows you to revise your judgments—maybe a unit that initially was placed in category X better belongs in category Z. For example, you started a category called "serious talk" in which you placed the "heart-to-heart" example above. But maybe, as your categories developed further, the "heart-to-heart" example better belongs in a category you later formed called "talk about the relationship between the speakers." Or maybe categories X and Z should be merged into a new, larger category. For example, in the dorm study, maybe you had two categories called "light chitchat" and "How are you?" which you now think should be joined into a broader category called "small talk." Or maybe category X needs to be subdivided into two new categories, to reflect the variation that exists in the units grouped initially into the same category. For example, maybe you realized that you should separate verbal conflict from more aggressive kinds of conflicts in which the parties threaten physical violence or actually use physical aggression in some way (e.g., slapping). Maybe your initial description of category X missed an important characteristic that you now see as common to all of the units grouped into the X category, so your memo needs to be revised. You may need to repeat this last step several times, depending on your confidence in your categories, the complexity of your data set, and when you initially undertook your categorizing work. Revision is the name of the game in this very important final step.

After reading these steps, it is clear why qualitative coding is often referred to as an emergent, iterative process. It is emergent in that categories emerge over time. It is iterative because you are analytically tacking back and forth, comparing a given unit to other units and a given category to other categories.

There's no magic number of categories you should have. The general advice is to have maximum homogeneity, or sameness, for the units placed within a given category combined with maximum heterogeneity, or difference, between categories (Lincoln & Guba, 1985). You should have as many categories as it takes to achieve this mix of homogeneity and heterogeneity.

Step 4: Plugging Holes

When a researcher revisits coding categories in the process just described, it is often necessary to "plug holes" with additional data gathering.

Let's suppose you have several units of text grouped into the same category, but your memoing is fuzzy or incomplete with respect to how the units fit together. The category seemed to make sense at the time you did the coding, but now that you look back on it, you really don't have a very clear grasp of what this category is all about. The problem may not rest in your brain but in your data—you may need to gather additional data that focus on this category in particular.

Maybe you have a category that has only a few textual units in it. You think that this category is interesting and important, but you just don't feel you have enough of the phenomenon to write a memo of the category's properties. You might want to gather more instances of this particular category.

Finally, suppose you see an emerging logic to several of your categories, but some categories appear to be missing. For example, suppose you are categorizing types of marriages and have identified two basic beliefs (we'll call them A and B) about marriage, upon which husbands and wives can agree or disagree. You have identified a category in your data in which husband and wife agree on both A and B, a category in your data in which husband and wife disagree on both A and B, and a category in which husband and wife agree on A but disagree on B. You wonder why you don't have any instances of what would logically complete the category set—husband-and-wife agreement on B and disagreement on A. You might want to go back to the field with the purpose of finding out whether this category is empirically present.

Additional, focused data gathering in response to perceived "soft spots" in the coding categories is very common in qualitative research. It's not a sign of untrustworthiness. Untrustworthiness would be failing to gather additional data.

Step 5: Checking

Because coding categories are the foundation of qualitative analysis, you should expend extra effort to ensure that your process meets the criteria of confirmability and credibility. Three procedures are employed by many qualitative researchers to check on the analysis at all points of the process, beginning with the development of coding categories: **negative case analysis, member checks,** and **triangulation.**

Negative Case Analysis Negative case analysis is a process of accounting for discrepancies in your data (Lincoln & Guba, 1985). As you develop initial coding categories, you gather additional data and "test" your categories against these new data. If you encounter a unit of data that disconfirms your categories—say, an instance that somehow challenges the integrity of your coding categories—you need to revise your coding categories accordingly. You keep considering new data until there are no new negative cases to account for. The goal is to have an analysis that accounts for 100 percent of your units of data.

Negative case analysis is not simply the iterative revision process we just described above. Negative case analysis obligates you to gather additional data, usually making an extra effort to locate deviant cases that don't fit the tidy categories you have identified to this point. In addition, negative case analysis is a method that applies to all kinds of analyses developed by the researcher, not just coding categories.

Negative case analysis is, according to Lindlof (1995, 240), "a stringent procedure, and not every analyst has the time or the patience to follow through on it." Negative case analysis means that you are accounting for 100 percent of your data incidents—a very high standard to achieve. Many qualitative researchers are content to account for the majority of their data incidents.

Member Checks As we have discussed in a prior chapter, member checking is a procedure in which you go back to participants with your analysis, seeking feedback on its credibility. Member checking applies to the development of coding categories as well as to subsequent analysis work. Member checks can vary in their directness and formality. For example, you could interview participants and ask them to comment on code categories you have developed. Or you could present them with several sample units of data and ask them to perform a categorization, determining the extent to which it matches your own category set.

Triangulation We have discussed this procedure in a prior chapter and won't repeat ourselves here, beyond noting that you can triangulate your coding categories in any of several ways. For example, you could triangulate different data sources, comparing, say, the coding categories you develop in interviews and those you develop in participant-observer field notes. You could triangulate multiple researcher perspectives, asking several researchers to derive code categories from the textual data, then compare their coding systems.

Negative case analysis, member checks, and triangulation are labor-intensive procedures used to enhance the confirmability and the credibility of all aspects of data analysis, including the development of coding categories. They share in common the acquisition of additional data beyond that used in initially developing the code categories. Not all qualitative researchers employ these procedures, but they are often present in the best qualitative work.

Step 6: Finding Exemplars

Put simply, **exemplars** are examples that illustrate vividly and concretely the abstract properties of each coding category. Exemplars, if used skillfully, bring the qualitative study alive for the reader. Exemplars help the researcher establish the confirmability and transferability of the qualitative study.

Exemplars should achieve what cultural anthropologist Clifford Geertz (1973, p. 6), borrowing from Gilbert Ryle, calls "thick description." We'll paraphrase the example used by Ryle, as summarized by Geertz (1973, pp. 6–7), because it is so elegant in capturing the difference between "thin" description and "thick" description. Suppose we see "two boys rapidly contracting the eyelids of their right eyes. In one, this is an involuntary twitch; in the other, a conspiratorial signal to a friend" (Geertz, 1973, p. 6). Suppose there is a third boy who, for purposes of amusing his friends, parodies the first boy's eye twitch, signaling perhaps through an exaggerated manner that he is making fun of the boy's inept winking. Further, let's imagine our teaser first practicing his exaggerated winking in front of a mirror, rehearsing his ability to pull off a humorous parody in front of his friends.

"Thin" description is the observation that in all four instances the same behavior is occurring—the rapid contracting and opening of the right eyelid. By contrast, "thick" description makes the differences apparent among a twitch, a wink of conspiracy, a parody of a wink, and a rehearsed wink, informing the reader of the meanings of the four actions. "Thick" description also provides us with an evocative rendering of each type of meaningful action, enabling readers to see the phenomenon in the mind's eye even though they weren't there to observe it first hand. Thick description, then, moves beyond a description of behaviors to a rich rendering of participant meanings and how those are produced through communicative action.

As you develop your coding categories and engage in memoing, you should get in the habit of identifying exemplars. Don't wait until you're all done with coding and then go back to locate exemplars—"flag" them as you go. It's easier. And in locating exemplars as you go, you force yourself to rethink in a very concrete way the abstract properties you have identified for a given category.

Step 7: Integrating Coding Categories

If all you do is create categories, your qualitative analysis is a listing enterprise. You need to take the next step—determining conceptual relationships between and among your various categories. This final step—integration or concept mapping—is crucial to a comprehensive qualitative analysis. There's no best way to accomplish integration. In the next section, we're going to illustrate two approaches to coding integration to give you a couple of systematic approaches that are frequently encountered in the communication research literature.

At a general level, integration is a kind of meta-coding activity: It is coding of coding categories. Thus, integration is an iterative and emergent process, like the coding activity we described above. Like coding, meta-coding activity will involve undertaking checks, locating exemplars, and perhaps additional focused data gathering in order to supplement empirical "soft spots" in the analysis.

In this section, we've described the qualitative analysis process of coding in general terms, giving you a generic "boilerplate" of the process. Next, we're going to review in some detail two specific models of qualitative data analysis that can be found in communication research: the **Developmental Research Sequence (DRS)** and **Grounded-Theory Development (GTD).** In discussing these two approaches, we'll flesh out our generic process in greater detail.

TWO ILLUSTRATIONS OF QUALITATIVE DATA ANALYSIS APPROACHES

We hesitate to provide you with only two illustrations of coding analysis for fear that you will conclude that these are the only ways to execute the qualitative analysis of data. There are many ways to accomplish qualitative data analysis, not just two. The two we are discussing are used frequently by communication researchers, and we thought it would be helpful to see them close up. Although both approaches follow the generic model we have just described, they are quite different from each other.

The Developmental Research Sequence (DRS) was developed by James Spradley (1979, 1980), and it is frequently employed by researchers from an ethnography of communication perspective and by interpretive scholars with a particular interest in language use. It is a model of qualitative data analysis that can inform us about both **semantic relationships** and communication **rules,** although the former is highlighted.

Grounded-Theory Development (GTD) is linked to the work of Barney Glaser and Anselm Strauss (e.g., Glaser & Strauss, 1967; Strauss & Corbin, 1990). It is used by researchers who take a grounded-theory perspective. The purpose of grounded-theory research is "to generate or discover a theory, an abstract analytical schema of a phenomenon, that relates to a particular situation" (Creswell, 1998, p. 56). The situation is one in which people "interact, take actions, or engage in a process in response to a phenomenon" (Creswell, 1998, p. 56). Researchers often use the term "grounded-theory approach" to refer more generally to any inductive theory construction that results from analysis of qualitative data. However, not all inductive theories are grounded theories in the sense in which Glaser and Strauss developed that term. Although GTD could inform us about semantic relationships, it probably features communication rules more centrally.

The Developmental Research Sequence

Let's begin with a hypothetical example, adapted from some research undertaken by one of us on kinds of talk differentiated by middle-class young adults in the United States (Baxter & Goldsmith, 1990; Goldsmith & Baxter, 1996). Suppose we're interested in finding out all of the different kinds of talk recognized by members of some cultural group. Let's suppose that we undertake participant-observation fieldwork, recording all of the different kinds of talk we see and participants' terms of reference for their everyday communication activities. Suppose we conduct interviews with people in which we ask them about all of the different kinds of talk they have enacted in the past couple of days. Suppose we ask participants to keep diary records for us, recording all of the different kinds of talk episodes in which they are involved for a two-week period. How do we go about analyzing this wealth of qualitative data? Let's go about the analysis process following the DRS model developed by Spradley (1979, 1980).

With respect to analysis, the DRS model involves four major kinds of activity: domain analysis, taxonomic analysis, componential analysis, and theme analysis. We'll illustrate each with our hypothetical example.

Domain Analysis   A domain is a category of meaning. The label for the category is its cover term. The elements in the category are included for membership in the category based on a semantic relationship. We discussed semantic relationships in Chapters 3 and 4. Spradley (1979, 1980) presents nine different semantic relationships that comprise systems of meaning. In our example, we'll start out with a semantic relationship of strict inclusion: X is a kind of Y. If Y is "talk," then we're going to analyze our data to produce a list of X's that hold category membership in our talk domain: X is a kind of talk.

Spradley recommends that you develop coding worksheets to assist you in domain construction. Figure 16-1 provides a sample worksheet for our domain of "talk."

Some of the terms in a domain analysis might be folk terms used by the participants themselves—we've placed these in quotation marks in Figure 16-1; these are first-order concepts. Other terms might be analytic terms generated by the researcher, what we earlier called second-order concepts. For example, our term "phatic communication" is not one used by our participants.

It should be evident that domain analysis is a process of code categorization. Domain analysis is an ongoing activity, subject to revision based on checks and additional focused data-gathering efforts. If we were to stop the analytic process here, however, we would have only a list before us. Let's complicate the analysis a bit.

Taxonomic Analysis   A taxonomy indicates the relationships among the members of a domain. It, too, is organized by a semantic relationship. Taxonomies are characterized by having different levels, or hierarchies.

Look again at the entries in Figure 16-1. Some of the entries appear to refer to kinds of talk that we might refer to as "small talk," or phatic communication—relatively superficial talk whose sole purpose is to massage social relations. By contrast, "having a fight" is a way to accomplish conflict. And the kind of talk initiated by the opener "Can we talk?" might be a way to accomplish serious relational business. Thus, we might find it useful to work with the means–end semantic relationship (X is a way to do Y), identifying all of the different ends served by talk. So far, we've identified three. If we developed a complete taxonomic analysis of our "talk" domain, based on the means–end semantic relationship, we would have analyzed the purposes served by talk in our cultural group.

We might find it helpful to devise a summary diagram of our taxonomy, indicating its various levels of cultural meaning. Figure 16-2 provides a partial taxonomy based on our hypothetical example. Through checking and additional focused data gathering, we would attempt to determine whether there were more ends served by talk (indicated by the "?" in the far right of the figure) and whether

1. Semantic relationship: <u>strict inclusion</u>
2. Form: <u>X (is a kind of) Y.</u>
3. Example: <u>Ice cream is a kind of dessert.</u>

Included Terms:	Semantic Relationship:	Cover Term:
"B.S.ing"		
"shooting the breeze"		
"chatting"		
	is a kind of	talk
"the kind of talk when someone says 'Can we talk?'"		
"having a fight"		

FIGURE 16-1　**Sample Domain Analysis Worksheet**

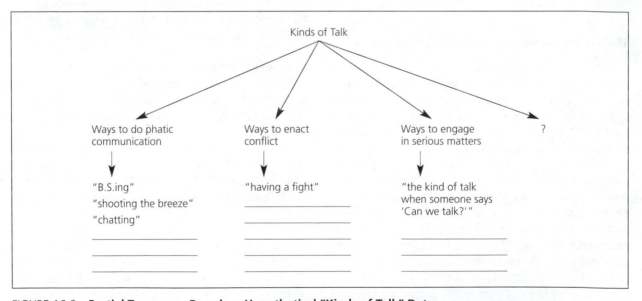

FIGURE 16-2　**Partial Taxonomy Based on Hypothetical "Kinds of Talk" Data**

there are more members within each identified end (indicated by the blank lines in the columns).

A taxonomy moves beyond a global list, providing an analysis of the relationship among included terms of a domain. With respect to the domain of kinds of talk, we now have a more complex portrait of the system of meaning of our participants.

Componental Analysis Meaning is based on differences or contrasts between things, not just on similarities between things. In part, our meaning of "sweets" comes not just through a mental category of all of the kinds of things that count as "sweets" (candy bars, decadent desserts, Mom's special raisin cinnamon bars) but also, by contrast, from things that are not "sweets" (salads, vegetables, etc.). Componential analysis zooms in on understanding contrasts. According to Spradley (1980, p. 131), componential analysis is "the systematic search for the attributes (components of meaning) associated with cultural categories." Attributes or components of meaning are based on contrasts among the members of a domain. As a qualitative analyst, you are searching your data for evidence of underlying dimensions that organize these contrasts.

For example, in the taxonomy presented in Figure 16-2, phatic communication appears to contrast with talk about serious matters—the former is light, superficial, lacking in seriousness, whereas the latter is characterized by its nontrivial, serious purposes. These two purposes of talk appear to be contrasted on an underlying dimension of seriousness, whose attribute endpoints are serious and nonserious. "Having a fight" is probably toward the serious end of the continuum. A second dimension might be valence—positivity and negativity. Whereas conflict might be experienced as a negative communication event by our participants, phatic communication might be experienced as positive. Talk about serious matters might be positive or negative, depending on other factors (e.g., a talk about asking someone to marry you could take either a positive or a negative direction). And so on.

In componential analysis, then, you determine the underlying dimensions by which domain members can be contrasted. When your componential analysis is complete, you should be able to indicate where each domain member is located for all of the underlying dimensions. Table 16-1 provides an example of a componential paradigm diagram based on our hypothetical domain of kinds of talk.

Of course, a componential analysis is subject to revision and refinement through checking and additional focused data gathering.

Theme Analysis A cultural theme is, according to Spradley (1980, p. 141), "any principle recurrent in a number of domains, tacit or explicit, and serving as a relationship among subsystems of cultural meaning." Themes might include such concepts as core values, core symbols, basic taken-for-granted premises, world views, or orientations.

Spradley suggests that themes can often be identified through dimensions that recur across domains. In our hypothetical example, we have examined only one domain—kinds of talk. In order to identify cultural themes, we would have to work with several domains at once, determining if similar dimensions of meaning surface again

TABLE 16-1   Sample Componential Paradigm Diagram for "Kinds of Talk" Data

Domain	Dimensions of Contrast	
	Seriousness	Valence
phatic communication	light	positive
conflict events	serious	negative
talk about serious matters	serious	positive or negative

and again. If so, we're probably stumbling into cultural themes.

Let's suppose that one dimension that we found for our domain of "kinds of talk" was personal expression; some kinds of talk are experienced by our participants as occasions to express their "true selves," whereas other kinds of talk are occasions where one's talk is constrained by the participants' roles (e.g., store clerk, professor).

Now suppose we analyzed another domain in the everyday lives of our cultural group—types of clothing. After conducting a domain analysis, taxonomic analysis, and componential analysis, we conclude that personal expression is an important dimension by which participants make sense of different kinds of clothing. There are clothes that are expressions of "who we are," and there are clothes that are "uniform straitjackets."

On the basis of identifying "personal expression" as a dimension of meaning in both cultural domains, we might conclude tentatively that this is an important cultural motif or theme for our participants.

We might seek triangulation of this conclusion by looking for other kinds of evidence of cultural themes. Spradley (1980) suggests that cultural themes sometimes appear as folk sayings, proverbs, or common expressions. We might, for example, hear reference to "do your own thing," "be all that you can be," and so forth—all of which suggest that personal expression is an important source of meaning to our participants.

Our presentation of Spradley's DRS has greatly oversimplified the analytic process, primarily through our partial rendering of but a single domain of meaning. To use a comprehensive DRS approach, the researcher would need to conduct domain, taxonomic, and componential analyses of all relevant domains of meaning, and then integrate them through a theme analysis.

Grounded-Theory Development

Our discussion of the grounded-theory model is adapted from Anselm Strauss and Juliet Corbin's (1990) comprehensive presentation of the procedures and techniques of developing grounded theory.

Grounded theory is conceived as an analytic process that culminates in the development of a formal, propositional theory. According to Glaser and Strauss (1967), this theory should fit the specific context from which it was developed, make sense to participants in that context, be abstract enough to allow generalizability to other similar contexts, and enable prediction and control. The focus on generalizability and control distinguishes the grounded-theory tradition from other qualitative approaches.

GTD involves four basic steps: open coding, axial coding, process analysis, and selective coding. (There's a fifth step—using a conditional matrix—that is more advanced than our introductory purposes here.) Each analytic step is punctuated by additional data gathering designed to check working hypotheses (i.e., coding decisions) as they emerge.

Let's work with another example. Suppose we're interested in studying the communication rules that guide the informal management of ethical issues in the workplace. We do participant-observation fieldwork in an organization, conduct interviews with employees, and consult a variety of social-text material, including formal organizational documents related to ethical issues such as published codes of ethics. Our goal is to develop a theory of everyday ethics management. The grounded-theory approach is just what we need to use.

Open Coding   GTD begins with open coding, which is "the process of breaking down, examining, comparing, conceptualizing, and categorizing data" (Strauss & Corbin, 1990, p. 61). This process involves the constant comparative method (Glaser & Strauss, 1967, pp. 101–116).

Let's suppose that our field notes contain this passage:

> Sat in the lounge all day, as various employees moved in and out, engaging in casual conversation with their co-workers or sitting alone. At 10:15 I saw someone use the candy machine to get a bag of chips. The person put in the money, made a selection, but nothing came out. After much frustration, the person left with nothing, not even a refund because the machine didn't give back the person's money. About fifteen minutes later, a different person went to the machine immediately after arriving in the lounge; the frustrated person had left by then. The person put in her money, made her selection, and to her surprise got not only her selection but the bag of chips selected by the prior person, as well as that person's change from the money slot. **The person laughed at receiving a bonus,**

then said for others to hear "Payback time for all of my lost quarters in this !@?! machine!" (1) She went and sat down by herself to eat. **After she was seated, she hesitated for a few seconds, then said to others around her, "Does anybody know whose chips these are? I got them just now when I selected my candy bar. Somebody else must have selected them, but didn't get them. And I got some change back, too—$.45." Nobody seemed to know whose chips they were. (2)** The person got up from her chair and placed the bag of chips on the countertop near the machine. She put the $.45 in the "coffee jar" that co-workers contribute to when they drink a cup of coffee from the communal pot. **Then she returned to her chair, saying to others "If anyone comes looking, those chips are on the counter there, and they get a 'free' cuppa coffee." (3)** Then she ate her selection (a candy bar), drank a can of soda, and returned, presumably, to work.

The first step in conducting open coding is to unitize. We might want to unitize our data by first locating all of the ethical issues that get managed communicatively. In this textual segment, one ethical issue would be identified: finding something that belongs to another person. We would then probably want to unitize our textual data for all of the communicative actions taken to manage the ethical issue. In this segment, we have identified three units, which we have emphasized and marked numerically at the conclusion of each unit. We might label these, respectively, Humorous Claim of Possession (1), Inquiry about Rightful Owner (2), and Public Giveback (3).

After unitizing and labeling all of our textual data, we would need to categorize our units, sorting similar units into the same category and generating a category label. We would engage in the constant comparative method. Because (1), (2), and (3) above strike us as different from one another, we have formed three categories with these three units. In categorizing additional data units, we might add incidents to these three categories, add more categories, and/or revise these three initial categories. Let's suppose that we have revised these categories based on additional data so that they represent larger classes of communicative actions: Possession Claims, Information Gathering, and Resolutions.

With each category, we create a memo that details the properties which characterize the category. These properties can then be dimensionalized by identifying the underlying dimension where a given property can be located. Strauss and Corbin (1990) give the example of the category "color." The properties of colors include shade, intensity, hue, and so forth. Each of these properties can be conceived along a dimension.

Let's suppose our category of Possession Claims contains the Humorous Claim of Possession incident and these additional incidents: an incident in which the person simply took possession of an object without saying anything, and an incident in which possession was taken of an object only after checking to see that nobody was looking. In all of these incidents, a person has taken possession of an object that does not belong to him or her, but this has been accomplished in different ways. The properties, and underlying dimensions, that might fit this category include public–private (whether the possession is witnessed by others) and verbal–nonverbal (whether the possession is accompanied by verbal expression).

Strauss and Corbin (1990, p. 73) present several generic properties, and associated dimensions, that might apply to a wide range of categories of action:

Properties	Dimensional Range
Frequency	often—never
Extent	more—less
Intensity	high—low
Duration	long—short

The open-coding step appears to synthesize features of Spradley's (1979, 1980) domain, taxonomic, and componential analyses.

Axial Coding   Axial coding involves an attempt to understand a phenomenon in terms of the conditions that give rise to it, the context in which it is embedded, any intervening conditions that affect responses to the phenomenon, the action/interaction strategies by which it is managed, and the consequences of those strategies.

As you undertake the constant comparative method, you will probably have categories that correspond to causes, contexts, conditions, actions/interactions, and consequences. If not, you need to create those categories in this step, identifying their properties and dimensions just as you did in open coding. In our example, our categories that capture different communication practices in the management of ethical issues fit well under "actions/interactions."

Some obvious overlaps exist between certain of Spradley's (1979, 1980) semantic relationships and the axial-coding categories. Here's a list of the correspondences we see:

Semantic Relationships (Spradley, 1979, 1980)	Axial-Coding Categories (Strauss & Corbin, 1990)
Cause–effect (X is a result of Y)	Causal conditions
Location-for-action (X is a place for doing Y)	Context
Means–end (X is a way to do Y)	Actions/interactions
Cause–effect	Consequences

Whereas Spradley would have us invoke a given semantic relationship only if it is present in the data, the grounded-theory approach obligates us to examine the axial-coding categories.

After you develop these categories, you will analyze how the categories relate to one another. Axial coding is the heart of grounded-theory development, because a grounded theory must address interconnections among causes, contexts, conditions, actions/interactions, and consequences.

Within the framework of our hypothetical example, the phenomenon we're dealing with is the category *types of ethical issues.* Our open coding of this category might look something like this:

Category: Type of Ethical Issues
    Properties:
    possession of object that belongs to the
      organization
    possession of object that belongs to a co-worker
    deception with client
    deception with co-worker
    deception with supervisor
    taking credit for co-worker's efforts
    etc.

Dimensions:
    magnitude of potential ethical violation (low–high)
    frequency (rare–often)
    etc.

In axial coding, our analytic task is to discern the causal conditions under which ethical dilemmas arise, the contexts in which ethical dilemmas arise, intervening conditions that affect their communicative management, the actions/interactions of communicative management, and the consequences of actions/interactions.

"Causal conditions" is a broad theoretical concept that includes events or incidents that lead up to an occurrence of the phenomenon, reasons for the phenomenon, and explanations and accounts of the phenomenon. We would read all of our textual data with an eye toward coding causal conditions. As with open coding, we would develop the properties and dimensions of each category of causal conditions.

For example, we might find that one condition under which ethical dilemmas arise is circumstances in which employees find themselves trapped between competing obligations—any action they take to meet an obligation positions them to engage in an unethical act. Another causal condition might be dispositional—some workers may perceive that ethical dilemmas are faced more so by some people than others because of their value systems, personalities, and so forth. For each causal condition we identified in our data, we would identify its underlying properties and dimensions. For example, the competing obligations cause might have dimensions that address the frequency with which employees encounter this situation (rarely–often) and the magnitude of what's at stake (minor–major).

"Contexts" refers to the locations (spatial and temporal) where the phenomenon is located. In analyzing our data to uncover the contexts where ethically related events take place, we might end up with these dimensions: public–private, frontstage–backstage, inside–outside normal working hours.

"Intervening conditions" refers to "the broad and general conditions bearing upon action/interactional strategies" (Strauss & Corbin, 1990, p. 103). For example, communicative management of ethical issues might be affected by perceptions of formal and informal guidelines and norms related to ethical conduct. Our coding with respect to this intervening condition might end up in the dimensions of formality of guideline (formal–informal), whether the perceived guidelines are sufficiently clear and specific (low–high), and whether any sanctions are perceived to accompany an act deemed unethical (none–minor–major).

"Actions" captures the responses of individuals, whereas "interactions" examines communication between at least two persons. Strauss and Corbin (1990, p. 104) tell us that actions/interactions are characterized by two general properties. First, they are process-oriented, and thus can be studied over time (we'll return to the matter of process in more detail below). Second, they are purposeful and goal-directed: They are in response to the phenomenon. We've already illustrated what this category might look like in our discussion above of open coding.

As one of us says (a lot) to her six-year-old, "Actions have consequences." Well, when you're engaging in axial coding, you need to read your textual data with an eye toward flagging all of the possible consequences that occur as a result of actions/interactions. With respect to our hypothetical example, we might note a range of consequences, including psychological (e.g., guilt), economic (e.g., getting fired), and social (e.g., losing/gaining co-workers' respect). Possible dimensions might include the magnitude of the consequence (low–high) and the duration of the consequence (short-term–long-term).

The "paradigm model" is the term Strauss and Corbin (1990, p. 99) use to refer to the interconnections you make among the coding categories of the axial-coding step. For example, are certain types of ethical issues systematically associated with certain types of communicative responses? Do communicative responses vary contingent on the presence of certain intervening conditions?

Paradigm analysis is a complex process of searching the data for patterns that link categories and their dimensions to other categories (and their dimensions). It is the final step in axial coding, and it moves us to the analytic task of integration, where we will continue to function in subsequent GTD steps.

Process Analysis Bringing process into the analytic picture is an important element of any grounded theory. Strauss and Corbin (1990, p. 143) define a process analysis in the following way: "By process we mean the linking of sequences of action/interaction as they pertain to the management of, control over, or response to, a phenomenon." A process analysis addresses change and the flow of events and actions over time.

In executing a process analysis, you systematically note several things in your textual data: (1) the changing conditions over time that influence actions/interactions, (2) the actions/interactions that are responses to those changing influences, (3) the consequences of actions/interactions over time, and (4) how consequences become conditions for the next actions/interactions (Strauss & Corbin, 1990).

If you execute open and axial coding adequately, process insights should appear naturally in your analysis. But Strauss and Corbin separate out this analytic focus because it is too easily lost.

How do you capture process? You could conceptualize it any number of ways, depending on the particulars of your data: incremental changes; discrete steps, stages, or phases; or repeating cycles or spirals. Important analytic dimensions in capturing change might include rate (fast–slow), shape (orderly–disorderly, progressive–nonprogressive), direction (forward–backward), and ability to control (low–high).

In the context of our hypothetical example, we might notice that workers change over time in how they respond to ethical dilemmas. For example, they might become less vigilant over time in protecting their public image as ethical persons because of their sense that it is a "losing battle." Important to our analysis of process would be an understanding of the conditions that account for the change, not simply a description of the form and pace of that change.

Selective Coding   You now have an elaborate system of code categories and have organized those categories into a Phenomenon-Cause-Context-Intervening Conditions-Actions/Interactions-Consequences framework. You have detected systematic patterning among your categories. In this step, you pull your analysis together, producing a descriptive narrative about the central phenomenon of the study. Selective coding is what positions you to write the story line of your narrative.

Selective coding refers to the process of selecting a core category, around which all of the other categories can be integrated. Your core category is the analytic heart of your findings—your "bottom line." As you examine the results of your axial coding, ask yourself these sorts of selective-coding questions: What is most striking in these categories and their patterning? What stands out as the "heart of the matter"?

Selective coding is challenging. It forces you to commit to a single core category and build a descriptive story of your data from that core seed.

When you think you have identified your core category, sit down and write a few sentences or a paragraph in which you pull it all together. With respect to our hypothetical example, we might end up with a story line something like this:

> The main story in these data is how people navigate everyday organizational life, attempting to sustain an identity as an "honest, trustworthy, and ethical person" in a minefield riddled with a variety of ethical challenges and dilemmas. Being ethical is an important feature of this organization's culture, and both formal and informal sanctions ensue when someone is perceived to be behaving "unethically." Workers engage in a variety of communicative practices designed to protect their public image as an ethical person. Yet this organization paradoxically positions its workers to face ethical dilemmas on an ongoing basis, mostly through competing expectations and obligations. Over time, workers become frustrated by how effortful it is to sustain their image as an ethical person, and they expend less communicative effort in managing their image.

If a story line successfully captures the heart of what is going on in the data, it provides the beginning point for writing up the study's conclusions and for grounding the more abstract theory that has been developed—a theory designed to apply to other similar organizations.

In elaborating upon the kernel story line, you fit other categories into the developing story line, fleshing out details accordingly. If you have successfully identified the core category, this fitting-together process will be fairly straightforward. However, if the category around which you built your story line is not a core, you will experience this process as a forced fit—an attempt to fit square pegs into round holes, so to speak. This is a sign that you may have misjudged your core category and that you need to return to the results of your axial coding in order to identify another core category around which a story line can be built.

The story line captures, in narrative form, the basic propositions of your grounded theory. An alternative way to express the theory would be in proposition form. Some hypothetical propositions that might accompany our example include the following:

- Proposition 1: When workers experience competing expectations or demands, ethical dilemmas increase.
- Proposition 2: Workers are motivated to sustain an identity as an ethical person, especially when the formal and informal culture of their organization values ethical conduct.

As with the DRS approach, our introduction to GTD has greatly oversimplified the analytic process. Our goal in presenting both DRS and GTD has been twofold: (1) to impress upon you the rigorous, systematic nature of qualitative data analysis and (2) to demonstrate that qualitative data analysis, while characterized by a core of basic analytic steps, can be executed in different ways depending on the purpose of the researcher.

COMPUTERS AND QUALITATIVE DATA ANALYSIS

Qualitative analysis software has revolutionized the processing of qualitative textual data, allowing you to do electronically what can still be done with paper, scissors, tape, and manila folders.

Most of the qualitative research software programs can be applied to textual data entered in a standard word-processing system. Once you've created a file of your notes using a word-processing system, you can access them with this software. These programs allow you to mark text passages with the electronic equivalent of the yellow highlighter pen. You can electronically create file folders, to which you can copy selected passages of marked text. You can write electronic memos that reflect your analytic thoughts and attach these memos to marked text passages, more or less as you might do with self-stick removable notes that you stick to sheets of paper.

Visit the web site http://www.soc.surrey.ac.uk/sru/SRU1.html, developed by sociologists at the University of Surrey, England, for an excellent list of qualitative data-analysis tools. This web site provides a brief description of each of the major qualitative data-analysis software packages, along with the price and contact information, if available: the Ethnograph, HyperQual, HyperResearch, HyperSoft, NUD*IST, QUALPRO, QUALOG, Textbase Alpha, SONAR, and Atlas-ti, among others.

In the end, these software packages help you only in processing your notes; they don't do the analysis part of the job. Whether working with electronic aids or with by-hand processing, your engaged mind is ultimately the tool that engages in the actual analysis of your qualitative data.

SUMMING UP

We began this chapter by indicating that our purpose was to demonstrate that qualitative data analysis is rigorous and systematic. At the same time, however, it is not a mechanical undertaking to be followed in a lockstep or cookie-cutter fashion. It is, in the end, an open-ended process that requires substantial flexibility, skills, and insight on the part of the researcher.

The qualitative analysis of textual data, like quantitative analysis of numerical data, has its strengths and limitations. Qualitative data analysis, done well, provides a richly textured understanding of the system of meanings in a text. The key to doing it well, we think, is appreciating that the process is as much art as science.

And herein lies the greatest challenge of qualitative data analysis: At the very least, there are no cut-and-dried steps that guarantee success. Although statistical analyses may intimidate some students, the steps involved can sometimes be learned by rote. That is, with practice, the rote exercise of quantitative skills can produce an ever-more-sophisticated understanding of the logic that lies behind those techniques. It is much more difficult to teach qualitative analysis as a series of rote procedures; understanding must precede practice.

It's a lot like learning how to paint with watercolors or compose a symphony. Instruction in such activities is certainly possible and helpful. But instruction can carry you only so far. The final product must come from you—your analytic ability to identify patterns in meanings and meaning making.

Of course, our position throughout the book has been that quantitative and qualitative research methods are by no means incompatible or in competition. Although we have discussed these methods separately, we think that you need to operate in both modes to explore your full potential as a communication researcher.

Main Points

◻ Qualitative data analysis is a systematic and rigorous process by which researchers interpret meanings and meaning making.

◻ The general process of qualitative data analysis involves seven steps: determining questions, unitizing textual data, developing coding categories, collecting additional focused data to fill analytic gaps, undertaking checks, locating exemplars, and integrating coding categories.

◻ Spradley's (1979, 1980) Developmental Research Sequence is a kind of qualitative analysis often used in communication research.

◻ Glaser and Strauss's (1967) Grounded-Theory Development is a second kind of qualitative analysis often found in communication research.

◻ Qualitative data analysis is not mechanistic; it is characterized by its open-ended nature and its demands for flexibility and insightful interpretation by the researcher.

Key Terms

coding	exemplars
unitizing	Developmental Research
constant comparative method	Sequence (DRS)
analytic induction	Grounded-Theory
negative case analysis	Development (GTD)
member checks	semantic relationship
triangulation	rules

Review Questions and Exercises

1. Select a textual domain of interest to you related to communication—for example, cards (birthday, graduation, etc.) in a card shop, magazines available at the local newsstand, advertisements in an issue of a magazine, commercials shown in one hour of prime-time television. Use the DRS method to conduct a qualitative analysis of your selected domain.

2. Suppose you are interested in understanding a certain domain of communicative acts—for example, kinds of questions posed by instructors to students or kinds of flirting in college bars. Take field notes on your selected phenomenon for at least a week. Perform a qualitative analysis of your textual data using the GTD method.

3. In the spirit of multi-method research, locate a qualitative study from one of the journals listed in Appendix A and then discuss how quantitative research methods could be used to conduct a complementary study on the same general topic. Now reverse this: Locate a quantitative study from one of the communication journals. Discuss how qualitative research methods could be used to conduct a complementary study.

Continuity Project

Create two domains as follows: domain 1 is a list of all the labels and terms that college students at your university use to describe kinds of women (e.g., "a total babe," "a witch"), and domain 2 is a list of all the labels and terms that college students at your university use to describe kinds of men (e.g., "a stud muffin," "a jock"). Conduct a qualitative analysis of each domain. Are the dimensions of meaning the same for both genders?

Additional Readings

Lincoln, Y. S., & Guba, E. G. (1985). *Naturalistic inquiry.* Newbury Park, CA: Sage. This is a classic on all facets of qualitative research methods. We think their treatment of data analysis is particularly strong.

Lofland, J., & Lofland, L. H. (1995). *Analyzing social settings: A guide to qualitative observation and analysis* (3rd ed.). New York: Wadsworth. Another classic book on qualitative methods. This book's treatment of qualitative data analysis is excellent, particularly the suggestions for generating questions to ask about data.

Miles, M. B., & Huberman, A. M. (1994). *Qualitative data analysis: An expanded sourcebook* (2nd ed.). Thousand Oaks, CA: Sage. A comprehensive practical guide on the how-tos of qualitative analysis.

Spradley, J. P. (1979). *The ethnographic interview.* New York: Holt, Rinehart and Winston; Spradley, J. P. (1980). *Participant observation.* New York: Holt, Rinehart and Winston. The two Spradley books are simply outstanding when it comes to a detailed and concrete presentation of the DRS method. The discussion of the DRS method is redundant in the two books, so you need to get your hands on only one of them.

Strauss, A., & Corbin, J. (1990). *Basics of qualitative research: Grounded theory procedures and techniques.* Newbury Park, CA: Sage. An outstanding book that lays out the GTD method in a detailed and concrete manner.

InfoTrac College Edition
http://www.infotrac-college.com/
wadsworth/access.html

Access the latest news and journal articles with Info-Trac College Edition, an easy-to-use online database of reliable, full-length articles from hundreds of top academic journals. Conduct an electronic search using the following search terms:

- semantic relationship
- analytic induction
- constant comparative method
- grounded theory
- open coding

APPENDIXES

APPENDIX A

Communication-Related Journals

If you want to learn more about the following journals, check their web sites.

JOURNALS SPONSORED BY THE INTERNATIONAL COMMUNICATION ASSOCIATION (ICA)

Communication Theory
Human Communication Research
Journal of Communication

JOURNALS SPONSORED BY THE NATIONAL COMMUNICATION ASSOCIATION (NCA) AND ITS REGIONAL AFFILIATE ORGANIZATIONS (CENTRAL STATES COMMUNICATION ASSOCIATION—CSCA, EASTERN COMMUNICATION ASSOCIATION—ECA, SOUTHERN STATES COMMUNICATION ASSOCIATION—SSCA, WESTERN STATES COMMUNICATION ASSOCIATION—WSCA)

Communication Education (formerly *Speech Teacher*)
Communication Monographs (formerly *Speech Monographs*)
Communication Quarterly (formerly *Today's Speech*)
Communication Reports
Communication Research Reports
Communication Studies (formerly *Central States Speech Journal*)
Critical Studies in Mass Communication
Journal of Applied Communication Research (formerly *Journal of Applied Communications Research*)
Quarterly Journal of Speech (formerly *Quarterly Journal of Public Speaking; Journal of Speech Education*)
The Review of Communication
Southern Communication Journal (formerly *Southern Speech Communication Journal; Southern Speech Journal*)

Text and Performance Quarterly (formerly *Literature in Performance*)
Western Journal of Communication (formerly *Western Journal of Speech Communication; Western Speech*)

JOURNALS WITH OTHER SPONSORSHIP

American Journalism Review
Argumentation and Advocacy (formerly *Journal of the American Forensic Association*)
Asian Journal of Communication
Australian Journal of Communication
Canadian Journal of Communication
College Composition and Communication
Columbia Journalism Review
Communication and Cognition
Communication and Research
Communication Review
Convergence: The Journal of Research into New Media Technologies
Discourse & Society
Discourse Processes
Discourse Studies
Electronic Journal of Communication
European Journal of Communication
Health Communication
Howard Journal of Communication
InterMedia
International Journal of Listening (formerly *Journal of the International Listening Association*)
Journal of Asian Pacific Communication
Journal of the Association for Communication Administration (formerly *Bulletin of the Association for Communication Administration; ACA Bulletin*)
Journal of Broadcasting & Electronic Media (formerly *Journal of Broadcasting*)
Journal of Business Communication
Journal of Business and Technical Communication (formerly *Iowa State JBTC*)
Journal of Communication & Religion (formerly *Religious Communication Today*)

Journal of Communication Inquiry
Journal of Computer-Mediated Communication
Journal of Development Communication
Journal of Educational Television
Journal of Family Communication
Journal of Film and Video
Journal of Health Communication
Journal of International Communication
Journal of Language and Social Psychology
Journal of Mass Media Ethics
Journal of Newspaper and Periodical History (formerly *Journal of Newspaper History*)
Journal of Popular Culture
Journal of Public Relations Research
Journal of Radio Studies
Journal of Social and Personal Relationships
Journal of Technical Writing and Communication
Journalism History
Journalism and Mass Communication Educator
Journalism and Mass Communication Quarterly
Journalism Monographs
Journalism Quarterly
Journalism: Theory, Practice & Criticism
Language & Communication
Management Communication Quarterly
Mass Comm Review
Mass Communication & Society
Media & Methods
Media, Culture, & Society
Media Studies Journal (formerly *Gannett Center Journal*)

National Forensic Journal
New Media & Society
Newspaper Research Journal
Personal Relationships
Philosophy & Rhetoric
Political Communication (formerly *Political Communication and Persuasion*)
Pre/Text: An Interdisciplinary Journal of Rhetoric
Public Opinion Quarterly
Public Relations Journal
Public Relations Review
Research in Language and Social Interaction
Rhetoric and Public Affairs
Rhetoric Review
Rhetoric Society Quarterly
Rhetorica
Science Communication (formerly *Knowledge*)
Small Group Research (formerly *Small Group Behavior*)
Studies in Communication
Symbolic Interaction
Technology and Culture
Text: An Interdisciplinary Journal for the Study of Discourse
Women and Language
Women's Studies in Communication (formerly *ORWAC Bulletin*)
World Communication (formerly *Communication, The Journal of the Communication Association of the Pacific; Communication*)
Written Communication

APPENDIX B

Using the Library

INTRODUCTION

Throughout this book we're assuming that you'll be reading reports of communication research. In this appendix, we want to talk a little about how you'll find reports to read.

As we've indicated repeatedly, you live in a world filled with social scientific research reports. Your daily newspaper, magazines, professional journals, alumni bulletins, club newsletters—virtually everything you pick up to read may carry reports dealing with a particular topic. This book is attempting to prepare you to read primary research published in scholarly journals, so we'll emphasize those references.

Today, there are two major approaches to finding library materials: the traditional paper route and electronically. Let's begin with the traditional method first and examine the electronic option afterward.

GETTING HELP

When you want to find something in the library, your best friend is the reference librarian, who's specially trained to find things in the library. Sometimes it's hard to ask people for help, but you'll do yourself a real service to make an exception in this case.

Some libraries have specialized reference librarians—for the social sciences, humanities, government documents, and so forth. Find the one you need and tell him or her what you're interested in. The reference librarian will probably put you in touch with some of the many available reference sources.

The reference librarian will probably be interested in your *keywords*—by subject, author, or title. When you begin your search for information, you need to identify several keywords relevant to your topic area. For example, if you were interested in how marital partners persuade each other, you might have the following subject-based keywords: "marriage," "persuasion," "social influence," "compliance-gaining." You might also have the names of

researchers who are identified with this topic area. You might have a title or two to specific scholarly articles or books.

How do you figure out your keywords? It seems like you have to know quite a bit on a topic area in order to identify keywords that will position you to locate existing research. It's kind of like when you were a kid and wondered how to spell a certain word and were told by the adults around you to "look it up in the dictionary." In order to look up the word in the dictionary, you needed to have some starting points on possible spellings. The same applies in using the library—you need some starting points, some keywords, that will serve as your gateway to available resources.

One very useful strategy to locate keywords is to see if someone has written a summary review of the literature on your topic area. *Communication Yearbook,* an annual volume published by the International Communication Association, contains chapter-length reviews on selected topic areas in communication research. In addition, topic-specific annual volumes provide summary reviews of literature, including the *Free Speech Yearbook* and the *International and Intercultural Communication Annual,* both of which are sponsored by the National Communication Association. An additional annual series that provides summary literature reviews is *Progress in Communication Sciences.*

There are also several handbooks published on specialized topics, including the *Handbook of Personal Relationships* (Duck, 1997), the *Handbook of Communication and Emotion* (Andersen & Guerrero, 1998), the *Handbook of Group Communication Theory and Research* (Frey, 1999), the *Handbook of Interpersonal Communication* (3rd ed.) (Knapp & Daly, 2002), the *New Handbook of Organizational Communication* (Jablin & Putnam, 2000), and the *Handbook of International and Intercultural Communication* (Gudykunst, Newmark, & Asante, 1994). Subject-specific scholarly dictionaries can also be helpful to you in identifying keywords, including *A Dictionary of Communication and Media Studies* (Watson & Hill, 1997) and *Webster's New World Dictionary of Media and Communications* (Weiner, 1996).

Subject-specific encyclopedias also provide useful introductions to various topics. You might, for example, consider the *International Encyclopedia of Communications* or, for more general treatment of the social sciences, the *International Encyclopedia of the Social Sciences*.

Once you have identified some useful keywords, you can begin your search for scholarly research in earnest. Probably the most important references sources will be indexes and abstracts of research published in scholarly journals.

INDEXES AND ABSTRACTS

The indexes and abstracts to scholarly journals are organized on the same principle as the *Readers' Guide to Periodical Literature*. The key difference is that the *Readers' Guide* provides an index of popular magazines and periodicals, whereas the scholarly indexes and abstracts cover the scholarly research journals.

Because you are interested in finding out information about communication research, you should first consult three databases designed specifically for communication studies:

- *ComIndex,* the online database maintained by CIOS (Communication Institute for Online Scholarship—www.cios.org). This reference database provides an index of more than 50 communication journals. Some services are available to the public, whereas others are available through membership only. Check to see if your institution's library provides you with member access.
- *Communication Abstracts,* a bimonthly publication that abstracts articles from more than 200 communication-related journals, available in hard-copy version.
- *CommSearch,* a CD database distributed by the National Communication Association that contains title, author, and keyword indexes for 26 communication-related journals through 1996, in addition to full text and abstracts for some other journals through 1997.

Because communication research is an interdisciplinary enterprise, you can often find additional relevant communication research in any number of additional indexes and abstracts. Here's a partial list of some of the most useful:

- *ABI/INFORM,* an index and abstracts of journals in business and management
- *Bibliographic Index,* an index of bibliographies on a wide range of topics
- *Business Periodical Index,* index and abstracts of business-related journals
- *CIS/Index,* an index and abstracts of congressional publications
- *Dissertation Abstracts,* an index and abstracts of all unpublished dissertations in all fields
- *Education Index,* an index and abstracts of journals broadly related to education
- *ERIC* (Educational Resources Information Center), an index of education-related resources, especially helpful in locating unpublished sources such as convention papers
- *Humanities Index,* an index and abstracts of journals in disciplines traditionally defined as "humanities"
- *International Indexes to Film & Television Periodicals,* an index of articles on film and television
- *Legal Resources Index,* an index and abstracts of law journals, of interest to scholars in legal communication
- *LEXIS,* an index of legal references in addition to full texts of laws and court cases of interest to scholars in legal communication
- *Linguistics and Language Behavior Abstracts,* an index and abstracts of journals in language and linguistics
- *Management Contents,* an index and abstracts of international publications in management and public administration
- *National Newspaper Index,* an index and abstracts of the *New York Times, Los Angeles Times, Wall Street Journal,* and *Christian Science Monitor*
- *Newspaper & Periodical Indexes,* indexes and abstracts of newspapers, broadcast news, and periodicals
- *NEXIS,* an index of full-text articles from newspapers, wire services, and other sources
- *Nursing and Applied Health Index,* an index and abstracts of health-related journals of relevance to scholars interested in health communication
- *Psychological Abstracts,* which provides an index and abstracts of psychology sources, including many communication journals
- *Social Science Citation Index,* an index of references used in articles from more than 1,400 social science journals
- *Social Science Index,* an index of more than 400 journals throughout the social sciences, including many communication journals
- *Sociological Abstracts,* an index and abstracts of sociology sources, including many communication journals

- *Transcript/Video Index,* an index and abstracts of more than 20,000 transcripts of broadcasting information and news programs available for purchase through Journal Graphics
- *UnCover,* an online searchable index of tables of contents of 15,000 periodicals in major libraries

Most of these are available online, as well as through hard-copy versions.

USING THE STACKS

For serious research, you must learn to use the stacks, where most of the library's books and journals are stored. In this section, we'll give you some information about finding books and journals in the stacks.

The Card Catalog

Your library's card catalog is the main reference system for finding out where books and journals are stored. Each book or journal is described with respect to author, title, and subject matter.

Most academic libraries have their card catalog available electronically. Somewhere on the screen for a given reference, you will see a call number, a number that helps you to locate the reference physically in the stacks.

Library of Congress Classifications

In most libraries, books and journals are arranged and numbered according to a subject matter classification developed by the Library of Congress. (Some follow the Dewey decimal system.) The following is a selected list of Library of Congress categories:

A	GENERAL WORKS	
B	PHILOSOPHY, PSYCHOLOGY, RELIGION	
	B–BD	Philosophy
	BF	Psychology
	BH	Aesthetics
	BJ	Ethics
C	HISTORY—AUXILIARY SCIENCES	
D	HISTORY (except America)	
E–F	HISTORY (America)	
G	GEOGRAPHY—ANTHROPOLOGY	
	GN	Anthropology
H	SOCIAL SCIENCES	
	HA	Statistics
	HB–HJ	Economics and business
	HM–HX	Sociology and social psychology

J	POLITICAL SCIENCE	
K	LAW	
L	EDUCATION	
M	MUSIC	
N	FINE ARTS	
P	LANGUAGE AND LITERATURE	
	PE	English language
	PG	Slavic language
	PJ–PM	Oriental language
	PN	Drama, oratory, journalism, speech communication
	PQ	Romance literature
	PR	English literature
	PS	American literature
	PT	Germanic literature
Q	SCIENCE	
R	MEDICINE	
	RT	Nursing
S	AGRICULTURE—PLANT AND ANIMAL INDUSTRY	
T	TECHNOLOGY	
U	MILITARY SCIENCE	
V	NAVAL SCIENCE	
Z	BIBLIOGRAPHY AND LIBRARY SCIENCE	

Your library will have a map that tells you where these classification categories can be located.

AFTER THE STACKS

Your search for relevant reference material doesn't end once you pass through the check-out counter at your library. In fact, you've hardly begun! You need to read the references you have checked out, with an eye toward implementing a kind of purposive snowball sampling. Read a given book, book chapter, or journal article for additional keywords, researchers whose names keep popping up, and articles or books that appear to be referenced often. Then look these materials up. Repeat the process for those materials. And so on. You will know that your library search can stop when you reach the point of bibliographical saturation—when you keep stumbling into the same references you have already uncovered.

ADDITIONAL READINGS

Rubin, R. B., Rubin, A. M., & Piele, L. J. (2000). *Communication research: Strategies and sources* (5th ed.). Belmont, CA: Wadsworth. An excellent reference volume on how to locate references in communication research.

APPENDIX C

Research in Cyberspace

A new resource has become a powerful tool for social scientists. Soon it will be indispensable. Since the Internet, the World Wide Web, and other elements of the "information superhighway" are changing month by month, we'll simply cover some basics that may be useful for readers new to cyberspace. Our aim is to orient you sufficiently for you to ask for help effectively.

We'll talk about three topics: e-mail, gophers, and the World Wide Web.

E-MAIL

The most common use of the Internet at present is as a substitute for telephone and postal services. *E-mail* is a hybrid of these two modes. As with a letter, you type out your communication on a computer. Then, rather than putting the letter in an envelope and mailing it, you send it over telephone lines. The recipient receives your message with his or her computer.

You'll need a computer account at your school or through some other provider to use e-mail or any of the other systems described in this appendix. If you can't obtain an account through your school, you may want to consider joining a commercial online service such as America Online or MSN. While subscribers to the same commercial service can communicate easily with each other, they can also communicate with other portions of the Internet. We'll illustrate how this is done.

Once you're connected, you send messages comprising the following elements: a message (just like a note, memo, or letter), a title (a fairly short heading to identify the message, such as "Travel Plans"), and the address where you want to send the message. Your own address will be attached automatically to all sent messages.

Let's look a little more carefully at the address. Each e-mail address contains three basic elements:

name. @ ,server. ,type

The name is usually fairly straightforward. Names are assigned when an account is opened. Our names, respectively, are "leslie-baxter" and "babbie." (What are the odds on that?) Thus, an e-mail address is typically a name at (@) a location.

The type of account is also fairly simple. A series of abbreviations indicate the type of installation providing access to the Net. Some common types used in the United States are these:

edu	an educational institution
com	a commercial provider such as a company
org	a nonprofit organization, such as NPR
gov	a government office

In place of these abbreviations, the address may be an international country abbreviation, such as *cn* for China, *uk* for United Kingdom, and *de* for Germany.

The middle portion of the address (the server, the local computer) varies greatly. For example, it's simply "aol" for America Online. An example of an America Online address might be

JDoe@aol.com

Some educational servers are pretty straightforward. For example, our respective addresses are: leslie-baxter@uiowa.edu (at the University of Iowa) and babbie@chapman.edu (at Chapman University). Some universities have more than one server (computer) handling e-mail, so a person's address may be slightly more complex than this example.

In addition to originating messages, most e-mail systems make it easy for you to reply to messages. When you do so, the computer automatically addresses your reply to the original sender and attaches your address as well. It may also automatically reprint the original message as a part of your reply, often identifying lines with "." marks.

Including the original message (or part of it) can be used to remind the original sender of what you're responding to. Sometimes, you can break up the original message, interspersing your responses to the different parts of it. Here's a brief example:

Original Message:
Pat:
Let's go to the movies Saturday night.
I'd prefer to go in your car if that's okay.
Let me know by Thursday.
Cheers, Jan

Automatic Reply Format:
.Pat:
.Let's go to the movies Saturday night.
.I'd prefer to go in your car if that's okay.
.Let me know by Thursday.
.Cheers, Jan

Edited Reply:
Jan:
.Let's go to the movies Saturday night.
Sure, that's great. What do you want to see?
.I'd prefer to go in your car if that's okay.
My car's in the shop. How about yours?
See ya, Pat

Since it's possible to reply to a reply, you may find yourself engaged in an unfolding conversation.

When replying to a message, it's generally a bad idea to resend the entire message you received, unless you have a reason to retain the entire chronology of message exchanges. Just include those portions (if any) that are useful in framing your response.

MAILING LISTS

In addition to person-to-person e-mail, you may find some of the thousands of electronic conversations useful. The most common of these go by the term *listserv*, though *listproc* and *majordomo* are major, alternate systems. There are several such mailing lists appropriate to social scientific research methods in general, as well as the various subspecialties within the communication studies discipline.

For example, METHODS is a mailing list created for people teaching social scientific research methods, though anyone can join. About 600 people from around the world belong as we write these words. Any of the subscribers can send a message to the list, and that message will appear in the mailboxes of all the other subscribers. If another subscriber wants to reply, that reply will also appear in the mailboxes of all subscribers. As a conse-

quence, methods instructors have been able to discuss common problems and share solutions.

To subscribe to a mailing list, you send an e-mail message to the computer that manages that list. In the case of METHODS, you do the following:

1. Send a message to listserv@unm.edu.
2. Do not put a title on the message.
3. Send this message: subscribe methods Jane Doe (but substitute your own name for "Jane Doe").

You can send messages to methods@unm.edu after you've subscribed.

This is a standard format, although there are some variations and exceptions. To subscribe to any of the lists that follow, send a subscribing message by substituting "listserv" for the name of the list and use the name of the list in the body of the message, as illustrated in the case of METHODS. Then, you can send messages to the list using the given address.

There's no charge for subscribing to mailing lists. You don't have to participate in the conversations; you can just listen if you want. And you can unsubscribe any time. Here are some other mailing lists you might find interesting. (Please note that addresses have no breaks or spaces, even though here they might have line breaks.)

CONTENT@gsu.edu
Content analysis

CRTNET@LISTS.PSU.EDU
Communication research and theory

FAMLYSCI@lsv.uky.edu
Family communication

por@gibbs.oit.unc.edu
Public opinion research

RhetNet@mizzoul.missouri.edu
Rhetoric

social-theory@mailbase.ac.uk
Social theory

qualrs-l@uga.cc.uga.edu
Qualitative research

qual-software@mailbase.ac.uk
Software for qualitative social research

qualnet@chimera.sph.umn.edu
Qualitative research discussion

sos-data@unc.edu
Social science data discussion

These are only a few of the mailing lists of interest to communication researchers. Moreover, the number increases daily. In the spirit of a snowball sample, however, you'll find that subscribing to one list will bring you references to others, and if you subscribe to them as well, they'll bring further references. Without a doubt, there is more useful information available to you than you'll be able to collect and read.

GOPHERS

Gophers, which execute *file transfer protocols (ftps),* allow you to download entire computer files. Programs such as Turbogopher or MacIP are designed to connect you to computers around the world. All you need (other than an ftp program) is the address ("host name") of an available computer.

Since this is a little more involved than sending e-mail or subscribing to a mailing list, you should get local assistance in connecting to a gopher site. Once you're connected with the distant computer, you'll find yourself looking at a directory of files available there. Your job is to select a file at the distant computer and copy it to your own. (You'll probably have to click a button labeled "Copy.")

The files available on computers around the world include text documents, computer games, check record programs, data analysis programs, and so forth. You won't be able to appreciate the volume and variety of materials available to you except by checking them out for yourself.

THE WORLD WIDE WEB

Perhaps the most exciting aspect of the Net today is the World Wide Web. It's something like the network of ftp sites—sources of information scattered around the world —but you can access information much more easily, and the presentation format is much fancier.

To access the Web, you'll need a "browser" such as Netscape Navigator or MSN Explorer. The commercial online services such as American Online provide their own web browser. Then you can enter Web URL (Uniform Resource Locator) addresses (typically beginning "http://"), and go visit. As you'll discover, nearly every Web location will contain buttons you can click, which will take you to other, related locations.

If you don't know what Internet resources are available on a given topic, you can search the Internet using a search engine. We list some of the most popular search engines below. We also provide you with some meta-search engines—search engines that search other search engines. The world of search engines changes frequently. Search Engine Watch (www.searchenginewatch.com) can help you keep track of these changes.

Here are just a few Web locations to get you started. Please be aware that these addresses may change. Happy surfing!

Communication—General Resources

American Communication Association directory of online resources
www.uark.edu/~aca/acastudiescenter.html
Communication, Cultural, Media Studies InfoBase
www.ccms-infobase.com
Communication Institute for Online Research (CIOS)
http://cios.org
Directory of Professional Communication Associations
http://ssca.net/resources/acadorg.htm
University of Iowa Libraries—Resources in Communication
www.arcade.uiowa.edu/gw/comm

Communication—Selected Subspecialty Resources

Center for Nonverbal Studies: The Nonverbal Dictionary
http://members.aol.com/nonverbal2/index.htm
Conflict Resolution
www.nova.edu/shss/DCAR/crwww.html
Family Communication
www.FamilyScholar.com
Freedom of Speech
www.freedomforum.org
Gender and Language
http://aitkenj.www7.50megs.com
Health Communication
www.roguecom.com/HCIG/linksindexes.html
Interpersonal and Small Group Communication Resources
http://empathy.colstate.edu/web_based_resources.htm
Language and Social Interaction
www.ohiou.edu/~scalsi
Mass Communication and Journalism Links
http://bailiwick.lib.uiowa.edu/journalism
www.mediastudies.rutgers.edu
www.sosu.edu/al/ct/ssca/mcwebresources.html

Organizational Communication
www.americancomm.org/~aca/studies/orgcomm.html

Relationship Communication
www.inpr.org
www.isspr.org

Rhetoric and Public Address
www.americanrhetoric.com/speechbank.htm
www.douglass.speech.nwu.edu
www.tulane.edu/~sscarpa/other.html

General Online References

APA Style Essentials
www.vanguard.edu/psychology/apa.html
Bartlett's Familiar Quotations, by H. Bartlett
www.bartleby.com/100
The Elements of Style, by W. Strunk
www.bartleby.com/141/index.htm
MSN Encarta online encyclopedia
www.encarta.msn.com
Foreign languages dictionaries
www.foreignword.com
INFOMINE (more than 11,000 links to scholarly Web resources)
http://lib-www.ucr.edu
Merriam WWWebster Dictionary
www.m-w.com/netdict.htm
U.S. Census Bureau's *Statistical Abstract of the United States*
www.census.gov/stat_abstract
U.S. Library of Congress Online Library
www.loc.gov

Popular Search and Metasearch Engines

AltaVista
www.altavista.com
Dogpile (metasearch engine)
www.dogpile.com
Excite
www.excite.com
Google
www.google.com
Hotbot
http://hotbot.lycos.com
Go.com
www.go.com
Inference Find (metasearch engine)
www.infind.com

Lycos
www.lycos.com
Northern Light (metasearch engine)
www.northernlight.com
Yahoo
www.yahoo.com

Research Applications and Studies

Be a participant in online research
www.socialpsychology.org/expts.htm#u
Jigsaw Classroom (breaking down stereotypes)
www.jigsaw.org
JoeChemo (persuasion directed at smoking cessation)
www.JoeChemo.org
Prisoner's Dilemma
www.miskatonic.org/pd.html
Stanford Prison Experiment
www.prisonexp.org

Research Institutes and Research Laboratories

Center for Sex Research
www.csun.edu/~sr2022/index.html
Institute for Social Research, University of Michigan
www.isr.umich.edu
Princeton University Survey Research Center
www.princeton.edu/~abelson/index.html
Social Research Laboratories
www.socialpsychology.org/labgroup.htm
UC–Berkeley Survey Research Center
http://srcweb.berkeley.edu:4229

Searchable Online Databases of Social Scientific Data

Harvard–MIT Data Center
http://data.fas.harvard.edu
Inter-University Consortium for Political & Social Research
www.icpsr.umich.edu
National Opinion Research Center (GSS)
www.norc.uchicago.edu
NCA/Roper Poll "How Americans Communicate"
www.natcom.org/research/Poll/how_americans_communicate.htm
Princeton University Data Library
www.princeton.edu/~data
Roper Center for Public Opinion Research
www.ropercenter.uconn.edu

Social Scientific Research Methods

ACA's megasite of communication research methods
www.uark.edu/~aca/studies/researchmethods.html

Content analysis resources
www.gsu.edu/~wwwcom/content.html

Social Psychology Network, megasite of social psychological methods
www.socialpsychology.org/methods.htm#methodology

Megasite of statistics resources
www.execpc.com/~helberg/statistics.html

Qualitative research resources on the Internet
www.nova.edu/ssss/QR/qualres.html

Random Numbers Generator
www.randomizer.org

Research ethics
www.socialpsychology.org/methods.htm#generalethics

Software Information Bank
www.gamma.rug.nl/query.html

Standardized measures of individual variables, Buros Institute of Mental Measurements
www.unl.edu/buros

Standardized measures—still more, Eric Clearinghouse on Assessment and Evaluation
www.ericae.net

Statistical calculations
http://members.aol.com/john71/javastat.html

USC's Ethnographic Lab
www.usc.edu/dept/elab/welcome

University of Surrey's list of social research methods
www.soc.surrey.ac.uk/sru/sru.htm

This list is not even the tip of the iceberg. If we could give you a complete listing of the web sites relevant to communication research, it would be out of date by the time our manuscript reached our publisher, let alone by the time it reached your hands. To give you a sense of how fast the Web is expanding, we'd like you to recall a time when you worked on a project that absolutely consumed you for days on end. You hardly thought about anything else while you were completing the project. Well, tonight, tens of thousands of individuals around the world are working with that level of passion on their web sites, and countless others are working at a less frantic pace. And they're doing it just for you.

Appendix D

A Sample Research Report/Proposal in APA Style

In this appendix, we provide you with portions of a hypothetical research report/proposal in order to describe some of the details of layout and organization that characterize the APA style. This sample is not complete, but it gives you a basic skeleton for organizing and formatting your own written work. Obviously, a research proposal will not have Results and Discussion sections, nor will it have any tables or figures in which findings are presented. Further, the Abstract will not include findings and implications. Last, the Method section will include subheadings for Schedule and Budget. In general terms, a report/proposal is typed on $8\frac{1}{2}'' \times 11''$ paper with at least 1" margins at the top, bottom, left, and right of every page. Double-spacing throughout is the standard. A serif typeface is preferred (e.g., 12-point Times Roman or 12-point Courier).

THE TITLE PAGE

This is a sample title page from a research proposal or research report. It contains four important pieces of information. First is the page header, which consists of the first two or three words from the paper's title and appears in the upper-right-hand corner above or five spaces to the left of the page number. A page header is a safety precaution should manuscript pages become separated. Second, the running head is an abbreviated title used for published articles; all papers written in APA are required to submit a running head. Running heads do not exceed 50 characters (including punctuation and spaces), and they appear flush left at the top of the title page. Third, the title of the proposal or report is centered in the upper half of the paper and double-spaced should it exceed one line (generally, titles are 10–12 words in length). Fourth, the byline (and institutional affiliation) of the author(s) are centered and double-spaced after the title. It is important to use upper and lower cases exactly as they have been illustrated in this sample title page.

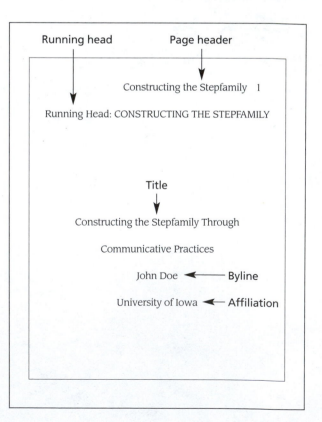

Running head · Page header

Constructing the Stepfamily   1

Running Head: CONSTRUCTING THE STEPFAMILY

Title

Constructing the Stepfamily Through

Communicative Practices

John Doe ← Byline

University of Iowa ← Affiliation

THE ABSTRACT PAGE

The second page of a manuscript is a double-spaced abstract of the (proposed) study. In Chapter 2, we discussed the content of a typical abstract for a research report. When you write an abstract of a proposal for research, your abstract should contain information about the study's purpose and proposed participants and methods. We draw your attention to some matters of presentation. First, the word "Abstract" is centered and typed in upper and lower case letters. Second, paragraphing is in block format (i.e., no indentation for paragraphs). Third, all numbers are written as arabic numerals unless they begin a sentence. Last, an abstract does not exceed 120 words.

Constructing the Stepfamily   2

Abstract

The communicative practices through which stepfamily members construct their identity as a stepfamily were investigated. Interviews and surveys were completed with the parents and stepchildren from 50 stepfamilies. The results indicated that stepfamily members constructed their stepfamily identity in several ways. The findings challenge existing views of stepfamily life.

THE INTRODUCTION

The double-spaced body of a report or proposal begins on page 3 of the manuscript. All paragraphs are indented $1/2''$ in their first lines. The title appears centered on the top of this page. The introduction to the (proposed) study begins on this page. There is no "Introduction" header. An introduction to a research report is very similar to how a proposed study is introduced. The introduction in a proposed study should introduce the problem area, state the purpose of the proposed study, review relevant research literature as part of an argument or rationale for the study, and formally present research questions or hypotheses that flow logically from the review of literature.

Constructing the Stepfamily   3

Constructing Stepfamilies
Through Communicative Practices

The stepfamily is arguably the fastest growing family form in the U.S. (Jones, 2002; Smith, 2001). It is also widely recognized as a highly unstable family system (Broadee, 2003). Thus, it is important to understand how stepfamilies function. The purpose of the current study was to investigate the communicative practices through which stepfamily members construct their family identity as a stepfamily. . . .

METHOD

A Method section does not begin on a new page and is paged continuously with the Introduction. It is centered in upper and lower case letters. Both a research report and a proposal for a study will have a Method section. In both, this section will include information about participants, materials and measures, and procedures (including methods of data analysis). However, the research proposal will generally have two additional subheadings: Schedule (or Timeline) and Budget. These subheadings are flush left in upper and lower case letters; they can be italicized or underlined. Whereas the past tense is used in research reports, a proposal discusses what will happen.

Constructing the Stepfamily   10

Method

Participants

Participants were the parents and children from 50 stepfamilies. The mean age of parents was 49.2 years, and the mean age of children was 15.4 years. Their stepfamilies had been formed a mean of 5.4 years at the time of data collection. . . .

Materials

The interviewer protocol used in the study consisted of 15 questions exploring issues. . . .

Procedure

Data were gathered in participant homes. . . .

RESULTS

A Results section does not automatically begin on a new page. The header is centered in upper and lower case letters. In Chapter 2, we discussed what appears in this section of a research report. If quantitative results are summarized in a table, it is referred to in the text and appended at the end of the paper (see the proper order below). For example, "Table 1 presents the mean scores for stepfamily parent and child perceptions of the intensity of their feelings of stepfamily identity." If findings are presented in a figure, the figure is referred to in the text, and it is presented at the end of the paper (see the proper order below).

Constructing the Stepfamily   13

Results

Five kinds of communication practices were identified through which stepfamily members constructed their identity as a stepfamily. Stepfamily parents and children differed in their reported use of these practices. Further, these practices correlated differently with the perceived strength of stepfamily identity for parents and for children. Results are organized by research question/ hypothesis. . . .

DISCUSSION

A Discussion section does not automatically begin on a new page. Its heading is centered in upper and lower case letters. In Chapter 2, we discussed the contents of a typical Discussion section. Obviously, a research proposal will not contain this section.

Constructing the Stepfamily   21

Discussion

The findings suggest that the construction of

stepfamily identity is a fluid process accomplished

through a variety of types of communicative

practices. Further, stepfamily parents and children

do not equally engage in these practices. . . .

This study has three important limitations. First,

interviews and surveys provide limited insight into

the details of enacted communication. . . .

In spite of these limitations, the findings have

interesting implications for practitioners who . . .

REFERENCES

The References section begins on a new page. The header is centered in upper and lower case letters. In Appendix E, we discuss the details of how to cite various kinds of sources. Here, we'll make some general comments about how citations are organized overall. Double-spacing is used throughout. Each entry is characterized by a hanging indent in which the first line is flush left and subsequent lines are indented. Entries are ordered alphabetically. One-author entries by the same author are arranged by year, the earliest first. For example, "Jones, A. B. (1998)" precedes "Jones, A. B. (1999)." One-author entries precede multiple-author entries. For example, "Jones, A. B. (1998)" precedes "Jones, A. B., & March, B. L. (1995)." References with the same first author and different second authors are ordered alphabetically by the surname of the second author. For example, "Jones, A. B., & March, B. L. (1995)" precedes "Jones, A. B., & Zoar, L. T. (2002)." If authorship and date of publication are the same for multiple citations, order them alphabetically according to the first substantive word of the title, and label each citation with an "a," "b," and so on in the text and in the References. For example, "Jones, A. B. (2002a). Differences . . . " precedes "Jones, A. B. (2002b). Factors. . . ."

Constructing the Stepfamily   25

References

Anderson, J. L., & Bradley, M. H. (2002). The

stepfamily in crisis. *Journal of Family Forms, 3,*

56–75.

Brown, J. T. (2000). *Intact families versus stepfamilies:*

The wrong comparison. New York: Family.

Clyde, M. J. (1999). Whose family is it anyway? In

J. L. Jones & P. L. Petry (Eds.), *Stepfamilies in*

transition (pp. 345–367). San Francisco:

Alternative.

OPTIONAL SECTIONS: APPENDIXES, AUTHOR NOTES, FOOTNOTES, TABLES, FIGURES

These are optional sections in a research report or proposal. Because tables generally present research findings, they are not relevant to a research proposal. Figures could be used to present theoretical models or visual charts and graphs of findings; if figures take the latter form, they obviously are not relevant to a research proposal. Pay attention to the details in how these various sections are laid out.

Constructing the Stepfamily   29

Author Note

Everything in this sample is hypothetical for purposes of illustrating some important features of the APA style. An actual author's note can contain a variety of information, including the history of the manuscript (e.g., "A prior version of this paper was presented at the 2002 conference of the NCA.") or an expression of thanks to people who assisted in the study (e.g., "The author would like to express her thanks to Ms. Em for her assistance in data collection.").

Constructing the Stepfamily   28

Appendix A

This report had no need for an appendix. If one had been necessary, it would have appeared here, following References. The header is centered in upper and lower case letters. The text of the paper would have referenced the appendix, as in "Appendix A provides a complete copy of the interview protocol questions."

Constructing the Stepfamily   30

Footnotes

[1] The sample you read didn't have any footnotes appearing in the text. If footnotes had been used, they would appear here, after the Author Note, on a separate page.

Constructing the Stepfamily   31

Table 1

Mean Correlations Between Number of Reported
Internal and External Communication Practices
and Stepfamily Identity for Stepfamily
Parents and Children

Stepfamily Member	Internal Practices	External Practices
Parents	.43*	.22
Children	.20	.56*

*p < .05.

Constructing the Stepfamily   33

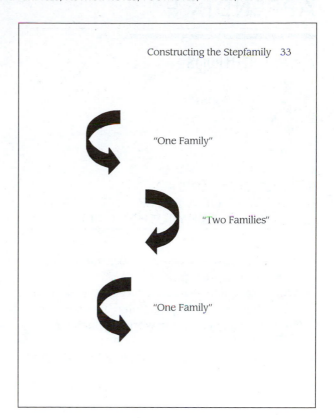

"One Family"

"Two Families"

"One Family"

Constructing the Stepfamily   32

Figure Caption

Figure 1.   A cyclical model of stepfamily identity
construction.

APPENDIX E

APA Citations

1. **As Smith (2002) explains, "We use reasoning in everyday life" (p. 24).**
   When you quote someone's words, you need to place those words in quotation marks and indicate the page(s) from the work in which the words appeared.

2. **"We use reasoning in everyday life" (Smith, 2002, p. 24).**
   This illustrates a different way in which you might include a quotation.

3. **Smith (2002) notes that reasoning is an everyday occurrence.**
   Smith was not quoted directly; thus, no quotation marks are necessary.

4. For quotations of more than 40 words, use the block format. This means that you quote the material exactly as it appears in the original source but indent it instead of using quotation marks. When you have finished with the block quotation, return to your authorial voice and comment about the quotation in some way:
   Smith (2002) argues that
   > **We use reasoning in everyday life. When you get up in the morning, you look outside to see if it's cloudy or not. Based on the sky, you infer the probability of rain and thus whether you should take an umbrella. (pp. 24–25)**
   Smith's point is well-taken. Scientific reasoning is thus nothing more than. . . .

5. **Smith (2002, pp. 24–25) presents a cogent example of how everyday our reasoning is. He describes how we reason in the morning whether or not to take an umbrella with us. He indicates that we look at the sky to find evidence of clouds. Based on our observations, we make an inference about the probability of rain.**

Notice that this citation includes page numbers even though we are not quoting Smith directly. When an author wants to provide a detailed paraphrase of someone's argument, rather than provide a general gloss of it, citing the exact pages relevant to the detailed paraphrase is a good practice.

6. **Smith, Black, and Blue (2002) found three important reasoning flaws in couple conflicts. Smith and his colleagues concluded their study by arguing for changes in training programs designed to help couples with their conflicts.**

   A number of scholars have argued that conflict training emphasizes emotional and relational issues to the relative neglect of reasoning issues (e.g., Smith et al., 2002; Zigler & Smith, 1998).
   This example is designed to illustrate several citation points. The first time a source is cited, you generally need to list all of the authors' surnames. If you refer to this same source subsequently, you only need to mention the first author by name, adding "et al." to replace the names of the other authors. If a subsequent citation appears in the same paragraph as the initial citation, you do not need the date of the reference. However, if subsequent citations appear in different paragraphs, you need to include a date. When multiple citations appear in parentheses, they are organized alphabetically using the same logic of ordering as we described in Appendix D for the References section of a report/proposal.

SAMPLE CITATIONS
IN THE REFERENCES SECTION
(ALL EXAMPLES HYPOTHETICAL)

1. Book:
   Smith, A. E. (2002). *Everyday and scientific reasoning.* New York: Hypothetical.

2. Journal article:
   Smith, A. E. (2002). Flaws in everyday reasoning. *Journal of Everyday Life, 16,* 345–378.

3. Book chapter:
   Smith, A. E. (2002). Fallacies in everyday reasoning: A review and commentary. In B. J. Jones & J. W. Pough (Eds.), *Handbook of reasoning* (pp. 56–79). Chicago: Windy City.

4. Magazine article:
   Smith, A. E. (2002, March). Reason isn't always reasonable. *Reading over Coffee,* pp. 67–70.

5. Internet source:
   Smith, A. E. (2002). *Flaws in reasoning in electronic chatrooms.* Retrieved May 29, 2002, from the Smith Reasoning Resources Web site: http://www.smithr&r.com/papers/flawchat.html.

6. Newspaper article:
   Smith, A. E. (2002, April 1). City Council displays common reasoning fallacies [Letter to the editor]. *Local Daily Newspaper,* p. A10.

7. An article with multiple authors:
   Smith, A. E., & Friendly, D. A. (2002). A small-space analysis of everyday reasoning forms. *Journal of Everyday Mathematics and Reasoning, 56,* 45–60.

APPENDIX F

Estimated Sampling Error

How to use this table: Find the intersection between the sample size and the approximate percentage distribution of the binomial in the sample. The number appearing at this intersection represents the estimated sampling error, at the 95-percent confidence level, expressed in percentage points (plus or minus).

Example: In a sample of 400 respondents, 60 percent answer yes and 40 percent answer no. The sampling error is estimated at plus or minus 4.9 percentage points. The confidence interval, then, is between 55.1 percent and 64.9 percent. We would estimate (95-percent confidence) that the proportion of the total population who would say yes is somewhere within that interval.

Sample Size	Binomial Percentage Distribution				
	50/50	60/40	70/30	80/20	90/10
100	10.0	9.8	9.2	8.0	6.0
200	7.1	6.9	6.5	5.7	4.2
300	5.8	5.7	5.3	4.6	3.5
400	5.0	4.9	4.6	4.0	3.0
500	4.5	4.4	4.1	3.6	2.7
600	4.1	4.0	3.7	3.3	2.4
700	3.8	3.7	3.5	3.0	2.3
800	3.5	3.5	3.2	2.8	2.1
900	3.3	3.3	3.1	2.7	2.0
1000	3.2	3.1	2.9	2.5	1.9
1100	3.0	3.0	2.8	2.4	1.8
1200	2.9	2.8	2.6	2.3	1.7
1300	2.8	2.7	2.5	2.2	1.7
1400	2.7	2.6	2.4	2.1	1.6
1500	2.6	2.5	2.4	2.1	1.5
1600	2.5	2.4	2.3	2.0	1.5
1700	2.4	2.4	2.2	1.9	1.5
1800	2.4	2.3	2.2	1.9	1.4
1900	2.3	2.2	2.1	1.8	1.4
2000	2.2	2.2	2.0	1.8	1.3

APPENDIX G

Random Numbers

10480	15011	01536	02011	81647	91646	69179	14194	62590	36207	20969	99570	91291	90700
22368	46573	25595	85393	30995	89198	27982	53402	93965	34095	52666	19174	39615	99505
24130	48360	22527	97265	76393	64809	15179	24830	49340	32081	30680	19655	63348	58629
42167	93093	06243	61680	07856	16376	39440	53537	71341	57004	00849	74917	97758	16379
37570	39975	81837	16656	06121	91782	60468	81305	49684	60672	14110	06927	01263	54613
77921	06907	11008	42751	27756	53498	18602	70659	90655	15053	21916	81825	44394	42880
99562	72905	56420	69994	98872	31016	71194	18738	44013	48840	63213	21069	10634	12952
96301	91977	05463	07972	18876	20922	94595	56869	69014	60045	18425	84903	42508	32307
89579	14342	63661	10281	17453	18103	57740	84378	25331	12566	58678	44947	05585	56941
85475	36857	53342	53988	53060	59533	38867	62300	08158	17983	16439	11458	18593	64952
28918	69578	88231	33276	70997	79936	56865	05859	90106	31595	01547	85590	91610	78188
63553	40961	48235	03427	49626	69445	18663	72695	52180	20847	12234	90511	33703	90322
09429	93969	52636	92737	88974	33488	36320	17617	30015	08272	84115	27156	30613	74952
10365	61129	87529	85689	48237	52267	67689	93394	01511	26358	85104	20285	29975	89868
07119	97336	71048	08178	77233	13916	47564	81056	97735	85977	29372	74461	28551	90707
51085	12765	51821	51259	77452	16308	60756	92144	49442	53900	70960	63990	75601	40719
02368	21382	52404	60268	89368	19885	55322	44819	01188	65255	64835	44919	05944	55157
01011	54092	33362	94904	31273	04146	18594	29852	71585	85030	51132	01915	92747	64951
52162	53916	46369	58586	23216	14513	83149	98736	23495	64350	94738	17752	35156	35749
07056	97628	33787	09998	42698	06691	76988	13602	51851	46104	88916	19509	25625	58104
48663	91245	85828	14346	09172	30168	90229	04734	59193	22178	30421	61666	99904	32812
54164	58492	22421	74103	47070	25306	76468	26384	58151	06646	21524	15227	96909	44592
32639	32363	05597	24200	13363	38005	94342	28728	35806	06912	17012	64161	18296	22851
29334	27001	87637	87308	58731	00256	45834	15398	46557	41135	10367	07684	36188	18510
02488	33062	28834	07351	19731	92420	60952	61280	50001	67658	32586	86679	50720	94953
81525	72295	04839	96423	24878	82651	66566	14778	76797	14780	13300	87074	79666	95725
29676	20591	68086	26432	46901	20849	89768	81536	86645	12659	92259	57102	80428	25280
00742	57392	39064	66432	84673	40027	32832	61362	98947	96067	64760	64584	96096	98253
05366	04213	25669	26422	44407	44048	37397	63904	45766	66134	75470	66520	34693	90449
91921	26418	64117	94305	26766	25940	39972	22209	71500	64568	91402	42416	07844	69618
00582	04711	87917	77341	42206	35126	74087	99547	81817	42607	43808	76655	62028	76630
00725	69884	62797	56170	86324	88072	76222	36086	84637	93161	76038	65855	77919	88006
69011	65795	95876	55293	18988	27354	26575	08625	40801	59920	29841	80150	12777	48501
25976	57948	29888	88604	67917	48708	18912	82271	65424	69774	33611	54262	85963	03547
09763	83473	73577	12908	30883	18317	28290	35797	05998	41688	34952	37888	38917	88050
91567	42595	27958	30134	04024	86385	29880	99730	55536	84855	29080	09250	79656	73211
17955	56349	90999	49127	20044	59931	06115	20542	18059	02008	73708	83517	36103	42791
46503	18584	18845	49618	02304	51038	20655	58727	28168	15475	56942	53389	20562	87338
92157	89634	94824	78171	84610	82834	09922	25417	44137	48413	25555	21246	35509	20468
14577	62765	35605	81263	39667	47358	56873	56307	61607	49518	89656	20103	77490	18062
98427	07523	33362	64270	01638	92477	66969	98420	04880	45585	46565	04102	46880	45709
34914	63976	88720	82765	34476	17032	87589	40836	32427	70002	70663	88863	77775	69348
70060	28277	39475	46473	23219	53416	94970	25832	69975	94884	19661	72828	00102	66794
53976	54914	06990	67245	68350	82948	11398	42878	80287	88267	47363	46634	06541	97809
76072	29515	40980	07391	58745	25774	22987	80059	39911	96189	41151	14222	60697	59583
90725	52210	83974	29992	65831	38857	50490	83765	55657	14361	31720	57375	56228	41546
64364	67412	33339	31926	14883	24413	59744	92351	97473	89286	35931	04110	23726	51900
08962	00358	31662	25388	61642	34072	81249	35648	56891	69352	48373	45578	78547	81788
95012	68379	93526	70765	10592	04542	76463	54328	02349	17247	28865	14777	62730	92277
15664	10493	20492	38391	91132	21999	59516	81652	27195	48223	46751	22923	32261	85653
16408	81899	04153	53381	79401	21438	83035	92350	36693	31238	59649	91754	72772	02338
18629	81953	05520	91962	04739	13092	97662	24822	94730	06496	35090	04822	86774	98289
73115	35101	47498	87637	99016	71060	88824	71013	18735	20286	23153	72924	35165	43040
57491	16703	23167	49323	45021	33132	12544	41035	80780	45393	44812	12515	98931	91202
30405	83946	23792	14422	15059	45799	22716	19792	09983	74353	68668	30429	70735	25499

16631	35006	85900	98275	32388	52390	16815	69298	82732	38480	73817	32523	41961	44437
96773	20206	42559	78985	05300	22164	24369	54224	35083	19687	11052	91491	60383	19746
38935	64202	14349	82674	66523	44133	00697	35552	35970	19124	63318	29686	03387	59846
31624	76384	17403	53363	44167	64486	64758	75366	76554	31601	12614	33072	60332	92325
78919	19474	23632	27889	47914	02584	37680	20801	72152	39339	34806	08930	85001	87820
03931	33309	57047	74211	63445	17361	62825	39908	05607	91284	68833	25570	38818	46920
74426	33278	43972	10119	89917	15665	52872	73823	73144	88662	88970	74492	51805	99378
09066	00903	20795	95452	92648	45454	09552	88815	16553	51125	79375	97596	16296	66092
42238	12426	87025	14267	20979	04508	64535	31355	86064	29472	47689	05974	52468	16834
16153	08002	26504	41744	81959	65642	74240	56302	00033	67107	77510	70625	28725	34191
21457	40742	29820	96783	29400	21840	15035	34537	33310	06116	95240	15957	16572	06004
21581	57802	02050	89728	17937	37621	47075	42080	97403	48626	68995	43805	33386	21597
55612	78095	83197	33732	05810	24813	86902	60397	16489	03264	88525	42786	05269	92532
44657	66999	99324	51281	84463	60563	79312	93454	68876	25471	93911	25650	12682	73572
91340	84979	46949	81973	37949	61023	43997	15263	80644	43942	89203	71795	99533	50501
91227	21199	31935	27022	84067	05462	35216	14486	29891	68607	41867	14951	91696	85065
50001	38140	19924	72163	09538	12151	06878	91903	18749	34405	56087	82790	70925
65390	05224	72958	28609	81406	39147	25549	48542	42627	45233	57202	94617	23772	07896
27504	96131	83944	41575	10573	08619	64482	73923	36152	05184	94142	25299	84387	34925
37169	94851	39117	89632	00959	16487	65536	49071	39782	17095	02330	74301	00275	48280
11508	70225	51111	38351	19444	66499	71945	05422	13442	78675	84081	66938	93654	59894
37449	30362	06694	54690	04052	53115	62757	95348	78662	11163	81651	50245	34971	52924
46515	70331	85922	38329	57015	15765	97161	17869	45349	61796	66345	81073	49106	79860
30986	81223	42416	58353	21532	30502	32305	86482	05174	07901	54339	58861	74818	46942
63798	64995	46583	09785	44160	78128	83991	42865	92520	83531	80377	35909	81250	54238
82486	84846	99254	67632	43218	50076	21361	64816	51202	88124	41870	52689	51275	83556
21885	32906	92431	09060	64297	51674	64126	62570	26123	05155	59194	52799	28225	85762
60336	98782	07408	53458	13564	59089	26445	29789	85205	41001	12535	12133	14645	23541
43937	46891	24010	25560	86355	33941	25786	54990	71899	15475	95434	98227	21824	19585
97656	63175	89303	16275	07100	92063	21942	18611	47348	20203	18534	03862	78095	50136
03299	01221	05418	38982	55758	92237	26759	86367	21216	98442	08303	56613	91511	75928
79626	06486	03574	17668	07785	76020	79924	25651	83325	88428	85076	72811	22717	50585
85636	68335	47539	03129	65651	11977	02510	26113	99447	68645	34327	15152	55230	93448
18039	14367	61337	06177	12143	46609	32989	74014	64708	00533	35398	58408	13261	47908
08362	15656	60627	36478	65648	16764	53412	09013	07832	41574	17639	82163	60859	75567
79556	29068	04142	16268	15387	12856	66227	38358	22478	73373	88732	09443	82558	05250
92608	82674	27072	32534	17075	27698	98204	63863	11951	34648	88022	56148	34925	57031
23982	25835	40055	67006	12293	02753	14827	23235	35071	99704	37543	11601	35503	85171
09915	96306	05908	97901	28395	14186	00821	80703	70426	75647	76310	88717	37890	40129
59037	33300	26695	62247	69927	76123	50842	43834	86654	70959	79725	93872	28117	19233
42488	78077	69882	61657	34136	79180	97526	43092	04098	73571	80799	76536	71255	64239
46764	86273	63003	93017	31204	36692	40202	35275	57306	55543	53203	18098	47625	88684
03237	45430	55417	63282	90816	17349	88298	90183	36600	78406	06216	95787	42579	90730
86591	81482	52667	61582	14972	90053	89534	76036	49199	43716	97548	04379	46370	28672
38534	01715	94964	87288	65680	43772	39560	12918	86537	62738	19636	51132	25739	56947

APPENDIX H

Constructing Indexes and Scales

INDEX CONSTRUCTION

Let's look at the several steps involved in the creation of an index: selecting possible items, examining their empirical relationships, combining some items into an index, and validating it. Because they're not all obvious, we've presented these steps in some detail. You should come away from this section able to create a composite measure that will fully support your subsequent analyses.

Item Selection

Face Validity The first step in creating an index is selecting items for a composite index, which is created to measure some variable. The first criterion for selecting items to be included in the index is *face validity* (or logical validity). The items should, on their face, be relevant to the variable you are seeking to measure. If, say, you are constructing a measure of communication competence, then each of your items must, on its face, relate to competence (or incompetence) in communicating.

Unidimensionality The methodological literature on conceptualization and measurement stresses the need for *unidimensionality* in scale and index construction: A composite measure should represent only one dimension. If you suspect that you have a multidimensional variable, then you will need to construct separate indexes or scales for each dimension.

General or Specific At the same time that you are working with a single dimension at a time, you should be aware of nuances that may exist within the general dimension you're attempting to measure. For example, communication competence may have a dimension of sensitivity to others. But this dimension could have many nuances to it—the extent to which a person listens to the other, the extent to which a person modifies his or her views to anticipate the reactions of the other, and so forth.

Variance In selecting items for an index, you must also be concerned with the amount of *variance* they provide. If a given item identified no one as a high scorer on your variable or everyone as a high scorer on your variable, that item would not be very useful in the construction of an index.

To guarantee variance, you have two options. First, you may select several items the responses to which divide people about equally in terms of the variable—for example, about half competent and half incompetent. Although no single response would justify the characterization of a person as very competent, a person who responded as competent on all items might be so characterized.

The second option is to select items differing in variance. One item might identify about half the respondents as competent while another might identify few of the respondents as competent. Note that this second option is necessary for scaling, and it is reasonable for index construction as well.

Bivariate Relationships among Items

The second step in index construction is to examine the *bivariate relationships* among the items being considered for inclusion. The basic issue involved is whether respondents' answers to one question—in a questionnaire, for example—give us any clue as to how respondents will answer other questions.

If any two items both reflect degrees of the same thing, we should expect responses to the two items to generally correspond with one another. If this expectation is met, we say there is a *bivariate relationship* between the two items.

You should examine all the possible bivariate relationships among the several items being considered for inclusion in an index to determine the relative strengths of relationships among the several pairs of items. Percentage tables, correlation coefficients, or both may be used for this purpose. The primary criterion for evaluating these several relationships is the strength of the relationships.

Be wary of items that are not related to one another empirically: It's unlikely they measure the same variable. You should probably drop any item that is not related to several other items.

At the same time, a very strong relationship between two items presents a different problem. If two items are perfectly related to each other, then only one is necessary for inclusion in the index, since it completely conveys the indications provided by the other. (This problem will become even clearer in the next section.)

Here's an example to illustrate the testing of bivariate relationships in index construction. One of us once conducted a survey of medical school faculty members to find out about the consequences of a "scientific perspective" on the quality of patient care provided by physicians. The primary intent was to determine whether scientifically inclined doctors treated patients more impersonally than did other doctors.

The survey questionnaire offered several possible indicators of respondents' scientific perspectives. Of those, three items appeared to provide especially clear indications of whether the doctors were scientifically oriented:

1. As a medical school faculty member, in what capacity do you feel you can make your greatest teaching contribution: as a practicing physician or as a medical researcher?
2. As you continue to advance your own medical knowledge, would you say your ultimate medical interests lie primarily in the direction of total patient management or the understanding of basic mechanisms? [The purpose of this item was to distinguish those who were mostly interested in overall patient care from those mostly interested in biological processes.]
3. In the field of therapeutic research, are you generally more interested in articles reporting evaluations of the effectiveness of various treatments or articles exploring the basic rationale underlying the treatments? [Similarly, the purpose of this item was to distinguish those more interested in articles dealing with patient care from those more interested in biological processes.] (Babbie, 1970, pp. 27–31)

For each of these items, we might conclude that those respondents who chose the second answer are more scientifically oriented than respondents who chose the first. Although this *comparative* conclusion is reasonable, we should not be misled into thinking that respondents who chose the second answer to a given item are scientists in any absolute sense. They are simply *more scientific* than those who chose the first answer to the item. To see this point more clearly, let's examine the distribution of responses to each item. From the first item—best teaching role—only about one-third of the respondents appeared scientifically oriented. (Approximately one-third said they could make their greatest teaching contribution as medical researchers.) In response to the second item—ultimate medical interests—approximately two-thirds chose the scientific answer, saying they were more interested in learning about basic mechanisms than learning about total patient management. In response to the third item—reading preferences—about 80 percent chose the scientific answer.

So these three questionnaire items cannot tell us how many "scientists" there are in the sample, for none of them is related to a set of criteria for what constitutes being a scientist in any absolute sense. Using the items for this purpose would present us with the problem of three quite different estimates of how many scientists there were in the sample.

However, these items do provide us with three independent indicators of respondents' *relative* inclinations toward science in medicine. Each item separates respondents into the *more* scientific and the *less* scientific. But each grouping of more or less scientific respondents will have a somewhat different membership from the others. Respondents who seem scientific in terms of one item will not seem scientific in terms of another. Nevertheless, to the extent that each item measures the same general dimension, we should find some correspondence among the several groupings. Respondents who appear scientific in terms of one item should be more likely to appear scientific in their response to another item than those who appeared nonscientific in their response to the first. We should find an association or correlation between the responses given to two items.

Figure H-1 shows the associations among the responses to the three items. Three bivariate tables are presented, showing the distribution of responses for each pair of items. Although each single item produces a different grouping of "scientific" and "nonscientific" respondents, we see in Figure H-1 that the responses given to each of the items correspond, to a degree, to the responses given to each of the other items.

An examination of the three bivariate relationships presented in Figure H-1 supports the suggestion that the three items all measure the same variable: *scientific orientations*. To see why this is so, let's begin by looking at the first bivariate relationship in the table. The table

FIGURE H-1   **Bivariate Relationships among Scientific Orientation Items**

shows that faculty who responded that "researcher" was their best teaching role were more likely to identify their ultimate medical interests as "basic mechanisms" than those who answered "physician." The data show that 87 percent of the "researchers" also chose the scientific response to the second item, as opposed to 51 percent of the "physicians." (*Note:* The fact that the "physicians" are about evenly split in their ultimate medical interests is irrelevant. It is only relevant that they are less scientific in their medical interests than the "researchers.") The strength of this relationship may be summarized as a 36-percentage-point difference.

The same general conclusion applies to the other bivariate relationships. The strength of the relationship between reading preferences and ultimate medical interests may be summarized as a 38-percentage-point difference, and the strength of the relationship between reading preferences and the two teaching roles as a 21-percentage-point difference.

Initially, the three items were selected on the basis of face validity—each appeared to give some indication of faculty members' orientations to science. By examining the bivariate relationship between the pairs of items, we found support for the expectation that they all measure basically the same thing. However, that support does not sufficiently justify including the items in a composite index.

Multivariate Relationships among Items

Before combining items in a single index, we need to examine the *multivariate relationships* among the several variables. Whereas a bivariate relationship deals with two variables at a time, a multivariate one uses more than two variables.

Recall that the primary purpose of index construction is to develop a method of classifying respondents in terms

Percentage Interested in Basic Mechanisms		Best Teaching Role	
		Physician	Researcher
Reading Preferences	Effectiveness	27% (66)	58% (12)
	Rationale	58% (219)	89% (130)

FIGURE H-2   **Trivariate Relationships among Scientific Orientation Items**

of some variable such as communication competence. An index of communication competence should identify those who are very competent, moderately competent, not very competent, and not at all competent (or moderately incompetent and very incompetent, respectively, in place of the last two categories). The several gradations of the variable are provided by the combination of responses given to the several items included in the index. Thus, the respondent who appeared competent on all items would be considered very competent overall.

For an index to provide meaningful gradations in this sense, each item must add something to the evaluation of each respondent. Recall from the preceding section that two items perfectly related to each other should not be included in the same index. If one item were included, the other would add nothing to our evaluation of respondents. The examination of multivariate relationships among the items is another way of eliminating deadwood. It also determines the overall power of the particular collection of items in measuring the variable under consideration.

The purposes of this multivariate examination will become clearer if we return to the earlier example of measuring scientific orientations among medical school faculty members. Figure H-2 presents the trivariate relationships among the three items. Presented somewhat differently from Figure H-1, Figure H-2 categorizes the sample respondents into four groups according to (1) their best teaching roles and (2) their reading preferences. The numbers in parentheses indicate the number of respondents in each group. (Thus, 66 of the faculty members who said they could best teach as physicians also said they preferred articles dealing with the effectiveness of treatments.) For each of the four groups, the percentage of those who say they are ultimately more interested in basic mechanisms has been presented. (Of the 66 faculty mentioned, 27 percent are primarily interested in basic mechanisms.)

The arrangement of the four groups is based on a previously drawn conclusion regarding scientific orien-

tations. The group in the upper-left corner of the table is presumably the least scientifically oriented, based on best teaching role and reading preferences. The group in the lower-right corner is presumably the most scientifically oriented in terms of those items.

Recall that expressing a primary interest in basic mechanisms was also taken as an indication of scientific orientations. As we should expect, then, those in the lower-right corner are the most likely to give this response (89 percent), and those in the upper-left corner are the least likely (27 percent). The respondents who gave mixed responses in terms of teaching roles and reading preferences have an intermediate rank in their concern for basic mechanisms (58 percent in both cases).

This figure tells us many things. First, we may note that the original relationships between pairs of items are not significantly affected by the presence of a third item. Recall, for example, that the relationship between teaching role and ultimate medical interest was summarized as a 36-percentage-point difference. Looking at Figure H-2, we see that among only those respondents who are most interested in articles dealing with the effectiveness of treatments, the relationship between teaching role and ultimate medical interest is 31 percentage points (58 percent minus 27 percent: first row), and the same is true among those most interested in articles dealing with the rationale for treatments (89 percent minus 58 percent: second row). The original relationship between teaching role and ultimate medical interest is essentially the same as in Figure H-1, even among those respondents judged as scientific or nonscientific in terms of reading preferences.

We can draw the same conclusion from the columns in Figure H-2. Recall that the original relationship between reading preferences and ultimate medical interests was summarized as a 38-percentage-point difference. Looking only at the "physicians" in Figure H-2, we see that the relationship between the other two items is now 31 percentage points. The same relationship is found among the "researchers" in the second column.

Percentage Interested in Basic Mechanisms		Best Teaching Role	
		Physician	Researcher
Reading Preferences	Effectiveness	51% (66)	87% (12)
	Rationale	51% (219)	87% (130)

FIGURE H-3 **Hypothetical Trivariate Relationship among Scientific Orientation Items**

The importance of these observations becomes clearer when we consider what might have happened. In Figure H-3, hypothetical data tell a much different story than do the actual data in Figure H-2. As you can see, Figure H-3 shows that the original relationship between teaching role and ultimate medical interest persists, even when reading preferences are introduced into the picture. In each row of the table the "researchers" are more likely to express an interest in basic mechanisms than are the "physicians." Looking down the columns, however, we note no relationship between reading preferences and ultimate medical interest. If we know whether a respondent feels he or she can best teach as a physician or as a researcher, knowing the respondent's reading preference adds nothing to our evaluation of his or her scientific orientation. If something like Figure H-3 resulted from the actual data, we would conclude that reading preference should not be included in the same index as teaching role, since it contributes nothing to the composite index.

This example used only three questionnaire items. If more were being considered, then more complex multivariate tables would be in order, constructed of four, five, or more variables. The purpose of this step in index construction, again, is to discover the simultaneous interaction of the items to determine which should be included in the same index.

Index Scoring

When you have chosen the best items for the index, you next assign scores for particular responses, thereby creating a single composite index out of the several items. There are two basic decisions to be made in this step.

First, you must decide the desirable range of the index scores. Certainly, a primary advantage of an index over a single item is the range of gradations it offers in the measurement of a variable. As noted earlier, communication competence might be measured from "very competent" to "not at all competent" (or "very incompetent"). How far to the extremes, then, should the index extend?

In this decision, the question of variance enters once more. Almost always, as the possible extremes of an index are extended, fewer cases are to be found at each end. The researcher who wishes to measure communication competence to its greatest extreme may find there is almost no one in that category.

The first decision, then, concerns the conflicting desire for (1) a range of measurement in the index and (2) an adequate number of cases at each point in the index. You'll be forced to reach some kind of compromise between these conflicting desires.

The second decision concerns the actual assignment of scores for each particular response. Basically, you must decide whether to give each item an equal weight in the index or to give them different weights. Although there are no firm rules, we suggest—and practice tends to support this method—that items be weighted equally unless there are compelling reasons for differential weighting. That is, the burden of proof should be on differential weighting; equal weighting should be the norm.

Of course, this decision must be related to the earlier issue regarding the balance of items chosen. If the index is to represent the composite of slightly different aspects of a given variable, then you should give each aspect the same weight. In some instances, however, you may feel that, say, two items reflect essentially the same aspect, and the third reflects a different aspect. If you wished to have both aspects equally represented by the index, you might decide to give the different item a weight equal to the combination of the two similar ones. In such a situation, you might want to assign a maximum score of 2 to the different item and a maximum score of 1 to each of the similar ones.

Although the rationale for scoring responses should take such concerns as these into account, you'll typically experiment with different scoring methods, examining the relative weights given to different aspects but at the same time worrying about the range and distribution of cases provided. Ultimately, the scoring method chosen will represent a compromise among these several demands. Of course, as in most research activities, such a decision is open to revision on the basis of later examinations. Validation of the index, to be discussed shortly, may lead you to recycle your efforts toward constructing a completely different index.

In the example taken from the medical school faculty survey, it was decided to weight the items equally, since they were chosen, in part, because they represented slightly different aspects of the overall variable *scientific orientation*. On each of the items, the respondents were given a score of 1 for choosing the "scientific" response to the item and a score of 0 for choosing the "nonscientific" response. Each respondent, then, could receive a score of 0, 1, 2, or 3. This scoring method provided what was considered a useful range of variation—four index categories—and also provided enough cases for analysis in each category.

Handling Missing Data

Regardless of your data-collection method, you'll frequently face the problem of missing data. In virtually every survey, some respondents fail to answer some questions (or choose a "don't know" response). Although missing data present problems at all stages of analysis, they're especially troublesome in index construction. However, there are several methods of dealing with these problems.

First, if there are relatively few cases with missing data, you may decide to exclude them from the construction of the index and the analysis. (This was done in the medical school faculty example.) The primary concerns in this instance are whether the numbers available for analysis will remain sufficient and whether the exclusion will result in a biased sample whenever the index is used in the analysis. The latter possibility can be examined through a comparison—on other relevant variables—of those who would be included and excluded from the index.

Second, you may sometimes have grounds for treating missing data as one of the available responses. For example, if a questionnaire has asked respondents to indicate their participation in a number of activities by checking "yes" or "no" for each, many respondents may have checked some of the activities "yes" and left the remainder blank. In such a case, you might decide that a failure to answer meant "no," and score missing data in this case as though the respondents had checked the "no" space.

Third, a careful analysis of missing data may yield an interpretation of their meaning. In constructing a measure of communication competence, for example, you may discover that respondents who failed to answer a given question were generally as competent on other items as those who gave the competent answer. Whenever the analysis of missing data yields such interpretations, then, you may decide to score such cases accordingly.

There are many other ways of handling this problem. If an item has several possible values, you might assign the middle value to cases with missing data; for example, you could assign a 2 if the values are 0, 1, 2, 3, and 4. For a continuous variable such as *age,* you could similarly assign the mean to cases with missing data. Or missing data can be supplied by assigning values at random. All of these are conservative solutions in that they work against any relationships you may expect to find.

If you're creating an index out of several items, you can sometimes handle missing data by using proportions based on what is observed. Suppose your index is composed of six indicators, and you have only four observations for a particular respondent. If the respondent has earned 4 points out of a possible 4, you might assign an index score of 6; if the respondent has 2 points (half the possible score on four items), you could assign a score of 3 (half the possible score on six observations).

The choice of a particular method to be used depends so much on the research situation that we can't reasonably suggest a single "best" method or rank the several we have described. Excluding all cases with missing data can bias the representativeness of the findings, but including such cases by assigning scores to missing data can influence the nature of the findings. The safest and best method is to construct the index using alternative methods and see whether the same findings follow from each. Understanding your data is the final goal of analysis anyway.

Index Validation

Up to this point, we've discussed all the steps in the selection and scoring of items that result in a composite index purporting to measure some variable. If each of the preceding steps is carried out carefully, the likelihood of the index actually measuring the variable is enhanced. To demonstrate success, however, there must be *validation* of the index. In the basic logic of validation, we assume that the composite index provides a measure of some variable—that is, the successive scores on the index arrange cases in a rank order in terms of that variable. An index of communication competence rank-orders people in terms of their relative competence. If the index does that successfully, then people scored as relatively competent on the index should appear relatively competent in all other indications of communication competence, such as questionnaire items. There are several methods for validating a composite index.

Item Analysis   The first step in index validation is an internal validation called *item analysis.* In item analysis, you examine the extent to which the composite index is related to (or predicts responses to) the individual items it comprises. Here's an illustration of this step.

In the index of scientific orientations among medical school faculty, for example, index scores ranged from 0 (most interested in patient care) to 3 (most interested in research). Now let's consider one of the items in the index: whether respondents wanted to advance their own knowledge more with regard to total patient management or more in the area of basic mechanisms. The latter were treated as being more scientifically oriented than the former. The following empty table shows how we would examine the relationship between the index and the individual item:

Index of Scientific Orientations

	0	1	2	3
Percentage who said they were more interested in basic mechanisms	??	??	??	??

If you take a minute to reflect on the table, you may see that we already know the numbers that go in two of the cells. To get a score of 3 on the index, respondents had to say "basic mechanisms" in response to this question and give the "scientific" answers to the other two items as well. Thus, 100 percent of the 3's on the index said "basic mechanisms." By the same token, all the 0's had to answer this item with "total patient management." Thus, 0 percent of those respondents said "basic mechanisms." Here's how the table looks with the information we already know:

Index of Scientific Orientations

	0	1	2	3
Percentage who said they could best teach as medical researcher	0	??	??	100

If the individual item is a good reflection of the overall index, we should expect the 1's and 2's to fill in a progression between 0 percent and 100 percent. More of the 2's should choose "basic mechanisms" than 1's. This is not guaranteed by the way the index was constructed, however; it is an empirical question—one we answer in

an item analysis. Here's how this particular item analysis turned out:

Index of Scientific Orientations

	0	1	2	3
Percentage who said they were more interested in basic mechanisms	0	16	91	100

As you can see, in accord with our assumption that the 2's are more scientifically oriented than the 1's, we find that a higher percentage of the 2's (91 percent) say "basic mechanisms" than the 1's (16 percent).

An item analysis of the other two components of the index yields similar results, as shown below:

Index of Scientific Orientations

	0	1	2	3
Percentage who said they were more interested in basic mechanisms	0	4	14	100
Percentage who said they preferred reading about rationales	0	80	97	100

Each of the items, then, seems an appropriate component in the index. Each seems to reflect the same quality that the index as a whole measures.

In a complex index containing many items, this step provides a convenient test of the independent contribution of each item to the index. If a given item is found to be poorly related to the index, it may be assumed that other items in the index cancel out the contribution of that item. If the item in question contributes nothing to the index's power, it should be excluded.

Although item analysis is an important first test of the index's validity, it is scarcely a sufficient test. If the index adequately measures a given variable, it should successfully predict other indications of that variable. To test this, we must turn to items not included in the index.

External Validation   People scored as communicatively competent on an index should appear competent in their responses to other items in the questionnaire. Of course, we're talking about relative competence, because we can't make an absolute definition of what constitutes communication competence. However, those respondents scored as the most competent on the index should be the most competent in answering other questions. Those scored as the least competent on the index should

TABLE H-1 **Validation of Scientific Orientation Index**

	Index of Scientific Orientation			
	Low 0	1	2	High 3
Percentage interested in attending scientific lectures at the medical school	34	42	46	65
Percentage who say faculty members should have experience as medical researchers	43	60	65	89
Percentage who would prefer faculty duties involving research activities only	0	8	32	66
Percentage who engaged in research during the preceding academic year	61	76	94	99

be the least competent on other items. Indeed, the ranking of groups of respondents on the index should predict the ranking of those groups in answering other questions dealing with communication competence.

In our example of the scientific orientation index, several questions in the questionnaire offered the possibility of such external validation. Table H-1 presents some of these items, which provide several lessons regarding index validation. First, we note that the index strongly predicts the responses to the validating items in the sense that the rank order of scientific responses among the four groups is the same as the rank order provided by the index itself. At the same time, each item gives a different *description* of scientific orientations overall. For example, the last validating item indicates that the great majority of *all* faculty were engaged in research during the preceding year. If this were the only indicator of scientific orientation, we would conclude that nearly all faculty were scientific. Nevertheless, those scored as more scientific on the index are more likely to have engaged in research than those who were scored as relatively less scientific. The third validating item provides a different descriptive picture: Only a minority of the faculty overall say they would prefer duties limited exclusively to research. Nevertheless, the percentages giving this answer correspond to the scores assigned on the index.

Bad Index versus Bad Validators Nearly every index constructor at some time must face the apparent failure of external items to validate the index. If the internal item analysis shows inconsistent relationships between the items included in the index and the index itself, something is wrong with the index. But if the index fails to predict strongly the external validation items, the conclusion to be drawn is more ambiguous. You must choose between two possibilities: (1) the index does not adequately measure the variable in question, or (2) the validation items do not adequately measure the variable and thereby do not provide a sufficient test of the index.

The researcher who has worked long and conscientiously on the construction of an index will find the second conclusion compelling. Typically, you will feel you have included the best indicators of the variable in the index; therefore, the validating items are second-rate indicators. Nevertheless, you should recognize that the index is purportedly a very powerful measure of the variable; thus, it should be somewhat related to any item that taps the variable even poorly.

When external validation fails, you should reexamine the index before deciding that the validating items are insufficient. One way is to examine the relationships between the validating items and the individual items included in the index. If you discover that some of the index items relate to the validators and others do not, you'll have improved your understanding of the index as it was initially constituted.

There is no cookbook solution to this dilemma; it is an agony that serious researchers must learn to survive. Ultimately, the wisdom of your decision to accept an index will be determined by the usefulness of that index in your later analyses. Perhaps you will initially decide that the index is a good one and that the validators are defective, and later find that the variable in question (as measured by the index) is not related to other variables in the ways you expected. Then you may have to compose a new index.

Now we'll turn our attention from the creation of cumulative indexes to an examination of scale construction. In particular, we'll talk about Guttman scaling as our illustration.

SCALE CONSTRUCTION

Researchers today often use the scale developed by Louis Guttman. Guttman scaling is based on the fact that some items under consideration may prove to be more extreme indicators of the variable than others.

For example, in the earlier example of measuring scientific orientations among medical school faculty members, a simple index was constructed. As it happens, however, the three items included in the index essentially form a Guttman scale.

The construction of a Guttman scale would begin with some of the same steps that initiate index construction. You would begin by examining the face validity of items available for analysis. Then you would examine the bivariate and perhaps multivariate relations among those items. In scale construction, however, you would also look for relatively "hard" and "easy" indicators of the variable being examined.

Suppose we are developing a media campaign for our client, a pro-choice organization, and need a way to determine people's attitudes toward abortion. We suspect that several conditions can affect people's opinions: whether the woman is married, whether her health is endangered, and so forth. These differing conditions provide an excellent illustration of Guttman scaling.

Here are the percentages of the people in the 1996 General Social Survey (GSS) sample who supported a woman's right to an abortion, under three different conditions:

Woman's health is seriously endangered	92%
Pregnant as a result of rape	86%
Woman is not married	48%

The different percentages supporting abortion under the three conditions suggest something about the different *levels* of support that each item indicates. For example, if someone would support abortion when the mother's life is seriously endangered, that's not a very strong indicator of general support for abortion, because almost everyone agreed with that. Supporting abortion for unmarried women seems a much stronger indicator of support for abortion in general—fewer than half the sample took that position.

Guttman scaling is based on the notion that anyone who gives a strong indicator of some variable will also give the weaker indicators. In this case, we would assume that anyone who supported abortion for unmarried women would also support it in the case of rape or of the woman's health being threatened. Table H-2 tests this assumption by presenting the number of respondents who gave each of the possible response patterns.

The first four response patterns in the table compose what we would call the *scale types:* those patterns that form a scalar structure. Following those respondents who

TABLE H-2 Scaling Support for Choice of Abortion

	Women's Health	Result of Rape	Woman Unmarried	Number of Cases
	+	+	+	612
Scale Types	+	+	−	448
	+	−	−	92
	−	−	−	79
			Total = 1231	
	−	+	−	15
Mixed Types	+	−	+	5
	−	−	+	2
	−	+	+	5
			Total = 27	

+ = favors woman's right to choose; − = opposes woman's right to choose

supported abortion under all three conditions (line 1), we see (line 2) that those with only two pro-choice responses have chosen the two easier ones; those with only one such response (line 3) chose the easiest of the three (the woman's health being endangered). Finally, there are some respondents who opposed abortion in all three circumstances (line 4).

The second part of the table presents those response patterns that violate the scalar structure of the items. The most radical departures from the scalar structure are the last two response patterns: those who accepted only the hardest item and those who rejected only the easiest one.

The final column in the table indicates the number of survey respondents who gave each of the response patterns. It's immediately apparent that the great majority (98 percent) of the respondents fit into one of the scale types. The presence of mixed types, however, indicates that the items do not form a *perfect* Guttman scale.

We should recall at this point that one of the chief functions of scaling is efficient data reduction. Scales provide a technique for presenting data in a summary form while maintaining as much of the original information as possible.

When the scientific orientation items were formed into an index in our earlier discussion, respondents were given one point for each scientific response they gave. If these same three items were scored as a Guttman scale, some respondents would be assigned scale scores that would permit the most accurate reproduction of their original responses to all three items.

Respondents fitting into the scale types would receive the same scores as were assigned in the index construction. Persons selecting all three pro-choice responses

TABLE H-3 **Index and Scale Scores**

	Response Pattern	Number of Cases	Index Scores	Scale Scores*	Total Scale Errors
	+ + +	612	3	3	0
Scale Types	+ + −	448	2	2	0
	+ − −	92	1	1	0
	− − −	79	0	0	0
	− + −	15	1	2	15
Mixed Types	+ − +	5	2	3	5
	− − +	2	1	0	2
	− + +	5	2	3	5

Total Scale Errors = 27

$$\text{Coefficient of reproducibility} = 1 - \frac{\text{number of errors}}{\text{number of gusses}}$$

$$= 1 - \frac{27}{1258 \times 3} = \frac{27}{3774}$$

$$= .993 = 99.3\%$$

*This table presents one common method for scoring mixed types, but you should be advised that other methods are also used.

would still be scored 3, those who selected pro-choice responses to the two easier items and were opposed on the hardest item would be scored 2, and so on. For each of the four scale types we could predict accurately all the actual responses given by all the respondents based on their scores.

The mixed types in the table present a problem, however. The first mixed type (2 1 2) was scored 1 on the index to indicate only one pro-choice response. But, if 1 were assigned as a scale score, we would predict that the 15 respondents in this group had chosen only the easiest item (approving abortion when the woman's life was endangered), and we would be making two errors for each such respondent. Therefore, scale scores are assigned with the aim of minimizing the errors that would be made in reconstructing the original responses.

Table H-3 illustrates the index and scale scores that would be assigned to each of the response patterns in our example. Note that one error is made for each respondent in the mixed types. This is the minimum we can hope for in a mixed-type pattern. In the first mixed type, for example, we would erroneously predict a pro-choice response to the easiest item for each of the 15 respondents in this group, making a total of 15 errors.

The extent to which a set of empirical responses form a Guttman scale is determined by the accuracy with which the original responses can be reconstructed from the scale scores. For each of the 1,258 respondents in this example, we will predict three questionnaire responses, for a total of 3,774 predictions. Table H-3 indicates that we will make 27 errors using the scale scores assigned. The percentage of correct predictions is called the coefficient of reproducibility: the percentage of original responses that could be *reproduced* by knowing the scale scores used to summarize them. In the present example, the coefficient of reproducibility is 3,747/3,774, or 99.3 percent.

Except for the case of perfect (100 percent) reproducibility, there is no way of saying that a set of items does or does not form a Guttman scale in any absolute sense. Virtually all sets of such items *approximate* a scale. As a general guideline, however, coefficients of 90 or 95 percent are the commonly used standards in this regard. If the observed reproducibility exceeds the level you've set, you'll probably decide to score and use the items as a scale.

The decision concerning criteria in this regard is, of course, arbitrary. Moreover, a high degree of reproducibility does not ensure that the scale constructed in fact measures the concept under consideration, although it increases confidence that all the component items measure the same thing. Also, you should realize that a high coefficient of reproducibility is most likely when few items are involved.

One concluding remark should be made in regard to Guttman scaling: It is based on the structure observed among the *actual data under examination*. This is an important point that is often misunderstood. It does not make sense to say that a set of questionnaire items (perhaps developed and used by a previous researcher) constitutes a Guttman scale. Rather, we can say only that they form a scale within a given body of data being analyzed. Scalability, then, is a sample-dependent, empirical matter. Although a set of items may form a Guttman scale among one sample of survey respondents, for example, there is no guarantee that this set will form such a scale among another sample. In this sense, then, a set of questionnaire items in and of themselves never forms a scale, but a set of empirical observations may.

In this appendix, we have emphasized index and scale construction with survey items. Other kinds of observations could also be used in forming indexes and scales. However, the basic logic presented here holds regardless of whether the data with which we are dealing are questions on a survey or another kind of observational data.

APPENDIX I

Distribution of Chi Square

			Probability				
df	.99	.98	.95	.90	.80	.70	.50
1	$.0^3157$	$.0^3628$	.00393	.0158	.0642	.148	.455
2	.0201	.0404	.103	.211	.446	.713	1.386
3	.115	.185	.352	.584	1.005	1.424	2.366
4	.297	.429	.711	1.064	1.649	2.195	3.357
5	.554	.752	1.145	1.610	2.343	3.000	4.351
6	.872	1.134	1.635	2.204	3.070	3.828	5.348
7	1.239	1.564	2.167	2.833	3.822	4.671	6.346
8	1.646	2.032	2.733	3.490	4.594	5.528	7.344
9	2.088	2.532	3.325	4.168	5.380	6.393	8.343
10	2.558	3.059	3.940	4.865	6.179	7.267	9.342
11	3.053	3.609	4.575	5.578	6.989	8.148	10.341
12	3.571	4.178	5.226	6.304	7.807	9.034	11.340
13	4.107	4.765	5.892	7.042	8.634	9.926	12.340
14	4.660	5.368	6.571	7.790	9.467	10.821	13.339
15	5.229	5.985	7.261	8.547	10.307	11.721	14.339
16	5.812	6.614	7.962	9.312	11.152	12.624	15.338
17	6.408	7.255	8.672	10.085	12.002	13.531	16.338
18	7.015	7.906	9.390	10.865	12.857	14.440	17.338
19	7.633	8.567	10.117	11.651	13.716	15.352	18.338
20	8.260	9.237	10.851	12.443	14.578	16.266	19.337
21	8.897	9.915	11.591	13.240	15.445	17.182	20.337
22	9.542	10.600	12.338	14.041	16.314	18.101	21.337
23	10.196	11.293	13.091	14.848	17.187	19.021	22.337
24	10.856	11.992	13.848	15.659	18.062	19.943	23.337
25	11.524	12.697	14.611	16.473	18.940	20.867	24.337
26	12.198	13.409	15.379	17.292	19.820	21.792	25.336
27	12.879	14.125	16.151	18.114	20.703	22.719	26.336
28	13.565	14.847	16.928	18.939	21.588	23.647	27.336
29	14.256	15.574	17.708	19.768	22.475	24.577	28.336
30	14.953	16.306	18.493	20.599	23.364	25.508	29.336

continued

For larger values of df, the expression $\sqrt{2\chi^2} - \sqrt{2df - 1}$ may be used as a normal deviate with unit variance, remembering that the probability of χ^2 corresponds with that of a single tail of the normal curve.

Source: We are grateful to the Literary Executor of the late Sir Ronald A. Fisher, F.R.S., to Dr. Frank Yates, F.R.S., and to Longman Group Ltd., London, for permission to reprint Table IV from their book *Statistical Tables for Biological, Agricultural, and Medical Research* (6th Edition, 1963).

			Probability				
df	.30	.20	.10	.05	.02	.01	.001
1	1.074	1.642	2.706	3.841	5.412	6.635	10.827
2	2.408	3.219	4.605	5.991	7.824	9.210	13.815
3	3.665	4.642	6.251	7.815	9.837	11.341	16.268
4	4.878	5.989	7.779	9.488	11.668	13.277	18.465
5	6.064	7.289	9.236	11.070	13.388	15.086	20.517
6	7.231	8.558	10.645	12.592	15.033	16.812	22.457
7	8.383	9.803	12.017	14.067	16.622	18.475	24.322
8	9.524	11.030	13.362	15.507	18.168	20.090	29.125
9	10.656	12.242	14.684	16.919	19.679	21.666	27.877
10	11.781	13.442	15.987	18.307	21.161	23.209	29.588
11	12.899	14.631	17.275	19.675	22.618	24.725	31.264
12	14.011	15.812	18.549	21.026	24.054	26.217	32.909
13	15.119	16.985	19.812	22.362	25.472	27.688	34.528
14	16.222	18.151	21.064	23.685	26.873	29.141	36.123
15	17.322	19.311	22.307	24.996	28.259	30.578	37.697
16	18.841	20.465	23.542	26.296	29.633	32.000	39.252
17	15.511	21.615	24.769	27.587	30.995	33.409	40.790
18	20.601	22.760	25.989	28.869	32.346	34.805	42.312
19	21.689	23.900	27.204	30.144	33.687	36.191	43.820
20	22.775	25.038	28.412	31.410	35.020	37.566	45.315
21	23.858	26.171	29.615	32.671	36.343	38.932	46.797
22	24.939	27.301	30.813	33.924	37.659	40.289	48.268
23	26.018	28.429	32.007	35.172	38.968	41.638	49.728
24	27.096	29.553	33.196	36.415	40.270	42.980	51.179
25	28.172	30.675	34.382	37.652	41.566	44.314	52.620
26	29.246	31.795	35.563	38.885	42.856	45.642	54.052
27	30.319	32.912	36.741	40.113	44.140	46.963	55.476
28	31.391	34.027	37.916	41.337	45.419	48.278	56.893
29	32.461	35.139	39.087	42.557	46.693	49.588	58.302
30	35.530	36.250	40.256	43.773	47.962	50.892	59.703

APPENDIX J

Distribution of *t*

							Probability						
n	.9	.8	.7	.6	.5	.4	.3	.2	.1	.05	.02	.01	.001
1	.158	.325	.510	.727	1.000	1.376	1.963	3.078	6.314	12.706	31.821	63.657	636.619
2	.142	.289	.445	.617	.816	1.061	1.386	1.886	2.920	4.303	6.965	9.925	31.598
3	.137	.277	.424	.584	.765	.978	1.250	1.638	2.353	3.182	4.541	5.841	12.924
4	.134	.271	.414	.569	.741	.941	1.190	1.533	2.132	2.776	3.747	4.604	8.610
5	.132	.267	.408	.559	.727	.920	1.156	1.476	2.015	2.571	3.365	4.032	6.869
6	.131	.265	.404	.553	.718	.906	1.134	1.440	1.943	2.447	3.143	3.707	5.959
7	.130	.263	.402	.549	.711	.896	1.119	1.415	1.895	2.365	2.998	3.499	5.408
8	.130	.262	.399	.546	.706	.889	1.108	1.397	1.860	2.306	2.896	3.355	5.041
9	.129	.261	.398	.543	.703	.883	1.100	1.383	1.833	2.262	2.821	3.250	4.781
10	.129	.260	.397	.542	.700	.879	1.093	1.372	1.812	2.228	2.764	3.169	4.587
11	.129	.260	.396	.540	.697	.876	1.088	1.363	1.796	2.201	2.718	3.106	4.437
12	.128	.259	.395	.539	.695	.873	1.083	1.356	1.782	2.179	2.681	3.055	4.318
13	.128	.259	.394	.538	.694	.870	1.079	1.350	1.771	2.160	2.650	3.012	4.221
14	.128	.258	.393	.537	.692	.868	1.076	1.345	1.761	2.145	2.624	2.977	4.140
15	.128	.258	.393	.536	.691	.866	1.074	1.341	1.753	2.131	2.602	2.947	4.073
16	.128	.258	.392	.535	.690	.865	1.071	1.337	1.746	2.120	2.583	2.921	4.015
17	.128	.257	.392	.534	.689	.863	1.069	1.333	1.740	2.110	2.567	2.898	3.965
18	.127	.257	.392	.534	.688	.862	1.067	1.330	1.734	2.101	2.552	2.878	3.922
19	.127	.257	.391	.533	.688	.861	1.066	1.328	1.729	2.093	2.539	2.861	3.883
20	.127	.257	.391	.533	.687	.860	1.064	1.325	1.725	2.086	2.528	2.845	3.850
21	.127	.257	.391	.532	.686	.859	1.063	1.323	1.721	2.080	2.518	2.831	3.819
22	.127	.256	.390	.532	.686	.858	1.061	1.321	1.717	2.074	2.508	2.819	3.792
23	.127	.256	.390	.532	.685	.858	1.060	1.319	1.714	2.069	2.500	2.807	3.767
24	.127	.256	.390	.531	.685	.857	1.059	1.318	1.711	2.064	2.492	2.797	3.745
25	.127	.256	.390	.531	.684	.856	1.058	1.316	1.708	2.060	2.485	2.787	3.725
26	.127	.256	.390	.531	.684	.856	1.058	1.315	1.706	2.056	2.479	2.779	3.707
27	.127	.256	.389	.531	.684	.855	1.057	1.314	1.703	2.052	2.473	2.771	3.690
28	.127	.256	.389	.530	.683	.855	1.056	1.313	1.701	2.048	2.467	2.763	3.674
29	.127	.256	.389	.530	.683	.854	1.055	1.311	1.699	2.045	2.462	2.756	3.659
30	.127	.256	.389	.530	.683	.854	1.055	1.310	1.697	2.042	2.457	2.750	3.646
40	.126	.255	.388	.529	.681	.851	1.050	1.303	1.684	2.021	2.423	2.704	3.551
60	.126	.254	.387	.527	.679	.848	1.046	1.296	1.671	2.000	2.390	2.660	3.460
120	.126	.254	.386	.526	.677	.845	1.041	1.289	1.658	1.980	2.358	2.617	3.373
∞	.126	.253	.385	.524	.674	.842	1.036	1.282	1.645	1.960	2.326	2.576	3.291

Probability values are two-tailed.

Source: We are grateful to the Literary Executor of the late Sir Ronald A. Fisher, F. R. S., to Dr. Frank Yates, F. R. S., and to Longman Group Ltd, London, for permission to reprint Table III from their book *Statistical Tables for Biological, Agricultural and Medical Research* (6th Edition, 1963).

APPENDIX K

Percentage Points of the F-Distribution

Upper 5% points

ν_2 \ ν_1	1	2	3	4	5	6	7	8	9	10	12	15	20	24	30	40	60	120	∞
1	161.4	199.5	215.7	224.6	230.2	234.0	236.8	238.9	240.5	241.9	243.9	245.9	248.0	249.1	250.1	251.1	252.2	253.3	254.3
2	18.51	19.00	19.16	19.25	19.30	19.33	19.35	19.37	19.38	19.40	19.41	19.43	19.45	19.45	19.46	19.47	19.48	19.49	19.50
3	10.13	9.55	9.28	9.12	9.01	8.94	8.89	8.85	8.81	8.79	8.74	8.70	8.66	8.64	8.62	8.59	8.57	8.55	8.53
4	7.71	6.94	6.59	6.39	6.26	6.16	6.09	6.04	6.00	5.96	5.91	5.86	5.80	5.77	5.75	5.72	5.69	5.66	5.63
5	6.61	5.79	5.41	5.19	5.05	4.95	4.88	4.82	4.77	4.74	4.68	4.62	4.56	4.53	4.50	4.46	4.43	4.40	4.36
6	5.99	5.14	4.76	4.53	4.39	4.28	4.21	4.15	4.10	4.06	4.00	3.94	3.87	3.84	3.81	3.77	3.74	3.70	3.67
7	5.59	4.74	4.35	4.12	3.97	3.87	3.79	3.73	3.68	3.64	3.57	3.51	3.44	3.41	3.38	3.34	3.30	3.27	3.23
8	5.32	4.46	4.07	3.84	3.69	3.58	3.50	3.44	3.39	3.35	3.28	3.22	3.15	3.12	3.08	3.04	3.01	2.97	2.93
9	5.12	4.26	3.86	3.63	3.48	3.37	3.29	3.23	3.18	3.14	3.07	3.01	2.94	2.90	2.86	2.83	2.79	2.75	2.71
10	4.96	4.10	3.71	3.48	3.33	3.22	3.14	3.07	3.02	2.98	2.91	2.85	2.77	2.74	2.70	2.66	2.62	2.58	2.54
11	4.84	3.98	3.59	3.36	3.20	3.09	3.01	2.95	2.90	2.85	2.79	2.72	2.65	2.61	2.57	2.53	2.49	2.45	2.40
12	4.75	3.89	3.49	3.26	3.11	3.00	2.91	2.85	2.80	2.75	2.69	2.62	2.54	2.51	2.47	2.43	2.38	2.34	2.30
13	4.67	3.81	3.41	3.18	3.03	2.92	2.83	2.77	2.71	2.67	2.60	2.53	2.46	2.42	2.38	2.34	2.30	2.25	2.21
14	4.60	3.74	3.34	3.11	2.96	2.85	2.76	2.70	2.65	2.60	2.53	2.46	2.39	2.35	2.31	2.27	2.22	2.18	2.13
15	4.54	3.68	3.29	3.06	2.90	2.79	2.71	2.64	2.59	2.54	2.48	2.40	2.33	2.29	2.25	2.20	2.16	2.11	2.07
16	4.49	3.63	3.24	3.01	2.85	2.74	2.66	2.59	2.54	2.49	2.42	2.35	2.28	2.24	2.19	2.15	2.11	2.06	2.01
17	4.45	3.59	3.20	2.96	2.81	2.70	2.61	2.55	2.49	2.45	2.38	2.31	2.23	2.19	2.15	2.10	2.06	2.01	1.96
18	4.41	3.55	3.16	2.93	2.77	2.66	2.58	2.51	2.46	2.41	2.34	2.27	2.19	2.15	2.11	2.06	2.02	1.97	1.92
19	4.38	3.52	3.13	2.90	2.74	2.63	2.54	2.48	2.42	2.38	2.31	2.23	2.16	2.11	2.07	2.03	1.98	1.93	1.88
20	4.35	3.49	3.10	2.87	2.71	2.60	2.51	2.45	2.39	2.35	2.28	2.20	2.12	2.08	2.04	1.99	1.95	1.90	1.84
21	4.32	3.47	3.07	2.84	2.68	2.57	2.49	2.42	2.37	2.32	2.25	2.18	2.10	2.05	2.01	1.96	1.92	1.87	1.81
22	4.30	3.44	3.05	2.82	2.66	2.55	2.46	2.40	2.34	2.30	2.23	2.15	2.07	2.03	1.98	1.94	1.89	1.84	1.78
23	4.28	3.42	3.03	2.80	2.64	2.53	2.44	2.37	2.32	2.27	2.20	2.13	2.05	2.01	1.96	1.91	1.86	1.81	1.76
24	4.26	3.40	3.01	2.78	2.62	2.51	2.42	2.36	2.30	2.25	2.18	2.11	2.03	1.98	1.94	1.89	1.84	1.79	1.73
25	4.24	3.39	2.99	2.76	2.60	2.49	2.40	2.34	2.28	2.24	2.16	2.09	2.01	1.96	1.92	1.87	1.82	1.77	1.71
26	4.23	3.37	2.98	2.74	2.59	2.47	2.39	2.32	2.27	2.22	2.15	2.07	1.99	1.95	1.90	1.85	1.80	1.75	1.69
27	4.21	3.35	2.96	2.73	2.57	2.46	2.37	2.31	2.25	2.20	2.13	2.06	1.97	1.93	1.88	1.84	1.79	1.73	1.67
28	4.20	3.34	2.95	2.71	2.56	2.45	2.36	2.29	2.24	2.19	2.12	2.04	1.96	1.91	1.87	1.82	1.77	1.71	1.65
29	4.18	3.33	2.93	2.70	2.55	2.43	2.35	2.28	2.22	2.18	2.10	2.03	1.94	1.90	1.85	1.81	1.75	1.70	1.64
30	4.17	3.32	2.92	2.69	2.53	2.42	2.33	2.27	2.21	2.16	2.09	2.01	1.93	1.89	1.84	1.79	1.74	1.68	1.62
40	4.08	3.23	2.84	2.61	2.45	2.34	2.25	2.18	2.12	2.08	2.00	1.92	1.84	1.79	1.74	1.69	1.64	1.58	1.51
60	4.00	3.15	2.76	2.53	2.37	2.25	2.17	2.10	2.04	1.99	1.92	1.84	1.75	1.70	1.65	1.59	1.53	1.47	1.39
120	3.92	3.07	2.68	2.45	2.29	2.17	2.09	2.02	1.96	1.91	1.83	1.75	1.66	1.61	1.55	1.50	1.43	1.35	1.25
∞	3.84	3.00	2.60	2.37	2.21	2.10	2.01	1.94	1.88	1.83	1.75	1.67	1.57	1.52	1.46	1.39	1.32	1.22	1.00

$F = \dfrac{s_1^2}{s_2^2} = \dfrac{S_1/\nu_1}{S_2/\nu_2}$, where $s_1^2 = \dfrac{S_1}{\nu_1}$ and $s_2^2 = \dfrac{S_2}{\nu_2}$ are independent mean squares estimating a common variance σ^2 and based on ν_1 and ν_2 degrees of freedom, respectively.

Upper 1% points

v_2 \ v_1	1	2	3	4	5	6	7	8	9	10	12	15	20	24	30	40	60	120	∞
1	4052	4999.5	5403	5625	5764	5859	5928	5981	6022	6056	6106	6157	6209	6235	6261	6287	6313	6339	6366
2	98.50	99.00	99.17	99.25	99.30	99.33	99.36	99.37	99.39	99.40	99.42	99.43	99.45	99.46	99.47	99.47	99.48	99.49	99.50
3	34.12	30.82	29.46	28.71	28.24	27.91	27.67	27.49	27.35	27.23	27.05	26.87	26.69	26.60	26.50	26.41	26.32	26.22	26.13
4	21.20	18.00	16.69	15.98	15.52	15.21	14.98	14.80	14.66	14.55	14.37	14.20	14.02	13.93	13.84	13.75	13.65	13.56	13.46
5	16.26	13.27	12.06	11.39	10.97	10.67	10.46	10.29	10.16	10.05	9.89	9.72	9.55	9.47	9.38	9.29	9.20	9.11	9.02
6	13.75	10.92	9.78	9.15	8.75	8.47	8.26	8.10	7.98	7.87	7.72	7.56	7.40	7.31	7.23	7.14	7.06	6.97	6.88
7	12.25	9.55	8.45	7.85	7.46	7.19	6.99	6.84	6.72	6.62	6.47	6.31	6.16	6.07	5.99	5.91	5.82	5.74	5.65
8	11.26	8.65	7.59	7.01	6.63	6.37	6.18	6.03	5.91	5.81	5.67	5.52	5.36	5.28	5.20	5.12	5.03	4.95	4.86
9	10.56	8.02	6.99	6.42	6.06	5.80	5.61	5.47	5.35	5.26	5.11	4.96	4.81	4.73	4.65	4.57	4.48	4.40	4.31
10	10.04	7.56	6.55	5.99	5.64	5.39	5.20	5.06	4.94	4.85	4.71	4.56	4.41	4.33	4.25	4.17	4.08	4.00	3.91
11	9.65	7.21	6.22	5.67	5.32	5.07	4.89	4.74	4.63	4.54	4.40	4.25	4.10	4.02	3.94	3.86	3.78	3.69	3.60
12	9.33	6.93	5.95	5.41	5.06	4.82	4.64	4.50	4.39	4.30	4.16	4.01	3.86	3.78	3.70	3.62	3.54	3.45	3.36
13	9.07	6.70	5.74	5.21	4.86	4.62	4.44	4.30	4.19	4.10	3.96	3.82	3.66	3.59	3.51	3.43	3.34	3.25	3.17
14	8.86	6.51	5.56	5.04	4.69	4.46	4.28	4.14	4.03	3.94	3.80	3.66	3.51	3.43	3.35	3.27	3.18	3.09	3.00
15	8.68	6.36	5.42	4.89	4.56	4.32	4.14	4.00	3.89	3.80	3.67	3.52	3.37	3.29	3.21	3.13	3.05	2.96	2.87
16	8.53	6.23	5.29	4.77	4.44	4.20	4.03	3.89	3.78	3.69	3.55	3.41	3.26	3.18	3.10	3.02	2.93	2.84	2.75
17	8.40	6.11	5.18	4.67	4.34	4.10	3.93	3.79	3.68	3.59	3.46	3.31	3.16	3.08	3.00	2.92	2.83	2.75	2.65
18	8.29	6.01	5.09	4.58	4.25	4.01	3.84	3.71	3.60	3.51	3.37	3.23	3.08	3.00	2.92	2.84	2.75	2.66	2.57
19	8.18	5.93	5.01	4.50	4.17	3.94	3.77	3.63	3.52	3.43	3.30	3.15	3.00	2.92	2.84	2.76	2.67	2.58	2.49
20	8.10	5.85	4.94	4.43	4.10	3.87	3.70	3.56	3.46	3.37	3.23	3.09	2.94	2.86	2.78	2.69	2.61	2.52	2.42
21	8.02	5.78	4.87	4.37	4.04	3.81	3.64	3.51	3.40	3.31	3.17	3.03	2.88	2.80	2.72	2.64	2.55	2.46	2.36
22	7.95	5.72	4.82	4.31	3.99	3.76	3.59	3.45	3.35	3.26	3.12	2.98	2.83	2.75	2.67	2.58	2.50	2.40	2.31
23	7.88	5.66	4.76	4.26	3.94	3.71	3.54	3.41	3.30	3.21	3.07	2.93	2.78	2.70	2.62	2.54	2.45	2.35	2.26
24	7.82	5.61	4.72	4.22	3.90	3.67	3.50	3.36	3.26	3.17	3.03	2.89	2.74	2.66	2.58	2.49	2.40	2.31	2.21
25	7.77	5.57	4.68	4.18	3.85	3.63	3.46	3.32	3.22	3.13	2.99	2.85	2.70	2.62	2.54	2.45	2.36	2.27	2.17
26	7.72	5.53	4.64	4.14	3.82	3.59	3.42	3.29	3.18	3.09	2.96	2.81	2.66	2.58	2.50	2.42	2.33	2.23	2.13
27	7.68	5.49	4.60	4.11	3.78	3.56	3.39	3.26	3.15	3.06	2.93	2.78	2.63	2.55	2.47	2.38	2.29	2.20	2.10
28	7.64	5.45	4.57	4.07	3.75	3.53	3.36	3.23	3.12	3.03	2.90	2.75	2.60	2.52	2.44	2.35	2.26	2.17	2.06
29	7.60	5.42	4.54	4.04	3.73	3.50	3.33	3.20	3.09	3.00	2.87	2.73	2.57	2.49	2.41	2.33	2.23	2.14	2.03
30	7.56	5.39	4.51	4.02	3.70	3.47	3.30	3.17	3.07	2.98	2.84	2.70	2.55	2.47	2.39	2.30	2.21	2.11	2.01
40	7.31	5.18	4.31	3.83	3.51	3.29	3.12	2.99	2.89	2.80	2.66	2.52	2.37	2.29	2.20	2.11	2.02	1.92	1.80
60	7.08	4.98	4.13	3.65	3.34	3.12	2.95	2.82	2.72	2.63	2.50	2.35	2.20	2.12	2.03	1.94	1.84	1.73	1.60
120	6.85	4.79	3.95	3.48	3.17	2.96	2.79	2.66	2.56	2.47	2.34	2.19	2.03	1.95	1.86	1.76	1.66	1.53	1.38
∞	6.63	4.61	3.78	3.32	3.02	2.80	2.64	2.51	2.41	2.32	2.18	2.04	1.88	1.79	1.70	1.59	1.47	1.32	1.00

$F = \dfrac{s_1^2}{s_2^2} = \dfrac{S_1/v_1}{S_2/v_2}$, where $s_1^2 = \dfrac{S_1}{v_1}$ and $s_2^2 = \dfrac{S_2}{v_2}$ are independent mean squares estimating a common variance σ^2 and based on v_1 and v_2 degrees of freedom, respectively.

Source: This table is abridged from Table 18 in E. S. Pearson and H. O. Hartley (Eds.) (1966), *Biometrika Tables for Statisticians*, Vol. 1, 3rd edition. Reproduced by permission of the Biometrika Trustees.

APPENDIX L

Values of the Correlation Coefficient for Different Levels of Significance

			Levels of Significance								
n	.1	.05	.02	.01	.001	n	.1	.05	.02	.01	.001
1	.98769	.99692	.999507	.999877	.9999988	16	.4000	.4683	.5425	.5897	.7084
2	.90000	.95000	.98000	.990000	.99900	17	.3887	.4555	.5285	.5751	.6932
3	.8054	.8783	.93433	.95873	.99116	18	.3783	.4438	.5155	.5614	.6787
4	.7293	.8114	.8822	.91720	.97406	19	.3687	.4329	.5034	.5487	.6652
5	.6694	.7545	.8329	.8745	.95074	20	.3598	.4227	.4921	.5368	.6524
6	.6215	.7067	.7887	.8343	.92493	25	.3233	.3809	.4451	.4869	.5974
7	.5822	.6664	.7498	.7977	.8982	30	.2960	.3494	.4093	.4487	.5541
8	.5494	.6319	.7155	.7646	.8721	35	.2746	.3246	.3810	.4182	.5189
9	.5214	.6021	.6851	.7348	.8471	40	.2573	.3044	.3578	.3932	.4896
10	.4973	.5760	.6581	.7079	.8233	45	.2428	.2875	.3384	.3721	.4648
11	.4762	.5529	.6339	.6835	.8010	50	.2306	.2732	.3218	.3541	.4433
12	.4575	.5324	.6120	.6614	.7800	60	.2108	.2500	.2948	.3248	.4078
13	.4409	.5139	.5923	.6411	.7603	70	.1954	.2319	.2737	.3017	.3799
14	.4259	.4973	.5742	.6226	.7420	80	.1829	.2172	.2565	.2830	.3568
15	.4124	.4821	.5577	.6055	.7246	90	.1726	.2050	.2422	.2673	.3375
						100	.1638	.1946	.2301	.2540	.3211

Probability values are for two-tailed tests.

Source: We are grateful to the Literary Executor of the late Sir Ronald A. Fisher, F. R. S., to Dr. Frank Yates, F. R. S., and to Longman Group Ltd., London, for permission to reprint Table VII from their book *Statistical Tables for Biological, Agricultural, and Medical Research* (6th Edition, 1963).

GLOSSARY

active member role   A kind of qualitative fieldwork in which the researcher engages in many, but not all, of the activities of the group being studied. See Chapter 13.

aggregate   The whole of something. Communication researchers study communication phenomena in whole populations rather than focusing on single individuals. See Chapter 1.

alternate-form reliability   A way in which *measurement reliability* can be demonstrated. When two forms of a measure produce comparable scores, the measure is said to have adequate alternate-form reliability. See Chapter 6.

analysis of variance (ANOVA)   A parametric, inferential statistic designed to examine differences among three or more groups, with one or more independent variables. See Chapter 12.

analytic induction   A method of qualitative data analysis in which the researcher derives categories inductively from textual data, accounting for 100 percent of cases through a systematic treatment of negative cases (i.e., cases that do not support the working hypothesis). See Chapter 16.

anonymity   A condition in which the researcher does not know the identity of a given participant. See Chapter 5.

ANOVA   Analysis of variance, a parametric statistical test designed to assess differences between more than two groups. One-way ANOVA involves three or more nominal groups on a single independent variable, whereas factorial ANOVA involves at least two independent groups, each of which has a minimum of two nominal groups. See Chapter 12.

APA style   The set of standards that guide the writing and publication of research, as elaborated in the *Publication Manual of the American Psychological Association*. See Chapter 2.

attributes   Characteristics of persons or things. See *variables* and Chapter 3.

bias   The quality of a measurement device that tends to result in a misrepresentation of what is being measured in a particular direction. For example, the questionnaire item "Don't you agree that the President is doing a good job?" would be *biased* in that it would generally encourage more favorable responses. See Chapter 8.

biographical study   A qualitative research perspective in which the researcher seeks to understand the life and experiences of an individual or group of individuals. See Chapter 14.

case study   A qualitative research perspective in which the researcher seeks in-depth understanding of a single concrete case. See Chapter 13.

causality   An independent variable (*X*) produces an effect in a dependent variable (*Y*). There are three conditions for making a causal claim: *X* occurs prior to *Y*; *X* and *Y* are correlated; alternative explanations of *Y* have been eliminated. See Chapter 3.

central tendency   A statistical term for what is typical or normal in a sample. It comes in three forms: *mean, median, mode.* See Chapter 11.

chi square   A nonparametric, inferential statistic designed to determine whether groups differ in the frequency with which a variable appears. See Chapter 12.

classical experiment   Also known as a "true" experiment. Participants are randomly assigned to an experimental group or a control group. See Chapter 9.

cleaning data   In quantitative data analysis, the process of checking data entered into a computer for entry errors—e.g., typing the wrong number. See Chapter 11.

cluster sampling   A multistage sample in which natural groups (*clusters*) are sampled initially, with the members of each selected group being subsampled afterward. For example, you might select a sample of U.S. colleges and universities from a directory, get lists of the students at all the selected schools, then draw samples of students from each. This procedure is discussed in Chapter 7.

codebook   The document used in quantitative data processing and analysis that tells the location of different data items in a data file. Typically, the codebook identifies the locations of data items and the meaning of the codes used to represent different attributes of variables. See Chapter 11.

coding The process of categorizing and sorting raw data. Used in quantitative data analysis and in qualitative data analysis. See Chapters 10 and 16.

coefficient of determination The square of a correlation coefficient, r^2. See Chapter 12.

cohort study A study in which some specific group is studied over time although data may be collected from different members in each set of observations. For example, a study of the occupational history of the class of 1970, in which questionnaires were sent every five years, would be a cohort study. See Chapter 2.

communication criticism A specific kind of case-study research in which the researcher seeks to understand (and perhaps evaluate) some public communication text(s)—for example, presidential State of the Union addresses or the discourse surrounding stem cell research. See Chapter 15.

communication studies A discipline of study that coheres around a focus on the production, transmission, uses, and effects of messages. See Chapter 1.

comparative judgment measure A survey method in which participants are asked to compare two or more phenomena, often with respect to their degree of similarity or difference. See Chapter 8.

complete-member role A kind of qualitative fieldwork in which the researcher occupies full membership in the group being studied. See Chapter 13.

complete-observer role A kind of qualitative fieldwork in which the researcher observes a group, with no participation in the group. Group members are unaware that they are being observed. See Chapter 13.

complete-participant role A kind of qualitative fieldwork in which the researcher participates fully in the activities of the group being studied, without their awareness of his or her status as a researcher. See Chapter 13.

composite measure A survey method in which multiple items are used to measure something. For example, if we have ten questions to assess attitude toward TV news credibility, we would have a composite measure. See Chapter 8.

concept An abstraction that refers to some feature or aspect of a communication phenomenon. See Chapter 6.

conceptualization The mental process whereby fuzzy and imprecise notions (concepts) are made more specific and precise. So you want to study *communication competence*. What do you mean by *com-petence*? Are there different kinds of competence in communication? What are they? See Chapter 6.

concurrent validity A form of criterion validity in which one measure of a given variable is compared to a second, established measure of the same variable. See Chapter 6.

confidence interval The range of values within which a population parameter is estimated to lie. For example, a survey may show 40 percent of a sample favoring Candidate A (poor devil). Although the best estimate of the support existing among all voters would also be 40 percent, we would not expect it to be exactly that. Therefore, we might compute a *confidence interval* (such as from 35 to 45 percent) within which the actual percentage of the population probably lies. Note that we must specify a *confidence level* in connection with every *confidence interval*. See Chapters 7 and 12.

confidence level The estimated probability that a population parameter lies within a given *confidence interval*. Thus, we might be 95-percent confident that between 35 and 45 percent of all voters favor Candidate A. See Chapters 7 and 12.

confidentiality A condition in which only the researcher knows the identity of given study participants. See Chapter 5.

confirmability One of four criteria by which the trustworthiness of qualitative research is evaluated. If a researcher's conclusions are well-reasoned from his or her textual data, the analysis is high in confirmability. See Part 3.

constant comparative method The process of deriving categories of meaning inductively from qualitative textual data. Very similar to *analytic induction*. See Chapter 16.

construct validity A way in which measurement validity is determined. In construct validity, the researcher asks whether a measure of a given variable correlates with other variables in a manner theoretically expected. It is established in two ways: *convergent construct validity* and *discriminant construct validity*. See Chapter 6.

content analysis A method of quantitative text analysis in which the researcher categorizes textual units into categories that have been inductively or deductively established. See Chapter 10.

content validity One of the ways in which measurement validity is demonstrated. Content validity refers to how well a measure captures the full scope of a given variable, as conceptualized by the researcher.

It, in turn, consists of *face validity* and *expert panel validity.* See Chapter 6.

contingency question   A survey question intended for only some respondents, determined by their responses to some other question. For example, all respondents might be asked whether they belong to the Cosa Nostra, and only those who said yes would be asked how often they go to company meetings and picnics. The latter would be a *contingency question.* See Chapter 8.

contingency table   A format for presenting the relationships among variables in the form of percentage distributions. See Chapter 11.

contrast question   A kind of question employed in qualitative interviewing in which the participant is asked to compare and contrast two or more phenomena. See Chapter 14.

control group   In experimentation, a group of participants to whom no experimental stimulus is administered but who should resemble the experimental group in all other respects. The comparison of the control group and the experimental group at the end of the experiment points to the effect of the experimental stimulus. See Chapter 9.

convenience sampling   A form of nonprobability-based sampling in which the researcher samples participants or other sampling units based on their easy availability. Generally, this form of sampling is not recommended if alternative sampling procedures can be employed. See Chapters 7 and 13.

convergent construct validity   A form of *construct validity* in which the researcher determines whether a measured variable is positively correlated with variables in a manner theoretically expected. See Chapter 6.

conversation analysis   A form of discourse analysis in which the qualitative researcher is interested in understanding how reality is constructed through the details of talk between communicators. See Chapter 15.

credibility   One of four criteria by which the trustworthiness of qualitative research is evaluated. It refers to whether the researcher's conclusions "ring true" to the people being studied. See Part 3.

criterion validity   A way in which measurement validity is determined. In criterion validity, the researcher compares a given measure to a criterion variable in one of two ways: *predictive validity* or *concurrent validity.* See Chapter 6.

critical case sampling   A kind of nonprobability sampling in which the researcher purposively seeks out instances that embody a given phenomenon in a dramatic way. Used in qualitative research. See Chapter 13.

critical paradigm   One of four primary systems of knowing in communication research. Scholars who adopt a critical paradigm are interested in understanding power relations between communicators. They typically adopt qualitative methods. See Chapter 3.

cross-sectional study   A study based on observations representing a single point in time. Contrasted with a *longitudinal study.* See Chapter 2.

data analysis   The process of drawing statistical or interpretive inferences about patterns in a data set. See Chapter 1.

data collection   The process of observing phenomena. A synonym for *observation.* See Chapter 1.

debriefing   A procedure in which study participants are informed after a study's completion on the details of the study. See Chapter 5.

deduction   The logical model in which specific expectations or *hypotheses* are developed on the basis of general principles. Starting from the general principle that all dogs are mean, you might anticipate that the new dog next door will bite. This anticipation would be the result of *deduction.* See also *induction* and Chapter 4.

degrees of freedom   A statistical term that refers to the possibilities for variation within a statistical model. See Chapter 12.

dependability   One of four criteria by which the trustworthiness of qualitative research is evaluated. Dependability refers to the trackability of a researcher's analysis and conclusions over the course of the study. See Part 3.

dependent variable   A variable assumed to depend on or be caused by another (called the *independent variable*). If you find that income is partly a function of one's level of communication anxiety, *income* is being treated as a *dependent variable.* See Chapter 3.

depth interview   A genre of qualitative interviewing characterized by its in-depth focus on the topic of interest. See Chapter 14.

descriptive question   A kind of question employed in qualitative interviewing in which the participant is asked to describe a given phenomenon or experience in his or her own words. See Chapter 14.

descriptive statistics   Statistical computations describing the characteristics of a sample. Descriptive statistics merely summarize a set of sample observations, whereas *inferential statistics* move beyond the description of specific observations to make inferences about the larger population from which the sample observations were drawn. See Chapter 11.

dimension   A specifiable aspect or facet of a concept. See Chapter 6.

discourse analysis   The qualitative analysis of discourse of any kind—whether verbal or nonverbal—with respect to its internal structure and its function. See Chapter 15.

discriminant construct validity   A form of *construct validity* in which the researcher determines whether a measured variable correlates negatively with other variables as theoretically expected. See Chapter 6.

dispersion   The distribution of values around some central value, such as a mean. The *range* is a simple example of a measure of *dispersion*. Thus, we may report that the *mean* age of a group is 37.9, and the *range* is from 12 to 89. See Chapter 11.

distributional structure   The frequency distribution of textual units across coding categories in content analysis and in interaction analysis. Distinct from *sequential analysis*. See Chapter 10.

double-blind experiment   An experiment in which neither the researcher nor the participants have knowledge during the study of which treatment group a given participant has been assigned to. See Chapter 9.

DRS   The developmental research sequence method of qualitative data analysis. See Chapter 16.

ecological fallacy   Erroneously drawing conclusions about individuals based solely on the observation of groups. See Chapter 2.

effect size   A statistical term that refers to the magnitude of the association between the independent variable and the dependent variable. If the association is slight, the effect size is small. If the association is substantial, the effect size is large. Related to *statistical power*. See Chapter 12.

empirical   In its most general sense, *empirical* means originating in or based on observation or experience. When a researcher engages in data collection through observation, the approach is empirical. See Chapter 1.

EPSEM   Equal probability of selection method. A sample design in which each member of a population has the same chance of being selected into the sample. See Chapter 7.

ethics   The professional standards that guide the research procedures acceptable for studying human beings. See Chapter 5.

ethnographic interview   A kind of qualitative interview in which the ethnographer engages participants in relatively short interviews that often seem like casual conversations. See Chapter 14.

ethnography of communication   A qualitative research perspective in which the researcher is interested in understanding the code of communication that organizes meaning in a given cultural group. See Chapter 13.

evaluation research   A form of applied research in which the researcher seeks to assess the effectiveness of some program, intervention, or other social action. This form of research often relies on *quasi-experiments*. See Chapter 9.

exemplar   A detailed and evocative example of a given category of meaning in qualitative data analysis. See Chapter 16.

experimental group   In experimentation, the participants who are exposed to the independent variable. Contrasted with the *control group*. See Chapter 9.

expert panel validity   A form of *content validity* in which a group of experts with knowledge of a given variable determine whether a given measure taps the full scope of the variable. See Chapter 6.

explanation   One of the primary goals of communication research. Positivist researchers are generally interested in cause–effect explanations. Systems researchers are generally interested in explanations of how variables function together. Interpretive and critical researchers are generally interested in explanation of what and how something means, or understanding. See Chapter 3.

external validity   One of four criteria by which the trustworthiness of quantitative research is evaluated. Refers to the extent to which conclusions drawn from a study are generalizable to the "real" world. See Part 2.

face validity   A form of *content validity* in which one asks whether a given measure, on its face, appears to tap the full range or scope of a variable, as conceptualized by the researcher. See Chapter 6.

factorial design   An experiment with more than one independent variable. See Chapter 9.

falsifiability   The extent to which a researcher's hypothesis can be falsified, or not supported. The hypothesis "The leader will or will not talk the most in the group meeting" is not falsifiable, whereas the hypothesis "The leader will talk the most in the group meeting" is falsifiable. See Chapter 4.

field experiment   In contrast to many experiments that take place in a lab, where the researcher manipulates independent variables, a field experiment involves taking advantage of natural occurrences of the independent variable. See Chapter 9.

field notes   Records kept by the researcher during participant-observation research. These notes are descriptions of what is going on in the field site, a record of the researcher's process, and the researcher's emerging analytic thoughts. See Chapter 13.

floating prompt   A kind of probe employed in qualitative interviewing in which the researcher asks a follow-up question that is based on what the participant has just said. See Chapter 14.

focus group   A group of individuals brought together by the researcher to participate in a "group interview." See Chapter 14.

frequency distribution   A description of the number of times the various attributes of a variable are observed in a sample. The report that 53 percent of a sample were men and 47 percent were women would be a simple example of a *frequency distribution.* See Chapter 11.

function explanation   In contrast to the cause–effect explanations characteristic of positivistic research, systems researchers ask how system parts function. See Chapter 3.

gatekeeper   In qualitative fieldwork, someone who gives the researcher access to the group by granting informed consent. See Chapter 13.

generalizability   The quality of a research finding that justifies the inference that it represents something more than the specific observations on which it was based. Sometimes, this involves the *generalization* of findings from a sample to a population. Generalizability, also referred to as *external validity,* is one of the four criteria by which the trustworthiness of quantitative research is evaluated. See Part 2.

grounded theory development (GTD)   A form of qualitative data analysis that culminates in a formal, propositional theory. See Chapter 16.

group interview   A form of qualitative interviewing in which participants are interviewed as a group so that the researcher can analyze the interaction that takes place among them. See *focus group* and Chapter 14.

Guttman scale   A type of *composite measure* used to summarize several discrete observations and to represent some more general variable. The items in a Guttman scale form a conceptual hierarchy. See Chapter 8 and Appendix H.

Hawthorne effect   A term coined in reference to a series of productivity studies at the Hawthorne plant of the Western Electric Company in Chicago, Illinois.

The researchers discovered that their presence affected the behavior of the workers being studied. The term now refers to any impact of research on the subject of study. See Chapter 9.

hypothesis   An expectation about the nature of things derived from a theory. It is a statement of something that ought to be observed in the real world if the theory is correct. See *deduction* and Chapter 4.

hypothesis testing   The determination of whether the expectations that a *hypothesis* represents are, indeed, found to exist in the real world. See Chapters 4 and 12.

ideology   In the context of critical research, an *ideology* refers to an integrated set of beliefs about the social world, usually with sociopolitical implications. See Chapter 3.

idiographic   An approach to explanation in which we seek to exhaust the idiosyncratic features of a particular condition or event. Imagine trying to list all the reasons why you chose to attend your particular college. Given all those reasons, it's difficult to imagine your making any other choice. By contrast, see *nomothetic.* See Chapter 3.

independent variable   An *independent variable* is presumed to cause or determine a *dependent variable.* If we discover that self-disclosure is partly a function of gender—women are more disclosive than men—gender is the *independent variable,* and self-disclosure is the *dependent variable.* Note that any given variable might be treated as independent in one part of an analysis and dependent in another part of it. See Chapter 3.

index   A type of composite measure that summarizes several specific observations and represents some more general dimension. Typical forms are based on Likert-type items and semantic differential items. Contrasted with *scale.* See Chapter 8.

indicator   An observation that we choose to consider as a reflection of a variable we wish to study. Thus, for example, hugging someone who is crying might be considered an *indicator* of social support. See Chapter 6.

induction   The logical model in which general principles are developed from specific observations. See also *deduction* and Chapter 4.

inferential statistics   The body of statistical computations relevant to making inferences from findings based on sample observations to some larger population. See also *descriptive statistics* and Chapters 4 and 12.

informant   Someone well versed in the phenomenon that you wish to study and who is willing to tell you what he or she knows. The term is often employed in the context of qualitative research. See Chapter 13.

informed consent   Written permission by study participants prior to involvement in a study. Usually required by IRBs to ensure voluntary participation by study participants. See Chapter 5.

interaction analysis   A method of quantitative text analysis in which the researcher examines the content and function of speech acts, who talks to whom, and what kinds of acts follow each other in face-to-face interaction. See Chapter 10.

interactive structure   A matrix of who talks to whom, derived by researchers as part of conducting an *interaction analysis.* See Chapter 10.

inter-coder reliability   A kind of measurement reliability in which two coders agree in how they categorize data. See also *inter-observer reliability* and Chapter 6.

interdependence   In the context of systems-oriented research, *interdependence* refers to how system parts both cause and affect one another in a reciprocal manner. See Chapter 3.

internal validity   Refers to the possibility that the conclusions drawn from a study's results may not accurately reflect what went on in the study itself. One of the four criteria by which the trustworthiness of quantitative research is evaluated. See Part 2.

inter-observer reliability   A kind of measurement reliability in which two observers agree on how they score a given variable. See also *inter-coder reliability* and Chapter 6.

interpretive paradigm   One of four primary systems of knowing in communication research. Interpretive researchers are interested in understanding meanings and how they are constructed. See Chapter 3.

interpretivism   An approach to qualitative research in which the researcher is interested in understanding participant experiences from the participant's point of view. See Chapter 14.

intersubjectivity   That quality of science (and other inquiries) whereby two different researchers studying the same problem arrive at the same conclusion. Ultimately, this is the practical criterion for what is called *objectivity.* We agree that something is "objectively true" if independent observers with different subjective orientations conclude that it is "true." See Chapter 3.

interval measure   A level of measurement describing a variable whose attributes are rank-ordered and have equal distances between adjacent attributes. The Fahrenheit temperature scale is an example of

this, since the distance between 17 and 18 is the same as that between 89 and 90. See also *nominal measure, ordinal measure, ratio measure,* and Chapter 6.

interview protocol   The questions to be employed by an interviewer. Protocols can be structured, semistructured, or unstructured. Quantitative research usually employs structured, standardized interview protocols. Qualitative research usually employs semistructured and unstructured protocols. See Chapter 8.

IRB (institutional review board)   The university group responsible for approving any research with humans with respect to ethical conduct. See Chapter 5.

item-total reliability   A kind of internal consistency measurement reliability in which the score on a given item is compared to the total score. If all of the items correlate positively with the total score, then the measure is said to have high item-total reliability. See Chapter 6.

iterative   A characteristic of qualitative data analysis. The researcher moves back and forth between working hypotheses and textual data in an effort to understand what is going on. See Chapters 4 and 16.

kappa   A statistic to assess inter-coder reliability in quantitative text analysis. See Chapter 10.

kurtosis   A statistical term that refers to the extent to which a frequency distribution departs from a *normal curve* with respect to its height. A normal curve has a height equal to three standard deviations. See Chapter 11.

latent content   As used in connection with content analysis, the underlying meaning of messages as distinguished from their *manifest content.* See Chapter 10.

laws   Generalized claims about how variables are patterned. In the context of positivistic quantitative research, a law is a generalized claim about a cause–effect relationship between variables. See Chapter 3.

level of significance   In the context of *tests of statistical significance,* the degree of likelihood that an observed, empirical relationship could be attributable to sampling error. A relationship is significant at the .05 level if the likelihood of its being only a function of sampling error is no greater than 5 out of 100. See Chapter 12.

Likert-type index   A type of composite measure developed by Rensis Likert in an attempt to improve the levels of measurement in social scientific research through the use of standardized response categories in survey *questionnaires*. Likert-type items are those using such response categories as strongly agree, agree, disagree, and strongly disagree. See Chapter 8.

logic The formal principles of reasoning that allow us to draw valid inferences. Reasoning is both inductive and deductive. See Chapter 1.

longitudinal study A study design involving the collection of data at different points in time, as contrasted with a *cross-sectional study*. See Chapter 2.

manifest content In connection with content analysis, the concrete terms contained in a communication message, as distinguished from *latent content*. See Chapter 10.

manipulation check In experimentation, the researcher should check to determine whether the intended independent variable was manipulated appropriately. See Chapter 9.

matching In connection with experimentation, the procedure whereby pairs of participants are matched on the basis of their similarities on one or more variables, and one member of the pair is assigned to the experimental group and the other to the *control group*. See Chapter 9.

maximum-variation sampling A kind of nonprobability sampling in which the researcher purposively seeks out cases that are different from one another. See Chapter 13.

mean An average, computed by summing the values of several observations and dividing by the number of observations. See Chapter 11.

measurement reliability One of four criteria by which the trustworthiness of quantitative research is evaluated. Reliability is the quality of measurement which suggests that the same data would have been collected each time in repeated observations of the same phenomenon. See Part 2.

measurement validity One of four criteria by which the trustworthiness of quantitative research is evaluated. The term refers to a measure that accurately reflects the concept it is intended to measure. See Part 2.

median Another *average*, representing the value of the "middle" case in a rank-ordered set of observations. If the ages of five men are 16, 17, 20, 54, and 88, the median would be 20. (The *mean* would be 39.) See Chapter 11.

member check A procedure employed by qualitative researchers to establish the credibility of their analysis. See Chapter 16.

mode Still another *average*, representing the most frequently observed value or attribute. If a sample con-

tains 1,000 people aged 65 or over, 275 people aged 45–64, and 33 persons aged 44 or younger, age 65+ is the *modal* category. See Chapter 11.

multi-method research Research in which more than one kind of method is employed, thereby resulting in a more comprehensive study of a phenomenon. Multi-method research can involve methods embedded in same or different paradigms. Quantitative–qualitative studies are one kind of multi-method research. See Chapter 3.

narrative A story, with setting, characters, and a plot. See Chapter 15.

narrative interview A kind of qualitative interview in which the researcher is interested in the participant's story or stories about some experience or phenomenon. See Chapter 14.

negative case analysis Part of analytic induction, a qualitative data analysis procedure in which the researcher adapts his or her working hypothesis in light of cases that challenge the hypothesis. See Chapter 16.

nominal measure A level of measurement describing a variable the different attributes of which are *only* different, as distinguished from *ordinal, interval,* or *ratio measures*. Sex is an example of a *nominal measure*. See Chapter 6.

nomothetic An approach to explanation in which we seek to identify a few features that generally characterize a class of conditions or events. Imagine the two or three key factors that determine which colleges students choose, such as proximity and reputation. By contrast, see *idiographic*. See Chapter 3.

nonparametric statistics The family of *inferential statistics* appropriate for nominal- or ordinal-level data, or for data that cannot otherwise meet the assumptions of *parametric statistics*. See Chapter 12.

nonprobability sampling A sample selected in some fashion other than any suggested by probability theory. Examples include *judgmental (purposive), quota,* and *snowball samples*. See Chapter 7.

nonsampling error Those imperfections of data quality that are a result of factors other than sampling error. Examples include misunderstandings of questions by respondents, erroneous recordings by interviewers and coders, and keypunch errors. See Chapter 12.

normal curve A frequency distribution of scores in which the majority of scores hover around the average with progressively fewer scores that depart from the average. In a normal curve, scores distribute themselves in known ways. In a normal curve, the mean, median, and mode are identical, and the curve has a kurtosis value of 3. See Chapter 11.

null hypothesis In connection with *hypothesis testing* and *tests of statistical significance,* the *null hypothesis* suggests that there is no relationship among the variables under study. You may conclude that the variables are related after having statistically rejected the *null hypothesis.* See Chapters 4 and 12.

objectivity Doesn't exist. See *intersubjectivity* and Chapter 3.

observation In its most general sense, *observation* refers to the gathering of data. Six modes of observation are discussed in this book: surveys, experiments, quantitative text analysis, participant observation, semistructured/unstructured interviewing, and qualitative text analysis. See Chapter 1.

observer-as-participant role A form of qualitative fieldwork in which a researcher has minimal involvement with group members, and group members are aware of the researcher's role. Interviewing is the foremost activity of the observer-as-participant role. See Chapter 13.

operational definition The concrete and specific definition of something in terms of the operations by which observations are to be categorized. The *operational definition* of "earning an *A* in this course" might be "correctly answering at least 90 percent of the final exam questions." See Chapter 6.

operationalization One step beyond *conceptualization. Operationalization* is the process of developing *operational definitions.* See chapters 4 and 6.

ordinal measure A level of measurement describing a variable with attributes you can rank-order along some dimension. An example would be *socioeconomic status* as composed of the attributes *high, medium, low.* See Chapter 6.

panel study A type of *longitudinal study* in which data are collected from the same sample (the *panel*) at several points in time. See Chapter 2.

paradigm A model or framework for observation and understanding that shapes both what we see and how we understand it. Four paradigms of knowing can be found in communication research: positivist, systems, interpretive, and critical. See Chapter 3.

parametric statistics The family of *inferential statistics* appropriate for interval- or ratio-level data, so long as other assumptions can be met. See Chapter 12.

participant Someone who is observed, measured, or studied in a research study. See also *respondent* and *informant. Participant* is a term that appears in all of this book's chapters.

participant-as-observer role A form of qualitative fieldwork in which the researcher participates in the activities of the group, with group members aware of the researcher role. See Chapter 13.

participant observation A method employed in qualitative research to study communication phenomena in their natural settings. The researcher can adopt any of several roles in the field. See Chapter 13.

Pearson product-moment correlation A parametric test of association to determine whether two variables, each measured at the interval or ratio level, are positively or negatively related to each other. See Chapter 12.

performance/dramatistic studies A qualitative research perspective in which the researcher understands social life by constructing performances and by studying others' performances. See Chapter 15.

peripheral member role A kind of qualitative fieldwork in which the researcher does not enact activities central to the group being studied. See Chapter 13.

phenomenology A qualitative research perspective in which the researcher seeks to understand the essence of meaning of an experience or phenomenon. See *interpretivism* and Chapter 14.

plagiarism Using someone's ideas or words without appropriate citation. See Chapter 5.

positivist paradigm One of four primary systems of knowing in communication research. The goal of positivist research is to understand cause-and-effect relations among variables. See Chapter 3.

postmodern interview A kind of qualitative interview in which the researcher strives to equalize the power relationship between the interviewer and the interviewee. See Chapter 14.

PPS (probability proportionate to size) This term refers to a type of multistage *cluster sample* in which clusters are selected not with equal probabilities (see *EPSEM*) but with probabilities proportionate to their sizes—as measured by the number of units to be subsampled. See Chapter 7.

predictive validity A form of *criterion validity* in which the researcher determines whether a measured variable predicts another variable. For example, if the GRE test predicts performance in graduate school, it has demonstrated adequate predictive validity. See Chapter 6.

pre-experimental designs Experimentation that lacks random assignment to experimental and control groups. See Chapter 9.

pretesting (1) In survey research, the practice of conducting a preliminary study, or pilot study, with a questionnaire or interview protocol to determine its adequacy. (2) In experimentation, pretest–posttest designs give participants a pretest prior to exposure to the independent variable; this pretest measures the dependent variable and is compared to the posttest score. See Chapter 8.

probability sampling   The general term for a sample selected in accord with probability theory, typically involving some random-selection mechanism. See Chapter 7.

probe   A technique employed in interviewing to solicit a more complete answer to a question. It is a nondirective phrase or question used to encourage a respondent to elaborate on an answer. Examples include "Anything more?" and "How is that?" See Chapter 8.

proprietary research   Research that is contracted by a client, typically not available in publication outlets available to the public. See Chapter 1.

purposive sampling   A kind of nonprobability sampling common in qualitative research. See Chapters 7 and 13.

qualitative data   Data whose form is textual—that is, nonnumerical. Typically, qualitative data is gathered by researchers who come from interpretivist or critical paradigms of knowing. See Chapters 3 and 13–16.

qualitative interviewing   Usually, semistructured or unstructured interviewing employed by qualitative researchers for purposes of understanding the system of meanings of the people being interviewed. See Chapter 14.

qualitative research   Research in which the data take nonnumerical (textual) form. See Chapter 2.

quantitative data   Data in numerical form, typically gathered by positivist or systems researchers for the purpose of describing and explaining the phenomena that those observations reflect. See Chapters 3 and 6–12.

quantitative research   Research in which the data take numerical form. See Chapter 2.

quasi-experimental designs   Experiments in which random assignment is not feasible. The experimental group is compared to itself at a different point in time or to a matched comparison group. Often used in evaluation research. See Chapter 9.

questionnaire   A written document containing questions and other types of items designed to solicit information appropriate to analysis. Questionnaires are primarily used in survey research. See Chapter 8.

quota sample   A type of nonprobability sample in which units are selected into the sample on the basis of prespecified characteristics so that the total sample will have the same distribution of characteristics assumed to exist in the population being studied. See Chapter 7.

random assignment   A technique for assigning experimental participants to *experimental groups* and *control groups* randomly. See Chapter 9.

range   A measure of *dispersion* composed of the highest and lowest values of a variable in some set of observations. In your class, for example, the *range* of ages might be from 17 to 37. See Chapter 11.

ratio measure   A level of measurement describing a variable the attributes of which have all the qualities of *nominal, ordinal,* and *interval measures* and are also based on a "true zero" point. Age is an example of a *ratio measure.* See Chapter 6.

reflexive journal   A form of field notes in which the researcher describes his or her research process and preliminary analysis. See Chapter 13.

reification   The process of regarding things that are not real as real. See Chapter 6.

reliability coefficient   A statistical index that describes the extent to which two sets of scores are associated. See *kappa* and Chapter 6.

replication   Generally, the duplication of a study to expose or reduce error. See *intersubjectivity* and Chapter 2.

representational validity   A form of *measurement validity* in which the researcher asks whether participant perceptions of a given variable correspond to how that variable is measured by the researcher. See Chapter 6.

representativeness   The quality of a sample of having the same distribution of characteristics as the population from which it was selected. By implication, descriptions and explanations derived from an analysis of the sample may be assumed to represent similar ones in the population. Representativeness is enhanced by *probability sampling* and provides for *generalizability* and the use of *inferential statistics.* See Chapter 7.

respondent   A person who provides data in survey research. See also *participant, informant,* and Chapter 8.

response rate   The number of people participating in a survey divided by the number selected in the sample, in the form of a percentage. This is also called the completion rate or, in self-administered surveys, the return rate: the percentage of *questionnaires* sent out that are returned. See Chapter 8.

review of literature   A summary of what is already known on a given topic, relevant to the argument a researcher is making to justify his or her own study. See Chapter 2.

rule   A commonly shared belief about appropriate action, including the action of attributing a given meaning to something. See Chapters 3 and 16.

sampling error   In probability sampling, a *sampling error* is a number that refers to how much the characteristics of a sample probably differ from the characteristics of the population as a whole. See Chapter 7.

sampling frame   The list or quasi-list of units composing a population from which a sample is selected. If the sample is to be *representative* of the population, it's essential that the sampling frame include all (or nearly all) members of the population. See Chapter 7.

sampling interval   The standard distance between elements selected from a population for a sample. Used in systematic sampling. See Chapter 7.

sampling ratio   The proportion of elements in the population that are selected to be in a sample. See Chapter 7.

saturation   In qualitative research, the point at which the researcher concludes that additional data gathering is no longer necessary. Saturation occurs when redundancy is achieved in the textual data. See Chapters 4 and 13.

scale   A type of composite measure composed of several items that have a logical or empirical structure among them. Examples of scales include *Guttman* and *Thurstone scales*. Contrasted with *index*. See also Chapter 8 and Appendix H.

scattergram   A plot of how each data point is measured with respect to two variables, *X* and *Y*. It is relevant to the calculation of a correlation coefficient. See Chapter 12.

scientific inquiry   A rigorous process in which both logic and observation are used to understand the social or natural world. See Chapter 1.

secondary analysis   A form of research in which the data collected and processed by one researcher are reanalyzed—often for a different purpose—by another researcher. This is especially appropriate in the case of survey data. Data archives are repositories or libraries for the storage and distribution of data for secondary analysis. See Chapter 8.

semantic differential   A questionnaire format in which the participant is asked to rate something in terms of two, opposite adjectives (e.g., rate textbooks as "boring" or "exciting"). See Chapter 8.

semantic relationship   A kernel of meaning, a primary unit of analysis for qualitative researchers. See Chapters 3 and 16.

semiotics   The study of symbols and their meanings. See Chapter 15.

semistructured interview   An interview, often employed in qualitative research, in which a researcher works with suggested questions whose wording and arrangement can vary from one participant to another. See Chapter 14.

sequential structure   The pattern of what follows what in interaction. Researchers who perform interaction analysis study sequential structure in addition to *distributional structure* and *interactive structure*. See Chapter 10.

simple random sampling   A type of *probability sampling* in which the units composing a population are assigned numbers. A set of random numbers is then generated, and the units having those numbers are included in the sample. Although probability theory and the calculations it provides assume this basic sampling method, it's seldom used, for practical reasons. An equivalent alternative is the *systematic sample* (with a random start). See Chapter 7.

skew   A statistical term to refer to a departure from a normal curve. The mean, median, and mode will not be equal. See Chapter 11.

snowball sampling   A *nonprobability sampling* method often employed in field research. Each person interviewed may be asked to suggest additional people for interviewing. See Chapters 7 and 13.

social regularities   Patterns of co-occurrence between variables or patterns of meaning or meaning making. See Chapter 1.

social text   A text used by the participants being studied—for example, an office report, a report card, a newspaper article. See Chapter 15.

specifications   Guidelines to interviewers on how best to clarify questions "on the spot" when interviewees have difficulty understanding a question. See Chapter 8.

split-half reliability   A kind of internal consistency measurement of reliability in which the scores from two halves of a given measure are correlated for a group of participants—for example, odd-numbered items and even-numbered items on a survey measure. See Chapter 6.

sponsor   In field research, someone who assists the researcher by functioning as his or her backer, supporter, or patron. See Chapter 13.

standard deviation   A statistical term that refers to the dispersion of a data set around the mean score. If the distribution is a normal curve, known percentages of scores can be found within one, two, and three standard deviations above and below the mean score. See Chapter 11.

standard error A statistical term that refers to the standard deviation of a sampling distribution. See Chapter 12.

standard score A statistical term that refers to how many *standard deviations* a given score is from the distribution's mean. See Chapter 11.

standardized interview Also known as a structured interview. An interview employed by quantitative researchers in which the same questions, worded identically and presented in the same order, are asked of participants in a uniform manner. See Chapter 8.

statistical power The probability of rejecting the null hypothesis when it is probably false. Statistical power is greater with larger *effect sizes.* See Chapter 12.

statistical significance A general term referring to the unlikeliness that relationships observed in a sample could be attributed to sampling error alone. See *tests of statistical significance* and Chapter 12.

stratification The grouping of the units composing a population into homogeneous groups (or strata) before sampling. This procedure, which may be used in conjunction with *simple random, systematic,* or *cluster sampling,* improves the representativeness of a sample, at least in terms of the stratification variables. See Chapter 7.

structural question In qualitative interviewing, a kind of question in which the participant is asked about how he or she mentally organizes a meaning domain. See Chapter 14.

structured interview Also known as a standardized interview—employed in survey research. An interview in which the same questions are asked in the same way, and in the same order, for all participants. Distinguished from *semistructured* and *unstructured* interviews. See Chapter 14.

subjectivity The process of knowing "reality" as it is perceived rather than believing in "reality" independent of the knower's mind. Qualitative researchers legitimate subjective knowing, whereas quantitative researchers generally do not. See Chapter 3.

system A group of interrelated parts that function as a whole. For example, an organization or a family is a system. See Chapter 3.

systematic sampling A type of *probability sampling* in which every kth unit in a list is selected for inclusion in the sample—for example, every 25th student in the college directory of students. See Chapter 7.

systems paradigm One of the primary systems of knowing found in communication research. Systems researchers are interested in studying how *systems* function. See Chapter 3.

test–retest reliability A kind of measurement reliability in which participants' scores at time 1 are comparable to their scores at time 2. See Chapter 6.

tests of statistical significance A class of statistical computations that indicate the likelihood that the relationship observed between variables in a sample can be attributed to sampling error only. See *inferential statistics* and Chapter 12.

text Any segment of symbol use—e.g., a TV ad, a newspaper editorial, a conversation between persons, a diary, or a visual image. See Chapter 10.

textualization The qualitative research process of constructing textual data from communicative messages. See Chapter 15.

theoretical construct sampling A kind of nonprobability sampling in which the researcher purposively seeks out instances based on their theoretical relevance. See Chapter 13.

theoretical sensitivity The qualitative researcher examines his or her textual data inductively while mindful of what has been found in existing research and theory. See Chapter 13.

theory A systematic explanation for the observations that relate to a particular aspect of life. Theories can deal with causal explanation, functional explanation, or understanding. See Chapters 1 and 4.

thick description In qualitative research, a textual description of some phenomenon in which its meaning is evoked in a richly detailed and textured manner. See Chapter 16.

Thurstone equal-appearing interval scale A type of composite measure, constructed in accord with the weights assigned by "judges" to various indicators of some variables. See Chapter 8.

transcription A written text of what was said, and how, between interactants. See Chapter 15.

transferability One of four criteria by which the trustworthiness of qualitative research is evaluated. A qualitative researcher needs to provide detailed information so that the reader is positioned to assess the applicability of the study's insights to another situation. See Part 3.

trend study A type of *longitudinal study* in which a given characteristic of some population is monitored over time. An example would be the series of Gallup polls showing the political-candidate preferences of the electorate over the course of a campaign, even though different samples were interviewed at each point. See Chapter 2.

triangulation   The process of comparing data gathered one way to data gathered using another method, using another researcher, or from different participants. See Chapters 2, 13, and 16.

trustworthiness   The standard by which quantitative and qualitative research should be judged. Quantitative research is evaluated by four criteria: *internal validity, measurement reliability, measurement validity,* and *external validity.* Qualitative research is evaluated by four other criteria: *credibility, dependability, confirmability,* and *transferability.* See Parts 2 and 3.

t-test   A parametric, inferential statistic designed to examine a difference between two groups. See Chapter 12.

Type I error   A statistical term that refers to an error in statistical decision making—also known as an alpha error. When researchers reject the null hypothesis, and it is probably true, they have made a Type I error. See Chapter 12.

Type II error   A statistical term that refers to an error in statistical decision making. When researchers fail to reject the null hypothesis when it is probably false, they have made a Type II error. See Chapter 12.

typical case sampling   A kind of nonprobability sampling in which the researcher purposively seeks out typical instances of the phenomenon of interest. See Chapter 13.

unitizing   The process of segmenting textual data into units for purposes of analysis. See Chapters 10 and 16.

units of analysis   The *what* or *whom* being studied. In social science research, the most typical units of analysis are individual people. See Chapter 2.

unobtrusive research   Research in which the participants are not aware of being observed. Content analysis and the analysis of social texts are examples of unobtrusive research. See Chapter 2.

unstructured interview   An interview, often employed in qualitative research, in which the researcher has few, if any, pre-formulated questions. See Chapter 14.

variables   Logical groupings of *attributes.* The variable *gender* is made up of the attributes *masculine* and *feminine.* See Chapter 3.

visual texts   Nonverbal texts such as photographs or films. See Chapter 13.

voluntary participation   In the context of the ethical protection of human subjects, *voluntary participation* refers to a participant's informed and prior consent to be involved in a research study. See Chapter 5.

z-score   A standard score, indicating the location of a score in terms of the number of standard deviations from the sample mean. See Chapter 11.

BIBLIOGRAPHY

Acosta-Alzuru, C., & Kreshel, P. J. (2002). "I'm an American girl . . . whatever *that* means": Girls consuming Pleasant Company's American Girl identity. *Journal of Communication, 52,* 139–161.

Adelman, M. B. (Producer), & Schultz, P. (Director) (1991). *The pilgrim must embark: Living in community* [Videotape]. (Available from Lawrence R. Frey, 2266 Washington Avenue, Memphis, TN 38104).

Adler, P. A., & Adler, P. (1987). *Membership roles in field research.* Newbury Park, CA: Sage.

American Psychological Association (2001). *Publication manual of the American Psychological Association* (5th ed.). Washington, DC: Author.

Andersen, P. A., & Guerrero, L. K. (Eds.) (1998). *Handbook of communication and emotion: Research, theory, applications, and contexts.* New York: Academic Press.

Anderson, A. B., Basilevsky, A., & Hum, D. (1983). Measurement: Theory and techniques. In P. H. Rossi, J. D. Wright, & A. B. Anderson (Eds.), *Handbook of survey research* (pp. 231–287). New York: Academic Press.

Anderson, W. (1990). *Reality isn't what it used to be: Theatrical politics, ready-to-wear religion, global myths, primitive chic, and other wonders of the postmodern world.* San Francisco: Harper.

Atkinson, J. M., & Heritage, J. (Eds.) (1984). *Structures of social action: Studies in conversation analysis.* New York: Cambridge University Press.

Ayres, J., & Crosby, S. (1995). Two studies concerning the predictive validity of the personal report of communication apprehension in employment interviews. *Communication Research Reports, 12,* 145–151.

Babbie, E. (1970). *Science and morality in medicine.* Berkeley: University of California Press.

Babbie, E., Halley, F., & Zaino, J. (2000). *Adventures in social research.* Newbury Park, CA: Pine Forge.

Bakeman, R., & Gottman, J. M. (1997). *Observing interaction: An introduction to sequential analysis* (2nd ed.). New York: Cambridge University Press.

Ballard, D. I., & Seibold, D. R. (2000). Time orientation and temporal variation across work groups: Implications for group and organizational communication. *Western Journal of Communication, 64,* 218–242.

Ballotti, J., & Kaid, L. L. (2000). Examining verbal style in presidential campaign spots. *Communication Studies, 51,* 258–273.

Bandura, A. (1994). Social cognitive theory of mass communication. In J. Bryant & D. Zillmann (Eds.), *Media effects: Advances in theory in research* (pp. 61–90). Hillsdale, NJ: Erlbaum.

Barnhurst, K. G., & Mutz, D. (1997). American journalism and the decline in event-centered reporting. *Journal of Communication, 47,* 27–53.

Bauman, R. (1977). *Verbal art as performance.* Prospect Heights, IL: Waveland.

Baxter, L. A. (1992). Root metaphors in accounts of developing romantic relationships. *Journal of Social and Personal Relationships, 9,* 253–276.

Baxter, L. A. (1993). "Talking things through" and "putting it in writing": Two codes of communication in an academic institution. *Journal of Applied Communication Research, 21,* 313–326.

Baxter, L. A. (1999). *Changes in drug narratives as a function of type of resistance skills intervention program and ethnicity.* Unpublished manuscript. University of Iowa.

Baxter, L. A., Braithwaite, D. O., Bryant, L., & Wagner, A. (2001, November). *Stepchildren's perceptions of the contradictions of blended family communication.* Paper presented at the annual convention of the National Communication Association, Atlanta, GA.

Baxter, L. A., Braithwaite, D. O., Golish, T. D., & Olson, L. N. (2002). Contradictions of interaction for wives of elderly husbands with adult dementia. *Journal of Applied Communication Research, 30,* 1–26.

Baxter, L. A., Braithwaite, D. O., & Nicholson, J. H. (1999). Turning points in the development of blended families. *Journal of Social and Personal Relationships, 16,* 291–313.

Baxter, L. A., Dun, T., & Sahlstein, E. (2001). Rules for relating communicated among social network members. *Journal of Social and Personal Relationships, 18,* 173–199.

Baxter, L. A., & Goldsmith, D. (1990). Cultural terms for communication events among some American high school adolescents. *Western Journal of Speech Communication, 54,* 377–394.

Baxter, L. A., & Pittman, G. (2001). Communicatively remembering turning points of relational development in heterosexual romantic relationships. *Communication Reports, 14,* 1–18.

Behnke, R. R., & Sawyer, C. R. (2001). Public speaking arousal as a function of anticipatory activation and autonomic reactivity. *Communication Reports, 14,* 73–86.

Belenky, M. F., Clinchy, B. M., Goldberger, N. R., & Tarule, J. M. (1986). *Women's ways of knowing: The development of self, voice, and mind.* New York: Basic.

Bellah, R. N. (1970). Christianity and symbolic realism. *Journal for the Scientific Study of Religion, 9,* 89–96.

Benoit, W. L., & Benoit, P. J. (1988). Factors influencing the accuracy of verbal reports of conversational behavior. *Central States Speech Journal, 39,* 219–232.

Benoit, W. L., & Hansen, G. J. (2001). Presidential debate questions and the public agenda. *Communication Quarterly, 49,* 130–141.

Benton, J. E., & Daly, J. L. (1991). A question order effect in a local government survey. *Public Opinion Quarterly, 55,* 640–642.

Berelson, B. (1952). *Content analysis in communication research.* New York: Free Press.

Berger, C. R. (2001). Making it worse than it is: Quantitative depictions of threatening trends in the news. *Journal of Communication, 51,* 655–677.

Berger, C. R., & Calabrese, R. J. (1975). Toward a developmental theory of interpersonal communication. *Human Communication Research, 1,* 99–112.

Bergvall, V. L., & Remlinger, K. A. (1996). Reproduction, resistance and gender in educational discourse: The role of critical discourse analysis. *Discourse & Society, 7,* 453–479.

Berlo, D. K., Lemert, J. B., & Mertz, R. J. (1970). Dimensions for evaluating the acceptability of message sources. *Public Opinion Quarterly, 33,* 563–576.

Bethea, L. S. (2002). The impact of an adult parent on communicative satisfaction and dyadic adjustment in the long-term marital relationship: Adult-children and spouses' retrospective accounts. *Journal of Applied Communication Research, 30,* 107–125.

Beveridge, W. I. B. (1950). *The art of scientific investigation.* New York: Vintage.

Bingham, S. G., & Burleson, B. R. (1996). The development of a sexual harassment proclivity scale: Construct validation and relationship to communication competence. *Communication Quarterly, 44,* 308–325.

Bingham, W. V. D., & Moore, B. V. (1959). *How to interview* (4th ed.). New York: Harper.

Blair, C., Brown, J. R., & Baxter, L. A. (1994). Disciplining the feminine. *Quarterly Journal of Speech, 80,* 383–409.

Blair, C., Jeppeson, M. S., & Pucci, E., Jr. (1991). Public memorializing in postmodernity: The Vietnam Veterans Memorial as prototype. *Quarterly Journal of Speech, 77,* 263–288.

Blair, J., Zhao, S., Bickart, B., & Kuhn, R. (1995). *Sample design for household telephone surveys: A bibliography 1949–1995.* College Park, MD: Survey Research Center, University of Maryland.

Blalock, H. M., Jr. (1979). *Social statistics.* New York: McGraw-Hill.

Bochner, A. P. (1985). Perspectives on inquiry: Representation, conversation, and reflection. In M. L. Knapp & G. R. Miller (Eds.), *Handbook of interpersonal communication* (pp. 27–58). Beverly Hills, CA: Sage.

Bochner, A. P. (1994). Perspectives on inquiry II: Theories and stories. In M. L. Knapp & G. R. Miller (Eds.), *Handbook of interpersonal communication* (2nd ed., pp. 21–41). Thousand Oaks, CA: Sage.

Bohrnstedt, G. W. (1983). Measurement. In P. H. Rossi, J. D. Wright, & A. B. Anderson (Eds.), *Handbook of survey research* (pp. 70–121). New York: Academic Press.

Bolstein, R. (1991). Comparison of the likelihood to vote among preelection poll respondents and nonrespondents. *Public Opinion Quarterly, 55,* 648–650.

Booth-Butterfield, S., & Gould, M. (1986). The communication anxiety inventory: Validation of state- and context-communication apprehension. *Communication Quarterly, 34,* 194–205.

Bormann, E. G., Bormann, E., & Harty, K. C. (1995). Using symbolic convergence theory and focus group interviews to develop communication designed to stop teenage use of tobacco. In L. R. Frey (Ed.), *Innovation in group facilitation: Applications in natural settings* (pp. 200–232). Cresskill, NJ: Hampton.

Bower, R. T., & de Gasparis, P. (1978). *Ethics in social research: Protecting the interests of human subjects.* New York: Praeger.

Boyd, J. (2000). Selling home: Corporate stadium names and the destruction of commemoration. *Journal of Applied Communication Research, 28,* 330–346.

Boyd, J. (2001). Corporate rhetoric participates in public dialogue: A solution to the public/private conundrum. *Southern Communication Journal, 66,* 279–292.

Braithwaite, C. A. (1997a). Blood money: The routine violation of conversational rules. *Communication Reports, 10,* 63–73.

Braithwaite, C. A. (1997b). Sa'ah Naaghai Bik'eh Hozhoon: An ethnography of Navajo educational communication practices. *Communication Education, 46,* 219–234.

Braithwaite, D. O. (1995). Ritualized embarrassment at "coed" wedding and baby showers. *Communication Reports, 8,* 145–157.

Braithwaite, D. O., & Baxter, L. A. (1995). "I do" again: The relational dialectics of renewing marriage vows. *Journal of Social and Personal Relationships, 12,* 177–198.

Braun, M. J. (2001). Using self-directed teams to integrate service-learning into an organizational communication course. *Southern Communication Journal, 66,* 226–238.

Briggs, C. L. (1986). *Learning how to ask: A sociolinguistic appraisal of the role of the interview in social science research.* New York: Cambridge University Press.

Brownlee, K. A. (1975). A note on the effects of nonresponse on surveys. *Journal of the American Statistical Association, 52,* 29–32.

Bruess, C. J. S., & Pearson, J. C. (1997). Interpersonal rituals in marriage and adult friendship. *Communication Monographs, 64,* 25–46.

Brummett, B., & Duncan, M. C. (1990). Theorizing without totalizing: Specularity and televised sports. *Quarterly Journal of Speech, 76,* 227–246.

Burgoon, J. K., & LePoire, B. A. (1999). Nonverbal cues and interpersonal judgments: Participant and observer perceptions of intimacy, dominance, composure and formality. *Communication Monographs, 66,* 105–124.

Burgoon, J. K., LePoire, B. A., & Rosenthal, R. (1995). Effects of preinteraction expectancies and target communication on perceiver recipocity and compensation in dyadic interaction. *Journal of Experimental Social Psychology, 31,* 287–321.

Buzzanell, P. M., Burrell, N. A., Stafford, R. S., & Berkowitz, S. (1996). When I call you up and you're not there: Application of communication accommodation theory to telephone answering machine messages. *Western Journal of Communication, 60,* 310–336.

Campbell, D. T., & Stanley, J. C. (1963). *Experimental and quasi-experimental designs for research.* New York: Houghton Mifflin.

Canary, D. J., Brossmann, B. G., & Seibold, D. R. (1987). Argument structures in decision-making groups. *Southern Speech Communication Journal, 53,* 18–37.

Carbaugh, D. (1999). "Just listen": "Listening" and landscape among the Blackfeet. *Western Journal of Communication, 63,* 250–270.

Carmines, E. G., & Zeller, R. A. (1979). *Reliability and validity assessment.* Beverly Hills, CA: Sage.

Caughlin, J. P. (2002). The demand/withdraw pattern of communication as a predictor of marital satisfaction over time. *Human Communication Research, 28,* 49–85.

Charmaz, K. (1983). The grounded theory method: An explication and interpretation. In R. M. Emerson (Ed.), *Contemporary field research: A collection of readings* (pp. 109–126). Prospect Heights, IL: Waveland.

Christophel, D. M. (1990). The relationships among teacher immediacy behaviors, student motivation, and learning. *Communication Education, 39,* 323–340.

Cohen, J. (1960). A coefficient of agreement for nominal scales. *Educational and Psychological Measurement, 20,* 37–46.

Cohen, J. (1988). *Statistical power analysis for the behavioral sciences* (2nd ed.). Hillsdale, NJ: Erlbaum.

Cohen, J. (1992). A power primer. *Psychological Bulletin, 112,* 155–159.

Coker, D. A., & Burgoon, J. K. (1987). The nature of conversational involvement and nonverbal encoding patterns. *Human Communication Research, 13,* 463–494.

Cole, S. (1992). *Making science: Between nature and society.* Cambridge, MA: Harvard University Press.

Collier, J., Jr. (1967). *Visual anthropology: Photography as a research method.* New York: Holt, Rinehart and Winston.

Collins, G. C., & Blodgett, T. B. (1981). Sexual harassment. . . Some see it. . . Some won't. *Harvard Business Review,* March–April, pp. 76–95.

Conquergood, D. (Producer), & Siegel, T. (Producer & Director) (1985). *Between two worlds: The Hmong shaman in America* [Videotape]. (Available from Filmmakers Library, 124 E. 40th St., Suite 901, New York, NY 10016).

Conquergood, D. (Producer), & Siegel, T. (Producer & Director) (1990). *The heart broken in half* [Videotape]. (Available from Filmmakers Library, 124 E. 40th St., Suite 901, New York, NY 10016).

Converse, J. M. (1987). *Survey research in the United States: Roots and emergence, 1980–1960.* Berkeley: University of California Press.

Converse, J. M., & Presser, S. (1986). *Survey questions: Handcrafting the standardized questionnaire.* Newbury Park, CA: Sage.

Conville, R. L. (1991). *Relational transitions: The evolution of personal relationships.* New York: Praeger.

Cook, T. D., & Campbell, D. T. (1979). *Quasi-experimentation: Design & analysis issues for field settings.* Boston: Houghton Mifflin.

Cooper, H. M. (1989). *Integrating research: A guide for literature reviews.* Newbury Park, CA: Sage.

Creswell, J. W. (1998). *Qualitative inquiry and research design: Choosing among five traditions.* Thousand Oaks, CA: Sage.

Crowne, D. P., & Marlowe, D. (1960). A new scale of social desirability independent of psychopathology. *Journal of Consulting Psychology, 24,* 349–354.

DeChaine, D. R. (2002). Affect and embodied understanding in musical experience. *Text and Performance Quarterly, 22,* 79–98.

Delgado, F. P. (1998). Chicano ideology revisited: Rap music and the (re)articulation of Chicanismo. *Western Journal of Communication, 62,* 95–113.

Della-Piana, C. K., & Anderson, J. A. (1995). Performing community: Community service as cultural conversation. *Communication Studies, 46,* 187–200.

Denzin, N. K. (1978). *Sociological methods.* New York: McGraw-Hill.

Denzin, N. K., & Lincoln, Y. S. (Eds.) (1994). *Handbook of qualitative research.* Thousand Oaks, CA: Sage.

Dickinson, G. (1997). Memories for sale: Nostalgia and the construction of identity in old Pasadena. *Quarterly Journal of Speech, 83,* 1–27.

Dillman, D. A. (1978). *Mail and telephone surveys: The total design method.* New York: Wiley.

Dimmick, J. W., Patterson, S., & Sikand, J. (1996). Personal telephone networks: A typology and two empirical studies. *Journal of Broadcasting & Electronic Media, 40,* 45–59.

Dinauer, L. D., & Ondeck, K. E. (1999). Gender and institutional affiliation as determinants of publishing in *Human Communication Research. Human Communication Research, 25,* 548–568.

Dindia, K. (1998). "Going into and coming out of the closet": The dialectics of stigma disclosure. In B. M. Montgomery & L. A. Baxter (Eds.), *Dialectical approaches to studying personal relationships* (pp. 83–108). Mahweh, NJ: Erlbaum.

Dindia, K., & Allen, M. (1992). Sex differences in self-disclosure: A meta-analysis. *Psychological Bulletin, 112,* 106–124.

Donald, M. N. (1960). Implications of nonresponse for the interpretation of mail questionnaire data. *Public Opinion Quarterly, 24,* 99–114.

Downs, C. W. (1988). *Communication audits.* Glenview, IL: Scott, Foresman.

Doyle, A. C. (1891/1892). A scandal in Bohemia. *The original illustrated Sherlock Holmes* (pp. 11–25). Secaucus, NJ: Castle. (First published in *The Strand,* July, 1891.)

Duck, S. (Ed.) (1997). *Handbook of personal relationships: Theory, research and interventions* (2nd ed.). New York: Wiley.

Edwards, J. A. (1993). Principles and contrasting systems of discourse transcription. In J. A. Edwards & M. D. Lampert (Eds.), *Talking data: Transcription and coding in discourse research* (pp. 3–32). Hillsdale, NJ: Erlbaum.

Edwards, J. A., & Lampert, M. D. (Eds.) (1993). *Talking data: Transcription and coding in discourse research.* Hillsdale, NJ: Erlbaum.

Elder, G. H., Jr., Pavalko, E. K., & Clipp, E. C. (1993). *Working with archival data: Studying lives.* Newbury Park, CA: Sage.

Ellis, B. H., & Miller, K. I. (1993). The role of assertiveness, personal control, and participation in the prediction of nurse burnout. *Journal of Applied Communication Research, 21,* 327–342.

Ellis, C. (1995). *Final negotiations: A story of love, loss, and chronic illness.* Philadelphia: Temple University Press.

Ellis, K. (2000). Perceived teacher confirmation: The development and validation of an instrument and two studies of the relationship to cognitive and affective learning. *Human Communication Research, 26,* 264–291.

Emerson, R. M. (Ed.) (1988). *Contemporary field research.* Boston: Little, Brown.

Emerson, R. M., Fretz, R. I., & Shaw, L. L. (1995). *Writing ethnographic fieldnotes.* Chicago: University of Chicago Press.

Emmert, P., & Barker, L. L. (Eds.) (1989). *Measurement of communication behavior.* New York: Longman.

Engelberg, M., Flora, J. A., & Nass, C. I. (1995). AIDS knowledge: Effects of channel involvement and interpersonal communication. *Health Communication, 7,* 73–91.

Erlandson, D. A., Harris, E. L., Skipper, B. L., & Allen, S. D. (1993). *Doing naturalistic inquiry: A guide to methods.* Newbury Park, CA: Sage.

Evans, W. (1996). Computer-supported content analysis: Trends, tools, and techniques. *Social Science Computer Review, 14,* 269–279.

Feick, L. F. (1989). Latent class analysis of survey questions that include don't know responses. *Public Opinion Quarterly, 53,* 525–547.

Finkel, S. E., Guterbok, T. M., & Borg, M. J. (1991). Race-of-interviewer effects in a preelection poll: Virginia 1989. *Public Opinion Quarterly, 55,* 313–330.

Fisher, R. A., & Yates, F. (1963). *Statistical tables for biological, agricultural, and medical research* (6th ed.). London: Longman.

Fiske, S. T. (1995). Social cognition. In A. Tesser (Ed.), *Advanced social psychology* (pp. 149–193). New York: McGraw-Hill.

Fitch, K. L. (1994). A cross-cultural study of direction sequences and some implications for compliance-gaining research. *Communication Monographs, 61,* 185–209.

Fitch, K. L. (1998). *Speaking relationally: Culture, communication, and interpersonal connection.* New York: Guilford.

Fitzpatrick, M. A. (1988). *Between husbands and wives: Communication in marriage.* Beverly Hills, CA: Sage.

Fitzpatrick, M. A., & Ritchie, L. D. (1994). Communication schemata within the family: Multiple perspectives on family interaction. *Human Communication Research, 20,* 275–301.

Floyd, K., & Voloudakis, M. (1999). Affectionate behavior in adult platonic friendships: Interpreting and evaluating expectancy violations. *Human Communication Research, 25,* 341–369.

Foddy, W. (1993). *Constructing questions for interviews and questionnaires: Theory and practice in social research.* New York: Cambridge University Press.

Fontana, A., & Frey, J. H. (1994). Interviewing: The art of science. In N. K. Denzin & Y. S. Lincoln (Eds.), *Handbook of qualitative research* (pp. 361–376). Thousand Oaks, CA: Sage.

Ford, L. A., Ray, E. B., & Ellis, H. B. (1999). Translating scholarship on intrafamilial sexual abuse: The utility of a dialectical perspective for adult survivors. *Journal of Applied Communication Research, 27,* 139–157.

Fowler, F. J., Jr. (1995). *Improving survey questions: Design and evaluation.* Thousand Oaks, CA: Sage.

Frankfort-Nachmias, C., & Leon-Guerrero, A. (1997). *Social statistics for a diverse society.* Thousand Oaks, CA: Pine Forge.

Frey, L. R. (Ed.) (1999). *The handbook of group communication theory and research.* Thousand Oaks, CA: Sage.

Gale directory of publications and broadcast media. (1999). Farmington Hills, MI: Author.

Gall, J. (1975). *Systemantics: How systems work and especially how they fail.* New York: Quadrangle.

Gallup, G. (1984, December 13). Where parents go wrong. *San Francisco Chronicle,* p. 7.

Gaziano, C., & McGrath, K. (1986). Measuring the concept of credibility. *Journalism Quarterly, 63,* 451–462.

Geertz, C. (1973). *The interpretation of cultures.* New York: Basic.

Gerbner, G., & Gross, L. (1976). Living with television: The violence profile. *Journal of Communication, 26,* 173–199.

Gibson, M. K., & Papa, M. J. (2000). The mud, the blood, and the beer guys: Organizational osmosis in blue-collar work groups. *Journal of Applied Communication Research, 28,* 68–88.

Giddens, A. (1984). *The constitution of society: Outline of the theory of structuration.* Berkeley: University of California Press.

Glaser, B., & Strauss, A. (1967). *The discovery of grounded theory.* Chicago: Aldine.

Goetz, J. P., & LeCompte, M. D. (1981). Ethnographic research and the problem of data reduction. *Anthropology and Education Quarterly, 12,* 51–70.

Goffman, E. (1959). *The presentation of self in everyday life.* New York: Doubleday.

Goffman, E. (1979). *Gender advertisements.* New York: Harper.

Gold, R. L. (1958). Roles in sociological field observations. *Social Forces, 36,* 217–223.

Goldsmith, D. J. (2000). Soliciting advice: The role of sequential placement in mitigating face threat. *Communication Monographs, 67,* 1–20.

Goldsmith, D. J., & Baxter, L. A. (1996). Constituting relationships in talk. *Human Communication Research, 23,* 87–114.

Goldsmith, D. J., & Fitch, K. (1997). The normative context of advice as social support. *Human Communication Research, 23,* 454–476.

Golish, T., & Caughlin, J. P. (2002). "I'd rather not talk about it": Adolescents' and young adults' use of topic avoidance in stepfamilies. *Journal of Applied Communication Research, 30,* 78–106.

Goodwin, M. J. (1990). *He-said-she-said: Talk as social organization among black children.* Bloomington: Indiana University Press.

Gottman, J. M. (1979). *Marital interaction: Experimental investigations.* New York: Academic Press.

Gottman, J. M. (1994). *What predicts divorce?* Hillsdale, NJ: Erlbaum.

Gottman, J., Levenson, R., & Woodin, E. (2001). Facial expressions during marital conflict. *Journal of Family Communication, 1,* 37–57.

Gould, J., & Kolb, W. (1964). *A dictionary of the social sciences.* New York: Free Press.

Graham, E. E. (1997). Turning points and commitment in post-divorce relationships. *Communication Monographs, 64,* 350–368.

Gring-Pemble, L. M. (2001). Are we going to now govern by anecdote? Rhetorical constructions of welfare recipients in Congressional hearings, debates, and legislation, 1992–1996. *Quarterly Journal of Speech, 87,* 341–365.

Gritching, W. (1986). Public opinion versus policy advice. *Australian Psychologist, 21,* 45–58.

Gubrium, J. F., & Holstein, J. A. (Eds.) (2002). *Handbook of interview research: Context & method.* Thousand Oaks, CA: Sage.

Gudykunst, W. B., Newmark, E., & Assante, M. K. (Eds.) (1994). *Handbook of international and intercultural communication* (2nd ed.). Newbury Park, CA: Sage.

Harper, D. (1994). On the authority of the image: Visual methods at the crossroads. In N. K. Denzin & Y. S. Lincoln (Eds.), *Handbook of qualitative research* (pp. 403–412). Thousand Oaks, CA: Sage.

Hart, R. P. (1984). *Verbal style and the presidency: A computer-based analysis.* San Francisco: Academic Press.

Hart, R. P. (1985). Systematic analysis of political discourse: The development of DICTION. In K. R. Sanders, L. L. Kaid, & D. Nimmo (Eds.), *Political communication yearbook I* (pp. 97–134). Carbondale: Southern Illinois University Press.

Hart, R. P. (1987). *The sound of leadership: Presidential communication in the modern age.* Chicago: University of Chicago Press.

Hart, R. P. (2000). *Campaign talk: Why elections are good for us.* Princeton, NJ: Princeton University Press.

Hart, R. P., & Jarvis, S. E. (1997). Political debate: Forms, styles, and media. *American Behavioral Scientist, 40,* 1095–1122.

Heath, S. B. (1983). *Ways with words: Language, life, and work in communities and classrooms.* New York: Cambridge University Press.

Hedrick, T. E., Bickman, L., & Rog, D. J. (1993). *Applied research design: A practical guide.* Newbury Park, CA: Sage.

Hendrick, S. S., & Hendrick, C. (1987). Multidimensionality of sexual attitudes. *Journal of Sex Research, 23,* 502–526.

Hendrick, S. S., & Hendrick, C. (1992). *Romantic love.* Newbury Park, CA: Sage.

Hirokawa, R. Y. (1982). Group communication and problem-solving effectiveness I: A critical review of inconsistent findings. *Communication Quarterly, 30,* 134–141.

Hirokawa, R. Y. (1988). Group communication research: Considerations for the use of interaction analysis. In C. H. Tardy (Ed.), *A handbook for the study of human communication: Methods and instruments for observing, measuring, and assessing communication processes* (pp. 229–246). Norwood, NJ: Ablex.

Hirschi, T., & Selvin, H. (1973). *Principles of survey analysis.* New York: Free Press.

Hodder, I. (1994). The interpretation of documents and material culture. In N. K. Denzin & Y. S. Lincoln (Eds.), *Handbook of qualitative research* (pp. 393–402). Thousand Oaks, CA: Sage.

Hoffman, E. W., & Heald, G. R. (2000). Tobacco and alcohol advertisements in popular African-American and general audiences magazines. *Communication Research Reports, 17,* 415–425.

Hogan, J. M., & Williams, G. (2000). Republican charisma and the American revolution: The textual persona of Thomas Paine's *Common Sense. Quarterly Journal of Speech, 86,* 1–18.

Hogelucht, K. S. B., & Geist, P. (1997). Discipline in the classroom: Communicative strategies for negotiating order. *Western Journal of Communication, 61,* 1–34.

Hopper, R., & Bell, R. A. (1984). Broadening the deception concept. *Quarterly Journal of Speech, 67,* 287–302.

Hopper, R., & LeBaron, C. (1998). How gender creeps into talk. *Research on Language and Social Interaction, 31,* 59–74.

How the poll was conducted (1995, October 1). *New York Times,* p. 15.

Howard, L. A., & Geist, P. (1995). Ideological positioning in organizational change: The dialectic of control in a merging organization. *Communication Monographs, 62,* 112–131.

Huck, S. W., & Sandler, H. M. (1979). *Rival hypotheses: Alternative interpretations of data based conclusions.* New York: Harper.

Humphreys, L. (1970). *Tearoom trade: Impersonal sex in public places.* Chicago: Aldine.

Huspek, M. (1989). Linguistic variability and power: An analysis of YOU KNOW/I THINK variation in working-class speech. *Journal of Pragmatics, 13,* 661–683.

Hymes, D. (1962). The ethnography of speaking. In T. Gladwin & W. C. Sturtevant (Eds.), *Anthropology and human behavior* (pp. 13–53). Washington, DC: Anthropology Society of Washington.

Hymes, D. (1972). Models of the interaction of language and social life. In J. Gumperz & D. Hymes (Eds.), *Directions in sociolinguistics: The ethnography of communication* (pp. 35–71). New York: Holt, Rinehart & Winston.

Infante, D. A., & Wigley, C. J., III (1986). Verbal aggressiveness: An interpersonal model and measure. *Communication Monographs, 53,* 61–69.

International encyclopedia of communications (1989). New York: Oxford University Press.

Jablin, F. M., & Putnam, L. L. (Eds.) (2000). *The new handbook of organizational communication.* Newbury Park, CA: Sage.

Janesick, V. J. (1994). The dance of qualitative research design: Metaphor, methodolatry, and meaning. In N. K. Denzin & Y. S. Lincoln (Eds.), *Handbook of qualitative research* (pp. 209–219). Thousand Oaks, CA: Sage.

Jarmon, L. (1996). Performance as a resource in the practice of conversation analysis. *Text and Performance Quarterly, 16,* 336–355.

Johnson, J. C. (1990). *Selecting ethnographic informants.* Newbury Park, CA: Sage.

Johnson, J. D., Meyer, M. E., Berkowitz, J. M., Ethington, C. T., & Miller, V. D. (1997). Testing two contrasting structural models of innovativeness in a contractual network. *Human Communication Research, 24,* 320–348.

Jones, J. H. (1981). *Bad blood: The Tuskegee syphilis experiments.* New York: Free Press.

Jones, S. R. G. (1990). Worker independence and output: The Hawthorne studies reevaluated. *American Sociological Review, 55,* 176–190.

Jorgenson, J. (1995). Re-relationalizing rapport in interpersonal settings. In W. Leeds-Hurwitz (Ed.), *Social approaches to communication* (pp. 155–170). New York: Guilford.

Kalbfleisch, P. J., & Davies, A. B. (1993). An interpersonal model for participation in mentoring relationships. *Western Journal of Communication, 57,* 399–415.

Kalton, G. (1983). *Introduction to survey sampling.* Newbury Park, CA: Sage.

Kanji, G. K. (1993). *100 statistical tests.* Newbury Park, CA: Sage.

Kaplan, A. (1964). *The conduct of inquiry.* San Francisco: Chandler.

Kasof, J. (1993). Sex bias in the naming of stimulus persons. *Psychological Bulletin, 113,* 140–163.

Katriel, T. (1994). Sites of memory: Discourses of the past in Israeli pioneering settlement museums. *Quarterly Journal of Speech, 80,* 1–20.

Katriel, T., & Farrell, T. (1991). Scrapbooks as cultural texts: An American art of memory. *Text and Performance Quarterly, 11,* 1–17.

Katzer, J., Cook, K. H., & Crouch, W. W. (1991). *Evaluating information: A guide for users of social science research* (3rd ed.). New York: McGraw-Hill.

Kiecolt, E. J., & Nathan, L. E. (1985). *Secondary analysis of survey data.* Beverly Hills, CA: Sage.

King, C. E., & Christensen, A. (1983). The relationship events scale: A Guttman scaling of progress in courtship. *Journal of Marriage and the Family, 45,* 671–678.

Kirby, E. L., & Krone, K. J. (2002). "The policy exists but you can't really use it": Communication and the structuration of work–family policies. *Journal of Applied Communication Research, 30,* 50–77.

Kish, L. (1965). *Survey sampling.* New York: Wiley.

Knapp, M. L., & Daly, J. A. (Eds.) (2002). *Handbook of interpersonal communication* (3rd ed.). Thousand Oaks, CA: Sage.

Koolstra, C. M., & Van Der Hoot, T. H. (1996). Longitudinal effects of television on childen's leisure-time reading: A test of three explanatory models. *Human Communication Research, 23,* 4–35.

Krippendorff, K. (1980). *Content analysis: An introduction to its methodology.* Beverly Hills, CA: Sage.

Krokoff, L. J. (1987). Recruiting representative samples for marital interaction research. *Journal of Social and Personal Relationships, 4,* 317–328.

Krueger, R. A. (1988). *Focus groups: A practical guide for applied research.* Newbury Park, CA: Sage.

Kuhn, T. (1970). *The structure of scientific revolutions.* Chicago: University of Chicago Press.

Kuhn, T., & Poole, M. S. (2000). Do conflict management styles affect group decision making? Evidence from a longitudinal field study. *Human Communication Research, 26,* 558–590.

Kvale, S. (1996). *InterViews: An introduction to qualitative research interviewing.* Thousand Oaks, CA: Sage.

Landon, 1,293,669: Roosevelt, 972,897 (1936a, October 31). *Literary Digest,* pp. 5–6.

Lannaman, J. J. (1991). Interpersonal communication research as ideological practice. *Communication Theory, 1,* 179–203.

LaPiere, R. T. (1934). Attitudes versus actions. *Social Forces, 13,* 230–237.

Larson, R., & Richards, M. H. (1994). *Divergent realities: The emotional lives of mothers, fathers, and adolescents.* New York: Basic.

Lazarsfield, P. F. (1959). Problems in methodology. In R. K. Merton (Ed.), *Sociology today.* New York: Basic.

Lee, R. (1993). *Doing research on sensitive topics.* Newbury Park, CA: Sage.

Lemert, J. B., Wanta, W., & Lee, T. (1999). Party identification and negative advertising in a U.S. Senate election. *Journal of Communication, 49,* 123–134.

Levy, P. E., & Steelman, L. A. (1996). Using advanced statistics. In F. T. L. Leong & J. T. Austin (Eds.), *The psychology research handbook: A guide for graduate students and research assistants* (pp. 219–228). Thousand Oaks, CA: Sage.

Lincoln, Y. S., & Guba, E. G. (1985). *Naturalistic inquiry.* Newbury Park, CA: Sage.

Lindlof, T. R. (1995). *Qualitative communication research methods.* Thousand Oaks, CA: Sage.

Lindsley, S. L. (1999). Communication and "the Mexican way": Stability and trust as core symbols in Maquiladoras. *Western Journal of Communication, 63,* 1–31.

Livingstone, S., & Leibes, T. (1995). "Where have all the mothers gone": Soap operas' replaying of the Oedipal story. *Critical Studies in Mass Communication, 12,* 155–175.

Lofland, J., & Lofland, L. H. (1995). *Analyzing social settings: A guide to qualitative observation and analysis* (3rd ed.). Belmont, CA: Wadsworth.

Lombard, M., Reich, R. D., Grabe, M. E., Bracken, C. C., & Ditton, T. B. (2000). Presence and television: The role of screen size. *Human Communication Research, 26,* 75–98.

Lull, J. (1990). *Inside family viewing.* London: Routledge.

MacLaine, S. (1983). *Out on a limb.* New York: Bantam.

Mandelbaum, J. (1989). Interpersonal activities in conversational storytelling. *Western Journal of Speech Communication, 53,* 114–126.

Manning, P. K. (1987). *Semiotics and fieldwork.* Newbury Park, CA: Sage.

Manning, P. K., & Cullum-Swan, B. (1994). Narrative, content, and semiotic analysis. In N. K. Denzin & Y. S. Lincoln (Eds.), *Handbook of qualitative research* (pp. 463–477). Thousand Oaks, CA: Sage.

Marquis, K. H. (1970). Effects of social reinforcement on health reporting in the household interview. *Sociometry, 33,* 203–215.

Marshall, C., & Rossman, G. B. (1995). *Designing qualitative research.* Thousand Oaks, CA: Sage.

McAlister, A., Perry, C., Killen, J., Slinkard, L. A., & Maccoby, N. (1980). Pilot study of smoking, alcohol, and drug abuse prevention. *American Journal of Public Health,* July, pp. 719–721.

McComb, M. (1995). Becoming a travelers aid volunteer: Communication in socialization and training. *Communication Studies, 46,* 297–316.

McCombs, M., & Bell, T. (1996). The agenda setting role of mass communication. In M. B. Salwen & D. W. Stacks (Eds.), *An integrated approach to communication theory and research* (pp. 93–110). Mahweh, NJ: Erlbaum.

McCracken, G. (1988). *The long interview.* Newbury Park, CA: Sage.

McCroskey, J. C., Hamilton, P. R., & Weiner, A. M. (1974). The effect of interaction behavior on source credibility, homophily, and interpersonal attraction. *Human Communication Research, 1,* 42–52.

McIver, J. P., & Carmines, E. G. (1981). *Unidimensional scaling.* Newbury Park, CA: Sage.

McKee, K. B., & Pardun, C. J. (1996). Mixed messages: The relationship between sexual and religious imagery in rock, country, and Christian videos. *Communication Reports, 9,* 163–171.

McLaurin, P. (1995). An examination of the effect of culture on pro-social messages directed at African-American at-risk youth. *Communication Monographs, 62,* 301–326.

Merton, R. K. (1987). The focused interview and focus groups. *Public Opinion Quarterly, 51,* 550–566.

Meyer, J. C. (1997). Humor in member narratives: Uniting and dividing at work. *Western Journal of Communication, 61,* 188–208.

Meyers, R. A., Seibold, D. R., & Brashers, D. E. (1991). Argument in initial group decision-making discussions: Refinement of a coding scheme and a descriptive quantitative analysis. *Western Journal of Speech Communication, 55,* 47–68.

Miles, M. B., & Huberman, A. M. (1994). *Qualitative data analysis: An expanded sourcebook* (2nd ed.). Thousand Oaks, CA: Sage.

Milgram, S. (1963). Behavioral study of obedience. *Journal of Abnormal Social Psychology, 67,* 371–378.

Milgram, S. (1965). Some conditions of obedience and disobedience to authority. *Human Relations, 18,* 57–76.

Miller, D. (1991). *Handbook of research design and social measurement.* Newbury Park, CA: Sage.

Miller, K., Joseph, L., & Apker, J. (2000). Strategic ambiguity in the role development process. *Journal of Applied Communication Research, 28,* 193–214.

Miller-Day, M., & Lee, J. W. (2001). Communicating disappointment: The viewpoint of sons and daughters. *Journal of Family Communication, 1,* 111–131.

Mishler, E. G. (1986). *Research interviewing: Context and narrative.* Cambridge, MA: Harvard University Press.

Mitofsky, W. J. (1999). Miscalls likely in 2000. *Public Perspective, 10,* 42–43.

Mohr, L. B. (1990). *Understanding significance testing.* Newbury Park, CA: Sage.

Montgomery, B. M., & Duck, S. (Eds.) (1991). *Studying interpersonal interaction.* New York: Guilford.

Morgan, D. L. (1988). *Focus groups as qualitative research.* Newbury Park, CA: Sage.

Morgan, D. L. (2002). Focus group interviewing. In J. F. Gubrium & J. A. Holstein (Eds.), *Handbook of interview research: Context & method* (pp. 141–160). Thousand Oaks, CA: Sage.

Morgan, M., & Shanahan, J. (1997). Two decades of cultivation research: An appraisal and meta-analysis. In B. R. Burleson & A. W. Kunkel (Eds.), *Communication yearbook 20* (pp. 1–45). Thousand Oaks, CA: Sage.

Morgan, S. E., & Miller, J. K. (2002). Communicating about gifts of life: The effect of knowledge, attitudes, and altruism on behavior and behavioral intentions regarding organ donation. *Journal of Applied Communication Research, 30,* 163–178.

Morman, M. T. (2000). The influence of fear appeals, message design, and masculinity on men's motivation to perform the testicular self-exam. *Journal of Applied Communication Research, 28,* 91–116.

Morse, J. M. (1994). Designing funded qualitative research. In N. K. Denzin & Y. S. Lincoln (Eds.), *Handbook of qualitative research* (pp. 220–235). Thousand Oaks, CA: Sage.

Moskowitz, M. (1981, May 23). The drugs that doctors order. *San Francisco Chronicle,* p. 33.

Murphy, A. G. (2001). The flight attendant dilemma: An analysis of communication and sensemaking during in-flight emergencies. *Journal of Applied Communication Research, 29,* 30–53.

Nicholls, W. L., II, Baker, R. P., & Martin, J. (1997). The effect of new data collection technology on survey data quality. In L. Lyberg, M. Collins, E. de Leeuw, C. Dippo, N. Schwarz, & D. Trewin (Eds.), *Survey measurement and process quality.* New York: Wiley.

Nisbett, R., & Ross, L. (1980). *Human inference: Strategies and shortcomings of social judgment.* Englewood Cliffs, NJ: Prentice-Hall.

Noelle-Neumann, E. (1970). Wanted: Rules for wording structured questionnaires. *Public Opinion Quarterly, 34,* 191–201.

Norton, C. S. (1989). *Life metaphors: Stories of ordinary survival.* Carbondale, IL: Southern Illinois University Press.

Norton, R. (1978). Foundation of a communicator style construct. *Human Communication Research, 4,* 99–112.

Norton, R. (1983). Measuring marital quality: A critical look at the dependent variable. *Journal of Marriage and the Family, 45,* 141–151.

Oetzel, J., Ting-Toomey, S., Masumoto, T., Yokochi, Y., Pan, X., Takai, J., & Wilcox, R. (2001). Face and facework in conflict: A cross-cultural comparison of China, Germany, Japan, and the United States. *Communication Monographs, 68,* 235–258.

O'Keefe, D. J., Shepherd, G. J., & Streeter, T. (1982). Role category questionnaire measures of cognitive complexity: Reliability and comparability of alternative forms. *Central States Speech Journal, 33,* 333–338.

Oliver, M. B. (1999). Caucasian viewers' memory of black and white criminal suspects in the news. *Journal of Communication, 49,* 46–60.

Osgood, C. E., Suci, C. J., & Tannenbaum, P. H. (1957). *The measurement of meaning.* Urbana: University of Illinois Press.

Papa, M. J., Singhal, A., Law, S., Pant, S., Sood, S., Rogers, E. M., & Shefner-Rogers, C. L. (2000). Entertainment-education and social change: An analysis of parasocial interaction, social learning, collective efficacy, and paradoxical communication. *Journal of Communication, 50,* 31–55.

Parrott, R., & Duggan, A. (1999). Using coaches as role models of sun protection for youth: Georgia's "Got Youth Covered" project. *Journal of Applied Communication Research, 27,* 107–119.

Patterson, B. R., Neupauer, N. C., Burant, P. A., Koehn, S. C., & Reed, A. T. (1996). A preliminary examination of conversation analytic techniques: Rates of inter-transcriber reliability. *Western Journal of Communication, 60,* 76–91.

Patton, M. Q. (1990). *Qualitative evaluation and research methods* (2nd ed.). Newbury Park, CA: Sage.

Pavitt, C., & Johnson, K. K. (2002). Scheidel and Crowell revisited: A descriptive study of group proposal sequencing. *Communication Monographs, 69,* 19–32.

Pearson, E. S., & Hartley, H. O. (Eds.) (1966). *Biometrika tables for statisticians* (3rd ed., Vol. 1). Cambridge, UK: The University Press.

Perinelli, P. (1986). Nonsuspecting public in TV call-in polls. *New York Times,* February 14, letter to the editor.

Peterson, R. A. (1984). Asking the age question: A research note. *Public Opinion Quarterly, 48,* 379–383.

Philipsen, G. (1975). Speaking "like a man" in Teamsterville: Culture patterns of role enactment in an urban neighborhood. *Quarterly Journal of Speech, 61,* 13–22.

Philipsen, G. (1992). *Speaking culturally: Explorations in social communication.* Albany: State University of New York Press.

Picou, J. S. (1996). Sociology and compelled disclosure: Protecting respondent confidentiality. *Sociological Spectrum, 16,* 209–232.

Planalp, S. (1993). Friends' and acquaintances' conversations II: Coded differences. *Journal of Social and Personal Relationships, 10,* 339–354.

Polkinghorne, D. (1983). *Methodology for the human sciences: Systems of inquiry.* Albany: State University of New York Press.

Pomerantz, A., & Fehr, B. J. (1997). Conversation analysis: An approach to the study of social action as sense making practices. In T. A. Van Dijk (Ed.), *Discourse as social interaction* (pp. 64–91). Thousand Oaks, CA: Sage.

Poole, M. S., & Folger, J. P. (1981). A new method of establishing the representational validity of interaction coding schemes: Do we see what they see? *Human Communication Research, 8,* 26–42.

Poole, M. S., Seibold, D. R., & McPhee, R. D. (1996). The structuration of group decisions. In R. Y. Hirokawa & M. S. Poole (Eds.), *Communication and group decision making* (2nd ed., pp. 114–146). Thousand Oaks, CA: Sage.

Potter, W. J. (1996). *An analysis of thinking and research about qualitative methods.* Mahweh, NJ: Erlbaum.

Presser, S., & Blair, J. (1994). Survey pretesting: Do different methods produce different results? In P. Marsden (Ed.), *Sociological methodology 1994* (pp. 73–104). San Francisco: Jossey-Bass.

Rasinski, K. A. (1989). The effect of question wording on public support for government spending. *Public Opinion Quarterly, 53,* 388–394.

Rasmussen, K., & Downey, S. D. (1991). Dialectical disorientation in Vietnam War films: Subversion of the mythology of war. *Quarterly Journal of Speech, 77,* 176–195.

Ray, W., & Ravizza, R. (2000). *Methods toward a science of behavior and experience* (6th ed.). Belmont, CA: Wadsworth.

Reinard, J. C., & Arsenault, D. J. (2000). The impact of forms of strategic and non-strategic *voir dire* questions on jury verdicts. *Communication Monographs, 67,* 158–177.

Reinharz, S. (1992). *Feminist methods in social research.* New York: Oxford University Press.

Richmond, V. P., Gorham, J. S., & McCroskey, J. C. (1987). The relationship between selected immediacy behaviors and cognitive learning. *Communication Yearbook, 10,* 574–590.

Riessman, C. K. (1993). *Narrative analysis.* Newbury Park, CA: Sage.

Riffe, D., Lacy, S., & Fico, F. G. (1998). *Analyzing media messages: Using quantitative content analysis in research.* Mahweh, NJ: Erlbaum.

Rimer, S. (1985, December 24). Poll sees landslide for Santa: Of U.S. children, 87% believe. *New York Times.*

Roberts, C. W. (1997). *Text analysis for the social sciences: Methods for drawing statistical inferences from texts and transcripts.* Mahweh, NJ: Erlbaum.

Roberts, J. (1974). *Seth speaks.* New York: Bantam.

Roethlisberger, F. J., & Dickson, W. J. (1939). *Management and the worker.* Cambridge, MA: Harvard University Press.

Rogers, E. M., Vaughan, P. W., Swalehe, R. M. A., Rao, N., & Sood, S. (1996). *Effects of an entertainment-education radio soap opera on family planning and HIV/AIDS prevention behavior in Tanzania.* Report presented at a technical briefing on the Tanzania Entertainment-Education Project, Rockefeller Foundation, New York, March 27.

Rogers, L. E., & Farace, R. V. (1975). Analysis of relational communication in dyads: New measurement procedures. *Human Communication Research, 1,* 222–239.

Rosenthal, R. (1966). *Experimenter effects in behavioral research.* New York: Meredith.

Rossi, P. H., & Freeman, H. E. (1993). *Evaluation: A systematic approach.* Newbury Park, CA: Sage.

Rossi, P. H., Wright, J. D., & Anderson, A. B. (Eds.) (1983). *Handbook of survey research.* New York: Academic Press.

Rossler, P., & Brosius, H. (2001). Do talk shows cultivate adolescents' views of the world? A prolonged-exposure experiment. *Journal of Communication, 51,* 143–163.

Rothman, E. (1981). The written record. *Journal of Family History,* Spring, pp. 47–56.

Rothman, E. K. (1984). *Hands and hearts: A history of courtship in America.* New York: Basic.

Rubin, A. M., Perse, E. M., & Powell, R. A. (1985). Loneliness, parasocial interaction, and local television news viewing. *Human Communication Research, 12,* 155–180.

Rubin, H. J., & Rubin, R. S. (1995). *Qualitative interviewing: The art of hearing data.* Thousand Oaks, CA: Sage.

Rubin, R. B., Palmgreen, P., & Sypher, H. E. (1994). *Communication research measures: A sourcebook.* New York: Guilford.

Rubin, R. B., Rubin, A. M., & Piele, L. J. (2000). *Communication research: Strategies and sources* (5th ed.). Belmont, CA: Wadsworth.

Sachs, H. (1995). Computer networks and the formation of public opinion: An ethnographic study. *Media, Culture & Society, 17,* 81–99.

Sacks, J. J., Krushat, W. M., & Newman, J. (1980). Reliability of the health hazard appraisal. *American Journal of Public Health,* July, pp. 730–732.

Salazar, A. J. (1997). Communication effects on small group decision-making: Homogeneity and task as moderators of the communication-performance relationship. *Western Journal of Communication, 61,* 35–65.

Salazar, A. J., Hirokawa, R. Y., Propp, K. M., Julian, K. M., & Leatham, G. B. (1994). In search of true causes: Examination of the effect of group potential and group interaction on decision performance. *Human Communication Research, 20,* 529–559.

Scarce, R. (1994). (No) trial, (but) tribulations: When courts and ethnography conflict. *Journal of Contemporary Ethnography, 23,* 123–149.

Schatzman, L., & Strauss, A. L. (1973). *Field research: Strategies for a natural sociology.* Englewood Cliffs, NJ: Prentice Hall.

Schiffrin, D. (1994). *Approaches to discourse.* Cambridge, MA: Blackwell.

Schuman, J., & Presser, S. (1981). *Questions and answers in attitude surveys: Experiments on question form, wording and context.* New York: Academic Press.

Schwarz, N., & Sudman, S. (Eds.) (1996). *Answering questions: Methodology for determining cognitive and communicative processes in survey research.* San Francisco: Jossey-Bass.

Scott, W. A. (1955). Reliability of content analysis: The case for nominal scale coding. *Public Opinion Quarterly, 19,* 321–325.

Shaffir, W. B., & Stebbins, R. A. (Eds.) (1991). *Experiencing field work: An inside view of qualitative research.* Newbury Park, CA: Sage.

Sheatsley, P. B. (1983). Questionnaire construction and item writing. In P. H. Rossi, J. D. Wright, & A. B. Anderson (Eds.), *Handbook of survey research* (pp. 195–230). New York: Academic Press.

Shimanoff, S. B. (1980). *Communication rules: Theory and research.* Beverly Hills, CA: Sage.

Siegel, S., & Castellan, N. J., Jr. (1988). *Nonparametric statistics for the behavioral sciences* (2nd ed.). New York: McGraw-Hill.

Sillars, A. L. (1991). Behavioral observations. In B. M. Montgomery & S. Duck (Eds.), *Studying interpersonal interaction* (pp. 197–218). New York: Guilford.

Sillars, A. L., & Scott, M. D. (1983). Interpersonal perception between intimates: An integrative review. *Human Communication Research, 10,* 153–176.

Sillars, M. O., & Gronbeck, B. E. (2001). *Communication criticism: Rhetoric, social codes, cultural studies.* Prospect Heights, IL: Waveland.

Sills, D. L. (Ed.) (1991). *International encyclopedia of the social sciences.* New York: Macmillan.

Simons, H. W. (2000). A dilemma-centered analysis of Clinton's August 17th apologia: Implications for rhetorical theory and method. *Quarterly Journal of Speech, 86,* 438–453.

Skill, T., & Wallace, S. (1990). Family interactions on prime-time television: A descriptive analysis of assertive power interactions. *Journal of Broadcasting & Electronic Media, 34,* 243–262.

Slater, M. E., Karan, D. N., Rouner, D., & Walters, D. (2002). Effects of threatening visuals and announcer differences on responses to televised alcohol. *Journal of Applied Communication Research, 30,* 27–49.

Smith, A. E., & Bishop, G. F. (1992, May). *The Gallup secret ballot experiments: 1944–1988.* Paper presented at the annual conference of the American Association for Public Opinion Research, St. Petersburg, FL.

Smith, E. R. A. N., & Squire, P. (1990). The effects of prestige names in question wording. *Public Opinion Quarterly, 54,* 97–116.

Smith, J. (1991). A methodology for twenty-first century sociology. *Social Forces, 70,* 1–17.

Smith, S. W., & Ellis, J. B. (2001). Memorable messages as guides to self-assessment of behavior: An initial investigation. *Communication Monographs, 68,* 154–168.

Smith, V., Siltanen, S. A., & Hosman, L. A. (1998). The effects of powerful and powerless speech styles and speaker expertise on impression formation and attitude change. *Communication Research Reports, 15,* 27–35.

Spangler, M. (2002). "A fadograph of a yestern scene": Performances promising authenticity in Dublin's Bloomsday. *Text and Performance Quarterly, 22,* 120–137.

Sparks, G. G., & Ogles, R. M. (1990). The difference between fear of victimization and the probability of being victimized: Implications for cultivation. *Journal of Broadcasting & Electronic Media, 34,* 351–358.

Spradley, J. P. (1979). *The ethnographic interview.* New York: Holt, Rinehart and Winston.

Spradley, J. P. (1980). *Participant observation.* New York: Holt, Rinehart and Winston.

Stafford, L., & Daly, J. A. (1984). Conversational memory: The effects of recall mode and memory expectancies on remembrances of natural conversations. *Human Communication Research, 10,* 379–402.

Stafford, L., Burggraf, C. S., & Sharkey, W. F. (1987). Conversational memory: The effects of time, recall, mode, and memory expectancies on remembrances of natural conversations. *Human Communication Research, 14,* 203–229.

Stake, R. E. (1994). Case studies. In N. K. Denzin & Y. S. Lincoln (Eds.), *Handbook of qualitative research* (pp. 236–247). Thousand Oaks, CA: Sage.

Standard periodical directory. (1999). New York: Oxbridge.

Stewart, D. W., & Shamdasani, P. N. (1990). *Focus groups: Theory and practice.* Newbury Park, CA: Sage.

Strauss, A., & Corbin, J. (1990). *Basics of qualitative research: Grounded theory procedures and techniques.* Newbury Park, CA: Sage.

Strunk, W., Jr., & White, E. B. (1979). *The elements of style* (3rd ed.). New York: Macmillan.

Sudman, S. (1983). Applied sampling. In P. H. Rossi, J. D. Wright, & A. B. Anderson (Eds.), *Handbook of survey research* (pp. 145–194). New York: Academic Press.

Surra, C. A., & Ridley, C. A. (1991). Multiple perspectives on interaction: Participants, peers, and observers. In B. M. Montgomery & S. Duck (Eds.), *Studying interpersonal interaction* (pp. 35–55). New York: Guilford.

Survey Sampling, Inc. (2000, November). *Increase response rates of online sampling.* Retrieved June 12, 2002 from http://www.worldopinion.com/the_frame/frame4.html

Tanner, E. (2001). Chilean conversations: Internet forum participants debate Augusto Pinochet's detention. *Journal of Communication, 51,* 383–403.

Tardy, C. H. (Ed.) (1988). *A handbook for the study of human communication: Methods and instruments for observing, measuring, and assessing communication processes.* Norwood, NJ: Ablex.

Taylor, H., & Terhanian, G. (1999). Heady days are here again: Online polling is rapidly coming of age. *Public Perspective, 10,* 20–23.

Taylor, P. J. (2002). A cylindrical model of communication behavior in crisis negotiation. *Human Communication Research, 28,* 7–48.

Thomas, W. I., & Znaniecki, F. (1918). *The Polish peasant in Europe and America.* Chicago: University of Chicago Press.

Thurstone, L. L. (1931). The measurement of social attitudes. *Journal of Abnormal and Social Psychology, 26,* 249–269.

Townsley, N. C., & Geist, P. (2000). The discursive enactment of hegemony: Sexual harassment and academic organizing. *Western Journal of Communication, 64,* 190–217.

Tracy, K., & Baratz, S. (1993). Intellectual discussion in the academy as situated discourse. *Communication Monographs, 60,* 300–320.

Trent, J. S. (Ed.) (1998). *Communication: Views from the helm for the 21st century.* Boston: Allyn and Bacon.

Tuckel, P. S., & Feinberg, B. M. (1991). The answering machine poses many questions for telephone survey researchers. *Public Opinion Quarterly, 55,* 200–217.

Van Dijk, T. A. (Ed.) (1997a). *Discourse as structure and process.* Thousand Oaks, CA: Sage.

Van Dijk, T. A. (Ed.) (1997b). *Discourse as social interaction.* Thousand Oaks, CA: Sage.

Van Maanen, J. (1979). The fact of fiction in organizational ethnography. In J. Van Maanen (Ed.), Qualitative methodology [Special issue]. *Administrative Science Quarterly, 24,* 535–550.

Van Maanen, J. (1988). *Tales of the field: On writing ethnography.* Chicago: University of Chicago Press.

Vangelisti, A. L. (1994). Couples' communication problems: The counselor's perspective. *Journal of Applied Communication Research, 22,* 106–126.

Vangelisti, A. L., Caughlin, J. P., & Timmerman, L. (2001). Criteria for revealing family secrets. *Communication Monographs, 68,* 1–27.

Veroff, J., Douvan, E., & Hatchett, S. J. (1995). *Marital instability: A social and behavioral study of the early years.* Greenwich, CT: Greenwood.

Wackwitz, L. A. (2002). Burger on *Miller:* Obscene effects and the filth of a nation. *Journal of Communication, 52,* 196–210.

Waggoner, C. E. (1997). The emancipatory potential of feminine masquerade in Mary Kay Cosmetics. *Text and Performance Quarterly, 17,* 256–272.

Walker, J. T. (1994). Fax machines and social surveys: Teaching an old dog new tricks. *Journal of Quantitative Criminology, 10,* 181–188.

Wallace, W. (1971). *The logic of science in sociology.* Chicago: Aldine.

Wang, J., & Chang, T. K. (1996). From class ideologue to state manager: TV programming and foreign imports in China, 1970–1990. *Journal of Broadcasting & Electronic Media, 40,* 196–207.

Wanta, W., & Foote, J. (1994). The president–news media relationship: A time series analysis of agenda-setting. *Journal of Broadcasting & Electronic Media, 38,* 437–448.

Watson, J., & Hill, A. (1997). *A dictionary of communication and media studies* (4th ed.). London: Edward Arnold.

Watzlawick, P., Beavin, J. H., & Jackson, D. D. (1967). *Pragmatics of human communication: A study of interactional patterns, pathologies, and paradoxes.* New York: Norton.

Webb, E. J., Campbell, D. T., Schwartz, R. D., Sechrest, L., & Grove, J. B. (1981). *Nonreactive measures in the social sciences* (2nd ed.). Boston: Houghton Mifflin.

Weber, M. (1925/1946). Science as a vocation. In *From Max Weber: Essays in sociology* (H. Gerth & C. W. Mills, Eds. & Trans.) (pp. 129–156). New York: Oxford University Press.

Weber, R. P. (1990). *Basic content analysis.* Newbury Park, CA: Sage.

Weiner, R. (1996). *Webster's New World dictionary of media and communications* (rev. ed.). New York: Webster's New World.

Weisberg, H. F. (1992). *Central tendency and variability.* Newbury Park, CA: Sage.

Weisberg, H. F., Krosnick, J. A., & Bowen, B. D. (1996). *An introduction to survey research, polling, and data analysis* (3rd ed.). Thousand Oaks, CA: Sage.

Weiss, C. (1972). *Evaluation research*. Englewood Cliffs, NJ: Prentice-Hall.

Weiss, R. L., & Summers, K. J. (1983). Marital interaction coding system III. In E. E. Filsinger (Ed.), *Marriage and family assessment* (pp. 85–115). Beverly Hills, CA: Sage.

What went wrong with the polls? (1936b, November 14). *Literary Digest*, pp. 7–8.

Wheeless, L. R., & Grotz, J. (1976). Conceptualization and measurement of reported self-disclosure. *Human Communication Research, 2*, 338–346.

Wheeless, L. R., & Grotz, J. (1977). The measurement of trust and its relationship to self-disclosure. *Human Communication Research, 3*, 250–257.

White, C. H., & Burgoon, J. K. (2001). Adaptation and communicative design: Patterns of interaction in truthful and deceptive conversations. *Human Communication Research, 27*, 9–37.

Wiemann, J. M. (1977). Explication and test of a model of communicative competence. *Human Communication Research, 3*, 195–213.

Wiener, M., & Mehrabian, A. (1968). *Language within language: Immediacy, a channel in verbal communication*. New York: Appleton-Century-Crofts.

Williams, F. (1992). *Reasoning with statistics: How to read quantitative research* (4th ed.). New York: Harcourt.

Wilson, B. J., Linz, D., Donnerstein, E., & Stipp, H. (1992). The impact of social issue television programming on attitudes toward rape. *Human Communication Research, 19*, 179–208.

Wonsek, P. L. (1992). College basketball on television: A study of racism in the media. *Media, Culture and Society, 14*, 449–461.

Wood, J. (1997). *Communication theories in action: An introduction*. New York: Wadsworth.

Wood, J. T. (2001). The normalization of violence in heterosexual romantic relationships: Women's narratives of love and violence. *Journal of Social and Personal Relationships, 18*, 239–262.

Worcester, R. (Winter, 2001, in press). Election eve polls reporting percentages of the population voting for U.S. presidential candidates, 2000. *WAPOR Newsletter*.

Wright, K. (2000). Computer-mediated social support, older adults, and coping. *Journal of Communication, 50*, 100–118.

Wright, K. (2002). Motives for communication within on-line support groups and antecedents for interpersonal use. *Communication Research Reports, 19*, 89–98.

Wrobbel, E. D. (1998). A conversation analyst's response to Patterson, Neupauer, Burant, Koehn, and Reed. *Western Journal of Communication, 62*, 209–216.

Wyatt, R. O., Katz, E., & Kim, J. (2000). Bridging the spheres: Political and personal conversation in public and private spaces. *Journal of Communication, 50*, 71–92.

Yammarino, F. J., Skinner, S. J., & Childers, T. L. (1991). Understanding mail survey response behavior: A meta-analysis. *Public Opinion Quarterly, 55*, 613–639.

Zaichkowsky, J. L. (1985). Measuring the involvement construct. *Journal of Consumer Research, 12*, 341–352.

Ziesel, H. (1957). *Say it with figures*. New York: Harper.

INDEX